THE COMPLETE POEMS
OF
WALTER DE LA MARE

THE COMPLETE POEMS OF

Walter de la Mare

ALFRED A. KNOPF

New York 1975

NOTE

The Literary Trustees of Walter de la Mare are greatly indebted to Mr Leonard Clark for much of the work that has gone into the preparation of this volume, to Mr Giles de la Mare, the poet's grandson, for his invaluable help with the final editing, and to Miss Dorothy Marshall for her work in tracking down uncollected poems, which has produced a surprising harvest. But the overall responsibility is theirs, including the selection of the poems that are printed here for the first time — a most difficult task. Their intention is that *Complete Poems* should be regarded as the definitive text for Walter de la Mare's poetry. An account of the principles on which the book has been compiled and arranged is to be found in the Editorial Introduction.

Richard de la Mare

CONTENTS

Contents

[x]

EDITORIAL INTRODUCTION

Walter de la Mare's first book of poems, *Songs of Childhood*, was published in February 1902. Of his last poems, at least one or two like 'A Lifetime: Epitaph for William Blake' seem to have been written in 1956, the year of his death. As the poems in *Songs of Childhood* were written around 1900–1901, this represents a continuous span of writing of nearly sixty years. During this long period Walter de la Mare published more than a thousand poems and verses.[1]

Complete Poems contains all the poems de la Mare published in book form during his lifetime; also all the uncollected poems that have been found and a selection of unpublished poems. There were in fact five volumes of 'collected' poems (gathering together poems from previous books) published during de la Mare's lifetime. *Poems 1901–1918* appeared in two volumes in 1920 and included most of his poems published to date, the second volume containing poems primarily intended for children. *Poems for Children* came in 1930 and had most of the poems written for children up to then, with twenty new ones. *Poems 1919–1934* (1935) consisted of most of the poems published between those two dates together with a few earlier ones — and also had eight new poems. All these volumes were published by Constable. *Collected Poems* was published in 1942, and *Collected Rhymes and Verses* in 1944, both by Faber and Faber — the latter volume being a collection made from de la Mare's various books of poems for children. But none of these earlier collected editions were ever complete. Nor were they intended to be. Not only did de la Mare omit the whole of *A Child's Day*[2] and all but three of the sixty verses in *Stuff and Nonsense* from them, but, in addition, nearly 150 poems from other previously published books. All these poems and verses are now included in the present volume.

At his death, de la Mare left behind a mass of material in manuscript and typescript form, some of which still remains undeciphered. Among this, there were a number of unpublished poems, some early, some late, some unfinished or fragmentary, some undecipherable, and some obviously not intended for publication. It is clear, though, that some of them were intended for publication. A good example is 'The Revenant', apparently written in about 1930 (and interesting for its glosses on 'The Listeners'), which was revised for publication in *The Burning-Glass* (1945), but was finally omitted at the galley stage, and then never published. There are several instances of poems being omitted

---

[1] For some of his comments on the distinction, see sections 31 and 32 in the Bibliographical Appendix, pp. 896–897, and the substantial introduction in *Poems for Children* (1930).
[2] See section 32 of the Bibliographical Appendix, however.

from the proofs of one collection and included in a later one. Four poems selected for inclusion in *Bells and Grass* (1941) (but not set up in type) were finally left out, probably for reasons of space, and three were never published; one, 'The Glutton', was serialized in 1956. 'I Wonder' was omitted from the page-proofs of *Memory* (1938) but was nonetheless serialized in April 1938 in the *Observer*. Also, a few poems seem never to have been considered for publication for purely personal reasons, no longer relevant, and to have been forgotten. All the unpublished poems have thus been carefully scrutinized, and from among them the Literary Trustees have chosen those that they think de la Mare would probably have wanted to include himself. These appear in the 'Unpublished Poems' section (p. 695). There are forty-seven of them. They have been arranged in approximate chronological order, and their texts have been checked against the manuscript and typescript versions. A certain amount of editing has been necessary, chiefly of punctuation.

De la Mare frequently serialized his poems in periodicals and magazines before including them in collections, often in revised form, sometimes completely rewritten, and sometimes many years later.[1] A diligent and arduous search has revealed that, whether by accident or design, many poems have remained 'uncollected' over the years. It is not surprising that there should be a big concentration of uncollected poems between *O Lovely England* (1953), his last collection, and his death. Had he lived longer, there would perhaps have been a new collection eventually. The earlier uncollected poems are less easy to explain, however. Probably a number of them were deliberately omitted; but equally probably a fairly high proportion of them were simply missed or forgotten through his not always being quite systematic in his collecting. As it is impossible to determine the exact reasons for poems remaining uncollected, all the poems found have been included—and it is hoped that there are not more than a few still to be discovered. With the poems from periodicals and magazines in the 'Uncollected Poems' section are grouped several poems that were printed privately or by themselves, and several that were contributions to books by other authors. The poems appear in the order in which they were first serialized or published, the most recent text being used in cases where they occur in more than one place. Just occasionally, the punctuation has required minor adjustments. All in all, there are 113 poems in this section.

Complete Poems should therefore be regarded as what it claims to

---

[1] E.g. in *The Burning-Glass* (1945), *Inward Companion* (1950) and *O Lovely England* (1953). There can also be a gap of anything up to fifty years between the writing of the earliest version of a poem and its first serialization. There is, for instance, evidence suggesting that 'Time, Love and Life', 'The Sun', and 'The Winnowing Dream' were originally written between about 1900 and 1906.

be. It is neither a selection of what the Literary Trustees consider to be the best of de la Mare's poetry, nor a collection omitting inferior work which some might consider would do harm to de la Mare's reputation. What it does is to make available in a single volume for the general reader and scholar all the poems and verses that he published in his lifetime — together with a number of unpublished poems chosen by the Literary Trustees.

With a few exceptions, the poems have been grouped chronologically according to the volumes in which they originally appeared. The chief exceptions are as follows. The uncollected and unpublished poems come at the end of the first main section; while the poems from the prose works and other miscellaneous works, the occasional verses written for *A Child's Day* (1912), *Flora* (1919), and *This Year: Next Year* (1937), and the volume of limericks and nonsense rhymes called *Stuff and Nonsense* (1927) are included in this order in the second main section. It was thought that poems torn from a prose context, or originally written to illustrations, and nonsense rhymes should remain separate from the rest, if only to emphasize their sometimes different character.

The text is based on *Collected Poems* (1942) and *Collected Rhymes and Verses* (1944) (these are abbreviated to CP (1942) and CRV (1944)) for poems found there — the majority — and on the latest versions printed for the rest.[1] Some minor corruptions have, however, been found in CP (1942) (e.g. 'Banquo') and CRV (1944) (e.g. 'Not I!'), and elsewhere (e.g. in the 1946 edition of *Stuff and Nonsense*); and in these cases reference has been made to the previous printed versions, or earlier ones, depending on how far back the corruptions go. Also, a very small number of textual emendations have been made where this seemed absolutely necessary (e.g. in 'The Idol of the World', line 24, where 'She' has been changed to 'Her' after examination of the original corrected typescript). A few significant textual variations, i.e. that completely change the sense or complexion of a line, stanza or whole poem, are mentioned in the footnotes. De la Mare was always changing and revising his poems at every opportunity, and to give all the variations in published versions — including punctuation, use of italics and capitals, indentation, spelling, division of stanzas, and so on — would clutter the text and distract one's attention from the poems themselves. Where poems or whole collections were radically revised at some stage, a mention of the fact is made in the Bibliographical Appendix — as also with changes in title, which are sometimes mentioned in the footnotes, too. Finally, the footnotes indicate the original date of publication of poems where this is not abundantly clear from the general arrangement, which is given on the next page.

[1] The Bibliographical Appendix shows which poems were omitted from CP (1942) and CRV (1944).

This, then, is the order in which the poems appear:

I   1. Poems in Collections
      2. Uncollected Poems
      3. Unpublished Poems

II 1. Poems from Prose and Miscellaneous Works
      2. Verses Written to Illustrations
      3. Nonsense Verses

And here is a summary of the poems contained in the six sections:

I 1. POEMS IN COLLECTIONS

These consist of all the poems in the following collections:

Songs of Childhood (1902) (1902, 1916, and 1923 editions used)
Poems (1906)
The Listeners and Other Poems (1912)
Peacock Pie (1913) (1924 edition used)
The Sunken Garden and Other Poems (1917)
Motley and Other Poems (1918)
Poems 1901–1918 (1920: 2 vols.)
Story and Rhyme (1921)
The Veil and Other Poems (1921)
Down-Adown-Derry (1922)
Poems for Children (1930)
The Fleeting and Other Poems (1933)
Poems 1919–1934 (1935)
Memory and Other Poems (1938)
Bells and Grass (1941)
Collected Poems (1942)
Collected Rhymes and Verses (1944)
The Burning-Glass and Other Poems (1945)
The Traveller (1945) (first separate edition, 1946)[1]
Inward Companion (1950)
Winged Chariot (1951)[1]
O Lovely England and Other Poems (1953)

2. UNCOLLECTED POEMS

These are poems not previously published by the author in book form that have appeared in periodicals and magazines, or have been printed privately, or by themselves, or as contributions to books by other authors. Verses primarily intended for children appear at the end of this section.

3. UNPUBLISHED POEMS

These are poems that have never appeared in print. Verses primarily intended for children again come at the end.

[1] Actually single poems, but included here for convenience. See pp. 898–899.

II 1. POEMS FROM PROSE AND MISCELLANEOUS WORKS

These consist of all the poems in the following books:

Henry Brocken (1904): a novel

The Three Royal Monkeys (1910) (originally called *The Three Mulla-Mulgars*): a story

The Return (1910): a novel

Memoirs of a Midget (1921): a novel

Crossings (1921): a fairy play

Come Hither (1923) (1928 edition used): an anthology of rhymes and poems

Ding Dong Bell (1924) (1936 edition used): short stories written around epitaphs

On the Edge (1930): short stories

The Lord Fish (1933): short stories

The Wind Blows Over (1936): short stories

Pleasures and Speculations (1940): essays

2. VERSES WRITTEN TO ILLUSTRATIONS

These consist of all the poems in the following collections:

A Child's Day (1912): rhymes to photographs by Carine and Will Cadby

Flora (1919): poems to drawings by Pamela Bianco

This Year: Next Year (1937): poems to drawings by Harold Jones

3. NONSENSE VERSES

Stuff and Nonsense, and So On (1927) (1946 edition used): limericks and nonsense rhymes

PART I

I. POEMS IN COLLECTIONS

Songs of Childhood (1902)[1]

SLEEPYHEAD[2]

As I lay awake in the white moon light,
I heard a faint singing in the wood,
    'Out of bed,
    Sleepyhead,
    Put your white foot now,
    Here are we,
    Neath the tree
    Singing round the root now!'

I looked out of window, in the white moon light,
The trees were like snow in the wood —
    'Come away,
    Child, and play
    Light with the gnomies;
    In a mound,
    Green and round,
    That's where their home is.
    Honey sweet,
    Curds to eat,
    Cream and fruménty,
    Shells and beads,
    Poppy seeds,
    You shall have plenty.'

But soon as I stooped in the dim moon light
To put on my stocking and my shoe,
The sweet sweet singing died sadly away,
And the light of the morning peeped through:
Then instead of the gnomies there came a red robin
To sing of the buttercups and dew.

---

[1] See Bibliographical Appendix, p. 889.
[2] Called 'The Gnomies' in *Songs of Childhood*, 1902.

[3]

O DEAR ME!

Here are crocuses, white, gold, grey!
'O dear me!' says Marjorie May;
Flat as a platter the blackberry blows:
'O dear me!' says Madeleine Rose;
The leaves are fallen, the swallows flown:
'O dear me!' says Humphrey John;
Snow lies thick where all night it fell:
'O dear me!' says Emmanuel.

BLUEBELLS

Where the bluebells and the wind are,
Fairies in a ring I spied,
And I heard a little linnet
Singing near beside.

Where the primrose and the dew are,
Soon were sped the fairies all:
Only now the green turf freshens,
And the linnets call.

LOVELOCKS

I watched the Lady Caroline
Bind up her dark and beauteous hair;
Her face was rosy in the glass,
And 'twixt the coils her hands would pass,
    White in the candleshine.

Her bottles on the table lay,
Stoppered, yet sweet of violet;
Her image in the mirror stooped
To view those locks as lightly looped
    As cherry-boughs in May.

The snowy night lay dim without,
I heard the Waits their sweet song sing;
The window smouldered keen with frost;
Yet still she twisted, sleeked and tossed
    Her beauteous hair about.

[4]

A-TISHOO

'Sneeze, Pretty: sneeze, Dainty,
Else the Elves will have you sure,
Sneeze, Light-of-Seven-Bright-Candles,
See they're tippeting at the door;
Tiny feet in measure falling,
All their little voices calling,
Calling, calling, calling, calling —
Sneeze, or never come no more!'
  '*A-tishoo!*'

TARTARY

If I were Lord of Tartary,
 Myself, and me alone,
My bed should be of ivory,
 Of beaten gold my throne;
And in my court should peacocks flaunt,
And in my forests tigers haunt,
And in my pools great fishes slant
  Their fins athwart the sun.

If I were Lord of Tartary,
 Trumpeters every day
To all my meals should summon me,
 And in my courtyards bray;
And in the evening lamps should shine,
Yellow as honey, red as wine,
While harp, and flute, and mandoline
  Made music sweet and gay.

If I were Lord of Tartary,
 I'd wear a robe of beads,
White, and gold, and green they'd be —
 And small and thick as seeds;
And ere should wane the morning star,
I'd don my robe and scimitar,
And zebras seven should draw my car
  Through Tartary's dark glades.

Lord of the fruits of Tartary,
  Her rivers silver-pale!
Lord of the hills of Tartary,
  Glen, thicket, wood, and dale!
Her flashing stars, her scented breeze,
Her trembling lakes, like foamless seas,
Her bird-delighting citron-trees,
    In every purple vale!

THE BUCKLE

I had a silver buckle,
I sewed it on my shoe,
And 'neath a sprig of mistletoe
I danced the evening through!

I had a bunch of cowslips,
I hid 'em in a grot,
In case the elves should come by night
And me remember not.

I had a yellow riband,
I tied it in my hair,
That, walking in the garden,
The birds might see it there.

I had a secret laughter,
I laughed it near the wall:
Only the ivy and the wind
May tell of it at all.

THE HARE

In the black furrow of a field
I saw an old witch-hare this night;
And she cocked a lissome ear,
And she eyed the moon so bright,
And she nibbled of the green;
And I whispered 'Whsst! witch-hare,'
Away like a ghostie o'er the field
She fled, and left the moonlight there.

[6]

BUNCHES OF GRAPES

'Bunches of grapes,' says Timothy;
'Pomegranates pink,' says Elaine;
'A junket of cream and a cranberry tart
    For me,' says Jane.

'Love-in-a-mist,' says Timothy;
'Primroses pale,' says Elaine;
'A nosegay of pinks and mignonette
    For me,' says Jane.

'Chariots of gold,' says Timothy;
'Silvery wings,' says Elaine;
'A bumpity ride in a wagon of hay
    For me,' says Jane.

JOHN MOULDY

I spied John Mouldy in his cellar,
Deep down twenty steps of stone;
In the dusk he sat a-smiling,
    Smiling there alone.

He read no book, he snuffed no candle;
The rats ran in, the rats ran out;
And far and near, the drip of water
    Went whisp'ring about.

The dusk was still, with dew a-falling,
I saw the Dog-star bleak and grim,
I saw a slim brown rat of Norway
    Creep over him.

I spied John Mouldy in his cellar,
Deep down twenty steps of stone;
In the dusk he sat a-smiling,
    Smiling there alone.

THE FLY

How large unto the tiny fly
    Must little things appear! —
A rosebud like a feather bed,
    Its prickle like a spear;

[7]

A dewdrop like a looking-glass,
A hair like golden wire;
The smallest grain of mustard-seed
As fierce as coals of fire;

A loaf of bread, a lofty hill;
A wasp, a cruel leopard;
And specks of salt as bright to see
As lambkins to a shepherd.

I SAW THREE WITCHES

I saw three witches
That bowed down like barley,
And took to their brooms 'neath a louring sky,
And, mounting a storm-cloud,
Aloft on its margin,
Stood black in the silver as up they did fly.

I saw three witches
That mocked the poor sparrows
They carried in cages of wicker along,
Till a hawk from his eyrie
Swooped down like an arrow,
And smote on the cages, and ended their song.

I saw three witches
That sailed in a shallop
All turning their heads with a truculent smile
Till a bank of green osiers
Concealed their grim faces,
Though I heard them lamenting for many a mile.

I saw three witches
Asleep in a valley,
Their heads in a row, like stones in a flood,
Till the moon, creeping upward,
Looked white through the valley,
And turned them to bushes in bright scarlet bud.

[8]

SONG

O for a moon to light me home!
O for a lanthorn green!
For those sweet stars the Pleiades,
That glitter in the twilight trees;
O for a lovelorn taper! O
For a lanthorn green!

O for a frock of tartan!
O for clear, wild, grey eyes!
For fingers light as violets,
'Neath branches that the blackbird frets;
O for a thistly meadow! O
For clear, wild, grey eyes!

O for a heart like almond boughs!
O for sweet thoughts like rain!
O for first-love like fields of grey,
Shut April-buds at break of day!
O for a sleep like music!
Dreams still as rain!

THE SILVER PENNY

'Sailorman, I'll give to you
My bright silver penny,
If out to sea you'll sail me
And my dear sister Jenny.'

'Get in, young sir, I'll sail ye
And your dear sister Jenny,
But pay she shall her golden locks
Instead of your penny.'

They sail away, they sail away,
O fierce the winds blew!
The foam flew in clouds
And dark the night grew!

And all the green sea-water
Climbed steep into the boat;
Back to the shore again
Sail they will not.

[9]

Drowned is the sailorman,
Drowned is sweet Jenny,
And drowned in the deep sea
A bright silver penny.

THE RAINBOW

I saw the lovely arch
Of Rainbow span the sky,
The gold sun burning
As the rain swept by.

In bright-ringed solitude
The showery foliage shone
One lovely moment,
And the Bow was gone.

THE NIGHT-SWANS

'Tis silence on the enchanted lake,
And silence in the air serene,
Save for the beating of her heart,
The lovely-eyed Evangeline.

She sings across the waters clear
And dark with trees and stars between,
The notes her fairy godmother
Taught her, the child Evangeline.

As might the unrippled pool reply,
Faltering an answer far and sweet,
Three swans as white as mountain snow
Swim mantling to her feet.

And still upon the lake they stay,
Their eyes black stars in all their snow,
And softly, in the glassy pool,
Their feet beat darkly to and fro.

She rides upon her little boat,
Her swans swim through the starry sheen,
Rowing her into Fairyland —
The lovely-eyed Evangeline.

'Tis silence on the enchanted lake,
And silence in the air serene;
Voices shall call in vain again
On earth the child Evangeline.

'Evangeline! Evangeline!'
Upstairs, downstairs, all in vain.
Her room is dim; her flowers faded;
She answers not again.

REVERIE

When slim Sophia mounts her horse
    And paces down the avenue,
It seems an inward melody
    She paces to.

Each narrow hoof is lifted high
    Beneath the dark enclustering pines,
A silver ray within his bit
    And bridle shines.

His eye burns deep, his tail is arched,
    And streams upon the shadowy air,
The daylight sleeks his jetty flanks,
    His mistress' hair.

Her habit flows in darkness down,
    Upon the stirrup rests her foot,
Her brow is lifted, as if earth
    She heeded not.

'Tis silent in the avenue,
    The sombre pines are mute of song,
The blue is dark, there moves no breeze
    The boughs among.

When slim Sophia mounts her horse
    And paces down the avenue,
It seems an inward melody
    She paces to.

THE THREE BEGGARS

'Twas autumn daybreak gold and wild
　While past St. Ann's grey tower they shuffled
Three beggars spied a fairy-child
　In crimson mantle muffled.

The daybreak lighted up her face
　All pink, and sharp, and emerald-eyed;
She looked on them a little space,
　And shrill as hautboy cried: —

'O three tall footsore men in rags
　Which walking this gold morn I see,
What will ye give me from your bags
　For fairy kisses three?'

The first, that was a reddish man,
　Out of his bundle takes a crust:
'La, by the tombstones of St. Ann
　There's fee, if fee ye must!'

The second, that was a chestnut man,
　Out of his bundle draws a bone:
'La, by the belfry of St. Ann,
　And all my breakfast gone!'

The third, that was a yellow man,
　Out of his bundle picks a groat,
'La, by the Angel of St. Ann,
　And I must go without.'

That changeling, lean and icy-lipped,
　Touched crust, and bone, and groat, and lo!
Beneath her finger taper-tipped
　The magic all ran through.

Instead of crust a peacock pie,
　Instead of bone sweet venison,
Instead of groat a white lily
　With seven blooms thereon.

And each fair cup was deep with wine:
　Such was the changeling's charity
The sweet feast was enough for nine,
　But not too much for three.

O toothsome meat in jelly froze!
O tender haunch of elfin stag!
Oh, rich the odour that arose!
    Oh, plump with scraps each bag!

There, in the daybreak gold and wild,
    Each merry-hearted beggar man
Drank deep unto the fairy child,
    And blessed the good St. Ann.

ALULVAN

The sun is clear of bird and cloud,
The grass shines windless, grey, and still,
In dusky ruin the owl dreams on,
The cuckoo echoes on the hill;
    Yet soft along Alulvan's walks
    The ghost at noonday stalks.

His eyes in shadow of his hat
Stare on the ruins of his house;
His cloak, up-fastened with a brooch,
Of faded velvet, grey as mouse,
    Brushes the roses as he goes:
    Yet wavers not one rose.

The wild birds in a cloud fly up
From their sweet feeding in the fruit;
The droning of the bees and flies
Rises gradual as a lute;
    Is it for fear the birds are flown,
    And shrills the insect-drone?

Thick is the ivy o'er Alulvan,
And crisp with summer-heat its turf;
Far, far across its empty pastures
Alulvan's sands are white with surf:
    And he himself is grey as the sea,
    Watching beneath an elder-tree.

All night the fretful, shrill Banshee
Lurks in the chambers' dark festoons,
Calling for ever, o'er garden and river,
Through magpie changing of the moons:
    'Alulvan, O, alas! Alulvan,
    The doom of lone Alulvan!'

THE PEDLAR

There came a Pedlar to an evening house;
Sweet Lettice, from her lattice looking down,
Wondered what man he was, so curious
His black hair dangled on his tattered gown:
Then lifts he up his face, with glittering eyes, —
'What will you buy, sweetheart? — Here's honeycomb,
And mottled pippins, and sweet mulberry pies,
Comfits and peaches, snowy cherry bloom,
To keep in water for to make night sweet:
All that you want, sweetheart, — come, taste and eat!'

Ev'n with his sugared words, returned to her
The clear remembrance of a gentle voice: —
'And Oh, my child, should ever a flatterer
Tap with his wares, and promise of all joys
And vain sweet pleasures that on earth may be;
Seal up your ears, sing some old happy song,
Confuse his magic who is all mockery:
His sweets are death.' Yet, still, how she doth long
But just to taste, then shut the lattice tight,
And hide her eyes from the delicious sight!

'What must I pay?' she whispered. 'Pay!' says he,
'Pedlar I am who through this wood do roam,
One lock of hair is gold enough for me,
For apple, peach, comfits, or honeycomb!'
But from her bough a drowsy squirrel cried,
'Trust him not, Lettice, trust, oh trust him not!'
And many another woodland tongue beside
Rose softly in the silence —'Trust him not!'
Then cried the Pedlar in a bitter voice,
'What, in the thicket, is this idle noise?'

A late, harsh blackbird smote him with her wings,
As through the glade, dark in the dim, she flew;
Yet still the Pedlar his old burden sings, —
'What, pretty sweetheart, shall I show to you?
Here's orange ribands, here's a string of pearls,
Here's silk of buttercup and pansy glove,
A pin of tortoiseshell for windy curls,
A box of silver, scented sweet with clove:
Come now,' he says, with dim and lifted face,
'I pass not often such a lonely place.'

'Pluck not a hair!' a hidden rabbit cried,
'With but one hair he'll steal thy heart away,
Then only sorrow shall your lattice hide:
Go in! all honest pedlars come by day.'
There was dead silence in the drowsy wood;
'Here's syrup for to lull sweet maids to sleep;
And bells for dreams, and fairy wine and food
All day your heart in happiness to keep'; —
And now she takes the scissors on her thumb, —
'O, then, no more unto my lattice come!'

Oh, sad the sound of weeping in the wood!
Now only night is where the Pedlar was;
And bleak as frost upon a quickling bud
His magic steals in darkness, O alas!
Why all the summer doth sweet Lettice pine?
And, ere the wheat is ripe, why lies her gold
Hid 'neath fresh new-pluckt sprigs of eglantine?
Why all the morning hath the cuckoo tolled,
Sad to and fro in green and secret ways,
With solemn bells the burden of her days?

And, in the market-place, what man is this
Who wears a loop of gold upon his breast,
Stuck heartwise; and whose glassy flatteries
Take all the townsfolk ere they go to rest
Who come to buy and gossip? Doth his eye
Remember a face lovely in a wood?
O people! hasten, hasten, do not buy
His woeful wares; the bird of grief doth brood
There where his heart should be; and far away
Dew lies on grave-flowers this selfsame day.

THE GREY WOLF

'A fagot, a fagot, go fetch for the fire, son!'
'O, Mother, the wolf looks in at the door!'
'Cry Shoo! now, cry Shoo! thou fierce grey wolf, fly, now;
Haste thee away, he will fright thee no more.'

'I ran, O, I ran but the grey wolf ran faster,
O, Mother, I cry in the air at thy door,
Cry Shoo! now, cry Shoo! but his fangs were so cruel,
Thy son (save his hatchet) thou'lt never see more.'

DAME HICKORY

'Dame Hickory, Dame Hickory,
Here's sticks for your fire,
Furze-twigs, and oak-twigs,
And beech-twigs, and briar!'
But when old Dame Hickory came for to see,
She found 'twas the voice of the False Faërie.

'Dame Hickory, Dame Hickory,
Here's meat for your broth,
Goose-flesh, and hare's flesh,
And pig's trotters both!'
But when old Dame Hickory came for to see,
She found 'twas the voice of the False Faërie.

'Dame Hickory, Dame Hickory,
Here's a wolf at your door,
His teeth grinning white,
And his tongue wagging sore!'
'Nay!' said Dame Hickory, 'ye False Faërie!'
But a wolf 'twas indeed, and famished was he.

'Dame Hickory, Dame Hickory,
Here's buds for your tomb,
Bramble, and lavender,
And rosemary bloom!'
'Whsst!' sighs Dame Hickory, 'you False Faërie,
You cry like a wolf, you do, and trouble poor me.'

THE FAIRIES DANCING

I heard along the early hills,
Ere yet the lark was risen up,
Ere yet the dawn with firelight fills
The night-dew of the bramble-cup, —
I heard the fairies in a ring
Sing as they tripped a lilting round
Soft as the moon on wavering wing.
The starlight shook as if with sound,

[16]

As if with echoing, and the stars
Pranked their bright eyes with trembling gleams;
While red with war the gusty Mars
Rained upon earth his ruddy beams.
He shone alone, low down the West,
While I, behind a hawthorn-bush,
Watched on the fairies flaxen-tressed
The fires of the morning flush.
Till, as a mist, their beauty died,
Their singing shrill and fainter grew;
And daylight tremulous and wide
Flooded the moorland through and through;
Till Urdon's copper weathercock
Was reared in golden flame afar,
And dim from moonlit dreams awoke
The towers and groves of Arroar.

THE MILLER AND HIS SON

A twangling harp for Mary,
    A silvery flute for John,
And now we'll play the livelong day,
    'The Miller and his Son.' . . .

'The Miller went a-walking
    All in the forest high,
He sees three doves a-flitting
    Against the dark blue sky:

'Says he, "My son, now follow
    These doves so white and free,
That cry above the forest,
    And surely cry to thee."

'"I go, my dearest Father,
    But Oh! I sadly fear,
These doves so white will lead me far,
    But never bring me near."

'He kisses the Miller,
    He cries, "Awhoop to ye!"
And straightway through the forest
    Follows the wood-doves three.

'There came a sound of weeping
   To the Miller in his Mill;
Red roses in a thicket
   Bloomed over near his wheel;

'Three stars shone wild and brightly
   Above the forest dim:
But never his dearest son
   Returns again to him.

'The cuckoo shall call "Cuckoo!"
   In vain along the vale,
The linnet, and the blackbird,
   The mournful nightingale;

'The Miller hears and sees not,
   He's thinking of his son;
His toppling wheel is silent;
   His grinding done.

'"O doves so white!" he weepeth,
   "O roses on the tree!
O stars that shine so brightly —
   You shine in vain for me!

'"I bade him, 'Follow, follow';
   He said, 'O Father dear,
These doves so white will lead me far
   But never bring me near!' " ' . . .

A twangling harp for Mary,
   A silvery flute for John,
And now we'll play the livelong day,
   'The Miller and his Son.'

THE OGRE

'Tis moonlight on Trebarwith Sands,
   And moonlight on their seas,
Lone in a cove a cottage stands
   Enclustered in with trees.

[18]

Snuffing its thin faint smoke afar
    An Ogre prowls, and he
Smells supper; for where humans are,
    Rich dainties too may be.

Sweet as a larder to a mouse,
    So to him staring down,
Seemed the small-windowed moonlit house,
    With jasmine overgrown.

He snorted, as the billows snort
    In darkness of the night,
Betwixt his lean locks tawny-swart
    He glowered on the sight.

Into the garden sweet with peas
    He put his wooden shoe,
And bending back the apple trees
    Crept covetously through;

Then, stooping, with an impious eye
    Stared through the lattice small,
And spied two children which did lie
    Asleep, against the wall.

Into their dreams no shadow fell
    Of his disastrous thumb
Groping discreet, and gradual,
    Across the quiet room.

But scarce his nail had scraped the cot
    Wherein these children lay,
As if his malice were forgot,
    It suddenly did stay.

For faintly in the ingle-nook
    He heard a cradle-song,
That rose into his thoughts and woke
    Terror them among.

For she who in the kitchen sat
    Darning by the fire,
Guileless of what he would be at,
    Sang sweet as wind or wire: —

'Lullay, thou little tiny child
By-by, lullay, lullie;
Jesu in glory, meek and mild,
This night remember thee!

'Fiend, witch, and goblin, foul and wild,
He deems them smoke to be;
Lullay, thou little tiny child,
By-by, lullay, lullie!'

The Ogre lifted up his eyes
Into the moon's pale ray,
And gazed upon her leopard-wise,
Cruel and clear as day;

He snarled in gluttony and fear —
The wind blows dismally —
'Jesu in storm my lambs be near,
By-by, lullay, lullie!'

And like a ravenous beast which sees
The hunter's icy eye,
So did this wretch in wrath confess
Sweet Jesu's mastery.

With gaunt locks dangling, crouched he, then
Drew backward from his prey,
Through tangled apple-boughs again
He wrenched and rent his way.

Out on Trebarwith Sands he broke,
The waves yelled back his cry,
Gannet and cormorant echo woke
As he went striding by.

THE GAGE

'Lady Jane, O Lady Jane!
Your hound hath broken bounds again,
And chased my timorous deer, O;
If him I see,
That hour he'll dee;
My brakes shall be his bier, O.'

'Hoots! lord, speak not so proud to me!
My hound, I trow, is fleet and free,
   He's welcome to your deer, O;
      Shoot, shoot you may,
      He'll gang his way,
Your threats we nothing fear, O.'

He's fetched him in, he's laid him low,
Drips his lifeblood red and slow,
   Darkens his dreary eye, O;
      'Here is your beast,
      And now at least
My herds in peace shall lie, O.'

'"In peace!" my lord, O mark me well!
For what my jolly hound befell
   You shall sup twenty-fold, O!
      For every tooth
      Of his, i'sooth,
A stag in pawn I hold, O.

'Huntsman and horn, huntsman and horn,
Shall scour your heaths and coverts lorn,
   Baying them shrill and clear, O:
      But lone and still
      Shall lift each hill,
Each valley wan and sere, O.

'Ride up you may, ride down you may,
Lonely or trooped, by night or day,
   One ghost shall haunt you ever:
      Bird, beast, and game
      Shall dread the same,
The fish of lake and river.'

Her cheek burns angry as the rose,
Her eye with wrath and pity flows:
   She gazes fierce and round, O.
      'Dear Lord!' he says,
      'What loveliness
To waste upon a hound, O!

'I'd give my stags, my hills and dales,
My stormcocks and my nightingales

[21]

To have undone this deed, O;
  For deep beneath
  My heart is death
Which for her love doth bleed, O.'

He wanders up, he wanders down,
On foot, on horse, by night and noon;
  His lands are bleak and drear, O;
  Forsook his dales
  Of nightingales,
Forsook his moors of deer, O.

Forsook his heart, ah me! of mirth;
There's nothing precious left on earth;
  All happy dreams seem vain, O,
  Save where remote
  The moonbeams gloat,
And sleeps the lovely Jane, O.

But happed one eve alone he went,
Gnawing his beard in dreariment —
  Lo! from a thicket hidden,
  Lovely as flower
  In April hour,
Steps forth a form unbidden.

'Get ye now down, my lord, to me!
I'm troubled so I'm like to dee,'
  She cries, 'twixt joy and grief, O;
  'The hound is dead,
  When all is said,
But love is past belief, O.

'Nights, nights I've lain your lands to see,
Forlorn and still — and all for me,
  All for a foolish curse, O;
  Pride may be well,
  But truth to tell,
To live unloved is worse, O!'

In faith, this lord, in that lone dale,
Hears now a sweeter nightingale,
  And lairs a tenderer deer, O;
  His sorrow goes
  Like mountain snows
In waters sweet and clear, O!

And now, what hound is this that fleet
Comes fawning to his mistress' feet,
And's bid forgive a master?
   How swiftly love
   May grief remove,
How happy make disaster!

Ay, as it were a bud did break
To loveliness for pity's sake,
  So she in beauty moving
   Rides at his hand
   Across his land,
Beloved as well as loving.

THE DWARF

'Now, Jinnie, my dear, to the dwarf be off,
   That lives in Barberry Wood,
And fetch me some honey, but be sure you don't laugh, —
   He hates little girls that are rude, are rude,
   He hates little girls that are rude.'

Jane tapped at the door of the house in the wood,
   And the dwarf looked over the wall,
He eyed her so queer, 'twas as much as she could
   To keep from laughing at all, at all,
   To keep from laughing at all.

His shoes down the passage came clod, clod, clod,
   And when he opened the door,
He croaked so harsh, 'twas as much as she could
   To keep from laughing the more, the more,
   To keep from laughing the more.

As there, with his bushy red beard, he stood
   Pricked out to double its size,
He squinted so cross, 'twas as much as she could
   To keep the tears out of her eyes, her eyes,
   To keep the tears out of her eyes.

He slammed the door, and went clod, clod, clod,
   But while in the porch she bides,
He squealed so fierce, 'twas as much as she could
   To keep from cracking her sides, her sides,
   To keep from cracking her sides.

He threw a pumpkin over the wall,
    And melons and apples beside,
So thick in the air that to see 'em all fall,
    She laughed, and laughed, till she cried, cried, cried,
    Jane laughed and laughed till she cried.

Down fell her teardrops a pit-apat-pat,
    And red as a rose she grew: —
'Kah! kah!' said the dwarf, 'is it crying you're at?
    It's the very worst thing you could do, do, do,
    It's the very worst thing you could do.'

He slipped like a monkey up into a tree,
    He shook her down cherries like rain;
'See now,' says he, cheeping, 'a blackbird I be,
    Laugh, laugh, little Jinnie, again-gain-gain,
    Laugh, laugh, little Jinnie, again!'

Ah me! what a strange, what a gladsome duet
    From a house in the deeps of a wood!
Such shrill and such harsh voices never met yet
    A-laughing as loud as they could, could, could,
    A-laughing as loud as they could.

Come Jinnie, come dwarf, cocksparrow, and bee,
    There's a ring gaudy-green in the dell,
Sing, sing, ye sweet cherubs, that flit in the tree;
    La! who can draw tears from a well, well, well,
    Who ever drew tears from a well!

THE PILGRIM

'Shall we help you with your bundle,
    You old grey man?
Over hill and dell and meadow
Lighter than an owlet's shadow
We will waft it through the air,
Through blue regions shrill and bare
So you may in comfort fare —
Shall we help you with your bundle,
    You old grey man?'

The Pilgrim lifted up his eyes
And saw three Fiends in the skies,
Stooping o'er that lonely place
    Evil in form and face.

[24]

'Nay', he answered, 'tempt me not,
    O three wild Fiends!
Long the journey I am wending,
Yet the longest hath an ending;
I must bear my bundle alone
    Till the day be done.'

The Fiends stared down with leaden eye,
Fanning the chill air duskily,
'Twixt their hoods they stoop and cry: —

'Shall we smooth the path before you,
    Weary old man?
Sprinkle it green with gilded showers,
Strew it o'er with painted flowers,
Lure bright birds to sing and flit
In the honeyed airs of it?
Shall we smooth the path before you,
    Sad old man?'

'O, 'tis better silence,
    Ye three wild Fiends!
Footsore am I, faint and weary,
Dark the way, forlorn and dreary,
Even so, at peace I be,
Nor want for ghostly company:
O, 'tis better silence,
    Ye three wild Fiends!'

It seemed a cloud obscured the air,
Lightning quivered in the gloom,
And a faint voice of thunder spake
Far in the high hill-hollows — 'Come!'
Then, half in fury, half in dread,
The Fiends drew closer down, and said:

'Nay, thou foolish fond old man,
    Hearken awhile!
Frozen, scorched, with ice and heat,
Tarry now, sit down and eat:
Juice of purple grape shall be
Joy and solace unto thee.

'Music of tambour, wire and wind,
Ease shall bring to heart and mind;
Wonderful sweet mouths shall sigh
Languishing and lullaby;

Turn then! Curse the dream that lures thee;
Turn thee, ere too late it be,
Lest thy three true Friends grow weary
    Of comforting thee!'

The Pilgrim crouches terrified
At stooping hood, and glassy face,
Gloating, evil, side by side,
Terror and hate brood o'er the place;
He flings his withered hands on high
With a bitter, breaking cry: —

'Pity have, and leave me, leave me,
    Ye three wild Fiends!
If I lay me down in slumber
Dark with death that sleep shall be;
All your fruits are fruits of evil —
Wrath and hate and treachery.
On mine eyes the darkness thickens,
Blind, in dread, I stumble on,
Cheat me not with false beguiling —
    Beseech ye, begone!'

And even as he spake, on high
Arrows of sunlight pierced the sky.
Bright streamed the rain. O'er burning snow
From hill to hill a wondrous Bow
Of colour and fire trembled in air,
Painting its heavenly beauty there.

Wild flung each Fiend a batlike hood
Against that flaming light, and stood
Beating the windless rain and then
Rose heavy and slow with cowering head,
Circled in company again,
And into darkness fled.

Marvellous sweet it was to hear
The waters gushing loud and clear;
Marvellous happy it was to be
Alone, and yet not solitary;
Oh, out of terror and dark to come
    In sight of home!

THE FIDDLERS

Nine feat Fiddlers had good Queen Bess
To play her music as she did dress.
Behind an arras of horse and hound
They sate there scraping delightsome sound.
Spangled, bejewelled, her skirts would she
Draw o'er a petticoat of cramasie;
And soft each string like a bird would sing
In the starry dusk of evening.
Then slow from the deeps the crisscross bows,
Crooning like doves, arose and arose.
When, like a cage, did her ladies raise
A stiff rich splendour o'er her ribbed stays,
Like bumbling bees those four times nine
Fingers in melodies loud did pine;
Last came her coif and her violet shoon
And her virgin face shone out like the moon:
Oh, then in a rapture those three times three
Fiddlers squealed shrill on their topmost C.

AS LUCY WENT A-WALKING

As Lucy went a-walking one morning cold and fine,
There sate three crows upon a bough, and three times three are
    nine:
Then 'O!' said Lucy, in the snow, 'it's very plain to see
A witch has been a-walking in the fields in front of me.'

Then stept she light and heedfully across the frozen snow,
And plucked a bunch of elder-twigs that near a pool did grow:
And, by and by, she comes to seven shadows in one place
Stretched black by seven poplar-trees against the sun's bright face.

She looks to left, she looks to right, and in the midst she sees
A little pool of water clear and frozen 'neath the trees;
Then down beside its margent in the crusted snow she kneels,
And hears a magic belfry, ringing with sweet bells.

Clear rang the faint far merry peal, then silence on the air,
And icy-still the frozen pool and poplars standing there:
Then, soft, as Lucy turned her head and looked along the snow
She sees a witch — a witch she sees, come frisking to and fro.

[27]

Her scarlet, buckled shoes they clicked, her heels a-twinkling high;
With mistletoe her steeple-hat bobbed as she capered by;
But never a dint, or mark, or print, in the whiteness there to see,
Though danced she light, though danced she fast, though danced
    she lissomely.

It seemed 'twas diamonds in the air, or tiny flakes of frost;
It seemed 'twas golden smoke around, or sunbeams lightly tossed;
It seemed an elfin music like to reeds' and warblers' rose:
'Nay!' Lucy said, 'it is the wind that through the branches flows.'

And as she peeps, and as she peeps, 'tis no more one, but three,
And eye of bat, and downy wing of owl within the tree,
And the bells of that sweet belfry a-pealing as before,
And now it is not three she sees, and now it is not four.

'O! who are ye,' sweet Lucy cries, 'that in a dreadful ring,
All muffled up in brindled shawls, do caper, frisk, and spring?'
'A witch and witches, one and nine,' they straight to her reply,
And look upon her narrowly, with green and needle eye.

Then Lucy sees in clouds of gold sweet cherry trees upgrow,
And bushes of red roses that bloomed above the snow;
She smells all faint the almond-boughs blowing so wild and fair,
And doves with milky eyes ascend fluttering in the air.

Clear flowers she sees, like tulip buds, go floating by like birds,
With wavering tips that warbled sweetly strange enchanted words;
And as with ropes of amethyst the twigs with lamps were hung,
And clusters of green emeralds like fruit upon them clung.

'O witches nine, ye dreadful nine, O witches three times three!
Whence come these wondrous things that I this Christmas
    morning see?'
But straight, as in a clap, when she of 'Christmas' says the word,
Here is the snow, and there the sun, but never bloom nor bird;

Nor warbling flame, nor gloaming-rope of amethyst there shows,
Nor bunches of green emeralds, nor belfry, well, and rose,
Nor cloud of gold, nor cherry-tree, nor witch in brindled shawl,
But like a dream which vanishes, so vanished were they all.

When Lucy sees, and only sees three crows upon a bough,
And earthly twigs, and bushes hidden white in driven snow,
Then 'O!' said Lucy, 'three times three are nine — I plainly see
Some witch has been a-walking in the fields in front of me.'

DOWN-ADOWN-DERRY

Down-adown-derry,
Sweet Annie Maroon,
Gathering daisies
In the meadows of Doone,
Sees a white fairy
Skip buxom and free
Where the waters go brawling
In rills to the sea;
  Singing down-adown-derry.

Down-adown-derry,
Sweet Annie Maroon
Through the green grasses
Peeps softly; and soon
Spies under green willows
A fairy whose song
Like the smallest of bubbles
Floats bobbing along;
  Singing down-adown-derry.

Down-adown-derry
Her cheeks are like wine,
Her eyes in her wee face
Like water-sparks shine,
Her niminy fingers
Her sleek tresses preen,
The which in the combing
She peeps out between;
  Singing down-adown-derry.

'Down-adown-derry,'
And shrill was her tune: —
'Come to my water-house,
Annie Maroon,
Come in your dimity,
Ribbon on head,
To wear siller seaweed
And coral instead;
  Singing down-adown-derry.'

'Down-adown-derry,
Lean fish of the sea,
Bring lanthorns for feasting
The gay Fäerie;

'Tis sand for the dancing,
A music all sweet
In the water-green gloaming
For thistledown feet;
    Singing down-adown-derry.'

Down-adown-derry,
Sweet Annie Maroon
Looked large on the fairy
Curled wan as the moon;
And all the grey ripples
To the Mill racing by,
With harps and with timbrels
Did ringing reply;
    Singing down-adown-derry.

'Down-adown-derry,'
Sang the Fairy of Doone,
Piercing the heart
Of sweet Annie Maroon;
And lo! when like roses
The clouds of the sun
Faded at dusk, gone
Was Annie Maroon;
    Singing down-adown-derry.

Down-adown-derry,
The daisies are few;
Frost twinkles powd'ry
In haunts of the dew;
And only the robin,
Perched on a thorn,
Can comfort the heart
Of a father forlorn;
    Singing down-adown-derry.

Down-adown-derry
Snow's on the air;
Ice where the lily
Bloomed waxen and fair;
He may call o'er the water,
Cry — cry through the Mill,
But Annie Maroon, alas!
Answer ne'er will;
    Singing down-adown-derry.

THE ENGLISHMAN

I met a sailor in the woods,
    A silver ring wore he,
His hair hung black, his eyes shone blue,
    And thus he said to me: —

'What country, say, of this round earth,
    What shore of what salt sea,
Be this, my son, I wander in,
    And looks so strange to me?'

Says I, 'O foreign sailorman,
    In England now you be,
This is her wood, and there her sky,
    And that her roaring sea.'

He lifts his voice yet louder,
    'What smell be this,' says he,
'My nose on the sharp morning air
    Snuffs up so greedily?'

Says I, 'It is wild roses
    Do smell so winsomely,
And winy briar too,' says I,
    'That in these thickets be.'

'And oh!' says he, 'what leetle bird
    Is singing in yon high tree,
So every shrill and long-drawn note
    Like bubbles breaks in me?'

Says I, 'It is the mavis
    That perches in the tree
And sings so shrill, and sings so sweet,
    When dawn comes up the sea.'

At which he fell a-musing,
    And fixed his eye on me,
As one alone 'twixt light and dark
    A spirit thinks to see.

'England!' he whispers soft and harsh,
    'England!' repeated he,
'And briar, and rose, and mavis,
    A-singing in yon high tree.

[31]

'Ye speak me true, my leetle son,
    So — so, it came to me,
A-drifting landwards on a spar,
    And grey dawn on the sea.

'Ay, ay, I could not be mistook;
    I knew them leafy trees,
I knew that land so witchery sweet,
    And that old noise of seas.

'Though here I've sailed a score of years,
    And heard 'em, dream or wake,
Lap small and hollow 'gainst my cheek,
    On sand and coral break;

' "Yet now," my leetle son, says I,
    A-drifting on the wave,
"That land I see so safe and green
    Is England, I believe.

' "And that there wood is English wood,
    And this here cruel sea,
The selfsame old blue ocean
    Years gone remembers me,

' "A-sitting with my bread and butter
    Down behind yon chitterin' mill;
And this same Marinere" — (that's me),
    "Is that same leetle Will! —

' "That very same wee leetle Will
    Eating his bread and butter there,
A-looking on the broad blue sea
    Betwixt his yaller hair!"

'And here be I, my son, throwed up
    Like corpses from the sea,
Ships, stars, winds, tempests, pirates past,
    Yet leetle Will I be!'

He said no more, that sailorman,
    But in a reverie
Stared like the figure of a ship
    With painted eye to sea.

THE PHANTOM

'Upstairs in the large closet, child,
This side the blue-room door,
Is an old Bible, bound in leather,
Standing upon the floor.

'Go with this taper, bring it me;
Carry it on your arm;
It is the book on many a sea
Hath stilled the waves' alarm!'

Late the hour; dark the night;
The house is solitary;
Feeble is a taper's light
To light poor Ann to see.

Her eyes are yet with visions bright
Of sylph and river, flower and fay,
Now through a narrow corridor
She goes her lonely way.

Vast shadows on the heedless walls
Gigantic loom, stoop low:
Each little hasty footfall calls
Hollowly to and fro.

Now in the dark clear glass there moves
A taper, mocking hers, —
A phantom face of light blue eyes,
Reflecting phantom fears.

Around her loom the vacant rooms,
Wind the upward stairs,
She climbs on into a loneliness
Only her taper shares.

Out in the dark a cold wind stirs,
At every window sighs;
A waning moon peers small and chill
From out the cloudy skies,

Casting faint tracery on the walls;
So stony still the house
From cellar to attic rings the shrill
Squeak of the hungry mouse.

[33]

Ann scarce can hear or breathe, so fast
　Her pent-up heart doth beat,
When, faint along the corridor,
　She hears the fall of feet: —

Sounds lighter than silk slippers make
　Upon a ballroom floor, when sweet
Violin and 'cello wake
　Music for twirling feet.

O! in an old unfriendly house,
　What shapes may not conceal
Their faces in the open day,
　At night abroad to steal!

Even her taper seems with fear
　To languish small and blue;
Far in the woods the winter wind
　Runs whistling through.

A dreadful cold plucks at each hair,
　Her mouth is stretched to cry,
But sudden, with a gush of joy,
　It narrows to a sigh.

'Tis but a phantom child which comes
　Soft through the corridor,
Singing an old forgotten song,
　This ancient burden bore: —

'Thorn, thorn, I wis,
And roses twain,
　A red rose and a white;
Stoop in the blossom, bee, and kiss
　A lonely child good-night.

'Swim fish, sing bird,
And sigh again,
　I that am lost am lone,
Bee in the blossom never stirred
　Locks hid beneath a stone!' —

Her eyes were of the azure fire
　That hovers in wintry flame;
Her raiment wild and yellow as furze
　That spouteth out the same;

[34]

And in her hand she bore no flower,
   But on her head a wreath
Of faded flowers that did yet
   Smell sweetly after death. . . .

Gloomy with night the listening walls
   Are now that she is gone,
Albeit this solitary child
   No longer seems alone.

Fast though her taper dwindles down,
   Though black the shadows come,
A beauty beyond fear to dim
   Haunts now her alien home.

Ghosts in the world, malignant, grim,
   Vex many a wood and glen,
And house and pool, — the unquiet ghosts
   Of dead and restless men.

But in her grannie's house this spirit —
   A child as lone as she —
Pining for love not found on earth,
   Ann dreams again to see.

Seated upon her tapestry-stool,
   Her fairy-book laid by,
She gazes into the fire, knowing
   She hath sweet company.

THE SLEEPING BEAUTY

The scent of bramble fills the air,
   Amid her folded sheets she lies,
The gold of evening in her hair,
   The blue of morn shut in her eyes.

How many a changing moon hath lit
   The unchanging roses of her face!
Her mirror ever broods on it
   In silver stillness of the days.

Oft flits the moth on filmy wings
　Into his solitary lair;
Shrill evensong the cricket sings
　From some still shadow in her hair.

In heat, in snow, in wind, in flood,
　She sleeps in lovely loneliness,
Half-folded like an April bud
　On winter-haunted trees.

HAUNTED

From out the wood I watched them shine, —
　The windows of the haunted house,
Now ruddy as enchanted wine,
　Now dark as flittermouse.

There went a thin voice piping airs
　Along the grey and crooked walks, —
A garden of thistledown and tares,
　Bright leaves, and giant stalks.

The twilight rain shone at its gates,
　Where long-leaved grass in shadow grew;
And back in silence to her mates
　A voiceless raven flew.

Lichen and moss the lone stones greened,
　Green paths led lightly to its door,
Keen from her lair the spider leaned,
　And dusk to darkness wore.

Amidst the sedge a whisper ran,
　The West shut down a heavy eye,
And like last tapers, few and wan,
　The watch-stars kindled in the sky.

THE SUPPER

A wolf he pricks with eyes of fire
Across the dark, frost-crusted snows,
   Seeking his prey,
   He pads his way
Where Jane benighted goes,
  Where Jane benighted goes.

He curdles the bleak air with ire,
Ruffling his hoary raiment through,
   And lo! he sees
   Beneath the trees
Where Jane's light footprints go,
  Where Jane's light footprints go.

No hound peals thus in wicked joy,
He snaps his muzzle in the snows,
   His five-clawed feet
   Now scamper fleet
Where Jane's bright lanthorn shows,
  Where Jane's bright lanthorn shows.

His hungry face stares out unseen
On hers as pure as wilding rose,
   Her amber eyes
   In fear's surprise
Watch largely as she goes,
  Watch largely as she goes.

Salt wells his hunger in his jaws,
His lust it revels to and fro
   Yet small beneath
   A soft voice saith,
'Jane shall in safety go,
  Jane shall in safety go.'

He lurched as if a fiery lash
Had scourged his hide, and through, and through
   His furious eyes
   O'erscanned the skies,
But nearer dared not go,
  But nearer dared not go.

He reared like wild Bucephalus,
His fangs like spears in him uprose,
    Ev'n to the town
    Jane's flitting gown
He grins on as she goes,
  He grins on as she goes.

In fierce lament he howls amain,
He scampers, marvelling in his throes
    What brought him there
    To sup on air,
While Jane unharmèd goes,
  While Jane unharmèd goes.

THE HORN

Hark! is that a horn I hear,
  In cloudland winding sweet —
And bell-like clash of bridle-rein,
  And silver-shod light feet?

Is it the elfin laughter
  Of fairies riding faint and high,
Beneath the branches of the moon,
  Straying through the starry sky?

Is it in the globèd dew
  Such sweet melodies may fall?
Wood and valley — all are still,
  Hushed the shepherd's call.

CAPTAIN LEAN

Out of the East a hurricane
  Swept down on Captain Lean —
That mariner and gentleman
  Will not again be seen.

[38]

He sailed his ship against the foes
   Of his own country dear,
But now in the trough of the billows
   An aimless course doth steer.

Powder was violets to his nostrils,
   Sweet the din of the fighting-line,
Now he is flotsam on the seas,
   And his bones are bleached with brine.

The stars move up along the sky,
   The moon she shines so bright,
And in that solitude the foam
   Sparkles unearthly white.

This is the tomb of Captain Lean,
   Would a straiter please his soul?
I trow he sleeps in peace,
   Howsoever the billows roll!

THE PORTRAIT OF A WARRIOR

His brow is seamed with line and scar;
   His cheek is red and dark as wine;
The fires as of a Northern star
   Beneath his cap of sable shine.

His right hand, bared of leathern glove,
   Hangs open like an iron gin,
You stoop to see his pulses move,
   To hear the blood sweep out and in.

He looks some king, so solitary
   In earnest thought he seems to stand,
As if across a lonely sea
   He gazed impatient of the land.

Out of the noisy centuries
   The foolish and the fearful fade;
Yet burn unquenched these warrior eyes,
   Time hath not dimmed nor death dismayed.

THE ISLE OF LONE

Three dwarfs there were which lived in an isle,
  And the name of that isle was Lone,
And the names of the dwarfs were Alliolyle,
  Lallerie, Muziomone.

Their house was small and sweet of the sea,
  And pale as the Malmsey wine;
Their bowls were three, and their beds were three,
  And their nightcaps white were nine.

Their beds they were made of the holly-wood,
  Their combs of the tortoise-shell,
Three basins of silver in corners there stood,
  And three little ewers as well.

Green rushes, green rushes lay thick on the floor,
  For light beamed a gobbet of wax;
There were three wooden stools for whatever they wore
  On their humpity-dumpity backs.

So each would lie on a drowsy pillow
  And watch the moon in the sky —
And hear the parrot scream to the billow,
  And the billow roar reply.

Parrots of sapphire and sulphur and amber,
  Amethyst, azure and green,
While apes in the palm trees would scramble and clamber,
  Hairy and hungry and lean.

All night long with bubbles a-glisten
  The ocean cried under the moon,
Till ape and parrot too sleepy to listen
  To sleep and slumber were gone.

Then from three small beds the dark hours' while
  In a house in the Island of Lone
Rose the snoring of Lallerie, Alliolyle,
  The snoring of Muziomone.

But soon as ever came peep of sun
  On coral and feathery tree,
Three night-capped dwarfs to the surf would run
  And soon were a-bob in the sea.

At six they went fishing, at nine to snare
   Young foxes in the dells,
At noon in the shade on sweet fruits would fare,
   And blew in their twisted shells.

Dark was the sea they gambolled in,
   And thick with silver fish,
Dark as green glass blown clear and thin
   To be a monarch's dish.

They sate to sup in a jasmine bower,
   Lit pale with flies of fire,
Their bowls the hue of the iris-flower,
   And lemon their attire.

Sweet wine in little cups they sipped,
   And golden honeycomb
Into their bowls of cream they dipped,
   Whipt light and white as foam.

Now Alliolyle where the sand-flower blows
   Taught three old apes to sing —
Taught three old apes to dance on their toes
   And caper around in a ring.

They yelled them hoarse and they croaked them sweet,
   They twirled them about and around,
To the noise of their voices they danced with their feet,
   They stamped with their feet on the ground.

But down to the shore skipped Lallerie,
   His parrot on his thumb,
And the twain they scritched in mockery,
   While the dancers go and come.

And, alas! in the evening, rosy and still,
   Light-haired Lallerie
Bitterly quarrelled with Alliolyle
   By the yellow-sanded sea.

The rising moon swam sweet and large
   Before their furious eyes,
And they rolled and rolled to the coral marge
   Where the surf for ever cries.

Too late, too late, comes Muziomone:
  Clear in the clear green sea
Alliolyle lies not alone,
  But clasped with Lallerie.

He blows on his shell low plaintive notes;
  Ape, perequito, bee
Flock where a shoe on the salt wave floats, —
  The shoe of Lallerie.

He fetches nightcaps, one and nine,
  Grey apes he dowers three,
His house as fair as the Malmsey wine
  Seems sad as the cypress-tree.

Three bowls he brims with sweet honeycomb
  To feast the bumble-bees,
Saying, 'O bees, be this your home,
  For grief is on the seas!'

He sate him down in a coral grot,
  At the flowing in of the tide;
When ebbed the billow, there was not,
  Save coral, aught beside.

So hairy apes in three white beds,
  And nightcaps, one and nine,
On moonlit pillows lay three heads
  Bemused with dwarfish wine.

A tomb of coral, the dirge of bee,
  The grey apes' guttural groan
For Alliolyle, for Lallerie,
  For thee, O Muziomone!

THE RAVEN'S TOMB

'Build me my tomb,' the Raven said
'Within the dark yew-tree,
So in the Autumn yewberries,
Sad lamps, may burn for me,
Summon the haunted beetle,

From twilight bud and bloom,
To drone a gloomy dirge for me
At dusk above my tomb.
Beseech ye too the glowworm
To rear her cloudy flame,
Where the small, flickering bats resort,
Whistling in tears my name.
Let the round dew a whisper make,
Welling on twig and thorn;
And only the grey cock at night
Call through his silver horn.
And you, dear sisters, don your black
For ever and a day,
To show how true a raven
In his tomb is laid away.'

THE CHRISTENING

The bells chime clear,
Soon will the sun behind the hills sink down;
Come, little Ann, your baby brother dear
Lies in his christening-gown.

His godparents
Are all across the fields stepped on before,
And wait beneath the crumbling monuments,
This side the old church door.

Your mammie dear
Leans frail and lovely on your daddie's arm;
Watching her chick, 'twixt happiness and fear,
Lest he should come to harm.

All to be blest
Full soon in the clear heavenly water, he
Sleeps on unwitting of't, his little breast
Heaving so tenderly.

I carried you,
My little Ann, long since on this same quest,
And from the painted windows a pale hue
Lit golden on your breast;

[43]

And then you woke,
Chill as the holy water trickled down,
And, weeping, cast the window a strange look,
Half smile, half infant frown.

I scarce could hear
The skylarks singing in the green meadows,
'Twas summertide, and, budding far and near,
The hedges thick with rose.

And now you're grown
A little girl; and this same helpless mite
Is come like such another bud half-blown,
Out of the wintry night.

Time flies, time flies!
And yet, bless me! 'tis little changed am I;
May Jesu keep from tears those infant eyes,
Be love their lullaby!

THE FUNERAL

They dressed us up in black,
Susan and Tom and me;
And, walking through the fields
All beautiful to see,
With branches high in the air
And daisy and buttercup,
We heard the lark in the clouds, —
In black dressed up.

They took us to the graves,
Susan and Tom and me,
Where the long grasses grow
And the funeral tree:
We stood and watched; and the wind
Came softly out of the sky
And blew in Susan's hair,
As I stood close by.

[44]

Back through the fields we came,
Tom and Susan and me,
And we sat in the nursery together,
And had our tea.
And, looking out of the window,
I heard the thrushes sing;
But Tom fell asleep in his chair.
He was so tired, poor thing.

THE MOTHER BIRD

Through the green twilight of a hedge
I peered, with cheek on the cool leaves pressed,
And spied a bird upon a nest:
Two eyes she had beseeching me
Meekly and brave, and her brown breast
Throbb'd hot and quick above her heart;
And then she opened her dagger bill, —
'Twas not the chirp that sparrows pipe
At early day; 'twas not the trill,
That falters through the quiet even;
But one sharp solitary note,
One desperate fierce and vivid cry
Of valiant tears, and hopeless joy,
One passionate note of victory.
Off, like a fool afraid, I sneaked,
Smiling the smile the fool smiles best,
At the mother bird in the secret hedge
Patient upon her lonely nest.

THE CHILD IN THE STORY GOES TO BED

I prythee, Nurse, come smooth my hair,
And prythee, Nurse, unloose my shoe,
And trimly turn my silken sheet
Upon my quilt of gentle blue.

My pillow sweet of lavender
Smooth with an amiable hand,
And may the dark pass peacefully by
As in the hour-glass droops the sand.

[45]

Prepare my cornered manchet sweet,
　　And in my little crystal cup
Pour out the blithe and flowering mead
　　That forthwith I may sup.

Withdraw my curtains from the night,
　　And let the crispèd crescent shine
Upon my eyelids while I sleep,
　　And soothe me with her beams benign.

Dark looms the forest far-away;
　　O, listen! through its empty dales
Rings from the solemn echoing boughs
　　The music of its nightingales.

Now quench my silver lamp, prythee,
　　And bid the harpers harp that tune
Fairies that haunt the meadowlands
　　Sing to the stars of June.

And bid them play, though I in dreams
　　No longer heed their pining strains,
For I would not to silence wake
　　When slumber o'er my senses wanes.

You Angels bright who me defend,
　　Enshadow me with curvèd wing,
And keep me in the long dark night
　　Till dawn another day shall bring.

THE CHILD IN THE STORY AWAKES

The light of dawn rose on my dreams,
　　And from afar I seemed to hear
In sleep the mellow blackbird call
　　Hollow and sweet and clear.

I prythee, Nurse, my casement open,
　　Wildly the garden peals with singing,
And hooting through the dewy pines
　　The goblins of the dark are winging.

O listen the droning of the bees,
　　That in the roses take delight!
And see a cloud stays in the blue
　　Like an angel still and bright.

[46]

The gentle sky is spread like silk,
    And, Nurse, the moon doth languish there,
As if it were a perfect jewel
    In the morning's soft-spun hair.

The greyness of the distant hills
    Is silvered in the lucid East,
See, now the sheeny-plumèd cock
    Wags haughtily his crest.

'O come you out, O come you out,
    Lily, and lavender, and lime;
The kingcup swings his golden bell,
    And plumpy cherries drum the time.

'O come you out, O come you out!
    Roses, and dew, and mignonette,
The sun is in the steep blue sky,
    Sweetly the morning star is set.'

CECIL

Ye little elves, who haunt sweet dells,
Where flowers with the dew commune,
I pray you hush the child, Cecil,
    With windlike song.

O little elves, so white she lieth,
Each eyelid gentler than the flow'r
Of the bramble, and her fleecy hair
    Like smoke of gold.

O little elves, her hands and feet
The angels muse upon, and God
Hath shut a glimpse of Paradise
    In each blue eye.

O little elves, her tiny body
Like a white flake of snow it is,
Drooping upon the pale green hood
    Of the chill snowdrop.

[47]

O little elves, with elderflower,
And pimpernel, and the white hawthorn,
Sprinkle the journey of her dreams:
  And, little elves,

Call to her magically sweet,
Lest of her very tenderness
She do forsake this rough brown earth
And return to us no more.

THE LAMPLIGHTER

When the light of day declineth,
And a swift angel through the sky
Kindleth God's tapers clear,
With ashen staff the lamplighter
Passeth along the darkling streets
To light our earthly lamps;

Lest, prowling in the darkness,
The thief should haunt with quiet tread,
Or men on evil errands set;
Or wayfarers be benighted;
Or neighbours bent from house to house
Should need a guiding torch.

He is like a needlewoman
Who deftly on a sable hem
Stitches in gleaming jewels;
Or, haply, he is like a hero,
Whose bright deeds on the long journey
Are beacons on our way.

And when in the East cometh morning,
And the broad splendour of the sun,
Then, with the tune of little birds
Ringing on high, the lamplighter
Passeth by each quiet house,
And putteth out the lamps.

[48]

I MET AT EVE

I met at eve the Prince of Sleep,
His was a still and lovely face,
He wandered through a valley steep,
   Lovely in a lonely place.

His garb was grey of lavender,
About his brows a poppy-wreath
Burned like dim coals, and everywhere
   The air was sweeter for his breath.

His twilight feet no sandals wore,
His eyes shone faint in their own flame,
Fair moths that gloomed his steps before
   Seemed letters of his lovely name.

His house is in the mountain ways,
A phantom house of misty walls,
Whose golden flocks at evening graze,
   And 'witch the moon with muffled calls.

Upwelling from his shadowy springs
Sweet waters shake a trembling sound,
There flit the hoot-owl's silent wings,
   There hath his web the silkworm wound.

Dark in his pools clear visions lurk,
And rosy, as with morning buds,
Along his dales of broom and birk
   Dreams haunt his solitary woods.

I met at eve the Prince of Sleep,
His was a still and lovely face,
He wandered through a valley steep,
   Lovely in a lonely place.

LULLABY

Sleep, sleep, thou lovely one!
The little mouse cheeps plaintively,
The nightingale in the chestnut-tree —
They sing together, bird and mouse,
In starlight, in darkness, lonely, sweet,
The wild notes and the faint notes meet —
  Sleep, sleep, thou lovely one!

Sleep, sleep, thou lovely one!
Amid the lilies floats the moth,
The mole along his galleries goeth
In the dark earth; the summer moon
Looks like a shepherd through the pane
Seeking his feeble lamb again —
  Sleep, sleep, thou lovely one!

Sleep, sleep, thou lovely one!
Time comes to keep night-watch with thee,
Nodding with roses, and the sea
Saith 'Peace! Peace!' amid his foam.
'O be still!'
The wind cries up the whispering hill —
  Sleep, sleep, thou lovely one!

ENVOY[1]

Child, do you love the flower
Shining with colour and dew
Lighting its transient hour?
  So I love you.

The lambs in the mead are at play,
'Neath a hurdle the shepherd's asleep,
From height to height of the day
  The sunbeams sweep.

[1] First published in *Songs of Childhood*, 1916.

Evening will come. And alone
The dreamer the dark will beguile;
All the world will be gone
  For a dream's brief while.

Then I shall be old; and away:
And you, with sad joy in your eyes,
Will brood over children at play
  With as loveful surmise.

ENVOY[1]

There clung three roses to a stem,
Did all their hues of summer don,
But came a wind and troubled them,
  And all were gone.

I heard three bells in unison
Clap out some transient heart's delight,
Time and the hour brought silence on
  And the dark night.

Doth not Orion even set!
O love, love, prove true alone,
Till youthful hearts ev'n love forget,
  Then, child, begone!

[1] Appeared only in *Songs of Childhood*, 1902.

Poems (1906)

FALSTAFF

'Twas in a tavern that with old age stooped
And leaned rheumatic rafters o'er his head —
A blowzed, prodigious man, which talked, and stared,
And rolled, as if with purpose, a small eye
Like a sweet Cupid in a cask of wine.
I could not view his fatness for his soul,
Which peeped like harmless lightnings and was gone;
As haps to voyagers of the summer air.
And when he laughed, Time trickled down those beams,
As in a glass; and when in self-defence
He puffed that paunch, and wagged that huge, Greek head,
Nosed like a Punchinello, then it seemed
A hundred widows wept in his small voice,
Now tenor, and now bass of drummy war.
He smiled, compact of loam, this orchard man;
Mused like a midnight, webbed with moonbeam snares
Of flitting Love; woke — and a King he stood,
Whom all the world hath in sheer jest refused
For helpless laughter's sake. And then, forfend!
Bacchus and Jove reared vast Olympus there;
And Pan leaned leering from Promethean eyes.
'Lord!' sighed his aspect, weeping o'er the jest,
'What simple mouse brought such a mountain forth?'

MACBETH

Rose, like dim battlements, the hills and reared
Steep crags into the fading primrose sky;
But in the desolate valleys fell small rain,
Mingled with drifting cloud. I saw one come,
Like the fierce passion of that vacant place,
His face turned glittering to the evening sky;
His eyes, like grey despair, fixed satelessly
On the still, rainy turrets of the storm;
And all his armour in a haze of blue.
He held no sword, bare was his hand and clenched,

As if to hide the inextinguishable blood
Murder had painted there. And his wild mouth
Seemed spouting echoes of deluded thoughts.
Around his head, like vipers all distort,
His locks shook, heavy-laden, at each stride.
If fire may burn invisible to the eye;
O, if despair strive everlastingly;
Then haunted here the creature of despair,
Fanning and fanning flame to lick upon
A soul still childish in a blackened hell.

BANQUO

What dost thou here far from thy native place?
What piercing influences of heaven have stirred
Thy heart's last mansion all-corruptible to wake,
To move, and in the sweets of wine and fire
Sit tempting madness with unholy eyes?
Begone, thou shuddering, pale anomaly!
The dark presses without on yew and thorn;
Stoops now the owl upon her lonely quest;
The pomp runs high here, and our beauteous women
Seek no cold witness — O, let murder cry,
Too shrill for human ear, only to God.
Come not in power to wreak so wild a vengeance!
Thou knowest not now the limit of man's heart;
He is beyond thy knowledge. Gaze not then,
Horror enthroned lit with insanest light!

MERCUTIO

Along an avenue of almond-trees
Came three girls chattering of their sweethearts three
And lo! Mercutio, with Byronic ease,
Out of his philosophic eye cast all
A mere flowered twig of thought, whereat —
Three hearts fell still as when an air dies out
And Venus falters lonely o'er the sea.
But when within the furthest mist of bloom
His step and form were hid, the smooth child Ann
Said, 'La, and what eyes he had!' and Lucy said,
'How sad a gentleman!' and Katherine,
'I wonder, now, what mischief he was at.'
And these three also April hid away,
Leaving the Spring faint with Mercutio.

JULIET

Sparrow and nightingale — did ever such
Strange birds consort in one untravelled heart?
And yet what signs of summer, and what signs
Of the keen snows humanity hath passed
To come to this wild apple-day! To think
So young a throat might rave so old a tune!
Youth's amber eyes reflect such ardent stars,
And capture heav'n with glancing! Was she not
Learn'd by some angel from her mother's womb
At last to be Love's mistress? doth not he
Rest all his arrows now and mutely adream
Seek his own peace in her Italian locks?
Cometh not Romeo singing in the night?—
Singing of youth — whose clust'ring locks do nod
And weave confusing shadows o'er his brow.
Sing on bright tongue and quench these fears of silence! —
But at the end waits Death to pluck his bloom,
Which is of yew the everlasting star.

JULIET'S NURSE

In old-world nursery vacant now of children,
With posied walls, familiar, fair, demure,
And facing southward o'er romantic streets,
Sits yet and gossips winter's dusk away
One gloomy, vast, glossy, and wise, and sly:
And at her side a cherried country cousin.
Her tongue claps ever like a ram's sweet bell;
There's not a name but calls a tale to mind —
Some marrowy patty of farce or melodram;
There's not a soldier but hath babes in view;
There's not on earth what minds not of the midwife:
'O, widowhood that left me still espoused!'
Beauty she sighs o'er, and she sighs o'er gold;
Gold will buy all things, even a sweet husband.
Else only Heaven is left and — farewell youth!
Yet, strangely, in that money-haunted head,
The sad, gemmed crucifix and incense blue
Is childhood come again. Her memory
Is like an ant-hill which a twig disturbs,
But twig stilled never. And to see her face,
Broad with sleek homely beams; her babied hands,

Ever like 'lighting doves, and her small eyes —
Blue wells a-twinkle, arch and lewd and pious —
To darken all sudden into Stygian gloom,
And paint disaster with uplifted whites,
Is life's epitome. She prates and prates —
A waterbrook of words o'er twelve small pebbles.
And when she dies — some grey, long, summer evening,
When the bird shouts of childhood through the dusk,
'Neath night's faint tapers — then her body shall
Lie stiff with silks of sixty thrifty years.

DESDEMONA

A stony tomb guards one who simply dreams
Of peace that shines, tho' love went down in storm—
Dreams ever a dark visage stoopeth o'er,
Whose darkness is not hatred but a mask
Love took for tend'rer loving. And when night
Steals thro' the sky to mock Othello, then
Rises she, counting at the windows high
Star after star till all her prayer be told,
And dawn repeat the glory of her end.
But on one day, in affluence of June,
At topmost flood of noon a shadow falls
Sweet at her side, chill head to snowy foot;
And then it seems the cypresses obscure
Whisper, 'O willow!'; and a shrill bird swoops,
As if the Moor had flown a silver soul
To take her captive at the key of Heaven!

IAGO

A dark lean face, a narrow, slanting eye,
Whose deeps of blackness one pale taper's beam
Haunts with a flitting madness of desire;
A heart whose cinder at the breath of passion
Glows to a momentary core of heat
Almost beyond indifference to endure:
So parched Iago frets his life away.
His scorn works ever in a brain whose wit
This world hath fools too many and gross to seek.

Ever to live incredibly alone,
Masked, shivering, deadly, with a simple Moor
Of idiot gravity, and one pale flower
Whose chill would quench in everlasting peace
His soul's unmeasured flame — O paradox!
Might he but learn the trick! — to wear her heart
One fragile hour of heedless innocence,
And then, farewell, and the incessant grave.
'O fool! O villain!'—'tis the shuttlecock
Wit never leaves at rest. It is his fate
To be a needle in a world of hay,
Where honour is the flattery of the fool;
Sin, a tame bauble; lies, a tiresome jest;
Virtue, a silly, whitewashed block of wood
For words to fell. Ah! but the secret lacking,
The secret of the child, the bird, the night,
Faded, flouted, bespattered, in days so far
Hate cannot bitter them, nor wrath deny;
Else were this Desdemona. . . . Why!
Woman a harlot is, and life a nest
Fouled by long ages of forked fools. And God —
Iago deals not with a tale so dull:
To have made the world! Fie on thee, Artisan!

CASCA

Butchers are honest though their agile knives
They wield with an engrossed dexterity.
To smile with natural hatred like a dog,
Dull, fretful, thirsty; — this is to be he
Who may unheated lave in burning blood
Hands white and large with idleness and sleep.
He is earth's hero — this plain, bloated Casca.
He glides like a great woman; while a hare
Squats in his shaggy breast, and stares, and trembles
If peeps the lightning in. So, let him pass;
His bloody hands his chosen orators.
There is much pig's flesh in a world of swine,
White as the lily.

IMOGEN

Even she too dead! all languor on her brow,
All mute humanity's last simpleness, —
And yet the roses in her cheeks unfallen!
Can death haunt silence with a silver sound?
Can death, that hushes all music to a close,
Pluck one sweet wire scarce-audible that trembles
As if a little child, called Purity,
Sang heedlessly on of his dear Imogen?
Surely if some young flowers of Spring were put
Into the tender hollow of her heart,
'Twould faintly answer, trembling in their petals.
Poise but a wild bird's feather, it will stir
On lips that even in silence wear the badge
Only of truth. Let but a cricket wake,
And sing of home, and bid her lids unseal
The unspeakable hospitality of her eyes.
O childless soul — call once her husband's name!
And even if indeed from these green hills
Of England, far, her spirit flits forlorn,
Back to its youthful mansion it will turn,
Back to the floods of sorrow these sweet locks
Yet heavy bear in drops; and Night shall see,
Unwearying as her stars, still Imogen,
Pausing 'twixt death and life on one hushed word.

POLONIUS

There haunts in Time's bare house an active ghost,
Enamoured of his name, Polonius.
He moves small fingers much, and all his speech
Is like a sampler of precisest words,
Set in the pattern of a simpleton.
His mirth floats eerily down chill corridors;
His sigh — it is a sound that loves a keyhole;
His tenderness a faint court-tarnished thing;
His wisdom prates as from a wicker cage;
His very belly is a pompous nought;
His eye a page that hath forgot his errand.
Yet in his bran — his spiritual bran —
Lies hid a child's demure, small, silver whistle
Which, to his horror, God blows, unawares.

And sets men staring. It is sad to think,
Might he but don indeed thin flesh and blood,
And pace important to Law's inmost room,
He would see, much marvelling, one immensely wise,
Named Bacon, who, at sound of his youth's step,
Would turn and call him Cousin — for the likeness.

OPHELIA

There runs a crisscross pattern of small leaves
Espalier, in a fading summer air,
And there Ophelia walks, an azure flower,
Whom wind, and snowflakes, and the sudden rain
Of love's wild skies have purified to heaven.
There is a beauty past all weeping now
In that sweet, crooked mouth, that vacant smile;
Only a lonely grey in those mad eyes,
Which never on earth shall learn their loneliness.
And when amid startled birds she sings lament,
Mocking in hope the long voice of the stream,
It seems her heart's lute hath a broken string.
Ivy she hath, that to old ruin clings;
And rosemary, that sees remembrance fade;
And pansies, deeper than the gloom of dreams;
But ah! if utterable, would this earth
Remain the base, unreal thing it is?
Better be out of sight of peering eyes;
Out — out of hearing of all-useless words,
Spoken of tedious tongues in heedless ears.
And lest, at last, the world should learn heart-secrets;
Lest that sweet wolf from some dim thicket steal;
Better the glassy horror of the stream.

HAMLET

Umbrageous cedars murmuring symphonies
Stooped in late twilight o'er dark Denmark's Prince:
He sat, his eyes companioned with dream —
Lustrous large eyes that held the world in view
As some entrancèd child's a puppet show.
Darkness gave birth to the all-trembling stars,
And a far roar of long-drawn cataracts,
Flooding immeasurable night with sound.

He sat so still, his very thoughts took wing,
And, lightest Ariels, the stillness haunted
With midge-like measures; but, at last, even they
Sank 'neath the influences of his night.
The sweet dust shed faint perfume in the gloom;
Through all wild space the stars' bright arrows fell
On the lone Prince — the troubled son of man —
On Time's dark waters in unearthly trouble:
Then, as the roar increased, and one fair tower
Of cloud took sky and stars with majesty,
He rose, his face a parchment of old age,
Sorrow hath scribbled o'er, and o'er, and o'er.

COME!

From an island of the sea
Sounds a voice that summons me, —
'Turn thy prow, sailor, come
  With the wind home!'

Sweet o'er the rainbow foam,
Sweet in the treetops, 'Come,
Coral, cliff, and watery sand,
  Sea-wave to land!

'Droop not thy lids at night,
Furl not thy sails from flight! . . .'
Cease, cease, above the wave,
  Deep as the grave!

O, what voice of the salt sea
Calls me so insistently?
Echoes, echoes, night and day, —
  'Come, come away!'

THE WINTER-BOY

I saw Jack Frost come louping o'er
  A hill of blinding snow;
And hooked upon his arm he bore
  A basket all aglow.

Cherries and damsons, peach and pear,
  The faint and moonlike quince;
Never before were fruits as rare,
  And never have been since.

[60]

'Come, will ye buy, ma'am?' says he sweet;
    And lo! began to fly
Flakes of bright, arrowy, frozen sleet
    From out the rosy sky.

'Silver nor pence, ma'am, ask I; but
    One kiss my cheek to warm, —
One with your scarlet lips tight shut
    Can do you, ma'am, no harm.'

O, and I stooped in that still place
    And pressed my lips to his;
And his cold locks about my face
    Shut darkness in my eyes.

Never, now never shall I be
    Lonely where snow is laid;
Sweet with his fruits comes louping he,
    And says the words he said.

His shrill voice echoes, slily creep
    His fingers cold and lean,
And lull my dazzled eyes asleep
    His icy locks between.

THEY TOLD ME[1]

They told me Pan was dead, but I
    Oft marvelled who it was that sang
Down the green valleys languidly
    Where the grey elder-thickets hang.

Sometimes I thought it was a bird
    My soul had charged with sorcery;
Sometimes it seemed my own heart heard
    Inland the sorrow of the sea.

But even where the primrose sets
    The seal of her pale loveliness,
I found amid the violets
    Tears of an antique bitterness.

[1] Called 'Tears' in *Poems*, 1906.

SORCERY

'What voice is that I hear
  Crying across the pool?'
'It is the voice of Pan you hear,
Crying his sorceries shrill and clear,
  In the twilight dim and cool.'

'What song is it he sings,
  Echoing from afar;
While the sweet swallow bends her wings,
Filling the air with twitterings,
  Beneath the brightening star?'

The woodman answered me,
  His faggot on his back: —
'Seek not the face of Pan to see;
Flee from his clear note summoning thee
  To darkness deep and black!

'He dwells in the thickest shade,
  Piping his notes forlorn
Of sorrow never to be allayed;
Turn from his coverts sad
  Of twilight unto morn!'

The woodman passed away
  Along the forest path;
His axe shone keen and grey
In the last beams of day:
  And all was still as death: —

Only Pan singing sweet
  Out of Earth's fragrant shade;
I dreamed his eyes to meet,
And found but shadow laid
  Before my tired feet.

Comes no more dawn to me,
  Nor bird of open skies.
Only his woods' deep gloom I see
  Till, at the end of all, shall rise,
Afar and tranquilly,
  Death's stretching sea.

THE CHILDREN OF STARE

Winter is fallen early
On the house of Stare;
Birds in reverberating flocks
Haunt its ancestral box;
Bright are the plenteous berries
In clusters in the air.

Still is the fountain's music,
The dark pool icy still,
Whereupon a small and sanguine sun
Floats in a mirror on,
Into a West of crimson,
From a South of daffodil.

'Tis strange to see young children
In such a wintry house;
Like rabbits' on the frozen snow
Their tell-tale footprints go;
Their laughter rings like timbrels
'Neath evening ominous:

Their small and heightened faces
Like wine-red winter buds;
Their frolic bodies gentle as
Flakes in the air that pass,
Frail as the twirling petal
From the briar of the woods.

Above them silence lours,
Still as an arctic sea;
Light fails; night falls; the wintry moon
Glitters; the crocus soon
Will open grey and distracted
On earth's austerity:

Thick mystery, wild peril,
Law like an iron rod: —
Yet sport they on in Spring's attire,
Each with his tiny fire
Blown to a core of ardour
By the awful breath of God.

AGE

This ugly old crone —
Every beauty she had
When a maid, when a maid.
Her beautiful eyes,
Too youthful, too wise
Seemed ever to come
To so lightless a home,
Cold and dull as a stone.
And her cheeks — who would guess
Cheeks cadaverous as this
Once with colours were gay
As the flower on its spray?
And who would believe
Life could bring one to grieve
So much as to make
Lips bent for love's sake
So thin and so grey?

O Youth, come away!
All she asks is her lone,
This old, desolate crone.
She needs us no more;
She is too old to care
For the charms that of yore
Made her body so fair.
Past repining, past care,
She lives but to bear
One or two fleeting years
Earth's indifference. Her tears
Have lost now their heat.
Her hands and her feet
Now shake but to be
Shed as leaves from a tree,
And her poor heart beats on
Like a sea — the storm gone.

THE GLIMPSE

Art thou asleep? or have thy wings
Wearied of my unchanging skies?
Or, haply, is it fading dreams
    Are in my eyes?

Not even an echo in my heart
Tells me the courts thy feet trod last,
Bare as a leafless wood it is,
    The summer past.

My inmost mind is like a book
The reader dulls with lassitude,
Wherein the same old lovely words
    Sound poor and rude.

Yet through this vapid surface, I
Seem to see old-time deeps; I see,
Past the dark painting of the hour,
    Life's ecstasy.

Only a moment; as when day
Is set, and in the shade of night,
Through all the clouds that compassed her,
    Stoops into sight.

Pale, changeless, everlasting Dian,
Gleams on the prone Endymion,
Troubles the dulness of his dreams:
    And then is gone.

REMEMBRANCE

The sky was like a waterdrop
    In shadow of a thorn,
Clear, tranquil, beautiful,
    Dark, forlorn.

Lightning along its margin ran;
    A rumour of the sea
Rose in profundity and sank
    Into infinity.

Lofty and few the elms, the stars
　In the vast boughs most bright;
I stood a dreamer in a dream
　In the unstirring night.

Not wonder, worship, not even peace
　Seemed in my heart to be:
Only the memory of one,
　Of all most dead[1] to me.

SHADOW

Even the beauty of the rose doth cast,
When its bright, fervid noon is past,
A still and lengthening shadow in the dust
　　Till darkness come
　　And take its strange dream home.

The transient bubbles of the water paint
'Neath their frail arch a shadow faint;
The golden nimbus of the windowed saint,
　　Till shine the stars,
　　Casts pale and trembling bars.

The loveliest thing earth hath, a shadow hath,
A dark and livelong hint of death,
Haunting it ever till its last faint breath . . .
　　Who, then, may tell
The beauty of heaven's shadowless asphodel?

UNREGARDING

Put by thy days like withered flowers
　In twilight hidden away:
Memory shall up-build thee bowers
　Sweeter than they.

Hoard not from swiftness of thy stream
　The shallowest cruse of tears:
Pools still as heaven shall lovelier dream
　In future years.

[1] Always printed thus. A misprint for 'dear'?

Squander thy love as she that flings
    Her soul away on night;
Lovely are love's far echoings,
    Height unto height.

O, make no compact with the sun,
    No compact with the moon!
Night falls full-cloaked, and light is gone
    Sudden and soon.

TREACHERY

She had amid her ringlets bound
Green leaves to rival their dark hue;
How could such locks with beauty bound
    Dry up their dew,
    Wither them through and through?

She had within her dark eyes lit
Sweet fires to burn all doubt away;
Yet did those fires, in darkness lit,
    Burn but a day,
    Not even till twilight stay.

She had within a dusk of words
A vow in simple splendour set;
How, in the memory of such words,
    Could she forget
    That vow — the soul of it?

IN VAIN

I knocked upon thy door ajar,
While yet the woods with buds were grey;
Nought but a little child I heard
    Warbling at break of day.

I knocked when June had lured her rose
To mask the sharpness of its thorn;
Knocked yet again, heard only yet
    Thee singing of the morn.

[67]

The frail convolvulus had wreathed
Its cup, but the faint flush of eve
Lingered upon thy Western wall;
    Thou hadst no word to give.

Once yet I came; the winter stars
Above thy house wheeled wildly bright;
Footsore I stood before thy door —
    Wide open into night.

THE MIRACLE

Who beckons the green ivy up
  Its solitary tower of stone?
What spirit lures the bindweed's cup
    Unfaltering on;
Calls even the starry lichen to climb
By agelong inches endless Time?

Who bids the hollyhock uplift
  Her rod of fast-sealed buds on high;
Fling wide her petals — silent, swift,
    Lovely to the sky?
Since as she kindled, so she will fade,
Flower above flower in squalor laid.

Ever the heavy billow rears
  All its sea-length in green, hushed wall;
But totters as the shore it nears,
    Foams to its fall;
Where was its mark? on what vain quest
Rose that great water from its rest? . . .

So creeps ambition on; so climb
  Man's vaunting thoughts. He, set on high,
Forgets his birth, small space, brief time,
    That he shall die;
Dreams blindly in his stagnant air;
Consumes his strength; strips himself bare;

Rejects delight, ease, pleasure, hope;
  Seeking in vain, but seeking yet,
Past earthly promise, earthly scope,
    On one aim set:
As if, like Chaucer's child, he thought
All but '*O Alma!*' nought.

EVEN ROSEMARY

I have seen a grave this day,
Yet no worm did therein lie; —
Only sweet Faith laid away,
　　Lonely to die,
Lonely as he lived, to die.

There's no buds. Ev'n rosemary
Hath sad dreams for smell withal;
Ev'n Hope's rose's leaf would be
　　Restless to fall;
To have done, and fade, and fall.

I will never walk again
Where such brittle dust doth lie;
Where to weep were quite in vain;
　　Vain too to sigh,
Only vain to weep and sigh.

Flee afar, then, heart, lest thou,
Quick with brooding on that spot,
Feign to see a dead face now,
　　Features forgot,
Eyes ev'n Heaven shall open not!

KEEP INNOCENCY

Like an old battle, youth is wild
With bugle and spear, and counter cry,
Fanfare and drummery, yet a child
Dreaming of that sweet chivalry,
The piercing terror cannot see.

He, with a mild and serious eye,
Along the azure of the years,
Sees the sweet pomp sweep hurtling by;
But he sees not death's blood and tears,
Sees not the plunging of the spears.

And all the strident horror of
Horse and rider, in red defeat,
Is only music fine enough
To lull him into slumber sweet
In fields where ewe and lambkin bleat.

O, if with such simplicity
Himself take arms and suffer war;
With beams his targe shall gilded be,
Though in the thickening gloom be far
The steadfast light of any star!

Though hoarse War's eagle on him perch,
Quickened with guilty lightnings — there
It shall in vain for terror search,
Where a child's eyes 'neath bloody hair
Gaze purely through the dingy air.

And when the wheeling rout is spent,
Though in the heaps of slain he lie;
Or lonely in his last content;
Quenchless shall burn in secrecy
The flame Death knows his victors by.

THE PHANTOM

Wilt thou never come again,
    Beauteous one?
Yet the woods are green and dim,
Yet the birds' deluding cry
Echoes in the hollow sky,
Yet the falling waters brim
The clear pool which thou wast fain
To paint thy lovely cheek upon,
    Beauteous one!

I may see the thorny rose
    Stir and wake
The dark dewdrop on her gold;
But thy secret will she keep
Half divulged — yet all untold,
Since a child's heart woke from sleep.

The faltering sunbeam fades and goes;
The night-bird whistles in the brake;
    The willows quake;
Utter quiet falls; the wind
    Sighs no more.
Yet it seems the silence yearns
But to catch thy fleeting foot;
Yet the wandering glow-worm burns
Lest her lamp should light thee not —
Thee whom I shall never find;
Though thy shadow lean before,
Thou thyself return'st no more —
    Never more.

All the world's woods, tree o'er tree,
    Come to nought.
Birds, flowers, beasts, how transient they,
Angels of a flying day.
Love is quenched; dreams drown in sleep;
Ruin nods along the deep:
Only thou immortally
    Hauntest on
This poor earth in Time's flux caught;
Hauntest on, pursued, unwon,
Phantom child of memory,
    Beauteous one!

VOICES[1]

Who is it calling by the darkened river
    Where the moss lies smooth and deep,

[1] *Poems*, 1906, had a 4th stanza:
    'So are we haunted; night and day
        Invisible witnesses
  Speak, or keep silent; watch and wait;
        Steadfast and slumberless: —
  Shades of the air, shades in the mind,
    Ghosts in the heart that weep
  In this thicket of all perplexities
        And tumult, "Sleep!"'

And the dark trees lean unmoving arms,
    Silent and vague in sleep,
And the bright-heeled constellations pass
    In splendour through the gloom;
Who is it calling o'er the darkened river
        In music, 'Come!'?

Who is it wandering in the summer meadows
    Where the children stoop and play
In the green faint-scented flowers, spinning
    The guileless hours away?
Who touches their bright hair? who puts
    A wind-shell to each cheek,
Whispering betwixt its breathing silences,
        'Seek! seek!'?

Who is it watching in the gathering twilight
    When the curfew bird hath flown
On eager wings, from song to silence,
    To its darkened nest alone?
Who takes for brightening eyes the stars,
    For locks the still moonbeam,
Sighs through the dews of evening peacefully
        Falling, 'Dream!'?

THULE

If thou art sweet as they are sad
    Who on the shores of Time's salt sea
Watch on the dim horizon fade
    Ships bearing love to night and thee;

If past all beacons Hope hath lit
    In the dark wanderings of the deep
They who unwilling traverse it
    Dream not till dawn unseal their sleep;

Ah, cease not in thy winds to mock
    Us, who yet wake, but cannot see
Thy distant shores; who at each shock
    Of the waves onset faint for thee!

THE BIRTHNIGHT: TO F.[1]

Dearest, it was a night
That in its darkness rocked Orion's stars;
A sighing wind ran faintly white
Along the willows, and the cedar boughs
Laid their wide hands in stealthy peace across
The starry silence of their antique moss:
No sound save rushing air
Cold, yet all sweet with Spring,
And in thy mother's arms, couched weeping there,
      Thou, lovely thing.

THE DEATH-DREAM

Who, now, put dreams into thy slumbering mind?
Who, with bright Fear's lean taper, crossed a hand
Athwart its beam, and stooping, truth maligned,
Spake so thy spirit speech should understand,
And with a dread 'He's dead!' awaked a peal
Of frenzied bells along the vacant ways
Of thy poor earthly heart; waked thee to steal,
Like dawn distraught upon unhappy days,
To prove nought, nothing? Was it Time's large voice
Out of the inscrutable future whispered so?
Or but the horror of a little noise
Earth wakes at dead of night? Or does Love know
When his sweet wings weary and droop, and even
In sleep cries audibly a shrill remorse?
Or, haply, was it I who out of dream
Stole but a little way where shadows course,
Called back to thee across the eternal stream?

'WHERE IS THY VICTORY?'

None, none can tell where I shall be
When the unclean earth covers me;
Only in surety if thou cry
Where my perplexèd ashes lie,
Know, 'tis but death's necessity
That keeps my tongue from answering thee.

[1] *Poems*, 1906, did not have 'To F.' in title. 'F.' was the poet's daughter, Florence.

Even if no more my shadow may
Lean for a moment in thy day;
No more the whole earth lighten, as if,
Thou near, it had nought else to give:
Surely 'tis but Heaven's strategy
To prove death immortality.

Yet should I sleep — and no more dream,
Sad would the last awakening seem,
If my cold heart, with love once hot,
Had thee in sleep remembered not:
How could I wake to find that I
Had slept alone, yet easefully?

Or should in sleep glad visions come:
Sick, in an alien land, for home
Would be my eyes in their bright beam;
Awake, we know 'tis not a dream;
Asleep, some devil in the mind
Might truest thoughts with false enwind.

Life is a mockery if death
Have the least power men say it hath.
As to a hound that mewing waits,
Death opens, and shuts to, his gates;
Else even dry bones might rise and say, —
'Tis *ye* are dead and laid away.'

Innocent children out of nought
Build up a universe of thought,
And out of silence fashion Heaven:
So, dear, is this poor dying even,
Seeing thou shalt be touched, heard, seen,
Better than when dust stood between.

FOREBODING

Thou canst not see him standing by —
    Time — with a poppied hand
Stealing thy youth's simplicity,
Even as falls unceasingly
    His waning sand.

He'll pluck thy childish roses, as
    Summer from her bush
Strips all the loveliness that was;
Even to the silence evening has
    Thy laughter hush.

Thy locks too faint for earthly gold,
    The meekness of thine eyes,
He will darken and dim, and to his fold
Drive, 'gainst the night, thy stainless, old
    Innocencies;

Thy simple words confuse and mar,
    Thy tenderest thoughts delude,
Draw a long cloud athwart thy star,
Still with loud timbrels heaven's far
    Faint interlude.

Thou canst not see; I see, dearest;
    O, then, yet patient be,
Though love refuse thy heart all rest,
Though even love wax angry, lest
    Love should lose *thee*!

THE HAPPY ENCOUNTER

I saw sweet Poetry turn troubled eyes
    On shaggy Science nosing on the grass,
    For by that way poor Poetry must pass
On her long pilgrimage to Paradise.
He snuffled, grunted, squealed; perplexed by flies,
    Parched, weatherworn, and near of sight, alas,
    From peering close where very little was
In dens secluded from the open skies.

But Poetry in bravery went down,
    And called his name, soft, clear, and fearlessly;
Stooped low, and stroked his muzzle overgrown;
    Refreshed his drought with dew; wiped pure and free
    His eyes: and lo! laughed loud for joy to see
In those grey deeps the azure of her own.

[75]

COUP DE GRÂCE

So Malice sharp'd his pen, and nibbled it,
  And leered 'neath faltering eyelids at the flame
  Of his calm candle till a notion came,
Coarse, acrid, with a distant hint of wit.
Once more he simmered, and once more he writ,
  Till not a dash was dull, a comma lame;
  Then exquisitely failed to sign his name,
Leaving the world to trace a slug by its spit.

Such was the barb, O Keats, (vain tongues would have),
  Troubled in its calm flight thy lovely art;
Cankered thy youth, thy faith; abashed the brave,
  Untarnishable sweetness of thy heart:
  How should these dullards dream *they* winged the dart
That pierced thee, silent, in th'unanswering grave!

APRIL

Come, then, with showers; I love thy cloudy face
  Gilded with splendour of the sunbeams thro'
  The heedless glory of thy locks. I know
The arch, sweet languour of thy fleeting grace,
The windy lovebeams of thy dwelling-place,
  Thy dim dells wherein azure bluebells blow,
  The brimming rivers where thy lightnings go
Harmless and full and swift from race to race.

Thou takest all young hearts captive with thine eyes;
  At rumour of thee the tongues of children ring
Louder than bees; the golden poplars rise
  Like trumps of peace; and birds, on homeward wing,
Fly mocking echoes shrill along the skies,
  Above the waves' grave diapasoning.

SEA-MAGIC
To R.I.[1]

My heart faints in me for the distant sea.
  The roar of London is the roar of ire
  The lion utters in his old desire
For Libya out of dim captivity.

[1] Roger Ingpen.

The long bright silver of Cheapside I see,
　Her gilded weathercocks on roof and spire
　　Exulting eastward in the western fire;
All things recall one heart-sick memory:—

Ever the rustle of the advancing foam,
　The surges' desolate thunder, and the cry
　　As of some lone babe in the whispering sky;
Ever I peer into the restless gloom
　To where a ship clad dim and loftily
Looms steadfast in the wonder of her home.

MESSENGERS

A few all-faithful words, a glance from eyes
　That in their deeps hide hosts they cannot see —
　Phantoms of loveliest simplicity;
A transient touch — some bird's that twittering flies
Into the primrose of the deepening skies;
　A child's pure cheek pressed cold and tranquilly
　Upon a brow ashamed, in misery;
A voice that sings easefully echo-wise:

Whence are they in a world so alien?
　Are they the waterdrops of that vast flood
Death shall unloose? Shall all they hint, again
　In fulness be retold? Shall this wild blood
That rocks to them, lull down to stillness when
　These light-wing messengers flit back to God?

IRREVOCABLE

I sometimes wonder what my life doth mean
　Now you are gone; the long, bright days, the nights
　Of silence, the vicissitudes, the sights,
The intrusive sounds, the dull, continuous scene —
It only minds me of the might-have-been,
　And in itself a taper is that lights
　Its own dark solitude: my spirit fights
In vain to pierce the veil and look within.

The fountain of my tears is sealed and dry;
  I do not grieve; my laughter is a jest;
My prayers an arid bitterness; each sigh
  The heedless habit of a tired breast.
My heart is dead; and when I come to die,
  Only to think of you no more were best.

WINTER COMING

O, thou art like an autumn to my days,
  Shining in still, sweet light on lonelier hours
  Of yellowing leaves, and well-nigh faded flowers;
In thy dear sight the birds renew their lays,
But with how faint a cheer! how meek their praise
  Rememb'ring April gone! — his crystal showers,
  His heav'n-surmounting wind-engirdled towers,
And all the graveness of his childlike ways.

The hours press closer on to winter now;
  In misty solitudes brief suns arise;
  And all the wonder now hath left my eyes,
And all my heart sinks to remember how
  Once, once we loved, we who are grown so wise —
Youth vanished, winter coming — I and thou!

THE MARKET-PLACE

My mind is like a clamorous market-place.
  All day in wind, rain, sun, its babel wells;
  Voice answering to voice in tumult swells.
Chaffering and laughing, pushing for a place,
My thoughts haste on, gay, strange, poor, simple, base;
  This one buys dust, and that a bauble sells:
  But none to any scrutiny hints or tells
The haunting secrets hidden in each sad face.

The clamour quietens when the dark draws near;
  Strange looms the earth in twilight of the West,[1]
Lonely with one sweet star serene and clear,
  Dwelling, when all this place is hushed to rest,
  On vacant stall, gold, refuse, worst and best,
Abandoned utterly in haste and fear.

[1] 'Ay, sad, 'neath sigh and smile, frown, laughter, jeer;
  Yet sad — like that still twilight in the West,'
                    (Poems, 1906)

ANATOMY

By chance my fingers, resting on my face,
  Stayed suddenly where in its orbit shone
  The lamp of all things beautiful; then on,
Following more heedfully, did softly trace
Each arch and prominence and hollow place
  That shall revealed be when all else is gone —
  Warmth, colour, roundness — to oblivion,
And nothing left but darkness and disgrace.

Life like a moment passed seemed then to be;
  A transient dream this raiment that it wore;
While spelled my hand out its mortality,
  Made certain all that had seemed doubt before:
Proved — O how vaguely, yet how lucidly! —
  How much death does: and yet can do no more.

EVEN IN THE GRAVE

I laid my inventory at the hand
  Of Death, who in his gloomy arbour sate;
  And while he conned it, sweet and desolate
I heard Love singing in that quiet land.
He read the record even to the end —
  The heedless, livelong injuries of Fate,
  The burden of foe, the burden of love and hate;
The wounds of foe, the bitter wounds of friend:

All, all, he read, ay, even the indifference,
  The vain talk, vainer silence, hope and dream.
He questioned me: 'What seek'st thou then instead?'
  I bowed my face in the pale evening gleam.
Then gazed he on me with strange innocence:
  'Even in the grave thou wilt have thyself,' he said.

OMNISCIENCE[1]

Why look'd'st thou on the beauties of the earth
So gravely in thy deep omniscience;
Turn'd'st from the dews of their unclouded birth
In woods where children call, and innocence
Broods like a dream within a lovely face,
To one wan hint, one backward glance on grief,
On darken'd eyes beyond Time's fleeting grace —
Death heavy and endless of a life too brief?

O love immeasurably meek that scanned,
Past all earth's fickle hopes, past beauty, lust,
The tottering palaces of wind and sand,
Pride and vain pomp, tears, ashes, rapture, dust,
The unearthly tomb whose fading stone shall keep
Man, till his Saviour come, at peace asleep!

BRIGHT LIFE

'Come now,' I said, 'put off these webs of death,
    Distract this leaden yearning of thine eyes
    From lichened banks of peace, sad mysteries
Of dust fallen-in where passed the flitting breath:
Turn thy sick thoughts from him that slumbereth
    In mouldered linen to the living skies,
    The sun's bright-clouded principalities,
The salt deliciousness the sea-breeze hath!

'Lay thy warm hand on earth's cold clods and think
    What exquisite greenness sprouts from these to grace
The moving fields of summer; on the brink
    Of archèd waves the sea-horizon trace,
Whence wheels night's galaxy; and in silence sink
    Thy pride in rapture of life's dwelling-place!'

[1] *Poems,* 1906, carried a quotation beneath the title:
      'Strew me o'er with maiden flowers.'
                                                    Henry VIII

HUMANITY

'Ever exulting in thyself; on fire
    To flaunt the purple of the Universe,
    To strut and strut, and thy great part rehearse;
Ever the slave of every proud desire;
Come now a little down where sports thy sire;
    Choose thy small better from thy abounding worse;
    Prove thou thy lordship who hadst dust for nurse,
And for thy swaddling the primeval mire!'

Then stooped our Manhood nearer, deep and still,
    As from earth's mountains an unvoyaged sea;
Hushed my faint voice in its great peace until
    It seemed but a bird's cry in eternity;
And in its future loomed the undreamable,
    And in its past slept simple men like me.

GLORIA MUNDI

Upon a bank, easeless with knobs of gold,
    Beneath a canopy of noonday smoke,
I saw a measureless Beast, morose and bold,
    With eyes like one from filthy dreams awoke,
Who stares upon the daylight in despair
For very terror of the nothing there.

This beast in one flat hand clutched vulture-wise
    A glittering image of itself in jet,
And with the other groped about its eyes
    To drive away the dreams that pestered it;
And never ceased its coils to toss and beat
The mire encumbering its feeble feet.

Sharp was its hunger, though continually
    It seemed a cud of stones to ruminate,
And often like a dog let glittering lie
    This meatless fare, its foolish gaze to sate;
Once more convulsively to stoop its jaw,
Or seize the morsel with an envious paw.

Indeed, it seemed a hidden enemy
    Must lurk within the clouds above that bank,

It strained so wildly its pale, stubborn eye,
   To pierce its own foul vapours dim and dank;
Till, wearied out, it raved in wrath and foam,
Daring that Nought Invisible to come.

Ay, and it seemed some strange delight to find
   In this unmeaning din, till, suddenly,
As if it heard a rumour on the wind,
   Or far away its freër children cry,
Lifting its face made-quiet, there it stayed,
Till died the echo its own rage had made.

That place alone was barren where it lay;
   Flowers bloomed beyond, utterly sweet and fair;
And even its own dull heart might think to stay
   In livelong thirst of a clear river there,
Flowing from unseen hills to unheard seas,
Through a still vale of yew and almond trees.

And then I spied in the lush green below
   Its tortured belly, One, like silver, pale,
With fingers closed upon a rope of straw,
   That bound the Beast, squat neck to hoary tail;
Lonely in all that verdure faint and deep,
He watched the monster as a shepherd sheep.

I marvelled at the power, strength, and rage
   Of this poor creature in such slavery bound;
Fettered with worms of fear; forlorn with age;
   Its blue wing-stumps stretched helpless on the ground;
While twilight faded into darkness deep,
And he who watched it piped its pangs asleep.

IDLENESS

I saw old Idleness, fat, with great cheeks
Puffed to the huge circumference of a sigh,
But past all tinge of apples long ago.
His boyish fingers twiddled up and down
The filthy remnant of a cup of physic
That thicked in odour all the while he stayed.
His eyes were sad as fishes that swim up
And stare upon an element not theirs

Through a thin skin of shrewish water, then
Turn on a languid fin, and dip down, down,
Into unplumbed, vast, oozy deeps of dream.
His stomach was his master, and proclaimed it;
And never were such meagre puppets made[1]
The slaves of such a tyrant, as his thoughts
Of that obese epitome of ills.

Trussed up he sat, the mockery of himself;
And when upon the wan green of his eye
I marked the gathering lustre of a tear,
Thought I myself must weep, until I caught
A grey, smug smile of satisfaction smirch
His pallid features at his misery.
And laugh did I, to see the little snares
He had set for pests to vex him: his great feet
Prisoned in greater boots; so narrow a stool
To seat such elephantine parts as his;
Ay, and the book he read, a Hebrew Bible;
And, to incite a gross and backward wit,
An old, crabbed, wormed, Greek dictionary; and
A foxy Ovid bound in dappled calf.

GOLIATH

Still as a mountain with dark pines and sun
He stood between the armies, and his shout
Rolled from the empyrean above the host:
'Bid any little flea ye have come forth,
And wince at death upon my finger-nail!'
He turned his large-boned face; and all his steel
Tossed into beams the lustre of the noon;
And all the shaggy horror of his locks
Rustled like locusts in a field of corn.
The meagre pupil of his shameless eye
Moved like a cormorant over a glassy sea.
He stretched his limbs, and laughed into the air,

---

[1] 'And never were such meagre pupils set
Before so vexed a tyrant, as his thoughts
Before that gross epitome of ills.
There seemed no notion i' him not of himself;' (*Poems*, 1906)

To feel the groaning sinews of his breast,
And the long gush of his swol'n arteries pause:
And, nodding, wheeled, towering in all his height.
Then, like a wind that hushes, he gazed and saw
Down, down, far down upon the untroubled green,
A shepherd-boy that swung a little sling.

Goliath shut his lids to drive that mote
Which vexed the eastern azure of his eye,
Out of his vision; and stared down again.
Yet stood the youth there, ruddy in the flare
Of his vast shield, nor spake, nor quailed, gazed up,
As one might scan a mountain to be scaled.
Then, as it were, a voice unearthly still
Cried in the cavern of his bristling ear,
'His name is Death!' . . . And, like the flush
That dyes Sahara to its lifeless verge,
His brows' bright brass flamed into sudden crimson;
And his great spear leapt upward, lightning-like,
Shaking a dreadful thunder in the air;
Span betwixt earth and sky, bright as a berg
That hoards the sunlight in a myriad spires,
Crashed: and struck echo through an army's heart.

Then paused Goliath, and stared down again.
And fleet-foot Fear from rolling orbs perceived
Steadfast, unharmed, a stooping shepherd-boy
Frowning upon the target of his face.
And wrath tossed suddenly up once more his hand;
And a deep groan grieved all his strength in him.
He breathed; and, lost in dazzling darkness, prayed —
Besought his reins, his gloating gods, his youth:
And turned to smite what he no more could see.

Then sped the singing pebble-messenger,
The chosen of the Lord from Israel's brooks,
Fleet to its mark, and hollowed a light path
Down to the appalling Babel of his brain.
And, like the smoke of dreaming Soufrière,
Dust rose in cloud, spread wide, slow silted down
Softly all softly on his armour's blaze.

YOUTH

With splendour shod sweeps Sirius through the night,
But Youth yet brightlier runs his course than he.
Youth hath the raiment of his childhood doffed
At morning-prime by life's resounding sea,
And lonely in beauty stands confronting Heaven.
He strides lithe-limbed, magnificently armed;
His young head helmeted with high desire;
His heart a haven of braveries fleet and eager;
His eyes like heroes never to be subdued,
And all man's passionate history in his blood.
Youth is Adonis, panting for the chase,
Scorning all languor, blandishment, all ease,
Scorning to dally while the noon slips by,
While rings the horn, fleets golden and sweet the hour,
And bursts untamed Ambition through the glades.
Oh, in what wrath he sees still Evening pour
Her crystal vial from the darkening West!
Now is an end to day's bright prowess come;
The flaming sunbeams multitudinous
Fade, as they kindled, on the unfolded rose.
He loves not Night's pale solitary brows,
Nor silver Hesper in the shadowy steep,
But like a panther fretteth in his lair,
Turning to slumb'r as to his strength's disgrace;
To sigh in dream 'neath moonlight's arrowy showers,
Marv'ling what makes Apollo's lute so still.
But dawn ascends. The night-watch'd stars shall not
Cry from heav'n's battlements in vain of day.
Earth wakens, cold with flowers, and the mists,
Smitten of light, fly, fall in radiant dew.
Birds mounting to the dayspring pour their throats;
And in like music she beguileth him: —
'Thou babe, here is my breast! Thou foolish one,
Strip off dull sleep; thy mother — here am I!'
And frowning up he leaps to her smooth arms,
As mounts the fledgling eagle tow'rd the sun . . .
How hasten his echoing feet when sweet tongues call,
And Love's unerring archery sings nigh!
Dim then with incense burns his heart of flame;
His thoughts are aisles where ever voices quire:
And silence is divine with folded wings.
He voyages at a hazard Arctic seas;
Scales, as for pastime, ice-encinctured Alps;
No torrent daunts him; no abyss appals;

[85]

Wind ne'er so faintly the far horn of danger,
Its echo tingles on a listening ear;
Whithersoever summon it he'll follow,
And vain were every bounty earth can squander
To salve the sorrow for a deed undared.
He pines to set desire beyond his scope,
And beauteous childhood wells into his soul
In covet of the fruits that droop and burn
Where rise th' unchanging terraces of death.
What worth renown when all that dawn conceived
Fades to a phantom in the chimes of night?
What worth the flattery of a myriad tongues
If mute be the proud umpire of his heart?
He'll strive him for an amaranthine crown
Outlasting laurel and the world's applause.
Earth but a shadow is of beauty cast
In trembling beams upon the stream of Time:
He'll set his heart no more on shadows now;
But brood in envy of those high summits Man
Hath left to sparkle in midmost heav'n alone;
Strive with smooth lead to plumb the unanswering deeps,
Where Wisdom heark'ns the music of her wells.
He'll walk in sure confederacy with truth.
Betwixt him and the Hills Celestial falls
Only a blinding avalanche of sun . . .
Flow'rs, birds, the river rushing in its strength,
The pine upon the mountains, the broad wind
Burdened with snowy coldness, the salt sea,
The shalms of morning — Youth's wild heart holds all; —
All glory, all wonder, purity, beauty, grace,
All things conceived of man, except defeat.
So spurns he hope: his hope is certainty.
And faith — while every act is faith transfigured,
How should through mournful shadows glance such eyes?
God walketh in His brightness on the hills,
And sitteth in the wonder of the bow,
And calleth o'er the waters of delight: —
What were all Time to prove all gratitude?
What life's brief dust to Heav'n's unfading rose? . . .
How fleet a foot then Youth's for long pursuit!
How high a courage to search wisdom out,
While he unwitting of't burns folly away!
Is aught too bold, too infinite, to dream
Fate's arm may guard for babes to spring from him,
Who flings his life down, drenched with rapture through,
To buy unchallenged honour for his bones?

THE VOICE OF MELANCHOLY

'Return from out thy stillness, though the dust
Lie thick upon thy earthly beauty, though
The ever-wandering shapes of Night creep through
Youth's fallen tabernacle! Now in long
Surge of recurrent light the days swing by,
Soundless above thine ears once musical,
Unnumbered by a heart expert in love,
Unmarked by those fall'n princes once thine eyes.—
Oh, what defeat, bright warrior, what disgrace,
To fret entwinèd in the bindweed's root,
And rot like manna, lovelier than the rose!
Once thou would'st turn thy face enriched with smiles,
Thy lips a thought asunder, and thy hair
Shining within the sun's magnificent ray;
Stand would'st thou like a beacon by deep seas: —
All light, all excellence, all joy, gone now;
Even the classic beauty of thy face
Melted like snow; dark as a moon eclipsed;
Never to bright'n again 'neath endless night . . .'
So did I brood, unanswered and alone,
Crying, 'Return, return!'
                    O simple fool!
What would'st thou out of the deep grave should rise?
What, from amid death's cypresses, awake;
Heave up the sod; press back the fruited boughs;
And lift his eyes across the tombs on thee?
Would love burn there, or measureless reproach?
Would Life's bright mantle, stiff with idiot pomp,
Lie easy on shoulders whence a shroud had fall'n?
Would Morn's shrill nightingale above his brows
Ring sweet on ears long-sealed in echoless peace?
Would those grey hands caress earth's tarnish'd orb,
And those still feet be amorous of spurs?
And that unutterably agèd head,
Darken'd with pansies fadeless, changeless, still,
How would it don again youth's triple crown,
Piercing the keenlier as its roses die?
Nay, but the very wind that stirred his hair
Would seem a tempest to sleep deep as his;
And the perplexèd galaxy of the stars
Intolerable cressets to his eyes,
Accustomed to a night as dark as his;
And the pale dew of daisied turf at dawn
The wine of madness to lips dry as his.

Oh, with what shuddering would those atoms meet!
With what a burning sluggardry that blood
Creep thro' its long disusèd channels from
The roaring chaos of his heart! What grief
Would wildly ring in the first words he said!
What sad astonishment besteep that brain,
And tears more pitiable than infancy's
Blur the estrangèd beauty of the dawn! . . .
Leave thou his memory, as his dust, at rest;
Nor burden peace with lamentable cries!
There lurks no shadow in the crypt of death;
Nor any shadow in the height of heaven:
Beyond the survey of the dark earth gone
He bides encloistered ev'n from love's surmise.
Cry then no more, 'Return, return!' — no more!
Thy thoughts are shallow, thy experience brief;
Whence learnedst *thou* of the riches of the grave?

'PORTRAIT OF A BOY'

Velazquez

At evens with the copious April clouds;
With meek, wild face he stands; and in his eye
Deeps where the empyrean ever broods,
And in his mouth some femininity.—
Ah! for we know his secret, hath not life
So strangely shod his feet lest, suddenly,
He should remember him — the babbling strife
Of Venus' sparrows — lest he stoop and fly,
Chafing at earth, into that April sky?

UNPAUSING

O sweetest, stay!
One moment in thy lonely play
    Turn, child, and look
Ev'n but a little on that great-leaf book,
Whose livelong record when thine eyes are old
Will seem, how lovely a tale, how briefly told!

VAIN FINDING

Ever before my face there went
  Betwixt earth's buds and me
A beauty beyond earth's content,
  A hope — half memory:
Till in the woods one evening —
  Ah! eyes as dark as they,
Fastened on mine unwontedly,
  Grey, and dear heart, how grey!

VIRTUE

Her breast is cold; her hands how faint and wan!
  And the deep wonder of her starry eyes
  Seemingly lost in cloudless Paradise,
And all earth's sorrows out of memory gone.
Yet sings her clear voice unrelenting on
  Of loveliest impossibilities;
  Though echo only answer her with sighs
Of effort wasted and delights forgone.

Spent, baffled, 'wildered, hated and despised,
  Her straggling warriors hasten to defeat;
By wounds distracted, and by night surprised,
  Fall where death's darkness and oblivion meet:
Yet, yet: O breast how cold! O hope how far!
Grant my son's ashes lie where these men are!

NAPOLEON

'What is the world, O soldiers?
    It is I:
  I, this incessant snow,
    This northern sky;
  Soldiers, this solitude
    Through which we go
      Is I.'

ENGLAND

No lovelier hills than thine have laid
　My tired thoughts to rest:
No peace of lovelier valleys made
　Like peace within my breast.

Thine are the woods whereto my soul,
　Out of the noontide beam,
Flees for a refuge green and cool
　And tranquil as a dream.

Thy breaking seas like trumpets peal;
　Thy clouds — how oft have I
Watched their bright towers of silence steal
　Into infinity!

My heart within me faints to roam
　In thought even far from thee:
Thine be the grave whereto I come,
　And thine my darkness be.

THE SEAS OF ENGLAND

The seas of England are our old delight;
　Let the loud billow of the shingly shore
　Sing freedom on her breezes evermore
To all earth's ships that sailing heave in sight!

The gaunt sea-nettle be our fortitude,
　Sturdily blowing where the clear wave sips;
　O, be the glory of our men and ships
Rapturous, woe-unheeding hardihood!

There is great courage in a land that hath
　Liberty guarded by the unearthly seas;
　And ev'n to find peace at the last in these
How many a sailor hath sailed down to death!

Their names are like a splendour in old song;
　Their record shines like bays along the years;
　Their jubilation is the cry man hears
Sailing sun-fronted the vast deeps among.

The seas of England are our old delight;
　Let the loud billow of the shingly shore
　Sing freedom on her breezes evermore
To all earth's ships that sailing heave in sight!

TRUCE

Far inland here Death's pinions mocked the roar
    Of English seas;
We sleep to wake no more,
    Hushed, and at ease;
Till sound a trump, shore on to echoing shore,
Rouse from a peace, unwonted then to war,
    Us and our enemies.

EVENING

When twilight darkens, and one by one,
The sweet birds to their nests have gone;
When to green banks the glow-worms bring
Pale lamps to lighten evening;
Then stirs in his thick sleep the owl,
Through the dewy air to prowl.

Hawking the meadows, swiftly he flits,
While the small mouse a-trembling sits
With tiny eye of fear upcast
Until his brooding shape be past,
Hiding her where the moonbeams beat,
Casting black shadows in the wheat.

Now all is still: the field-man is
Lapped deep in slumbering silentness.
Not a leaf stirs, but clouds on high
Pass in dim flocks across the sky,
Puffed by a breeze too light to move
Aught but these wakeful sheep above.

O, what an arch of light now spans
These fields by night no longer Man's!
Their ancient Master is abroad,
Walking beneath the moonlight cold:
His presence is the stillness, He
Fills earth with wonder and mystery.

NIGHT

All from the light of the sweet moon
Tired men now lie abed;
Actionless, full of visions, soon
Vanishing, soon sped.

The starry night aflock with beams
Of crystal light scarce stirs:
Only its birds — the cocks, the streams,
Call 'neath heaven's wanderers.

All's silent; all hearts still;
Love, cunning, fire, fallen low:
When faint morn straying on the hill
Sighs, and his soft airs flow.

THE UNIVERSE

I heard a little child beneath the stars
Talk as he ran along
To some sweet riddle in his mind that seemed
A-tiptoe into song.

In his dark eyes lay a wild universe, —
Wild forests, peaks, and crests;
Angels and fairies, giants, wolves and he
Were that world's only guests.

Elsewhere was home and mother, his warm bed: —
Now, only God alone
Could, armed with all His power and wisdom, make
Earths richer than his own.

O Man! — thy dreams, thy passions, hopes, desires! —
He in his pity keep
A homely bed where love may lull a child's
Fond Universe asleep!

REVERIE

Bring not bright candles, for his eyes
   In twilight have sweet company;
Bring not bright candles, else they fly —
   His phantoms fly —
Gazing aggrieved on thee!

Bring not bright candles, startle not
   The phantoms of a vacant room,
Flocking above a child that dreams —
   Deep, deep in dreams, —
Hid, in the gathering gloom!

Bring not bright candles to those eyes
   That between earth and stars descry,
Lovelier for the shadows there,
   Children of air,
Palaces in the sky!

THE MASSACRE

The shadow of a poplar tree
   Lay in that lake of sun,
As I with my little sword went in —
   Against a thousand, one.

Haughty, and infinitely armed,
   Insolent in their wrath,
Plumed high with purple plumes they held
   The narrow meadow path.

The air was sultry; all was still;
   The sun like flashing glass;
And snip-snap my light-whispering steel
   In arcs of light did pass.

Lightly and dull fell each proud head,
  Spiked keen without avail,
Till swam my uncontented blade
  With ichor green and pale.

And silence fell: the rushing sun
  Stood still in paths of heat,
Gazing in waves of horror on
  The dead about my feet.

Never a whir of wing, no bee
  Stirred o'er the shameful slain;
Nought but a thirsty wasp crept in
  Stooped, and came out again.

The very air trembled in fear;
  Eclipsing shadow seemed
Rising in crimson waves of gloom —
  On one who dreamed.

ECHO

'Who called?' I said, and the words
  Through the whispering glades,
Hither, thither, baffled the birds —
  'Who called? Who called?'

The leafy boughs on high
  Hissed in the sun;
The dark air carried my cry
  Faintingly on:

Eyes in the green, in the shade,
  In the motionless brake,
Voices that said what I said,
  For mockery's sake:

'Who cares?' I bawled through my tears;
  The wind fell low:
In the silence, 'Who cares? Who cares?'
  Wailed to and fro.

FEAR

I know where lurk
The eyes of Fear;
I, I alone,
Where shadowy-clear,
Watching for me,
Lurks Fear.

'Tis ever still
And dark, despite
All singing and
All candlelight,
'Tis ever cold,
And night.

He touches me;
Says quietly,
'Stir not, nor whisper,
I am nigh;
Walk noiseless on,
I am by!'

He drives me
As a dog a sheep;
Like a cold stone
I cannot weep.
He lifts me,
Hot from sleep,

In marble hands
To where on high
The jewelled horror
Of his eye
Dares me to struggle
Or cry.

No breast wherein
To chase away
That watchful shape!
Vain, vain to say,
'Haunt not with night
The day!'

THE MERMAIDS

Sand, sand; hills of sand;
  And the wind where nothing is
Green and sweet of the land;
  No grass, no trees,
  No bird, no butterfly,
But hills, hills of sand,
  And a burning sky.

Sea, sea; mounds of the sea,
  Hollow, and dark, and blue,
Flashing incessantly
  The whole sea through;
  No flower, no jutting root,
Only the floor of the sea,
  With foam afloat.

Blow, blow, winding shells;
  And the watery fish,
Deaf to the hidden bells,
  In the waters plash;
No streaming gold, no eyes,
  Watching along the waves,
But far-blown shells, faint bells,
  From the darkling caves.

MYSELF

There is a garden, grey
  With mists of autumntide;
Under the giant boughs,
  Stretched green on every side,

Along the lonely paths,
  A little child like me,
With face, with hands, like mine,
  Plays ever silently;

On, on, quite silently,
  When I am there alone,
Turns not his head; lifts not his eyes;
  Heeds not as he plays on.

After the birds are flown
    From singing in the trees,
When all is grey, all silent,
    Voices, and winds, and bees;

And I am there alone:
    Forlornly, silently,
Plays in the evening garden
    Myself with me.

AUTUMN

There is a wind where the rose was;
Cold rain where sweet grass was;
    And clouds like sheep
    Stream o'er the steep
Grey skies where the lark was.

Nought gold where your hair was;
Nought warm where your hand was;
    But phantom, forlorn,
    Beneath the thorn,
Your ghost where your face was.

Sad winds where your voice was;
Tears, tears where my heart was;
    And ever with me,
    Child, ever with me,
Silence where hope was.

WINTER

Green Mistletoe!
Oh, I remember now
A dell of snow,
Frost on the bough;
None there but I:
Snow, snow, and a wintry sky.

[97]

None there but I,
And footprints one by one,
Zigzaggedly,
Where I had run;
Where shrill and powdery
A robin sat in the tree.

And he whistled sweet;
And I in the crusted snow
With snow-clubbed feet
Jigged to and fro,
Till, from the day,
The rose-light ebbed away.

And the robin flew
Into the air, the air,
The white mist through;
And small and rare
The night-frost fell
Into the calm and misty dell.

And the dusk gathered low,
And the silver moon and stars
On the frozen snow
Drew taper bars,
Kindled winking fires
In the hooded briers.

And the sprawling Bear
Growled deep in the sky;
And Orion's hair
Streamed sparkling by:
But the North sighed low:
'*Snow, snow, more snow!* '

TO MY MOTHER[1]

Thine is my all, how little when 'tis told
    Beside thy gold!
Thine the first peace, and mine the livelong strife;
Thine the clear dawn, and mine the night of life;
    Thine the unstained belief,
    Darkened in grief.

Scarce even a flower but thine its beauty and name,
    Dimmed, yet the same;
Never in twilight comes the moon to me,
Stealing thro' those far woods, but tells of thee,
    Falls, dear, on my wild heart,
    And takes thy part.

Thou art the child, and I — how steeped in age!
    A blotted page
From that clear, little book life's taken away:
How could I read it, dear, so dark the day?
    Be it all memory
    'Twixt thee and me!

[1] Called 'Envoy: To my Mother' in *Poems*, 1906.

The Listeners and Other
Poems (1912)

THE THREE CHERRY TREES

There were three cherry trees once,
Grew in a garden all shady;
And there for delight of so gladsome a sight,
Walked a most beautiful lady,
Dreamed a most beautiful lady.

Birds in those branches did sing,
Blackbird and throstle and linnet,
But she walking there was by far the most fair —
Lovelier than all else within it,
Blackbird and throstle and linnet.

But blossoms to berries do come,
All hanging on stalks light and slender,
And one long summer's day charmed that lady away,
With vows sweet and merry and tender;
A lover with voice low and tender.

Moss and lichen the green branches deck;
Weeds nod in its paths green and shady:
Yet a light footstep seems there to wander in dreams,
The ghost of that beautiful lady,
That happy and beautiful lady.

OLD SUSAN

When Susan's work was done, she'd sit,
With one fat guttering candle lit,
And window opened wide to win
The sweet night air to enter in.
There, with a thumb to keep her place,
She'd read, with stern and wrinkled face,
Her mild eyes gliding very slow
Across the letters to and fro,
While wagged the guttering candle flame
In the wind that through the window came.

And sometimes in the silence she
Would mumble a sentence audibly,
Or shake her head as if to say,
'You silly souls, to act this way!'
And never a sound from night I'd hear,
Unless some far-off cock crowed clear;
Or her old shuffling thumb should turn
Another page; and rapt and stern,
Through her great glasses bent on me,
She'd glance into reality;
And shake her round old silvery head,
With —'You! — I thought you was in bed!'—
Only to tilt her book again,
And rooted in Romance remain.

OLD BEN

Sad is old Ben Thistlethwaite,
    Now his day is done,
And all his children
    Far away are gone.

He sits beneath his jasmined porch,
    His stick between his knees,
His eyes fixed, vacant,
    On his moss-grown trees.

Grass springs in the green path,
    His flowers are lean and dry,
His thatch hangs in wisps against
    The evening sky.

He has no heart to care now,
    Though the winds will blow
Whistling in his casement,
    And the rain drip through.

He thinks of his old Bettie,
    How she would shake her head and say,
'You'll live to wish my sharp old tongue
    Could scold — some day.'

But as in pale high autumn skies
    The swallows float and play,
His restless thoughts pass to and fro,
    But nowhere stay.

Soft, on the morrow, they are gone;
    His garden then will be
Denser and shadier and greener,
    Greener the moss-grown tree.

MISS LOO

When thin-strewn memory I look through,
I see most clearly poor Miss Loo;
Her tabby cat, her cage of birds,
Her nose, her hair, her muffled words,
And how she'd open her green eyes,
As if in some immense surprise,
Whenever as we sat at tea
She made some small remark to me.
It's always drowsy summer when
From out the past she comes again;
The westering sunshine in a pool
Floats in her parlour still and cool;
While the slim bird its lean wires shakes,
As into piercing song it breaks;

Till Peter's pale-green eyes ajar
Dream, wake; wake, dream, in one brief bar.
And I am sitting, dull and shy,
And she with gaze of vacancy,
And large hands folded on the tray,
Musing the afternoon away;
Her satin bosom heaving slow
With sighs that softly ebb and flow,
And her plain face in such dismay,
It seems unkind to look her way:
Until all cheerful back will come
Her gentle gleaming spirit home:
And one would think that poor Miss Loo
Asked nothing else, if she had you.

THE TAILOR

Few footsteps stray when dusk droops o'er
The tailor's old stone-lintelled door.
There sits he, stitching, half asleep,
Beside his smoky tallow dip.
'*Click, click*,' his needle hastes, and shrill
Cries back the cricket beneath the sill.
Sometimes he stays, and over his thread
Leans sidelong his old tousled head;
Or stoops to peer with half-shut eye
When some strange footfall echoes by;
Till clearer gleams his candle's spark
Into the dusty summer dark.
Then from his cross legs he gets down,
To find how dark the evening's grown;
And hunched up in his door he'll hear
The cricket whistling crisp and clear;
And so beneath the starry grey
He'll mutter half a seam away.

MARTHA

'Once . . . once upon a time . . .'
    Over and over again,
Martha would tell us her stories,
    In the hazel glen.

Hers were those clear grey eyes
    You watch, and the story seems
Told by their beautifulness
    Tranquil as dreams.

She'd sit with her two slim hands
    Clasped round her bended knees;
While we on our elbows lolled,
    And stared at ease.

Her voice and her narrow chin,
    Her grave small lovely head,
Seemed half the meaning
    Of the words she said.

'Once . . . once upon a time . . .'
  Like a dream you dream in the night,
Fairies and gnomes stole out
  In the leaf-green light.

And her beauty far away
  Would fade, as her voice ran on,
Till hazel and summer sun
  And all were gone:

All fordone and forgot;
  And like clouds in the height of the sky,
Our hearts stood still in the hush
  Of an age gone by.

THE SLEEPER

As Ann came in one summer's day,
  She felt that she must creep,
So silent was the clear cool house,
  It seemed a house of sleep.
And sure, when she pushed open the door,
  Rapt in the stillness there,
Her mother sat, with stooping head,
  Asleep upon a chair;
Fast — fast asleep; her two hands laid
  Loose-folded on her knee,
So that her small unconscious face
  Looked half unreal to be:
So calmly lit with sleep's pale light
  Each feature was; so fair
Her forehead — every trouble was
  Smoothed out beneath her hair.
But though her mind in dream now moved,
  Still seemed her gaze to rest —
From out beneath her fast-sealed lids,
  Above her moving breast —
On Ann; as quite, quite still she stood;
  Yet slumber lay so deep
Even her hands upon her lap
  Seemed saturate with sleep.
And as Ann peeped, a cloudlike dread
  Stole over her, and then,
On stealthy, mouselike feet she trod,
  And tiptoed out again.

[105]

THE KEYS OF MORNING

While at her bedroom window once,
  Learning her task for school,
Little Louisa lonely sat
  In the morning clear and cool,
She slanted her small bead-brown eyes
  Across the empty street,
And saw Death softly watching her
  In the sunshine pale and sweet.

His was a long lean sallow face;
  He sat with half-shut eyes,
Like an old sailor in a ship
  Becalmed 'neath tropic skies.
Beside him in the dust he had set
  His staff and shady hat;
These, peeping small, Louisa saw
  Quite clearly where she sat —
The thinness of his coal-black locks,
  His hands so long and lean
They scarcely seemed to grasp at all
  The keys that hung between:
Both were of gold, but one was small,
  And with this last did he
Wag in the air, as if to say,
  'Come hither, child, to me!'

Louisa laid her lesson book
  On the cold window-sill;
And in the sleepy sunshine house
  Went softly down, until
She stood in the half-opened door,
  And peeped. But strange to say,
Where Death just now had sunning sat
  Only a shadow lay:
Just the tall chimney's round-topped cowl,
  And the small sun behind,
Had with its shadow in the dust
  Called sleepy Death to mind.
But most she thought how strange it was
  Two keys that he should bear,
And that, when beckoning, he should wag
  The littlest in the air.

RACHEL

Rachel sings sweet —
  Oh, yes, at night,
Her pale face bent
  In the candle-light,
Her slim hands touch
  The answering keys,
And she sings of hope
  And of memories:
Sings to the little
  Boy that stands
Watching those slim,
  Light, heedful hands.
He looks in her face;
  Her dark eyes seem
Dark with a beautiful
  Distant dream;
And still she plays,
  Sings tenderly
To him of hope,
  And of memory.

ALONE

A very old woman
Lives in yon house.
The squeak of the cricket,
The stir of the mouse,
Are all she knows
Of the earth and us.

Once she was young,
Would dance and play,
Like many another
Young popinjay;
And run to her mother
At dusk of day.

And colours bright
She delighted in;
The fiddle to hear,
And to lift her chin,
And sing as small
As a twittering wren.

But age apace
Comes at last to all;
And a lone house filled
With the cricket's call;
And the scampering mouse
In the hollow wall.

THE BELLS

Shadow and light both strove to be
The eight bell-ringers' company,
As with his gliding rope in hand,
Counting his changes, each did stand;
While rang and trembled every stone,
To music by the bell-mouths blown:
Till the bright clouds that towered on high
Seemed to re-echo cry with cry.
Still swang the clappers to and fro,
When, in the far-spread fields below,
I saw a ploughman with his team
Lift to the bells and fix on them
His distant eyes, as if he would
Drink in the utmost sound he could;
While near him sat his children three,
And in the green grass placidly
Played undistracted on: as if
What music earthly bells might give
Could only faintly stir their dream,
And stillness make more lovely seem.
Soon night hid horses, children, all,
In sleep deep and ambrosial.
Yet, yet, it seemed, from star to star,
Welling now near, now faint and far,
Those echoing bells rang on in dream,
And stillness made even lovelier seem.

THE SCARECROW

All winter through I bow my head
    Beneath the driving rain;
The North Wind powders me with snow
    And blows me black again;
At midnight in a maze of stars
    I flame with glittering rime,

[108]

And stand, above the stubble, stiff
  As mail at morning-prime.
But when that child, called Spring, and all
  His host of children, come,
Scattering their buds and dew upon
  These acres of my home,
Some rapture in my rags awakes;
  I lift void eyes and scan
The skies for crows, those ravening foes,
  Of my strange master, Man.
I watch him striding lank behind
  His clashing team, and know
Soon will the wheat swish body high
  Where once lay sterile snow;
Soon shall I gaze across a sea
  Of sun-begotten grain,
Which my unflinching watch hath sealed
  For harvest once again.

NOD

Softly along the road of evening,
  In a twilight dim with rose,
Wrinkled with age, and drenched with dew,
  Old Nod, the shepherd, goes.

His drowsy flock streams on before him,
  Their fleeces charged with gold,
To where the sun's last beam leans low
  On Nod the shepherd's fold.

The hedge is quick and green with brier,
  From their sand the conies creep;
And all the birds that fly in heaven
  Flock singing home to sleep.

His lambs outnumber a noon's roses,
  Yet, when night's shadows fall,
His blind old sheep-dog, Slumber-soon,
  Misses not one of all.

His are the quiet steeps of dreamland,
  The waters of no-more-pain,
His ram's bell rings 'neath an arch of stars,
  'Rest, rest and rest again.'

THE BINDWEED

The bindweed roots pierce down
   Deeper than men do lie,
Laid in their dark-shut graves
   Their slumbering kinsmen by.

Yet what frail thin-spun flowers
   She casts into the air,
To breathe the sunshine, and
   To leave her fragrance there.

But when the sweet moon comes,
   Showering her silver down,
Half-wreathèd in faint sleep,
   They droop where they have blown.

So all the grass is set,
   Beneath her trembling ray,
With buds that have been flowers,
   Brimmed with reflected day.

WINTER

Clouded with snow
   The bleak winds blow,
And shrill on leafless bough
The robin with its burning breast
   Alone sings now.

The rayless sun,
   Day's journey done,
Sheds its last ebbing light
On fields in leagues of beauty spread
   Unearthly white.

Thick draws the dark,
   And spark by spark,
The frost-fires kindle, and soon
Over that sea of frozen foam
   Floats the white moon.

THERE BLOOMS NO BUD IN MAY

There blooms no bud in May
   Can for its white compare
With snow at break of day,
   On fields forlorn and bare.

For shadow it hath rose,
   Azure, and amethyst;
And every air that blows
   Dies out in beauteous mist.

It hangs the frozen bough
   With flowers on which the night
Wheeling her darkness through
   Scatters a starry light.

Fearful of its pale glare
   In flocks the starlings rise;
Slide through the frosty air,
   And perch with plaintive cries.

Only the inky rook,
   Hunched cold in ruffled wings,
Its snowy nest forsook,
   Caws of unnumbered Springs.

NOON AND NIGHT FLOWER

Not any flower that blows
   But shining watch doth keep;
Every swift changing chequered hour it knows
Now to break forth in beauty; now to sleep.

   This for the roving bee
   Keeps open house, and this
Stainless and clear is, that in darkness she
May lure the moth to where her nectar is.

Lovely beyond the rest
Are these of all delight: —
The tiny pimpernel that noon loves best,
The primrose palely burning through the night.

One 'neath day's burning sky
With ruby decks her place,
The other when eve's chariot glideth by
Lifts her dim torch to light that dreaming face.

ESTRANGED

No one was with me there —
Happy I was — alone;
Yet from the sunshine suddenly
    A joy was gone.

A bird in an empty house
Sad echoes makes to ring,
Flitting from room to room
    On restless wing:

Till from its shades he flies,
And leaves forlorn and dim
The narrow solitudes
    So strange to him.

So, when with fickle heart
I joyed in the passing day,
A presence my mood estranged
    Went grieved away.

THE TIRED CUPID

The thin moonlight with trickling ray,
Thridding the boughs of silver may,
Trembles in beauty, pale and cool,
On folded flower, and mantled pool.
All in a haze the rushes lean —
And he — he sits, with chin between
His two cold hands; his bare feet set
Deep in the grasses, green and wet.

About his head a hundred rings
Of gold loop down to meet his wings,
Whose feathers, arched their stillness through,
Gleam with slow-gathering drops of dew.
The mouse-bat peers; the stealthy vole
Creeps from the covert of its hole;
A shimmering moth its pinions furls,
Grey in the moonshine of his curls;
'Neath the faint stars the night-airs stray,
Scattering the fragrance of the may;
And with each stirring of the bough
Shadow beclouds his childlike brow.

DREAMS

Be gentle, O hands of a child;
Be true: like a shadowy sea
In the starry darkness of night
    Are your eyes to me.

But words are shallow, and soon
Dreams fade that the heart once knew;
And youth fades out in the mind,
    In the dark eyes too.

What can a tired heart say,
Which the wise of the world have made dumb?
Save to the lonely dreams of a child,
    'Return again, come!'

FAITHLESS

The words you said grow faint;
    The lamp you lit burns dim;
Yet, still be near your faithless friend
    To urge and counsel him.

Still with returning feet
    To where life's shadows brood,
With steadfast eyes made clear in death
    Haunt his vague solitude.

So he, beguiled with earth,
    Yet with its vain things vexed,
Keep even to his own heart unknown
    Your memory unperplexed.

[113]

THE SHADE

Darker than night; and, oh, much darker, she
Whose eyes in deep night darkness gaze on me.
No stars surround her; yet the moon seems hid
Afar somewhere, beneath that narrow lid.
She darkens against the darkness; and her face
Only by adding thought to thought I trace,
Limmed shadowily: O dream, return once more
To gloomy Hades and the whispering shore!

BE ANGRY NOW NO MORE!

Be angry now no more!
  If I have grieved thee — if
Thy kindness, mine before,
No hope may now restore:
  Only forgive, forgive!

If still resentment burns
  In thy cold breast, oh, if
No more to pity turns,
No more, once tender, yearns
  Thy love; oh, yet forgive! ...

Ask of the winter rain
June's withered rose again:
Ask grace of the salt sea:
She will not answer thee.
God would ten times have shriven
A heart so riven;
In her cold care thou wouldst be
Still unforgiven.

SPRING

Once when my life was young,
I, too, with Spring's bright face
By mine, walked softly along,
  Pace to his pace.

Then burned his crimson may,
Like a clear flame outspread,
Arching our happy way:
  Then would he shed

Strangely from his wild face
Wonderful light on me —
Like hounds that keen in chase
  Their quarry see.

Oh, sorrow now to know
What shafts, what keenness cold
His are to pierce me through,
  Now that I'm old.

EXILE

Had the gods loved me I had lain
  Where darnel is, and thorn,
And the wild night-bird's nightlong strain
  Trembles in boughs forlorn.

Nay, but they loved me not; and I
  Must needs a stranger be,
Whose every exiled day gone by
  Aches with their memory.

WHERE?

Where is my love —
In silence and shadow she lies,
Under the April-grey calm waste of the skies;
  And a bird above,
In the darkness tender and clear,
Keeps saying over and over, Love lies here!

  Not that she's dead;
Only her soul is flown
Out of its last pure earthly mansion;
  And cries instead
In the darkness, tender and clear,
Like the voice of a bird in the leaves, Love —
  Love lies here.

[115]

MUSIC UNHEARD

Sweet sounds, begone —
　　Whose music on my ear
Stirs foolish discontent
　　Of lingering here;
When, if I crossed
　　The crystal verge of death,
Him I should see
　　Who these sounds murmureth.

Sweet sounds, begone —
　　Ask not my heart to break
Its bond of bravery for
　　Sweet quiet's sake;
Lure not my feet
　　To leave the path they must
Tread on, unfaltering,
　　Till I sleep in dust.

Sweet sounds, begone!
　　Though silence brings apace
Deadly disquiet
　　Of this homeless place;
And all I love
　　In beauty cries to me,
'We but vain shadows
　　And reflections be.'

ALL THAT'S PAST

Very old are the woods;
　　And the buds that break
Out of the brier's boughs,
　　When March winds wake,
So old with their beauty are —
　　Oh, no man knows
Through what wild centuries
　　Roves back the rose.

Very old are the brooks;
  And the rills that rise
Where snow sleeps cold beneath
  The azure skies
Sing such a history
  Of come and gone,
Their every drop is as wise
  As Solomon.

Very old are we men;
  Our dreams are tales
Told in dim Eden
  By Eve's nightingales;
We wake and whisper awhile,
  But, the day gone by,
Silence and sleep like fields
  Of amaranth lie.

WHEN THE ROSE IS FADED

When the rose is faded,
  Memory may still dwell on
Her beauty shadowed,
  And the sweet smell gone.

That vanishing loveliness,
  That burdening breath
No bond of life hath then
  Nor grief of death.

'Tis the immortal thought
  Whose passion still
Makes of the changing
  The unchangeable.

Oh, thus thy beauty,
  Loveliest on earth to me,
Dark with no sorrow, shines
  And burns, with Thee.

SLEEP

Men all, and birds, and creeping beasts,
  When the dark of night is deep,
From the moving wonder of their lives
  Commit themselves to sleep.

Without a thought, or fear, they shut
  The narrow gates of sense;
Heedless and quiet, in slumber turn
  Their strength to impotence.

The transient strangeness of the earth
  Their spirits no more see:
Within a silent gloom withdrawn,
  They slumber in secrecy.

Two worlds they have — a globe forgot,
  Wheeling from dark to light;
And all the enchanted realm of dream
  That burgeons out of night.

THE STRANGER

Half-hidden in a graveyard,
  In the blackness of a yew,
Where never living creature stirs,
  Nor sunbeam pierces through,

Is a tomb-stone, green and crooked —
  Its faded legend gone —
With one rain-worn cherub's head
  To sing of the unknown.

There, when the dusk is falling,
  Silence broods so deep
It seems that every air that breathes
  Sighs from the fields of sleep.

Day breaks in heedless beauty,
  Kindling each drop of dew,
But unforsaking shadow dwells
  Beneath this lonely yew.

And, all else lost and faded,
Only this listening head
Keeps with a strange unanswering smile
Its secret with the dead.

NEVER MORE, SAILOR

Never more, Sailor,
Shalt thou be
Tossed on the wind-ridden,
Restless sea.
Its tides may labour;
All the world
Shake 'neath that weight
Of waters hurled:
But its whole shock
Can only stir
Thy dust to a quiet
Even quieter.
Thou mock'st at land
Who now art come
To such a small
And shallow home;
Yet bore the sea
Full many a care
For bones that once
A sailor's were.
And though the grave's
Deep soundlessness
Thy once sea-deafened
Ear distress,
No robin ever
On the deep
Hopped with his song
To haunt thy sleep.

THE WITCH

Weary went the old Witch,
Weary of her pack,
She sat her down by the churchyard wall,
And jerked it off her back.

The cord brake, yes, the cord brake,
Just where the dead did lie,
And Charms and Spells and Sorceries
Spilled out beneath the sky.

Weary was the old Witch;
She rested her old eyes
From the lantern-fruited yew trees,
And the scarlet of the skies;

And out the dead came stumbling,
From every rift and crack,
Silent as moss, and plundered
The gaping pack.

They wish them, three times over,
Away they skip full soon:
Bat and Mole and Leveret,
Under the rising moon;

Owl and Newt and Nightjar:
They take their shapes and creep
Silent as churchyard lichen,
While she squats asleep.

All of these dead were stirring:
Each unto each did call,
'A Witch, a Witch is sleeping
Under the churchyard wall;

'A Witch, a Witch is sleeping . . .'
The shrillness ebbed away;
And up the way-worn moon clomb bright,
Hard on the track of day.

She shone, high, wan, and silvery;
Day's colours paled and died:
And, save the mute and creeping worm,
Nought else was there beside.

Names may be writ; and mounds rise;
   Purporting, Here be bones:
But empty is that churchyard
   Of all save stones.

Owl and Newt and Nightjar,
   Leveret, Bat, and Mole
Haunt and call in the twilight
   Where she slept, poor soul.

ARABIA

Far are the shades of Arabia,
   Where the Princes ride at noon,
'Mid the verdurous vales and thickets,
   Under the ghost of the moon;
And so dark is that vaulted purple
   Flowers in the forest rise
And toss into blossom 'gainst the phantom stars
   Pale in the noonday skies.

Sweet is the music of Arabia
   In my heart, when out of dreams
I still in the thin clear mirk of dawn
   Descry her gliding streams;
Hear her strange lutes on the green banks
   Ring loud with the grief and delight
Of the dim-silked, dark-haired Musicians
   In the brooding silence of night.

They haunt me — her lutes and her forests;
   No beauty on earth I see
But shadowed with that dream recalls
   Her loveliness to me:
Still eyes look coldly upon me,
   Cold voices whisper and say —
'He is crazed with the spell of far Arabia,
   They have stolen his wits away.'

THE MOUNTAINS

Still and blanched and cold and lone
  The icy hills far off from me
With frosty ulys overgrown
  Stand in their sculptured secrecy.

No path of theirs the chamois fleet
  Treads, with a nostril to the wind;
O'er their ice-marbled glaciers beat
  No wings of eagles in my mind —

Yea, in my mind these mountains rise,
  Their perils dyed with evening's rose;
And still my ghost sits at my eyes
  And thirsts for their untroubled snows.

QUEEN DJENIRA

When Queen Djenira slumbers through
  The sultry noon's repose,
From out her dreams, as soft she lies,
  A faint thin music flows.

Her lovely hands lie narrow and pale
  With gilded nails, her head
Couched in its banded nets of gold
  Lies pillowed on her bed.

The little Nubian boys who fan
  Her cheeks and tresses clear,
Wonderful, wonderful, wonderful voices
  Seem afar to hear.

They slide their eyes, and nodding, say,
  'Queen Djenira walks to-day
The courts of the lord Pthamasar
  Where the sweet birds of Psuthys are.'

And those of earth about her porch
  Of shadow cool and grey
Their sidelong beaks in silence lean,
  And silent flit away.

NEVER-TO-BE

Down by the waters of the sea
Reigns the King of Never-to-be.
His palace walls are black with night;
His torches star and moon's light,
And for his timepiece deep and grave
Beats on the green unhastening wave.

Windswept are his high corridors;
His pleasance the sea-mantled shores;
For sentinel a shadow stands
With hair in heaven, and cloudy hands;
And round his bed, king's guards to be,
Watch pines in iron solemnity.

His hound is mute; his steed at will
Roams pastures deep with asphodel;
His queen is to her slumber gone;
His courtiers mute lie, hewn in stone;
He hath forgot where he did hide
His sceptre in the mountain-side.

Grey-capped and muttering, mad is he —
The childless King of Never-to-be;
For all his people in the deep
Keep, everlasting, fast asleep;
And all his realm is foam and rain,
Whispering of what comes not again.

THE DARK CHÂTEAU

In dreams a dark château
  Stands ever open to me,
In far ravines dream-waters flow,
  Descending soundlessly;
Above its peaks the eagle floats,
  Lone in a sunless sky;
Mute are the golden woodland throats
  Of the birds flitting by.

[123]

No voice is audible. The wind
    Sleeps in its peace.
No flower of the light can find
    Refuge beneath its trees;
Only the darkening ivy climbs
    Mingled with wilding rose,
And cypress, morn and evening, time's
    Black shadow throws.

All vacant, and unknown;
    Only the dreamer steps
From stone to hollow stone,
    Where the green moss sleeps,
Peers at the river in its deeps,
    The eagle lone in the sky,
While the dew of evening drips,
    Coldly and silently.

Would that I could steal in! —
    Into each secret room;
Would that my sleep-bright eyes could win
    To the inner gloom;
Gaze from its high windows,
    Far down its mouldering walls,
Where amber-clear still Lethe flows,
    And foaming falls.

But ever as I gaze,
    From slumber soft doth come
Some touch my stagnant sense to raise
    To its old earthly home;
Fades then that sky serene;
    And peak of ageless snow;
Fades to a paling dawn-lit green,
    My dark château.

THE DWELLING-PLACE

Deep in a forest where the kestrel screamed,
    Beside a lake of water, clear as glass,
The time-worn windows of a stone house gleamed
    Named only 'Alas'.

Yet happy as the wild birds in the glades
  Of that green forest, thridding the still air
With low continued heedless serenades,
  Its heedless people were.

The throbbing chords of violin and lute,
  The lustre of lean tapers in dark eyes,
Fair colours, beauteous flowers, faint-bloomed fruit
  Made earth seem Paradise

To them that dwelt within this lonely house:
  Like children of the gods in lasting peace,
They ate, sang, danced, as if each day's carouse
  Need never pause, nor cease.[1]

Some to the hunt would wend, with hound and horn,
  And clash of silver, beauty, bravery, pride,
Heeding not one who on white horse upborne
  With soundless hoofs did ride.

Dreamers there were who watched the hours away
  Beside a fountain's foam. And in the sweet
Of phantom evening, 'neath the night-bird's lay,
  Did loved with loved-one meet.

All, all were children, for, the long day done,
  They barred the heavy door against lightfoot fear;
And few words spake though one known face was gone,
  Yet still seemed hovering near.

They heaped the bright fire higher; poured dark wine;
  And in long revelry dazed the questioning eye;
Curtained three-fold the heart-dismaying shine
  Of midnight streaming by.

They shut the dark out from the painted wall,
  With candles dared the shadow at the door,
Sang down the faint reiterated call
  Of those who came no more.

---

[1] Stanza 5 in the original version read:
  'Some might cry, Vanity! to a weeping lyre,
  Some in that deep pool mock their longings vain,
  Came yet at last long silence to the wire,
  And dark did dark remain.'   (*The Listeners*, 1912)
This stanza was omitted from later editions.

Yet clear above that portal plain was writ,
   Confronting each at length alone to pass
Out of its beauty into night star-lit,
   That worn 'Alas!'

THE LISTENERS

'Is there anybody there?' said the Traveller,
   Knocking on the moonlit door;
And his horse in the silence champed the grasses
   Of the forest's ferny floor:
And a bird flew up out of the turret,
   Above the Traveller's head:
And he smote upon the door again a second time;
   'Is there anybody there?' he said.
But no one descended to the Traveller;
   No head from the leaf-fringed sill
Leaned over and looked into his grey eyes,
   Where he stood perplexed and still.
But only a host of phantom listeners
   That dwelt in the lone house then
Stood listening in the quiet of the moonlight
   To that voice from the world of men:
Stood thronging the faint moonbeams on the dark stair,
   That goes down to the empty hall,
Hearkening in an air stirred and shaken
   By the lonely Traveller's call.
And he felt in his heart their strangeness,
   Their stillness answering his cry,
While his horse moved, cropping the dark turf,
   'Neath the starred and leafy sky;
For he suddenly smote on the door, even
   Louder, and lifted his head: —
'Tell them I came, and no one answered,
   That I kept my word,' he said.
Never the least stir made the listeners,
   Though every word he spake
Fell echoing through the shadowiness of the still house
   From the one man left awake:
Ay, they heard his foot upon the stirrup,
   And the sound of iron on stone,
And how the silence surged softly backward,
   When the plunging hoofs were gone.

TIME PASSES

There was nought in the Valley
But a Tower of Ivory,
Its base enwreathed with red
Flowers that at evening
Caught the sun's crimson
As to Ocean low he sped.

Lucent and lovely
It stood in the morning
Under a trackless hill;
With snows eternal
Muffling its summit,
And silence ineffable.

Sighing of solitude
Winds from the cold heights
Haunted its yellowing stone;
At noon its shadow
Stretched athwart cedars
Whence every bird was flown.

Its stair was broken,
Its starlit walls were
Fretted; its flowers shone
Wide at the portal,
Full-blown and fading,
Their last faint fragrance gone.

And on high in its lantern
A shape of the living
Watched o'er a shoreless sea,
From a Tower rotting
With age and weakness,
Once lovely as ivory.

BEWARE!

An ominous bird sang from its branch,
'Beware, O Wanderer!
Night 'mid her flowers of glamourie spilled
Draws swiftly near:

'Night with her darkened caravans,
Piled deep with silver and myrrh,
Draws from the portals of the East,
O Wanderer, near.

'Night who walks plumèd through the fields
Of stars that strangely stir —
Smitten to fire by the sandals of him
Who walks with her.'

THE JOURNEY[1]

Heart-sick of his journey was the Wanderer;
Footsore and parched was he;
And a Witch who long had lurked by the wayside,
Looked out of sorcery.

'Lift up your eyes, you lonely Wanderer,'
She peeped from her casement small;
'Here's shelter and quiet to give you rest, young man,
And apples for thirst withal.'

And he looked up out of his sad reverie,
And saw all the woods in green,
With birds that flitted feathered in the dappling,
The jewel-bright leaves between.

And he lifted up his face towards her lattice,
And there, alluring-wise,
Slanting through the silence of the long past,
Dwelt the still green Witch's eyes.

And vaguely from the hiding-place of memory
Voices seemed to cry:
'What is the darkness of one brief life-time
To the deaths thou hast made us die?

---

[1] Stanza 13 in the original version read:
'His shoulders were bowed with his knapsack;
His staff trailed heavy in the dust;
His eyes were dazed, and hopeless of the white road
Which tread all pilgrims must.'

(*The Listeners*, 1912)

This stanza was omitted from later editions.

[128]

'Heed not the words of the Enchantress
Who would us still betray!'
And sad with the echo of their reproaches,
Doubting, he turned away.

'I may not shelter beneath your roof, lady,
Nor in this wood's green shadow seek repose,
Nor will your apples quench the thirst
A homesick wanderer knows.'

'"Homesick" forsooth!' she softly mocked him:
And the beauty in her face
Made in the sunshine pale and trembling
A stillness in that place.

And he sighed, as if in fear, that young Wanderer,
Looking to left and to right,
Where the endless narrow road swept onward,
Till in distance lost to sight.

And there fell upon his sense the brier,
Haunting the air with its breath,
And the faint shrill sweetness of the birds' throats,
Their tent of leaves beneath.

And there was the Witch, in no wise heeding;
Her arbour, and fruit-filled dish,
Her pitcher of well-water, and clear damask —
All that the weary wish.

And the last gold beam across the green world
Faltered and failed, as he
Remembered his solitude and the dark night's
Inhospitality.

And he looked upon the Witch with eyes of sorrow
In the darkening of the day;
And turned him aside into oblivion;
And the voices died away. . . .

And the Witch stepped down from her casement:
In the hush of night he heard
The calling and wailing in dewy thicket
Of bird to hidden bird.

And gloom stole all her burning crimson,
    Remote and faint in space
As stars in gathering shadow of the evening
    Seemed now her phantom face.

And one night's rest shall be a myriad,
    Mid dreams that come and go;
Till heedless fate, unmoved by weakness, bring him
    This same strange by-way through:

To the beauty of earth that fades in ashes,
    The lips of welcome, and the eyes
More beauteous than the feeble shine of Hesper
    Lone in the lightening skies:

Till once again the Witch's guile entreat him;
    But, worn with wisdom, he
Steadfast and cold shall choose the dark night's
    Inhospitality.

HAUNTED

The rabbit in his burrow keeps
No guarded watch, in peace he sleeps;
The wolf that howls in challenging night
Cowers to her lair at morning light;
The simplest bird entwines a nest
Where she may lean her lovely breast,
Couched in the silence of the bough: —
But thou, O man, what rest hast thou?

Thy emptiest solitude can bring
Only a subtler questioning
In thy divided heart. Thy bed
Recalls at dawn what midnight said.
Seek how thou wilt to feign content,
Thy flaming ardour's quickly spent;
Soon thy last company is gone,
And leaves thee — with thyself — alone.

Pomp and great friends may hem thee round,
A thousand busy tasks be found;
Earth's thronging beauties may beguile
Thy longing lovesick heart awhile;
And pride, like clouds of sunset, spread
A changing glory round thy head;
But fade with all; and thou must come,
Hating thy journey, homeless, home.

Rave how thou wilt; unmoved, remote,
That inward presence slumbers not,
Frets out each secret from thy breast,
Gives thee no rally, pause, nor rest,
Scans close thy very thoughts, lest they
Should sap his patient power away;
Answers thy wrath with peace, thy cry
With tenderest taciturnity.

SILENCE

With changeful sound life beats upon the ear;
    Yet, striving for release,
    The most seductive string's
        Sweet jargonings,
        The happiest throat's
    Most easeful, lovely notes
Fall back into a veiling silentness.

Ev'n 'mid the rumour of a moving host,
    Blackening the clear green earth,
    Vainly 'gainst that thin wall
        The trumpets call,
        Or with loud hum
    The smoke-bemuffled drum:
From that high quietness no reply comes forth.

When, all at peace, two friends at ease alone
    Talk out their hearts — yet still,
    Between the grace-notes of
        The voice of love
        From each to each
    Trembles a rarer speech,
And with its presence every pause doth fill.

[131]

Unmoved it broods, this all-encompassing hush
  Of one who stooping near,
  No smallest stir will make
    Our fear to wake;
    But yet intent
  Upon some mystery bent
Hearkens the lightest word we say, or hear.

WINTER DUSK

Dark frost was in the air without,
  The dusk was still with cold and gloom,
When less than even a shadow came
  And stood within the room.

But of the three around the fire,
  None turned a questioning head to look,
Still read a clear voice, on and on,
  Still stooped they o'er their book.

The children watched their mother's eyes
  Moving on softly line to line;
It seemed to listen too — that shade,
  Yet made no outward sign.

The fire-flames crooned a tiny song,
  No cold wind stirred the wintry tree;
The children both in Faërie dreamed
  Beside their mother's knee.

And nearer yet that spirit drew
  Above that heedless one, intent
Only on what the simple words
  Of her small story meant.

No voiceless sorrow grieved her mind,
  No memory her bosom stirred,
Nor dreamed she, as she read to two,
  'Twas surely three who heard.

Yet when, the story done, she smiled
  From face to face, serene and clear,
A love, half dread, sprang up, as she
  Leaned close and drew them near.

AGES AGO

Launcelot loved Guinevere,
  Ages and ages ago,
Beautiful as a bird was she,
Preening its wings in a cypress tree,
Happy in sadness, she and he,
  They loved each other so.

Helen of Troy was beautiful
  As tender flower in May,
Her loveliness from the towers looked down,
With the sweet moon for silver crown,
Over the walls of Troy Town,
  Hundreds of years away.

Cleopatra, Egypt's Queen,
  Was wondrous kind to ken,
As when the stars in the dark sky
Like buds on thorny branches lie,
So seemed she too to Antony,
  That age-gone prince of men.

The Pyramids are old stones,
  Scarred is that grey face,
That by the greenness of Old Nile
Gazes with an unchanging smile,
Man with all mystery to beguile
  And give his thinking grace.

HOME

Rest, rest — there is no rest,
Until the quiet grave
Comes with its narrow arch
  The heart to save
From life's long cankering rust,
From torpor, cold and still —
The loveless, saddened dust,
  The jaded will.

And yet, be far the hour
Whose haven calls me home;
Long be the arduous day
  Till evening come;

[133]

What sureness now remains
But that through livelong strife
Only the loser gains
    An end to life?

Then in the soundless deep
Of even the shallowest grave
Childhood and love he'll keep,
    And his soul save;
All vext desire, all vain
Cries of a conflict done
Fallen to rest again;
    Death's refuge won.

THE GHOST

Peace in thy hands,
Peace in thine eyes,
Peace on thy brow;
Flower of a moment in the eternal hour,
Peace with me now.

Not a wave breaks,
Not a bird calls,
My heart, like a sea,
Silent after a storm that hath died,
Sleeps within me.

All the night's dews,
All the world's leaves,
All winter's snow
Seem with their quiet to have stilled in life's dream
All sorrowing now.

AN EPITAPH

Here lies a most beautiful lady,
Light of step and heart was she;
I think she was the most beautiful lady
That ever was in the West Country.

But beauty vanishes; beauty passes;
However rare — rare it be;
And when I crumble, who will remember
This lady of the West Country?

'THE HAWTHORN HATH A DEATHLY SMELL'

The flowers of the field
   Have a sweet smell;
Meadowsweet, tansy, thyme,
   And faint-heart pimpernel;
But sweeter even than these,
   The silver of the may
Wreathed is with incense for
   The Judgment Day.

An apple, a child, dust,
   When falls the evening rain,
Wild brier's spicèd leaves,
   Breathe memories again;
With further memory fraught,
   The silver of the may
Wreathed is with incense for
   The Judgment Day.

Eyes of all loveliness —
   Shadow of strange delight,
Even as a flower fades
   Must thou from sight;
But, oh, o'er thy grave's mound,
   Till come the Judgment Day,
Wreathed shall with incense be
   Thy sharp-thorned may.

Peacock Pie:
A Book of Rhymes (1913)[1]

THE HORSEMAN

I heard a horseman
  Ride over the hill;
The moon shone clear,
  The night was still;
His helm was silver,
  And pale was he;
And the horse he rode
  Was of ivory.

KINGS AND QUEENS

Eight Henries, one Mary,
  One Elizabeth;
Crowned and throned Kings and Queens
  Now lie still in death.

Four Williams, one Stephen,
  Anne, Victoria, John:
Sceptre and orb are laid aside;
  All are to quiet gone.
And James and Charles, and Charles's sons —
  They, too, have journeyed on.

Three Richards, seven Edwards
  Their royal hour did thrive;
They sleep with Georges one to four:
  And we praise God for five.

UP AND DOWN

Down the Hill of Ludgate,
  Up the Hill of Fleet,
To and fro and East and West
  With people flows the street;
Even the King of England
  On Temple Bar must beat
For leave to ride to Ludgate
  Down the Hill of Fleet.

[1] See Bibliographical Appendix, p. 891.

[137]

MRS. EARTH

Mrs. Earth makes silver black,
  Mrs. Earth makes iron red,
But Mrs. Earth cannot stain gold
  Nor ruby red.
Mrs. Earth the slenderest bone,
  Whitens in her bosom cold,
But Mrs. Earth can change my dreams
  No more than ruby or gold.
Mrs. Earth and Mr. Sun
  Can tan my skin, and tire my toes,
But all that I'm thinking of, ever shall think,
  Why, neither knows.

ALAS, ALACK!

Ann, Ann!
  Come! quick as you can!
There's a fish that *talks*
  In the frying-pan.
Out of the fat,
  As clear as glass,
He put up his mouth
  And moaned 'Alas!'
Oh, most mournful,
  'Alas, alack!'
Then turned to his sizzling,
  And sank him back.

TIRED TIM

Poor tired Tim! It's sad for him.
He lags the long bright morning through,
Ever so tired of nothing to do;
He moons and mopes the livelong day,
Nothing to think about, nothing to say;
Up to bed with his candle to creep,
Too tired to yawn, too tired to sleep:
Poor tired Tim! It's sad for him.

MIMA

Jemima is my name,
  But oh, I have another;
My father always calls me Meg,
  And so do Bob and mother;
Only my sister, jealous of
  The strands of my bright hair,
'Jemima — Mima — Mima!'
  Calls, mocking, up the stair.

THE HUNTSMEN

Three jolly gentlemen,
  In coats of red,
Rode their horses
  Up to bed.

Three jolly gentlemen
  Snored till morn,
Their horses champing
  The golden corn.

Three jolly gentlemen,
  At break of day,
Came clitter-clatter down the stairs
  And galloped away.

THE BANDOG

Has anybody seen my Mopser? —
  A comely dog is he,
With hair of the colour of a Charles the Fifth,
  And teeth like ships at sea,
His tail it curls straight upwards,
  His ears stand two abreast,
And he answers to the simple name of Mopser,
  When civilly addressed.

[139]

I CAN'T ABEAR

I can't abear a Butcher,
   I can't abide his meat,
The ugliest shop of all is his,
   The ugliest in the street;
Bakers' are warm, cobblers' dark,
   Chemists' burn watery lights;
But oh, the sawdust butcher's shop,
   That ugliest of sights!

THE DUNCE

Why does he still keep ticking?
   Why does his round white face
Stare at me over the books and ink,
   And mock at my disgrace?
Why does that thrush call, 'Dunce, dunce, dunce!'?
   Why does that bluebottle buzz?
Why does the sun so silent shine? —
   And what do I care if it does?

CHICKEN

Clapping her platter stood plump Bess,
   And all across the green
Came scampering in, on wing and claw,
   Chicken fat and lean: —
Dorking, Spaniard, Cochin China,
   Bantams sleek and small,
Like feathers blown in a great wind,
   They came at Bessie's call.

SOME ONE

Some one came knocking
   At my wee, small door;
Some one came knocking,
   I'm sure — sure — sure;

[140]

I listened, I opened,
　I looked to left and right,
But nought there was a-stirring
　In the still dark night;
Only the busy beetle
　Tap-tapping in the wall,
Only from the forest
　The screech-owl's call,
Only the cricket whistling
　While the dewdrops fall,
So I know not who came knocking,
　At all, at all, at all.

BREAD AND CHERRIES

'Cherries, ripe cherries!'
　The old woman cried,
In her snowy white apron,
　And basket beside;
And the little boys came,
　Eyes shining, cheeks red,
To buy bags of cherries
　To eat with their bread.

OLD SHELLOVER

'Come!' said Old Shellover.
'What?' says Creep.
'The horny old Gardener's fast asleep;
The fat cock Thrush
To his nest has gone;
And the dew shines bright
In the rising Moon;
Old Sallie Worm from her hole doth peep:
Come!' said Old Shellover.
'Ay!' said Creep.

[141]

HAPLESS

Hapless, hapless, I must be
All the hours of life I see,
Since my foolish nurse did once
Bed me on her leggen bones;
Since my mother did not weel
To snip my nails with blades of steel.
Had they laid me on a pillow
In a cot of water willow,
Had they bitten finger and thumb,
Not to such ill hap I had come.

THE LITTLE BIRD

My dear Daddie bought a mansion
  For to bring my Mammie to,
In a hat with a long feather,
  And a trailing gown of blue;
And a company of fiddlers
  And a rout of maids and men
Danced the clock round to the morning,
  In a gay house-warming then.
And when all the guests were gone — and
  All was still as still can be,
In from the dark ivy hopped a
  Wee small bird. And that was Me.

CAKE AND SACK

Old King Caraway
  Supped on cake,
And a cup of sack
  His thirst to slake;
Bird in arras,
  And hound in hall
Watched very softly
  Or not at all;
Fire in the middle,
  Stone all round
Changed not, heeded not,
  Made no sound;
All by himself
  At the Table High
He'd nibble and sip
  While his dreams slipped by;

And when he had finished,
   He'd nod and say,
  'Cake and sack
   For King Caraway!'

THE SHIP OF RIO

There was a ship of Rio
   Sailed out into the blue,
And nine and ninety monkeys
   Were all her jovial crew.
From bo'sun to the cabin boy,
   From quarter to caboose,
There weren't a stitch of calico
   To breech 'em — tight or loose;
From spar to deck, from deck to keel,
   From barnacle to shroud,
There weren't one pair of reach-me-downs
   To all that jabbering crowd.
But wasn't it a gladsome sight,
   When roared the deep-sea gales,
To see them reef her fore and aft,
   A-swinging by their tails!
Oh, wasn't it a gladsome sight,
   When glassy calm did come,
To see them squatting tailor-wise
   Around a keg of rum!
Oh, wasn't it a gladsome sight,
   When in she sailed to land,
To see them all a-scampering skip
   For nuts across the sand!

TILLIE

Old Tillie Turveycombe
Sat to sew,
Just where a patch of fern did grow;
There, as she yawned,
And yawn wide did she,
Floated some seed
Down her gull-e-t;
And look you once,

[143]

And look you twice,
Poor old Tillie
Was gone in a trice.
But oh, when the wind
Do a-moaning come,
'Tis poor old Tillie
Sick for home;
And oh, when a voice
In the mist do sigh,
Old Tillie Turveycombe's
Floating by.

MR. ALACADACCA

Mr. Alacadacca's
Long strange name
Always filled his heart
With shame.
'I'd much — much — rather
Be called,' said he,
'Plain "Mr. A,"
Or even "Old B";
What can Alacadacca
Mean to me!'
Nobody answered;
Nobody said
Plain 'Mr. A';
'Old B,' instead.
They merely smiled
At his dismay —
A-L-A-C-A-D-A-
C-C-A.

THE HORSEMAN

There was a Horseman rode so fast
The Sun in heaven stayed still at last.

On, on, and on, his galloping shoon
Gleamed never never beneath the Moon.

The People said, 'Thou must be mad, O
Man with a never-lengthening shadow!

'Mad and bad! Ho! stay thy course,
Thou and thy never-stabled horse!

'Oh, what a wild and wicked sight —
A Horseman never dark with night!

'Depart from us, depart from us,
Thou and thy lank-maned Pegasus!' . . .

They talked into declining day,
Since both were now leagues — leagues away.

JIM JAY

Do diddle di do,
  Poor Jim Jay
Got stuck fast
  In Yesterday.
Squinting he was,
  On cross-legs bent,
Never heeding
  The wind was spent.
Round veered the weathercock,
  The sun drew in —
And stuck was Jim
  Like a rusty pin. . . .
We pulled and we pulled
  From seven till twelve,
Jim, too frightened
  To help himself.
But all in vain.
  The clock struck one,
And there was Jim
  A little bit gone.
At half-past five
  You scarce could see
A glimpse of his flapping
  Handkerchee.
And when came noon,
  And we climbed sky-high,
Jim was a speck
  Slip — slipping by.
Come to-morrow,
  The neighbours say,
He'll be past crying for:
  Poor Jim Jay.

[145]

MISS T.

It's a very odd thing —
  As odd as can be —
That whatever Miss T. eats
  Turns into Miss T.;
Porridge and apples,
  Mince, muffins and mutton,
Jam, junket, jumbles —
  Not a rap, not a button
It matters; the moment
  They're out of her plate,
Though shared by Miss Butcher
  And sour Mr. Bate;
Tiny and cheerful,
  And neat as can be,
Whatever Miss T. eats
  Turns into Miss T.

THE CUPBOARD

I know a little cupboard,
With a teeny tiny key,
And there's a jar of Lollipops
  For me, me, me.

It has a little shelf, my dear,
As dark as dark can be,
And there's a dish of Banbury Cakes
  For me, me, me.

I have a small fat grandmamma,
With a very slippery knee,
And she's Keeper of the Cupboard,
  With the key, key, key.

And when I'm very good, my dear,
As good as good can be,
There's Banbury Cakes, and Lollipops
  For me, me, me.

[146]

THE BARBER'S

Gold locks, and black locks,
  Red locks, and brown,
Topknot to love-curl
  The hair wisps down;
Straight above the clear eyes,
  Rounded round the ears,
Snip-snap and snick-a-snick,
  Clash the Barber's shears;
Us, in the looking-glass,
  Footsteps in the street,
Over, under, to and fro,
  The lean blades meet;
Bay Rum or Bear's Grease,
  A silver groat to pay —
Then out a-shin-shan-shining
  In the bright, blue day.

HIDE AND SEEK

Hide and seek, says the Wind,
  In the shade of the woods;
Hide and seek, says the Moon,
  To the hazel buds;
Hide and seek, says the Cloud,
  Star on to star;
Hide and seek, says the Wave
  At the harbour bar;
Hide and seek, say I,
  To myself, and step
Out of the dream of Wake
  Into the dream of Sleep.

NOT I!

As I came out of Wiseman's Street,
The air was thick with driven sleet;
Crossing over Proudman's Square
Cold louring clouds obscured the air;
But as I entered Goodman's Lane
The burning sun came out again;
And on the roofs of Children's Row
In solemn glory shone the snow.
There did I lodge; there hope to die:
Envying no man — no, not I.

THEN

Twenty, forty, sixty, eighty,
    A hundred years ago,
All through the night with lantern bright
    The Watch trudged to and fro.
And little boys tucked snug abed
    Would wake from dreams to hear —
'Two o' the morning by the clock,
    And the stars a-shining clear!'
Or, when across the chimney-tops
    Screamed shrill a North-East gale,
A faint and shaken voice would shout,
    'Three! — and a storm of hail!'

THE WINDOW

Behind the blinds I sit and watch
The people passing — passing by;
And not a single one can see
    My tiny watching eye.

They cannot see my little room,
All yellowed with the shaded sun,
They do not even know I'm here;
    Nor'll guess when I am gone.

POOR HENRY

Thick in its glass
  The physic stands,
Poor Henry lifts
  Distracted hands;
His round cheek wans
  In the candlelight,
To smell that smell!
  To see that sight!

Finger and thumb
  Clinch his small nose,
A gurgle, a gasp,
  And down it goes;
Scowls Henry now;
  But mark that cheek,
Sleek with the bloom
  Of health next week!

FULL MOON

One night as Dick lay fast asleep,
  Into his drowsy eyes
A great still light began to creep
  From out the silent skies.
It was the lovely moon's, for when
  He raised his dreamy head,
Her surge of silver filled the pane
  And streamed across his bed.
So, for awhile, each gazed at each —
  Dick and the solemn moon —
Till, climbing slowly on her way,
  She vanished, and was gone.

THE BOOKWORM

'I'm tired — oh, tired of books,' said Jack,
  'I long for meadows green,
And woods where shadowy violets
  Nod their cool leaves between;

[149]

I long to see the ploughman stride
    His darkening acres o'er,
To hear the hoarse sea-waters drive
    Their billows 'gainst the shore;
I long to watch the sea-mew wheel
    Back to her rock-perched mate;
Or, where the breathing cows are housed,
    Lean, dreaming, at the gate.
Something has gone, and ink and print
    Will never bring it back;
I long for the green fields again,
    I'm tired of books,' said Jack.

THE QUARTETTE

Tom sang for joy and Ned sang for joy and old Sam sang for joy;
All we four boys piped up loud, just like one boy;
And the ladies that sate with the Squire — their cheeks were all wet,
For the noise of the voice of us boys, when we sang our Quartette.

Tom he piped low and Ned he piped low and old Sam he piped low;
Into a sorrowful fall did our music flow;
And the ladies that sate with the Squire vowed they'd never forget,
How the eyes of them cried for delight, when we sang our Quartette.

SNOW

No breath of wind,
No gleam of sun —
Still the white snow
Whirls softly down —
Twig and bough
And blade and thorn
All in an icy
Quiet, forlorn.
Whispering, rustling,
Through the air,
On sill and stone,
Roof — everywhere,
It heaps its powdery

Crystal flakes,
Of every tree
A mountain makes;
Till pale and faint
At shut of day,
Stoops from the West
One wintry ray.
And, feathered in fire,
Where ghosts the moon,
A robin shrills
His lonely tune.

MISTLETOE

Sitting under the mistletoe
(Pale-green, fairy mistletoe),
One last candle burning low,
All the sleepy dancers gone,
Just one candle burning on,
Shadows lurking everywhere:
Some one came, and kissed me there.

Tired I was; my head would go
Nodding under the mistletoe
(Pale-green, fairy mistletoe);
No footsteps came, no voice, but only,
Just as I sat there, sleepy, lonely,
Stooped in the still and shadowy air
Lips unseen — and kissed me there.

THE LOST SHOE

Poor little Lucy
  By some mischance,
Lost her shoe
  As she did dance:
'Twas not on the stairs,
  Not in the hall;
Not where they sat
  At supper at all.
She looked in the garden,
  But there it was not;

[151]

Henhouse, or kennel,
　　Or high dovecote.
Dairy and meadow,
　　And wild woods through
Showed not a trace
　　Of Lucy's shoe.
Bird nor bunny
　　Nor glimmering moon
Breathed a whisper
　　Of where 'twas gone.
It was cried and cried,
　　Oyez and *Oyez!*
In French, Dutch, Latin
　　And Portuguese.
Ships the dark seas
　　Went plunging through,
But none brought news
　　Of Lucy's shoe;
And still she patters,
　　In silk and leather,
Snow, sand, shingle,
　　In every weather;
Spain, and Africa,
　　Hindustan,
Java, China,
　　And lamped Japan,
Plain and desert,
　　She hops — hops through,
Pernambuco
　　To gold Peru;
Mountain and forest,
　　And river too,
All the world over
　　For her lost shoe.

THE TRUANTS

Ere my heart beats too coldly and faintly
　　To remember sad things, yet be gay,
I would sing a brief song of the world's little children
　　Magic hath stolen away.

The primroses scattered by April,
　　The stars of the wide Milky Way,
Cannot outnumber the hosts of the children
　　Magic hath stolen away.

The buttercup green of the meadows,
　　The snow of the blossoming may,
Lovelier are not than the legions of children
　　Magic hath stolen away.

The waves tossing surf in the moonbeam,
　　The Albatross lone on the spray,
Alone know the tears wept in vain for the children
　　Magic hath stolen away.

In vain: for at hush of the evening,
　　When the stars twinkle into the grey,
Seems to echo the far-away calling of children
　　Magic hath stolen away.

THE SEA BOY

Peter went — and nobody there —
Down by the sandy sea,
And he danced a jig, while the moon shone big,
All in his lone danced he;
And the surf splashed over his tippeting toes,
And he sang his riddle-cum-ree,
With hair a-dangling,
Moon a-spangling
The bubbles and froth of the sea.
He danced him to, and he danced him fro,
And he twirled himself about,
And now the starry waves tossed in,
And now the waves washed out;
Bare as an acorn, bare as a nut,
Nose and toes and knee,
Peter the sea-boy danced and pranced,
And sang his riddle-cum-ree.

BERRIES

There was an old woman
  Went blackberry picking
Along the hedges
  From Weep to Wicking.
Half a pottle —
  No more she had got,
When out steps a Fairy
  From her green grot;
And says, 'Well, Jill,
  Would 'ee pick 'ee mo?'
And Jill, she curtseys,
  And looks just so.
'Be off,' says the Fairy,
  'As quick as you can,
Over the meadows
  To the little green lane,
That dips to the hayfields
  Of Farmer Grimes:
I've berried those hedges
  A score of times;
Bushel on bushel
  I'll promise 'ee, Jill,
This side of supper
  If 'ee pick with a will.'
She glints very bright,
  And speaks her fair;
Then lo, and behold!
  She had faded in air.

Be sure Old Goodie
  She trots betimes
Over the meadows
  To Farmer Grimes.
And never was queen
  With jewellery rich
As those same hedges
  From twig to ditch;
Like Dutchmen's coffers,
  Fruit, thorn, and flower —
They shone like William
  And Mary's bower.
And be sure Old Goodie
  Went back to Weep

[154]

So tired with her basket
    She scarce could creep.

When she comes in the dusk
    To her cottage door,
There's Towser wagging
    As never before,
To see his Missus
    So glad to be
Come from her fruit-picking
    Back to he.
As soon as next morning
    Dawn was grey,
The pot on the hob
    Was simmering away;
And all in a stew
    And a hugger-mugger
Towser and Jill
    A-boiling of sugar,
And the dark clear fruit
    That from Faërie came,
For syrup and jelly
    And blackberry jam.

Twelve jolly gallipots
    Jill put by;
And one little teeny one,
    One inch high;
And that she's hidden
    A good thumb deep,
Half way over
    From Wicking to Weep.

MUST AND MAY

Must and May they were two half-brothers,
    And Must — a giant was he:
And May but a wisp of a flibbetigibbet,
    A mere minikin manikinee.

They dwelt in a mansion called Oughtoo, yes, Oughtoo,
    And a drearisome house was she.
In an hundred great chambers Must wallowed in comfort,
    All at his ease to be.

And the hundred and first was a crack of a cupboard,
　　With nought but a hole for the key,
Where the glint of a glimmer of a quickle of sunshine
　　Gleamed in about half-past three.

And there our May, smiling up at the window —
　　At the place where the window should be;
As he sang to a harp with a top and a bottom string —
　　A—B—C—D—E—F— and G.

But if there was one thing Must could not instomach,
　　'Twas a treble-shrill fiddlededee,
And he vowed a great vow he would learn May his manners,
　　And he did — as you'll shortly agree.

Down—down—he collumbered; and with ear to the keyhole
　　He crouched upon bended knee;
And he roared with a roar that drowned the sweet harp-strings,
　　He roared like a storm at sea.

And he catched little May by the twist of his breeches
　　Where the slack is snipped out in a V;
And swallowed him whole; and he scrunched up his harp, too,
　　He was so an—ga—ree.

Now mutterers say that that Oughtoo is haunted,
　　Exactly at half-past three,
By the phantom of poor little May to fey harp-strings
　　Singing A, B, C, D, E. F. G.

OFF THE GROUND

Three jolly Farmers
Once bet a pound
Each dance the others would
Off the ground.
Out of their coats
They slipped right soon,
And neat and nicesome,
Put each his shoon.

One — Two — Three! —
And away they go,
Not too fast,
And not too slow;

Out from the elm–tree's
Noonday shadow,
Into the sun
And across the meadow.
Past the schoolroom,
With knees well bent
Fingers a-flicking,
They dancing went.
Up sides and over,
And round and round,
They crossed click-clacking,
The Parish bound.
By Tupman's meadow
They did their mile,
Tee-to-tum
On a three-barred stile.
Then straight through Whipham,
Downhill to Week,
Footing it lightsome,
But not too quick,
Up fields to Watchet,
And on through Wye,
Till seven fine churches
They'd seen skip by —
Seven fine churches,
And five old mills,
Farms in the valley,
And sheep on the hills;
Old Man's Acre
And Dead Man's Pool
All left behind,
As they danced through Wool.

And Wool gone by,
Like tops that seem
To spin in sleep
They danced in dream:
Withy — Wellover —
Wassop — Wo —
Like an old clock
Their heels did go.
A league and a league
And a league they went,
And not one weary,
And not one spent.
And lo, and behold!

Past Willow-cum-Leigh
Stretched with its waters
The great green sea.

Says Farmer Bates,
'I puffs and I blows,
What's under the water,
Why, no man knows!'
Says Farmer Giles,
'My wind comes weak,
And a good man drownded
Is far to seek.'
But Farmer Turvey,
On twirling toes
Up's with his gaiters,
And in he goes:
Down where the mermaids
Pluck and play
On their twangling harps
In a sea-green day;
Down where the mermaids,
Finned and fair,
Sleek with their combs
Their yellow hair. . . .

Bates and Giles —
On the shingle sat,
Gazing at Turvey's
Floating hat.
But never a ripple
Nor bubble told
Where he was supping
Off plates of gold.
Never an echo
Rilled through the sea
Of the feasting and dancing
And minstrelsy.
They called — called — called:
Came no reply:
Nought but the ripples'
Sandy sigh.
Then glum and silent
They sat instead,
Vacantly brooding
On home and bed,
Till both together

Stood up and said: —
'Us knows not, dreams not,
Where you be,
Turvey, unless
In the deep blue sea;
But axcusing silver —
And it comes most willing —
Here's us two paying
Our forty shilling;
For it's sartin sure, Turvey,
Safe and sound,
You danced us square, Turvey;
Off the ground!'

THE THIEF AT ROBIN'S CASTLE

There came a Thief one night to Robin's Castle,
    He climbed up into a Tree;
And sitting with his head among the branches,
    A wondrous Sight did see.

For there was Robin supping at his table,
    With Candles of pure Wax,
His Dame and his two beauteous little Children,
    With Velvet on their backs.

Platters for each there were shin-shining,
    Of Silver many a pound,
And all of beaten Gold, three brimming Goblets,
    Standing the table round.

The smell that rose up richly from the Baked Meats
    Came thinning amid the boughs,
And much that greedy Thief who snuffed the night air —
    His Hunger did arouse.

He watched them eating, drinking, laughing, talking,
    Busy with finger and spoon,
While three most cunning Fiddlers, clad in crimson,
    Played them a supper-tune.

And he waited in the tree-top like a Starling,
    Till the Moon was gotten low;
When all the windows in the walls were darkened,
    He softly in did go.

[159]

There Robin and his Dame in bed were sleeping,
    And his Children young and fair;
Only Robin's Hounds from their warm kennels
    Yelped as he climbed the stair.

All, all were sleeping, page and fiddler,
    Cook, scullion, free from care;
Only Robin's Stallions from their stables
    Neighed as he climbed the stair.

A wee wan light the Moon did shed him,
    Hanging above the sea,
And he counted into his bag (of beaten Silver)
    Platters thirty-three.

Of Spoons three score; of jolly golden Goblets
    He stowed in four save one,
And six fine three-branched Cupid Candlesticks,
    Before his work was done.

Nine bulging bags of Money in a cupboard,
    Two Snuffers and a Dish
He found, the last all studded with great Garnets
    And shapen like a Fish.

Then tiptoe up he stole into a Chamber,
    Where on Tasselled Pillows lay
Robin and his Dame in dreaming slumber,
    Tired with the summer's day.

That Thief he mimbled round him in the gloaming,
    Their Treasures for to spy,
Combs, Brooches, Chains, and Rings, and Pins and **Buckles**
    All higgledy piggle-dy.

A Watch shaped in the shape of a flat Apple
    In purest Crystal set,
He lifted from the hook where it was ticking
    And crammed in his Pochette.

He heaped the pretty Baubles on the table,
    Trinkets, Knick-knackerie,
Pearls, Diamonds, Sapphires, Topazes, and Opals —
    All in his bag put he.

And there in night's pale Gloom was Robin dreaming
   He was hunting the mountain Bear,
While his Dame in peaceful slumber in no wise heeded
   A greedy Thief was there.

And that ravenous Thief he climbed up even higher,
   Till into a chamber small
He crept where lay poor Robin's beauteous Children,
   Lovelier in sleep withal.

Oh, fairer was their Hair than Gold of Goblet,
   'Yond Silver their Cheeks did shine,
And their little hands that lay upon the linen
   Made that Thief's hard heart to pine.

But though a moment there his hard heart faltered,
   Eftsoons he took the twain,
Slipped them into his Bag with all his Plunder,
   And softly stole down again.

Spoon, Platter, Goblet, Ducats, Dishes, Trinkets,
   And those two Children dear,
A-quaking in the clinking and the clanking,
   And half bemused with fear,

He carried down the stairs into the Courtyard,
   But there he made no stay,
He just tied up his Garters, took a deep breath,
   And ran like the wind away.

Past Forest, River, Mountain, River, Forest —
   He coursed the whole night through,
Till morning found him come into a Country,
   Where none his bad face knew.

Past Mountain, River, Forest, River, Mountain —
   That Thief's lean shanks sped on,
Till Evening found him knocking at a Dark House,
   His breath now well-nigh gone.

There came a little maid and asked his Business;
   A Cobbler dwelt within;
And though she much disliked the Bag he carried,
   She led the Bad Man in.

He bargained with the Cobbler for a lodging
  And soft laid down his Sack —
In the Dead of Night, with none to spy or listen —
  From off his weary Back.

And he taught the little Chicks to call him Father,
  And he sold his stolen Pelf,
And bought a Palace, Horses, Slaves, and Peacocks,
  To ease his wicked self.

And though the Children never really loved him,
  He was rich past all belief;
While Robin and his Dame o'er Delf and Pewter
  Spent all their Days in Grief.

A WIDOW'S WEEDS

A poor old Widow in her weeds
Sowed her garden with wild-flower seeds;
Not too shallow, and not too deep,
And down came April — drip — drip — drip.
Up shone May, like gold, and soon
Green as an arbour grew leafy June.
And now all summer she sits and sews
Where willow-herb, comfrey, bugloss blows,
Teasel and tansy, meadowsweet,
Campion, toadflax, and rough hawksbit;
Brown bee orchis, and Peals of Bells;
Clover, burnet, and thyme she smells;
Like Oberon's meadows her garden is
Drowsy from dawn till dusk with bees.
Weeps she never, but sometimes sighs,
And peeps at her garden with bright brown eyes;
And all she has is all she needs —
A poor old Widow in her weeds.

'SOOEEP!'

Black as a chimney is his face,
And ivory white his teeth,
And in his brass-bound cart he rides,
The chestnut blooms beneath.

'Sooeep, Sooeep!' he cries, and brightly peers
This way and that, to see
With his two light-blue shining eyes
What custom there may be.

And once inside the house, he'll squat,
And drive his rods on high,
Till twirls his sudden sooty brush
Against the morning sky.

Then, 'mid his bulging bags of soot,
With half the world asleep,
His small cart wheels him off again,
Still hoarsely bawling, 'Sooeep!'

MRS. MACQUEEN[1]

With glass like a bull's-eye,
    And shutters of green,
Down on the cobbles
    Lives Mrs. MacQueen.

At six she rises;
    At nine you see
Her candle shine out
    In the linden tree;

And at half-past nine
    Not a sound is nigh,
But the bright moon's creeping
    Across the sky;

Or a far dog baying;
    Or a twittering bird
In its drowsy nest,
    In the darkness stirred;

Or like the roar
    Of a distant sea,
A long-drawn *S-s-sh!*
    In the linden tree.

[1] Called 'Mrs. MacQueen (or The Lollie-Shop)' in *Peacock Pie*, 1913.

THE LITTLE GREEN ORCHARD

Some one is always sitting there,
  In the little green orchard;
Even when the sun is high,
In noon's unclouded sky,
And faintly droning goes
The bee from rose to rose,
Some one in shadow is sitting there,
  In the little green orchard.

Yes, and when twilight's falling softly
  On the little green orchard;
When the grey dew distils
And every flower-cup fills;
When the last blackbird says,
'What — what!' and goes her way — ssh!
I have heard voices calling softly
  In the little green orchard.

Not that I am afraid of being there,
  In the little green orchard;
Why, when the moon's been bright,
Shedding her lonesome light,
And moths like ghosties come,
And the horned snail leaves home:
I've sat there, whispering and listening there,
  In the little green orchard;

Only it's strange to be feeling there,
  In the little green orchard;
Whether you paint or draw,
Dig, hammer, chop, or saw;
When you are most alone,
All but the silence gone . . .
Some one is waiting and watching there,
  In the little green orchard.

POOR 'MISS 7'

Lone and alone she lies,
　Poor Miss 7,
Five steep flights from the earth,
　And one from heaven;
Dark hair and dark brown eyes, —
Not to be sad she tries,
Still — still it's lonely lies
　Poor Miss 7.

One day-long watch hath she,
　Poor Miss 7,
Not in some orchard sweet
　In April Devon, —
Just four blank walls to see,
And dark come shadowily,
No moon, no stars, ah me!
　Poor Miss 7.

And then to wake again,
　Poor Miss 7,
To the cold night — to have
　Sour physic given —
Out of some dream of pain;
Then strive long hours in vain
Deep dreamless sleep to gain:
　Poor Miss 7.

Yet memory softly sings
　Poor Miss 7
Songs full of love and peace
　And gladness even;
Clear flowers and tiny wings,
All tender, lovely things,
Hope to her bosom brings —
　Happy Miss 7.

SAM

When Sam goes back in memory,
　It is to where the sea
Breaks on the shingle, emerald-green
　In white foam, endlessly;
He says — with small brown eye on mine —
　'I used to keep awake,
And lean from my window in the moon,
　Watching those billows break.

[165]

And half a million tiny hands,
　And eyes, like sparks of frost,
Would dance and come tumbling into the moon,
　On every breaker tossed.
And all across from star to star,
　I've seen the watery sea,
With not a single ship in sight,
　Just ocean there, and me;
And heard my father snore . . . And once,
　As sure as I'm alive,
Out of those wallowing, moon-flecked waves
　I saw a mermaid dive;
Head and shoulders above the wave,
　Plain as I now see you,
Combing her hair, now back, now front,
　Her two eyes peeping through;
Calling me, "Sam!" — quietlike — "Sam!" . . .
　But me . . . I never went,
Making believe I kind of thought
　'Twas someone else she meant . . .
Wonderful lovely there she sat,
　Singing the night away,
All in the solitudinous sea
　Of that there lonely bay.
P'raps,' and he'd smooth his hairless mouth,
　'P'raps, if 'twere *now*, my son,
P'raps, if I heard a voice say, "Sam!" . . .
　Morning would find me gone.'

LATE

Three small men in a small house,
　And none to hear them say,
'One for his nob,' and 'One for his noddle,'
　And 'One for his dumb dog Stray!'
'Clubs are trumps — and he's dealt and bluffed':
　'And Jack of diamonds led':
'And perhaps the cullie has dropped a shoe;
　He tarries so late,' they said.

Three small men in a small house,
　And one small empty chair,
One with his moleskin over his brows,
　One with his crany bare,

And one with a dismal cast in his eye,
    Rocking a heavy head . . .
'And perhaps the cullie's at *The Wide World's End*;
    He tarries so late,' they said.

Three small men in a small house,
    And a candle guttering low,
One with his cheek on the ace of spades,
    And two on the boards below.
And a window black 'gainst a waste of stars,
    And a moon five dark nights dead . . .
'Who's that a-knocking and a-knocking and a-knocking?'
    One stirred in his sleep and said.

THE OLD SOLDIER

There came an Old Soldier to my door,
Asked a crust, and asked no more;
The wars had thinned him very bare,
Fighting and marching everywhere,
    With a Fol rol dol rol di do.

With nose stuck out, and cheek sunk in,
A bristling beard upon his chin —
Powder and bullets and wounds and drums
Had come to that Soldier as suchlike comes —
    With a Fol rol dol rol di do.

'Twas sweet and fresh with blossoming May,
Flowers springing from every spray;
And when he had supped the Old Soldier trolled
The song of youth that never grows old,
    Called Fol rol dol rol di do.

Most of him rags, and all of him lean,
And the belt round his belly drawn tightly in,
He lifted his peaked old grizzled head,
And these were the very same words he said —
    A Fol-rol-dol-rol-*di*-do.

THE PENNY OWING[1]

Poor blind Tam, the beggar man,
I'll give a penny to as soon as I can.
Where he stood at the corner in his rags, and cried,
The sun without shadow does now abide.

Safe be my penny till I come some day
To where Tam's waiting. And then I'll say,
'Here is my ghost, Tam, from the fire and dew,
And the penny I grudged kept safe for you.'

THE PICTURE

Here is a sea-legged sailor,
Come to this tottering inn,
Just when the bronze on its signboard is fading,
And the black shades of evening begin.

With his head on his paws sleeps a sheepdog,
There stoops the shepherd, and see,
All follow-my-leader the ducks waddle homeward,
Under the sycamore tree.

Burned brown is the face of the sailor;
His bundle is crimson; and green
Are the thick leafy boughs that hang dense o'er the tavern;
And blue the far meadows between.

But the crust, ale and cheese of the sailor,
His mug and his platter of Delf,
And the crescent to light home the shepherd and sheepdog
The painter has kept to himself.

---

[1] Called 'Blind Tam' in *Peacock Pie*, 1924.

THE LITTLE OLD CUPID

'Twas a very small garden;
The paths were of stone,
Scattered with leaves,
With moss overgrown;
And a little Old Cupid
Stood under a tree,
With a small broken bow
He stood aiming at me.

The dog-rose in briars
Hung over the weeds,
The air was aflock
With the floating of seeds;
And a little old Cupid
Stood under a tree,
With a small broken bow
He stood aiming at me.

The dovecote was tumbling,
The fountain dry,
A wind in the orchard
Went whispering by;
And a little old Cupid
Stood under a tree,
With a small broken bow
He stood aiming at me.

KING DAVID

King David was a sorrowful man:
  No cause for his sorrow had he:
And he called for the music of a hundred harps,
  To solace his melancholy.

They played till they all fell silent:
  Played — and play sweet did they;
But the sorrow that haunted the heart of King David
  They could not charm away.

He rose; and in his garden
  Walked by the moon alone,
A nightingale hidden in a cypress-tree
  Jargoned on and on.

[169]

King David lifted his sad eyes
Into the dark-boughed tree —
'Tell me, thou little bird that singest,
Who taught my grief to thee?'

But the bird in no wise heeded;
And the king in the cool of the moon
Hearkened to the nightingale's sorrowfulness,
Till all his own was gone.

THE OLD HOUSE

A very, very old house I know —
And ever so many people go,
Past the small lodge, forlorn and still,
Under the heavy branches, till
Comes the blank wall, and there's the door.
Go in they do; come out no more.
No voice says aught; no spark of light
Across that threshold cheers the sight;
Only the evening star on high
Less lonely makes a lonely sky,
As, one by one, the people go
Into that very old house I know.

UNSTOOPING

Low on his fours the Lion
    Treads with the surly Bear;
But Men straight upward from the dust
    Walk with their heads in air;
The free sweet winds of heaven,
    The sunlight from on high
Beat on their clear bright cheeks and brows
    As they go striding by;
The doors of all their houses
    They arch so they may go,
Uplifted o'er the four-foot beasts,
    Unstooping, to and fro.

ALL BUT BLIND

All but blind
   In his chambered hole
Gropes for worms
   The four-clawed Mole.

All but blind
   In the evening sky
The hooded Bat
   Twirls softly by.

All but blind
   In the burning day
The Barn-Owl blunders
   On her way.

And blind as are
   These three to me,
So, blind to Some-One
   I must be.

NICHOLAS NYE

Thistle and darnel and dock grew there,
   And a bush, in the corner, of may,
On the orchard wall I used to sprawl
   In the blazing heat of the day;
Half asleep and half awake,
   While the birds went twittering by,
And nobody there my lone to share
   But Nicholas Nye.

Nicholas Nye was lean and grey,
   Lame of a leg and old,
More than a score of donkey's years
   He had seen since he was foaled;
He munched the thistles, purple and spiked,
   Would sometimes stoop and sigh,
And turn his head, as if he said,
   'Poor Nicholas Nye!'

Alone with his shadow he'd drowse in the meadow,
   Lazily swinging his tail,
At break of day he used to bray,—
   Not much too hearty and hale;

But a wonderful gumption was under his skin,
 And a clear calm light in his eye,
And once in a while: he'd smile . . .
 Would Nicholas Nye.

Seem to be smiling at me, he would,
 From his bush in the corner, of may, —
Bony and ownerless, widowed and worn,
 Knobble-kneed, lonely and grey;
And over the grass would seem to pass
 'Neath the deep dark blue of the sky,
Something much better than words between me
 And Nicholas Nye.

But dusk would come in the apple boughs,
 The green of the glow-worm shine,
The birds in nest would crouch to rest,
 And home I'd trudge to mine;
And there, in the moonlight, dark with dew
 Asking not wherefore nor why,
Would brood like a ghost, and as still as a post,
 Old Nicholas Nye.

THE PIGS AND THE CHARCOAL-BURNER

The old Pig said to the little pigs,
 'In the forest is truffles and mast,
Follow me then, all ye little pigs,
 Follow me fast!'

The Charcoal-burner sat in the shade,
 His chin on his thumb,
And saw the big Pig and the little pigs,
 Chuffling come.

He watched 'neath a green and giant bough,
 And the pigs in the ground
Made a wonderful grizzling and gruzzling
 And greedy sound.

And when, full-fed, they were gone, and Night
 Walked her starry ways,
He stared with his cheeks in his hands
 At his sullen blaze.

[172]

FIVE EYES

In Hans' old Mill his three black cats
Watch his bins for the thieving rats.
Whisker and claw, they crouch in the night,
Their five eyes smouldering green and bright:
Squeaks from the flour sacks, squeaks from where
The cold wind stirs on the empty stair,
Squeaking and scampering, everywhere.
Then down they pounce, now in, now out,
At whisking tail, and sniffing snout;
While lean old Hans he snores away
Till peep of light at break of day;
Then up he climbs to his creaking mill,
Out come his cats all grey with meal —
Jekkel, and Jessup, and one-eyed Jill.

GRIM

Beside the blaze, as of forty fires,
Giant Grim doth sit,
Roasting a thick-woolled mountain sheep
Upon an iron spit.
Above him wheels the winter sky,
Beneath him, fathoms deep,
Lies hidden in the valley mists
A village fast asleep —
Save for one restive hungry dog
That, snuffing towards the height,
Smells Grim's broiled supper-meat, and spies
His watch-fire twinkling bright.

TIT FOR TAT

Have you been catching of fish, Tom Noddy?
  Have you snared a weeping hare?
Have you whistled, 'No Nunny,' and gunned a poor bunny,
  Or a blinded bird of the air?

Have you trod like a murderer through the green woods,
  Through the dewy deep dingles and glooms,
While every small creature screamed shrill to Dame Nature,
  'He comes — and he comes!'?

Wonder I very much do, Tom Noddy,
  If ever, when off you roam,
An Ogre from space will stoop a lean face
  And lug you home:

Lug you home over his fence, Tom Noddy,
  Of thorn-sticks nine yards high,
With your bent knees strung round his old iron gun
  And your head dan-dangling by:

And hang you up stiff on a hook, Tom Noddy,
  From a stone-cold pantry shelf,
Whence your eyes will glare in an empty stare,
  Till you are cooked yourself!

SUMMER EVENING

The sandy cat by the Farmer's chair
Mews at his knee for dainty fare;
Old Rover in his moss-greened house
Mumbles a bone, and barks at a mouse.
In the dewy fields the cattle lie
Chewing the cud 'neath a fading sky;
Dobbin at manger pulls his hay:
Gone is another summer's day.

EARTH FOLK

The cat she walks on padded claws,
The wolf on the hills lays stealthy paws,
Feathered birds in the rain-sweet sky
At their ease in the air, flit low, flit high.

The oak's blind, tender roots pierce deep,
His green crest towers, dimmed in sleep,
Under the stars whose thrones are set
Where never prince hath journeyed yet.

AT THE KEYHOLE

'Grill me some bones,' said the Cobbler,
  'Some bones, my pretty Sue;
I'm tired of my lonesome with heels and soles,
Springsides and uppers too;
A mouse in the wainscot is nibbling;
A wind in the keyhole drones;
And a sheet webbed over my candle, Susie, —
  Grill me some bones!

'Grill me some bones,' said the Cobbler,
  'I sat at my tic-tac-to;
And a footstep came to my door and stopped,
And a hand groped to and fro;
And I peered up over my boot and last;
And my feet went cold as stones: —
I saw an eye at the keyhole, Susie! —
  Grill me some bones!'

THE OLD STONE HOUSE

Nothing on the grey roof, nothing on the brown,
Only a little greening where the rain drips down;
Nobody at the window, nobody at the door,
Only a little hollow which a foot once wore;
But still I tread on tiptoe, still tiptoe on I go,
Past nettles, porch, and weedy well, for oh, I know
A friendless face is peering, and a clear still eye
Peeps closely through the casement as my step goes by.

THE RUIN

When the last colours of the day
Have from their burning ebbed away,
About that ruin, cold and lone,
The cricket shrills from stone to stone;
And scattering o'er its darkened green,
Bands of the fairies may be seen,
Chattering like grasshoppers, their feet
Dancing a thistledown dance round it:
While the great gold of the mild moon
Tinges their tiny acorn shoon.

THE RIDE-BY-NIGHTS

Up on their brooms the Witches stream,
Crooked and black in the crescent's gleam;
One foot high, and one foot low,
Bearded, cloaked, and cowled, they go.
'Neath Charlie's Wain they twitter and tweet,
And away they swarm 'neath the Dragon's feet,
With a whoop and a flutter they swing and sway,
And surge pell-mell down the Milky Way.

Between the legs of the glittering Chair
They hover and squeak in the empty air.
Then round they swoop past the glimmering Lion
To where Sirius barks behind huge Orion;
Up, then, and over to wheel amain
Under the silver, and home again.

PEAK AND PUKE

From his cradle in the glamourie
They have stolen my wee brother,
Housed a changeling in his swaddlings
For to fret my own poor mother.
Pules it in the candle light
Wi' a cheek so lean and white,
Chinkling up its eyne so wee
Wailing shrill at her an' me.
It we'll neither rock nor tend
Till the Silent Silent send,
Lapping in their waesome arms
Him they stole with spells and charms,
Till they take this changeling creature
Back to its own fairy nature —
Cry! Cry! as long as may be,
Ye shall ne'er be woman's baby!

THE CHANGELING

'Ahoy, and ahoy!'
    'Twixt mocking and merry —
'Ahoy and ahoy, there,
    Young man of the ferry!'

She stood on the steps
    In the watery gloom —
That Changeling — 'Ahoy, there!'
    She called him to come.
He came on the green wave,
    He came on the grey,
Where stooped that sweet lady
    That still summer's day.

[176]

He fell in a dream
Of her beautiful face,
As she sat on the thwart
And smiled in her place.
No echo his oar woke,
Float silent did they,
Past low-grazing cattle
In the sweet of the hay.
And still in a dream
At her beauty sat he,
Drifting stern foremost
Down — down to the sea.
Come you, then: call,
When the twilight apace
Brings shadow to brood
On the loveliest face;
You shall hear o'er the water
Ring faint in the grey —
'Ahoy, and ahoy, there!'
And tremble away;
'Ahoy, and ahoy! . . .'
And tremble away.

THE MOCKING FAIRY

'Won't you look out of your window, Mrs. Gill?'
Quoth the Fairy, nidding, nodding in the garden;
'*Can't* you look out of your window, Mrs. Gill?'
Quoth the Fairy, laughing softly in the garden;
But the air was still, the cherry boughs were still,
And the ivy-tod neath the empty sill,
And never from her window looked out Mrs. Gill
On the Fairy shrilly mocking in the garden.

'What have they done with you, you poor Mrs. Gill?'
Quoth the Fairy brightly glancing in the garden;
'Where have they hidden you, you poor old Mrs. Gill?'
Quoth the Fairy dancing lightly in the garden;
But night's faint veil now wrapped the hill,
Stark 'neath the stars stood the dead-still Mill,
And out of her cold cottage never answered Mrs. Gill
The Fairy mimbling, mambling in the garden.

BEWITCHED

I have heard a lady this night,
  Lissome and jimp and slim,
Calling me — calling me over the heather,
  'Neath the beech boughs dusk and dim.

I have followed a lady this night,
  Followed her far and lone,
Fox and adder and weasel know
  The ways that we have gone.

I sit at my supper 'mid honest faces,
  And crumble my crust and say
Nought in the long-drawn drawl of the voices
  Talking the hours away.

I'll go to my chamber under the gable,
  And the moon will lift her light
In at my lattice from over the moorland
  Hollow and still and bright.

And I know she will shine on a lady of witchcraft,
  Gladness and grief to see,
Who has taken my heart with her nimble fingers,
  Calls in my dreams to me;

Who has led me a dance by dell and dingle
  My human soul to win,
Made me a changeling to my own, own mother,
  A stranger to my kin.

THE HONEY ROBBERS

There were two Fairies, Gimmul and Mel,
Loved Earth Man's honey passing well;
Oft at the hives of his tame bees
They would their sugary thirst appease.

When even began to darken to night,
They would hie along in the fading light,
With elf-locked hair and scarlet lips,
And small stone knives to slit the skeps,

So softly not a bee inside
Should hear the woven straw divide.
And then with sly and greedy thumbs
Would rifle the sweet honeycombs.
And drowsily drone to drone would say,
'A cold, cold wind blows in this way';
And the great Queen would turn her head
From face to face, astonishèd,
And, though her maids with comb and brush
Would comb and soothe and whisper, 'Hush!'
About the hive would shrilly go
A keening — keening, to and fro;
At which those robbers 'neath the trees
Would taunt and mock the honey-bees,
And through their sticky teeth would buzz
Just as an angry hornet does.
And when this Gimmul and this Mel
Had munched and sucked and swilled their fill,
Or ever Man's first cock should crow
Back to their Faërie Mounds they'd go.
Edging across the twilight air,
Thieves of a guise remotely fair.

LONGLEGS[1]

Longlegs — he yelled 'Coo-ee!'
   And all across the combe
Shrill and shrill it rang — rang through
   The clear green gloom.
Fairies there were a-spinning,
   And a white tree-maid
Lifted her eyes, and listened
   In her rain-sweet glade.
Bunnie to bunnie stamped; old Wat
   Chin-deep in bracken sate;
A throstle piped, 'I'm by, I'm by!'
   Clear to his timid mate.
And there was Longlegs straddling,
   And hearkening was he,
To distant Echo thrilling back
   A thin 'Coo-ee!'

[1] Inscribed '(To E.T.)' (Edward Thomas) in *Down-Adown-Derry*, 1922.

MELMILLO

Three and thirty birds there stood
In an elder in a wood;
Called Melmillo — flew off three,
Leaving thirty in the tree;
Called Melmillo — nine now gone,
And the boughs held twenty-one;
Called Melmillo — and eighteen
Left but three to nod and preen;
Called Melmillo — three — two — one
Now of birds were feathers none.

Then stole slim Melmillo in
To that wood all dusk and green,
And with lean long palms outspread
Softly a strange dance did tread;
Not a note of music she
Had for echoing company;
All the birds were flown to rest
In the hollow of her breast;
In the wood — thorn, elder, willow —
Danced alone — lone danced Melmillo.

TREES

Of all the trees in England,
  Her sweet three corners in,
Only the Ash, the bonnie Ash
  Burns fierce while it is green.

Of all the trees in England,
  From sea to sea again,
The Willow loveliest stoops her boughs
  Beneath the driving rain.

Of all the trees in England,
  Past frankincense and myrrh,
There's none for smell, of bloom and smoke,
  Like Lime and Juniper.

Of all the trees in England,
  Oak, Elder, Elm and Thorn,
The Yew alone burns lamps of peace
  For them that lie forlorn.

SILVER

Slowly, silently, now the moon
Walks the night in her silver shoon;
This way, and that, she peers, and sees
Silver fruit upon silver trees;
One by one the casements catch
Her beams beneath the silvery thatch;
Couched in his kennel, like a log,
With paws of silver sleeps the dog;
From their shadowy cote the white breasts peep
Of doves in a silver-feathered sleep;
A harvest mouse goes scampering by,
With silver claws, and silver eye;
And moveless fish in the water gleam,
By silver reeds in a silver stream.

NOBODY KNOWS

Often I've heard the Wind sigh
  By the ivied orchard wall,
Over the leaves in the dark night,
  Breathe a sighing call,
And faint away in the silence,
  While I, in my bed,
Wondered, 'twixt dreaming and waking,
    What it said.

Nobody knows what the Wind is,
  Under the height of the sky,
Where the hosts of the stars keep far away house
  And its wave sweeps by —
Just a great wave of the air,
  Tossing the leaves in its sea,
And foaming under the eaves of the roof
    That covers me.

And so we live under deep water,
  All of us, beasts and men,
And our bodies are buried down under the sand,
  When we go again;
And leave, like the fishes, our shells,
  And float on the Wind and away,
To where, o'er the marvellous tides of the air,
    Burns day.

[181]

WANDERERS

Wide are the meadows of night,
And daisies are shining there,
Tossing their lovely dews,
Lustrous and fair;
And through these sweet fields go,
Wand'rers 'mid the stars —
Venus, Mercury, Uranus, Neptune,
Saturn, Jupiter, Mars.

'Tired in their silver, they move,
And circling, whisper and say,
Fair are the blossoming meads of delight
Through which we stray.

GROAT NOR TESTER

No groat for a supper,
No tester for a bed:
Ay, some poor men for taper have
The light stars shed;
And some poor men for pillow have
A mossy wayside stone,
Beneath a bough where sits and sings
The night-bird lone;
And some poor men for coverlid
Lie 'neath the mists of night —
Heavy the dew upon their breasts
At pierce of morning light;
And some poor men for valance have
Bracken whose spicy smell
Haunts the thick stillness of the dark
And brings sweet dreams as well;
And some poor men for bellman have
The farm cocks grey and red —
Who paid no groat for supper
Nor had tester for a bed.

MANY A MICKLE

A little sound —
Only a little, a little —
The breath in a reed,
A trembling fiddle;
A trumpet's ring,
The shuddering drum;
So all the glory, bravery, hush
Of music come.

A little sound —
Only a stir and a sigh
Of each green leaf
Its fluttering neighbour by;
Oak on to oak,
The wide dark forest through —
So o'er the watery wheeling world
The night winds go.

A little sound,
Only a little, a little —
The thin high drone
Of the simmering kettle,
The gathering frost,
The click of needle and thread;
Mother, the fading wall, the dream,
The drowsy bed.

WILL EVER?

Will he ever be weary of wandering,
    The flaming sun?
Ever weary of waning in lovelight,
    The white still moon?
Will ever a shepherd come
    With a crook of simple gold,
And lead all the little stars
    Like lambs to the fold?

Will ever the Wanderer sail
  From over the sea,
Up the river of water,
  To the stones to me?
Will he take us all into his ship,
  Dreaming, and waft us far,
To where in the clouds of the West
  The Islands are?

THE SONG OF THE SECRET

Where is beauty?
  Gone, gone:
The cold winds have taken it
  With their faint moan;
The white stars have shaken it,
  Trembling down,
Into the pathless deeps of the sea:
  Gone, gone
  Is beauty from me.

The clear naked flower
  Is faded and dead;
The green-leafed willow,
  Drooping her head,
Whispers low to the shade
  Of her boughs in the stream,
    Sighing a beauty
    Secret as dream.

THE SONG OF SOLDIERS

As I sat musing by the frozen dyke,
There was one man marching with a bright steel pike,
Marching in the dayshine like a ghost came he,
And behind me was the moaning and the murmur of the sea.

As I sat musing, 'twas not one but ten —
Rank on rank of ghostly soldiers marching o'er the fen,
Marching in the misty air they showed in dreams to me,
And behind me was the shouting and the shattering of the sea.

As I sat musing, 'twas a host in dark array,
With their horses and their cannon wheeling onward to the fray,
Moving like a shadow to the fate the brave must dree,
And behind me roared the drums, rang the trumpets of the sea.

THE BEES' SONG

Thousandz of thornz there be
On the Rozez where gozez
The Zebra of Zee:
Sleek, striped, and hairy,
The steed of the Fairy
Princess of Zee.

Heavy with blossomz be
The Rozez that growzez
In the thickets of Zee,
Where grazez the Zebra
Marked *Abracadeeebra*
Of the Princess of Zee.

And he nozez the poziez
Of the Rozez that growzez
So luvez'm and free,
With an eye, dark and wary,
In search of a Fairy,
Whose Rozez he knowzez
Were not honeyed for he,
But to breathe a sweet incense
To solace the Princess
Of far-away Zzzee.

A SONG OF ENCHANTMENT

A Song of Enchantment I sang me there,
In a green — green wood, by waters fair,
Just as the words came up to me
I sang it under the wild wood tree.

Widdershins turned I, singing it low,
Watching the wild birds come and go;
No cloud in the deep dark blue to be seen
Under the thick-thatched branches green.

Twilight came; silence came;
The planet of evening's silver flame;
By darkening paths I wandered through
Thickets trembling with drops of dew.

But the music is lost and the words are gone
Of the song I sang as I sat alone,
Ages and ages have fallen on me —
On the wood and the pool and the elder tree.

DREAM-SONG

Sunlight, moonlight,
Twilight, starlight —
Gloaming at the close of day,
And an owl calling,
Cool dews falling
In a wood of oak and may.

Lantern-light, taper-light,
Torchlight, no-light:
Darkness at the shut of day,
And lions roaring,
Their wrath pouring
In wild waste places far away.

Elf-light, bat-light,
Touchwood-light and toad-light,
And the sea a shimmering gloom of grey,
And a small face smiling
In a dream's beguiling
In a world of wonders far away.

[186]

THE SONG OF SHADOWS

Sweep thy faint strings, Musician,
  With thy long lean hand;
Downward the starry tapers burn,
  Sinks soft the waning sand;
The old hound whimpers couched in sleep,
  The embers smoulder low;
Across the walls the shadows
    Come, and go.

Sweep softly thy strings, Musician,
  The minutes mount to hours;
Frost on the windless casement weaves
  A labyrinth of flowers;
Ghosts linger in the darkening air,
  Hearken at the open door;
Music hath called them, dreaming,
    Home once more.

THE SONG OF THE MAD PRINCE

Who said, 'Peacock Pie'?
  The old King to the sparrow:
Who said, 'Crops are ripe'?
  Rust to the harrow:
Who said, 'Where sleeps she now?
  Where rests she now her head,
Bathed in eve's loveliness'? —
  That's what I said.

Who said, 'Ay, mum's the word'?
  Sexton to willow:
Who said, 'Green dusk for dreams,
  Moss for a pillow'?
Who said, 'All Time's delight
  Hath she for narrow bed;
Life's troubled bubble broken'? —
  That's what I said.

[187]

THE SONG OF FINIS

At the edge of All the Ages
  A Knight sate on his steed,
His armour red and thin with rust,
  His soul from sorrow freed;
And he lifted up his visor
  From a face of skin and bone,
And his horse turned head and whinnied
  As the twain stood there alone.

No Bird above that steep of time
  Sang of a livelong quest;
No wind breathed,
      Rest:
'Lone for an end!' cried Knight to steed,
  Loosed an eager rein —
Charged with his challenge into Space:
  And quiet did quiet remain.

Motley and Other Poems (1918)[1]

THE LITTLE SALAMANDER
To Margot[2]

When I go free,
I think 'twill be
A night of stars and snow,
And the wild fires of frost shall light
My footsteps as I go;
Nobody — nobody will be there
With groping touch, or sight,
To see me in my bush of hair
Dance burning through the night.

THE LINNET

Upon this leafy bush
    With thorns and roses in it,
Flutters a thing of light,
    A twittering linnet,
And all the throbbing world
    Of dew and sun and air
By this small parcel of life
    Is made more fair:
As if each bramble-spray
    And mounded gold-wreathed furze,
Harebell and little thyme,
    Were only hers;
As if this beauty and grace
    Did to one bird belong,
And, at a flutter of wing,
    Might vanish in song.

THE SUNKEN GARDEN

Speak not — whisper not;
Here bloweth thyme and bergamot;
Softly on the evening hour,
Secret herbs their spices shower.
Dark-spiked rosemary and myrrh,
Lean-stalked purple lavender;

[1] See Bibliographical Appendix p. 891.
[2] Margot Loines.

Hides within her bosom, too,
All her sorrows, bitter rue.

Breathe not — trespass not;
Of this green and darkling spot,
Latticed from the moon's beams,
Perchance a distant dreamer dreams;
Perchance upon its darkening air,
The unseen ghosts of children fare,
Faintly swinging, sway and sweep,
Like lovely sea-flowers in the deep;
While, unmoved, to watch and ward,
Amid its gloomed and daisied sward,
Stands with bowed and dewy head
That one little leaden Lad.

THE RIDDLERS

'Thou solitary!' the Blackbird cried,
'I, from the happy Wren,
Linnet and Blackcap, Woodlark, Thrush,
Perched all upon a sweetbrier bush,
Have come at cold of midnight-tide
To ask thee, Why and when
Grief smote thy heart so thou dost sing
In solemn hush of evening,
So sorrowfully, lovelorn Thing —
Nay, nay, not sing, but rave, but wail,
Most melancholy Nightingale?
Do not the dews of darkness steep
All pinings of the day in sleep?
Why, then, when rocked in starry nest
We mutely couch, secure, at rest,
Doth thy lone heart delight to make
Music for sorrow's sake?'

A Moon was there. So still her beam,
It seemed the whole world lay in dream,
Lulled by the watery sea.
And from her leafy night-hung nook
Upon this stranger soft did look
The Nightingale: sighed he: —

"'Tis strange, my friend; the Kingfisher
But yestermorn conjured me here
Out of his green and blue to say
Why thou, in splendour of the day,
Wearest, of colour, but bill gold-gay,
And else dost thee array
In a most sombre suit of black?
"Surely," he sighed, "some load of grief,
Past all our thinking — and belief —
Must weigh upon his back!"
Do, then, in turn, tell me, If joy
Thy heart as well as voice employ,
Why dost thou now, most Sable, shine
In plumage woefuller far than mine?
Thy silence is a sadder thing
Than any dirge I sing!'

Thus, then, these two small birds, perched there,
Breathed a strange riddle both did share
Yet neither could expound.
And we — who sing but as we can,
In the small knowledge of a man —
Have we an answer found?
Nay, some are happy whose delight
Is hid even in themselves from sight;
And some win peace who spend
The skill of words to sweeten despair
Of finding consolation where
Life has but one dark end;
Who, in rapt solitude, tell o'er
A tale as lovely as forelore,
Into the midnight air.

MOONLIGHT

The far moon maketh lovers wise
  In her pale beauty trembling down,
Lending curved cheeks, dark lips, dark eyes,
  A strangeness not her own.
And, though they shut their lids to kiss,
  In starless darkness peace to win,
Even on that secret world from this
  Her twilight enters in.

THE BLIND BOY

'I have no master,' said the Blind Boy,
  'My mother, "Dame Venus" they do call;
Cowled in this hood she sent me begging
  For whate'er in pity may befall.

'Hard was her visage, me adjuring, —
  "Have no fond mercy on the kind!
Here be sharp arrows, bunched in quiver,
  Draw close ere striking — thou art blind."

'So stand I here, my woes entreating,
  In this dark alley, lest the Moon
Point with her sparkling my barbed armoury,
  Shine on my silver-lacèd shoon.

'Oh, sir, unkind this Dame to me-ward;
  Of the salt billow was her birth. . . .
In your sweet charity draw nearer
  The saddest rogue on Earth!'

THE QUARRY

You hunted me with all the pack,
  Too blind, too blind, to see
By no wild hope of force or greed
  Could you make sure of me.

And like a phantom through the glades,
  With tender breast aglow,
The goddess in me laughed to hear
  Your horns a-roving go.

She laughed to think no mortal ever
  By dint of mortal flesh
The very Cause that was the Hunt
  One moment could enmesh:

That though with captive limbs I lay,
  Stilled breath and vanquished eyes,
He that hunts Love with horse and hound
  Hunts out his heart and eyes.

[192]

MRS. GRUNDY

'Step very softly, sweet Quiet-foot,
Stumble not, whisper not, smile not:
By this dark ivy stoop cheek and brow.
Still even thy heart! What seest thou? . . .'

'High-coifed, broad-browed, aged, suave yet grim,
A large flat face, eyes keenly dim,
Staring at nothing — that's me! — and yet,
With a hate one could never, no, never forget . . .'

'This is my world, my garden, my home,
Hither my father bade mother to come
And bear me out of the dark into light,
And happy I was in her tender sight.

'And then, thou frail flower, she died and went,
Forgetting my pitiless banishment,
And that Old Woman — an Aunt — she said,
Came hither, lodged, fattened, and made her bed.

'Oh, yes, thou most blessed, from Monday to Sunday,
Has lived on me, preyed on me, Mrs. Grundy:
Called me, "dear Nephew"; on each of those chairs
Has gloated in righteousness, heard my prayers.

'Why didst thou dare the thorns of the grove,
Timidest trespasser, huntress of love?
Now thou hast peeped, and now dost know
What kind of creature is thine for foe.

'Not that she'll tear out thy innocent eyes,
Poison thy mouth with deviltries.
Watch thou, wait thou: soon will begin
The guile of a voice: hark! . . .' 'Come in. Come in!'

THE TRYST

Flee into some forgotten night and be
Of all dark long my moon-bright company:
Beyond the rumour even of Paradise come,
There, out of all remembrance, make our home:

[193]

Seek we some close hid shadow for our lair,
Hollowed by Noah's mouse beneath the chair
Wherein the Omnipotent, in slumber bound,
Nods till the piteous Trump of Judgment sound.
Perchance Leviathan of the deep sea
Would lease a lost mermaiden's grot to me,
There of your beauty we would joyance make —
A music wistful for the sea-nymph's sake:
Haply Elijah, o'er his spokes of fire,
Cresting steep Leo, or the heavenly Lyre,
Spied, tranced in azure of inanest space,
Some eyrie hostel, meet for human grace,
Where two might happy be — just you and I —
Lost in the uttermost of Eternity.
Think! In Time's smallest clock's minutest beat
Might there not rest be found for wandering feet?
Or, 'twixt the sleep and wake of Helen's dream,
Silence wherein to sing love's requiem?

No, no. Nor earth, nor air, nor fire, nor deep
Could lull poor mortal longingness asleep.
Somewhere there Nothing is; and there lost Man
Shall win what changeless vague of peace he can.

ALONE

The abode of the nightingale is bare,
Flowered frost congeals in the gelid air,
The fox howls from his frozen lair:
    Alas, my loved one is gone,
    I am alone;
    It is winter.

Once the pink cast a winy smell,
The wild bee hung in the hyacinth bell,
Light in effulgence of beauty fell:
    Alas, my loved one is gone,
    I am alone;
    It is winter.

My candle a silent fire doth shed,
Starry Orion hunts o'erhead;
Come moth, come shadow, the world is dead:
    Alas, my loved one is gone,
    I am alone;
    It is winter.

THE EMPTY HOUSE[1]

See this house, how dark it is
Beneath its vast-boughed trees!
Not one trembling leaflet cries
To that Watcher in the skies —
'Remove, remove thy searching gaze,
Innocent of heaven's ways,
Brood not, Moon, so wildly bright,
On secrets hidden from sight.'

'Secrets,' sighs the night-wind,
'Vacancy is all I find;
Every keyhole I have made
Wails a summons, faint and sad,
No voice ever answers me,
      Only vacancy.'
'Once, once . . .' the cricket shrills,
And far and near the quiet fills
With its tiny voice, and then
      Hush falls again.

Mute shadows creeping slow
Mark how the hours go.
Every stone is mouldering slow.
And the least winds that blow
Some minutest atom shake,
Some fretting ruin make
In roof and walls. How black it is
Beneath these thick-boughed trees!

MISTRESS FELL

'Whom seek you here, sweet Mistress Fell?'
'One who loved me passing well.
Dark his eye, wild his face —
Stranger, if in this lonely place
Bide such an one, then, prythee, say
I am come here to-day.'

[1] Called 'The Dark House' in *The Sunken Garden and Other Poems*, 1917.

'Many his like, Mistress Fell?'
'I did not look, so cannot tell.
Only this I surely know,
When his voice called me, I must go;
Touched me his fingers, and my heart
Leapt at the sweet pain's smart.'

'Why did he leave you, Mistress Fell?'
'Magic laid its dreary spell —
Stranger, he was fast asleep;
Into his dream I tried to creep;
Called his name, soft was my cry;
He answered — not one sigh.

'The flower and the thorn are here;
Falleth the night-dew, cold and clear;
Out of her bower the bird replies,
Mocking the dark with ecstasies,
See how the earth's green grass doth grow,
Praising what sleeps below!

'Thus have they told me. And I come,
As flies the wounded wild-bird home.
Not tears I give; but all that he
Clasped in his arms, sweet charity;
All that he loved — to him I bring
For a close whispering.'

THE GHOST

'Who knocks?' 'I, who was beautiful,
  Beyond all dreams to restore,
I, from the roots of the dark thorn am hither.
  And knock on the door.'

'Who speaks?' 'I — once was my speech
  Sweet as the bird's on the air,
When echo lurks by the waters to heed;
  'Tis I speak thee fair.'

'Dark is the hour!' 'Ay, and cold.'
  'Lone is my house.' 'Ah, but mine?'
'Sight, touch, lips, eyes yearned in vain.'
  'Long dead these to thine . . .'

Silence. Still faint on the porch
  Brake the flames of the stars.
In gloom groped a hope-wearied hand
  Over keys, bolts, and bars.

A face peered. All the grey night
  In chaos of vacancy shone;
Nought but vast sorrow was there —
  The sweet cheat gone.

THE STRANGER

In the woods as I did walk,
  Dappled with the moon's beam,
I did with a Stranger talk,
  And his name was Dream.

Spurred his heel, dark his cloak,
  Shady-wide his bonnet's brim;
His horse beneath a silvery oak
  Grazed as I talked with him.

Softly his breast-brooch burned and shone;
  Hill and deep were in his eyes;
One of his hands held mine, and one
  The fruit that makes men wise.

Wondrously strange was earth to see,
  Flowers white as milk did gleam;
Spread to Heaven the Assyrian Tree,
  Over my head with Dream.

Dews were still betwixt us twain;
  Stars a trembling beauty shed;
Yet, not a whisper comes again
  Of the words he said.

[197]

BETRAYAL

She will not die, they say,
She will but put her beauty by
  And hie away.

Oh, but her beauty gone, how lonely
Then will seem all reverie,
  How black to me!

All things will sad be made
And every hope a memory,
  All gladness dead.

Ghosts of the past will know
My weakest hour, and whisper to me,
  And coldly go.

And hers in deep of sleep,
Clothed in its mortal beauty I shall see,
  And, waking, weep.

Naught will my mind then find
In man's false Heaven my peace to be:
  All blind, and blind.

THE CAGE

Why did you flutter in vain hope, poor bird,
  Hard-pressed in your small cage of clay?
'Twas but a sweet, false echo that you heard,
  Caught only a feint of day.

Still is the night all dark, a homeless dark.
  Burn yet the unanswering stars. And silence brings
The same sea's desolate surge — sans bound or mark —
  Of all your wanderings.

Fret now no more; be still. Those steadfast eyes,
  Those folded hands, they cannot set you free;
Only with beauty wake wild memories —
  Sorrow for where you are, for where you would be.

THE REVENANT

O all ye fair ladies with your colours and your graces,
    And your eyes clear in flame of candle and hearth,
Toward the dark of this old window lift not up your smiling faces,
    Where a Shade stands forlorn from the cold of the earth.

God knows I could not rest for one I still was thinking of;
    Like a rose sheathed in beauty her spirit was to me;
Now out of unforgottenness a bitter draught I'm drinking of,
    'Tis sad of such beauty unremembered to be.

Men all are shades, O Women. Winds wist not of the way they
    blow.
    Apart from your kindness, life's at best but a snare.
Though a tongue, now past praise, this bitter thing doth say, I
    know
    What solitude means, and how, homeless, I fare.

Strange, strange, are ye all — except in beauty shared with her —
    Since I seek one I loved, yet was faithless to in death.
Not life enough I heaped, so thus my heart must fare with her,
    Now wrapt in the gross clay, bereft of life's breath.

MUSIC

When music sounds, gone is the earth I know,
And all her lovely things even lovelier grow;
Her flowers in vision flame, her forest trees
Lift burdened branches, stilled with ecstasies.

When music sounds, out of the water rise
Naiads whose beauty dims my waking eyes,
Rapt in strange dreams burns each enchanted face,
With solemn echoing stirs their dwelling-place.

When music sounds, all that I was I am
Ere to this haunt of brooding dust I came;
While from Time's woods break into distant song
The swift-winged hours, as I hasten along.

THE REMONSTRANCE

I was at peace until you came
And set a careless mind aflame.
I lived in quiet; cold, content;
All longing in safe banishment,
Until your ghostly lips and eyes
    Made wisdom unwise.

Naught was in me to tempt your feet
To seek a lodging. Quite forgot
Lay the sweet solitude we two
In childhood used to wander through;
Time's cold had closed my heart about;
    And shut you out.

Well, and what then? . . . O vision grave,
Take all the little all I have!
Strip me of what in voiceless thought
Life's kept of life, unhoped, unsought! —
Reverie and dream that memory must
    Hide deep in dust!

This only I say: — Though cold and bare
The haunted house you have chosen to share,
Still 'neath its walls the moonbeam goes
And trembles on the untended rose;
Still o'er its broken roof-tree rise
The starry arches of the skies;
And in your lightest word shall be
The thunder of an ebbing sea.

NOCTURNE

'Tis not my voice now speaks; but as a bird
In darkling forest hollows a sweet throat —
Pleads on till distant echo too hath heard
    And doubles every note:
So love that shrouded dwells in mystery
    Would cry and waken thee.

Thou Solitary, stir in thy still sleep!
All the night waits thee, must thou still dream on?
Furtive the shadows that about thee creep,
And cheat the shining footsteps of the moon:
Unseal thine eyes, it is my heart that sings,
    And beats in vain its wings.

Lost in heaven's vague, the stars burn softly through
The world's dark latticings, we prisoned stray
Within its lovely labyrinth, and know
    Mute seraphs guard the way
Even from silence unto speech, from love
To that self's self it still is dreaming of.

THE EXILE

I am that Adam who, with Snake for guest,
Hid anguished eyes upon Eve's piteous breast.
I am that Adam who, with broken wings,
Fled from the Seraph's brazen trumpetings.
Betrayed and fugitive, I still must roam
A world where sin, and beauty, whisper of Home.

Oh, from wide circuit, shall at length I see
Pure daybreak lighten again on Eden's tree?
Loosed from remorse and hope and love's distress,
Enrobe me again in my lost nakedness?
No more with worldless grief a loved one grieve,
But to Heaven's nothingness re-welcome Eve?

THE UNCHANGING

After the songless rose of evening,
    Night quiet, dark, still,
In nodding cavalcade advancing
    Starred the deep hill:
You, in the valley standing,
    In your quiet wonder took

[201]

All that glamour, peace, and mystery
    In one grave look.
Beauty hid your naked body,
    Time dreamed in your bright hair,
In your eyes the constellations
    Burned far and fair.

NIGHTFALL

The last light fails — that shallow pool of day!
The coursers of the dark stamp down to drink,
Arch their wild necks, lift their wild heads and neigh;
Their drivers, gathering at the water-brink,
With eyes ashine from out their clustering hair,
Utter their hollow speech, or gaze afar,
Rapt in irradiant reverie, to where
Languishes, lost in light, the evening star.
Come the wood-nymphs to dance within the glooms,
Calling these charioteers with timbrels' din;
Ashen with twilight the dark forest looms
O'er the nocturnal beasts that prowl within.
'O glory of beauty which the world makes fair!'
Pant they their serenading on the air.

Sound the loud hooves, and all abroad the sky
The lusty charioteers their stations take;
Planet to planet do the sweet Loves fly,
And in the zenith silver music wake.
Cities of men, in blindness hidden low,
Fume their faint flames to that arched firmament,
But all the dwellers in the lonely know
The unearthly are abroad, and weary and spent,
With rush extinguished, to their dreaming go.
And world and night and star-enclustered space
The glory of beauty are in one enravished face.

INVOCATION

The burning fire shakes in the night,
    On high her silver candles gleam,
With far-flung arms enflamed with light,
    The trees are lost in dream.

Come in thy beauty! 'tis my love,
    Lost in far-wandering desire,
Hath in the darkling deep above
    Set stars and kindled fire.

EYES

O strange devices that alone divide
The seër from the seen —
The very highway of earth's pomp and pride
That lies between
The traveller and the cheating, sweet delight
Of where he longs to be,
But which, bound hand and foot, he, close on night,
Can only see.

LIFE

Hearken, O dear, now strikes the hour we die;
We, who in one strange kiss
Have proved a dream the world's realities,
Turned each from other's darkness with a sigh,
Need heed no more of life, waste no more breath
On any other journey, but of death.

And yet: Oh, know we well
How each of us must prove Love's infidel;
Still out of ecstasy turn trembling back
To earth's same empty track
Of leaden day by day, and hour by hour, and be
Of all things lovely the cold mortuary.

THE DISGUISE[1]

Why in my heart, O Grief,
Dost thou in beauty hide?
Dead is my well-content,
And buried deep my pride.
Cold are their stones, beloved,
To hand and side.

The shadows of evening are gone,
Shut are the day's clear flowers,
Now have her birds left mute
Their singing bowers,
Lone shall we be, we twain,
In the night hours.

[1] Called 'The Tryst' in *The Sunken Garden and Other Poems*, 1917.

Thou with thy cheek on mine,
And dark hair loosed, shalt see
Take the far stars for fruit
The cypress tree,
And in the yew's black
Shall the moon be.

We will tell no old tales,
Nor heed if in wandering air
Die a lost song of love
Or the once fair;
Still as well-water be
The thoughts we share!

And, while the ghosts keep
Tryst from chill sepulchres,
Dreamless our gaze shall sleep,
And sealed our ears;
Heart unto heart will speak,
Without tears.

O, thy veiled, lovely face —
Joy's strange disguise —
Shall be the last to fade
From these rapt eyes,
Ere the first dart of daybreak
Pierce the skies.

VAIN QUESTIONING

What needest thou? — a few brief hours of rest
Wherein to seek thyself in thine own breast;
A transient silence wherein truth could say
Such was thy constant hope, and this thy way? —
    O burden of life that is
    A livelong tangle of perplexities!

What seekest thou? — a truce from that thou art;
Some steadfast refuge from a fickle heart;
Still to be thou, and yet no thing of scorn,
To find no stay here, and yet not forlorn? —
    O riddle of life that is
    An endless war 'twixt contrarieties.

Leave this vain questioning. Is not sweet the rose?
Sings not the wild bird ere to rest he goes?
Hath not in miracle brave June returned?
Burns not her beauty as of old it burned?
    O foolish one to roam
    So far in thine own mind away from home!

Where blooms the flower when her petals fade,
Where sleepeth echo by earth's music made,
Where all things transient to the changeless win,
There waits the peace thy spirit dwelleth in.

VIGIL

Dark is the night,
    The fire burns faint and low,
Hours — days — years,
    Into grey ashes go;
I strive to read,
    But sombre is the glow.

Thumbed are the pages,
    And the print is small;
Mocking the winds
    That from the darkness call;
Feeble the fire that lends
    Its light withal.

O ghost, draw nearer;
    Let thy shadowy hair
Blot out the pages
    That we cannot share;
Be ours the one last leaf
    By Fate left bare!

Let's Finis scrawl,
    And then Life's book put by;
Turn each to each
    In all simplicity:
Ere the last flame is gone
    To warm us by.

THE OLD MEN[1]

Old and alone, sit we,
    Caged, riddle-rid men;
Lost to Earth's 'Listen!' and 'See!'
    Thought's 'Wherefore?' and 'When?'

Only far memories stray
    Of a past once lovely, but now
Wasted and faded away,
    Like green leaves from the bough.

Vast broods the silence of night,
    The ruinous moon
Lifts on our faces her light,
    Whence all dreaming is gone.

We speak not; trembles each head;
    In their sockets our eyes are still;
Desire as cold as the dead;
    Without wonder or will.

And One, with a lanthorn, draws near,
    At clash with the moon in our eyes:
'Where art thou?' he asks: 'I am here,'
    One by one we arise.

And none lifts a hand to withhold
    A friend from the touch of that foe:
Heart cries unto heart, 'Thou art old!'
    Yet, reluctant, we go.

THE DREAMER

O thou who giving helm and sword,
    Gav'st too the rusting rain,
And starry dark's all tender dews
    To blunt and stain:

Out of the battle I am sped,
    Unharmed, yet stricken sore;
A living shape amid whispering shades
    On Lethe's shore.

---

[1] First published in 1913 as a Flying Fame sheet, decorated by C. Lovat Fraser.

No trophy in my hands I bring,
   To this sad, sighing stream,
The neighings and the trumps and cries
   Were but a dream.

Traitor to life, of life betrayed
   O, of thy mercy deep,
A dream my all, the all I ask
   Is sleep.

HAPPY ENGLAND

Now each man's mind all Europe is:
   Boding and fear in dread array
Daze every heart: O grave and wise,
   Abide in hope the judgment day.

This war of millions in arms
   In myriad replica we wage;
Unmoved, then, Soul, by earth's alarms
   The dangers of the dark engage.

Remember happy England: keep
   For her bright cause thy latest breath;
Her peace that long hath lulled to sleep,
   May now exact the sleep of death.

Her woods and wilds, her loveliness,
   With harvest now are richly at rest;
Safe in her isled securities,
   Thy children's heaven is her breast.

O what a deep contented night
   The sun from out her Eastern seas
Would bring the dust which in her sight
   Had given its all for these!

MOTLEY

Come, Death, I'd have a word with thee;
And thou, poor Innocency;
And Love — a Lad with broken wing;
And Pity, too:
The Fool shall sing to you,
As Fools will sing.

Ay, music hath small sense,
And a tune's soon told,
And Earth is old,
And my poor wits are dense;
Yet have I secrets, — dark, my dear,
To breathe you all. Come near.
And lest some hideous listener tells,
I'll ring my bells.

They are all at war! —
Yes, yes, their bodies go
'Neath burning sun and icy star
To chaunted songs of woe,
Dragging cold cannon through a mire
Of rain and blood and spouting fire,
The new moon glinting hard on eyes
Wide with insanities!

Ssh! . . . I use words
I hardly know the meaning of;
And the mute birds
Are glancing at Love
From out their shade of leaf and flower,
Trembling at treacheries
Which even in noonday cower.
Heed, heed not what I said
Of frenzied hosts of men,
More fools than I,
On envy, hatred fed,
Who kill, and die —
Spake I not plainly, then?
Yet Pity whispered, 'Why?'

And Death — no ears hath. He hath supped where
   creep

Eyeless worms in hush of sleep;
Yet, when he smiles, the hand he draws
Athwart his grinning jaws —
Faintly the thin bones rattle, and — there, there!
Hearken how my bells in the air
Drive away care! . . .

Nay, but a dream I had
Of a world all mad.
Not simple happy mad like me,
Who am mad like an empty scene
Of water and willow tree,
Where the wind hath been;
But that foul Satan-mad,
Who rots in his own head,
And counts the dead,
Not honest one — and two —
But for the ghosts they were,
Brave, faithful, true,
When, head in air,
In Earth's clear green and blue
Heaven they did share
With beauty who bade them there. . . .

There, now! Death goes —
Mayhap I've wearied him.
Ay, and the light doth dim;
And asleep's the rose;
And tired Innocence
In dreams is hence. . . .
Come, Love, my lad,
Nodding that drowsy head,
'Tis time thy prayers were said!

THE MARIONETTES

Let the foul Scene proceed:
    There's laughter in the wings;
'Tis sawdust that they bleed,
    Only a box Death brings.

[209]

How rare a skill is theirs —
  These extreme pangs to show,
How real a frenzy wears
  Each feigner of woe!

Gigantic dins uprise!
  Even the gods must feel
A smarting of the eyes
  As these fumes upsweel.

Strange, such a Piece is free,
  While we Spectators sit,
Aghast at its agony,
  Yet absorbed in it!

Dark is the outer air,
  Coldly the night draughts blow,
Mutely we stare, and stare
  At the frenzied Show.

Yet heaven hath its quiet shroud
  Of deep, immutable blue —
We cry 'An end!' We are bowed
  By the dread, 'It's true!'

While the Shape who hoofs applause
  Behind our deafened ear,
Hoots — angel-wise — 'the Cause!'
  And affrights even fear.

TO E.T.: 1917[1]

You sleep too well — too far away,
  For sorrowing word to soothe or wound;
Your very quiet seems to say
  How longed-for a peace you have found.

Else, had not death so lured you on,
  You would have grieved — 'twixt joy and fear —
To know how my small loving son
  Had wept for you, my dear.

[1] E.T. was Edward Thomas.

APRIL MOON

Roses are sweet to smell and see,
   And lilies on the stem;
But rarer, stranger buds there be,
   And she was like to them.

The little moon that April brings,
   More lovely shade than light,
That, setting, silvers lonely hills
   Upon the verge of night —

Close to the world of my poor heart
   So stole she, still and clear;
Now that she's gone, O dark, and dark,
   The solitude, the fear.

THE FOOL'S SONG

Never, no never, listen too long,
To the chattering wind in the willows, the night bird's song.

   'Tis sad in sooth to lie under the grass,
But none too gladsome to wake and grow cold where life's
     shadows pass.

   Dumb the old Toll-Woman squats,
And, for every green copper battered and worn, doles out
     Nevers and Nots.

   I know a Blind Man, too,
Who with a sharp ear listens and listens the whole world
     through.

   Oh, sit we snug to our feast,
With platter and finger and spoon — and good victuals
     at least.

CLEAR EYES

Clear eyes do dim at last,
  And cheeks outlive their rose.
Time, heedless of the past,
  No loving-kindness knows;
Chill unto mortal lip
  Still Lethe flows.

Griefs, too, but brief while stay,
  And sorrow, being o'er,
Its salt tears shed away,
  Woundeth the heart no more.
Stealthily lave those waters
  That solemn shore.

Ah, then, sweet face, burn on,
  While yet quick memory lives!
And Sorrow, ere thou art gone,
  Know that my heart forgives —
Ere yet, grown cold in peace,
  It loves not, nor grieves.

DUST TO DUST

Heavenly Archer, bend thy bow;
Now the flame of life burns low,
Youth is gone; I, too, would go.

Ever Fortune leads to this:
Harsh or kind, at last she is
Murderess of all ecstasies.

Yet the spirit, dark, alone,
Bound in sense, still hearkens on
For tidings of a bliss foregone.

Sleep is well for dreamless head,
At no breath astonishèd,
From the Gardens of the Dead.

I the immortal harps hear ring,
By Babylon's river languishing.
Heavenly Archer, loose thy string.

THE THREE STRANGERS

Far are those tranquil hills,
  Dyed with fair evening's rose;
On urgent, secret errand bent,
  A traveller goes.

Approach him strangers three,
  Barefooted, cowled; their eyes
Scan the lone, hastening solitary
  With dumb surmise.

One instant in close speech
  With them he doth confer:
God-sped, he hasteneth on,
  That anxious traveller . . .

I was that man — in a dream:
  And each world's night in vain
I patient wait on sleep to unveil
  Those vivid hills again.

Would that they three could know
  How yet burns on in me
Love — from one lost in Paradise —
  For their grave courtesy.

ALEXANDER

It was the Great Alexander,
  Capped with a golden helm,
Sate in the ages, in his floating ship,
  In a dead calm.

Voices of sea-maids singing
  Wandered across the deep:
The sailors labouring on their oars
  Rowed, as in sleep.

All the high pomp of Asia,
  Charmed by that siren lay,
Out of their weary and dreaming minds,
  Faded away.

[213]

Like a bold boy sate their Captain,
  His glamour withered and gone,
In the souls of his brooding mariners,
  While the song pined on.

Time, like a falling dew,
  Life, like the scene of a dream,
Laid between slumber and slumber,
  Only did seem. . . .

O Alexander, then,
  In all us mortals too,
Wax thou not bold — too bold
  On the wave dark-blue!

Come the calm, infinite night,
  Who then will hear
Aught save the singing
  Of the sea-maids clear?

THE REAWAKENING

Green in light are the hills, and a calm wind flowing
  Filleth the void with a flood of the fragrance of Spring;
Wings in this mansion of life are coming and going,
  Voices of unseen loveliness carol and sing.

Coloured with buds of delight the boughs are swaying,
  Beauty walks in the woods, and wherever she rove
Flowers from wintry sleep, her enchantment obeying,
  Stir in the deep of her dream, reawaken to love.

Oh, now begone, sullen care — this light is my seeing;
  I am the palace, and mine are its windows and walls;
Daybreak is come, and life from the darkness of being
  Springs, like a child from the womb, when the lonely one calls.

THE VACANT DAY

As I walked out in meadows green
  I heard the summer noon resound
With call of myriad things unseen
  That leapt and crept upon the ground.

High overhead the windless air
  Throbbed with the homesick coursing cry
Of swifts that ranging everywhere
  Woke echo in the sky.

Beside me, too, clear waters coursed
  Which willow branches, lapsing low,
Breaking their crystal gliding forced
  To sing as they did flow.

I listened; and my heart was dumb
  With praise no language could express;
Longing in vain for him to come
  Who had breathed such blessedness

On this fair world, wherein we pass
  So chequered and so brief a stay;
And yearned in spirit to learn, alas,
  What kept him still away.

THE FLIGHT

How do the days press on, and lay
  Their fallen locks at evening down,
While the clear stars in darkness play
  And moonbeams weave a crown —

A crown of flower-like light in heaven,
  Where in the hollow arch of space
Morn's mistress dreams, and the Pleiads seven
  Stand watch about her place.

Stand watch — O days, no number keep
  Of hours when this dark clay is blind.
When the world's clocks are dumb in sleep
  'Tis then I seek my kind.

[215]

THE TWO HOUSES[1]

In the strange city of Life
Two houses I know well:
One wherein Silence a garden hath,
And one where Dark doth dwell.

Roof unto roof they stand,
Shadowing the dizzied street,
Where Vanity flaunts her gilded booths
In the noontide glare and heat.

Green-graped upon their walls
An ancient, hoary vine
Hath clustered their carven, lichenous stones
With tendril serpentine.

And ever and anon,
Dazed in that clamorous throng,
I thirst for the soundless fount that stills
Those orchards mute of song.

Knock, knock, nor knock in vain:
Heart all thy secrets tell
Where Silence a fast-sealed garden hath,
Where Dark doth dwell.

FOR ALL THE GRIEF

For all the grief I have given with words
  May now a few clear flowers blow,
In the dust, and the heat, and the silence of birds,
  Where the friendless go.

For the thing unsaid that heart asked of me
  Be a dark, cool water calling — calling
To the footsore, benighted, solitary,
  When the shadows are falling.

[1] A later version on p. 457 has the title 'Nostalgia'.

[216]

O, be beauty for all my blindness,
  A moon in the air where the weary wend,
And dews burdened with loving-kindness
  In the dark of the end.

THE SCRIBE

What lovely things
  Thy hand hath made:
The smooth-plumed bird
  In its emerald shade,
The seed of the grass,
  The speck of stone
Which the wayfaring ant
  Stirs — and hastes on!

Though I should sit
  By some tarn in thy hills,
Using its ink
  As the spirit wills
To write of Earth's wonders,
  Its live, willed things,
Flit would the ages
  On soundless wings
Ere unto Z
  My pen drew nigh;
Leviathan told,
  And the honey-fly:
And still would remain
  My wit to try —
My worn reeds broken,
  The dark tarn dry,
All words forgotten —
  Thou, Lord, and I.

FARE WELL

When I lie where shades of darkness
Shall no more assail mine eyes,
Nor the rain make lamentation
    When the wind sighs;
How will fare the world whose wonder
Was the very proof of me?
Memory fades, must the remembered
    Perishing be?

Oh, when this my dust surrenders
Hand, foot, lip, to dust again,
May these loved and loving faces
    Please other men!
May the rusting harvest hedgerow
Still the Traveller's Joy entwine,
And as happy children gather
    Posies once mine.

Look thy last on all things lovely,
Every hour. Let no night
Seal thy sense in deathly slumber
    Till to delight
Thou have paid thy utmost blessing;
Since that all things thou wouldst praise
Beauty took from those who loved them
    In other days.

Story and Rhyme (1921)[1]

SAM'S THREE WISHES:
OR LIFE'S LITTLE WHIRLIGIG[2]

'I'm thinking and thinking,' said old Sam Shore,
''Twere somebody *knocking* I heard at the door.'

From the clock popped the cuckoo and cuckooed out eight,
As there in his chair he wondering sate . . .
'There's no-one I knows on would come so late,
A-clicking the latch of an empty house
With nobbut inside 'un but me and a mouse. . . .
Maybe a-waking in sleep I be,
And 'twere out of a dream came that tapping to me.'
At length he cautiously rose, and went,
And with thumb upon latch awhile listening bent,
Then slowly drew open the door. And behold!
There stood a Fairy — all green and gold,
Mantled up warm against dark and cold,
And smiling up into his candle shine,
Lips like wax, and cheeks like wine,
As saucy and winsome a thing to see
As are linden buds on a linden tree.

Stock-still in the doorway stood simple Sam,
A-ducking his head, with 'Good-e'en to 'ee, Ma'am.'

Dame Fairy she nods, and cries clear and sweet,
''Tis a *very* good-e'en, sir, when such folks meet.
I know thee, Sam, though thou wist not of me,
And I come in late gloaming to speak with thee;
Though my eyes do dazzle at glint of your rush,
All under this pretty green fuchsia bush.'

Sam ducked once more, smiling simple and slow.
Like the warbling of birds her words did flow,
And she laughed, very merry, to see how true
Shone the old man's kindness his courtesy through.
And she nodded her head, and the stars on high
Sparkled down on her smallness from out of the sky.

[1] Subtitle: 'A Selection from the Writings of Walter de la Mare Chosen by the Author.'
[2] First published in *Twelve Poets: A Miscellany of New Verse*, London, 1918; and later included in *Down-Adown-Derry*, 1922.

'A friend is a friend, Sam, and wonderful pleasant,
And I'm come for old sake's sake to bring thee a present.
Three wishes, three wishes are thine, Sam Shore,
Just three wishes — and wish no more.
All for because, ruby-ripe to see,
The pixy-pears burn in yon hawthorn tree,
And the old milch cow, wheresoever she goes,
Never crops over the fairy-knowes.
Ay, Sam, thou art old and thy house is lone,
But there's Potencies round thee, and here is one!'

Poor Sam, he stared: and the stars o'erhead
A shimmering light on the elm-tops shed.
Like rilling of water her voice rang sweet,
And the night-wind sighed at the sound of it.
He frowned — glanced back at the empty grate,
And shook very slowly his grey old pate:
'Three wishes, my dear! Why, I scarcely knows
Which be my crany and which my toes.
But I thank 'ee, Ma'am, kindly, and this I'd say,
That the night of your passing is Michaelmas Day;
And if it were company come on a sudden,
Why, I'd ax for a fat goose to fry in the oven!'

And lo, and forsooth! as the words he was uttering,
A rich puff of air set his candle a-guttering,
And there rose in the kitchen a sizzling and sputtering,
With a crackling of sparks and of flames a great fluttering,
And — of which there could not be two opinions —
A smoking-hot savour of sage and onions.
Beam, wall and flagstones the kitchen was lit,
Every dark corner and cranny of it,
With the blaze from the hearthstone. Copper and brass
Winked back the winking of platter and glass.
And a wonderful squeaking of mice went up
At the smell of a Michaelmas supper to sup —
Unctuous odours that wreathed and swirled
Where'er frisked a whisker or mouse-tail twirled,
While out of the chimney up into the night
That ne'er-to-be-snuffed-too-much smoke took flight.

'That's one,' says the Fairy, finger on thumb,
'So now, Mister Sam, there's but two to come!'
She leaned her head sidelong; she lifted her chin,
With a twinkling of eye from the radiance within.

[220]

Poor Sam stood stounded; he says, says he,
'I *wish* my old Mother was back with me,
For if there was one thing she couldn't refuse
'Twas a sweet thick slice from the breast of a goose.'
But his cheek grew stiff, and his eyes stared bright,
For there, on her stick, pushing out of the night,
Tap-tapping along, herself and no other,
Came who but the shape of his dear old Mother!
Straight into the kitchen she hastened and went,
Her breath coming quick as if all but spent:
'Why, Sam,' says she, 'the bird be turning,
For my nose tells I that the skin's a-burning!'
And down at the oven the ghost of her sat,
And basted the goose with the boiling fat.

'Oho,' cries the Fairy, sweet and small,
'Another wish gone will leave nothing at all.'
And Sam sighs, 'Bless 'ee, Ma'am, keep the other,
There's nowt that I want now I have my Mother.'
But the Fairy laughs softly, and says, says she,
'There's one wish left, Sam, I promised 'ee three.
Hasten thy wits, the hour creeps on,
There's calling afield, and I'm soon to be gone.
Soon as haps midnight the cocks will crow,
And me to the gathering and feasting must go.'

Sam gazed at his Mother — withered and wan,
The rose in her cheek, her bright hair, gone,
And her poor old back bent double with years —
And he scarce could speak for the salt, salt tears.
'Well, well,' he says, 'I'm unspeakable glad:
But — it bain't quite the same as when I was a lad.
There's joy and there's joy, Ma'am, but to tell 'ee the truth
There's none can compare with the joy of one's youth.
And if it was possible, how could I choose
But be back in boy's breeches to eat the goose;
And all the old things — and my Mother the most,
To shine again real as my own gatepost.
What wouldn't I give, too, to see again wag
The dumpity tail of my old dog, Shag!
Your kindness, Ma'am: but all wishing was vain
Unless us can both be young again.'

A shrill, faint laughter from nowhere came . . .
Empty the dark in the candle-flame. . . .

And there stood our Sam, about four foot high,
Snub nose, shock hair, and round blue eye.
Breeches and braces, and coat of him too,
Shirt on his back, and each clodhopping shoe
Had shrunk to a nicety — button and hem
To fit the small Sammie tucked up into them.
There was his Mother, too; smooth, clear cheek,
Lips as smooth as a blackbird's beak,
Pretty arched eyebrows, the daintiest nose —
While the smoke of the baking deliciously rose.

'Come, Sammie,' she cries, 'your old Mammikin's joy,
Climb up on your stool, supper's ready, my boy.
Bring in the candle, and shut out the night;
There's goose, baked taties and cabbage to bite.
Why, bless the wee lamb, he's all shiver and shake,
And you'd think from the look of him scarcely awake!
If 'ee glour wi' those eyes, Sam, so dark and round,
The elves will away with 'ee, I'll be bound!'

So Sam and his mother by wishes three
Were made just as happy as happy can be.
And there — with a bumpity tail to wag —
Sat laughing, with tongue out, their old dog, Shag.
To clatter of platter, bones, giblets, and juice,
Between them they ate up the whole of the goose.

But time is a river for ever in flow,
The weeks went by as the weeks must go.
Soon fifty-two to a year did grow.
The long years passed, one after another,
Making older and older our Sam and his Mother;
And, alas and alack, with nine of them gone,
Poor Shag lay asleep again under a stone.
And a sorrowful dread would sometimes creep
Into Sam's dreams, as he lay asleep,
That his Mother was lost, and away he'd fare,
Calling her, calling her, everywhere,
In dark, in rain, by roads unknown,
Under echoing hills, and alone, alone.
What bliss in the morning to wake and see
The sun shining green in the linden tree,
And out of that dream's dark shadowiness
To slip in on his Mother and give her a kiss,
Then go whistling off in the dew to hear
The thrushes all mocking him, sweet and clear.

Still, moon after moon from heaven above
Shone on Mother and son, and made light of love.
Her roses faded, her pretty brown hair
Had sorrowful grey in it everywhere.
And at last she died, and was laid to rest,
Her tired hands crossed on her shrunken breast.
And Sam, now lonely, lived on and on
Till most of his workaday life seemed gone.

Yet spring came again with its green and blue,
And presently summer's wild roses too,
Pinks, Sweet William, and sops-in-wine,
Blackberry, lavender, eglantine.
And when these had blossomed and gone their way
'Twas apples, and daisies and Michaelmas Day —
Yes, spider-webs, dew, and haws in the may,
And seraphs singing in Michaelmas Day.

Sam worked all morning and *couldn't* get rest
For a kind of a feeling of grief in his breast.
And yet, not grief, but something more
Like the thought that what happens has happened before.
He fed the chickens, he fed the sow,
On a three-legged stool sate down to the cow,
With a pail 'twixt his legs in the green of the meadow,
Under the elm trees' lengthening shadow;
And woke at last with a smile and a sigh
To find he had milked his poor Jingo dry.

As dusk set in, the birds did seem
To be calling and whistling from out of a dream.
He chopped up kindling, shut up his shed,
In a bucket of well-water soused his head
To freshen his eyes up a little and make
The drowsy old wits of him wider awake.
As neat as a womanless creature is able
He swept up his hearthstone, and laid the table.
And then o'er his platter and mug, if you please,
Sate gloomily gooming at loaf and cheese —
Gooming and gooming as if the mere sight
Of his victuals could satisfy appetite!
And the longer and longer he looked at them,
The slimmer slimmed upward his candle flame,
Blue in the air. And when squeaked a mouse
'Twas loud as a trump in the hush of the house.
Then, sudden, a soft little wind puffed by,

[223]

'Twixt the thick-thatched roof and the star-sown sky;
And died . . . And then
That deep, dead, wonderful silence again.

Then — soft as a rattle counting her seeds
In the midst of a tangle of withered-up weeds —
Came a faint, faint knocking, a rustle like silk,
And a breath at the keyhole as soft as milk —
Still as the flit of a moth. And then . . .
That infinitesimal knocking again.

Sam lifted his chin from his fists. He listened.
His wandering eyes in the candle glistened.
Then slowly, slowly, rolled round by degrees —
And there sat a mouse on the top of his cheese.
He stared at this Midget, and it at him,
Over the edge of his mug's round rim,
And — as if it were Christian — he says, 'Did 'ee hear
A faint little tap-tap-tap–tapping, my dear?
You was at supper, and me in a maze,
'Tis dark for a caller in these lone days,
There's nowt in the larder. We're both of us old,
And all of my loved ones sleep under the mould,
And yet — and yet — as I've told 'ee before . . .'

But if Sam's story you'd read to the end,
Turn back to page 1, and press onward, dear friend;
Yes, if you would stave the last note of this song,
Turn back to page primus, and warble along!
For all sober records of life (come to write 'em),
Are bound to continue — well — ad infinitum!

The Veil and Other Poems (1921)

THE IMP WITHIN

'Rouse now, my dullard, and thy wits awake;
'Tis first of the morning. And I bid thee make —
No, not a vow; we have munched our fill of these
From crock of bone-dry crusts and mouse-gnawn cheese —
Nay, just one whisper in that long, long ear —
Awake; rejoice. Another Day is here! —

'A virgin wilderness, which, hour by hour,
Mere happy idleness shall bring to flower.
Barren and arid though its sands now seem,
Wherein oasis becks not, shines no stream,
Yet wake — and lo, 'tis lovelier than a dream!

'Plunge on, thy every footprint shall make fair
Its thirsty waste; and thy forecome despair
Undarken into sweet birds in the air,
Whose coursing wings and love-crazed summoning cries
Into infinity shall attract thine eyes.

'No . . .? Well, lest promise in performance faint,
A less inviting prospect will I paint.
I bid thee adjure thy Yesterday, and say:
"As *thou* wast, Enemy, so be To-day! —
Immure me in the same close narrow room;
Be hated toil the lamp to light its gloom;
Make stubborn my pen; sift dust into my ink;
Forbid mine eyes to see, my brain to think.
Scare off the words whereon the mind is set.
Make memory the power to forget.
Constrain imagination; bind its wing;
Forbid the unseen Enchantresses to sing.
Ay, do thy worst!"
     'Vexed Spectre, prythee smile.
Even though that yesterday was bleak and sour,
Art thou a slave beneath its thong to cower?
Thou hast survived! And hither am I — again,
Kindling with mockery thy o'erlaboured brain.

[225]

Though scant the moments be wherein we meet,
Think what dark months would even one make sweet!

'Thy pen? Thy paper? Ah, my dear, be true.
Come quick To-morrow. Until then, Adieu.'

THE OLD ANGLER

Twilight leaned mirrored in a pool
   Where willow boughs swept green and hoar,
Silk-clear the water, calm and cool,
   Silent the weedy shore:

There in abstracted, brooding mood
   One fishing sate. His painted float
Motionless as a planet stood;
   Motionless his boat.

A melancholy soul was this,
   With lantern jaw, gnarled hand, vague eye;
Huddled in pensive solitariness
   He had fished existence by.

Empty his creel; stolen his bait —
   Impassively he angled on,
Though mist now showed the evening late
   And daylight wellnigh gone.

Suddenly, like a tongueless bell,
   Downward his gaudy cork did glide;
A deep, low-gathering, gentle swell
   Spread slowly far and wide.

Wheeped out his tackle from noiseless winch,
   And furtive as a thief, his thumb,
With nerve intense, wound inch by inch
   A line no longer numb.

What fabulous spoil could thus unplayed
   Gape upward to a mortal air? —
He stoops engrossed; his tanned cheek greyed;
   His heart stood still: for there,

Wondrously fairing, beneath the skin
  Of secretly bubbling water seen,
Swims, not the silver of scale and fin —
  But gold inmixt with green.

Deeply astir in oozy bed,
  The darkening mirror ripples and rocks:
And lo — a wan-pale, lovely head,
  Hook tangled in its locks!

Cold from her haunt — a Naiad slim.
  Shoulder and cheek gleamed ivory white;
Though now faint stars stood over him,
  The hour hard on night.

Her green eyes gazed like one half-blind
  In sudden radiance; her breast
Breathed the sweet air, while gently twined,
  'Gainst the cold water pressed,

Her lean webbed hands. She floated there,
  Light as a scentless petalled flower,
Water-drops dewing from her hair
  In tinkling beadlike shower.

So circling sidelong, her tender throat
  Uttered a grieving, desolate wail;
Shrill o'er the dark pool lapsed its note,
  Piteous as nightingale.

Ceased Echo. And he? — a life's remorse
  Welled to a tongue unapt to charm,
But never a word broke harsh and hoarse
  To quiet her alarm.

With infinite stealth his twitching thumb
  Tugged softly at the tautened gut,
Bubble-light, fair, her lips now dumb,
  She moved, and struggled not;

But with set, wild, unearthly eyes
  Pale-gleaming, fixed as if in fear,
She couched in the water, with quickening sighs
  And floated near.

In hollow heaven the stars were at play;
  Wan glow-worms greened the pool-side grass;
Dipped the wide-bellied boat. His prey
  Gazed on; nor breathed. Alas! —

Long sterile years had come and gone;
  Youth, like a distant dream, was sped;
Heart, hope, and eyes had hungered on. . . .
  He turned a shaking head,

And clumsily groped amid the gold,
  Sleek with night dews, of that tangling hair,
Till pricked his finger keen and cold
  The barb imbedded there.

Teeth clenched, he drew his knife —'Snip, snip,'—
  Groaned, and sate shivering back; and she,
Treading the water with birdlike dip,
  Shook her sweet shoulders free:

Drew backward, smiling, infatuate fair,
  His life's disasters in her eyes,
All longing and folly, grief, despair,
  Daydreams and mysteries.

She stooped her brow; laid low her cheek,
  And, steering on that silk-tressed craft,
Out from the listening, leaf-hung creek,
  Tossed up her chin, and laughed —

A mocking, icy, inhuman note.
  One instant flashed that crystal breast,
Leaned, and was gone. Dead-still the boat:
  And the deep dark at rest.

Flits moth to flower. A water-rat
  Noses the placid ripple. And lo!
Streams a lost meteor. Night is late,
  And daybreak zephyrs flow. . . .

And he — the cheated? Dusk till morn,
  Insensate, even of hope forsook,
He muttering squats, aloof, forlorn,
  Dangling a baitless hook.

THE WILLOW

Leans now the fair willow, dreaming
Amid her locks of green.
In the driving snow she was parched and cold,
And in midnight hath been
Swept by blasts of the void night,
Lashed by the rains.
Now of that wintry dark and bleak
No memory remains.

In mute desire she sways softly;
Thrilling sap up-flows;
She praises God in her beauty and grace,
Whispers delight. And there flows
A delicate wind from the Southern seas,
Kissing her leaves. She sighs.
While the birds in her tresses make merry;
Burns the Sun in the skies.

TITMOUSE

If you would happy company win,
Dangle a palm-nut from a tree,
Idly in green to sway and spin,
Its snow-pulped kernel for bait; and see
A nimble titmouse enter in.

Out of earth's vast unknown of air,
Out of all summer, from wave to wave,
He'll perch, and prank his feathers fair,
Jangle a glass-clear wildering stave,
And take his commons there —

This tiny son of life; this spright,
By momentary Human sought,
Plume will his wing in the dappling light,
Clash timbrel shrill and gay —
And into Time's enormous Nought,
Sweet-fed, will flit away.

[229]

THE VEIL

I think and think; yet still I fail —
Why does this lady wear a veil?
Why thus elect to mask her face
Beneath that dainty web of lace?
The tip of a small nose I see,
And two red lips, set curiously
Like twin-born cherries on one stem,
And yet she has netted even them.
Her eyes, it's plain, survey with ease
All that to glance upon they please.
Yet, whether hazel, grey, or blue,
Or that even lovelier lilac hue,
I cannot guess: why — why deny
Such beauty to the passer-by?
Out of a bush a nightingale
May expound his song; beneath that veil
A happy mouth no doubt can make
English sound sweeter for its sake.
But then, why muffle in, like this,
What every blossomy wind would kiss?
Why in that little night disguise
A daylight face, those starry eyes?

THE FAIRY IN WINTER[1]

There was a Fairy — flake of winter —
Who, when the snow came, whispering, Silence,
Sister crystal to crystal sighing,
Making of meadow argent palace,
　　Night a star-sown solitude,
Cried 'neath her frozen eaves, 'I burn here!'

Wings diaphanous, beating bee-like,
Wand within fingers, locks enspangled,
Icicle foot, lip sharp as scarlet,
She lifted her eyes in her pitch-black hollow —
Green as stalks of weeds in water —
Breathed: stirred.

[1] With subtitle '(For a drawing by Dorothy Pulis Lathrop)' (*The Veil and Other Poems*, 1921)

[230]

Rilled from her heart the ichor, coursing,
Flamed and awoke her slumbering magic.
Softlier than moth's her pinions trembled;
Out into blackness, light-like, she flittered,
Leaving her hollow cold, forsaken.

In air, o'er crystal, rang twangling night-wind.
Bare, rimed pine-woods murmured lament.

THE FLOWER

Horizon to horizon, lies outspread
The tenting firmament of day and night;
Wherein are winds at play; and planets shed
Amid the stars their gentle gliding light.

The huge world's sun flames on the snow-capped hills;
Cindrous his heat burns in the sandy plain;
With myriad spume-bows roaring ocean swills
The cold profuse abundance of the rain.

And man — a transient object in this vast,
Sighs o'er a universe transcending thought,
Afflicted by vague bodings of the past,
Driven toward a future, unforeseen, unsought.

Yet, see him, stooping low to naked weed
That meeks its blossom in his anxious eye,
Mark how he grieves, as if his heart did bleed,
And wheels his wondrous features to the sky;
As if, transfigured by so small a grace,
He sought Companion in earth's dwelling-place.

BEFORE DAWN

Dim-berried is the mistletoe
With globes of sheenless grey,
The holly mid ten thousand thorns
Smoulders its fires away;
And in the manger Jesu sleeps
    This Christmas Day.

[231]

Bull unto bull with hollow throat
Makes echo every hill,
Cold sheep in pastures thick with snow
The air with bleatings fill;
While of his mother's heart this Babe
    Takes His sweet will.

All flowers and butterflies lie hid,
The blackbird and the thrush
Pipe but a little as they flit
Restless from bush to bush;
Even to the robin Gabriel hath
    Cried softly, 'Hush!'

Now night's astir with burning stars
In darkness of the snow;
Burdened with frankincense and myrrh
And gold the Strangers go
Into a dusk where one dim lamp
    Burns faintly, Lo!

No snowdrop yet its small head nods,
In winds of winter drear;
No lark at casement in the sky
Sings matins shrill and clear;
Yet in this frozen mirk the Dawn
    Breathes, Spring is here!

THE SPECTRE

In cloudy quiet of the day,
While thrush and robin perched mute on spray,
A spectre by the window sat,
    Brooding thereat.

He marked the greenness of the Spring,
Daffodil blowing, bird a-wing —
Yet dark the house the years had made
    Within that Shade.

Blinded the rooms wherein no foot falls.
Faded the portraits on the walls.
Reverberating, shakes the air
    A river there.

Coursing in flood, its infinite roars;
From pit to pit its water pours;
And he, with countenance unmoved,
    Hears cry: —'Beloved,

'Oh, ere the day be utterly spent,
Return, return, from banishment.
The night thick-gathers. Weep a prayer
    For the true and fair!'

THE VOICE

'We are not often alone, we two,'
Mused a secret voice in my ear,
As the dying hues of afternoon
Lapsed into evening drear.

A withered leaf, wafted on in the street,
Like a wayless spectre, sighed;
Aslant on the roof-tops a sickly moon
Did mutely abide.

Yet waste though the shallowing day might seem,
And fainter than hope its rose,
Strangely that speech in my thoughts welled on;
As water in-flows:

Like remembered words once heard in a room
Wherein death kept far-away tryst;
'Not often alone, we two; but thou,
How sorely missed!'

THE HOUR-GLASS

Thou who know'st all the sorrows of this earth —
I pray Thee, ponder, ere again Thou turn
Thine hour-glass o'er again, since one sole birth,
To poor clay-cold humanity, makes yearn
A heart at passion with life's endless coil.
Thou givest thyself too strait a room therein.
For so divine a tree too poor a soil.
For so great agony what small peace to win.

[233]

Cast from that Ark of Heaven which is Thy home
The raven of hell may wander without fear;
But sadly wings the dove o'er floods to roam,
Nought but one tender sprig his eyes to cheer.
Nay, Lord, I speak in parables. But see!
'Tis stricken Man in Men that pleads with Thee.

IN THE DOCK

Pallid, mis-shapen he stands. The World's grimed thumb,
Now hooked securely in his matted hair,
Has haled him struggling from his poisonous slum
And flung him, mute as fish, close-netted there.

His bloodless hands entalon that iron rail.
He gloats in beastlike trance. His settling eyes
From staring face to face rove on — and quail.
Justice for carrion pants; and these the flies.

Voice after voice in smooth impartial drone
Erects horrific in his darkening brain
A timber framework, where agape, alone,
Bright life will kiss good-bye the cheek of Cain.

Sudden like wolf he cries; and sweats to see
When howls man's soul, it howls inaudibly.

THE WRECK

Storm and unconscionable winds once cast
On grinding shingle, masking gap-toothed rock,
This ancient hulk. Rent hull, and broken mast,
She sprawls sand-mounded, of sea birds the mock.
Her sailors, drowned, forgotten, rot in mould,
Or hang in stagnant quiet of the deep —
The brave, the afraid into one silence sold;
Their end a memory fainter than of sleep.
She held good merchandise. She paced in pride
The uncharted paths men trace in ocean's foam.
Now laps the ripple in her broken side,
And zephyr in tamarisk softly whispers, Home.

The dreamer scans her in the sea-blue air,
And, sipping of contrast, finds the day more fair.

THE SUICIDE

Did these night-hung houses,
Of quiet, starlit stone,
Breathe not a whisper — 'Stay,
Thou unhappy one;
Whither so secret away?'

Sighed not the unfriending wind,
Chill with nocturnal dew,
'Pause, pause, in thy haste,
O thou distraught! I too
Tryst with the Atlantic waste.'

Steep fell the drowsy street;
In slumber the world was blind:
Breathed not one midnight flower
Peace in thy broken mind? —
'Brief, yet sweet, is life's hour.'

Syllabled thy last tide —
By as dark moon stirred,
And doomed to forlorn unrest —
Not one compassionate word? . . .
'Cold is this breast.'

DRUGGED

Inert in his chair,
In a candle's guttering glow;
His bottle empty,
His fire sunk low;
With drug-sealed lids shut fast,
Unsated mouth ajar,
This darkened phantasm walks
Where nightmares are:

In a frenzy of life and light,
Crisscross — a menacing throng —
They gibe, they squeal at the stranger,
Jostling along,
Their faces cadaverous grey:
While on high from an attic stare
Horrors, in beauty apparelled,
Down the dark air.

[235]

A stream gurgles over its stones,
The chambers within are a-fire.
Stumble his shadowy feet
Through shine, through mire;
And the flames leap higher.
In vain yelps the wainscot mouse;
In vain beats the hour;
Vacant, his body must drowse
Until daybreak flower —

Staining these walls with its rose,
And the draughts of the morning shall stir
Cold on cold brow, cold hands.
And the wanderer
Back to flesh house must return.
Lone soul — in horror to see,
Than dream more meagre and awful,
Reality.

WHO'S THAT?

Who's that? Who's that? . . .
Oh, only a leaf on the stone;
And the sigh of the air in the fire.
    Yet it seemed, as I sat,
Came company — not my own;
Stood there, with ardent gaze over dark, bowed shoulder
        thrown,
    Till the dwindling flames leaped higher,
    And showed fantasy flown.

Yet, though the cheat is clear —
From transient illusion grown;
In the vague of my mind those eyes
    Still haunt me. One stands so near
I could take his hand, and be gone: —
No more in this house of dreams to sojourn aloof, alone:
    Could sigh, with full heart, and arise,
    And choke, 'Lead on!'

HOSPITAL

Welcome! Enter! This is the Inn at the Cross Roads,
Sign of the *Rising Sun*, of the *World's End*:
Ay, O Wanderer, footsore, weary, forsaken,
    Knock, and we will open unto thee — Friend.

Gloomy our stairs of stone, obscure the portal;
Burdened the air with a breath from the further shore;
Yet in our courtyard plays an invisible fountain,
    Ever flowers unfading nod at the door.

Ours is much company, and yet none is lonely;
Some with a smile may pay and some with a sigh;
So all be healed, restored, contented — it is no matter;
    So all be happy at heart to bid good-bye.

But know, our clocks are the world's; Night's wings are leaden;
Pain languidly sports with the hours: have courage, sir!
We wake but to bring thee slumber, our drowsy syrups
    Sleep beyond dreams on the weary will confer.

Ghosts may be ours; but gaze thou not too closely
If haply in chill of the dark thou rouse to see
One silent of foot, hooded, and hollow of visage,
    Pause, with secret eyes, to peer out at thee.

He is the Ancient Tapster of this Hostel,
To him at length even we all keys must resign;
And if he beckon, Stranger, thou too must follow —
    Love and all peace be thine.

A SIGN

How shall I know when the end of things is coming?
The dark swifts flitting, the drone-bees humming;
The fly on the window-pane bedazedly strumming;
Ice on the waterbrooks their clear chimes dumbing —
How shall I know that the end of things is coming?

The stars in their stations will shine glamorous in the black:
Emptiness, as ever, haunt the great Star Sack;
And Venus, proud and beautiful, go down to meet the day,
Pale in phosphorescence of the green sea spray —
How shall I know that the end of things is coming?

Head asleep on pillow; the peewits at their crying;
A strange face in dreams to my rapt phantasma sighing;
Silence beyond words of anguished passion;
Or stammering an answer in the tongue's cold fashion —
How shall I know that the end of things is coming?

Haply on strange roads I shall be, the moorland's peace around me;
Or counting up a fortune to which Destiny hath bound me;
Or — Vanity of Vanities — the honey of the Fair;
Or a greybeard, lost to memory, on the cobbles in my chair —
How shall I know that the end of things is coming?

The drummers will be drumming; the fiddlers at their thrumming;
Nuns at their beads; the mummers at their mumming;
Heaven's solemn Seraph stoopt weary o'er his summing;
The palsied fingers plucking, the way-worn feet numbing —
        And the end of things coming.

GOOD-BYE

The last of last words spoken is, Good-bye —
The last dismantled flower in the weed-grown hedge,
The last thin rumour of a feeble bell far ringing,
The last blind rat to spurn the mildewed rye.

A hardening darkness glasses the haunted eye,
Shines into nothing the watcher's burnt-out candle,
Wreathes into scentless nothing the wasting incense,
Faints in the outer silence the hunting-cry.

Love of its muted music breathes no sigh,
Thought in her ivory tower gropes in her spinning,
Toss on in vain the whispering trees of Eden,
Last of all last words spoken is, Good-bye.

THE MONOLOGUE

Alas, O Lovely One,
    Imprisoned here,
I tap; thou answerest not,
    I doubt, and fear.
Yet transparent as glass these walls,
    If thou lean near.

Last dusk, at those high bars
    There came, scarce-heard,
Claws, fluttering feathers,
    Of deluded bird —
With one shrill, scared, faint note
    The silence stirred.

Rests in that corner,
    In puff of dust, a straw —
Vision of harvest-fields
    I never saw,
Of strange green streams and hills,
    Forbidden by law.

These things I whisper,
    For I see — in mind —
Thy caged cheek whiten
    At the wail of wind,
That thin breast wasting; unto
    Woe resigned.

Take comfort, listen!
    Once we twain were free;
There was a Country —
    Lost the memory . . .
Lay thy cold brow on hand,
    And dream with me.

Awaits me torture;
    I have smelt their rack;
From spectral groaning wheel
    Have turned me back;
Thumbscrew and boot, and then —
    The yawning sack.

Lean closer, then!
    Lay palm on stony wall.

[239]

Let but thy ghost beneath
      Thine eyelids call:
'Courage, my brother!' Nought
      Can then appal.

Yet coward, coward am I,
      And drink I must
When clanks the pannikin
      With the longed-for crust;
Though heart within is sour
      With disgust.

Long hours there are,
      When mutely tapping — well,
Is it to Vacancy
      I these tidings tell?
Knock these numb fingers against
      An empty cell?

Nay, answer not.
      Let still mere longing make
Thy presence sure to me,
      While in doubt I shake:
Be but my Faith in thee,
      For sanity's sake.

AWAKE!

Why hath the rose faded and fallen, yet these eyes have not seen?
Why hath the bird sung shrill in the tree — and this mind deaf
            and cold?
Why have the rains of summer veiled her flowers with their sheen
      And this black heart untold?

Here is calm Autumn now, the woodlands quake,
And, where this splendour of death lies under the tread,
The spectre of frost will stalk, and a silence make,
      And snow's white shroud be spread.

O self! O self! Wake from thy common sleep!
Fling off the destroyer's net. He hath blinded and bound thee.
In nakedness sit; pierce thy stagnation, and weep;
      Or corrupt in thy grave — all Heaven around thee.

NOT THAT WAY

No, no. Guard thee. Get thee gone.
    Not that way.
See; the louring clouds glide on,
Skirting West to South; and see,
The green light under that sycamore tree —
    Not that way.

There the leaden trumpets blow,
    Solemn and slow.
There the everlasting walls
Frown above the waterfalls
    Silver and cold;
    Timelessly old:
    Not that way.

Not toward Death, who, stranger, fairer,
Than any siren turns his head —
Than sea-couched siren, arched with rainbows,
Where knell the waves of her ocean bed.
Alas, that beauty hangs her flowers
For lure of his demoniac powers:
Alas, that from these eyes should dart
Such piercing summons to thy heart;
That mine in frenzy of longing beats,
Still lusting for these gross deceits.
    Not that way!

FOG

Stagnant this wintry gloom. Afar
The farm-cock bugles his 'Qui vive?'
The towering elms are lost in mist;
Birds in the thorn-trees huddle a-whist;
    The mill-race waters grieve.
      Our shrouded day
      Dwindles away
    To final black of eve.

Beyond these shades in space of air
Ride exterrestrial beings by?
Their colours burning rich and fair,

Where noon's sunned valleys lie?
With inaudible music are they sweet —
Bell, hoof, soft lapsing cry?

Turn marvellous faces, each to each? —
Lips innocent of sigh,
Or groan or fear, sorrow and grief,
Clear brow and falcon eye;
Bare foot, bare shoulder in the heat,
And hair like flax? Do their horses beat
Their way through wildernesses infinite
Of starry-crested trees, blue sward,
And gold-chasm'd mountain, steeply shored
O'er lakes of sapphire dye?

Mingled with lisping speech, faint laughter,
Echoes the Phoenix' scream of joyance
      Mounting on high? —
Light-bathed vistas and divine sweet mirth,
Beyond dream of spirits penned to earth,
Condemned to pine and die? . . .
Hath serving Nature, bidden of the gods,
Thick-screened Man's narrow sky,
And hung these Stygian veils of fog
      To hide his dingied sty? —
The gods who yet, at mortal birth,
      Bequeathed him Fantasy?

SOTTO VOCE

To Edward Thomas

The haze of noon wanned silver-grey
The soundless mansion of the sun:
The air made visible in his ray,
Like molten glass from furnace run,
Quivered o'er heat-baked turf and stone
And the flower of the gorse burned on —
Burned softly as gold of a child's fair hair
Along each spiky spray, and shed
Almond-like incense in the air
Whereon our senses fed.

At foot — a few sparse harebells: blue
And still as were the friend's dark eyes
That dwelt on mine, transfixèd through
With sudden ecstatic surmise.

'Hst!' he cried softly, smiling, and lo,
Stealing amidst that maze gold-green,
I heard a whispering music flow
From guileful throat of bird, unseen: —
So delicate the straining ear
Scarce carried its faint syllabling
Into a heart caught up to hear
That inmost pondering
Of bird-like self with self. We stood,
In happy trance-like solitude,
Hearkening a lullay grieved and sweet —
As when on isle uncharted beat
'Gainst coral at the palm-tree's root,
With brine-clear, snow-white foam afloat,
The wailing, not of water or wind —
A husht, far, wild, divine lament,
When Prospero his wizardry bent
Winged Ariel to bind. . . .

Then silence, and o'er-flooding noon.
I raised my head; smiled too. And he —
Moved his great hand, the magic gone —
Gently amused to see
My ignorant wonderment. He sighed.
'It was a nightingale,' he said,
'That *sotto voce* cons the song
He'll sing when dark is spread;
And Night's vague hours are sweet and long,
And we are laid abed.'

THE IMAGINATION'S PRIDE

Be not too wildly amorous of the far,
    Nor lure thy fantasy to its utmost scope.
Read by a taper when the needling star
    Burns red with menace in heaven's midnight cope.
Friendly thy body: guard its solitude.
    Sure shelter is thy heart. It once had rest
Where founts miraculous thy lips endewed,
    Yet nought loomed further than thy mother's breast.

[243]

O brave adventure! Ay, at danger slake
   Thy thirst, lest life in thee should, sickening, quail;
But not toward nightmare goad a mind awake,
   Nor to forbidden horizons bend thy sail —
Seductive outskirts whence in trance prolonged
   Thy gaze, at stretch of what is sane-secure,
Dreams out on steeps by shapes demoniac thronged
   And vales wherein alone the dead endure.

Nectarous those flowers, yet with venom sweet.
   Thick-juiced with poison hang those fruits that shine
Where sick phantasmal moonbeams brood and beat,
   And dark imaginations ripe the vine.
Bethink thee: every enticing league thou wend
   Beyond the mark where life its bound hath set
Will lead thee at length where human pathways end
   And the dark enemy spreads his maddening net.

Comfort thee, comfort thee. Thy Father knows
   How wild man's ardent spirit, fainting, yearns
For mortal glimpse of death's immortal rose,
   The garden where the invisible blossom burns.
Humble thy trembling knees; confess thy pride;
   Be weary. Oh, whithersoever thy vaunting rove,
His deepest wisdom harbours in thy side,
   In thine own bosom hides His utmost love.

THE WANDERERS

Within my mind two spirits strayed
From out their still and purer air,
And there a moment's sojourn made;
As lovers will in woodlands bare.
Nought heeded they where now they stood,
Since theirs its alien solitude
Beyond imagination fair.

The light an earthly candle gives,
When it is quenched leaves only dark;
Theirs yet in clear remembrance lives
And, still within, I whispered, 'Hark';
As one who faintly on high has heard
The call note of a hidden bird
Even sweeter than the lark.

[244]

Yet 'twas their silence breathed only this —
'I love you.' As if flowers might say,
'Such is our natural fragrantness';
Or dewdrop at the break of day
Cry, 'Thus I beam.' Each turned a head,
But each its own clear radiance shed
With joy and peace at play.

So in a gloomy London street
Princes from Eastern realms might pause
In secret converse, then retreat.
Yet without haste passed these from sight;
As if a human mind were not
Wholly a dark and dismal spot —
At least in their own light.

THE CORNER STONE

Sterile these stones
By time in ruin laid.
Yet many a creeping thing
Its haven has made
In these least crannies, where falls
Dark's dew, and noonday shade.

The claw of the tender bird
Finds lodgement here;
Dye-winged butterflies poise;
Emmet and beetle steer
Their busy course; the bee
Drones, laden, near.

Their myriad-mirrored eyes
Great day reflect.
By their exquisite farings
Is this granite specked;
Is trodden to infinite dust;
By gnawing lichens decked.

Toward what eventual dream
Sleeps its cold on,
When into ultimate dark
These lives shall be gone,
And even of man not a shadow remain
Of all he has done?

[245]

THE SPIRIT OF AIR

Coral and clear emerald,
And amber from the sea,
Lilac-coloured amethyst,
Chalcedony;
The lovely Spirit of Air
Floats on a cloud and doth ride,
Clad in the beauties of earth
Like a bride.

So doth she haunt me; and words
Tell but a tithe of the tale.
Sings all the sweetness of Spring
Even in the nightingale?
Nay, but with echoes she cries
Of the valley of love;
Dews on the thorns at her feet,
And darkness above.

THE UNFINISHED DREAM

Rare-sweet the air in that unimagined country —
My spirit had wandered far
From its weary body close-enwrapt in slumber
Where its home and earth-friends are;

A milk-like air — and of light all abundance;
And there a river clear
Painting the scene like a picture on its bosom,
Green foliage drifting near.

No sign of life I saw, as I pressed onward,
Fish, nor beast, nor bird,
Till I came to a hill clothed in flowers to its summit,
Then shrill small voices I heard.

And I saw from concealment a company of elf-folk
With faces strangely fair,
Talking their unearthly scattered talk together,
A bind of green-grasses in their hair,

Marvellously gentle, feater far than children,
In gesture, mien and speech,
Hastening onward in translucent shafts of sunshine
And gossiping each with each.

[246]

Straw-light their locks, on neck and shoulder falling,
  Faint of almond the silks they wore,
Spun not of worm, but as if inwoven of moonbeams
  And foam on rock-bound shore;

Like lank-legged grasshoppers in June-tide meadows,
  Amalillios of the day,
Hungrily gazed upon by me — a stranger,
  In unknown regions astray.

Yet, happy beyond words, I marked their sunlit faces,
  Stealing soft enchantment from their eyes,
Tears in my own confusing their small image,
  Hearkening their bead-like cries.

They passed me, unseeing, a waft of flocking linnets;
  Sadly I fared on my way;
And came in my dream to a dreamlike habitation,
  Close-shut, festooned, and grey.

Pausing, I gazed at the porch dust-still, vine-wreathèd,
  Worn on the stone steps thereto,
Mute hung its bell, whence a stony head looked downward,
  Grey 'gainst the sky's pale-blue —

Strange to me: strange. . . .

MUSIC

O restless fingers — not that music make!
Bidding old griefs from out the past awake,
And pine for memory's sake.

Those strings thou callest from quiet to yearn,
Of other hearts did hapless secrets learn,
And thy strange skill will turn

To uses that thy bosom dreams not of:
Ay, summon from their dark and dreadful grove
The chaunting, pale-cheeked votaries of love.

Stay now, and hearken! From that far-away
Cymbal on cymbal beats, the fierce horns bray,
Stars in their sapphire fade, 'tis break of day.

[247]

Green are those meads, foam-white the billow's crest,
And Night, withdrawing in the cavernous West,
Flings back her shadow on the salt sea's breast.

Snake-haired, snow-shouldered, pure as flame and dew,
Her strange gaze burning slumbrous eyelids through,
Rises the Goddess from the waves dark blue.

THE SON OF MELANCHOLY

Unto blest Melancholy's house one happy day
    I took my way:
Into a chamber was shown, whence could be seen
Her flowerless garden, dyed with sunlit green
    Of myrtle, box, and bay.

Cool were its walls, shade-mottled, green and gold.
    In heavy fold
Hung antique tapestries, from whose fruit and flower
Light had the bright hues stolen, hour by hour,
    And time worn thin and old.

Silence, as of a virginal laid aside,
    Did there abide.
But not for voice or music was I fain,
Only to see a long-loved face again —
    For her sole company sighed.

And while I waited, giving memory praise,
    My musing gaze
Lit on the one sole picture in the room,
Which hung, as if in hiding, in the gloom
    From evening's stealing rays.

Framed in fast-fading gilt, a child gazed there,
    Lovely and fair;
A face whose happiness was like sunlight spent
On some poor desolate soul in banishment,
    Mutely his grief to share.

Long, long I stood in trance of that glad face,
    Striving to trace
The semblance that, disquieting, it bore
To one whom memory could not restore,
    Nor fix in time and space.

Sunk deep in brooding thus, a voice I heard
      Whisper its word:
I turned — and, stooping in the threshold, stood
She — the dark mistress of my solitude,
      Who smiled, nor stirred.

Her ghost gazed darkly from her pondering eyes
      Charged with surmise;
Challenging mine, between mockery and fear,
She breathed her greeting, '*Thou*, my only dear!
      Wherefore such heavy sighs?'

'But this?' One instant lids her scrutiny veiled;
      Her wan cheek paled.
'This child?' I asked. 'Its picture brings to mind
Remembrance faint and far, past thought to find,
      And yet by time unstaled.'

Smiling, aloof, she turned her narrow head,
'Make thou my face thy glass,' she cried and said.
'What wouldst thou see therein — thine own, or mine?
O foolish one, what wonder thou didst pine?

'Long thou hast loved me; yet hast absent been.
See now: Dark night hath pressed an entrance in.
Jealous! thou dear? Nay, come; by taper's beam
Share thou this pictured Joy with me, though only a dream.'

THE QUIET ENEMY

Hearken! — now the hermit bee
Drones a quiet threnody;
Greening on the stagnant pool
The criss-cross light slants silken-cool;
In the venomed yew tree wings
Preen and flit. The linnet sings.

Gradually the brave sun
Droops to a day's journey done;
In the marshy flats abide
Mists to muffle midnight-tide.
Puffed within the belfry tower
Hungry owls drowse out their hour. . . .

Walk in beauty. Vaunt thy rose.
Flaunt thy transient loveliness.
Pace for pace with thee there goes
A shape that hath not come to bless.
I thine enemy? . . . Nay, nay.
I can only watch and wait
Patient treacherous time away,
Hold ajar the wicket gate.

THE FAMILIAR

'Are you far away?'
'Yea, I am far — far;
Where the green wave shelves to the sand,
And the rainbows are;
And an ageless sun beats fierce
From an empty sky:
There, O thou Shadow forlorn,
Is the wraith of thee, I.'

'Are you happy, most Lone?'
'Happy, forsooth!
Who am eyes of the air; the voice of the foam;
Ah, happy in truth.
My hair is astream, this cheek
Glistens like silver, and see,
As the gold to the dross, the ghost in the mirk,
I am calling to thee.'

'Nay, I am bound.
And your cry faints out in your mind.
Peace not on earth have I found,
Yet to earth am resigned.
Cease thy shrill mockery, Voice,
Nor answer again.'
'O Master, thick cloud shuts thee out
And cold tempests of rain.'

MAERCHEN

Soundless the moth-flit, crisp the death-watch tick;
Crazed in her shaken arbour bird did sing;
Slow wreathed the grease adown from soot-clogged wick:
   The Cat looked long and softly at the King.

Mouse frisked and scampered, leapt, gnawed, squeaked;
Small at the window looped cowled bat a-wing;
The dim-lit rafters with the night-mist reeked:
   The Cat looked long and softly at the King.

O wondrous robe enstarred, in night dyed deep:
O air scarce-stirred with the Court's far junketing:
O stagnant Royalty — A-swoon? Asleep?
   The Cat looked long and softly at the King.

GOLD

Sighed the wind to the wheat: —
'The Queen who is slumbering there,
Once bewildered the rose;
Scorned, "Thou un-fair!"
Once, from that bird-whirring court,
Ascended the ruinous stair.
Aloft, on that weed-hung turret, suns
Smote on her hair —
Of a gold by Archíac sought,
Of a gold sea-hid,
Of a gold that from core of quartz
No flame shall bid
Pour into light of the air
For God's Jews to see.'

Mocked the wheat to the wind: —
'Kiss me! Kiss me!'

THE GALLIASS

'Tell me, tell me,
   Unknown stranger,
When shall I sight me
   That tall ship
On whose flower-wreathed counter is gilded, *Sleep*?'

'Landsman, landsman,
Lynx nor kestrel
Ne'er shall descry from
Ocean steep
That midnight-stealing, high-pooped galliass, *Sleep*.'

'Promise me, Stranger,
Though I mark not
When cold night-tide's
Shadows creep
Thou wilt keep unwavering watch for *Sleep*.'

'Myriad the lights are,
Wayworn landsman,
Rocking the dark through
On the deep:
She alone burns none to prove her *Sleep*.

THE DECOY

'Tell us, O pilgrim, what strange She
Lures and decoys your wanderings on?
Cheek, eye, brow, lip, you scan each face,
Smile, ponder — and are gone.

'Are we not flesh and blood? Mark well,
We touch you with our hands. We speak
A tongue that may earth's secrets tell:
Why further will you seek?'

'Far have I come, and far must fare.
Noon and night and morning-prime,
I search the long road, bleak and bare,
That fades away in Time.

'On the world's brink its wild weeds shake,
And there my own dust, dark with dew,
Burns with a rose that, sleep or wake,
Beacons me —"Follow true!"'

'Her name, crazed soul? And her degree?
What peace, prize, profit in her breast?'
'A thousand cheating names hath she;
And none fore-tokens rest.'

SUNK LYONESSE

In sea-cold Lyonesse,
When the Sabbath eve shafts down
On the roofs, walls, belfries
Of the foundered town,
The Nereids pluck their lyres
Where the green translucency beats,
And with motionless eyes at gaze
Make minstrelsy in the streets.

And the ocean water stirs
In salt-worn casemate and porch.
Plies the blunt-snouted fish
With fire in his skull for torch.
And the ringing wires resound;
And the unearthly lovely weep,
In lament of the music they make
In the sullen courts of sleep:
Whose marble flowers bloom for aye:
And — lapped by the moon-guiled tide —
Mock their carver with heart of stone,
Caged in his stone-ribbed side.

THE CATECHISM

'Hast thou then nought wiser to bring
Than worn-out songs of moon and of rose?'
'Cracked my voice, and broken my wing,
          God knows.'

'Tell'st thou no truth of the life that *is*;
Seek'st thou from heaven no pitying sign?'
'Ask thine own heart these mysteries,
          Not mine.'

'Where then the faith thou hast brought to seed?
Where the sure hope thy soul would feign?'
'Never ebbed sweetness — even out of a weed —
          In vain.'

'Fool. The night comes. . . . 'Tis late. Arise.
Cold lap the waters of Jordan stream.'
'Deep be their flood, and tranquil thine eyes
          With a dream.'

FUTILITY

Sink, thou strange heart, unto thy rest.
Pine now no more, to pine in vain.
Doth not the moon on heaven's breast
Call the floods home again?

Doth not the summer faint at last?
Do not her restless rivers flow
When that her transient day is past
To hide them in ice and snow?

All this — thy world — an end shall make,
Planet to sun return again;
The universe, to sleep from wake,
In a last peace remain.

Alas, the futility of care
That, spinning thought to thought, doth weave
An idle argument on the air
We love not, nor believe.

WHO?

1st Stranger: Who walks with us on the hills?
2nd Stranger: I cannot see for the mist.
3rd Stranger: Running water I hear,
Keeping lugubrious tryst
With its cresses and grasses and weeds,
In the white obscure light from the sky.
2nd Stranger: *Who walks with us on the hills?*
Wild Bird: Ay! ... Aye! ... *Ay!* ...

A RIDDLE

The mild noon air of Spring again
Lapped shimmering in that sea-lulled lane.
Hazel was budding; wan as snow
The leafless blackthorn was a-blow.

A chaffinch clankt, a robin woke
An eerie stave in the leafless oak.
Green mocked at green; lichen and moss
The rain-worn slate did softly emboss.

From out her winter lair, at sigh
Of the warm South wind, a butterfly
Stepped, quaffed her honey; on painted fan
Her labyrinthine flight began.

Wondrously solemn, golden and fair,
The high sun's rays beat everywhere;
Yea, touched my cheek and mouth, as if,
Equal with stone, to me 'twould give

Its light and life.
                    O restless thought,
Contented not! With 'Why' distraught.
Whom asked you then your riddle small? —
'If hither came no man at all

'Through this grey-green, sea-haunted lane,
Would it mere blackened naught remain?
Strives it this beauty and life to express
Only in human consciousness?

'Or, rather, idly breaks he in
To an Eden innocent of sin;
And, prouder than to be afraid,
Forgets his Maker in the made?'

THE OWL

What if to edge of dream,
When the spirit is come,
Shriek the hunting owl,
And summon it home —
To the fear-stirred heart
And the ancient dread
Of man, when cold root or stone
Pillowed roofless head?

Clangs not at last the hour
When roof shelters not;
And the ears are deaf,
And all fears forgot:
Since the spirit too far has fared
For summoning scream
Of any strange fowl on earth
To shatter its dream?

THE LAST COACHLOAD

To Colin[1]

Crashed through the woods that lumbering Coach. The dust
Of flinted roads bepowdering felloe and hood.
Its gay paint cracked, its axles red with rust,
It lunged, lurched, toppled through a solitude

Of whispering boughs, and feathery, nid-nod grass.
Plodded the fetlocked horses. Glum and mum,
Its ancient Coachman recked not where he was,
Nor into what strange haunt his wheels were come.

Crumbling the leather of his dangling reins;
Worn to a cow's tuft his stumped, idle whip;
Sharp eyes of beast and bird in the trees' green lanes
Gleamed out like stars above a derelict ship.

'Old Father Time — Time — Time!' jeered twittering throat.
A squirrel capered on the leader's rump,
Slithered a weasel, peered a thief-like stoat,
In sandy warren beat on the coney's thump.

[1] The author's younger son.

[256]

Mute as a mammet in his saddle sate
The hunched Postilion, clad in magpie trim;
The bright flies buzzed around his hairless pate;
Yaffle and jay squawked mockery at him.

Yet marvellous peace and amity breathed there.
Tranquil the labyrinths of this sundown wood.
Musking its chaces, bloomed the brier-rose fair;
Spellbound as if in trance the pine-trees stood.

Through moss and pebbled rut the wheels rasped on;
That Ancient drowsing on his box. And still
The bracken track with glazing sunbeams shone;
Laboured the horses, straining at the hill. . . .

But now — a verdurous height with eve-shade sweet;
Far, far to West the Delectable Mountains glowed.
Above, Night's canopy; at the horses' feet
A sea-like honied waste of flowers flowed.

There fell a pause of utter quiet. And —
Out from one murky window glanced an eye,
Stole from the other a lean, groping hand,
The padded door swung open with a sigh.

And — *Exeunt Omnes!* None to ask the fare —
A myriad human Odds in a last release
Leap out incontinent, snuff the incensed air;
A myriad parched-up voices whisper, 'Peace.'

On, on, and on — a stream, a flood, they flow.
O wondrous vale of jocund buds and bells!
Like vanishing smoke the rainbow legions glow,
Yet still the enravished concourse sweeps and swells.

All journeying done. Rest now from lash and spur —
Laughing and weeping, shoulder and elbow — 'twould seem
That Coach capacious all Infinity were,
And these the fabulous figments of a dream.

Mad for escape; frenzied each breathless mote,
Lest rouse the Old Enemy from his death-still swoon,
Lest crack that whip again — they fly, they float,
Scamper, breathe — 'Paradise!' abscond, are gone. . . .

AN EPITAPH

Last, Stone, a little yet;
And then this dust forget.
But thou, fair Rose, bloom on.
For she who is gone
Was lovely too; nor would she grieve to be
Sharing in solitude her dreams with thee.

Down-Adown-Derry:
A Book of Fairy Poems (1922)

THE DOUBLE

I curtseyed to the dovecote.
I curtseyed to the well.
I twirled me round and round about,
The morning scents to smell.
When out I came from spinning so,
Lo, betwixt green and blue
Was the ghost of me — a fairy child —
A-dancing — dancing, too.

Nought was of her wearing
That is the earth's array.
Her thistledown feet beat airy fleet,
Yet set no blade astray.
The gossamer shining dews of June
Showed grey against the green;
Yet never so much as a bird-claw print
Of footfall to be seen.

Fading in the mounting sun,
That image soon did pine.
Fainter than moonlight thinned the locks
That shone as clear as mine.
Vanished! Vanished! O, sad it is
To spin and spin — in vain;
And never to see the ghost of me
A-dancing there again.

THE STRANGER

In the nook of a wood where a pool freshed with dew
Glassed, daybreak till evening, blue sky glimpsing through,
Then a star; or a slip of May-moon silver-white
Thridding softly aloof the quiet of night,
      Was a thicket of flowers.

Willow-herb, mint, pale speedwell and rattle,
Water hemlock and sundew — to the wind's tittle-tattle
They nodded, dreamed, swayed in jocund delight,
In beauty and sweetness arrayed, still and bright.
By turn scampered rabbit; trotted fox; bee and bird
Paused droning, sang shrill, and the fair water stirred.
Plashed green frog, or some brisk little flickering fish —
Gudgeon, stickleback, minnow — set the ripples a-swish.

A lone pool, a pool grass-fringed, crystal-clear:
Deep, placid, and cool in the sweet of the year;
Edge-parched when the sun to the Dog Days drew near;
And with winter's bleak rime hard as glass, robed in snow,
The whole wild-wood sleeping, and nothing a-blow
But the wind from the North — bringing snow.

That is all. Save that one long, sweet, June night-tide straying,
The harsh hemlock's pale umbelliferous bloom
Tenting nook, dense with fragrance and secret with gloom,
In a beaming of moon-coloured light faintly raying,
On buds orbed with dew phosphorescently playing,
Came a Stranger — still-footed, feat-fingered, clear face,
Unhumanly lovely . . . and supped in that place.

THE ENCHANTED HILL

From height of noon, remote and still,
The sun shines on the empty hill.
No mist, no wind, above, below;
No living thing strays to and fro.
No bird replies to bird on high,
Cleaving the skies with echoing cry.
Like dreaming water, green and wan,
Glassing the snow of mantling swan,
Like a clear jewel encharactered
With secret symbol of line and word,
Asheen, unruffled, slumbrous, still,
The sunlight streams on the empty hill.

But soon as Night's dark shadows ride
Across its shrouded Eastern side,
When at her kindling, clear and full,
Star beyond star stands visible;
Then course pale phantoms, fleet-foot deer
Lap of its waters icy-clear.
Mounts the large moon, and pours her beams
On bright-fish-flashing, singing streams.
Voices re-echo. Coursing by,
Horsemen, like clouds, wheel silently.
Glide then from out their pitch-black lair
Beneath the dark's ensilvered arch,
Witches becowled into the air;
And iron pine and emerald larch,
Tents of delight for ravished bird,
Are by loud music thrilled and stirred.
Winging the light, with silver feet,
Beneath their bowers of fragrance met,
In dells of rose and meadowsweet,
In mazy dance the fairies flit;
While drives his share the Ploughman high
Athwart the daisy-powdered sky:
Till far away, in thickening dew,
Piercing the Eastern shadows through,
Rilling in crystal clear and still,
Light 'gins to tremble on the hill.
And like a mist on faint winds borne,
Silent, forlorn, wells up the morn.
Then the broad sun with burning beams
Steeps slope and peak and gilded streams.
Then no foot stirs; the brake shakes not;
Soundless and wet in its green grot
As if asleep, the leaf hangs limp;
The white dews drip untrembling down,
From bough to bough, orblike, unblown;
And in strange quiet, shimmering and still,
Morning enshrines the empty hill.

THE LITTLE CREATURE

Twinkum, twankum, twirlum and twitch —
My great grandam — She was a Witch;
Mouse in wainscot, Saint in niche —
My great grandam — She was a Witch;
Deadly nightshade flowers in a ditch —
My great grandam — She was a Witch;
Long though the shroud, it grows stitch by stitch —
My great grandam — She was a Witch;
Wean you weakling before you breech —
My great grandam — She was a Witch;
The fattest pig's but a double flitch —
My great grandam — She was a Witch;
Nightjars rattle, owls scritch —
My great grandam — She was a Witch.

Pretty and small,
A mere nothing at all,
Pinned up sharp in the ghost of a shawl,
She'd straddle her down to the kirkyard wall,
And mutter and whisper and call,
And call. . . .

Red blood out and black blood in,
My Nannie says I'm a child of sin.
How did I choose me my witchcraft kin?
Know I as soon as dark's dreams begin
Snared is my heart in a nightmare's gin;
Never from terror I out may win;
So dawn and dusk I pine, peak, thin,
Scarcely knowing t'other from which —
My great grandam — She was a Witch.

THE OLD KING

Woke — the old King of Cumberland:
    Yet breathed not nor stirred,
But crouched in the darkness, hearkening after
    A voice he had heard.

He leaned upon his foursquare bed,
    Thumb beneath bristling chin;
'Alas, alas! — the woeful dream —
    The dream that I was in!'

The old, old King of Cumberland
    Muttered, ''Twas not the sea
Gushing upon Schlievlisskin rocks
    That wakened me.

'Thunder from midmost night it was not,
    For yonder at those bars
Burn fiercely toward the Eastern deeps
    The summer stars.'

The old, old King of Cumberland
    Mused yet, 'Rats ever did
Ramp, rustle, clink my spurs, and gnaw
    My coverlid.

'Oft hath a furtive midnight breeze
    Along this valance skirred;
But in this stagnant calm 'twas not
    The wind I heard.

'Some keener, stranger, quieter, closer
    Voice it was me woke . . .'
And silence, like a billow, drowned
    The word he spoke.

Fixed now his stare, for limned in dark,
    Gazing from cowl-like hood,
Stark in the vague, all-listening night,
    A shadow stood.

Sudden a gigantic hand he thrust
    Into his bosom cold,
Where now no surging restless beat
    Its long tale told.

[263]

Swept on him then, as there he sate,
  Terror icy chill:
'Twas silence that had him awoke —
  His heart stood still.

Poems for Children (1930)

THE O.M.O.R.E.

'Tis years fourscore
Since Rory O'More —
He and his brothers three,
Patrick, Seumas, and Timothy Tim,
With the Pole Star shining free,
Sailed with a sail, and an oar for a rudder,
Bound for an Unknown Sea.

Bound for that Unknown Sea forlore
Mariners many have sailed before;
Into the evening mist they swing,
Daring what ever the dark may bring;
And so went Timothy, Seumas and Pat,
Each with a sprig of yew in his hat,
And so sailed Rory O'More.

Sailed . . . But a wind came out of the cloud,
Piping shrill and long and loud,
Smote on their boat as they did float,
Stretched their cloaks on the stoop o' the wave,
Violet, azure, and green-grass-green,
And Rory's of scarlet brave;
Tossed them adrift on the foam of the main;
Bowed on them, fawned on them, bowed again,
Roared them to slumber, deep, serene,
Made of their sail their shroud . . .

Yet still 'tis whispered and still 'tis said
That fishermen weary and sore bestead,
Hauling their nets on the watery deep,
Numb with the cold and half asleep,
Will lift their eyes from the spray and spy
Ghosts in the glint of the moon pass by —
Phantoms four of the name of O'More,
Lifting their heads they see —
Patrick, Seumas, and Timothy Tim,
And Rory walking free,
Arm in arm where the petrels skim,
Over the billow's hissing rim,

Swinging their feet through the surge they go,
Four jolly ghosts in a glimmering row,
Four abreast, and nodding their heads,
Walking the waves these ghostly lads,
Haunting the wind with their voices four,
Timothy, Patrick, Seumas and Ror —
Rory O'More.

Striding the sea-drifts leagues from shore,
Ghosts of his brothers and Rory O'More
Fishermen white
In that haze of light
Dazed with its radiance, see,
And sigh in a breath,
Their beards beneath,
'See! there! — the O.M.O.R.E.!
We have seen the O.M.O.R.E.!'

THE APPLE CHARM

I plucked an apple, sleek and red,
I took his three black pips,
Stuck two upon my cheek, and brow,
    And t'other on my lips.

Dick on my cheek, the other Tom,
But O — my love to be —
Robin that couched upon my lip
    Was truest unto me.

WHO REALLY?

When Winter's o'er, the Bear once more
Rolls from his hollow tree
And pokes about, and in and out,
Where dwells the honey-bee.
Then all the little creatures go,
And to their Queen they say:
'Here's that old Bruin, hark, what he's doing,
Let's drive the beast away!'
Old Bruin smiles, and smooths his hair
Over a sticky nose;
'That Thieves should hate a Thief,' he smirks,
'Who really would suppose!'

JENNY WREN

That farthing bird, J. Wren,
The cruel boys pursue;
Hunt her with sticks and stones
Hedge and green coppice through.

A farthing bird. Amen.
Ay, two brown sparrows can
For as easy a sum be bought
By heedless chaffering man.

Yet not for all earthbound gold,
Or argosies under the sea,
Can one moment's pity of pitiful child
Be marketed for, perdie.

CRUMBS

You little birds, I bring my crumbs,
For now the cold of winter comes.
The North Wind blows down frozen rain;
The fields are white with snow again;
The worm's in house; the bare-twigged trees
Are thick with frost instead of bees;
From running brooks all noise is gone;
And every pool lies still as stone.

THE ROBIN

As little Bess was walking home
She saw a robin on a stone.
He looked at her with bead-bright eye —
These two alone there, no one by.

She gave him bread-crumbs dipped in milk,
She stroked his feathers soft as silk.
Then leaning sidelong her fair head,
'Sing sweet! I'm listening,' she said.

And he, the dainty imp, he skips,
And pecks a crumb between her lips
And then, to his own wild being gone,
Left empty the round pebble-stone.

[267]

HI!

Hi! handsome hunting man
Fire your little gun.
Bang! Now the animal
Is dead and dumb and done.
Nevermore to peep again, creep again, leap again,
Eat or sleep or drink again, Oh, what fun!

PUSS

Puss loves man's winter fire
Now that the sun so soon
Leaves the hours cold it warmed
In burning June.

She purrs full length before
The heaped-up hissing blaze,
Drowsy in slumber down
Her head she lays.

While he with whom she dwells
Sits snug in his inglenook,
Stretches his legs to the flames
And reads his book.

SEEDS

The seeds I sowed —
For weeks unseen —
Have pushed up pygmy
Shoots of green;
So frail you'd think
The tiniest stone
Would never let
A glimpse be shown.
But no; a pebble
Near them lies,
At least a cherry-stone
In size,
Which that mere sprout
Has heaved away,
To bask in sunshine,
See the Day.

EDEN[1]

I wonder if from Noah's Ark
Ever was heard the bobtail's bark.
If ever o'er the empty Flood
Our English ash-boughs stood in bud.
'Tis sure when Eve and Adam sate
Smiling within green Eden's gate
And gave its birds, beasts, fishes, names
Somewhere flowed clear our English Thames.
And when they both in woe were driven
Beyond the shining bounds of heaven,
Simply for grief that outcast morn
Broke into bloom our English thorn.
And — far from Eden — our nightingale
Did their sad banishment bewail:
While we, asleep within her dust,
Hearkened — as all poor humans must.

BABEL

The sea washes England,
Where all men speak
A language rich
As ancient Greek.

The wide world over
Man with man
Has talked his own tongue
Since speech began.

Yet still must sorrow
Move the mind,
He understands
But his own kind.

The voices lovely,
Hollow, drear,
Of beast and bird
Beat on his ear:

[1] First published in *New Paths*, ed. C. W. Beaumont and M. T. H Sadler, London, 1918, under the title of 'Noah's Ark'.

Eye into eye
Gaze deep he may;
Yet still through Babel
Gropes his way.

THAMES

There flows a wonderful water
Where lofty vessels glide
To take up their home-come stations
By the dark wharves' side.
And their masts tip up over the roofs,
With their lean long pennons a-blow,
While ant-like the men on the stones of the quay
Swarm to and fro.
And their spars lean slant on the sky,
And strange are the sounds of their names,
Gilded on counters afloat from remote
Sea-havens to Thames.

THE HOLLY

The sturdiest of forest-trees
With acorns is inset;
Wan white blossoms the elder brings
To fruit as black as jet;
But O, in all green English woods
Is aught so fair to view
As the sleek, sharp, dark-leaved holly tree
And its berries burning through?

Towers the ash; and dazzling green
The larch her tassels wears;
Wondrous sweet are the clots of may
The tangled hawthorn bears;
But O, in heath or meadow or wold
Springs aught beneath the blue
As brisk and trim as a holly-tree bole
With its berries burning through?

[270]

When hither, thither, falls the snow,
And blazes small the frost,
Naked amid the winter stars
The elm's vast boughs are tossed;
But O, of all that summer showed
What now to winter's true
As the prickle-beribbed dark holly tree,
With its berries burning through!

LONE

Shrill rang the squeak in the empty house
Of the sharp-nosed mouse, the hungry mouse.

'Sing, sing: here none doth dwell!'
Dripped the water in the well.

A robin on the shepherd's grave
Whistled a solitary stave.

And, 'Lone-lone!' the curlew cried,
Scolding the sheep-strewn mountain's side.

THE FOUR BROTHERS

Hithery, hethery — I love best
The wind that blows from out the West,
Breathing balm, and sweet of musk,
Rosy at morning, rosy at dusk.

Wind from the North, Oho, and Oho!
Climbs with his white mules laden with snow,
Up through the mirk plod muffled by
Master and mules through the louring sky.

Wind from the South lags back again
With bags of jewels from out of Spain;
A hole in the corner, and out they come —
May-bud, apple-bud, bramble-bloom.

Black runs the East, with clouted hair,
Grim as a spectre through the air,
And, with his lash, drives in again
Beasts to stall; to their fireside, men.

AS I WENT TO THE WELL-HEAD

As I went to the well-head
I heard a bird sing:
'Lie yonder, lie yonder
The Islands of Ling.

'Leagues o'er the water
Their shores are away,
In a darkness of stars,
And a foaming of spray.'

WILD ARE THE WAVES

Wild are the waves when the wind blows;
But fishes in the deep
Live in a world of waters,
Still as sleep.

Wild are the skies when Winter
Roars at the doors of Spring;
But when his lamentation's lulled
Then sweet birds sing.

ECHOES

The sea laments
The livelong day,
Fringing its waste of sand;
Cries back the wind from the whispering shore —
No words I understand:
Yet echoes in my heart a voice,
As far, as near, as these —
The wind that weeps,
The solemn surge
Of strange and lonely seas.

TO BED

Candle lank and lean and pale
Light me to bed,
Rearing aloft thy flaming hair
Above thy head.

Red is the tip of thy long nose;
As if from weeping
Tears that shall in the night congeal
When I am sleeping.

Up, up the peevish stair we go;
Silent as death
Thy smoke trails back along the air
Like frosty breath.

Circling around thy tapering head
Pale colours bloom,
While shadows watch thee from their lair
Of ghostly gloom.

At every wink they crouch and spring —
I conjure thee
Droop not a languid eyelid till
In bed I be.

And while the mice make romping stir,
I do entreat
Twine not thy spectral body with
A winding sheet.

But steadfast as a sentinel,
Vigilant, stark,
Guard thou the battlements of light
Against the dark!

SHE IN THY DREAMS WATCH OVER THEE![1]

She in thy dreams watch over thee!
Who in the dark and cold
Keeps all her buds of earth fast-sealed,
Her meek sheep safe in fold;
Who comes with dew and goes with dew;
And lulls the winds to rest;
And hushes the weary birds of eve
To silence on her breast.

She of the ages of the night,
The childhood of the morn,
Solace the sadness of thy thoughts
Long waking made forlorn;
Stoop with the stillness of her smile,
The safety of her hand,
Charm with the clear call of her voice,
Thee, in the shadowy land!

The daisy will unfold in light
The fairness of her face,
The lark from his green furrow course
Back to his sun-wild place;
Then she, whose drowsy cheek by thine
Lonely all night hath lain,
Will toss her dark locks from thy sweet eyes,
Loose thee to earth again!

[1] Called 'Lullaby' in *Poems for Children*, 1930.

The Fleeting and Other Poems (1933)

IN THE GARDEN

A mild parochial talk was ours;
The air of afternoon was sweet
With burthen of the sun-parched flowers;
His fiery beams in fury beat
From out the O of space, and made,
Wherever leaves his glare let through,
Circlets of brilliance in the shade
Of his unfathomable blue.

Old Dr. Salmon sat pensive and grey,
And Archie's tongue was never still,
While dear Miss Arbuthnot fanned away
The stress of walking up the hill.
And little Bertha? — how bony a cheek!
How ghast an eye! Poor mite. . . . That pause —
When not even tactful tongues could speak! . . .
The drowsy Cat pushed out her claws.

A bland, unvexing talk was ours —
Sharing that gentle gilded cage —
Manners and morals its two brief hours
Proffered alike to youth and age.
Why break so pleasing a truce? — forfend!
Why on such sweetness and light intrude?
Why bid the child, 'Cough, "*Ah!*" ' — and end
Our complaisance; her solitude?

PEEPING TOM

I was there — by the curtains
When some men brought a box:
And one at the house of
    Miss Emily knocks:

[275]

A low *rat-tat-tat*.
The door opened — and then,
Slowly mounting the steps, stooped
   In the strange men.

Then the door darkly shut,
And I saw their legs pass,
Like an insect's, Miss Emily's
   Window-glass —

Though why all her blinds
Have been hanging so low
These dumb foggy days,
   I don't know.

Yes, only last week
I watched her for hours,
Potting out for the winter her
   Balcony flowers.

And this very Sunday
She mused there a space,
Gazing into the street, with
   The vacantest face:

Then turned her long nose
And looked up at the skies —
One you would not have thought
   Weather-wise!

Yet . . . well, out stepped the men —
One ferrety-fair —
With gentlemen's hats, and
   Whiskers and hair;

And paused in the porch.
Then smooth, solemn, grey,
They climbed to their places,
   And all drove away

In their square varnished carriage,
The horse full of pride,
With a tail like a charger's:
   They all sate outside.

Then the road became quiet:
Her house stiff and staid —
Like a Stage — while you wait
  For the Harlequinade ...

But what can Miss Emily
Want with a box
So long, narrow, shallow,
  And without any locks?

EPISODES

'Oh! Raining! Look!' she whispered —
    Gazing out
On wheat-fields parched with drought,
And trees that yet in prime
Even of summertime
Showed yellow in their green;
But now, as with delight,
Showered down their withered leaves
Among the untimely sheaves
Of harvest, poor and lean:
    'And I, alas!'
      She sighed,
'This day to be a bride!'

Fair shone the sick man's moon
    Upon his bed,
And her cold silver shed.
Glazed eyes, in wasted face,
He marked her solemn pace,
As on, from height to height,
She to her zenith won,
And the wide fields below
Made lovely — as with snow —
Transfiguring the night.
    'Thou courtesan!'
    Mocked he,
'Would'st thou, then, lie with *me*!'

Loud sounded out the Trump:
    In vestry chill.
Its every stone a thrill,
The parson leaned an ear,
With pouted lip, to hear.

[277]

But now a silence wells,
As of a sea at rest,
Stilling the honeyed air —
With fruit and flowers made fair —
As mute as his own bells.
      He frowned. He sighed.
        'To come
Just now! — at Harvest Home!'

ON THE ESPLANADE[1]

The autumnal gales had wreaked their will;
Now lipped the wave its idle stones;
And winter light lay grey and chill;
Snow-capped the town's one distant hill,
Snow-cloaked its churchyard bones.

Sole farers on the esplanade,
A mother with her daughter walked.
Across a sea of pallid jade
The air thin fretful music made
And whimpered while they talked: —

'It's not the *present* that I dread,
No vulgar talk of chances lost.
Your heart seems stranger to your head,
And time wears on,' the elder said;
'My only fear, the cost.

'Sheer habit numbs the mind, my dear;
And lips by lover never kissed
Taste only at last the bitter cheer
Repining memory brings near
Of sweetness they have missed.

'You frown. Ah, yes! But why forget
I too was once in youth astray?
If ghosts at noonday could be met
And suns have heat that long have set —
Well, well, I have had my day.

[1] First published in *The Captive and Other Poems* in a limited edition of 600 copies, Bowling Green Press, New York, 1928.

'And now for you alone I live.
Think not I speak to pry, or vex;
Mere cold advice not mine to give;
Be truth and love between us, if
We share one heart, one sex!'

Awhile these two in silence paced,
Vacant the windows shoreward set.
Thin-screened with cloud the West they faced,
No glint of sun their shadows traced
On the flat flags; and yet

A burning, proud, defiant flare
Gleamed in the younger's eyes, as she
'Neath louring brows, as cold as fair,
Gazed straightly through the wintry air
Over the restless sea.

'Yes, Mother, all you say is true.'
She shrugged her slender shoulders. 'I —
Well, nothing I can say, or do
Has any meaning through and through;
What use to question, why?

'Infatuated bees may spend
Their silly lives of droning trance
In gathering nectar without end,
For other busy bees to blend,
And die in like mischance —

'The old, old tale. You say we share
One sex. It's that has gone askew.
The butterflies still dance on air
Without an instant's thought or care
And "sip the morning dew";

'As for the rest, they ape the Man,
And sacrifice their shapes and skin;
In freedom's blaze their faces tan;
Utopian revolutions plan;
Bemoan the Might-have-been.

'Not I. I loathe them both. I know
My very instincts are at war —
Another kind of neuter. So,
Whatever now may come or go,
There's nothing I deplore.

[279]

'Pity I laugh at. Flatterer
Flatters not twice the self-same way!
And when at last I come to where
Mere growing old brings solace — there!
I shall have had my day.

'A day as deadly black as night
For fatuous dream of a strange fate —
That long, long since has taken flight —
A lover not of sense or sight:
For him I used to wait.

'I ask you, Mother, how could a mind
Farced up with all I have learned and read —
The lies that curious fools have spread —
A vestige of him hope to find?
Enough of that!' she said.

Turned then the twain about to see
An East as rayless, grey, and bland,
Stretching into infinity,
And vacant windows glassily
Edging the pebbled strand;

While, poised in air, a bird of snow
Faltered on lifted wing — to glide
And glance at this strange to-and-fro,
That greying hair, that cheek's young glow —
And shrill, sad challenge cried.

THE FAT WOMAN

Massed in her creaseless black,
She sits; vast and serene;
Light — on glossed hair, large knees,
Huge bust — a-sheen.

A smile lurks deep in her eyes,
Thick-lidded, motionless, pale,
Taunting a world grown old,
Faded, and stale.

Enormous those childless breasts:
God in His pity knows
Why, in her bodice stuck,
Reeks a mock rose.

THE FECKLESS DINNER-PARTY

'Who are we waiting for?' '*Soup* burnt?' '... Eight —'
'Only the tiniest party.— Us!'
'Darling! Divine!' 'Ten minutes late —'
'And my digest —' 'I'm *rav*enous!'
'"Toomes"?' — 'Oh, he's new.' 'Looks crazed, I guess.'
'"Married" — *Again*!' 'Well; more or less!'

'Dinner is *served*!' '"Dinner is served"!'
'Is served?' 'Is served.' 'Ah, yes.'

'Dear Mr. Prout, will you take down
   The Lilith in leaf-green by the fire?
Blanche Ogleton? ...' 'How coy a frown! —
   Hasn't she borrowed *Eve's* attire?'
'Morose Old Adam!' 'Charmed — I vow.'
   'Come then, and meet her now.'

'Now, Dr. Mallus — would you please? —
   Our daring poetess, Delia Seek?'
'The lady with the bony knees?'
   'And — *entre nous* — less song than beak.'
'Sharing her past with Simple Si —'
   '*Bare* facts! He'll blush!' 'Oh, fie!'

'And *you*, Sir Nathan — false but fair! —
   That fountain of wit, Aurora Pert.'
'More wit than It, poor dear! But there ...'
   'Pitiless Pacha! *And* such a flirt!'
'"Flirt"! *Me*?' 'Who else?' 'You here.... Who can ...?'
   'In*corr*igible man!'

'And now, Mr. Simon — little me! —
   Last and —' 'By no means least!' 'Oh, come!
What naughty, naughty flattery!

[281]

Honey! — I *hear* the creature hum!'
'Sweets for the sweet, *I* always say!'
' "Always"? . . . We're last.' '*This* way?' . . .

'No, sir; straight on, please.' 'I'd have vowed! —
I came the other . . .' 'It's queer; I'm sure . . .'
'What frightful pictures!' 'Fiends!' 'The *crowd!*'
'Such nudes!' 'I can't endure . . .'

'Yes, *there* they go.' 'Heavens! *Are* we right?'
'Follow up closer!' ' "Prout"? — sand-blind!'
'This endless . . .' 'Who's turned down the light?'
'Keep calm! They're close behind.'

'Oh! Dr. Mallus; what dismal stairs!'
'I hate these old Victor . . .' 'Dry rot!'
'Darker and darker!' 'Fog!' 'The air's . . .'
'Scarce breathable!' 'Hell!' '*What?*'

'The banister's gone!' 'It's deep; keep close!'
'We're going down and down!' 'What fun!'
'Damp! Why, my shoes . . .' 'It's slimy . . . Not *moss!*'
'I'm freezing cold!' 'Let's run.'

'. . . Behind us. I'm giddy. . . .' 'The catacombs . . .'
'That shout!' 'Who's there?' 'I'm *alone!*' 'Stand back!'
'She said, Lead . . .' 'Oh!' 'Where's Toomes?' '*Toomes!*'
    'Toomes!'
'Stifling!' 'My skull will crack!'

'Sir Nathan! *Ai!*' 'I *say! Toomes!* Prout!'
'Where? Where?' ' "Our silks and fine array" . . .'
'She's mad.' 'I'm dying!' 'Oh, Let me *out!*'
'My God! We've lost our way!' . . .

And now how sad-serene the abandoned house,
Whereon at dawn the spring-tide sunbeams beat;
And time's slow pace alone is ominous,
And naught but shadows of noonday therein meet;
Domestic microcosm, only a Trump could rouse:
And, pondering darkly, in the silent rooms,
He who misled them all — the butler, Toomes.

COMFORT

As I mused by the hearthside,
    Puss said to me:
'There burns the Fire, man,
    And here sit we.

'Four Walls around us
    Against the cold air;
And the latchet drawn close
    To the draughty Stair.

'A Roof o'er our heads
    Star-proof, moon immune,
And a wind in the chimney
    To wail us a tune.

'What Felicity!' miaowed he,
    'Where none may intrude;
Just Man and Beast — met
    In this Solitude!

'Dear God, what security,
    Comfort and bliss!
And to think, too, what ages
    Have brought us to this!

'You in your sheep's-wool coat,
    Buttons of bone,
And me in my fur-about
    On the warm hearthstone.'

THE SLUM CHILD

No flower grew where I was bred,
No leafy tree
Its canopy of greenness spread
Over my youthful head.

My woodland walk was gutter stone.
Nowhere for me
Was given a place where I alone
Could to myself be gone.

In leafless Summer's stench and noise
I'd sit and play
With other as lean-faced girls and boys,
And sticks and stones for toys —

Homeless, till evening dark came down;
And street lamp's ray
On weary skulking beggary thrown
Flared in the night-hung town.

Then up the noisome stairs I'd creep
For food and rest,
Or, empty-bellied, lie, and weep
My wordless woes to sleep:

And wept in silence — shaken with fear —
But cautious lest
Those on the mattress huddled near
Should, cursing, wake and hear. . . .

O wondrous Life! though plainly I see,
Thus looking back,
What evil, and filth, and poverty,
In childhood harboured me,

And marvel that merciless man could so
The innocent rack;
Yet, in bare truth, I also know
A well-spring of peace did flow,

Secretly blossomed, along that street;
And — foul-mouthed waif —
Though I in no wise heeded it
In the refuse at my feet,

Yet, caged within those spectral bones,
Aloof and safe,
Some hidden one made mock of groans,
Found living bread in stones.

O mystery of mysteries!
Between my hands I take that face,
Bloodless and bleak, unchildlike wise —
Epitome of man's disgrace —

I search its restless eyes,
And, from those woe-flecked depths, at me
Looks back through all its misery
A self beyond surmise.

NEWS[1]

'Hearken! 'Tis news I cry!'
The shades drift by . . .
'Strange and ominous things:
A four-foot Beast upon Wings,
Thieves in a burning Mill,
An empty Cross on a Hill,
Ravin of swine in Beauty's places,
And a Woman with two Faces!
News! — News! I call. . . .'

But a wind from the cold unknown
Scatters the words as they fall —
Into naught they are blown.
What do these Walkers seek,
Pranked up in silk and in flax,
With a changeless rose on the cheek,
And Hell's hump on their backs?
These of the mincing gait,
And an ape in each sidelong leer;
These for the Way that is strait
To the pomp-hung bier;
These of the wasted dream,
Of the loveless silver and gold,
And the worm of disgust in them
That shall never grow old?

'Not unto such I cry,
But to thee, O Solitary! . . .
The world founders in air,
Plague-stricken Vanity Fair
Dyed hath its booths with blood;
Quenched are its stars in mud;
Come now the Mourners to chaunt
End and lament.'

[1] First published as Ariel Poem, No. 31, 1930, where it was in 7 stanzas.

There is a stream I know,
Sullen in flood its waters flow,
Heavy with secrets, slow,
Leaden and lightless, deep
With slumber and sleep.
Shall not even Innocence find
Peace of body and mind?

'Ay, but thou also art old,
And there's news to be told.
News, strange to hearing and sight . . .
It is Winter. And Night.
An icy and pitiless moon
Witched hath our sea-tides. And soon
The Nymph in her grottoes will hear
The loud trumpet of fear!
She weepeth cold tears in the sea! . . .
You shall *buy* not such tidings of me:
Stoop an ear, bow a desolate head:
It is breathed, "Love is dead".'

I SIT ALONE[1]

I sit alone,
And clear thoughts move in me,
Pictures, now near, now far,
Of transient fantasy.
Happy I am, at peace
In my own company.

Yet life is a dread thing, too,
Dark with horror and fear.
Beauty's fingers grow cold,
Sad cries I hear,
Death with a stony gaze
Is ever near.

Lost in myself I hide
From the cold unknown:
Lost, like a world cast forth
Into space star-sown:
And the songs of the morning are stilled,
And delight in them flown.

[1] First published as Ariel Poem, No. 4, 1927.

So even the tender and dear
Like phantoms through memory stray —
Creations of sweet desire,
That faith can alone bid stay:
They cast off the cloak of the real
And vanish away.

Only love can redeem
This truth, that delight;
Bring morning to blossom again
Out of plague-ridden night;
Restore to the lost the found,
To the blinded, sight.

FORESTS

Turn, now, tired mind, unto your rest,
Within your secret chamber lie,
Doors shut, and windows curtained, lest
Footfall or moonbeam, stealing by,
Wake you, or night-wind sigh.

Now, Self, we are at peace — we twain;
The house is silent, except that — hark!
Against its walls wells out again
That rapture in the empty dark;
Where, softly beaming, spark by spark,

The glow-worms stud the leaves with light;
And unseen flowers, refreshed with dew —
Jasmine, convolvulus, glimmering white,
The air with their still life endue,
And sweeten night for me and you.

Be mute all speech; and not of love
Talk we, nor call on hope, but be —
Calm as the constant stars above —
The friends of fragile memory,
Shared only now by you and me.

[287]

Thus hidden, thus silent, while the hours
From gloom to gloom their wings beat on,
Shall not a moment's peace be ours,
Till, faint with day, the East is wan,
And terrors of the dark are gone?

Nay — in the forest of the mind
Lurk beasts as fierce as those that tread
Earth's rock-strown wilds, to night resigned,
There stars of heaven no radiance shed —
Bleak-eyed Remorse, Despair becowled in lead.

With dawn these ravening shapes will go —
Though One at watch will still remain:
Till knell the sunset hour, and lo!
The listening soul once more will know
Death and his pack are hot afield again.

THE BOTTLE

Of green and hexagonal glass,
    With sharp, fluted sides —
Vaguely transparent these walls,
    Wherein motionless hides
A simple so potent it can
    To oblivion lull
The weary, the racked, the bereaved,
    The miserable.

Flowers in silent desire
    Their life-breath exhale —
Self-heal, hellebore, aconite,
    Chamomile, dwale:
Sharing the same gentle heavens,
    The sun's heat and light,
And, in the dust at their roots,
    The same shallow night.

Each its own livelihood hath,
    Shape, pattern, hue;
Age on to age unto these
    Keeping steadfastly true;

[288]

And, musing amid them, there moves
  A stranger, named Man,
Who of their ichor distils
  What virtue he can;

Plucks them ere seed-time to blazon
His house with their radiant dyes;
Prisons their attar in wax;
Candies their petals; denies
Them freedom to breed in their wont;
Buds, fecundates, grafts them at will;
And with cunningest leechcraft compels
  Their good to his ill.

Intrigue fantastic as this
  Where shall we find?
Mute in their beauty they serve him,
  Body and mind.
And one — but a weed in his wheat —
Is the poppy — frail, pallid, whose juice
With its saplike and opiate fume
  Strange dreams will induce

Of wonder and horror. And none
  Can silence the soul,
Wearied of self and of life,
  Earth's darkness and dole,
More secretly, deeply . . . But finally? —
  Waste not thy breath;
The words that are scrawled on this phial
  Have for synonym, *death* —

Wicket out into the dark
  That swings but one way;
Infinite hush in an ocean of silence
  Aeons away —
Thou forsaken! — even thou! —
  The dread good-bye;
The abandoned, the thronged, the watched,
  the unshared —
  Awaiting me — I!

WHAT?

What dost thou surely know?
What will the truth remain,
When from the world of men thou go
To the unknown again?

What science — of what hope?
What heart-loved certitude won
From thought shall then for scope
Be thine — thy thinking done?

'Tis said, that even the wise,
When plucking at the sheet,
Have smiled with swift-darkening eyes,
As if in vision fleet

Of some mere flower, or bird,
Seen in dream, or in childhood's play;
And then, without sign or word,
Have turned from the world away.

RECONCILIATION[1]

Leave April now, and autumn having,
Leave hope to fade, and darkness braving,
    Take thine own soul
    Companion,
    And journey on.

The cresset fire of noon is waning,
Shadow the lonelier hills is staining;
    Watch thou the West
    Whence pale shall shine
    Hesper divine!

Beauty, what is it but love's vision?
Earth's fame, the soul's supreme derision?
    O ardent dust,
    Turn to thy grave,
    And quiet have!

[1] First published in *The Captive and Other Poems,* New York, 1928.

THE HOUSE

'Mother, it's such a lonely house,'
The child cried; and the wind sighed.
'A narrow but a lovely house,'
The mother replied.

'Child, it is such a narrow house,'
The ghost cried; and the wind sighed.
'A narrow and a lonely house,'
The withering grass replied.

THE TACITURN

Countless these crosses and these ruinous stones,
Which taunt the living with but sighs and groans!
Thou canst not in this quiet a moment stray
    But dust cries, *Vanity!* and, *Welladay!*
Not mine such tedious tidings, Stranger. Yet,
Think not because I am silent, I forget.

THE THORN

O thou who pausest here,
With naught but some thorned wilding near
To tell of beauty; be not sad.
For he who in this grave is laid
Would give the all on earth he had
One moment but by thee to stand
And with warm hand touch hand.

ARIEL

This lad, when but a child of six,
Had learned how earth and heaven may mix —
At this so innocent an age
He, as light Ariel, trod the stage;
So nimble-tongued, and silver-fleet,
Air, fire, did in one body meet.
Ay; had he hied to where the bones
Of Shakespeare lie 'neath Stratford's stones,
And whispered: 'Master, hearken!'— so:
One might have answered — Prospero!

BENEATH A MOTIONLESS YEW

Beneath a motionless yew, and tower,
Hoary with age, whose clock's one bell
Of Sexton Time had hour by hour
As yet in vain rung out the knell,

A worn old woman, in her black,
Knelt in the green churchyard alone;
And, self-forgotten, crook'd arm, bent back,
Scrubbed at her husband's burial stone.

Here lies J——— H———: Aged 34:
'*He giveth his beloved sleep*':
Fainter the letters than of yore —
Where lichens had begun to creep —

Showed 'neath the pale-blue vacant sky,
Under that dust-dry shadowiness;
She stayed to read — with a long sigh,
Less of regret than weariness.

Evening's last gleam now tinged the yew;
The gilded hand jerked on; a bird
Made stony rattle; and anew
She scanned the tombstone's every word.

For forty years she had kept her tryst,
And grief long since had ceased to upbraid
Him whose young love she had sorely missed,
And at whose side she would soon be laid.

Tired out, and old; past hope or thought,
She pined no more to meet some day
Her dead; and yet, still faithfully sought
To wash the stains of Time away.

GOOD COMPANY

The stranger from the noisy inn
Strode out into the quiet night,
Tired of the slow sea-faring men.

The wind blew fitfully in his face;
He smelt the salt, and tasted it,
In that sea-haunted, sandy place.

Dim ran the road down to the sea
Bowered in with trees, and solitary;
Ever the painted sign swang slow —
An Admiral staring moodily.

The stranger heard its silly groan;
The beer-mugs rattling to and fro;
The drawling gossip: and the glow
Streamed thro' the door on weed and stone.

Better this star-sown solitude,
The empty night-road to the sea,
Than company so dull and rude.

He smelt the nettles sour and lush,
About him went the bat's shrill cry,
Pale loomed the fragrant hawthorn-bush.

And all along the sunken road —
Green with its weeds, though sandy dry —
Bugloss, hemlock and succory —
The night-breeze wavered from the sea.
And soon upon the beach he stood.

A myriad pebbles in the faint
Horned radiance of a sinking moon
Shone like the rosary of a saint —
A myriad pebbles which, through time,
The bitter tides had visited,
Flood and ebb, by a far moon led,
Noon and night and morning-prime.

He stood and eyed the leaping sea,
The long grey billows surging on,
Baying in sullen unison
Their dirge of agelong mystery.

And, still morose, he went his way,
Over the mounded shingle strode,
And reached a shimmering sand that lay
Where transient bubbles of the froth
Like eyes upon the moonshine glowed,
Faint-coloured as the evening moth.

But not on these the stranger stared,
Nor on the stars that spanned the deep,
But on a body, flung at ease,
As if upon the shore asleep,
Hushed by the rocking seas.

Of a sudden the air was wild with cries —
Shrill and high and violent,
Fled fast a soot-black cormorant,
'Twixt ocean and the skies.

It seemed the sea was like a heart
That stormily a secret keeps
Of what it dare to none impart.
And all its waves rose, heaped and high —
And communed with the moon-grey sky.

The stranger eyed the sailor there,
Mute, and stark, and sinister —
His stiffening sea-clothes grey with salt;
His matted hair, his eyes ajar,
And glazed after the three-fold fear.

And ever the billows cried again
Over the rounded pebble stones,
Baying that heedless sailor-man.

He frowned and glanced up into the air —
Where star with star all faintly shone,
Cancer and the Scorpion,
In ancient symbol circling there:

Gazed inland over the vacant moor;
But ancient silence, and a wind
That whirls upon a sandy floor,
Were now its sole inhabitants.

Forthwith, he wheeled about — away
From the deep night's sad radiance;
The yells of gulls and cormorants
Rang shrilly in his mind.

Pursued by one who noiseless trod,
Whose sharp scythe whistled as he went,
O'er sand and shingle, tuft and sod,
Like hunted hare he coursing ran,
Nor stayed until he came again
Back to the old convivial inn —
The mugs, the smoke, the muffled din —
Packed with its slow-tongued sailor-men.

THE RAILWAY JUNCTION

From here through tunnelled gloom the track
Forks into two; and one of these
Wheels onward into darkening hills,
And one toward distant seas.

How still it is; the signal light
At set of sun shines palely green;
A thrush sings; other sound there's none,
Nor traveller to be seen —

Where late there was a throng. And now,
In peace awhile, I sit alone;
Though soon, at the appointed hour,
I shall myself be gone.

But not their way: the bow-legged groom,
The parson in black, the widow and son,
The sailor with his cage, the gaunt
Gamekeeper with his gun,

That fair one, too, discreetly veiled —
All, who so mutely came, and went,
Will reach those far nocturnal hills,
Or shores, ere night is spent.

I nothing know why thus we met —
Their thoughts, their longings, hopes, their fate:
And what shall I remember, except —
The evening growing late —

That here through tunnelled gloom the track
Forks into two; of these
One into darkening hills leads on,
And one toward distant seas?

REFLECTIONS

Three Sisters — and the youngest
    Was yet lovelier to see
Than wild flower palely blooming
    Under Ygdrasil Tree,

Than this well at the woodside
    Whose waters silver show,
Though in womb of the blind earth
    Ink-like, ebon, they flow.

Creeps on the belled bindweed;
    The bee, in hoverings nigh,
Sucks his riches of nectar;
    Clouds float in the sky;

And she, O pure vanity,
    Newly-wakened, at that brink,
Crouches close, smiling dreamlike,
    To gaze, not to drink.

She sees not earth's morning
    Darkly framed in that cold deep:
Naught, naught but her beauty
    Made yet fairer by sleep.

And though glassed in that still flood
    She peer long, and long,
As faithful stays that image,
    As echo is to song . . .

Anon — in high noontide
    Comes her sister, wan with fear,
Lest the love in her bosom
    Even the bright birds should hear

Wail divine grieved enchantment.
   She kneels; and, musing, sighs;
Unendurable strangenesses
   Darken the eyes

That meet her swift searchings.
   From her breast there falls a flower.
Down, down — as she ponders —
   The fair petals shower,

Hiding brow, mouth, cheek — all
   That reflected there is seen.
And she gone, that Mirror
   As of old rests serene. . . .

Comes moth-light, faint dusk-shine,
   The green woods still and whist;
And their sister, the eldest
   To keep her late tryst.

Long thought and lone broodings
   Have wanned, have withered, lined
A face, without beauty,
   Which no dream hath resigned

To love's impassioned grieving.
   She stands. The louring air
Breathes cold on her cheekbone,
   Stirs thief-like her hair;

And a still quiet challenge
   Fills her dark, her flint-grey eyes,
As she lifts her bowed head
   To survey the cold skies.

Wherein stars, hard and restless,
   Burn in station fore-ordained,
As if mocking for ever
   A courage disdained.

And she stoops wearied shoulders,
   Void of scorn, of fear, or ruth,
To confront in that well-spring
   The dark gaze of Truth.

SELF TO SELF[1]

Wouldst thou then happy be
On earth, where woes are many?
Where naught can make agree
Men paid for wage a penny?
Wherein ambition hath
Set up proud gate to Death;
And fame with trump and drum
Cannot undeaf the dumb
Who unto dust are come?
Wouldst thou then happy be? —
Impossibility?

Maybe, when reasons rule
Dunces kept in at school;
Or while mere Logic peers
Sand-blind at her bright shears
Snip-snapping this, and this,
Ay, on my soul, it is —
Till, looking up, thou see
Noonday's immensity,
And, turning back, see too
That in a bead of dew.

Heart-near or fancy-far,
All's thine to make or mar.
Thine its sole consciousness,
Whether thou ban or bless.
Loving delight forgot,
Life's very roots must rot.
Be it for better or worse,
Thou art thy universe.
If then at length thou must
Render them both to dust,
Go with their best in trust.
If thou wake never — well:
But if perchance thou find
Light, that brief gloom behind,
Thou'lt have wherewith to tell
If thou'rt in heaven or hell.

[1] First published as Ariel Poem, No. 11, 1928.

THE SLEEPER

The Lovely, sleeping, lay in bed,
  Her limbs, from quiet foot to chin,
Still as the dust of one that's dead
  Whose spirit waits the entering-in.

Yet her young cheek with life's faint dye
  Was mantled o'er; her gentle breast
Like sea at peace with starry sky,
  Moved with a heart at rest.

Fair country of a thousand springs,
  Calm hill and vale! Those hidden eyes
And tongue that daylong talks and sings,
  Wait only for the sun to rise.

Let but a bird call in that ear,
  Let beam of day that window wan,
This hidden one will, wakening, hear,
  And deathlike slumber-swoon be gone:

Her ardent eyes once more will shine,
  She will uplift her hair-crowned head;
At lip, miraculous, life's wine,
  At hand, its wondrous bread.

THE HUNTER

'Why wilt thou take my heart? It fawnlike flies,
'Frighted at clarion of thy hunting cries,
And shrinks benumbed beneath thy jealous eyes.

'Shun those green solitudes, these paths and vales
Where winds the grasses tell their faint-sung tales
Of distant Ocean's secret nightingales;

'Of frail foam-bubbles, spun of light and air,
From glass wherein sirens braid their sun-gilt hair,
Watching their round mouths chaunt a dying air. . . .

'O arrows, pierce me not! O horns, be still!
Sweet God, divine compassion have: or kill!'

[299]

THE VISIONARY

There is a pool whose waters clear
Reflect not what is standing near;
The silver-banded birch, the grass
Find not therein a looking-glass;
Nor doth Orion, pacing night,
Scatter thereon his wintry light.
Nor ever to its darnelled brink
Comes down the hare or deer to drink;
Sombre and secret it doth keep
Stilled in unshaken, crystal sleep.

But once, a Wanderer, parched, forlorn,
Worn with night-wayfaring, came at morn,
By pathless thickets grey with dew;
And stooping at its margent blue
To lave his wearied eyes, discerned
Somewhat that in the water burned —
A face like amber, pale and still,
With eyes of light, unchangeable,
Whose grave and steadfast scrutiny
Pierced through all earthly memory.
Voiceless and windless the green wood,
Above its shadowy quietude,
Sighed faintly through its unfading leaves;
And still he stooped; and still he yearned
To kiss the lips that therein burned;
To close those eyes that from the deep
Gazed on him, wearied out for sleep.

He drank; he slumbered; and he went
Back into life's wild banishment,
Like one whose every thought doth seem
The wreckage of a wasting dream;
All savour gone from life, delight
Charged with foreboding dark as night;
Love but the memory of what
Woke once, but reawakens not.

THE CAPTIVE[1]

I twined a net; I drove a stake; I laid a glittering bait.
With still of dewfall stepped my prey; cried — and cried too late.
I clutched him by his golden curls: I penned his flutterings.
Secure within a golden cage he beats in vain his wings.

But why is now their beauty gone
From woods where once it happy shone?
Why is my bosom desolate,
When entering in at fall of eve,
I listen at the wicket gate,
And hear my captive grieve?

THUS HER TALE[2]

Spake the fire-tinged bramble, bossed with gleaming fruit and
        blossoming,
    Gently serpentining in the air a blunted tongue: —
'Far too long these bones I hide have blackened in my covert here,
    Too long their noxious odour to my sweetness now hath clung.
Would they were gross clay, and their evil spell removed from me;
    How much lovelier I, if my roots not thence had sprung.'

Breathed the wind of sundown, 'Ay, this haunt is long years sour to
        me;
    But naught on earth that's human can my fancy free beguile.
Wings are mine far fleeter than the birds' that clip these branches;
    Arabian rich the burden which for honeyed mile on mile
Is wafted on my bosom, hill to ocean, wood to valeland.
    Anathema on relics that my fragrances defile!'

Stirred a thousand frondlets and the willow tree replied to it: —
    'Sty and mixen, foetid pool, and carrion-shed — whose these?
Yet earth makes sweet the foulest; naught — naught stays long
        unclean to her;
    Thou, too, howe'er reluctant, art her servant, gliding Breeze.
Restrain thy fretting pudency; in pity sigh for one I knew —
    The woman whose unburied bones in thornbrake take their
        ease.'

[1] First published in *The Captive and Other Poems*, New York, 1928.
[2] First published as a separate poem by The Porpoise Press, Edinburgh, 1923.

'*Urkkh:* when dark hath thicked to night,' croaked vermin toad that
    crouched near-by,
  'And the stars that mock in heaven unto midnight's cope have
    clomb,
When the shades of all the humans that in life were brutal foes to me
    Lift thready lamentation from the churchyard's rancid loam —
Return doth she in mortal guise 'gainst whom I bear no enmity,
  Foredoomed by fate this treacherous field for aye to haunt and
    roam.'

'*Pictured* once her image I,' sang sliding brook its rushes from,
  'That sallow face, and eyes that seemed to stare as if in dream,
Narrow shoulders, long lean hands, and hair like withered grass in
    hue,
  Pale lips drawn thwart with grieving in stars' silver mocking beam.
Once, too, I heard her story, but little I remember now,
  Though the blood that gave her power to suffer them imbrued my
    stream.'

Stony rock groaned forth its voice, 'No mirror featly shattered I,
  Blind I am by nature, but, I boast, not deaf or dumb,
Small truck I pay to Time's decay, nor mark what wounds black
    winter makes.
  Not mine to know what depths of snow have thawed and left
    me numb —
Since an eve when flowers had cast their seed, and evening cooled my
    brow again.
  And I echoed to a voice that whispered, "Loved one, I have
    come."'

Wafting through the woodland swept an owl from out the silentness,
  '*Too wittoo woo,*' she hooted. 'A human comes this way,
Gliding as on feathered heel, so tenuous that the thorns she skirts
  To eyes bright-glassed for glooms like mine show black beyond
    her grey.
A tryst she keeps. Beware, good friends, not mine day's mortal
    company,
  Hungry my brood for juicier fare,' she squawked, and plumed
    away.

Lone, in a shoal of milk-white cloud, bathed now the punctual
    fickle moon
  That nook of brook and willow, long unpolled, with silvery
    glare: —
'Unstilled yet tranquil Phantom, see, thou canst not hide thy form
    from me:

When last thy anguished body trod these meadows fresh and fair,
I, the ringing sand-dunes of the vast Sahara hoared with light:
  What secret calls thee from the shades; why hither dost thou
      fare?' . . .

Small beauty graced the spectre pondering mute beneath the
      willow-boughs
  O'er relics long grown noisome to the bramble and the breeze;
A hand upon her narrow breast, her head bent low in shadowiness;
  'I've come,' sighed voice like muted bell of nightbird in the trees,
'To tell again for all to hear, the wild remorse that suffers me,
  No single thought of rest or hope whereon to muse at ease.

'Self-slaughtered I, for one I loved, who could not give me love
      again,
  Uncounted now the Autumns since that twilight hour malign
When, insensate for escape from a hunger naught could satisfy,
  I vowed to God no more would I in torment live and pine.
Alas! He turned His face away, and woeful penance laid on me —
  That every night make tryst must I till life my love resign.'

Furtive fell the anxious glance she cast that dreadful hiding-place;
  Strangely still and muted ceased the tones in which she spake.
Shadow filled her vacant place. The moon withdrew in cloud again.
  Hushed the ripples grieving to the pebbles in their wake.
'Thus her *tale*!' quoth sod to sod. 'Not ours, good friends, to
      challenge it;
Though her blood still cries for vengeance on her murderer from
      this brake!'

ADIEU

Had these eyes never seen you,
This heart kept its paces,
If this mind — flooded river —
Had glassed not your graces;
Though lone my cold pillow,
In peace I had slumbered,
Whose hours now of waking
By moments are numbered.

You came; ice-still, asp-like;
You glanced 'neath your lashes;
You smiled — and you sighed out
Life's flame into ashes.

[303]

No compassion you showed me,
Void breast, cheating laughter:
Now I swing to my tryst
From this night-clotted rafter.

Peep out with your eyes.
Pout your mouth. Tilt your nose.
'Gainst the stench and the flies
Cull a balm-sprig, a rose.
This tongue that is stilled —
Not a tremor! Oh, else,
The whole roof of heaven
　　Would cry, False!

THE OUTSKIRTS

The night was cloyed with flowers
In the darkness deep and sweet,
When, at the window of the World,
I heard the dancing feet;
And viol and tambour
Made musical the air,
While yet a voice within me cried,
　　　Beware!

My eyes upon the glow were set
From out that thorny grot:
I hungered for the lips and eyes
And hearts remembering not;
And still the thrill and thud beat on
With sorcery in the air;
And, luring, leaping, called to me,
　　　Beware!

O all you hapless souls, like birds
Within night's branching may,
Hearken the words of him who speaks,
And fly from hence — away.
These dancers with their wiles and gauds,
That music on the air —
'Tis the swart Fowler with his nets
To play you false, though fair;
Hearken — an outcast I — I cry,
　　　Beware!

ROSE

Three centuries now are gone
Since Thomas Campion
Left men his airs, his verse, his heedful prose.
Few other memories
Have we of him, or his,
And, of his sister, none, but that her name was Rose.

Woodruff, far moschatel
May the more fragrant smell
When into brittle dust their blossoming goes.
His, too, a garden sweet,
Where rarest beauties meet,
And, as a child, he shared them with this Rose.

Faded, past changing, now,
Cheek, mouth, and childish brow.
Where, too, her phantom wanders no man knows.
Yet, when in undertone
That eager lute pines on,
Pleading of things he loved, it sings of Rose.

LUCY[1]

Strange — as I sat brooding here,
While memory plied her quiet thread,
Your once-loved face came back, my dear,
Amid the distant dead.

That pleasant cheek, hair smooth and brown,
Clear brows, and wistful eyes — yet gay:
You stand, in your alpaca gown,
And ghost my heart away.

I was a child then; nine years old —
And you a woman. Well, stoop close,
To heed a passion never told
Under how faded a rose!

Do you remember? Few my pence:
I hoarded them with a miser's care,
And bought you, in passionate innocence,
A birthday maidenhair.

[1] First published as Ariel Poem No. 33, 1931.

I see its fronds. Again I sit,
Hunched up in bed, in the dark, alone,
Crazed with those eyes that, memory-lit,
    Now ponder on my own.

You gave me not a thought, 'tis true —
Precocious, silly child; and yet,
Perhaps of all you have loved — loved you,
    I may the last forget.

And though no single word of this
You heed — a lifetime gone — at rest;
I would that all remembrances
    As gently pierced my breast!

A YOUNG GIRL

I search in vain your childlike face to see
The thoughts that hide behind the words you say;
I hear them singing, but close-shut from me
Dream the enchanted woods through which they stray.
Cheek, lip, and brow — I glance from each to each,
And watch that light-winged Mercury, your hand;
And sometimes when brief silence falls on speech
I seem your hidden self to understand.

Mine a dark fate. Behind his iron bars
The captive broods, with ear and heart a-strain
For jangle of key, for glimpse of moon or stars,
Grey shaft of daylight, sighing of the rain.
Life built these walls. Past all my dull surmise
Must burn the inward innocence of your eyes.

TWILIGHT

When to the inward darkness of my mind
I bid your face come, not one hue replies
Of that curved cheek, no, nor the faint-tinged rose
Of lips, nor smile between the mouth and eyes:
Only the eyes themselves, past telling, seem
To break in beauty in the twilight there,
And out of solitude your very ghost
Steals through the scarce-seen shadow of your hair.

THE TRYST

Faint now the colours in the West;
   And, stilled with lapse of day,
All life within it laid to rest,
   The wintry wood grows grey.

Frost enlines the withered flower,
   Its hips and haws now blackening are,
The slender naked tree-tops cower
   Beneath the evening-star.

Pace we then softly, you and I,
   Nor stir one England-wintering bird —
Start not! — 'twas but some wild thing's cry,
   No wailing ghost you heard.

Yet ghosts there are, remote and chill,
   Waiting the moon's phantasmal fire,
But not for us to heed, until
   We too doff Earth's attire.

Oh, far from home we both shall be,
   When we, with them, shall coldly brood
On lovers twain, like you and me,
   Trespassing in this wood.

THE ENCOUNTER

'Twixt dream and wake we wandered on,
Thinking of naught but you and me;
And lo, when day was nearly gone,
    A wondrous sight did see.

There, in a bed of rushes, lay
A child all naked, golden and fair —
Young Eros dreaming time away,
    With roses in his hair.

Tender sleep had o'ertaken him,
Quenched his bright arrows, loosed his bow,
And in divine oblivion dim
    Had stilled him through and through.

Never have I such beauty seen
As burned in his young dreaming face,
Cheek, hair, and lip laid drowsily
    In slumber's faint embrace.

Oh, how he started, how his eyes
Caught back their sudden shiningness
To see you stooping, loving-wise,
    Him, slumbering, to caress!

How flamed his brow, what childish joy
Leapt in his heart at sight of thee,
When, 'Mother, mother!' cried the boy:
    And — frowning — turned on me!

FULL CIRCLE[1]

When thou art as little as I am, Mother,
And I as old as thou,
I'll feed thee on wild-bee honeycomb,
And milk from my cow.
I'll make thee a swan's-down bed, Mother;
Watch over thee then will I.
And if in a far-away dream you start
I'll sing thee lullaby.
It's many — Oh, ages and ages, Mother,
We've shared, we two. Soon, now:
Thou shalt be happy, grown again young,
And I as old as thou.

[1] Title in *Bells and Grass*, 1941. It was called 'Karma' in *The Fleeting and Other Poems*, 1933.

THE GLANCE

Dearest one, daughter! at glance of your brow-shaded eye,
Fixed gravely in all its young scrutiny dark on my own,
Lone seemed my soul as this earth was itself 'neath the sky,
When at word of creation the trumps of the angels were blown.

They rang to the verge of the universe, solemn and deep,
Clanging untellable joy to the heavens above,
And, at core of that clangour, in silence profounder than sleep,
Adam and Eve lay adream in their Eden of love.

But you, in your bird-eyed wonder, gazed steadily on,
Knowing naught of the tempest so stirred. I stooped down my
head,
And, shutting my eyes to a prayer whereof words there are none,
Could but clasp your cold hand in my own and was dumb as the
dead.

HOW BLIND!

How blind 'twas to be harsh, I know —
    And to be harsh to *thee*;
To let one hour in anger go,
    And unforgiven be!

And now — O idiot tongue to dart
    That venomed fang, nor heed
Not thine but mine the stricken heart
    Shall never cease to bleed.

MAKING A FIRE

Scatter a few cold cinders into the empty grate;
    On these lay paper puffed into airy balloon,
Then wood — parched dry by the suns of Summer drowsy and
    sweet;
A flash, a flare, a flame; and a fire will be burning soon —

    Fernlike, fleet, and impetuous. But unless you give heed,
    It will faint, fade, fall, lose fervour, ash away out.
So it is with anger in heart and in brain; the insensate seed
Of dangerous fiery enkindling leaps into horror and rout;

[309]

But remaining untended, it dies. And the soul within
Is refreshed by the dews of sweet amity, pity's cool rain.
Not so with the flames Hell has kindled for unassoiled sin,
As soon as God's mercy would quench them, Love, weeping,
    lights them again.

THE ROUND

I watched, upon a vase's rim,
An earwig — strayed from honeyed cell —
Circling a track once strange to him,
    But now known far too well.

With vexed antennae, searching space,
And giddy grope to left and right,
On — and still on — he pressed apace,
    Out of, and into, sight.

In circumambulation drear,
He neither wavered, paused nor stayed;
But now kind Providence drew near —
    A slip of wood I laid

Across his track. He scaled its edge:
And soon was safely restored to where
A sappy, dew-bright, flowering hedge
    Of dahlias greened the air.

Ay, and as apt may be my fate! . . .
Smiling, I turned to work again:
But shivered, where in shade I sate,
    And idle did remain.

THE OMEN

Far overhead — the glass set fair —
I heard a raven in the air;
'Twixt roof and stars it fanning went,
And croaked in sudden dreariment.

Over the pages of my book
I, listening, cast a sidelong look.
Curtained the window; shut the door;
I turned me to my book once more;
But in that quiet strove in vain
To win its pleasure back again.

WHICH WAY?

Wander, spirit? — *I!*
Who do not even know
Which way I'd go:
Yet sigh:

Who cannot even, first,
What far-off living well
I pine for, tell:
Yet thirst!

Unfailing joys I share;
No hour, however fleet,
But brings its sweet
And fair:

And yet — scoff not! — day gone,
Some silly ghost creeps back,
'What do you lack?'
To groan.

MIST

Sometimes in moods of gloom — like mist
  Enswathing hill and wood —
A miracle of sunshine breaks
  Into my solitude.

In scattered splendour burns the dew;
  Still as in dream, the trees
Their vaulted branches echo make
  To the birds' ecstasies.

What secret influence was this
  Made all dark brooding vain?
Has then the mind no inward sun? —
  The mists cloud down again:

Stealthily drape the distant heights
  Blot out the songless tree:
Into cold silence flit the thoughts
  That sang to me.

[311]

THE ARGUMENT

Why, then, if love is all there is need to give,
    All love be thine.
Thine the bright wonder of this life I live,
    Its doubt's dark broodings mine.

Serene that marvellous waste of crystal sky,
    And that gaunt crook-backed tree!
Hush! breathes the wind invisibly rippling by,
    Hush! to the wild bird's cry . . .

Yet even as mind vowed no more to grieve,
    Heart answered with a sigh.

DAWN

Near, far, unearthly, break the birds
From spectral bush and tree,
Into a strange and drowsy praise,
The flush of dawn to see.

Old ashen rooks, on ragged wing,
And heads with sidling eye,
Sweep in the silvery heights of daybreak,
Silent through the sky.

The restless robin — like a brook
Tinkling in frozen snow —
Shakes his clear, sudden, piercing bells,
Flits elf-like to and fro.

Cock to cock yells, the enormous earth
Lies like a dream outspread
Under the canopy of space,
Stretched infinite overhead.

[312]

Light on the wool-fleeced ewes pours in;
Meek-faced, they snuff the air;
The glint-horned oxen sit agaze;
The east burns orient-fair.

The milk-white mists of night wreathe up
From meadows greenly grey —
Their every blade of grass ablaze
With dewdrops drenched in day.

THE SPARK

Calm was the evening, as if asleep,
But sickled on high with brooding storm,
Couched in invisible space. And, lo!
I saw in utter silence sweep
Out of that darkening starless vault
A gliding spark, as blanched as snow,
That burned into dust, and vanished in
A hay-cropped meadow, brightly green.

A meteor from the cold of space,
Lost in Earth's wilderness of air? —
Presage of lightnings soon to shine
In splendour on this lonely place? —
I cannot tell; but only how fair
It glowed within the crystalline
Pure heavens, and of its strangeness lit
My mind to joy at sight of it.

Yet what is common as lovely may be:
The petalled daisy, a honey bell,
A pebble, a branch of moss, a gem
Of dew, or fallen rain — if we
A moment in their beauty dwell;
Entranced, alone, see only them.
How blind to wait, till, merely unique,
Some omen thus the all bespeak!

JENNY WREN

Of all the birds that rove and sing,
    Near dwellings made for men,
None is so nimble, feat, and trim
    As Jenny Wren.

With pin-point bill, and tail a-cock,
    So wildly shrill she cries,
The echoes on their roof-tree knock
    And fill the skies.

Never was sweeter seraph hid
    Within so small a house —
A tiny, inch-long, eager, ardent,
    Feathered mouse.

THE SNAIL[1]

All day shut fast in whorled retreat
You slumber where — no wild bird knows;
While on your rounded roof-tree beat
The petals of the rose.
The grasses sigh above your house;
Through drifts of darkest azure sweep
The sun-motes where the mosses drowse
That soothe your noonday sleep.

But when to ashes in the west
Those sun-fires die; and, silver, slim,
Eve, with the moon upon her breast,
Smiles on the uplands dim;
Then, all your wreathèd house astir,
Horns reared, grim mouth, deliberate pace,
You glide in silken silence where
The feast awaits your grace.

Strange partners, Snail! Then I, abed,
Consign the thick-darked vault to you,
Nor heed what sweetness night may shed
Nor moonshine's slumbrous dew.

---

[1] First published in *The Captive and Other Poems*, New York, 1928.

SPEECH

The robin's whistled stave
Is tart as half-ripened fruit;
Wood-sooth from bower of leaves
The blackbird's flute;
Shrill-small the ardent wren's;
And the thrush, and the long-tailed tit —
Each hath its own apt tongue,
    Shrill, harsh, or sweet.

The meanings they may bear
Is long past ours to guess —
What sighs the wind, of the past,
In the wilderness?
Man also in ancient words
His thoughts may pack,
But if he not sing them too,
    Music they lack.

Oh, never on earth was bird,
Though perched on Arabian tree,
Nor instrument echoing heaven
Made melody strange as he;
Since even his happiest speech
Cries of his whither and whence,
And in mere sound secretes
    His inmost sense.

TOM'S ANGEL

No one was in the fields
But me and Polly Flint,
When, like a giant across the grass,
The flaming angel went.

It was budding time in May,
And green as green could be,
And all in his height he went along
Past Polly Flint and me.

We'd been playing in the woods,
And Polly up, and ran,
And hid her face, and said,
'Tom! Tom! The Man! The Man!'

And I up-turned; and there.
Like flames across the sky,
With wings all bristling, came
The Angel striding by.

And a chaffinch overhead
Kept whistling in the tree
While the Angel, blue as fire, came on
Past Polly Flint and me.

And I saw his hair, and all
The ruffling of his hem,
As over the clovers his bare feet
Trod without stirring them.

Polly — she cried; and, oh!
We ran, until the lane
Turned by the miller's roaring wheel,
And we were safe again.

ENGLISH DOWNS

Here, long ere kings to battle rode
  In thunder of the drum,
And trumps fee-faughed defiance,
  And taut bow-strings whistled, 'Come!' —

This air breathed milky sweet
  With nodding columbine,
Dangled upon the age-gnarled thorn
  The clematis twine;

Meek harebell hung her head
  Over the green-turfed chalk,
And the lambs with their dams forgathered
  Where the shepherds talk.

'HOW SLEEP THE BRAVE'

Bitterly, England must thou grieve —
  Though none of these poor men who died
But did within his soul believe
  That death for thee was glorified.

[316]

Ever they watched it hovering near —
  A mystery beyond thought to plumb —
And often, in loathing and in fear,
  They heard cold danger whisper, Come! —

Heard, and obeyed. Oh, if thou weep
  Such courage and honour, woe, despair;
Remember too that those who sleep
  No more remorse can share.

THE IMAGE

Faint sighings sounded, not of wind, amid
That chasmed waste of boulder and cactus flower,
Primeval sand its sterile coverlid,
Unclocked eternity its passing hour.

Naught breathed or stirred beneath its void of blue,
Save when in far faint dying whisper strained
Down the sheer steep, where not even lichen grew,
Eroded dust, and, where it fell, remained.

Hewn in that virgin rock, nude 'gainst the skies,
Loomed mighty Shape — of granite brow and breast,
Its huge hands folded on its sightless eyes,
Its lips and feet immovably at rest.

Where now the wanderers who this image scored
For age-long idol here? — Death? Destiny? Fame? —
Mute, secret, dreadful, and by man adored;
Yet not a mark in the dust to tell its name?

A ROBIN

Ghost-grey the fall of night,
    Ice-bound the lane,
Lone in the dying light
    Flits he again;
Lurking where shadows steal,
Perched in his coat of blood,
Man's homestead at his heel,
    Death-still the wood.

[317]

Odd restless child; it's dark;
    All wings are flown
But this one wizard's — hark!
    Stone clapped on stone!
Changeling and solitary,
Secret and sharp and small,
Flits he from tree to tree,
    Calling on all.

SNOWING

Snowing; snowing;
Oh, between earth and sky
A wintry wind is blowing,
Scattering with its sigh
Petals from trees of silver that shine
Like invisible glass, when the moon
In the void of night on high
Paces her orchards divine.

Snowing; snowing;
Ah me, how still, and how fair
The air with flakes interflowing,
The fields crystal and bare,
When the brawling brooks are dumb
And the parched trees matted with frost,
And the birds in this wilderness stare
    Dazzled and numb!

Snowing . . . snowing . . . snowing:
Moments of time through space
Into hours, centuries growing,
Till the world's marred lovely face,
Wearied of change and chance,
Radiant in innocence dream —
Lulled by an infinite grace
To rest in eternal trance.

MEMORY

When summer heat has drowsed the day
With blaze of noontide overhead,
And hidden greenfinch can but say
What but a moment since it said;

When harvest fields stand thick with wheat,
And wasp and bee slave — dawn till dark —
Nor home, till evening moonbeams beat,
Silvering the nightjar's oaken bark:
How strangely then the mind may build
A magic world of wintry cold,
Its meadows with frail frost-flowers filled —
Bright-ribbed with ice, a frozen wold! . . .

When dusk shuts in the shortest day,
And huge Orion spans the night;
Where antlered fireflames leap and play
Chequering the walls with fitful light —
Even sweeter in mind the summer's rose
May bloom again; her drifting swan
Resume her beauty; while rapture flows
Of birds long since to silence gone:
Beyond the Nowel, sharp and shrill,
Of Waits from out the snowbound street,
Drums to their fiddle beneath the hill
June's mill wheel where the waters meet . . .

O angel Memory that can
Double the joys of faithless Man!

A BALLAD OF CHRISTMAS[1]

It was about the deep of night,
  And still was earth and sky,
When in the moonlight, dazzling bright,
  Three ghosts came riding by.

Beyond the sea — beyond the sea,
  Lie kingdoms for them all:
I wot their steeds trod wearily —
  The journey is not small.

By rock and desert, sand and stream,
  They footsore late did go:
Now, like a sweet and blessed dream,
  Their path was deep with snow.

[1] First published as a separate poem, *A Ballad of Christmas*, in an edition of
100 copies, London, 1924.

Shining like hoarfrost, rode they on,
　　Three ghosts in earth's array:
It was about the hour when wan
　　Night turns at hint of day.

Oh, but their hearts with woe distraught
　　Hailed not the wane of night,
Only for Jesu still they sought
　　To wash them clean and white.

For bloody was each hand, and dark
　　With death each orbless eye; —
It was three Traitors mute and stark
　　Came riding silent by.

Silver their raiment and their spurs,
　　And silver-shod their feet,
And silver-pale each face that stared
　　Into the moonlight sweet.

And he upon the left that rode
　　Was Pilate, Prince of Rome,
Whose journey once lay far abroad,
　　And now was nearing home.

And he upon the right that rode,
　　Herod of Salem sate,
Whose mantle dipped in children's blood
　　Shone clear as Heaven's gate.

And he, these twain betwixt, that rode
　　Was clad as white as wool,
Dyed in the Mercy of his God,
　　White was he crown to sole.

Throned mid a myriad Saints in bliss
　　Rise shall the Babe of Heaven
To shine on these three ghosts, i-wis,
　　Smit through with sorrows seven;

Babe of the Blessed Trinity
　　Shall smile their steeds to see:
Herod and Pilate riding by,
　　And Judas, one of three.

THE SNOWDROP[1]

Now — now, as low I stooped, thought I,
I will see what this snowdrop *is*;
So shall I put much argument by,
    And solve a lifetime's mysteries.

A northern wind had frozen the grass;
Its blades were hoar with crystal rime,
Aglint like light-dissecting glass
    At beam of morning-prime.

From hidden bulb the flower reared up
Its angled, slender, cold, dark stem,
Whence dangled an inverted cup
    For tri-leaved diadem.

Beneath these ice-pure sepals lay
A triplet of green-pencilled snow,
Which in the chill-aired gloom of day
    Stirred softly to and fro.

Mind fixed, but else made vacant, I,
Lost to my body, called my soul
To don that frail solemnity,
    Its inmost self my goal.

And though in vain — no mortal mind
Across that threshold yet hath fared! —
In this collusion I divined
    Some consciousness we shared.

Strange roads — while suns, a myriad, set —
Had led us through infinity;
And where they crossed, there then had met
    Not two of us, but three.

[1] First published as Ariel Poem, No. 20, 1929.

THE FLEETING[1]

The late wind failed; high on the hill
The pine's resounding boughs were still:
Those wondrous airs that space had lent
To wail earth's night-long banishment
From heat and light and song of day
In a last sighing died away.

Alone in the muteness, lost and small,
I watched from far-off Leo fall
An ebbing trail of silvery dust,
And fade to naught; while, near and far,
Glittered in quiet star to star;
And dreamed, in midnight's dim immense,
Heaven's universal innocence.

O transient heart that yet can raise
To the unseen its pang of praise,
And from the founts in play above
Be freshed with that sweet love!

HERESY

Enter on to a prodigious headland, a little before noon, two men in alien dress, and between them a third, younger than they, blindfold, and in the raiment of a prince. They remove the bandage from his eyes, and seat themselves on the turf. His hands bound behind his back, the Prince stands between them, looking out to sea. Dazed for a moment by the sudden glare, he stays silent.

Prince. What place is this?
                            All's strange to me, and I
Had fallen at last accustomed to the dark.
Why, then, to this vast radiance bring me blindfold?
Hangman. Why, Prince, a happy surprise!
  First coach-room; then,
A steady creeping upward; and now — this.
Once died — and lived — a corse named Lazarus:
Remember, then, to all men else than they
Who will not blab, you have been three days dead —
And, that far gone, even princes are soon forgot.
Lo, then, your resurrection! — take your fill.
Nor need we three have joy in it alone.
Legions of listeners surround us here,

First published in *Poems for Children*, 1930.

Alert, though out of hearing and of sight.
　Prince. Like many journeys, this is best being done.
My lungs ache with the ascent and the thin air.
After your souring 'coach-room' it smells sweet.

(He turns away.)

How wondrous a scene of universal calm,
These last days' troubles and distractions done!
Look, how that pretty harebell nods her head,
Whispering, *ay, ay*. How fresh the scent of thyme!
The knife-winged birds that haunt this sea-blue vault
Even in their droppings mock the eye with flowers
Whiter than snow.
　Hangman. Yes, and as bleached have picked
This coney's bones that dared their empire here.
　Prince. How dark a shadow in so little a head
Peers from its thin-walled skull.
　Hangman. 　　　　　　　By Gis,
Not thyme but stark Eternity domes this perch;
And who needs hempseed when his ghost's gone home?
　Courtier. When yours goes home, the bitterest weed earth fats
Would taste more savoury to the hawks of hell.
　Hangman. Meanwhile, a civil tongue hang in your head!
You've bribed your coming hither; let it rest.
　Prince. I pray you cut these ropes from off my wrists.
Here's neither need nor hour to challenge why
And by whose tyranny I have endured
Monstrous humiliations. That may wait.
But I am faint, and have no hope in flight.
In quiet we'll sit, and you shall then rehearse
What wrongs are yours a little thought may right.
We all are human, and the heavens be judge.
　Hangman (*as he picks up the skull of the rabbit from the turf*).
'We all are human, and the heavens be judge'! —
A dainty saying, Prince, in either part;
Come noon, and ample proof is yours of both!
I've heard of hermits drowned so deep in silence
Their hairy ears dreamed voices in their brains.
I'd be a hermit too, if in my cell
A homelier music than this bleaching wind's
In these sharp-bladed grasses lulled me asleep.
It seemed an instant gone a halting voice
Sighed, *flight* — as if in envy of these mews
That scream defiance o'er our innocent heads.
Alackaday, the dirge they seem to sing!
　Courtier. This is sole solitude. It utterly dwarfs
Not merely man's corporeal girth and stature,

[323]

But melts to naught the imaginings of his soul.

    Hangman (mocking him). So empty this wide salt-tang'd vast of air
'Twould gobble up the cries of all the dying
As artlessly as God Man's sabbath prayers!
Raved here some fell she-Roc a shrill lament
Over her brood struck cold by heedless thunder,
The nearest listener would softly smile
Dreaming him lulled by sigh of passing zephyr!
(To the Prince.) So, sir, our talk has edged again to'rd you.

    Prince. Ay, has it so? What would you?

    Hangman.   Our sole selves,
And a something motionless in a huddle of clothes,
Which soon air's birds, earth's ants will disinfect,
Leaving it naught more talkative than bones.

    Prince. Murder is in your thoughts?

    Hangman.   Ah, sir, a boy
That lugs poor Puss close-bagged and stone-companioned
Off to her first — and only — watery bath
May have misgivings; but not so grown men.
Murder's no worse a thing when it's called Justice.
We promise you your remorse shall vex no ear
Unwonted to reproaches. Scan this height!

    Courtier (sotto voce). It is a table open to the eye of heav'n:
And lo, beyond that girdle of huge egg-boulders,
Sun-shivering waters to the horizon's verge —
The Ocean Sea — self-lulled, like full-fed babe
That mumbles its mother's nipple in its dreams.

    Hangman. You see, sir, though Fate may on Kings cry, 'Check!',
Princes she merely pushes off the board.
Ay, and one broken down there, upon those stones,
Frenzied with thirst and pain, need not despair!
The lapping comfort of the inning tide,
Though of a languid pace as tardy as time's,
Will, at its leisure, muffle all lamentings.
And what care lobsters if their supper talk?

    Prince. You speak as if some devil in your brains
Had stolen their sanity.

    Hangman (smiling closely into his face). There runs a silly saying in
      my mind,
Moaned by poor lovers cheated of desire,
Two's company; three's none!

    Prince (ironically).   So be it, my friend.
Adieu. I will turn back without delay!
Doubtless the paths by which you have led me blindfold
Some instinct of direction will recall.

    Hangman. I'm told that cats have such a sense of home

They'll dog their would-be murderers twenty miles,
To miaow defiance.
    Prince (facing him, eye to eye). Yes. And so would I!
Wait but till I am free from fleshly bonds!
    Hangman (laughing hollowly). An assignation past the post of
       death!
So be it! tho' night grows cold to'rd crow of cock!
    Courtier (to the Hangman). Hold now your festering tongue awhile,
       and wait;
A few more minutes, and it's final noon.
        (*He cuts the ropes that bind the Prince's wrists. The Prince seats
        himself on the turf. The Courtier paces the edge of the cliff,
        pausing at times to peer into the abyss.*)
    Courtier. This three days gone — and now no hope can help me —
A last brief message from the King's been mine
To bring you, Prince. In vain, in vain I stayed,
Pining in misery it might harmless prove,
Since Fate the while held all things in the balance.
The waiting's over; and the balance down.
The wild resolve I neither loved nor shared
Has fallen to worse than nothing; and the foes
That hated you can now feed full on scorn.
    Prince. Cut to the bone, friend; I am sick of snippets.
    Hangman. Well said, cut softly to the very bone.
The minutes dwindle, and the tide has turned.
    Courtier. I'll keep my Master's pace. . . . There was a realm,
A state, a hive, a human emmet heap,
Ruled over by a king whose sceptre of iron
He wielded wisely, and bade kiss or crush,
According to his kingdom's need and crisis.
Merciful he when mercy he knew well
Could virtue serve, his People, justice, peace;
But swift and pitiless when his anxious gaze
Pierced to the cancer of that People's ill.
Such rulers win more confidence than love.
None ever assailed his lealty to the good
That in his inmost soul he deemed the best —
Best for the most, less, least — since best for all.
    Hangman. A pleasing purge — and kingly common sense.
Think now, had this bold rabbit, gone to dust,
Ruled o'er his warren — why, this bright green turf
Were now a rodents' Golgotha of bones.
He who brews poison should be first to taste it.
    Prince. Of your twin voices one is wolfish bass,
But keeps the nearer to the tune they share.

Courtier. But little more of *that*, God knows — then none.
    (*He continues almost as if he were talking to himself.*)
In hives of Bees, whose summer is all spent
Toiling and moiling against wintry want,
It's not the worker, or the fatted drone,
May breed disaster, but some royal she
Fed only on nectar in her nymphal cell,
And yet uniquely sensed, who issues out
Into the whispering business of the hive,
Intent on some pre-natal paradise,
To find it but a maze of servile instinct.
What wonder if in heat of youth she rove,
Plagued and impatient at a fate so pinched,
Lusting to free her kind, to entice them on —
On to some dreamed chimera of workless bliss!
Treason! she trumps to her contented kin.
'*Awake! Arouse! Fools, fools, your Queen is mad!*'
But skeps of straw are not of the weaving of heaven,
And Nature's neutral tyranny is such
She'll sate with sunshine, and then starve in ice.
This jade I tell of, ardent, selfless, rash,
May of truth's essence have sucked, but what of that?
One born too wise within a polity
As ancient as the Bee's is curse more dire
Than countless generations of the dull.
    Hangman. All that this prating means is, Look at me! —
Crafty enough to feign I have few wits,
But yet can do with skill the things I'm bid.
And after, bloody-fingered, fist my wages.
    Prince. So plain the gallows shows upon your face
You need no hangman tongue to draw the trap.
(*To the other.*) Of you I ask only a moment's peace
To be alone in commune with myself.
I weary of your parables and am dumb.
Were I led hither again, again, again,
And at this bleak abyss which now I face
My bowels in a frenzy of fear should melt —
Again, again; I would no word recant,
No act recall, nor one ideal betray
Which these last few vain hours have brought to naught.
Oh, I am weary, give me leave to die.
Words may worse torture wreak than screw or rack.
    Hangman. And that's why we have given you words in plenty.
    Courtier (*still ignoring him*). One other grief — to share; and *I* have done.
This She I spoke of was, in fact, a prince;
The hive, his father's realm: a prince held dear

Beyond idolatry; the wonder and hope
Of this wise monarch's soul. No Absalom —
Since thrones in time began — was more endued
With beauty, genius, grace, fame, fortune, zeal.
He'd but to turn his head to be beloved.
The dumb-tongued stones that paved his palace court
Echoed of glory when he trod; no bliss
Was past his full achievement. Yes, my lord,
Our royal master grudged you nothing; and
He bade me breathe you peace on this account;
Avow again — though you are past his pity —
That not one blotch of envy in his blood
Did ever incite him to a thought's revenge.
He loved you . . . So, 'tis done. And I am here
To bring his blessing ere your feet go on
Into the dark unknown. There this world's kings
May find them less in rank than scullions
In service of the gods; who yet decreed
That they reign faithfully and reign unmoved
By any hope too high for human practice.
To call men equal is a heresy;
And worse — denial of the divine. Think you,
Doth jealousy green the hyssop in the wall
That with the cedar shares her mote of sunlight?
Is pain the blesseder for being shared?
Is aught in life worth having but what the mind
Hath sealed its own within its secret silence?
What is heart's ease — ambition, or the peace
That only comes of loving its poor best? . . .
When death is in the pulpit — thus he speaks!
And I, alas, his deputy. But now
I cease. No more the mouthpiece of my Master,
I stay to keep you company to the end.

> (*With a gesture the Hangman bids the Prince stand. He leads
> him to the brink of the abyss.*)

Prince. So wild a light, and then the little dark.
This is the end, then. And, to you, farewell.
What was between my father and his son
I gave you never warranty to share.
What was between my inmost self and me
Yours never the faintest insight to descry.
He gave me life — scant born in world half-dead.
And now he craves it of me, since his seed
Has fruited past his liking. Tell him this —
When you from your day's pleasuring have gone back:
I died remorseless, yet in shame — for one

So rich in magnanimity who yet
Refused his realm the very elixir of life;
And sick with terror of what the truth might tell,
Uncharged, untried, has chos'n me *this* for end.
I am gone forth on my high errand; he
Breathes on in infamy.
    Hangman. Ha, ha, *ha, ha!* The pity that a roost
So fecund as this gives the young cock no hens!
    Courtier. Great deeds great crimes may be; and so
Of their extravagance win doom at last,
Commensurate in scope, in kind, in awe,
With him whose blinded wisdom brought them forth.
Hence this immensity on which we stand.
Such was his edict.
    Prince.   And is *this* the sot
He of his own sole choice bade bring me here?
We two — though at this pass — are of a kin;
I loved you; love you yet, but —
    Courtier. I know not, sir. The King's mouth now says nothing.
I came at no man's orders; only lest
This hangman here . . .
        (*A triple fanfare of trumpets is heard echoing up from where beyond
          view of the headland the three legions of soldiery have been
          awaiting noon.*)
                    But hark, we're for a journey
Beyond the talisman of our wits to scan.
    Hangman (*spitting upon the ground in contempt of both of them*).
    'Ware, then! Lift princely eyes into the void
And watch as 'twere your soul's winged silver slide
Into the empyrean. Get you gone!
    Prince (*leaping out into space*). Away!
    Courtier. And I! . . . Away! . . .
        (*A triple roll of drums reverberates in the parched air of noonday
        from out of the valley, ascends into the heavens, ceases.*)

BREAK OF MORNING

Sound the invisible trumps. In circuit vast
    The passive earth, like scene in dream, is set.
The small birds flit and sing, their dark hours past,
    And their green sojournings with dewdrops wet.

With giant boughs outspread, the oaks on high
    Brood on in slumbrous quiet in the air.
Sole in remote inane of vacant sky
    Paling Arcturus sparkles wildly fair.

Sound the invisible trumps. The waters weep.
  A stealing wind breathes in the meads, is gone.
Into their earthen burrows the wild things creep;
  Cockcrow to thinning cockcrow echoes on.

Avert thine eyes, sleep-ridden face! Nor scan
  Those seraph hosts that in divine array
Girdle the mortal-masked empyrean:
  Their sovereign beauty is this break of day.

Theirs is the music men call silence here;
  What wonder grief distorts thy burning eyes?
Turn to thy pillow again — in love and fear;
  Not thine to see the Son of Morning rise.

THE OWL

'Well, God 'ild you! They say the owle was a baker's daughter'. Hamlet, IV, v

The door-bell jangled in evening's peace,
Its clapper dulled with verdigris.
Lit by the hanging lamp's still flame
Into the shop a beggar came,
Glanced gravely around him — counter, stool,
Ticking clock and heaped-up tray
Of bakers' dainties, put to cool;
And quietly turned his eyes away.

Stepped out the goodwife from within —
Her blandest smile from brow to chin
Fading at once to blank chagrin
As she paused to peer, with keen blue eyes
Sharpened to find a stranger there,
And one, she knew, no customer.
'We never give . . .' she said, and stayed;
Mute and intent, as if dismayed
At so profoundly still a face.
'What do you want?' She came a pace
Nearer, and scanned him, head to foot.
He looked at her, but answered not.

[329]

The tabby-cat that, fathom deep,
On the scoured counter lay asleep,
Reared up its head to yawn, and then,
Composing itself to sleep again,
With eyes by night made black as jet,
Gazed on the stranger. 'A crust,' he said.
   'A crust of bread.'
Disquiet in the woman stirred —
No plea, or plaint, or hinted threat —
So low his voice she had scarcely heard.
She shook her head; he turned to go.
'We've nothing here for beggars. And so . . .
If we gave food to all who come
They'd eat us out of house and home —
Where charity begins, they say;
And ends, as like as not — or may.'

Still listening, he answered not,
His eyes upon the speaker set,
Eyes that she tried in vain to evade
   But had not met.
She frowned. 'Well, that's my husband's rule;
But stay a moment. There's a stool —
Sit down and wait. Stale bread we've none.
And else . . .' she shrugged. 'Still, rest awhile,'
Her smooth face conjured up a smile,
'And I'll go see what can be done.'

He did as he was bidden. And she
Went briskly in, and shut the door;
To pause, in brief uncertainty,
Searching for what she failed to find.
Then tiptoed back to peer once more
In through the ribboned muslin blind,
And eyed him secretly, askance,
With a prolonged, keen, searching glance;
As if mere listening might divine
Some centuries-silent countersign . . .
Scores of lean hungry folk she had turned
Even hungrier from her door, though less
From stint and scorn than heedlessness.
Why then should she a scruple spare
For one who, in a like distress,
Had spoken as if in heart he yearned
Far more for peace than bread? But now

[330]

No mark of gloom obscured his brow,
No shadow of darkness or despair.
Still as an image of age-worn stone
That from a pinnacle looks down
Over the seas of time, he sat;
His stooping face illumined by
The burnished scales that hung awry
Beside the crusted loaves of bread.
Never it seemed shone lamp so still
  On one so sore bestead.
'Poor wretch,' she muttered, 'he minds me of . . .'
A footfall sounded from above;
And, hand on mouth, immovable,
She watched and pondered there until,
Stepping alertly down the stair,
Her daughter — young as she was fair —
Came within earshot.
           'H'st,' she cried.
'A stranger here! And Lord betide,
He may have been watching till we're alone,
Biding his time, your father gone.
Come, now; come quietly and peep! —
Rags! — he would make a Christian weep!
I've promised nothing; but, good lack!
What shall I say when I go back?'

Her daughter softly stepped to peep.
'Pah! begging,' she whispered; 'I know that tale.
Money is all he wants — for ale!'
Through the cold glass there stole a beam
Of lamplight on her standing there,
Stilling her beauty as in a dream.
It smote to gold her wing-soft hair,
It scarleted her bird-bright cheek,
With shadow tinged her childlike neck,
Dreamed on her rounded bosom, and lay —
Like a sapphire pool at break of day,
Where martin and wagtail preen and play —
In the shallow shining of her eye.

'T't, mother,' she scoffed, with a scornful sigh,
And peeped again, and sneered — her lip
Drawn back from her small even teeth,
Showing the bright-red gums beneath.
'Look, now! The wretch has fallen asleep —

[331]

Stark at the counter, there; still as death.
As I sat alone at my looking-glass,
I heard a footstep — watched him pass,
Turn, and limp thief-like back again.
Out went my candle. I listened; and then
Those two faint *dings*. Aha! thought I,
Honest he may be, though old and blind,
But *that's* no customer come to buy.
So down I came — too late! I knew
He'd get less comfort from me than you!
I warrant, a pretty tale he told!
"Alone"! Lord love us! Leave him to me.
I'll teach him manners. Wait and see.'
She nodded her small snake-like head,
Sleeked with its strands of palest gold,
'Waste not, want not, say I,' she said.

Her mother faltered. Their glances met —
Furtive and questioning; hard and cold —
In mute communion mind with mind,
Though little to share could either find.
'Save us!' she answered, 'sharp eyes you have,
If in the dark you can see the blind!
He was as tongueless as the grave.
"Tale"! Not a sigh. Not one word said.
    Except that he asked for bread.'

Uneasy in her thoughts, she yet
Knew, howsoever late the hour,
And none in call, small risk they ran
From any homeless beggar-man.
While as for this — worn, wasted, wan —
    A nod, and he'd be gone.
Waste not, want not, forsooth! The chit —
To think that she should so dictate!

' "Asleep" you say? Well, what of that?
What mortal harm can come of it?
A look he gave me; and his eyes . . .
Leave him to me, Miss Worldly-wise!
Trouble him not. Stay here, while I
See how much broken meat's put by.
God knows the wretch may have his fill.
And you — keep watch upon the till!'

She hastened in, with muffled tread.
Meanwhile her daughter, left alone,
Waited, watching, till she was gone;
Then softly drew open the door, to stare
More nearly through the sombre air
At the still face, dark matted hair,
Scarred hand, shut eyes, and silent mouth,
Parched with the long day's bitter drouth;
Now aureoled in the lustre shed
From the murky lamp above his head.
Her tense young features distorted, she
Gazed on, in sharpening enmity,
Her eager lips tight shut, as if
The very air she breathed might be
Poisoned by this foul company.
That such should be allowed to live!
Yet, as she watched him, needle-clear,
  Beneath her contempt stirred fear.
Fear, not of body's harm, or aught
Instinct or cunning may have taught
Wits edged by watchful vanity:
It seemed her inmost soul made cry —
Wild thing, bewildered, the huntsmen nigh —
Of hidden ambush, and a flood
Of vague forebodings chilled her blood.
Kestrel keen, her eyes' bright blue
Narrowed, as she stole softly through.

'H'st, you!' she whispered him. 'Waken! **Hear!**
I come to warn you. Danger's near!'
Cat-like she scanned him, drew-to the door,
'She is calling for help. No time to wait! —
Before the neighbours come — before
They hoick their dogs on, and it's too late!'
The stranger listened; turned; and smiled:
'But whither shall I go, my child?
All ways are treacherous to those
Who, seeking friends, find only foes.'

My child! — the words like poison ran
Through her quick mind. 'What!' she began,
In fuming rage; then stayed; for, lo,
This visage, for all its starven woe,
That now met calmly her scrutiny,
Of time's corruption was wholly free.

[333]

The eyes beneath the level brows,
Though weary for want of sleep, yet shone
With strange directness, gazing on.
In her brief life she had never seen
A face so eager yet serene,
And, in its deathless courage, none
To bear with it comparison.

'I will begone,' at length he said.
  'All that I asked was bread.'

Her anger died away; she sighed;
Pouted; then laughed. 'So Mother tried
To scare me? Told me I must stop
In there — some wretch was in the shop
Who'd come to rob and . . . Well, thought I,
Seeing's believing; I could but try
To keep *her* safe. What else to do —
Till help might come?' She paused, and drew
A straying lock of yellow hair
Back from her cheek — as palely fair —
In heedless indolence; as when
A wood-dove idly spreads her wing
Sunwards, and folds it in again.
Aimless, with fingers slender and cold,
She fondled the tress more stealthily
  Than miser with his gold.
And still her wonder grew: to see
A man of this rare courtesy
So sunken in want and poverty.
What was his actual errand here?
And whereto was he journeying?
A silence had fallen between them. Save
The weight-clock's ticking, slow and grave,
No whisper, in or out, she heard;
The cat slept on; and nothing stirred.
'Is it only hungry?' she cajoled,
In this strange quiet made more bold.
'Far worse than hunger seems to me
The cankering fear of growing old.
That is a kind of hunger too —
Which even *I* can share with you.
And, heaven help me, always alone!
Mother cares nothing for that. But wait;
See now how dark it is, and late;
Nor any roof for shelter. But soon

Night will be lovely — with the moon.
When all is quiet, and she abed,
Do you come back, and click the latch;
And I'll sit up above, and watch.
A supper then I'll bring,' she said,
'Sweeter by far than mouldy bread!'

Like water chiming in a well
Which uncropped weeds more sombre make,
The low seductive syllables fell
    Of every word she spake —
Music lulling the listening ear,
Note as of nightbird, low and clear,
    That yet keeps grief awake.
But still he made no sign. And she,
Now, fearing his silence, scoffed mockingly,
'God knows I'm not the one to give
For the mere asking. As I live
I loathe the cringing skulking scum,
Day in, day out, that begging come;
Sots, tramps, who pester, whine, and shirk —
They'd rather starve to death than work.
And lie!'— She aped, '"God help me, m'm;
'Tisn't myself but them at home!
Crying for food they are. Yes, seven! —
And their poor mother safe in heaven!"' '
Glib as a prating parrot she
Mimicked the words with sidling head,
Bright-red tongue and claw-like hands.
'But — I can tell you — when *I*'m there
There's little for the seven to share!'
She raised her eyebrows; innocent, mild —
Less parrot now than pensive child;
Her every movement of body and face,
As of a flower in the wind's embrace,
    Born of a natural grace.
A vagrant moth on soundless plume,
Lured by the quiet flame within,
Fanned darkling through the narrow room,
Out of the night's obscurity.
    She watched it vacantly.
'If we gave food to *all*, you see
We might as well a Workhouse be!
I've not much patience with beggary.
What use is it to whine and wail? —
Most things in this world are made for sale!

[335]

But one who really needs . . .' She sighed.
'I'd hate for him to be denied.'
She smoothed her lips, then smiled, to say:
'Have you yourself come far to-day?'
Like questing call, where shallows are
And sea-birds throng, rang out that *far* —
Decoy to every wanderer.

The stranger turned, and looked at her.
'Far, my child; and far must fare.
My only home is everywhere;
      And that the homeless share:
The vile, the lost, in misery —
      Where comfort cannot be.
You are young, your life's your own to spend;
May it escape as dark an end.'

Her fickle heart fell cold, her eyes
Stirred not a hair's breadth, serpent-wise.
'You say', she bridled, 'that to me!
Meaning you'd have their company
Rather than mine? Why, when a friend
Gives for the giving, there's an end
To that dull talk! *My child!* — can't you
See who you are talking to?
Do you suppose because I stop
Caged up in this dull village shop
With none but clods and numskulls near,
Whose only thought is pig and beer,
And sour old maids that pry and leer,
I am content? Me! Never pine
For what by every right is mine?
Had I a wild-sick bird to keep,
Is this where she should mope and cheep?
Aching, starving, for love and light,
Eating her heart out, dawn to night!
Oh, yes, they say that safety's sweet;
And groundsel — something good to eat!
But, Lord! I'd outsing the morning stars,
For a lump of sugar between the bars!
I loathe this life. "*My Child!*" *You* see!
Wait till she's dead — and I am free!'
Aghast, she stayed — her young cheeks blenched,
Mouth quivering, and fingers clenched —
'What right have you . . .?' she challenged, and then,

With a stifled sob, fell silent again.
'And now,' she shuddered, frowned, and said,
'It's closing time. And I'm for bed.'
She listened a moment, crossed the floor,
And, dumbing on tiptoe — thumb on latch —
The clapper-bell against its catch,
    Stealthily drew wide the door.

All deathly still, the autumnal night
Hung starry and radiant, height to height,
Moon-cold hills and neighbouring wood.
Black shadows barred the empty street,
Dew-bright its cobbles at her feet,
And the dead leaves that sprinkled it.
With earthy, sour-sweet smell endued
The keen air coldly touched her skin —
Alone there, at the entering in.
Soon would the early frosts begin,
And the long winter's lassitude,
Mewed up, pent in, companionless.
No light in her mind to soothe and bless;
Only unbridled bitterness
Drummed in her blood against her side.
Her eyelids drooped, and every sense
Languished in secret virulence.
She turned and looked. 'You thought,' she cried
Small and dull as a toneless bell,
'A silly, country wench like me,
Goose for the fox, befooled could be
By your fine speeches! "Hungry"? Well,
I've been in streets where misery is
Common as wayside blackberries —
Been, and come back; less young than wise.
Go to the parson, knock him up;
He'll dole you texts on which to sup.
Or if his tombstones strike too cold,
Try the old Squire at Biddingfold:
Ask there! He thinks the village pond's
The drink for rogues and vagabonds!'
The Hunter's Moon from a cloudless sky
In pallid splendour earthward yearned;
Dazzling in beauty, cheek and eye:
And her head's gold to silver turned.
Her fierce young face in that wild shine
Showed like a god's, morose, malign.

He rose: and face to face they stood
In sudden, timeless solitude.
The fevered frenzy in her blood
Ebbed, left enfeebled body and limb.
     Appalled, she gazed at him,
Marvelling in horror of stricken heart,
In this strange scrutiny, at what
She saw but comprehended not.
Out of Astarte's borrowed light
She couched her face, to hide from sight
The tears of anguish and bitter pride
That pricked her eyes. 'My God,' she cried,
Pausing in misery on the word,
As if another's voice she had heard,
'Give — if you can — the devil his due —
I'd rather sup with him than you!
So get you gone; no more I want
     Of you, and all your cant!' . . .
A hasty footstep neared; she stayed,
Outwardly bold, but sore afraid.
'Mother!' she mocked. 'Now we shall see
What comes of asking charity.'

Platter in hand, the frugal dame
Back to the counter bustling came.
Something, she saw, had gone amiss.
And one sharp look her daughter's way
Warned her of what she had best not say.
Fearing her tongue and temper, she
Spoke with a smiling asperity.
'Look, now,' she said, 'I've brought you this.
That slut of mine's an hour abed;
The oven chilled, the fire half dead,
The bellows vanished. . . . Well, you have seen
The mort of trouble it has been.
Still, there it is; and food at least.
My husband does not hold with waste;
That's been his maxim all life through.
What's more, it's in the Scriptures too.
By rights we are shut; it's growing late;
And as you can't bring back the plate,
Better eat here — if eat you must!
And now — ah, yes, you'll want a crust.
All this bread is for sale. I'll in
And see what leavings are in the bin.'

Their glances met. Hers winced, and fell;
But why it faltered she could not tell.

The slumbering cat awoke, arose —
Roused by the savour beneath his nose,
Arched his spine, with tail erect,
Stooped, gently sniffing, to inspect
The beggar's feast, gazed after her,
And, seeing her gone, began to purr.
Her daughter then, who had watched the while,
Drew near, and stroked him — with a smile
As sly with blandishment as guile.
Daintily, finger and thumb, she took
A morsel of meat from off the plate,
And with a sidling crafty look
Dangled it over him for a bait:
'No, no; say, please!' The obsequious cat
Reared to his haunches, with folded paws,
Round sea-green eyes, and hook-toothed jaws,
Mewed, snapped, and mouthed it down; and then
Up, like a mammet, sat, begging again.
'Fie, now; he's famished! Another bit?
Mousers by rights should hunt their meat!
That's what the Master says: isn't it?'
The creature fawned on her, and purred,
As if he had pondered every word.
Yet, mute the beggar stood, nor made
A sign he grudged this masquerade.
'I dote on cats,' the wanton said.
'Dogs grovel and cringe at every nod;
Making of man a kind of God!
Beat them or starve them, as you choose,
They crawl to you, whining, and lick your shoes.
Cats know their comfort, drowse and play,
And, when the dark comes, steal away —
Wild to the wild. Make *them* obey!
As soon make water run uphill.
I'm for the night; I crave the dark;
Would wail the louder to hear them bark;
Pleasure myself till the East turns grey.'
She eyed the low window; 'Welladay!
You the greyhound, and I the hare,
I warrant of coursing you'd have your share.'
Scrap after scrap she dangled, until
The dainty beast had gorged his fill,
And, lithe as a panther, sheened like silk,

Minced off to find a drink of milk.
'There! That's cat's thanks! His feasting done,
He's off — and half your supper gone! . . .
But, wise or foolish, you'll agree
You had done better to sup with me!'

The stranger gravely raised his head.
'Once was a harvest thick with corn
When I too heard the hunting-horn;
I, too, the baying, and the blood,
And the cries of death none understood.
He that in peace with God would live
Both hunter is and fugitive.
I came to this house to ask for bread,
We give but what we have,' he said;
'Are what grace makes of us, and win
The peace that is our hearts within.'
He ceased, and, yet more gravely, smiled.
'I would that ours were reconciled!'
So sharply intent were sense and ear
On his face and accents, she failed to hear
          The meaning his words conveyed.
'"*Peace!*"' she mocked him. 'How pretty a jibe!
So jows the death-bell's serenade.
          Try a less easy bribe!'

The entry darkly gaped. And through
The cold night air, a low *a-hoo*,
A-hoo, a-hoo, from out the wood,
Broke in upon their solitude;
A call, a bleak decoy, a cry,
Half weird lament, half ribaldry.
She listened, shivered; 'Pah!' whispered she,
'No peace of yours, my God, for me!
I have gone my ways, have eyes, and wits.
Am I a cat to feed on bits
Of dried-up Bible-meat? I know
What kind of bread has that for dough;
Yes, and how honey-sweet the leaven
That starves, on earth, to glut, in heaven!
Dupe was I? Well, come closer, look,
Is my face withered? Sight fall'n in?
Beak-sharp nose and gibbering chin?
Lips that no longer can sing, kiss, pout?
Body dry sinews, the fire gone out?
So it may be with me, Judgment Day;

[340]

And, men being men, of hope forsook,
Gold all dross — hair gone grey,
Love burnt to ashes.
        Yet, still, I'd say —
Come then, to taunt me, though you may —
I'd treat hypocrites Pilate's way!
False, all false! — Oh, I can see,
You are not what you pretend to be!'

Weeping, she ceased; as flowerlike a thing
As frost ever chilled in an earthly spring.
Mingling moonlight and lamplight played
On raiment and hair; and her beauty arrayed
In a peace profound, as when in glade
On the confines of Eden, unafraid,
Cain and his brother as children strayed.

'What am I saying! I hear it. But none —
None is — God help me! — my own.'

Her mother, listening, had heard
That last low passionate broken word.
What was its meaning? Shame or fear —
It knelled its misery on her ear
      Like voices in a dream.
And, as she brooded, deep in thought,
Trembling, though not with cold, she sought
In her one twinkling candle's beam
From stubborn memory to restore
Where she had seen this man before;
What, in his marred yet tranquil mien —
Dimmed by the veils of time between —
Had conjured the past so quickly back:
Hours when by hopes, proved false, beguiled,
She too had stubborn been and wild,
As vain; but not as lovely. Alas!
And, far from innocent, a child.
A glass hung near the chimney shelf —
She peered into its shadows, moved
By thoughts of one in youth beloved,
Long tongueless in the grave, whom yet
Rancour could shun, but not forget.
Was this blowsed woman here herself?
No answer made the image there —
      Bartered but stare for stare.

[341]

She turned aside. What use to brood
On follies gone beyond recall —
Nothing to do the living good,
Secrets now shared by none; and all
Because this chance-come outcast had
Asked for alms a crust of bread.
Clean contrary to common sense,
She'd given him shelter, fetched him food —
Old scraps, maybe, but fit, at worst,
For her goodman; and warmed them first!
And this for grace and gratitude!
Charity brings scant recompense
This side of Jordan — from such as he!

But then; what meant that frenzied speech,
Cry of one loved, lost — out of reach,
From girlhood up unheard before,
And past all probing to explore?
What was between them — each with each?
What in the past lay hid?
Long since the tongue of envy had
Whispered its worst about her child;
Arrogant, beautiful, and wild;
And beauty tarnished may strive in vain
To win its market back again . . .
To what cold furies is life betrayed
When the ashes of youth begin to cool,
When things of impulse are done by rule,
When, sickened of faiths, hopes, charities,
The soul pines only to be at ease;
And — moulting vulture in stony den —
Waits for the end, Amen!

Thus, in the twinkling of an eye,
This heart-sick reverie swept by;
She must dissemble — if need be — lie:
Rid house and soul of this new pest,
Prudence would do the rest.
Muffling her purpose, aggrieved in mind,
In she went, and, knee on stool,
Deigning no glance at either, leant
Over the tarnished rail of brass
That curtained off the window-glass,
And, with a tug, drew down the blind.
'Lord's Day, to-morrow,' she shrugged. 'No shop!
Come, child, make haste; it's time to sup;
High time to put the shutters up.'

The shutters up: The shutters up —
Ticked the clock the silence through,
And a yet emptier silence spread.
Shunning the effort, she raised her head;
'And *you'll* be needing to go,' she said.
She seized a loaf, broke off a crust,
Turned, and, 'There's no stale left . . .' began
Coldly, and paused — her haunted eyes
Fixed on the grease-stains, where the cat,
Mumbling its gobbets, had feasting sat.
All doubting gone, pierced to the quick
At hint of this malignant trick,
Like spark in tinder, fire in rick,
A sudden rage consumed her soul,
Beyond all caution to control.
Ignored, disdained, deceived, defied! —
'Have you, my God!' she shrilled, 'no pride?
    No shame?
Stranger, you say — and now, a friend!
Cheating and lies, from bad to worse —
Fouling your father's honest name —
Make *me*, you jade, your stalking-horse!
I've watched you, mooning, moping — ay,
    And now, in my teeth, know why!'

A dreadful quiet spread, as when
Over Atlantic wastes of sea,
Black, tempest-swept, there falls a lull,
As sudden as it is momentary,
In the maniac tumult of wind and rain,
Boundless, measureless, monstrous: and then
The insensate din begins again.

    The damsel stirred.
Jade — she had caught the bitter word;
Shame, cheating, lies. Crouched down, she stood,
Lost in a lightless solitude.
No matter; the words were said; all done.
And yet, how strange this woman should,
Self-blinded, have no heart to see
The secret of her misery;
Should think that she — all refuge gone,
And racked with hatred and shame, could be
The *friend* of this accursèd one!
The anguished blood had left her cheek
White as a leper's. With shaking head,

And eyes insanely wide and bleak,
Her body motionless as the dead,
At bay against a nameless fear,
She strove awhile in vain to speak.
Then, 'Thank you for *that*!' she whispered. 'Who
Betrayed me into a world like this,
Swarming with evil and deviltries?
Gave me these eyes, this mouth, these feet,
Flesh to hunger — and tainted meat?
Pampered me — flattered — yet taunted me when
Body and soul became prey to men,
And dog to its vomit returned again?
Ask me my name! *You?* Magdalen!
Devils? So be it. What brought me here? —
A stork in the chimney-stack, mother dear?
Oh, this false life! An instant gone
A voice within me said, *See! Have done,*
Take to you wings, and, ravening, flee,
Far from this foul hypocrisy!'
Like an old beldame's her fingers shook,
Mouth puckered, and the inning moon
Gleamed, as she cowered, on brow and eye,
Fixed now in torment on one near by.
'*Friend!* did you say? You heard that? You! —
Forsaken of God, a wandering Jew!
With milk for blood! Speak! Is it true?'

Beyond the threshold a stealthy breeze,
Faint with night's frost-cold fragrancies,
    Stirred in the trees.
Ghostlike, on moon-patterned floor there came
A scamper of leaves. The lamp's dim flame
Reared smoking in the sudden draught.
He gazed, but answered not the Jew.
Woe, beyond mortal eye to trace,
Watched through compassion in his face.
And though — as if the spirit within
Were striving through fleshly bonds to win
Out to its chosen — fiery pangs
Burned in her breast like serpent's fangs,
She lifted her stricken face, and laughed:
Hollowly, ribaldly, *Heugh, heugh, heugh!*
    'A Jew! A Jew!'—
Ran, clawed, clutched up the bread and meat,
    And flung them at his feet.
And then was gone; had taken her flight

Out through the doorway, into the street,
Into the quiet of the night,
On through the moon-chequered shadowy air;
    Away, to where
In woodland of agelong oak and yew,
Echoing its vaulted dingles through,
Faint voices answered her — *Hoo! A-hoo!*
A-hoo! A-hoo!
A-hoo!

THE STRANGE SPIRIT[1]

Age shall not daunt me, nor sorrow for youth that is gone,
If thou lead on before me;
If thy voice in the darkness and bleak of that final night
Still its enchantment weave o'er me.
Thou hauntest the stealing shadow of rock and tree;
Hovering on wings invisible smilest at me;
Fannest the secret scent of the moth-hung flower;
Making of musky eve thy slumber-bower.

But not without danger thy fleeting presence abides
In a mind lulled in dreaming.
Lightning bepictures thy gaze. When the thunder raves,
And the tempest rain is streaming,
Betwixt cloud and earth thy falcon-head leans near —
Menacing earth-bound spirit betrayed to fear.
Cold then as shadow of death, that icy glare
Pierces the window of sense to the chamber bare.

Busied o'er dust, engrossed o'er the clod-close root,
Fire of the beast in conflict bleeding,
Goal of the coursing fish on its ocean tryst,
Wind of the weed's far seeding,
Whose servant art thou? Who gave thee earth, sky and sea
For uttermost kingdom and ranging? Who bade thee to be
Bodiless, lovely; snare, and delight of the soul,
Fantasy's beacon, of thought the uttermost goal?

When I told my love thou wert near, she bowed, and sighed.
With passion her pale face darkened.
Trembling the lips that to mine in silence replied;
Sadly that music she hearkened.

[1] First published in *The Captive and Other Poems*, New York, 1928.

Miracle thine the babe in her bosom at rest,
Flowerlike, hidden loose-folded on gentle breast —
And we laughed together in quiet, unmoved by fear,
Knowing that, life of life, thou wast hovering near.

TO K.M.[1]

And there was a horse in the king's stables: and the name of the horse was, Genius

We sat and talked . . . It was June, and the summer light
Lay fair upon ceiling and wall as the day took flight.
Tranquil the room — with its colours and shadows wan,
Cherries, and china, and flowers: and the hour slid on.
Dark hair, dark eyes, slim fingers — you made the tea,
Pausing with spoon uplifted, to speak to me.
Lulled by our thoughts and our voices, how happy were we!

And, musing, an old, old riddle crept into my head.
'Supposing I just say, *Horse in a field,*' I said,
'What do you *see*?' And we each made answer: 'I —
A roan — long tail, and a red-brick house, near by.'
'I — an old cart-horse and rain!' 'Oh no, not rain;
A mare with a long-legged foal by a pond — oh plain!'
'And I, a hedge — and an elm — and the shadowy green
Sloping gently up to the blue, to the west, I mean!' . . .

And now: on the field that I see night's darkness lies.
A brook brawls near: there are stars in the empty skies.
The grass is deep, and dense. As I push my way,
From sour-nettled ditch sweeps fragrance of clustering may.
I come to a stile. And lo, on the further side,
With still, umbrageous, night-clad fronds, spread wide,
A giant cedar broods. And in crescent's gleam —
A horse, milk-pale, sleek-shouldered, engendered of dream!
Startled, it lifts its muzzle, deep eyes agaze,
Silk-plaited mane . . .
            'Whose pastures are thine to graze?
Creature, delicate, lovely, with woman-like head,
Sphinx-like, gazelle-like? Where tarries thy rider?' I said.
And I scanned by that sinking ship's thin twinkling shed
A high-pooped saddle of leather, night-darkened red,
Stamped with a pattern of gilding; and over it thrown
A cloak, chain-buckled, with one great glamorous stone,

[1] First published in *The Captive and Other Poems*, New York, 1928, but
without the quotation at the head of the poem. 'K.M.' was Katherine Mansfield.

Wan as the argent moon when o'er fields of wheat
Like Dian she broods, and steals to Endymion's feet.
Interwoven with silver that cloak from seam to seam.
And at toss of that head from its damascened bridle did beam
Mysterious glare in the dead of the dark. . . .
     'Thy name,
Fantastical steed? Thy pedigree?
Peace, out of Storm, is the tale? Or *Beauty, of Jeopardy?*'
The water grieves. Not a footfall — and midnight here.
Why tarries Darkness's bird? Mounded and clear
Slopes to yon hill with its stars the moorland sweet.
There sigh the airs of far heaven. And the dreamer's feet
Scatter the leagues of paths secret to where at last meet
Roads called Wickedness, Righteousness, broad-flung or strait,
And the third that leads on to the Queen of fair Elfland's gate. . . .

This then the horse that I see; swift as the wind;
That none may master or mount; and none may bind —
But she, his Mistress: cloaked, and at throat that gem —
Dark hair, dark eyes, slim shoulder. . . .
    God-speed, K.M.!

DREAMS

Ev'n one who has little travelled in
This world of ample land and sea;
Whose Arctic, Orient, tropics have been —
Like Phœnix, siren, jinn, and *Sidhe* —
But of his thoughts' anatomy —
Each day makes measureless journeys twain:
From wake to dream; to wake again.

At night he climbs a quiet stair,
Secure within its pictured wall;
His clothes, his hands, the light, the air,
Familiar objects one and all —
Accustomed, plain, and natural.
He lays him down: and, ages deep,
Flow over him the floods of sleep.

[347]

Lapped in this influence alien
To aught save sorcery could devise,
Heedless of *Sesame* or *Amen*,
He is at once the denizen
Of realms till then beyond surmise;
Grotesque, irrational, and sans
All law and order known as Man's.

Though drowsy sentries at the gate
Of eye and ear dim watch maintain,
And, at his absence all elate,
His body's artisans sustain
Their toil in sinew, nerve, and brain:
Nothing recks he; he roves afar,
Past compass, chart, and calendar.

Nor is he the poor serf who shares
One self alone where'er he range,
Since in the seven-league Boots he wears
He may, in scores of guises, change
His daily ego — simple or strange;
Stand passive looker-on; or be
A paragon of energy.

Regions of beauty, wonder, peace
By waking eyes unscanned, unknown.
Waters and hills whose loveliness,
Past mortal sense, are his alone.
There flow'rs by the shallows of Lethe sown
Distil their nectar, drowsy and sweet,
And drench the air with news of it.

Or lost, betrayed, forlorn, alas!
Gaunt terror leads him by the hand
Through demon-infested rank morass;
O'er wind-bleached wilderness of sand;
Where cataracts rave; or bleak sea-strand
Shouts at the night with spouted spume;
Or locks him to rot in a soundless tomb.

Here, too, the House of Folly is,
With gates ajar, and windows lit,
Wherein with foul buffooneries
A spectral host carousing sit.
'Hail, thou!' they yelp. 'Come, taste and eat!'
And so, poor zany, sup must he
The nightmare dregs of idiocy.

[348]

All this in vain? Nay, thus abased,
Made vile in the dark's incontinence,
Though even the anguish of death he taste,
The murderer's woe — his penitence,
And pangs of the damned experience —
Will he God's mercy less esteem
When dayspring prove them only a dream?

What bliss to clutch, when thus beset,
The folded linen of his sheet;
Or hear, without, more welcome yet,
A footfall in the dawnlit street;
The whist of the wind; or, far and sweet,
Some small bird's daybreak rhapsody,
That bids him put all figments by.

Oh, when, at morning up, his eyes
Open to earth again, then, lo!
An end to all dream's enterprise! —
It melts away like April snow.
What night made false now true doth show;
What day discloses night disdained;
And who shall winnow real from feigned?

But men of learning little heed
Problems that simple folk perplex;
And some there are who have decreed
Dreams the insidious wiles of sex;
That slumber's plain is wake's complèx;
And, plumbing their own minds, profess
Them quagmires of unconsciousness.

Sad fate it is, like one who is dead,
To lie inert the long night through,
And never by dream's sweet fantasy led
To lave tired eyes in heavenly dew!
But worse — the prey of a gross taboo
And sport of a Censor — to squat and make
Pies of a mud forbidd'n the awake!

Nay, is that Prince of the Dust — a man,
But a tissue of parts, dissectable?
Lancet, balances, callipers — can
The least of his actions by human skill
Be measured as so much Sex, Want, Will? —
Fables so dull would the sweeter be
With extract of humour for company!

Once was a god whose lovely face,
Wan as the poppy and arched in wings,
So haunted a votary with his grace
And the still wonder that worship brings,
That, having sipped of Helicon's springs,
He cast his beauty in bronze. And now
Eternal slumber bedims his brow —

Hypnos: and Dream was his dear son.
Not ours these follies. We haunt instead
Tropical jungles drear and dun,
And see in some fetish of fear and dread
Our symbol of dream — that brooding head!
And deem the wellspring of genius hid
In a dark morass that is dubbed the Id.

Sacred of old was the dyed baboon,
Though least, of the monkeys, like man is he.
Yet, rank the bones of his skeleton
With *homo sapiens*': will they be
Void of design, form, symmetry?
To each his calling. Albeit we know
Apes father no Michelangelo!

In truth, a destiny undivined
Haunts every cell of bone and brain;
They share, to time and space resigned,
All passions that to earth pertain,
And twist man's thoughts to boon or bane;
Yet, be he master, need we ban
What the amoeba's made of man?

Who of his thoughts can reach the source?
Who in his life-blood's secret share?
By knowledge, artifice, or force
Compel the self within declare
What fiat bade it earthward fare?
Or proof expound this journey is
Else than a tissue of fantasies?

See, now, this butterfly, its wing
A dazzling play of patterned hues;
Far from the radiance of Spring,
From every faltering flower it choose
'Twill dip to sip autumnal dews:
So flit man's happiest moments by,
Daydreams of selfless transiency.

[350]

Was it by cunning the curious fly
That preys in a sunbeam schooled her wings
To ride her in air all motionlessly,
Poised on their myriad winnowings?
Where conned the blackbird the song he sings?
Was Job the instructor of the ant?
Go bees for nectar to Hume and Kant?

Who bade the scallop devise her shell?
Who tutored the daisy at cool of eve
To tent her pollen in floreted cell?
What dominie taught the dove to grieve;
The mole to delve; the worm to weave?
Does not the rather their life-craft seem
A tranced obedience to a dream?

Thus tranced, too, body and mind, will sit
A winter's dawn to dark, alone,
Heedless of how the cold moments flit,
The worker in words, or wood, or stone:
So far his waking desires have flown
Into a realm where his sole delight
Is to bring the dreamed-of to mortal sight.

Dumb in its wax may the music sleep —
In a breath conceived — that, with ardent care,
Note by note, in a reverie deep,
Mozart penned, for the world to share.
Waken it, needle! And then declare
How, invoked by thy tiny tang,
Sound such strains as the Sirens sang!

Voyager dauntless on Newton's sea,
Year after year still brooding on
His algebraical formulae,
The genius of William Hamilton
Sought the square root of *minus* one;
In vain; till — all thought of it leagues away —
The problem flowered from a dream one day.

Our restless senses leap and say,
'How marvellous this! — How ugly **that!'**
And, at a breath, will slip away
The very thing they marvel at.
Time is the tyrant of their fate;
And frail the instant which must be
Our all of actuality.

[351]

If then to Solomon the Wise
Some curious priest stooped low and said,
'Thou, with thy lidded, sleep-sealed eyes,
This riddle solve from out thy bed:
Art thou — am I — by phantoms led?
Where is the real? In dream? Or wake?'
I know the answer the King might make!

And teeming Shakespeare: would he avow
The creatures of his heart and brain,
Whom, Prospero-like, he could endow
With all that mortal souls contain,
Mere copies that a fool can feign
Out of the tangible and seen? —
This the sole range of his demesne?

Ask not the Dreamer! See him run,
Listening a shrill and gentle neigh,
Foot into stirrup, he is up, he has won
Enchanted foothills far away.
Somewhere? Nowhere? Who need say?
So be it in secrecy of his mind
He some rare delectation find.

Ay, once I dreamed of an age-wide sea
Whereo'er three moons stood leper-bright;
And once — from agony set free —
I scanned within the womb of night,
A hollow inwoven orb of light,
Thrilling with beauty no tongue could tell,
And knew it for Life's citadel.

And — parable as strange — once, I
Was lured to a city whose every stone,
And harpy human hastening by
Were spawn and sport of fear alone —
By soulless horror enthralled, driven on:
Even the waters that, ebon-clear,
Coursed through its dark, raved only of *Fear*!

Enigmas these; but not the face,
Fashioned of sleep, which, still at gaze
Of daybreak eyes, I yet could trace,
Made lovelier in the sun's first rays;
Nor that wild voice which in amaze,
Wide-wok'n, I listened singing on —
All memory of the singer gone.

[352]

O Poesy, of wellspring clear,
Let no sad Science thee suborn,
Who art thyself its planisphere!
All knowledge is foredoomed, forlorn —
Of inmost truth and wisdom shorn —
Unless imagination brings
Its skies wherein to use its wings.

Two worlds have we: without; within;
But all that sense can mete and span,
Until it confirmation win
From heart and soul, is death to man.
Of grace divine his life began;
And — Eden empty proved — in deep
Communion with his spirit in sleep

The Lord Jehovah of a dream
Bade him, past all desire, conceive
What should his solitude redeem;
And, to his sunlit eyes, brought Eve.
Would that my day-wide mind could weave
Faint concept of the scene from whence
She awoke to Eden's innocence!

Starven with cares, like tares in wheat,
Wildered with knowledge, chilled with doubt,
The timeless self in vain must beat
Against its walls to hasten out
Whither the living waters fount;
And — evil and good no more at strife —
Seek love beneath the tree of life.

When then in memory I look back
To childhood's visioned hours I see
What now my anxious soul doth lack
Is energy in peace to be
At one with nature's mystery:
And Conscience less my mind indicts
For idle days than dreamless nights.

Poems 1919-1934 (1935)

ST. ANDREWS[1]

September 1925

Fickle of choice is Memory:
But hidden in her secret deeps
She guards whatever in life may be
Vivid and sweet perpetually;
And of the loved strict treasury keeps.

There childhood's flowers bloom for aye;
There, in a quiet grave, profound,
Those whom dark death hath lured away
Live on, with peace unchanging crowned,
Immune from time's decay.

Keeps she for me, then, safe-enshrined —
Cold of the North — those bleached grey streets;
Grey skies, a glinting sun, a wind
From climes where sea with ocean meets,
And ruinous walls by tempests pined.

There, history and romance abide:[2]
Martyr and saint, Pict, Scot, Culdees.
They dared, fought, suffered, dreamed and died,
Yet of their long wild centuries
Left but these stones their bones beside.

Ghosts in that sunlight come and go:
Columba, David, Margaret,
Bothwell the fierce, dark Rizzio,
And she, caught fast in fate's fell net,
Mary, the twice-queened, fair as snow . . .

The winter daylight wanes. The tide
Lays a cold wreath of foam upon
Its sea-worn rocks. The billows ride
In endless cavalcade — are gone.
The rose of eve burns far and wide.

[1] First published in *St. Andrews*, 1926, two poems specially contributed by
Rudyard Kipling and Walter de la Mare. Called 'A Memory' there and 'A
Memory (from *St. Andrews)*' in *Poems 1919–1934*, 1935; and it had the title above
in *O Lovely England and Other Poems*, 1953.
[2] 'There history in romance doth hide:' (1926)

WINTER

Mute now the music that made me
    Its earthly echo be.
Flown now the tender hovering wing
    To its own further Spring.
And fallen to the dust they were —
    Flowers of a rarer air.

O winter of my heart, keep yet
    Thy cold snows over it;
Those flowers fast-sealed; that music asleep
    In darkened silence keep;
Baffle me not with beams that stir
    Too anxious a wanderer
Only to lift distracted sight
    On empty fields forlorn with night.

ROMANCE

Well, then, you ask me what is *real*,
    And I — poor thief — I say,
See, what wild gold the tide-drifts steal
    To pour into this bay!

Those emeralds, opals, pearls to land
    Washed in by wave on wave;
That heat-struck swoon of shimmering sand,
    That music-echoing cave!

Salt? Bubbles? Cheating mist and light?
    Quartz ground by surge to dust?
Call *me* mere brittle bones — and sight —
    Illusion if you must;

Yet still some seraph in my mind
    His praises cries, has flown
Into a region unconfined
    Man, baffled, calls the unknown.

Desire leaps up, and poised on high
    Love's gaze — from eyes askance —
Scans in delight of sea and sky
    The vineyards of Romance.

AFRAID[1]

Here lies, but seven years old, our little maid,
Once of the darkness Oh, so sore afraid!
Light of the World — remember that small fear,
And when nor moon nor stars do shine, draw near!

A STAVE

O my dear one,
Do not repine
Their rose hath left
Those cheeks of thine.
In memory hid
Blooms yet, how clear,
Past fading now,
Its beauty, dear.
Yet — fallen a little
In time, soon gone,
Is the heart that yearned
Their fragrance on;
And much is quenched
Of that wild fire
That did from dust
To thee aspire.

It is our fate.
Like tapers, we
Life's pure wax waste
Unheedingly.
Till Love, grown weary
Of its light,
Frowns, puffs his cheek,
And sighs, good night.

QUACK

What said the drake to his lady-love
    But *Quack*, then *Quack*, then QUACK!
And she, with long love-notes as sweet as his,
    Said *Quack* — then, softlier, QUACK
And Echo that lurked by the old red barn,
    Beyond their staddled stack,
Listening this love-lorn pair's delight,
    Quacked their quacked *Quack*, *Quack*, *Quacks* back.

[1] Called 'An Epitaph' in *Poems 1919–1934*, 1935; it had the title above in *Inward Companion*, 1950.

[357]

OH, YES, MY DEAR

Oh, yes, my dear, you have a mother,
And she, when young, was loved by another,
And in that mother's nursery
Played *her* mamma, like you and me.
When that mamma was tiny as you
She had a happy mother too:
On, on . . . Yes, presto! Puff! Pee-fee! —
And Grandam Eve and the apple-tree.
O, into distance, smalling, dimming,
Think of that endless row of women,
Like beads, like posts, like lamps, they seem —
Grey-green willows, and life a stream —
Laughing and sighing and lovely; and, oh,
You to be next in that long row!

SEEN AND HEARD[1]

Lovely things these eyes have seen —
Dangling cherries in leaves dark-green;
Ducks as white as winter snow,
Which quacked as they webbed on a-row;
The wren that, with her needle note,
Through blackthorn's foam will flit and float;
Clear dews whereon the moonbeams softly gloat
    And sun will sheen.

Lovely music my ears have heard —
Catkined twigs in April stirred
By the same air that carries true
Two notes from Africa, *Cuck-oo*;
And then, when night has darkened again,
The lone wail of the willow-wren,
And cricket rasping on, 'Goode'n — goode'n',
    Shriller than mouse or bird.

Ay, and all praise would I, please God, dispose
For but one faint-hued cowslip, one wild rose.

---

[1] As printed in *Inward Companion*, 1950, except for line 7, which was omitted in error.

Memory and Other Poems (1938)

A SUNDAY

A child in the Sabbath peace, there —
Down by the full-bosomed river;
Sun on the tide-way, flutter of wind,
Water-cluck, — *Ever ... for ever ...*

Time itself seemed to cease there —
The domed, hushed city behind me;
Home how distant! The morrow would come —
But here, no trouble could find me.

A respite, a solacing, deep as the sea,
Was mine. Will it come again? ... Never? ...
Shut in the past is that Sabbath peace, there —
Down by the full-bosomed river.

A POT OF MUSK

A glance — and instantly the small meek flower
Whispered of what it had to childhood meant;
But kept the angel secret of that far hour
    Ere it had lost its scent.

BROTHER AND SISTER

A turn of head, that searching light,
And — was it fancy? — a faint sigh:
I know not what; there leapt the thought,
We are old, now — she and I.

Old, though those eager clear blue eyes,
And lines of laughter along the cheek,
Far less of time than time's despite
    To one who loves her speak. ...

[359]

Besides, those pale and smiling lips,
That once with beauty were content,
Now wisdom too have learned; and that
    No clock can circumvent. . . .

Nor is this world of ours a toy
That woe should darken when bed-time nears;
Still memory-sweet its old decoy,
    And — well, what use in tears?

So limped the brittle argument;
Yet — had I Prospero's wizardry,
She should at once have back her youth,
    Whatever chanced to me.

POLLIE

Pollie is a simpleton;
'Look!' she cries, 'that *lovely* swan!'
And, even before her transports cease,
    Adds, 'But I do love geese.'

When a lark wings up the sky,
She'll sit with lips ajar, then sigh —
For rapture; and the rapture o'er,
    Whisper, 'What's music *for*?'

Every lesson I allot,
As soon as learned is clean forgot.
'L-O-V . . .?' I prompt. And she
    Smiles, but I catch no 'E'.

It seems in her round head you come
As if to a secret vacuum;
Whence then the wonder, love and grace
    Shining in that small face?

THE IRREVOCABLE

Weep no more, thou weary one;
Tears — and so beloved a face!
Raindrops on a daybreak flower —
Token of cold midnight's grace —
No more radiant are than these.
Both of transient darkness tell;
And but one last beam of morning
    Either will dispel.

I thy midnight was. . . . Yet word,
Easy, innocent of guile,
Weeping eyes and childlike lips
    Have conjured to a smile.
All forgotten, all forgiven.
Why remorse, then? . . . Well I know
The few clear stars still mine in heaven
Never shall now as brightly show.

ABSALOM

Vain, proud, rebellious Prince, thy treacherous hair,
Though thirty centuries have come and gone,
Still in that bitter oak doth thee ensnare;
Rings on that broken-hearted, *Son, my son!* . . .

And though, with childhood's tragic gaze, I see
Thee — idol of Israel — helpless in the tree,
Thy dying eyes turned darkened from the Sun;
Yet, of all faces in far memory's shrine —
Paris, Adonis, pale Endymion —
    The loveliest still is thine.

IN A LIBRARY[1]

Would — would that there were
A book on that shelf
To teach an old man
To teach himself! —

The joy of some scribe,
Brush in service to quill,
Who, with bird, flower, landscape,
Emblem and vision,
Loved his margins to fill.

Then might I sit,
By true learning beguiled,
Far into the night
Even with self reconciled,
Retrieving the wisdom
I lost, when a child.

[1] First published in *Two Poems*, privately printed in an edition of 200 copies
for Arthur Rogers, Newcastle-upon-Tyne, 1938.

IN DISGRACE

The fear-dulled eyes in the pallid face
Stared at the darkening window-pane;
Sullen, derided, in disgrace —
They watched night narrowing in again:
Far-away shoutings; a furtive wind
Which a keyhole had found; a star aloof;
A heart at war with a blunted mind;
    And a spout dripping rain from the roof: —

Drip — drip . . . till the light is gone;
But a heart not so hard as a stone.

'UNHEARD MELODIES'

A minstrel came singing in the way;
            And the children,
            Nothing saying,
            Gathered round him,
            From their playing,
In a bower of the shadowy may.

He stood in a loop of the green;
            And his fingers
            On the wires
            Feigned their heart's deep,
            Hidden desires
For a country that never was seen.

Like moonbeams in forests of trees,
            Like brook water
            Dropping sweetness,
            Like the wild hare
            In her fleetness,
Like the wings of the honey-sucking bees;

He drew each pure heart with his skill;
            With his beauty,
            And his azure,
            And his topaz,
            Gold for pleasure,
And his locks wet with dew of April.

Time sped; and night's shadows grew deep,
    Came owl-hoot
    From the thicket,
    And the shrill note
    Of the cricket
Called the children to silence and sleep. . . .

Strange, strange! though the minstrel is gone,
    Yet that hawthorn
    Fair and lonely
    Stoops mutely
    Waiting only
Till the clamour of noonday is done —

Until, in the faint skies of eve,
    Far and sweetly,
    Like a river,
    Silver wires seem
    Throbbing ever
As if echo in sorrow would grieve

In ears dulled with wrath and rebuke;
    And like snowdrops
    After winter,
    Tired feet pause there,
    And then enter
That bower by the midsummer brook.

O minstrel, keep thy tryst, sound thine airs
    In a heart that
    Oft forgets thee,
    Scorns, reviles thee,
    Tires, and frets thee
With the burden of silence it bears.

A CHILD ASLEEP

Angel of Words, in vain I have striven with thee,
Nor plead a lifetime's love and loyalty;
Only, with envy, bid thee watch this face,
    That says so much, so flawlessly,
      And in how small a space!

RESERVED

...'I was thinking, Mother, of that poor old horse
    They killed the other day;
Nannie *says* it was only a bag of bones,
    But I hated it taken away.'
'Of course, sweet; but now the baker's man
Will soon have a nice new motor van.'

'Yes, Mother. But when on our walk a squirrel
    Crept up to my thumb to be fed,
She shoo'd it away with her gloves — like this!
    They ought to be shot, she said.'
'She may have been reading, darling, that
Squirrels are only a kind of *rat*.'

'Goldfinches, Mother, owls and mice,
    Tom-tits and bunnies and jays —
Everything in my picture-books
    Will soon be gone, she says.'
'You see, my precious, so many creatures,
    Though exquisitely made,
Steal, or are dirty and dangerous,
    Or else they are bad for Trade.'

'I wonder, Mother, if when poor Noah
    Was alone in the rain and dark,
He can ever have thought what wicked things
    Were round him in the Ark. . . .
And are all children — like the rest —
Like me, as Nannie says, a pest?

'I woke last night from a dreadful dream
    Of a place — it was all of stone;
And dark. And the walls went up, and up —
    And oh, I was lost: alone!
I was *terrified*, Mother, and tried to call;
    But a gabble, like echoes, came back.
It will soon, I suppose, be bedtime again?
    And I hate lying there awake.'

'You mustn't, angel.' She glanced at the window —
  Smiled at the questioning mite.
'There's nothing to fear.' A wild bird scritched.
  The sun's last beam of light
Gilded the Globe, reserved for Man,
  Preparing for the Night.

DRY AUGUST BURNED

Dry August burned. A harvest hare
Limp on the kitchen table lay,
Its fur blood-blubbered, eyes astare,
While a small child that stood near by
Wept out her heart to see it there.

Sharp came the *clop* of hoofs, the clang
Of dangling chain, voices that rang.
Out like a leveret she ran,
To feast her glistening bird-clear eyes
On a team of field artillery,
Gay, to manœuvres, thudding by.
Spur and gun and limber plate
Flashed in the sun. Alert, elate,
Noble horses, foam at lip,
Harness, stirrup, holster, whip,
She watched the sun-tanned soldiery,
Till dust-white hedge had hidden away —
Its din into a rumour thinned —
The laughing, jolting, wild array:
And then — the wonder and tumult gone —
Stood nibbling a green leaf, alone,
Her dark eyes, dreaming. . . . She turned, and ran,
Elf-like, into the house again.
The hare had vanished. . . . 'Mother,' she said,
Her tear-stained cheek now flushed with red,
'Please, may I go and see it skinned?'

'OF A SON'

A garish room — oil-lamped; a stove's warm blaze;
Gilt chairs drawn up to candles, and green baize:
The doctor hastened in — a moment stayed,
Watching the cards upon the table played —
Club, and sharp diamond, and heart, and spade.
And — still elated — he exclaimed, '*Parbleu*,
A thousand pardons, friends, for keeping you;
I feared I'd never see the lady through.
A boy, too! *Magnifique* the fight she made!
Ah, well, she's happy now!' Said one, '"She"? — who?'
   'A woman called Landru.'

Gentle as flutter of dove's wing, the cards
Face downwards fell again; and fever-quick,
Topped by old Time and scythe, a small brass clock
In the brief hush of tongues resumed its tick.

SHADOW

*B*eware! — breathes the faint evening wind?
Omen! — sighs dayspring's innocent air?
Stalks out from shadow, when drawn's the blind,
A warning Nothing, to shake the mind
   And touch the soul with care?
   At midnight on thy stair?

Lurks there in every rose's sweet
A murderous whisper, *Fade must I?*
Mutters the vagrant in the street,
Edging his way with anxious feet —
   Thou too art hastening by.
   Drones on the carrion fly?

Oh, climb thou down from fool's disdain;
Stoop thy cold lips to rag and sore;
Kiss the gaunt cheek while yet remains
Life's blood in it. Ay, hearken; again! —
   Thou art the thief, the murderer,
   The outcast at thy door.

ONE IN THE PUBLIC GALLERY

The Seraph scanned the murderer in the dock —
The motionless Judge, beneath the court-room clock,
The listening jury, warders, counsel, Clerk;
Ay, one and all who shared that deepening dark:
    And then, as I shunned to see,
He turned his burning eyes and looked at me.

THE BRIDGE

With noble and strange devices Man hath spanned
River and torrent, raging in flood beneath;
But one more subtle than he ever planned
    Will exhaust my last faint breath:
A bridge, now nearing, I shall walk alone —
One pier on earth, the other in the unknown:
    And there, a viewless wraith —
Prince of the wreckage of the centuries,
Yet still past thought's fixed scrutiny, heart's surmise,
    And nought but a name, yet: Death.

SOLITUDE

Ghosts there must be with me in this old house,
Deepening its midnight as the clock beats on.
Whence else upwelled — strange, sweet, yet ominous —
That moment of happiness, and then was gone?

Nimbler than air-borne music, heart may call
A speechless message to the inward ear,
As secret even as that which then befell,
Yet nought that listening could make more clear.

Delicate, subtle senses, instant, fleet! —
But oh, how near the verge at which they fail!
In vain, self hearkens for the fall of feet
Soft as its own may be, beyond the pale.

THE 'SATIRE'

The dying man on his pillow
   Turned slowly his head.
'Five years on my Satire on Man
   I spent,' he said.
'But, lying alone, I have mused
   On myself, of late!'

Smiling, he nodded; and glanced
   At the ash in the grate.

INCANTATION

Vervain . . . basil . . . orison —
Whisper their syllablings till all meaning is gone,
And sound all vestige loses of mere word. . . .
'Tis then as if, in some far childhood heard,
A wild heart languished at the call of a bird,
Crying through ruinous windows, high and fair,
A secret incantation on the air:
   A language lost; which, when its accents cease,
   Breathes, voiceless, of a pre-Edenic peace.

A ROSE IN CANDLELIGHT

The oil in wild Aladdin's lamp
   A witching radiance shed;
But when its Genie absent was
   It languished, dull and dead.

Lo, now, the light that bathes this rose,
   That wondrous red its cheek to give!
It breathes, 'We, too, a secret share;
   Fleeting we are, however fair;
   And only representative.'

DEFEAT

The way on high burned white beneath the sun,
Crag and gaunt pine stood stark in windless heat,
With sun-parched weeds its stones were over-run,
And he who had dared it, his long journey done,
Lay sunken in the slumber of defeat.

A raven low in the air, with stagnant eyes,
Poised in the instant of alighting gust,
Rent the thin silence with his hungry cries,
Voicing his greed o'er this far-scented prize,
Stiff in the invisible movement of the dust.

He lay, sharp-boned beneath his skin, half-nude,
His black hair tangled with a blackening red,
His gaze wide-staring in his solitude,
O'er which a bristling cloud of flies did brood,
In mumbling business with his heedless head.

Unfathomable drifts of space below,
Stretched, like grey glass, an infinite low sea,
Whereon a conflict of bright beams did flow,
In fiery splendour trembling to and fro —
The noon sun's angel-loosened archery.

And still on high, the way, a lean line, wound,
Wherefrom the raven had swooped down to eat,
To mortal eyes without an end, or bound,
Nor any creeping shadow to be found
To cool the sunken temples of defeat.

Defeat was scrawled upon each naked bone,
Defeat in the glazed vacancy of his eye,
Defeat his hand clutched in that waste of stone,
Defeat the bird yelped, and the flies' mazed drone
Lifted thanksgiving for defeat come by.

Lost in eternal rumination stare
Those darkened sockets of a dreamless head,
That cheek and jaw with the unpeopled air,
With smile immutable, unwearying, share
The subtle cogitations of the dead.

Yet, dwindling mark upon fate's viewless height,
For sign and token above the infinite sea,
'Neath the cold challenge of the all-circling night
Shall lie for witness in the Invisible's sight
The mockless victory that defeat may be.

AT EASE

Most wounds can Time repair;
But some are mortal — these:
For a broken heart there is no balm,
No cure for a heart at ease —

At ease, but cold as stone,
Though the intellect spin on,
And the feat and practised face may show
Nought of the life that is gone;

But smiles, as by habit taught;
And sighs, as by custom led;
And the soul within is safe from damnation,
Since it is dead.

AN ABANDONED CHURCH

Roofless and eyeless, weed-sodden, dank, old, cold —
Fickly the sunset glimmered through the rain,
Gilded the gravestones — faded out again;
A storm-cock shrilled its aeon-old refrain,
Lambs bleated from their fold.

A ROSE IN WATER

A rose, in water, to its stem
Decoys a myriad beads of air;
And, lovely with the light on them,
Gives even its thorns their share.

NOT ONLY

Not only ruins their lichen have;
Nor tombs alone, their moss.
Implacable Time, in markless grave,
Turns what seemed gold to dross.

Yet — a mere ribbon for the hair,
A broken toy, a faded flower
A passionate deathless grace may wear,
Denied its passing hour.

EVENING

The little cirque, horizon-wide,
Of earth now swiftly draws away,
Though fulling moon aloft doth ride
Into the sun's perpetual day.

Little? It's all I have. For space
Than time itself's no less confined:
Its only being is what has place
At pin-point moment in the mind.

All history, knowledge, wisdom, power,
All man has said, or done, or made —
As transitory as a flower —
For me on this scant thread is stayed.

The all, the one; their better and worse,
Interdependent ever remain;
Each instant is my universe;
Which at a nod may fade again.

At the last slumber's nod, what then?

THE ASSIGNATION

Echoes of voices stilled may linger on
Until a lapse of utter quiet steal in;
As 'tis hushed daybreak — the dark night being gone —
That calls small birds their matins to begin. . . .

Felled with such sickness I had lain that life
Nightmare's phantasmagoria seemed to be.
Alas, poor body, racked with woe and strife,
Its very weakness set my spirit free.

Wondrous the regions then through which I strayed,
Spectre invisible as the wind and air,
Regions that midnight fantasy had made,
And clear cold consciousness can seldom share.

But of these wanderings one remembered best
Nothing exotic showed — no moon-drenched vale,
Where in profound ravines dark forests rest,
The wild-voiced cataracts their nightingale;

But only a sloping meadow, rimed with frost;
Bleak pollard willows, and a frozen brook,
All tinkle of its waters hushed and lost,
Its sword-sharp rushes by the wind forsook:

An icy-still, grey-heavened, vacant scene,
With whin and marron hummocked, and flowerless gorse. . . .
And in that starven upland's winter green,
Stood grazing in the silence a white horse.

No marvel of beauty, or strangeness, or fable, this —
Una — *la Belle Dame* — hero — or god might ride;
Worn, aged with time and toil, and now at peace,
It cropped earth's sweetmeats on the stark hill's side.

Spellbound, I watched it — hueless mane and tail
Like wraith of foam upon an un-named sea;
Until, as if at mute and inward hail,
It raised its gentle head and looked at me —

Eyes blue as speedwell, tranquil, morning-fair:
It was as if for aeons these and I
Had planned this mystic assignation there,
In this lone waste, beneath that wintry sky. . . .

Strange is man's soul, which solace thus can win,
When the poor body lies at woe's extreme —
Yea, even where the shades of death begin —
In secret symbol, and painted by a dream!

THE MOMENT

O Time — the heedless child you are!
A daisy, the most distant star
Fall to your toying scimitar.
And I? And this loved face? We too
Are things but of a moment. True:
But then, poor youngling, so are you!

Dream on! In your small company
We are contented merely to be —
Yes, even to Eternity.

MEMORY

Ah, Memory — that strange deceiver!
Who can trust her? How believe her —
While she hoards with equal care
The poor and trivial, rich and rare;
Yet flings away, as wantonly,
Grave fact and loveliest fantasy?

When I call her — need her most,
Lo, she's in hiding, or is lost!
Or, capricious as the wind,
Brings stalks — and leaves the flowers behind!
Of all existence — as I live —
She can no more than moments give.
Thousands of dew-clear dusks in Spring
Were mine, time gone, to wander in,
But of their fragrance, music, peace,
What now is left my heart to bless?
Oases in a wilderness!
Nor could her tongue tell o'er the tale
Even of one June nightingale.
And what of the strange world that teems —
Where brooding Hypnos reigns — with dreams?
Twenty years in sleep I have spent —
Horror, delight, grief, wonderment;
Through what wild wizard scenes lured on!
Where are they? . . . In oblivion.
Told she her all, 'twould reach an end
Ere nodded off the drowsiest friend!

She has, it's true, a sovereign skill
A wounded heart to salve and heal;
Can lullaby to sorrow sing;
Shed balm on grief and suffering;
And guard with unremitting care
Secrets that we alone can share.
Ay, so bewitched her amber is
'Twill keep enshrined the tiniest flies —
Instants of childhood, fresh as when
My virgin sense perceived them then —
Daisy or rainbow, a look, a kiss,
As safe as if Eternity's;
And can, with probe as keen, restore
Some fear, or woe, when I was four.
Fleeter than Nereid, plummet-deep,

Enticed by some long-sunken ship,
She, siren-wise, laughs out to see
The treasure she retrieves for me —
Gold foundered when I was a boy,
Now cleansed by Time from all alloy.
And think what priceless boons I owe
Her whimsical punctilio!

Nothing would recognition bring
Should she forsake me. Everything
I will, or want, or plan, or say
Were past conceiving, she away.
Only her exquisite vigilance
Enables me to walk, sing, dance.
Tree and bird would name-less pine
Did she the twain refuse to entwine.
And where, sad dunce, if me she shun,
My A B C? my twice times one?
Fancy her nurseling is; and thought
Can solely in her toils be caught.
Ev'n who and where and what I am
Await her whisper to proclaim.

If only — what the infinite loss! —
I had helped her sever gold from dross!
Since now she is — for better or worse —
The relics of my Universe.
But, ah, how scant a heed she pays
To much well-meaning Conscience says!
And good intentions? Alas for them!
They are left to languish on the stem.
The mort of promises idly made —
Where now their husks, the fickle jade?
Where, too, the jilt so gaily resigned
To out-of-sight being out-of-mind?
And, Love? — I would my heart and she
Were more attuned to constancy!

Musing, she sits, at ease, in peace,
Unchanged by age or time's caprice,
And quietly cons again with me
Some well-loved book of poetry,
Her furtive finger putting by,
With a faint smile, or fainter sigh,
The withered flowers that mark a place
Once over-welled with grief or grace.

Yes, and, as though the wanton tried
Once bitter pangs to gloss, or hide,
She stills a voice fall'n harsh and hoarse
With sudden ill-concealed remorse.
I scan the sphinx-like face, and ask
What still lies hid beneath that mask? —
The sins, the woes, the perfidy —
O murderous taciturnity!
I am the *all* I have ever been,
Why gild the cage thou keep'st me in?
Sweet, sweet! she mocks me, the siren; and then
Its very bars shine bright again.

Yet, of my life, from first to last,
This wayward mistress of the Past —
Soundless foot, and tarn-dark eyes —
Keeps safe for me what most I prize.
The sage may to the Future give
Their *Now*, however fugitive;
Mine savours less of rue and myrrh
When spent, in solitude, with her;
When, kingfisher, on leafy spray,
I while the sunshine hours away
In tranquil joy — as in a dream —
Not of its fish, but of the stream;
Whose gliding waters then reflect
Serener skies, in retrospect,
And flowers, ev'n fairer to the eye
Than those of actuality.

And with what grace she has dealt with me —
What patience, insight, sorcery!
Why, every single word here writ
Was hers, till she surrendered it;
And where, without her — I? for lo,
When she is gone I too must go.

CLAVICHORD

Hearken! Tiny, clear, discrete:
The listener within deems solely his,
A music so remote and sweet
It all but lovely as silence is.

[375]

FAINT MUSIC

The meteor's arc of quiet; a voiceless rain;
The mist's mute communing with a stagnant moat;
The sigh of a flower that has neglected lain;
  That bell's unuttered note:

A hidden self rebels, its slumber broken;
Love secret as crystal forms within the womb;
The heart may as faithfully beat, the vow unspoken;
  All sounds to silence come.

WAITING

  'Waiting to . . .'
  'Who is?'
  'We are . . .
Was that the night-owl's cry?'
'I heard not. But see! the evening star;
And listen! — the ocean's solacing sigh.'
'You mean the surf at the harbour bar?'
  'What did you say?'
  'Oh, "waiting".'
  '"Waiting?"—
  Waiting what for?'
  'To die.'

EUPHRASY

Hope, wreathed with roses,
Led sand-blind Despair
To a clear babbling wellspring
And laved his eyes there —
Dark with long brooding
In dungeon-like keep —
Hope laved his eyes,
And he fell fast asleep.

He fell fast asleep
By the willows green-grey,
While the child on his pipes
Piped twilight away.

[376]

So that when he awoke
The skies were outspread
With a powder of stars
Strewn in myriads o'erhead.

And Despair lifted up
His gaunt cavernous face;
He said, 'I see Suns
Like wild beacons, in space;
I cannot endure
The blaze, dazzle, flare!'
But the child — he saw only
Faint stars glinting there.

And he flung back his head
With laughter at sight
Of that lantern-jawed face
Dazed with fear at the Night.
And he counselled Despair
Some sly shift to devise
Lest daybreak brought blindness
Again — to his eyes.

And he his young brows
Sprinkled cold in the brook
For the magic of starshine
Which them had forsook.

THE STRATAGEM

Here's the cave where Sorrow dwells
Weeping in his courts of yew!
Foot then lightly in these dells,
Let not plash one drop of dew.
Bring your chains of pimpernels,
Bring your silvery honeydew.

Lay your nets deliciously,
Set the bait in that sweet beam —
One grey tear to lure him by
When he wakens from his dream,
And the breath of a faint sigh,
That shall ev'n less be than seem.

[377]

Hide you, hide you, not a note,
From the little birds you are!
Let not the least laughter float
Near or far, near or far.
See he wakens! scare him not —
Wild with weeping as a star.

Hie away, ah, hie away!
Woe is all! see, how the sun
Ruddies through his filmy grey,
Turns to light the dreaming one —
Mist and dew of a Spring day
Trembling a night-nothing on.

Fold your nets and mew your bait!
Come, sweet spirits, how shall we
Watch and, never ending, wait
For a wraith of transiency?
Fly ere yet the day grow late,
Else we too grow shadowy!

HOMESICK

O homesick, brood no more!
Lovely that sky; haunted the wandering wind;
Strange the dark breakers beating on the shore
That never rest, nor any respite find,
Yet ever call to the lone ghost in thee,
'Where is thy peace, where thy tranquillity?'

Only a wasting fire
Is this remembrance, cheating day and night
With vain and unassuageable desire,
And fleeting phantom pictures of delight.
And yet, O sleep — friend of my body — be
Friend to the soul also that thirsts for thee!

NIGHT

That shining moon — watched by that one faint star:
Sure now am I, beyond the fear of change,
The lovely in life is the familiar,
And only the lovelier for continuing strange.

OUT OF BOUNDS

Why covet what eye cannot see;
    Or earthly longing know?
Decoyed by cheating fantasy —
    This restless ranging to and fro?

Would wildlier sing dark's nightingale
    Where Hera's golden apples grow?
Would lovelier be the swallow's flight
In wastes of wild auroral night,
    Wondrous with falling snow?

PEACE

Night is o'er England, and the winds are still;
Jasmine and honeysuckle steep the air;
Softly the stars that are all Europe's fill
Her heaven-wide dark with radiancy fair;
That shadowed moon now waxing in the west
Stirs not a rumour in her tranquil seas;
Mysterious sleep has lulled her heart to rest,
Deep even as theirs beneath her churchyard trees.

Secure, serene; dumb now the night-hawk's threat;
The guns' low thunder drumming o'er the tide;
The anguish pulsing in her stricken side. . . .
All is at peace. . . . But, never, heart, forget:
For this her youngest, best, and bravest died,
These bright dews once were mixed with bloody sweat.

THE WIDOW

Grief now hath pacified her face;
Even hope might share so still a place.
Yet, if — in silence of her heart —
A memoried voice or footstep start,
Or a chance word of ecstasy
Cry through dim-cloistered memory,
Into her eyes her soul will steal
To gaze on the irrevocable —
As if death had not power to keep
One, who had loved her long, so long asleep.

[379]

Now all things lovely she looks on
Wear the mute aspect of oblivion;
   And all things silent seem to be
   Richer than any melody.
   Her narrow hands, like birds that make
   A nest for some old instinct's sake,
   Have hollowed a refuge for her face —
   A narrow and a darkened place —
   Where, far from the world's light, she may
   See clearer what is passed away:
   And only little children know
Through what dark half-closed gates her smile may go.

THE LAST CHAPTER

I am living more alone now than I did;
This life tends inward, as the body ages;
And what is left of its strange book to read
Quickens in interest with the last few pages.

Problems abound. Its authorship? A sequel?
Its hero-villain, whose ways so little mend?
The plot? still dark. The style? a shade unequal.
And what of the dénouement? And, the end?

No, no, have done! Lay the thumbed thing aside;
Forget its horrors, folly, incitements, lies;
In silence and in solitude abide,
And con what yet may bless your inward eyes.

Pace, still, for pace with you, companion goes,
Though now, through dulled and inattentive ear,
No more — as when a child's — your sick heart knows
His infinite energy and beauty near.

His, too, a World, though viewless save in glimpse;
He, too, a book of imagery bears;
And, as your halting foot beside him limps,
Mark you whose badge and livery he wears.

COURAGE

O heart, hold thee secure
In this blind hour of stress,
Live on, love on, endure,
Uncowed, though comfortless.

Life's still the wondrous thing
It seemed in bygone peace,
Though woe now jar the string,
And all its music cease.

Even if thine own self have
No haven for defence;
Stand not the unshaken brave
To give thee confidence?

Worse than all worst 'twould be,
If thou, who art thine all,
Shatter ev'n their reality
    In thy poor fall!

MARTINS: SEPTEMBER

At secret daybreak they had met —
   Chill mist beneath the welling light
Screening the marshes green and wet —
   An ardent legion wild for flight.

Each preened and sleeked an arrowlike **wing**;
   Their eager throats with lapsing cries
Praising whatever fate might bring —
   Cold wave, or Africa's paradise.

Unventured, trackless leagues of air;
   England's sweet summer narrowing on;
Her lovely pastures: nought their care —
   Only this ardour to be gone.

A tiny, elfin, ecstatic host . . .
   And 'neath them, on the highway's crust,
Like some small mute belated ghost,
   A sparrow pecking in the dust.

SUNRISE

Bliss it is at break of day
To watch the night-mists thin away:
Like wraiths, of light distilled, they seem —
Phantoms of beauty from a forgotten dream.

As if to a new world new-bidden,
The risen sun shines through the gates of heaven;
And, since the meagrest face with joy may shine,
His glory greets the candle-flame in mine.

THE DREAMER

The woods were still. No breath of air
    Stirred in leaf or brake.
Cold hung the rose, unearthly fair;
    The nightingale, awake,
In rusted coverts of the may
    Shook out his bosom's down;

Alone, upon her starry way,
    The moon, to fulness grown,
Moved, shining, through her misty meads;
    And, roofless from the dew,
Knelt way-worn Love, with idle beads,
    And dreamed of you.

SALLIE'S MUSICAL BOX

Once it made music, tiny, frail, yet sweet —
Bead-note of bird where earth and elfland meet.
Now its thin tinkling stirs no more, since she
Whose toy it was, has gone; and taken the key.

A PORTRAIT[1]

A solemn plain-faced child stands gazing there,
Her small hand resting on a purple chair.
Her stone-grey waisted gown is looped with black;
Linked chain and star encircle a slender neck;
Knots of bright red deck wrist, breast, flaxen hair;
Shoulder to waist falls band of lettered gold:
Round-eyed, she watches me — this eight-year-old,
The ghost of her father in her placid stare.

[1] For the later, revised version of this poem called 'Paint', see Uncollected
Poems, p. 658.

Darkness beyond. A moment she and I
Engage in some abstruse small colloquy —
On time, art, beauty, life, mortality!
But of one secret not a hint creeps out —
What grave Velasquez talked to her about;
And from that shadow not a clapper cries
Where now the fowler weaves his subtleties.

BRUEGHEL'S WINTER

Jagg'd mountain peaks and skies ice-green
Wall in the wild cold scene below.
Churches, farms, bare copse, the sea
In freezing quiet of winter show;
Where ink-black shapes on fields in flood
Curling, skating, and sliding go.
To left, a gabled tavern; a blaze;
Peasants; a watching child; and lo,
Muffled, mute — beneath naked trees
In sharp perspective set a-row —
Trudge huntsmen, sinister spears aslant,
Dogs snuffling behind them in the snow;
And arrowlike, lean, athwart the air
    Swoops into space a crow.

But flame, nor ice, nor piercing rock,
Nor silence, as of a frozen sea,
Nor that slant inward infinite line
Of signboard, bird, and hill, and tree,
Give more than subtle hint of him
Who squandered here life's mystery.

O CHILDISH MIND!

O childish mind! — last night to rapture won
In marvel of wild Orion; now to sink
Earthward; and by the flames of a dwarf sun
Find a like happiness in a single pink!

UNFORESEEN

Darkness had fallen. I opened the door:
And lo, a stranger in the empty room —
A marvel of moonlight upon wall and floor . . .
The quiet of mercy? Or the hush of doom?

[383]

TWICE LOVELY

Chalk-white, light dazzled on the stone,
And there a weed, a finger high,
Bowed its silvery head with every
Breath of wind that faltered by.

Twice lovely thing! For when there drifted
A cloud across the radiant sun,
Not only that had it forsaken,
Its tiny shadow too was gone.

THE DAISY

Oh, saw I there —
Under bleak shadow of a towering wall,
From its great height let fall,
Dense-historied, and, echoing from its stone,
Ruinous, mossed, and lone,
The crying fowls of the air —
Set in a smooth, cool flood of agelong green,
Reared up on inch-high stalk, to see, be seen,
A pygmy daisy, with a silver face,
Shining in that dark place.

FOREBODING

The sycamore, by the heap of dead
    Summer's last flowers that rot below,
Will suddenly in the stillness shed
    A cockled leaf from a bud–tight bough:
So ghostlike the sound that I turn my head
As if at a whisper — at something said;
    'What! And still happy? Thou!'

That is this captious phantom's way —
    Omens, monitions, hints of fate,
On a quiet, air-sweet October day
    Of beauty past estimate!
Is it age; or conscience; or mind now fey
At a world from love so far astray
    That can only falter, 'Wait'?

WHICH?

'What did you say?'
'I? Nothing.' 'No?...
What was that sound?'
'When?'
'Then.'
'I do not know.'
'Whose eyes were those on us?'
'Where?'
'There.'
'No eyes I saw.'
'Speech, footfall, presence — how cold the night may be!'
'Phantom or fantasy, it's all one to *me*.'

THE WINDOW

Sunlit, the lashes fringe the half-closed eyes
With hues no bow excels that spans the skies;
As magical the meteor's flight o'erhead,
And daybreak shimmering on a spider's thread...
Thou starry Universe — whose breadth, depth, height
Contracts to such strait entry as mere sight!

THE DOVE

How often, these hours, have I heard the monotonous crool
   of a dove —
Voice, low, insistent, obscure, since its nest it has hid in a grove —
Flowers of the linden wherethrough the hosts of the honeybees rove.

And I have been busily idle: no problems; nothing to prove;
No urgent foreboding; but only life's shallow habitual groove:
Then why, if I pause to listen, should the languageless note of a dove
So dark with disquietude seem? And what is it sorrowing of?

SWALLOWS FLOWN

Whence comes that small continuous silence
   Haunting the livelong day?
This void, where a sweetness, so seldom heeded,
   Once ravished my heart away?
As if a loved one, too little valued,
   Had vanished — could not stay?

[385]

A QUEEN WASP

Why rouse from thy long winter sleep?
And sound that witchcraft drone in air?
The frost-bound hours of darkness creep,
    The night is cold, and bare

Of all that gave thee power to rear
Thy myriad Amazonian host.
All, all are dust. I only, here;
    And thou — untimely ghost! —

Prowling, black-orbed, disconsolate,
Questing antennae, quivering wing,
Unwitting of the mortal fate
    A human thought might bring

To the mute marvels in thy womb,
Tarrying only summer's heat
To breed a Babylon from the tomb —
    As wondrous and exquisite!

Still, now. Thou'rt safe and hidden again;
Thy sombre, astonished piping done . . .
And I, with the hosts that flock the brain,
    Back to my self am gone.

A HARE

Eyes that glass fear, though fear on furtive foot
    Track thee, in slumber bound;
Ears that whist danger, though the wind sigh not,
    Nor Echo list a sound;
Heart — oh, what hazard must thy wild life be,
With sapient Man for thy cold enemy!

Fleet Scatterbrains, thou hast thine hours of peace
    In pastures April-green,
Where the shrill skylark's raptures never cease,
And the clear dew englobes the white moon's beam.
All happiness God gave thee, albeit thy foe
Roves Eden, as did Satan, long ago.

THE CHERRY TREES

Under pure skies of April blue I stood,
Where, in wild beauty, cherries were in blow;
And, as sweet fancy willed, see there I could
Boughs thick with blossom, or inch-deep in snow.

A DREAM

Idle I sat — my book upon my knee,
The Tyro's Outline of Biology.
Drowsy the hour: and wits began to roam
Far, far from gene, as far from chromosome.
Sweet sleep stole over me. . . .
                                        A valley in Spring! —
Wherein a river of water crystal clear
In rarer beauty imaged all things near —
Green grass, and leaf; lithe leopard, swift gazelle —
Gihon? Euphrates? No, I could not tell,
But knew it was Eden by the asphodel,
The painted birds, the songs I heard them sing.

There, where heaven's sunbeams with earth's shade inwove —
This side a slumber-solemn cedar grove,
A clear green twilight underneath a tree,
(Of Life? Of Knowledge? it was strange to me)
Two mortals sat: a sage, dome-headed, grey,
Who looked a child, albeit in age astray —
Talking, it seemed, his very heart away;
And one even lovelier than woods in May.

She, as if poesy haunted all he said —
Eyes blue as chicory flower, and braided head —
Showed silent as snow against the tender grass,
For naked she as Aphrodite was.
And, at her shoulder, mid its coils near by,
A subtle Serpent couched, with lidless eye,
Which, its tongue flickering, else motionlessly,
Raised its rune-blazoned head, and gazed at me . . .

Whereat, although it harmless seemed, I woke;
My dream-cleansed eyes now fixed upon my book;
Nor could by any stealth I entry win
Into that paradisal scene again —
Fruit so much sweeter to a childish love
Than any knowledge I had vestige of.

[387]

THOMAS HARDY

Mingled the moonlight with daylight — the last in the narrowing
    west;
Silence of nightfall lay over the shallowing valleys at rest
        In the Earth's green breast:
Yet a small multitudinous singing, a lully of voices of birds,
Unseen in the vague shelving hollows, welled up with my
    questioning words:
All Dorsetshire's larks for connivance of sweetness seemed trysting
    to greet
Him in whose song the bodings of raven and nightingale meet.

Stooping and smiling, he questioned, 'No birdnotes myself do I
    hear?
Perhaps 'twas the talk of chance farers, abroad in the hush with us
    here —
        In the dusk-light clear?'
And there peered from his eyes, as I listened, a concourse of
    women and men,
Whom his words had made living, long-suffering — they flocked
    to remembrance again;
'O Master,' I cried in my heart, 'lorn thy tidings, grievous thy
    song;
Yet thine, too, this solacing music, as we earthfolk stumble along.'

THE OLD SUMMERHOUSE[1]

This blue-washed, old, thatched summerhouse —
Paint scaling, and fading from its walls —
How often from its hingeless door
I have watched — dead leaf, like the ghost of a mouse,
Rasping the worn brick floor —
The snows of the weir descending below,
And their thunderous waterfall.

Fall — fall: dark, garrulous rumour,
Until I could listen no more.
Could listen no more — for beauty with sorrow
Is a burden hard to be borne:
The evening light on the foam, and the swans, there;
That music, remote, forlorn.

[1] First printed privately, Christmas 1937.

ROOKS IN OCTOBER

They sweep up, crying, riding the wind,
  Ashen on blue outspread —
Gilt-lustred wing, sharp light-glazed beak,
  And low flat ravenous head.

Claws dangling, down they softly swoop
  Out of the eastern sun
Into the yellowing green-leaved boughs —
  Their morning feast begun.

Clasping a twig that even a linnet
  Might bend in song, they clip
Pat from the stalked embossed green cup
  Its fruitage bitter-ripe.

Oh, what divine far hours their beauty
  Of old for me beguiled,
When — acorn, oak, untarnished heavens —
  I watched them as a child!

THE CAGE

Thou angel face! — like a small exquisite cage,
  Such as some old Chinese
Once spent his love and skill on — youth to age,
In hope its destined prisoner to please;
And then had empty left; since he had heard
What death would do in setting free the bird.

QUIET

Mutely the mole toils on;
The worm in silk cocoon
Stealthily as spider spins,
  As glides the moon.
But listen where envy peers 'neath the half-closed lid;
Where peeping vanity lurks; where pride lies hid;
And peace beyond telling share with the light-stilled eye,
When nought but an image of the loved one's nigh.

THE CAPTIVE

When gloaming droops
To the raven's croak,
And the nightjar churs
From his time-gnarled oak
In the thunder-stricken wood:

When the drear dark waters
'Neath sallows hoar
Shake the veils of night
With their hollow roar,
Plunging deep in flood;

Spectral, wan
From unquiet rest,
A phantom walks
With anguished breast,
Doomed to love's solitude.

Her footstep is leaf-like,
Light as air,
Her raiment scarce stirs
The gossamer.
While from shadowy hood

In the wood-light pale
Her dream-ridden eyes,
Without sorrow or tear,
Speculation, surmise,
Wildly, insanely brood.

AN INTERLUDE[1]

A small brook gushed on stones hard by,
Waste-lorn it babbled; alone was I,
Dawn's ever-changing alchemy
   Low in the eastern sky.

Ghost that I was, by dream waylaid,
Benighted, and yet unafraid,
I sat, in those brief hours, long-lost,
   And communed with the sea.

[1] For the earlier, longer version of this poem called 'The Might-have-been', see Uncollected Poems, p. 638.

[390]

Faint, o'er its shingly murmuring,
The secret songs I had hoped to sing —
When I on earth was sojourning —
Of which poor words, alas, can bring
Only a deadened echoing
 Of what they meant to me —

Rose in my throat; and poured their dew —
A hymn of praise — my being through;
Shed peace on a mind that never knew
 Peace in that mind could be.

Only a soundless voice was I,
Yet sweeter that than man can hear
When, latticed in by moonbeams clear,
The bird of darkness to its fere
 Tells out love's mystery.

No listener there — a dream; but ne'er
Sang happier heart in heaven fair
 To lyre or psaltery. . . .

Oh, futile vanity to mourn
What the day's waking leaves forlorn!
Doth not earth's strange and lovely mean
Only, 'Come, see, O son of man,
All that you hope, the nought you can,
 The glory that might have been?'

A PRAYER

When with day's woes night haunts wake-weary eyes,
How deep a blessing from the heart may rise
On the happy, the beautiful, the good, the wise!

The poor, the outcast, knave, child, stranger, fool
Need no commending to the merciful;
But, in a world grieved, ugly, wicked, or dull,

Who could the starry influences surmise —
What praises ardent enough could prayer devise
For the happy, the beautiful, the good, the wise?

[391]

HERE SLEEPS

Here sleeps, past earth's awakening,
A woman, true and pretty,
Who was herself in everything —
Tender, and grave, and witty.
Her smallest turn of foot, hand, head,
Was way of wind with water;
So with her thoughts and all she said —
It seemed her heart had taught her.
O thou most dear and loving soul
Think not I shall forget thee;
Nor take amiss what here is writ
For those who never met thee!

THE LAST ARROW

There came a boy,
Full quiver on his back —
Tapped at my door ajar.

'No, no, my child,' said I,
'I nothing lack;
And see! — the evening star!'

Finger on string,
His dangerous eyes
Gazed boldly into mine:

'Know thou my mother
An Immortal is!
Guard thee, and hope resign!'

'But patience,' I pleaded,
Pointing to a shelf,
Where rusting arrows lay.

'All these, times gone,
You squandered on myself,
Why come — so late, to-day?'

These words scarce uttered,
I discerned a Shade
Shadow till then had hid;

Clang went that bowstring,
And past wit to evade,
Into my bosom slid

His final dart.
He shook his rascal head,
Its curls by the lamp-shine gilt:

'Thank thou the Gods!
Here's One, I vow,' he said,
'Not even thee shall jilt.'

AWAY

There is no sorrow
Time heals never;
No loss, betrayal,
Beyond repair.
Balm for the soul, then,
Though grave shall sever
Lover from loved
And all they share;
See, the sweet sun shines,
The shower is over,
Flowers preen their beauty,
The day how fair!
Brood not too closely
On love, or duty;
Friends long forgotten
May wait you where
Life with death
Brings all to an issue;
None will long mourn for you,
Pray for you, miss you,
Your place left vacant,
You not there.

OH, WHY?

Oh, why make such ado —
This fretful care and trouble?
The sun in noonday's blue
Pours radiance on earth's bubble.
What though the heart-strings crack,
And sorrow bid thee languish,
Dew falls; the night comes back;
Sleep, and forget thine anguish.
Oh, why in shadow haunt?
Shines not the evening flower?
Hark, how the sweet birds chaunt,
The lovely light their bower.
Water her music makes,
Lulling even these to slumber;
And only dead of darkness wakes
    Stars without number.

THE LOOKING-GLASS

'Nothing is so sure that it
May not in a moment flit:
Quench the candle, gone are all
The wavering shadows on the wall.
Eros, like Time, is winged. And, why?
To warn us, dear, he too can fly.
Watch, now, your bright image here
In this water, calm and fair —
Those clear brown eyes, that dark brown hair.
See, I fling a pebble in;
What distortions now begin!
Refluent ripples sweep and sway,
Chasing all I love away.
But, imagine a strange glass
Which, to gaze, gave back, alas,
Nothing but a crystal wall,
And else, no hint of you at all:
No rose on cheek, no red on lip,
No trace of beauty's workmanship.
That, my dear, for me, for you,
Precisely is what life might do.
Might, I say. . . . Oh, then, how sweet

Is it by this stream to sit,
And in its molten mirror see
All that is now reality:
The interlacing boughs, the sun's
Tiny host of flickering moons,
That rainbow kingfisher, and these
Demure, minute anemones —
Cherubim, in heaven's blue,
Leaning their wizard faces too —
Lost in delight at seeing you.'

SNOW

This meal-white snow —
Oh, look at the bright fields!
What crystal manna
Death-cold winter yields!

Falling from heavens
Earth knows little of,
Yet mantling it
As with a flawless love —

A shining cloak —
It to the naked gives,
Wooing all sorrow
From the soul it shrives.

Adam no calmer vales
Than these descried;
Leda a shadow were
This white beside.

Water stays still for wonder;
Herb and flower,
Else starved with cold,
In warmth and darkness cower.

Miracle, far and near,
That starry flake
Can of its myriads
Such wide pastures make,

[395]

For sun to colour,
And for moon to wan,
And day's vast vault of blue
To arch upon!

A marvel of light,
Whose verge of radiance seems
Frontier of paradise,
The bourne of dreams.

O tranquil, silent, cold —
Such loveliness to see:
The heart sighs answer,
Benedicite!

Bells and Grass:
A Book of Rhymes (1941)

MARY

Mary! Mary! *Mary!*
Come to the dairy, please!
Give me some butter to spread on my bread,
Give me a morsel of cheese.
The cows in the meadow are chewing the cud,
Some of them deep in the stream —
Give me a suppet of curds and whey,
Or a wee little bowl of cream!
It's half a week since breakfast,
And cook won't spare a crumb;
Fol-di-diddle-O, starve I shall,
Unless, you dear, you come!
A hungry wolf's inside me,
Though I wouldn't for worlds just tease;
Mary! Mary! *Mary!*
Come to the dairy, *please*!

THUNDER

Call the cows home!
Call the cows home!
Louring storm clouds
Hitherward come;
East to West
Their wings are spread;
Lost in the blue
Is each heaven-high head;
They've dimmed the sun;
Turned day to night;
With a whistling wind
The woods are white;

[397]

Down streams the rain
On farm, barn, byre,
Bright green hill,
And bramble and brier,
Filling the valley
With glimmer and gloom:
Call the cows home!
Call the cows home!

GRACE

For every sip the Hen says grace;
The Rabbit twinkles his small face;
Ev'n to the Fox, stol'n safely home,
A crafty grin of thanks must come;
Even the Spider, plump in net,
His manners cannot quite forget,
And when he's supped upon a fly
Puts what is over neatly by.
Oh, *any* one with tongue and wits
Who crowded up with victuals sits
Through breakfasts, luncheons, dinners, teas,
With never a *Thank you* or a *Please*,
Eating not what he should but can,
Can *not* be a well-mannered man.

No doubt if Cows and Sheep were able
To draw their chairs up to the table,
It's only common sense to say
They'd keep on stuffing there all day,
They need such quantities of hay.
But though they never could let pass
A dainty dish of greens or grass,
Even the littlest Lambkin would
Express a sheepish gratitude;
While sager beasts, however staid,
Might smile upon the parlourmaid.

TOM'S LITTLE DOG

Tom told his dog called Tim to beg,
And up at once he sat,
His two clear amber eyes fixed fast,
His haunches on his mat.

Tom poised a lump of sugar on
His nose; then, 'Trust!' says he;
Stiff as a guardsman sat his Tim;
Never a hair stirred he.

'Paid for!' says Tom; and in a trice
Up jerked that moist black nose;
A snap of teeth, a crunch, a munch,
And down the sugar goes!

FOR MOPSA

Ah, would I were a Pastrycook!
My Mopsa then I'd make
A Sallie Lunn, a Crumpet, and a
Cake.

Ah, would I were a Grocer!
How happy she should be
With Jars of Honey, Raisins, Currants,
Tea.

Ah, would I were an Oilman!
She should never, never mope
For Clothes Pegs, Candles, Soda, or for
Soap.

Ah, would I were a Pothecary!
For Possets she'd not pine,
Or Pills, or Ipecacuanha
Wine.

Or, just suppose, a Fishmonger!
The *pains* I would be at
To pick her out a Whitebait, or a
Sprat!

Or a green-baize-aproned Fruiterer —
The punnets that should come
Of Cherries, Apples, Peach, and Pear, and
Plum!

There's a small dark shop I know of too,
In another place, called Sleep;
And there's nothing sold in Dreams it doesn't
Keep.

But as it's only rhymes I make,
I can but dower my Dove
With scribbles, and with kisses, and with
    Love.

A—APPLE PIE

Little Pollie Pillikins
Peeped into the kitchen,
'H'm,' says she, 'Ho,' says she,
   'Nobody there!'
Only little meeny mice,
Miniken and miching
On the big broad flagstones, empty and bare.

Greedy Pollie Pillikins
Crept into the pantry,
There stood an Apple Pasty,
   Sugar white as snow.
Off the shelf she toppled it,
Quick and quiet and canty,
And the meeny mice they watched her
   On her tip-tap-toe.

'Thief, Pollie Pillikins!'
Crouching in the shadows there,
Flickering in the candle-shining,
   Fee, fo, fum!
Munching up the pastry,
Crunching up the apples,
'Thief!' squeaked the smallest mouse,
   'Pollie, spare a crumb!'

QUACK!

The duck is whiter than whey is,
His tail tips up over his back,
The eye in his head is as round as a button,
And he says, *Quack! Quack!*

He swims on his bright blue mill-pond,
By the willow tree under the shack,
Then stands on his head to see down to the bottom,
And says, *Quack! Quack!*

[400]

When Mollie steps out of the kitchen,
For apron — pinned round with a sack;
He squints at her round face, her dish, and what's in it,
And says, *Quack! Quack!*

He preens the pure snow of his feathers
In the sun by the wheat-straw stack;
At dusk waddles home with his brothers and sisters,
And says, *Quack! Quack!*

DONE FOR

Old Ben Bailey
He's been and done
For a small brown bunny
With his long gun.

Glazed are the eyes
That stared so clear,
And no sound stirs
In that hairy ear.

What was once beautiful
Now breathes not,
Bound for Ben Bailey's
Smoking pot.

MISS CHERRY

Once — once I loved:
And Miss Cherry was she
Who took my heart captive,
And set my heart free.

I'd sing, and I'd sing
What no words ever meant,
And never felt lonely
Wherever I went.

No bird in the air,
No fish in the sea,
No skylark in heaven
Could happier be.

[401]

Never hungry or tired,
From breakfast to bed;
I just nibbled, and thought
Of Miss Cherry instead.

All night I would sleep
Like a top, until day
With a shower of sunbeams
Washed slumber away.

And it seemed that the World
Was a Wonder to see,
Since I loved Miss Cherry,
And Miss Cherry loved me.

NICOLETTA

Oh, my pretty Nicoletta,
Come away, come away!
There's a linnet in the willow,
And the moon is up to-day,
When the one is sleepy silent
And the other wildly clear,
I know a hazel thicket
Where I'll kiss you, dear.

Ah, sweetheart Nicoletta,
Come away, come away!
There are rabbits in the warren,
There is blossom on the may;
And when the first are nibbling
And the other's cold with dew,
I'll tell you tales of magic,
And of moonshine, and of you.

Come away, Nicoletta,
Nicoletta-likkalay!
There's a secret I must sigh you
And a hidden thing to say;
Creep out as soon as evening comes,
Not a wink your eyelids close,
And I'll show you where on hills of dream
The wild thyme blows.

SALLIE

When Sallie with her pitcher goes
Down the long lane where the hawthorn blows
   For water from the spring,
I watch her bobbing sun-bright hair,
In the green leaves and blossoms there,
Shining and gleaming primrose-fair;
Till back again, like bird on wing,
Her pitcher, brimmed, she turns to bring —
   Oh, what a joy to see!
And her clear voice, the birds' above,
Rings sweet with joy, entranced with love —
   Ah! would 'twere love for me!

THE OLD SAILOR

There came an old sailor
Who sat to sup
Under the trees
Of the *Golden Cup*.

Beer in a mug
And a slice of cheese
With a hunk of bread
He munched at his ease.

Then in the summer
Dusk he lit
A little black pipe,
And sucked at it.

He thought of his victuals,
Of ships, the sea,
Of his home in the West,
And his children three.

And he stared and stared
To where, afar,
The lighthouse gleamed
At the harbour bar;

Till his pipe grew cold,
And down on the board
He laid his head,
And snored, snored, snored.

WHITE

Once was a Miller, and he would say,
'I go as *white* as lambs in May!
I go as white as rose on bush!
White as the white convolvulus!'

He snapped his fingers, began to sing: —
'White, by my beard, is everything!
Meal, and chalk, and frost, and hail;
Clouds and surf and ships in sail.

'There's nowt on earth that brighter shines
Than daisies, pinks and columbines;
But what of *ME* when full moon doth show
And mill and meadows are deep in snow!'

SAMBO

Nigger-boy Sambo who scours the pots
    Dazzles them up so bright,
The metal shines like a looking-glass,
    And his face in it black as night.

Two coal-black eyes stare steadily back,
    Where its deepest dark begins,
Then — fuzz-wigged head, wide nose, thick lips —
    He grins and grins and grins.

THE OLD TAILOR

There was once an old Tailor of Hickery Mo,
Too tired at evening to sew, to sew;
He put by his needle, he snapped his thread,
And, cross-legged, sang to his fiddle instead.
His candle bobbed at each note that came
And spat out a spark from the midst of its flame;
His catgut strings they yelped and yawled,
The wilder their scrapings the louder he bawled;
The grease trickled over at every beat,
Welled down to the stick in a winding-sheet —
Till up sprang Puss from the fire, with a *WOW*!
'A *fine* kakkamangul you're making now!'

BONUM OMEN

As we sailed out of London river,
  Sing a lo lay and a lo lay lone,
I heard a Maid sing —'Come back, never!'
  And a lo lay lone.

Her hair was yellow as sea-maids' hair is,
  Sing a lo lay and a lo lay lone,
And she'd corn for the chicks that are Mother Carey's;
  And a lo lay lone.

Sam Murphy's grog went cold as water,
  Sing a lo lay and a lo lay lone,
And our hearts to our boots went tumbling after:
  And a lo lay lone.

When we're there and back — by gum, we'll see her,
  Sing a lo lay and a lo lay lone,
Buy cheap she may, but she sells de-ar:
  And a lo lay lone.

THE SHEPHERD[1]

When I was out one morning —
In a meadow, white with sheep,
Lay a shepherd by a haystack
  Fast asleep.

With me the lark was carolling,
There was gold and green and blue;
But what, you drowsy shepherd,
  Was with you?

Was it night and water gushing
And moonbeams cold and clear
On the softly silver-slipping
  Dripping weir?

Was it childhood, was it sweetheart,
Was it distant isles and seas,
Day of Judgment, Harvest Home, or
  Bread and cheese?

---

[1] Originally called 'The Miller', and given this new title in the American edition of *Bells and Grass*, 1942, and *Rhymes and Verses: Collected Poems for Young People*, New York, 1947.

POOH!

Dainty Miss Apathy
Sat on a sofa,
Dangling her legs,
And with nothing to do;
She looked at a drawing of
Old Queen Victoria,
At a rug from far Persia —
An exquisite blue;
At a bowl of bright tulips;
A needlework picture
Of doves caged in wicker
You could almost hear coo;
She looked at the switch
That evokes e-
Lectricity;
At the coals of an age
B.C. millions and two —
When the trees were like ferns
And the reptiles all flew;
She looked at the cat
Asleep on the hearthrug,
At the sky at the window, —
The clouds in it, too;
And a marvellous light
From the West burning through:
And the one silly word
In her desolate noddle
As she dangled her legs,
Having nothing to do,
Was not, as you'd guess,
Of dumbfoundered felicity,
But contained just four letters,
And these pronounced *POOH!*

WON'T

See, Master Proud-Face!
Cold as a stone;
Light, life, love
From his bright eyes gone;
Pale as a pudding
His smooth round cheek;

[406]

His head like a block
On his stiff, wooden neck.

Won't, says his cherry mouth;
Won't, says his chin;
Won't, says the Spectre,
His bosom within;
Won't, says his clenched fist;
Won't, says his foot;
Every single inch of him
Shouts, I will *NOT!* ...

Poor, poor Mamma —
She mopes in her room,
Pining and pining
For the moment to come
When her short sharp you *SHALL!*
She can safely unsay,
And the sun sparkle out,
And the tears dry away;

Yes, her whole heart is sighing
In passionate trust
For a kiss from those *Won'ts*
To make hay of her Must!

THE HAREBELL

In the clear summer sunshine, hour by hour,
I've toiled, but toiled in vain, to paint this flower;
Brushes, and box of colours from their shelf,
And nought else with me but the flower itself.

Nothing alive — so steadfast yet so frail —
Could ever bloom on paper, I know well;
But poor and clumsy though the copy be,
I could not wish for happier company.

It seems it might, if I gazed on and on —
That wiry stalk, those petals, blue yet wan,
The solemn beauty of that marvellous cup —
At last, for very love, give its strange secret up.

SILLY SALLIE

Silly Sallie! Silly Sallie!
Called the boys down Blind Man's Alley;
But she, still smiling, never made
A sign she had heard, or answer gave;
Her blue eyes in her skimpy hair
Seemed not to notice they were there;
Seemed still to be watching, rain or shine,
Some other place, not out, but in:
Though it pleased the boys in Blind Man's Alley
Still to be shouting *Silly Sallie!*

DAYBREAK

After the dark of night
Spreads slowly up the glow
Into the starry height
Of daybreak piercing through.

Now gin the cocks to crow;
Runs lapwing, claw and crest;
From her green haunt the hare
Lopes wet with dew. The east

Gathers its cloudy host
Into its soundless pen;
Stirring in their warm sleep,
Beasts rise and graze again.

Now, with his face on fire,
And drenched with sunbeams through,
Sam, with his dappled team,
Drags out the iron plough.

Glistens with drops the grass;
Sighing, with joy, the trees
Stoop their green leafiness
Into the breeze.

Earth's wake now: every heart,
Wing, foot, and eye
Revels in light and heat:
The Sun's in the sky!

[408]

COME — GONE

Gone the snowdrop — comes the crocus;
With the tulip blows the squill;
Jonquil white as wax between them,
And the nid-nod daffodil.

Peach, plum, cherry, pear and apple,
Rain-sweet lilac on the spray;
Come the dog-rose in the hedges —
Gone's the sweetness of the may.

BLACKBIRDS

In April, when these orchards blow,
The boughs are white as driven snow.
Dark-leafed in May, like beads are seen
Hard little berries of a bright clear green.
A rosy flush steals through the skin,
While the small almond kernel swells within.
The Sun pours down his golden rain;
And soon comes honeyed June again:
Listen! — the Wood-boy's drowsy flute! —
Or is it some wild blackbird in the ripe red fruit?

BLINDMAN'S IN[1]

'*Applecumjockaby*, blindfold eye!
How many rooks come sailing by,
Caw — caw, in the deep blue sky?'

'*Applecumjockaby, you* tell me!
I can listen though I can't see;
Twenty soot-black rooks there be.'

'*Applecumjockaby*, I say, No!
Who can tell what he don't know?
Blindman's in, and round we go.'

[1] For the earlier version of this poem called 'Twinkum', see Uncollected Poems, p. 689.

THE ORCHARD

Lapped in the light and heat of noon,
I saw an orchard — glorious
With countless, cup-shaped, coloured flowers
Of intertwined convolvulus.

At sun-down, I came back again —
Faint shadows in the twilight wan;
A hundred aging apple trees;
But they? — all gone.

A WARBLER[1]

In the sedge a tiny song
Wells and trills the whole day long;
In my heart another bird
Has its music heard.

As I watch and listen here,
Each to each pipes low and clear;
But when one has ceased to sing,
Mine will still be echoing.

A GOLDFINCH

This feather-soft creature,
Tail to head,
Is golden yellow,
And black, and red.

A sip of water,
A twig to sing on,
A prong for nest,
The air to wing on,

A mate to love,
Some thistledown seed
Are all his joy, life,
Beauty, need.

[1] For another version of this poem called 'The Two Birds', see Unpublished Poems, p. 710.

THE FEATHER

A feather, a feather! —
I wonder whether
Of Wren? Or Sparrow?
Or poor Cock Robin,
Shot with an arrow?

A learnèd man
Would tell me whether
This airy scrap
Of down — this feather,
Was of Wren, or Sparrow —
From thorn or willow,
Ivy or gorse,
Or grey-leafed sallow —
Or poor Cock Robin's,
Shot with an arrow.

The beak nibs in,
A wind-puff blows,
Off and away
The morsel goes,
Tiny, delicate,
Downy, narrow,
Preened and sleek —
The dainty fellow!

So I can't help asking,
Wren? Or Sparrow?
Or — it would fill
My heart with sorrow —
Poor Cock Robin's,
Slain with an arrow?

POOR BIRD!

Poor bird! —
No hands, no fingers thine;
Two angel-coloured wings instead:
But where are mine?

Cold voiceless fish! —
No hands, no spindly legs, no toes;
But fins and a tail,
And a mouth for nose.

Wild weed! —
Not even an eye with which to see!
Or ear, or tongue,
For sigh or song;
Or heart to beat,
Or mind to long.

And yet — ah, would that I,
In sun and shade, like thee,
Might no less gentle, sweet,
And lovely be!

WHERE

Houses! houses! — Oh, I know
Where the clovers are in blow;
Where the bee for nectar goes
From the clovers to the rose;
Where the rose that was a bud
Stands wide open in the wood;
Where the wood is thick with trees
Tossed to sunshine in the breeze;
Where the breezes whisper, 'Come!
Listen, far one, here is home.'

SUPPER

I supped where bloomed the red red rose,
    And a bird in the tree
Looked on my sweet white bread and whistled
    Tunes to me.

And a wasp prowled in the evening light,
    My honey all about;
And the martin to her sun-baked nest
    Swept in and out.

I sat so still in the garden
    That wasp and leaf and bird
Seemed as I dreamed the only things
    That had ever stirred.

[412]

THE SHADOW

When the last of gloaming's gone,
When the world is drowned in Night,
Then swims up the great round Moon,
Washing with her borrowed light
Twig, stone, grass-blade — pin-point bright —
Every tiniest thing in sight.

Then, on tiptoe,
Off go I
To a white-washed
Wall near by,
Where, for secret
Company,
My small shadow
Waits for me.

Still and stark,
Or stirring — *so*,
All I'm doing
He'll do too.
Quieter than
A cat he mocks
My walk, my gestures,
Clothes and looks.

I twist and turn,
I creep, I prowl,
Likewise does he,
The crafty soul,
The Moon for lamp,
And for music, owl.

'*Sst!*' I whisper,
'Shadow, come!'
No answer:
He is blind and dumb —
Blind and dumb.
And when I go,
The wall will stand empty,
White as snow.

SOMEWHERE

Would you tell me the way to Somewhere?
   Somewhere, *Some*where,
   I have heard of a place called Somewhere —
   But know not where it can be.
      It makes no difference,
      Whether or not
      I go in dreams
      Or trudge on foot:
Could you tell me the way to Somewhere,
   The Somewhere meant for me?

There's a little old house in Somewhere —
   *Some*where, *Some*where,
A queer little house, with a Cat and a Mouse —
   Just room enough for three.
      A kitchen, a larder,
      A bin for bread,
      A string of candles,
      Or stars instead,
      A table, a chair,
      And a four-post bed —
There's room for us all in Somewhere,
   For the Cat and the Mouse and Me.

Puss is called *Skimme* in Somewhere,
   In *Some*where, *Some*where;
   Miaou, miaou, in Somewhere,
   S — K — I — M — M — E.
      Miss Mouse is scarcely
      One inch tall,
      So *she* never needed
      A name at all;
      And though you call,
      And call, and call,
      There squeaks no answer,
      Great or small —
Though her tail is a sight times longer
   Than this is likely to be: —

FOR

I want to be *off* to Somewhere,
To far, lone, lovely Somewhere,
No matter where Somewhere be.

[414]

It makes no difference
Whether or not
I flit in sleep
Or trudge on foot,
Or this time to-morrow
How far I've got,
Summer or Winter,
Cold, or hot,
Where, or When,
Or Why, or What —
Please, tell me the way to Somewhere —
    *Some*where, *Somewhere;*
Somewhere, *Some*where, *Somewhere*, SOMEWHERE —
    The Somewhere meant for me!

DREAMLAND

Annie has run to the mill dam,
Annie is down by the weir;
Who was it calling her name, then?
Nobody else to hear?
Cold the water, calm and deep,
Honey-sweet goldilocks half-asleep,
Where the green-grey willows weep,
Annie is down by the weir.

ECHO

Seven sweet notes
In the moonlight pale
Warbled a leaf-hidden
Nightingale:
And Echo in hiding
By an old green wall
Under the willows
Sighed back them all.

EVER[1]

Ever, ever
Stir and shiver
The reeds and rushes
By the river:
Ever, ever,
As if in dream,
The lone moon's silver
Sleeks the stream.
What old sorrow,
What lost love,
Moon, reeds, rushes,
Dream you of?

SHADOWS

The horse in the field,
The cows in the meadow,
Each browses and swishes
Plumb over its shadow —

It is noon . . . And beneath
That old thorn on the steep
A shepherd and sheepdog
Sit watching their sheep.

It is cool by the hedgerow,
A thorn for a tent,
Her flowers a snowdrift,
The air sweet with scent.

But oh, see already
The shade has begun
To incline to'rds the East,
As the earth and the sun

Change places, like dancers
In dance: for at morn
They stretched to the West —
When the new day was born.

[1] Called 'Why?' in *Bells and Grass*, 1941.

THE VOICE

As I sat in the gloaming
I heard a voice say,
Weep no more, sigh no more;
Come, come away!

It was dusk at the window;
From down in the street
No rumble of carts came,
No passing of feet.

I sat very still,
Too frightened to play;
And again the voice called me,
Little boy, come away!

Dark, darker it grew;
Stars came out, and the moon
Shone clear through the glass
The carpet upon.

I listened and listened;
But no more would it say —
The voice that had called me,
Come, come away!

NO JEWEL

No jewel from the rock
Is lovely as the dew,
Flashing with flamelike red
With sea-like blue.

No web the merchant weaves
Can rival hers —
The silk the spider spins
Across the furze.

THE WIND

The wind — yes, I hear it — goes wandering by,
Willow and beech stir their branches and sigh;
Each leaf to its sisters lisps softly, and then,
The air being stilled, they are silent again.

Alone with the stars stands a thorn on the height,
The snow of his flowers perfuming the night;
But so sharp are his prickles, so gnarled his old bole,
When the wind calls to him, he just whimpers, poor soul!

THE MAGNIFYING GLASS

With this round glass
I can make *Magic* talk —
A myriad shells show
In a scrap of chalk;

Of but an inch of moss
A forest — flowers and trees;
A drop of water
Like a hive of bees.

I lie in wait and watch
How the deft spider jets
The woven web-silk
From his spinnerets;

The tigerish claws he has!
And oh! the silly flies
That stumble into his net —
With all those eyes!

Not even the tiniest thing
But this my glass
Will make more marvellous,
And itself surpass.

Yes, and with lenses like it,
Eyeing the moon,
'Twould seem you'd walk there
In an afternoon!

KIPH

My Uncle Ben, who's been
To Bisk, Bhir, Biak —
Been, and come back:
To Tab, Tau, Tze, and Tomsk,
And home, by Teneriffe:
Who, brown as desert sand,
Gaunt, staring, slow and stiff,
Has chased the Unicorn
And Hippogriff,
Gave me a smooth, small, shining stone,
Called *Kiph*.

'Look'ee, now, Nevvy mine,'
He told me —'*If*
You'd wish a wish,
Just rub this smooth, small, shining stone,
Called *Kiph*.'

Hide it did I,
In a safe, secret spot;
Slept, and the place
In dreams forgot.

One wish *alone*
Now's mine: Oh, if
I could but find again
That stone called *Kiph!*

COALS

In drowsy fit
I hear the flames
Syllabling o'er
Their ancient names:
The coals — a glory
Of gold — blaze on,
Drenched with the suns
Of centuries gone;
While, at the window,
This rainy day
In darkening twilight
Dies away.

[419]

THE FIRE

Loud roared the flames
On Bonner's heath,
But all was crudded
Snow beneath,
Save where in shadow
Clip — clop — clupp,
He stumbled down
Who had stolen up.

RAIN

I woke in the swimming dark
And heard, now sweet, now shrill,
The voice of the rain-water,
    Cold and still,

Endlessly sing; now faint,
In the distance borne away;
Now in the air float near,
    But nowhere stay;

Singing I know not what,
Echoing on and on;
Following me in sleep,
    Till night was gone.

LOB-LIE-BY-THE-FIRE

Keep me a crust
Or starve I must;
Hoard me a bone
Or I am gone;
A handful of coals
Leave red for me;
Or the smouldering log
Of a wild-wood tree;
Even a kettle
To sing on the hob
Will comfort the heart
Of poor old Lob:
Then with his hairy
Hands he'll bless
Prosperous master,
And kind mistress.

[420]

MISSEL THRUSH

When from the brittle ice the fields
Begin to spring with green,
Then sits the storm-cock tree-top high,
And shrills the blasts between.

And when the sun, with thinning ray,
Tells winter's drawing nigh,
Still, this wild bird, of valiant heart,
Shouts wild against the sky.

THE SNOWFLAKE

Before I melt,
Come, look at me!
This lovely icy filigree!
Of a great forest
In one night
I make a wilderness
Of white:
By skyey cold
Of crystals made,
All softly, on
Your finger laid,
I pause, that you
My beauty see:
Breathe, and I vanish
Instantly.

WHERE

Monkeys in a forest,
Beggarmen in rags,
Marrow in a knucklebone,
Gold in leather bags;

Dumplings in the oven,
Fishes in a pool,
Flowers in a parlour,
Dunces in a school;

Feathers in a pillow,
Cattle in a shed,
Honey in a beehive,
And Babs in bed.

WHY

'Why do you weep, Mother? Why do you weep?
The evening light has ceased to shine,
   The wind has fallen asleep;
Try as I may, the dreams will come,
   Yet still awake you keep;
Why do you weep, Mother? Why do you weep?

'Why do you sigh, Mother? Why do you sigh?
The world is silent; it is night;
   The stars are in the sky;
No knock would come as late as this,
   No footsteps go by;
I want us now to be alone,
   Just you and I.
Why do you sigh, Mother? Why do you sigh?'

LULLY

Nay, ninny, shut those sleepy eyes,
   The robin from his spray
Long since to his cold winter roost
   Has flown away.

Hush, now, and fold those gentle hands;
   Across the fields the snow
Has hidden the bleating sheep from sight,
   And heaped the hedges through.

Wail not so shrill, thou tiny voice;
   These shadows mean no harm;
'Tis but the flames this wintry night
   To keep thee safe and warm;
Lully, and rest then, pretty soul,
   Safe on thy mother's arm.

HARK!

My little Charles is afraid of the dark;
Stares at the window, stiff and stark,
Sits up in bed, with tousled head,
White as chalk, scarce able to talk....
   '*Listen!*' he whispers; '*Hark!*'....

'My dear, my dear, my dear, my *dear*!
See, you are safe; just us.
It's only the wind at the keyhole,
It's only a nibbling mouse;
Only the creak of an empty stair;
And the moon looking into the house;
It's only a moth on the ceiling;
Or a little screech owl in the wood.
There's nothing behind the door ajar.
Stop breathing as long as you could,
You still wouldn't hear what you think you hear;
There's nothing to fear in what you fear —
    Lying alone in the dark.'

Poor little Charles, he weeps at me;
Begs and prays he may sleep with me;
Tear-dabbled cheeks, wild eyes I see;
And a silence falls in the vacancy. . . .

    '*Listen!* . . .' he whispers. '*Hark!* . . .'

NO BED

No bed! no bed! we shouted,
And wheeled our eyes from home
To where the green and golden woods
    Cried, Come!

Wild sang the evening birds,
The sun-clouds shone in our eyes,
A silver snippet of moon hung low
    In the skies.

We ran, we leapt, we sang,
We yodelled loud and shrill,
Chased Nobody through the valley and
    Up the hill.

We laughed, we quarrelled, we drank
The cool sweet of the dew,
Beading on bud and leaf the dim
    Woods through.

We stayed, we listened, we looked —
Now dark was on the prowl!
Too-whit-a-woo, from its hollow called
An owl. . . .

O Sleep, at last to slide
Into eyes made drunk with light;
Call in thy footsore boys to harmless
Night!

STRANGERS

The sad bells sound;
Night hastens on apace;
Oh, leave me not to languish
In this place!

I stand, I know,
Beside you, weeping not,
Pressing my childish Why?
My stubborn What?

I would forgive
If only a dream you are,
If only a little I'm to stay,
And wake afar.

Cold is this church,
Cold the high arches, cold
With dazzling light, and Oh,
How old! how old!

Under the hollow roof
The strangers' voices come —
'The night is dark, and I
Am far from home'.

THE BEAD MAT

We had climbed the last steep flight of stairs;
Alone were she and I:
'It's something I wanted to give to you,'
She whispered, with a sigh.

There, in her own small room she stood —
  Where the last beam of sun
Burned in the glass — and showed me what
  For me she had done: —

An oblong shining mat of beads,
  Yellow and white and green,
And where the dark-blue middle was
  A gold between.

I heard no far-off voice, no sound:
  Only her clear grey eyes
Drank in the thoughts that in my face
  Passed shadow-wise.

She clasped her hands, and turned her head,
  And in the watchful glass
She saw how many things had seen
  All that had passed.

She snatched her gift away; her cheek
  With scarlet was aflame;
'It isn't *anything*,' she said,
  If *we*'re the same!'

Her eyes were like a stormy sea,
  Forlorn, and vast, and grey;
Wherein a little beaten ship
  Flew through the spray.

THE PLAYMATE

Weep no more, nor grieve, nor sigh;
Wet and cold with tears is yet
The saddened lustre of thine eye;
Tears, dear, do darken it.

Weep no more, thy grief hath made
Too wild an autumn for so small
And meek a mouth, and tears have laid
Shadow where they fall.

Weep no more; how dark a face
In thy hair! Oh, I shall see
How many years, this silent place
Where I was cruel to thee!

THE HOUSE

A lane at the end of Old Pilgrim Street
Leads on to a sheep-track over the moor,
Till you come at length to where two streams meet,
The brook called Liss, and the shallow Stour.

Their waters mingle and sing all day —
Rushes and kingcups, rock and stone;
And aloof in the valley, forlorn and gray,
Is a house whence even the birds have flown.

Its ramshackle gate swings crazily; but
No sickle covets its seeding grass;
There's a cobbled path to a door close-shut;
But no face shows at the window-glass.

No smoke wreathes up in the empty air
From the chimney over its weed-green thatch;
Briar and bryony ramble there;
And no thumb tirls at the broken latch.

Even the warbling water seems
To make lone music for none to hear;
Else is a quiet found only in dreams,
And in dreams this foreboding, though not of fear.

Yes, often at dusk-fall when nearing home —
The hour of the crescent and evening star —
Again to the bridge and the streams I come,
Where the sedge and the rushes and kingcups are:

And I stand, and listen, and sigh — in vain;
Since only of Fancy's the face I see;
Yet its eyes in the twilight on mine remain,
And it seems to be craving for company.

THE BIRD

As poor old Biddie[1]
Sat by the hearth,
Chilled to the bone
By the cold in the earth,
Under the eaves —
Biddie nodding and napping —[2]
Came a beak at the casement,
Tap — tapping — and tapping:
Dark creeping in,
The fields all thick
With hoar-frost — still tapping
That restless beak.
But Biddie, as deaf
As a post, drowsed on;
And at last in the starlight
The tapping was gone.
Three mortal days
Lagged wintrily through,
But at midnight on Thursday
Gone was old Biddie too.

SUPPER

Her pinched grey body,
In widow's fur,
Mousey daren't
From her wainscot stir;
Twitching nose,
And hollow ear,
She stoops and listens,
Stark with fear:
There, like a tiger,
Sleek and sly,
Grimalkin's crouched
With gloating eye,
Watching her door —
While over the crumbs
The dusk of deepening
Evening comes.

[1] 'As poor old Goodie' (*Bells and Grass*, 1941)
[2] 'Goodie nodding and napping —' (*Bells and Grass*, 1941)

[427]

THE PRINCE

Sweet Peridarchus was a Prince,
The Prince he was of — Mouses;
He roved and roamed the haunts of Men,
And ranged about their houses.

He gnawed his way along a street,
Through holes in every wainscot,
Fandangoed in the attics and
From basement on to basement.

His eyes like bits of rubies shone;
His coat, as sleek as satin,
With teeth as sharp as needle-points
He kept to keep him fat in.

His squeak so sharp in the small hours rang
That ever waker wondered;
He trimmed his whiskers stiff as wire,
Had sweethearts by the hundred.

He'd gut a Cheshire cheese with ease,
Plum cake devoured in slices,
Lard, haggis, suet, sausages,
And everything that nice is.

Cork out, he'd dangle down his tail
For oil that was in bottle;
Nothing too sweet, nothing too fat
For Peridarchus' throttle.

He'd dance upon a chimney-pot,
The merry stars a-twinkling;
Or, scampering up a chandelier,
Set all the lustres tinkling.

He'd skip into a pianoforte
To listen how it sounded;
He bored into a butt of wine,
And so was nearly drownded.

At midnight when he sat at meat,
Twelve saucy sonsy maidens,
With bee-sweet voices ditties sang,
Some sad ones, and some gay ones.

For bodyguard he had a score
Of warriors grim and hardy;
They raided every larder round,
From Peebles to Cromàrty.

Grimalkin — deep in dreams she lay,
Comes he, with these gay friskers,
Steals up and gnaws away her claws,
And plucks out all her whiskers.

He scaled a bell-rope where there snored
The Bailiff and his Lady;
Danced on his nose, nibbled her toes,
And kissed the squalling Baby.

A merry life was his, I trow,
Despite it was a short one;
One night he met a mort of rats —
He bared his teeth, and fought one:

A bully ruffian, thrice his size;
But when the conflict ended,
He sighed, 'Alack, my back is broke,
And that can ne'er be mended.'

They laid him lifeless on a bier,
They lapped him up in ermine;
They lit a candle, inches thick,
His Uncle preached the sermon: —

'O Mouseland, mourn for him that's gone,
Our noble Peridarchus!
In valiant fight but yesternight,
And now, alas, a carcass!

'A Hero — Mouse or Man — is one
Who never wails or winces;
Friends, shed a tear for him that's here,
The Princeliest of Princes!'

THE CORNER

Good News to tell!
Oh, mark it well!
Old Mister Jones,
Once all but bones —
There never was
A sight forlorner —
At last, at last,
All danger past,
Has been and gone and
Turned the corner;
And every hour
Is growing younger.

A week ago,
By Almanac,
His long white beard
Went jetty black,
The red into his cheeks
Came back.
His teeth were sharp
And thirty-two,
His faded eyes
A bright bird-blue.
When two-three days
Were scarcely run,
He slips from forty
To twenty-one;
He skips and dances,
Heel and toe;
He couldn't downwards
Quicker grow.
All that he'd learned
Began to go;
His memory melted
Just like snow.

At plump four foot
He burst his stitches,
His trousers dwindled
Back to breeches;
The breeches gone,
There came short clothes,
Two dumpling cheeks,
A button nose,

[430]

A mop of curls,
Ten crinkled toes.
And now as fast
As he is able,
He's nestling down
Into his cradle.

Old Mrs. Jones,
With piping eye,
She rocks, and croons
Him *Hushaby*.
Last Sunday gone,
He turned the corner,
And still grows
Younger, younger, younger . . .
Old Mister Jones.

ALL THE WAY

All the way from Adam
You came, my dear, to me;
The wind upon your cheek
Wafted Noah on the sea,
The daisy in your hand —
Silver petals, stud of gold,—
Just such another starred the grass,
  In Eden, of old.

It's a long, long way to Abel,
And a path of thorns to Cain,
And men less wise than Solomon
Must tread them both again;
But those fountains still are spouting,
And the Serpent twines the bough,
And lovely Eve is sleeping
  In our orchard, *now*.

ME

As long as I live
I shall always be
My Self — and no other,
Just me.

Like a tree —
Willow, elder,
Aspen, thorn,
Or cypress forlorn.

Like a flower,
For its hour —
Primrose, or pink,
Or a violet —
Sunned by the sun,
And with dewdrops wet.

Always just me.
Till the day come on
When I leave this body,
It's all then done,
And the spirit within it
Is gone.

TWO DEEP CLEAR EYES

Two deep clear eyes,
Two ears, a mouth, a nose,
Ten supple fingers,
And ten nimble toes,
Two hands, two feet, two arms, two legs,
And a heart through which love's blessing flows.

Eyes bid ears
Hark:
Ears bid eyes
Mark:
Mouth bids nose
Smell:
Nose says to mouth,
I will:
Heart bids mind
Wonder:
Mind bids heart
Ponder.

Arms, hands, feet, legs,
Work, play, stand, walk;
And a jimp little tongue in a honey-sweet mouth,
With rows of teeth due North and South,
Does nothing but talk, talk, talk.

THE BORDER BIRD

As if a voice had called, I woke,
The world in silence lay;
The winter sun was not yet up,
The moon still in the sky.

A strange sea bird had hither flown,
Out of the last of night,
While yet the Dog Star in the west
Shone palely bright.

His wings came like a *hush* of wind,
His feet were coral red,
No mantling swan has softer down,
No blackcap blacker head.

He lighted on the frozen snow;
Trod here, and there, and then
Lifted his gentle neck and gazed
Up at my window-pane.

[433]

And I, from out of dream, looked down,
This lovely thing to see;
The world a wilderness of white,
Nought living there but he.

Then with a sweet low call, he raised
Dark head and pinions wan,
Swept up into the gold of day,
    Was gone.

TINY EENANENNIKA

Tiny Eenanennika
Was like a little bird;
If the least whisper sounded,
She heard, oh, she heard!
Claw or wing, in bush or brake,
However soft it stirred.

Tiny Eenanennika
Had bright gold hair;
Fair as a field of wheat,
Like sunshine, fair,
Like flame, like gilded water — oh,
Past words to declare!

And every sing-song bird there is,
Titmouse to wren,
In springtime, in nesting-time,
Would watch keep; and when
She chanced to look the other way
Would steal up, and then —

Snip from her shining head
Just one hair, or twain,
A gleaming, glistening, shimmering thread,
And fly off again —
A gossamer of glittering gold,
And flit off again.

AT LAST

A mound in a corner,
A sprinkle of snow
To tell how in summer
The daisies will blow;
And a thorn, a bare thorn
Whereto he may flit —
That lone bird, the redbreast,
To whistle on it;
No warmth but the sun's
Brief wintry red ray,
Ere the dark with all heaven
Wheels cold above day.
I shall stay fast asleep —
This poor dust that I am,
In the plentiful earth,
Naked, just as I came;
With all my strange dreams,
Passions, sorrow, delight,
Like the seed of the wild flowers,
Hid deep out of sight;
Like the song of the bird
In the silence of night.

PIGS

A cock it was, in the stable yard,
That reared its crest with shimmering plume,
And crowed till all the fields around
        Re-echoed in the gloom.

Up got the landlord, and looked out —
'What ails the bird! So shrill he cries!'
How should he dream this farmyard prince
        Was more than earthly wise?

How should he dream that over the bridge
That spans the lilies of Ullone
The Witch of the Woods now winsome rides
        Her milk-white ass upon?

And down she comes with nodding flowers
Into the Inn's cool quietness;
'Heh, bring me butter and honeycomb,
        And I th's house will bless!'

She breaks with finger and with thumb
The waxen honeycomb; she quaffs
Of the sweet buttermilk; and turns —
 Turns to the house and laughs:

'Mimsey and mo, I thirsty was!'
Then looks she on the garden fruits,
Which hung upon the branches green
 Bowed almost to the roots.

'Prythee,' she says, 'my pigs let come
Into your orchard when the moon
Eyes with a red and fiery face
 The harvest of Ullone.'

Says he, 'Small custom comes this way.
Can man make cider out of mast!
With all my apples fattening pigs,
 What's left for me at last?

With all my codlins crunched for ham —'
His rage broke out, his green eyes shone —
'Thou muncher of poor man's honeycomb!
 Begone, thou Witch, begone!'

He frowned upon her waxen cheek,
Her sloe-black eyes, her smooth-drawn hair;
And she looked back, the woeful witch,
 Straddling her saddle there.

She lightly plucked her bridle rein,
She wheeled her milk-white ass aside,
And, stooping in her laughter, turned:
 But not one word replied. . . .

And soon it was the midnight hour;
And large the moon was mounted up
Into the night's dark hollow roof,
 When came her pigs to sup.

They pattered like hailstones over the bridge,
And, like the mandrake, squealed: and soon
In the deep orchard-grasses lay
 No fruit beneath the moon.

[436]

Then cried the landlord, peeping out —
'Oddslife! and I no payment take!' —
And out into the yard he stole,
    His burning ire to slake.

Sticks — sticks he in his knife, plumb-deep. . . .
When, suddenly, like a story told,
Age, like a withered mantle, falls,
    And all things doth enfold.

He sees his Inn a ruin hoar,
Mantled with ivy thick and close,
Wherein a host of fearless birds
    In tumult comes and goes.

He sees his gnarled grey apple trees
Bent like old men, and fruitless all;
He sees a broken bridge lead down
    To a wild waterfall.

And on the hand that holds his knife
Age hath turned white the scattered hairs;
And in his ear a wind makes moan
    In drear and dreamy airs. . . .

Still stoops that green and mantled Inn;
Still o'er the mixen, lank doth range
Old Chanticleer with wattles wan,
    And whoop unearthly strange.

The old fox skulks, more grey than red,
Between the lichen-cankered boles;
And all about the blackened thatch
    The starlings make their holes.

And from a window dense in leaves
And smitten with the first moonbeam,
An owl-face peers, whose real is now
    The sorcery of a dream.

And still, when autumn spiders spin,
And Michael's daisy spreads its mauve,
Out from the gloom of dark Ullone
    Ramp piglings, drove on drove.

Then dwindles one lone ghostly crow;
Hesper a silver arrow flings;
And faint from out of the far-away,
    A snow-white blackbird sings.

[437]

THE SONG OF SEVEN

Far away, and long ago —
May sweet Memory be forgiven!
Came a Wizard in the evening,
And he sang the Song of Seven.
Yes, he plucked his jangling harp-strings
With fingers smooth and even;
And his eyes beneath his dangling hair
Were still as is the sea;
But the Song of Seven has never yet,
One note, come back to me.

The Song of One I know,
A rose its thorns between;

The Song of Two I learned
Where only the birds have been;

The Song of Three I heard
When March was fleet with hares;

The Song of Four was the wind's — the wind's,
Where wheat grew thick with tares;

The Song of Five, ah me!
Lovely the midmost one;

The Song of Six, died out
Before the dream was done. . . .

One — two — three — four — five, six —
And all the grace notes given:
But *widdershins*, and witchery-sweet,
Where is the Song of Seven?

WILL-O'-THE-WISP

'Will-o'-the-Wisp,
Come out of the fen,
And vex no more
Benighted men!'
Pale, blue,
Wavering, wan,
'Will-o'-the-Wisp,
Begone, begone!'

But the trees weep,
The mist-drops hang,
Light dwindles
The bents among.
Oh, and he hovers,
Oh, and he flies,
Will-o'-the-Wisp,
With the baleful eyes.

MERMAIDS

Leagues, leagues over
The sea I sail
Couched on a wallowing
Dolphin's tail:
The sky is on fire
The waves a-sheen;
I dabble my foot
In the billows green.

In a sea-weed hat
On the rocks I sit
Where tern and sea-mew
Glide and beat,
Where dark as shadows
The cormorants meet.

In caverns cool
When the tide's a-wash,
I sound my conch
To the watery splash.

From out their grottoes
At evening's beam
The mermaids swim
With locks agleam

To where I watch
On the yellow sands;
And they pluck sweet music
With sea-cold hands.

[439]

They bring me coral
And amber clear;
But when the stars
In heaven appear
Their music ceases,
They glide away,
And swim to their grottoes
Across the bay.

Then listen only
To my shrill tune
The surfy tide,
And the wandering moon.

THE STORM

First there were two of us, then there were three of us,
Then there was one bird more,
Four of us — wild white sea-birds,
Treading the ocean floor;
And the *wind* rose, and the *sea* rose,
To the angry billows' roar —
With one of us — two of us — three of us — four of us
Sea-birds on the shore.

Soon there were five of us, soon there were nine of us,
And lo! in a trice sixteen!
And the yeasty surf curdled over the sands,
The gaunt grey rocks between;
And the tempest raved, and the lightning's fire
Struck blue on the spindrift hoar —
And on four of us — ay, and on four times four of us
Sea-birds on the shore.

And our sixteen waxed to thirty-two,
And they to past three score —
A wild, white welter of winnowing wings,
And ever more and more;
And the winds lulled, and the sea went down,
And the sun streamed out on high,
Gilding the pools and the spume and the spars
'Neath the vast blue deeps of the sky;

And the isles and the bright green headlands shone,
As they'd never shone before,
Mountains and valleys of silver cloud,
Wherein to swing, sweep, soar —
A host of screeching, scolding, scrabbling
Sea-birds on the shore —
A snowy, silent, sun-washed drift
Of sea-birds on the shore.

GONE

Bright sun, hot sun, oh, to be
Where beats on the restless sea!
To hear the sirens of the deep
Chaunting old Ocean's floods to sleep!
And shadowed wave to sunlit wave
Call from the music-haunted cave!
There, with still eyes, their watch they keep,
While, at horizon mark, a ship,
With cloudlike sails glides slowly on,
    Smalls, vanishes, is gone.

CAW

Ho, ho, ho, ho!
Now old Winter's winds do blow!
Driving down his flocks of snow.
All the fields where daisies were
He has frozen bleak and bare;
Every bush and hedge he decks
With a myriad shining flakes.
Waiting for the sun to rise,
They stand up like hills of ice;
Glisten, gleam, and flame and burn
Every dazzling hue in turn.
Now the farmer's boy he goes,
Scarlet ears, and redder nose,
Whistling as he shuffles by —
A sea of white, a cloudless sky.

Now the hare peeps out to see
What strange wonder this can be;
And the solemn-headed rook,
Perched above his hooded oak,
Hoarsely caws, and shakes the snow
From his sooty wing; and '*Caw!*'
Cries again: 'What have we here,
    Neighbours dear!
The Magician, in one night,
Has changed a world that's green to white!'

THE GHOST CHASE

What sight is this? . . . on dazzling snow,
Cold as a shroud beneath the sky,
Swoop into view, the valley through,
Fox, horsemen, hounds — in soundless cry!
    Hullà! Hullo! Hulla-hoo!

Reynard himself, muzzle to brush,
Is whiter than the crystal track
He races over in the hush
Of woods that cast no rumour back.

The voiceless hounds are white as he;
Huntsman and horse — no scarlet theirs;
No fleck, mark, dapple, or spot to see,
White as the North — horses and mares.

They move as in a dream — no stir,
No hoof-fall, music, tongue or steel —
Swift as a noiseless scimitar
Cutting the snows the winds congeal.

Now they are gone. O dove-white yews!
O sleep-still vale! All silent lies
The calm savanna of the snows,[1]
Beneath the blue of arctic skies!
    Hullà! Hullo! Hulla-hoo!

---

[1] 'The tranquil pasture of the snows,' (*Bells and Grass*, 1941)

NOTHING

*Wh*sst, and away, and over the green,
Scampered a shape that never was seen.
It ran without sound, it ran without shadow,
Never a grass-blade in unmown meadow
Stooped at the thistledown fall of its foot.
I watched it vanish, yet saw it not —
A moment past, it had gazed at me;
Now nought but myself and the spindle tree.
A nothing! — Of air? Of earth? Of sun? —
From emptiness come, into vacancy gone! ...
Whsst, and away, and over the green,
Scampered a shape that never was seen.

SOLITUDE

'Wish! and it's thine!' the changeling piped,
    Shrill from her thorn.
And I with dew-soaked shoes could only
    Stare in return.

High up above me sang the lark,
    Beneath me lay the sea,
Gorse, bramble, rock and whinchat were
    My only company.

Her tiny voice fell faint, and lo,
    Where she had been
Leaned but a few-days-budded rose
    Out of the green.

NEVER

'Take me, or leave me — I'm not thine,'
The fairy mocked on the sands of Lyne —

Frail as Phosphor over the sea:
'Seven long years shalt thou toil for me.'

Full seven I laboured, teen and tine:
But —'Take me, or leave me, I'm not thine!'

[443]

IN THE DYING OF DAYLIGHT[1]

In the dying of the daylight —
With my book, and alone —
Of a sudden my heart
Paused, still as a stone.

I watched, I listened;
There was nothing to hear;
Yet I knew, in the silence,
Some living thing near.

I crept to the staircase,
And stayed — there to see
A child at the window
Who not yet had seen me.

She had stooped her small head,
In the darkening air,
Low over the flowers
In a bowl that was there,

Her chin on their petals;
Her clear, sidelong eyes
Gazing out of the glass
At the light in the skies.

She was not of this earth —
Lost, solitary,
In the stealth of the house
She was sharing with me:

Yet never have I,
Awake, or at night,
Seen in any strange face
So intense a delight;

So hungry a gaze,
Fixed, enraptured and still,
On the green of the grass,
And the light on the hill;

[1] Called 'The Small Phantom' in *Bells and Grass*, 1941.

As if parched up with thirst
For the loved that no more
To a heart, lost to earth,
Earth could ever restore.

And yet — when I turned,
But scarcely had stirred,
At a sound, like the note
Of a late evening bird,
Then looked back — she was gone;
As if she, too, had heard.

THEN AS NOW

Then as Now; and Now as Then,
Spins on this World of Men.
White — Black — Yellow — Red:
They wake, work, eat, play, go to bed.
Black — Yellow — Red — White:
They talk, laugh, weep, dance, morn to night.
Yellow — Red — White — Black:
Sun shines, moon rides, clouds come back.
Red — White — Black — Yellow:
Count your hardest, who could tell o'
The myriads that have come and gone,
Stayed their stay this earth upon,
And vanished then, their labour done?
Sands of the wilderness, stars in heaven,
Solomon could not sum them even:
Then as Now; Now as Then
Still spins on this World of Men.

EEKA, NEEKA

Eeka, Neeka, Leeka, Lee —
Here's a lock without a key;
Bring a lantern, bring a candle,
Here's a door without a handle;
Shine, shine, you old thief Moon,
Here's a door without a room;
Not a whisper, moth or mouse,
Key — lock — door — room: where's the house?

Say nothing, creep away,
And live to knock another day!

[445]

A LANTERN

A lantern lighted me to bed
  Because I had no candle;
Across the frozen fields it shone
  And danced upon the Wandle.

Cock robin in the icy hedge,
  Nor blackbird, bill in feather,
Nor snail tucked snug in close-shut house
  Will ever now know whether

A lantern lighted me to bed,
  Because I had no candle,
And from my frozen window-pane
  Beamed clean across the Wandle.

THE STRANGER

A little after twilight,
When the Bear was high in heaven,
And Venus in her beauty
Stood shining in the even;
Still and hushed was the dell
And she came like a flame —
A Stranger, clad in cramoisy,
And danced in the same.

Dew wells not more quietly,
More softly doth shine,
She danced till her cheek
Was red as red wine,
Light like a little taper
Burned small in her eye;
Like snow, like waterdrops, her feet
Twirled softly by.

Not a sound. Not a bird
Stirred a soft folded wing,
While deep in the woodland
She only did sing
Who hath night for her arbour,
For playmate the moon,
And a brook for babbling music there,
Murmuring alone.

Hours scattered their dust,
Night wanned and drew on
A veil of pale silver,
And lo, it was dawn!
Green, green glowed the dell,
And the leaves over, green:
But where was She in cramoisy
Who'd danced in the same?

I DREAM OF A PLACE

I dream of a place where I long to live always:
Green hills, shallow sand dunes, and nearing the sea;

The house is of stone; there are twelve lattice windows,
And a door, with a keyhole — though lost is the key.

Thick-thatched is the roof; it has low, white-washed chimneys,
Where doves preen their wings, and coo, *Please*, love: love *me*!

There martins are flitting; the sun shines; the moon shines;
Drifts of bright flowers are adrone with the bee;

And a wonderful music of bird-song at daybreak
Wells up from the bosom of every tree.

A brook of clear water encircles the garden,
With kingcups, and cress, and the white *fleur de lys* —

Moorhens and dabchicks; the wild duck at evening
Wing away to the sun, in the shape of a V;

And the night shows the stars, shining in at the windows,
Brings nearer the far-away sigh of the sea.

Oh, the quiet, the green of the grass, the grey willows,
The light, and the shine, and the air sweet and free! —

That dream of a place where I long to live always:[1]
Low hills, shallow sand dunes — at peace there to be!

[1] These lines do not appear in the original.
  The following lines appear at this point instead:
    'I would toil for a lifetime, my heart never weary,
    If at last, with one loved, there at peace I might be.'
                                    (*Bells and Grass*, 1941)

THE HOUSE OF DREAM

Candle, candle, burning clear,
Now the House of Dream draws near;
See what shadowy flowers move
The solitary porch above;
Hark, how still it is within,
Though so many guests go in.

No faint voice will answer make
While thy tapering flame's awake.
Candle, candle, burning low,
It is time for me to go.
Music, faint and distant, wells
From those far-off dales and dells.

Now in shoes of silence I
Stand by the walls of witchery;
Out then, earthly flame, for see,
Sleep's unlatched her door to me.

GONE

Where's the Queen of Sheba?
Where King Solomon?
Gone with Boy Blue who looks after the sheep,
Gone and gone and gone.

Lovely is the sunshine;
Lovely is the wheat;
Lovely the wind from out of the clouds
Having its way with it.

Rise up, Old Green-stalks!
Delve deep, Old Corn!
But where's the Queen of Sheba?
Where King Solomon?

KNOWN OF OLD

'I dream, and I dream. . . .'

'Speak! what do you dream?'

'That I see Phantoms walking,
Translucent as flame,
In a place, known of old,
Though now lost is its name —
A place of a peace
So profound that I seem
As serenely at rest
As a leaf on stream. —
I dream, and I dream. . . .

'Yet no strangers are these
Who in ecstasy stray
Where the moon high in heaven,
Shines open as day.
Their robes are of light,
And each calm solemn face,
In the crystalline night,
Of grief shows no trace,
But shines with the joy
Of an infinite grace.
So, with gladness I weep,
As in rapture and silence,
Aloof, and yet near me,
They move in my sleep;
And their voices repeat
Words ancient and sweet —
A rune once I knew,
But, alas, now forget,
A rune known of old
Which, alas, I forget.—
I dream, and I dream . . .

'And that is my dream.'

UNDER THE ROSE

The Song of the Wanderer

Nobody, nobody told me
What nobody, nobody knows:
But now I know where the Rainbow ends,
I know where there grows
A Tree that's called the Tree of Life,
I know where there flows
The River of All-Forgottenness,
And where the Lotus blows,
And I — I've trodden the forest, where
In flames of gold and rose,
To burn, and then arise again,
    The Phoenix goes.

Nobody, nobody told me
What nobody, nobody knows:
Hide thy face in a veil of light,
Put on thy silver shoes,
Thou art the Stranger I know best,
Thou art the sweet heart, who
Came from the Land between Wake and Dream,
Cold with the morning dew.

Collected Rhymes and Verses (1944)

KINGS

King Canute
   Sat down by the sea,
Up washed the tide
   And away went he.

Good King Alfred
   Cried, 'My sakes!
Not five winks,
   And look at those cakes!'

Lackland John
   Were a right royal Tartar
Till he made his mark
   Upon *Magna Carta*:

Ink, seal, table,
   On Runnymede green,
Anno Domini
   12–15.

NOON

Few and faint a bird's small notes
Stirred on the air and died away
Among the wind-enticing leaves;
And everywhere the crimson may
Lapped in the sun-sweet silence bloomed;
And, lost in lovely reverie,
A mirrored swan upon a pool
Floated beneath a willow tree.

The Burning-Glass and Other Poems
(1945)

A PORTRAIT

Old: yet unchanged; — still pottering in his thoughts;
Still eagerly enslaved by books and print;
Less plagued, perhaps, by rigid musts and oughts,
But no less frantic in vain argument;

Still happy as a child, with its small toys,
Over his inkpot and his bits and pieces, —
Life's arduous, fragile and ingenuous joys,
Whose charm failed never — nay, it even increases!

Ev'n happier in watch of bird or flower,
Rainbow in heaven, or bud on thorny spray,
A star-strewn nightfall, and that heart-break hour
Of sleep-drowsed senses between dawn and day;

Loving the light — laved eyes in those wild hues! —
And dryad twilight, and the thronging dark;
A Crusoe ravished by mere solitude —
And silence — edged with music's faintest *Hark!*

And any chance-seen face whose loveliness
Hovers, a mystery, between dream and real;
Things usual yet miraculous that bless
And overwell a heart that still can feel;

Haunted by questions no man answered yet;
Pining to leap from A clean on to Z;
Absorbed by problems which the wise forget;
Avid for fantasy — yet how staid a head!

Senses at daggers with his intellect;
Quick, stupid; vain, retiring; ardent, cold;
Faithful and fickle; rash and circumspect;
And never yet at rest in any fold;

Punctual at meals; a spendthrift, close as Scot;
Rebellious, tractable, childish — long gone grey!
Impatient, volatile, tongue wearying not —
Loose, too: which, yet, thank heaven, was taught to pray;

'Childish' indeed! — a waif on shingle shelf
Fronting the rippled sands, the sun, the sea;
And nought but his marooned precarious self
For questing consciousness and will-to-be;

A feeble venturer — in a world so wide!
So rich in action, daring, cunning, strife!
You'd think, poor soul, he had taken Sloth for bride, —
Unless the imagined is the breath of life;

Unless to speculate bring virgin gold,
And *Let's-pretend* can range the seven seas,
And dreams are not mere tales by idiot told,
And tongueless truth may hide in fantasies;

Unless the alone may their own company find,
And churchyards harbour phantoms 'mid their bones,
And even a daisy may suffice a mind
Whose bindweed can redeem a heap of stones;

Too frail a basket for so many eggs —
Loose-woven: Gosling? cygnet? Laugh or weep?
Or is the cup at richest in its dregs?
The actual realest on the verge of sleep?

One yet how often the prey of doubt and fear,
Of bleak despondence, stark anxiety;
Ardent for what is neither now nor here,
An Orpheus fainting for Eurydice;

Not yet inert, but with a tortured breast
At hint of that bleak gulf — his last farewell;
Pining for peace, assurance, pause and rest,
Yet slave to what he loves past words to tell;

A foolish, fond old man, his bed-time nigh,
Who still at western window stays to win
A transient respite from the latening sky,
And scarce can bear it when the Sun goes in.

IN THE LOCAL MUSEUM

They stood — rain pelting at window, shrouded sea —
Tenderly hand in hand, too happy to talk;
And there, its amorous eye intent on me,
Plautus impennis, the extinct Great Auk.

THE RAPIDS

Grieve must my heart. Age hastens by.
No longing can stay Time's torrent now.
Once would the sun in eastern sky
Pause on the solemn mountain's brow.
Rare flowers he still to bloom may bring,
But day approaches evening;
And ah, how swift their withering!

The birds, that used to sing, sang then
As if in an eternal day;
Ev'n sweeter yet their grace notes, when
Farewell . . . farewell is theirs to say.
Yet, as a thorn its drop of dew
Treasures in shadow, crystal clear,
All that I loved I love anew,
    Now parting draweth near.

ARIEL

Ariel! Ariel! —
But the glittering moon
Sank to the curve of the world,
Down, down:
And the curlew cried,
And the nightjar stirred in her rest,
And Ariel on the cool high steep of heaven
Leaned his breast.

Ariel! Ariel! —
His curv'd wings whist,
With the bliss of the star-shaking breeze
'Gainst his pinions prest.
Lower the great globe
Rolled her icy snows:
Lone is the empty dark, and the moonless heart
When the Bright One goes.

[455]

THE SUMMONS

'What bodiless bird so wildly sings,
Albeit from no earthly tree?
Whence rise again those Phoenix wings
To waken from prolonged unease —
Isle of the Lost Hesperides!
    A self long strange to me?'

'Red coral in the sea may shine,
And rock-bound Sirens, half divine,
Seduced Ulysses: but to find
Music as rare as childhood's thrush
Yet lorn as curlew's at the hush
    Of dewfall in the mind!'

'O shallow questioner! Know you not
That notes like these, sad, urgent, sweet,
Call from an Egypt named the heart,
Which with a deeper life doth beat
Than any wherein thought hath part;
And of whose wisdom, Love knows well,
    Only itself could tell?'

A DULL BOY

'Work?' Well, not *work* — this stubborn desperate quest
To conjure life, love, wonder into words;
Far happier songs than any me have blest
Were sung, at ease, this daybreak by the birds.

I watch with breathless envy in her glass
The dreamlike beauty of the silent swan;
As mute a marvel is the bladed grass
Springing to life again, June's sickle gone.

What music could be mine compared with that
The idling wind woos from the sand-dune's bent?
What meaning deeper than the smile whereat
A burning heart conceives the loved intent?

'And what did'st *thou*' . . . I see the vaulted throng,
The listening heavens in that dread array
Fronting the Judge to whom all dooms belong:—
Will the lost child in me cry bravely, 'Play'?

[456]

TWO GARDENS

Two gardens see! — this, of enchanted flowers,
Strange to the eye, and more than earthly-sweet;
Small rivulets running, song-reëchoing bowers;
And green-walled pathways which, ere parting, meet;
And there a lion-like sun in heaven's delight
Breathes plenitude from dayspring to the night.

The other: — walls obscure, and chaces of trees,
Ilex and yew, and dream-enticing dark,
Hid pools, moths, creeping odours, silentness,
Luna its deity, and its watchward, *Hark!*
A still and starry mystery, wherein move
Phantoms of ageless wonder and of love.

Two gardens for two children — in one mind:
But ah, how seldom open now their gates I find!

NOSTALGIA[1]

In the strange city of life
A house I know full well —
That wherein Silence a refuge has,
Where Dark doth dwell.

Gable and roof it stands,
Fronting the dizzied street,
Where Vanity flaunts her gilded booths
In the noontide glare and heat.

Green-graped upon its walls
Earth's ancient hoary vine
Clusters the carven lichenous stone
With tendril serpentine.

[1] A different earlier version called 'The Two Houses' appears on p. 216.

Deafened, incensed, dismayed,
Dazed in the clamorous throng,
I thirst for the soundless fount that rills
As if from my inmost heart, and fills
The stillness with its song.

As yet I knock in vain:
Nor yet what is hidden can tell;
Where Silence perpetual vigil keeps,
Where Dark doth dwell.

THE SECRET

I bless the hand that once held mine,
The lips that said:
'No heart, though kiss were Circe's wine,
Can long be comforted.'

Ay, though we talked the long day out
Of all life marvels at,
One thing the soul can utter not,
Or self to self relate.

We gazed, enravished, you and I,
Like children at a flower;
But speechless stayed, past even a sigh . . .
Not even Babel Tower

Heard language strange and close enough
To tell that moment's peace,
Where broods the Phoenix, timeless Love,
And divine silence is.

WINTER COMPANY

Blackbird silent in the snow;
Motionless crocus in the mould;
Naked tree; and, cold and low,
Sun's wintry gold . . .
Lost for the while in their strange beauty — self how far! —
Lulled were my senses into a timeless dream;
As if the inmost secret of what they are
Lay open in what they seem.

THE SOLITARY BIRD

Why should a bird in that solitary hollow
    Flying from east to west
Seem in the silence of the snow-blanched sunshine
    Gilding the valley's crest
Envoy and symbol of a past within me
    Centuries now at rest?

Shallowly arched the horizon looms beyond it,
    Turquoise green and blue;
Not even a whisper irks the magic of the evening
    The narrowing valley through;
No faintest echo brings a syllable revealing
    The secret once I knew:
Down *whsts* the snow again, cloud masks the
    sunshine —
    Bird gone, and memory too.

AND SO TO BED

'Night-night, my Precious!'; '*Sweet* dreams, Sweet!'
'Heaven bless you, Child!'— the accustomed grown-ups said.
Two eyes gazed mutely back that none could meet,
Then turned to face Night's terrors overhead.

ISRAFEL

To Alec McLaren
1940

Sleepless I lay, as the grey of dawn
Through the cold void street stole into the air,
When, in the hush, a solemn voice
Pealed suddenly out in Connaught Square.

Had I not heard notes wild as these
A thousand times in childhood ere
This chill March daybreak they awoke
The echoing walls of Connaught Square,

[459]

I might have imagined a seraph — strange
In such bleak days! — had deigned to share,
For joy and love, the haunts of man —
An Israfel in Connaught Square!

Not that this singer eased the less
A human heart surcharged with care —
Merely a blackbird, London-bred,
Warbling of Spring in Connaught Square!

It was the contrast with a world
Of darkness, horror, grief, despair,
Had edged with an irony so sharp
That rapturous song in Connaught Square.

HARVEST HOME

A bird flies up from the hayfield;
Sweet, to distraction, is the new-mown grass:
But I grieve for its flowers laid low at noonday —
    And only this poor *Alas!*

I grieve for War's innocent lost ones —
The broken loves, the mute goodbye,
The dread, the courage, the bitter end,
The shaken faith, the glazing eye?

O bird, from the swathes of that hayfield —
The rancid stench of the grass!
And a heart stricken mute by that Harvest Home —
    And only this poor *Alas!*

THE UNUTTERABLE
September 1940

What! jibe in ignorance, and scold
The Muses when, the earth in flame,
They hold their peace, and leave untolled
Ev'n Valour's deathless requiem?

Think you a heart in misery,
Riven with pity, dulled with woe,
Could weep in song its threnody,
And to such tombs with chaunting go?

Think you that all-abandoning deeds
Of sacrifice by those whose love
Must barren lie in widow's weeds,
Gone all their youth was dreaming of,

Can be revealed in words? Alas!
No poet yet in Fate's dark count
Has ever watched Night dread as this,
Or seen such evils to surmount.

We stand aghast. Pride, rapture, grief
In storm within; on fire to bless
The daybreak; but yet wiser if
We bide that hour in silentness.

THE SPECTACLE

Scan with calm bloodshot eyes the world around us,
Its broken stones, its sorrows! No voice could tell
The toll of the innocent crucified, weeping and wailing,
In this region of torment ineffable, flame and derision —
      What wonder if we believe no longer in Hell?

            And Heaven? That daybreak vision?
In the peace of our hearts we learn beyond shadow of
      doubting
That our dream of this vanished kingdom lies sleeping
      within us;
Its gates are the light we have seen in the hush of the
      morning,
When the shafts of the sunrise break in a myriad
      splendours;
Its shouts of joy are those of all earthly creatures,
Their primal and innocent language — the song of the
      birds:
Thrush in its rapture, ecstatic wren, and wood-dove
      tender,
Calling on us poor mortals to put our praise into words.

Passionate, sorrowful hearts, too — the wise, the true
    and the gentle;
Minds that outface all fear, defy despair, remain faithful,
Endure in silence, hope on, assured in their selfless
    courage,
Natural and sweet in a love no affliction or doubt could
    dispel.
If, as a glass reflecting its range, we have these for our
    guidance,
If, as our love creates beauty, we exult in that transient
    radiance,
This is the garden of paradise which in our folly
        We abandoned long ages gone.

Though, then, the wondrous divine were ev'n nebulae-
    distant,
The little we make of our all is our earthly heaven.
        Else we are celled in a darkness,
Windowless, doorless, alone.

AN ISLAND

Parched, panting, he awoke; phantasmal light
Blueing the hollows of his fevered eyes;
And strove to tell of what he had dreamed that night —
In stumbling words its meaning to devise: —

An island, lit with beauty, like a flower
Its sea of sapphire fringed with ocean's snow,
Whose music and beauty with the changing hour
Seemed from some inward source to ebb and flow;
A heart, all innocence and innately wise,
Well-spring of very love appeared to be —
'A candle whose flame', he stammered, 'never dies,
But feeds on light itself perpetually.
Me! This! A thing corrupt on the grave's cold brink,
And into outer darkness soon to sink!'

The tired nurse yawned. 'A strange dream that!' she said.
'But now you are awake. And see, it's day!'
She smoothed the pillow for his sweat-dark head,
Smiled, frowned; 'There, sleep again!'— and turned away.

[462]

THE SCARECROW

In the abandoned orchard — on a pole,
The rain-soaked trappings of that scarecrow have
Usurped the semblance of a man — poor soul —
    Haled from a restless grave.

Geese for his company this fog-bound noon,
He eyeless stares. And I with eyes reply.
Lifting a snakelike head, the gander yelps
    '*Ware!*' at the passer-by.

It is as though a few bedraggled rags
Poised in this wintry waste were lure enough
To entice some aimless phantom here to mime
    All it is image of . . .

Once Man in grace divine all beauty was;
And of his bone God made a lovelier Eve;
Now even the seraphs sleep at sentry-go;
    The swine break in to thieve

Wind-fallen apples from the two old Trees.
Oh see, Old Adam, once of Eden! Alas!
How is thy beauty fallen: fallen thine Eve,
    Who did all life surpass!

Should in the coming nightfall the Lord God,
Goose-challenged, call, 'My Creature, where art *thou*?'
Scarecrow of hate and vengeance, wrath and blood,
    What would'st thou answer now?

THE BURNING-GLASS

No map shows my Jerusalem,
    No history my Christ;
Another language tells of them,
    A hidden evangelist.

Words may create rare images
    Within their narrow bound;
'Twas speechless childhood brought me these,
    As music may, in sound.

[463]

Yet not the loveliest song that ever
   Died on the evening air
Could from my inmost heart dissever
   What life had hidden there.

It is the blest reminder of
   What earth in shuddering bliss
Nailed on a cross — that deathless Love —
   Through all the eternities.

I am the Judas whose perfidy
   Sold what no eye hath seen,
The rabble in dark Gethsemane,
   And Mary Magdalene.

To very God who day and night
   Tells me my sands out-run,
I cry in misery infinite,
   'I am thy long-lost son.'

EDGES

Think you your heart is safely at rest,
Contemptuous, calm, disdainful one?
Maybe a stone is in your breast
   From whence all motion's gone.

Undauntable soldier, vent no scorn
On him who in terror faced the foe;
There is a radiant core of rapture
   None but the fearful know.

And you, sweet poet? Heaven might kiss
The miracles you dreamed to do;
But waste not your soul on self-sought bliss,
   Since no such dream comes true.

SWIFTS

1943

No; they are only birds — swifts, in the loft of the morning,
Coursing, disporting, courting, in the pale-blue arc of the
    sky.
There is no venom for kin or for kind in their wild-winged
    archery,
Nor death in their innocent droppings as fleet in their
    mansions they fly;
Swooping, with flicker of pinion to couple, the loved with the
    loved one,
Never with malice or hate, in their vehement sallies
    through space.
Listen! that silken rustle, as they charge on their beehive
    houses,
Fashioned of dried-up mud daubed each in its chosen place.
Hunger — not fear — sharps the squawk of their featherless
    nestlings;
From daybreak into the dark their circuitings will not cease:
How beautiful they! — and the feet on earth's heavenly
    mountains
Of him that bringeth good tidings, proclaimeth the gospel of
    peace!

THE VISITANT

A little boy leaned down his head
    Upon his mother's knee;
'Tell me the old, old tale', he said,
    'You told last night to me.'

It was in dream. For when at dawn
    She woke, and raised her head,
Still haunted her sad face forlorn
    The beauty of the dead.

THE FIELD

Yes, there was once a battle here:
There, where the grass takes on a shade
Of paradisal green, sun-clear —
    There the last stand was made.

[465]

LULLAY

'Now lullay, my sweeting,
What hast thou to fear?
It is only the wind
In the willows we hear,
And the sigh of the waves
By the sand dunes, my dear.
Stay thy wailing. Let sleep be
Thy solace, thou dear;
And dreams that shall charm
From that cheek every tear.
See, see, I am with thee
No harm can come near.
Sleep, sleep, then, my loved one,
My lorn one, my dear!' ...

I heard that far singing
With pining oppressed,
When grief for one absent
My bosom distressed,
When the star of the evening
Was low in the West.
And I mused as I listened,
With sorrow oppressed,
Would that heart were *my* pillow,
That safety my rest!
Ah, would I could slumber —
A child laid to rest —
Could abide but a moment
Assoiled, on that breast,
While the planet of evening
Sinks low in the west:
Could wake, and dream on,
At peace and at rest;
Ere fall the last darkness,
When silence is best.

For alas, love is mortal;
And night must come soon;
And another, yet deeper,
When — no more to roam —
The lost one within me
Shall find its long home,
In a sleep none can trouble,
The hush of the tomb.

Cold, sombre, eternal,
Dark, narrow that room;
But no grief, no repining
Will deepen its gloom;
Though of voice, once adored,
Not an echo can come;
Of hand, brow, and cheek,
My rapture and doom,
Once my all, and adored,
No least phantom can come. . . .

'Now lullay, my sweeting,
There is nothing to fear.
It is only the wind
In the willows we hear,
And the sigh of the waves
On the sand dunes, my dear.
Stay thy wailing. Let sleep be
Thy solace, thou dear;
And dreams that shall charm
From that cheek every tear.
See, see, I am with thee,
No harm can come near.
Sleep, sleep, then, my loved one,
My lorn one, my dear!'

THE CHART[1]

That mute small face, but twelve hours here,
Maps secrets stranger than the seas',
In hieroglyphics more austere,
And wiser far than Rameses'.

TO A CANDLE

Burn stilly, thou; and come with me.
I'll screen thy rays. Now . . . Look, and see,
Where, like a flower furled,
Sealed from this busy world,
Tranquil brow, and lid, and lip,
One I love lies here asleep.

[1] As printed in *Inward Companion*, 1950.

Low upon her pillow is
A head of such strange loveliness —
Gilded-brown, unwoven hair —
That dread springs up to see it there:
Lest so profound a trance should be
Death's momentary alchemy.

Venture closer, then. Thy light
Be little day to this small night!
Fretting through her lids it makes
The lashes stir on those pure cheeks;
The scarcely-parted lips, it seems,
Pine, but in vain, to tell her dreams.

Every curve and hollow shows
In faintest shadow — mouth and nose;
Pulsing beneath the silken skin
The milk-blue blood rills out and in:
A bird's might be that slender bone,
Magic itself to ponder on.

Time hath spread its nets in vain;
The child she was is home again;
Veiled with Sleep's seraphic grace.
How innocent yet how wise a face!
Mutely entreating, it seems to sigh, —
'Love made me. It is only I.

'Love made this house wherein there dwells
A thing divine, and homeless else.
Not mine the need to ponder why
In this sweet prison I exult and sigh.
Not mine to bid you hence. God knows
It was for joy he shaped the rose.'

See, she stirs. A hand at rest
Slips from above that gentle breast,
White as winter-mounded snows,
Summer-sweet as that wild rose . . .
Thou lovely thing! Ah, welladay!
Candle, I dream. Come, come away!

SAFETY FIRST

Do not mention this young child's beauty as he stands there
    gravely before you;
Whisper it not, lest there listeners be. Beware, the evil eye!
Only as humming-bird, quaffing the delicate glory
Of the flow'r that it lives by — gaze: yes, but make no reply
To the question, What is it? Whence comes it, this innocent
    marvel?
Those features past heart to dissever from the immanent truth
    they imply?
No more than the star of the morning its image in reflex can
    ponder
Can he tell of, delight in, this beauty and promise. Oh, sigh of
    a sigh;
Be wise! Let your love through thought's labyrinths happily
    wander;
Let your silence its intricate praises, its gratitude squander;
But of speech, not a word: just a smile. Beware of the evil
    eye!

THE BLIND BOY

A spider her silken gossamer
In the sweet sun began to wind;
The boy, alone in the window-seat,
    Saw nought of it. He was blind.

By a lustre of glass a slender ray
Was shattered into a myriad tints —
Violet, emerald, primrose, red —
    Light's exquisite finger-prints.

Unmoved, his face in the shadow stayed,
Rapt in a reverie mute and still.
The ray stole on; but into that mind
    No gem-like atom fell.

It paused to ponder upon a moth,
Snow-hooded, delicate past belief,
Drowsing, a spelican from his palm . . .
    O child of tragedy — if

[469]

Only a moment you might gaze out
On this all-marvellous earth we share! . . .
A smile stole into the empty eye,
    And features fair,

As if an exquisite whisper of sound,
Of source as far in time and space,
And, no less sovran than light, had found
    Its recompense in his face.

THE TOMTIT

Twilight had fallen, austere and grey,
The ashes of a wasted day,
When, tapping at the window-pane,
My visitor had come again,
To peck late supper at his ease —
A morsel of suspended cheese.

What ancient code, what Morse knew he —
This eager little mystery —
That, as I watched, from lamp-lit room,
Called on some inmate of my heart to come
Out of its shadows — filled me then
With love, delight, grief, pining, pain,
Scarce less than had he angel been?

Suppose, such countenance as that,
Inhuman, deathless, delicate,
Had gazed this winter moment in —
Eyes of an ardour and beauty no
Star, no Sirius could show!

Well, it were best for such as I
To shun direct divinity;
Yet not stay heedless when I heard
The tip-tap nothings of a tiny bird.

THE OWL

Owl of the wildwood I:
Muffled in sleep I drowse,
Where no fierce sun in heaven
Can me arouse.

My haunt's a hollow
In a half-dead tree,
Whose strangling ivy
Shields and shelters me.

But when dark's starlight
Thrids my green domain,
My plumage trembles and stirs,
I wake again:

A spectral moon
Silvers the world I see;
Out of their daylong lairs
Creep thievishly

Night's living things.
Then I,
Wafted away on soundless pinions
Fly;
Curdling her arches
With my hunting-cry:

A-hooh! a-hooh:
Four notes; and then,
Solemn, sepulchral, cold,
Four notes again,
The listening dingles
Of my woodland through:
A-hooh! A-hooh! —
    A-hooh!

ONCE

Once would the early sun steal in through my eastern
    window,
        A sea of time ago;
Tracing a stealthy trellis of shadow across the pictures
        With his gilding trembling glow;
Brimming my mind with rapture, as though of some
    alien spirit,
        In those eternal hours
I spent with my self as a child; alone, in a world of
    wonder —
        Air, and light and flowers;
Tenderness, longing, grief, intermingling with bodiless
    beings
        Shared else with none:
How would desire flame up in my soul; with what
    passionate yearning
        As the rays stole soundlessly on! —
Rays such as Rembrandt adored, such as dwell on the
    faces of seraphs,
        Wings-folded, solemn head,
Piercing the mortal with sorrow past all
    comprehension. . . .

        Little of that I read
In those shadowy runes in my bedroom. But one wild
    notion
        Made my heart with tears overflow —
The knowledge that love unsought, unspoken,
    unshared, unbetokened,
        Had mastered me through and through:
And yet — the children we are! — that naught of its
    ardour and beauty
        Even the loved should know.

A RECLUSE

Here lies (where all at peace may be)
A lover of mere privacy.
Graces and gifts were his; now none
Will keep him from oblivion;
How well they served his hidden ends
Ask those who knew him best, his friends.

He is dead; but even among the quick
This world was never his candlestick.
He envied none; he was content
With self-inflicted banishment.
'Let your light shine!' was never his way:
What then remains but, Welladay!

And yet his very silence proved
How much he valued what he loved.
There peered from his hazed, hazel eyes
A self in solitude made wise;
As if within the heart may be
All the soul needs for company:
And, having that in safety there,
Finds its reflection everywhere.

Life's tempests must have waxed and waned:
The deep beneath at peace remained.
Full tides that silent well may be
Mark of no less profound a sea.
Age proved his blessing. It had given
The all that earth implies of heaven;
And found an old man reconciled
To die, as he had lived, a child.

'PHILIP'

A flattened orb of water his,
  Pent in by brittle glass
Through which his little jet-black eyes
  Observe what comes to pass:
I watch him, but how hard it is
  To estimate his size.

The further off he fins away
  The larger he appears,
And, having wheeled and turned about,
Grows smaller as he nears!
The Great, we lesser folk agree,
Suffer from like propinquity.

But great and small like Philip swim
In shallow waters, clear or dim;
  And few seem fully aware
Whose bounty scatters ants' eggs there;
And all — O Universe! — poor souls,
Remain cooped up in finite bowls;
Whose psychic confines are, alas,
  Seldom as clear as glass.

What truth, then, from the vast Beyond
Is theirs (in so minute a pond)
Concerning Space, or Space-*plus*-Time,
Or metaphysics more sublime,
Eludes, I fear, poor Philip's rhyme.

STILL LIFE

Bottle, coarse tumbler, loaf of bread,
Cheap paper, a lean long kitchen knife:
No moral, no problem, sermon, or text,
No hint of a Why, Whence, Whither, or If;
Mere workaday objects put into paint —
Bottle and tumbler, loaf and knife. . . .
And engrossed, round-spectacled Chardin's
    Passion for life.

THE OUTCASTS

*The Brazen Trompe of iron-wingèd fame
That mingleth truth with forgèd lies*

Grunting, he paused. Dead-cold the balustrade.
Full-flood the river flowed, and black as night.
Amorphous bundle poised, he listening stayed,
Then peered, pushed, stooped, and watched it out of sight.

A faint, far plunge — and silence. Then the *whirr*
Menacing, stealthy, of a vast machine.
Midnight; but still the city was astir,
And clock to clock announced the old routine.

Trembling and fevered, light of heart and head,
He turned to hasten away; but stayed — to stare:
A paint-daubed woman bound for lonely bed,
Wide mouth, and sluggish gaze, and tinsel hair,

Stood watching him. 'That's that,' she said, and laughed.
'The dead — they tell no tales. Nor living *might*.
Nor need good money talk . . . What's more,' she chaffed,
'Much better out of mind what's out of sight.

'*And — who?*' she added, shrugging, with a nod,
Callous and cold, towards the granite shelf.
'Not for the first time have I wished, by God,
That I had long since gone that way myself!' . . .

His puke-stained face twitched upwards in a smile.
'My friend,' he said, 'behold one who at last
From lifelong bondage is now freed a while.
The sack you saw contained, in fact, my Past.

'I was a writer — and of some repute,
(Candour, just now of all times, nothing burkes) —
Fiction, *belles lettres*; and I twanged the lute;
Yes, added poesy to my other works.

'Year after year the burden grew apace;
Fame, that old beldame, shared my bed and board;
No Christian, in his pilgrimage to grace,
Bore on his back a burden so abhorred.

[475]

'"What was she?" Chiefly of mere fantasy made;
Seeming divine, but Lamia accursed.
She cared no more for me, insidious jade,
Than drunkard needs for quickening his thirst.

'Fattened on praise, she like a vampire sat,
Sucking my life-blood, having slain my youth;
And on her hated body I begat
Twenty abortions, but not one called Truth.

'Not, mind you, friend, it ever seemed that I
Spared of my sweat to conjure from my ink
What one might hope time would not falsify —
The most my heart could feel, my poor mind think.

'And yet by slow sour torturing degree
There crept the vile conviction in that I —
Victim of heinous anthropophagy —
Lived on my Self, as spider lives on fly.

'Ay, and that madam, sprawling in my sheets,
Vain beyond hell, a pride that knew no ebb,
Mistress, by Satan taught, of all deceits,
Never ceased weaving her mephitic web.

'At my last gasp, my door one midnight stirred.
There showed a face there, tranquil as a dove.
As if a dream had spoken — yet no word:
With some lost ghost in me I fell in love . . .

'There came this moonless night. And, see, high tide! . . .
They say when Nature brings to fruitage twins —
At jutting thigh, at spine, or elsewise tied —
And one to'rds death his pilgrimage begins,

'Severance ends both. And that may be my fate.
But now,' the grey face paled, the thin voice broke,
'I am at peace again. Myself — though late;
My last days freed from an atrocious yoke . . .'

The painted woman stared. Her glittering eyes
Weasel-wise watched him; then, to left and right,
Under the dull lead pallor of the skies,
Searched the dark bridge — but not a soul in sight . . .

ARROGANCE

I saw bleak Arrogance, with brows of brass,
Clad nape to sole in shimmering foil of lead,
Stark down his nose he stared; a crown of glass
Aping the rainbow, on his tilted head.

His very presence drained the vital air;
He sate erect — stone-cold, self-crucified;
On either side of him an empty chair;
And sawdust trickled from his wounded side.

LIKE SISTERS

There is a thicket in the wild
By waters deep and dangerous,
Where — close as loveless sisters — grow
Nightshade and the convolvulus.

Tangled and clambering, stalk and stem,
Its tendrils twined against the sun,
The bindweed has a heart-shaped leaf,
Nightshade a triple-pointed one.

The one bears petals pure as snow —
A beauty lingering but a day;
The other's, violet and gold,
Into bright berries shed away;

And these a poisonous juice distil.
Yet both are lovely too — as might
Those rival hostile sisters be:
Different as day is from the night
When darkness is its dead delight; —
As love is from unchastity.

THE DITCH

Masked by that brilliant weed's deceitful green,
No glint of the dark water can be seen
Which, festering, slumbers, with this scum for screen.

It is as though a face, as false as fair,
Dared not, by smiling, show the evil there.

[477]

THE DEAD JAY

A witless, pert, bedizened fop,
  Man scoffs, resembles you:
Fate levels all — voice harsh or sweet —
  Ringing the woodlands through:
But, O, poor hapless bird, that broken death-stilled wing,
  That miracle of blue!

LAID LOW

Nought else now stirring my sick thoughts to share,
Laid low, I watched the house-flies in the air;
Swarthy, obscene, they angled, gendering there.
And Death, who every daybreak now rode by —
Dust-muffled hoofs, lank animal, and he —
A mocking adept in telepathy,
Jerked in his saddle, and laughed into the sky ...

'Where is this Blind Man's stable? Where, his grain?
What starved fowls peck his cobblestones between?
Where stews his hothouse? Why must shut remain
His iron-hinged door to those who may not bide —
As welcome guests may — for one night, then go?
What lacqueys they who at the windows hide?
And whose that scarce-heard traipsing to and fro?

Façade! — that reeks of nightmare-dread and gloom!
Dwale, henbane, hemlock in its courtyard bloom;
Dumb walls; the speechless silence of the tomb.
No smoke its clustered chimney-shafts emit;
No taper stars at attic window-pane;
Who enters, enters once — comes not again;
A vigilant vacancy envelops it....'

So chattered boding to a menaced bed;
While in the east earth's sunrise broadened out.
Its pale light gilt the ceiling. My heart said,
'Nay, there is nought to fear'— yet shook with dread:
Wept, 'Call him back!': groaned, 'Ah! that eyeless head!'
Impassioned by its beauty; sick with doubt: —
'Oh God, give life!' and, 'Would that I were dead!'

EUREKA

Lost in a dream last night was I.
I dreamed that, from this earth set free,
In some remote futurity
I had reached the place prepared for me.

A vault, it seemed, of burnished slate,
Whose planes beyond the pitch of sight
Converged — unswerving, immaculate —
Bathed in a haze of blinding light;

Not of the sun, or righteousness.
No cherub here, o'er lute-string bowed,
Tinkled some silly hymn of peace,
But, '*Silence! No loitering allowed!*'

In jet-black characters I read
Incised upon the porcelain floor.
Ay, and the silence of the dead
No sentient heart could harrow more.

There, stretching far as eye could see,
Beneath that flat and leprous glare
A maze of immense machinery
Hummed in the ozoned air —

Prodigious wheels of steel and brass;
And — ranged along the un-windowed walls —
Engrossed in objects of metal and glass,
Stooped spectres, in spotless over-alls.

Knees quaking, dazed affrighted eyes,
I turned to the Janitor and cried,
'Is this, friend, Hell or Paradise?'
And, sneering, he replied,

'Terms trite as yours the ignorant
On earth, it seems, may yet delude.
Here, "sin" and "saint" and "hierophant"
Share exile with "the Good".

'Be grateful that the state of bliss
Henceforth, perhaps, reserved for thee,
Is sane and sanative as this,
And void of fatuous fantasy.

[479]

'Here God, the Mechanist, reveals,
As only mechanism can,
Mansions to match the new ideals
Of his co-worker, Man.

'On strict probation, you are now
To toil with yonder bloodless moles —
These skiagrams will show you how —
On mechanizing human souls . . .'

At this I woke: and, cold as stone,
Lay quaking in the hazardous light
    Of earth's familiar moon;
A clothes-moth winged from left to right,
    A tap dripped on and on;
And there, my handmade pot, my jug
Beside the old grained washstand stood;
There, too, my once-gay threadbare rug,
    The flattering moonlight wooed:
And — Heaven forgive a dream-crazed loon! —
    I found them very good.

BUT OH, MY DEAR

Hearts that too wildly beat —
    Brief is their epitaph!
Wisdom is in the wheat,
    Not in the chaff.
But Oh, my dear, how rich and rare, and root-down-
deep and wild and sweet
    It is to laugh!

THE FROZEN DELL

How still it is! How pure and cold
The air through which the wood-birds glide
From frost-bound tree to tree —
Veiled with so thin a mist that through
Its meshes steals that dayspring blue!

No other life. All motion gone —
As though a spectre, night being down,
Had through this darkened dingle trod
And frozen all he touched to stone.

Where art thou, mole? Where, busy ant?
Each in its earthen fastness is
As passive as the hive-bound bees,
As squirrel drowsing free from want,
And silken-snug chrysalides,
Queens of the wasps with ash-dark eyes —
Tranced exquisite complexities —
    And buds of the slumbering trees.

Yet human lovers, astray in this
Unfathomable silentness,
Into such dreamlike beauty come,
Though it seem lifeless as the tomb,
Might pause a moment here to kiss,
Their cold hands clasped; might even weep
For joy at their own ecstasy —
This crystal cage, sleep's wizardry,
    And secret as the womb!

BIRDS IN WINTER

I know not what small winter birds these are,
Warbling their hearts out in that dusky glade
While the pale lustre of the morning star
    In heaven begins to fade.

Not me they sing for, this — earth's shortest — day,
A human listening at his window-glass;
They would, affrighted, cease and flit away
    At glimpse even of my face.

And yet how strangely mine their music seems,
As if of all things loved my heart was heir,
Had helped create them — albeit in my dreams —
    And they disdained my share.

FEBRUARY

Whence is the secret of these skies,
Their limpid colours, deeper light,
That ardent dovelike tenderness,
Hinting at hidden mysteries
Beyond the reach of sight?

The risen sun's not half an hour
Earlier than on St. Lucy's Day;
And scarcely twice as long as that
In loftier arch, like opening flower,
His chariot loiters on the way;

But ev'n the rain upon the cheek
A kindlier message seems to bring;
There's sweetness in the moving air,
The stars of cold December's dark
Wheel on to their last westering;

And Earth herself this secret shares.
The sap is welling in her veins;
She to the heavens her bosom bares;
Snowdrop and crocus pierce the sod;
A brightening green the meadow stains.

And at her still, enticing call
The honeysuckle leaves untwine;
A softly-warbling thrush replies;
Mosses begem the orchard wall —
A fortnight from St. Valentine!

All this in open bliss appears;
Is it but fancy that within
The heart a resurrection stirs,
Some secret listener also hears
The hosannas of the Spring? . . .

And Oh, the wonder of a face —
Darkened by illness, grief and pain —
Love scarce can breathe its speechless Grace
When, mystery of all mysteries,
That heaven-sent life steals back again!

THESE SOLEMN HILLS

These solemn hills are silent now that night
Steals softly their green valleys out of sight;
The only sound that through the evening wells
  Is new-born lambkin's bleat;
    And — with soft rounded wings,
    Silvered in day's last light,
      As on they beat —
The lapwing's slow, sad, anguished
    Pee-oo-eet.

SHEEP

Early sunbeams shafting the beech-boles,
  An old oak fence, and in pasture deep —
Dark, and shapeless, dotting the shadows —
  A grazing and motionless flock of sheep;

So strangely still as they munched the grasses
  That I, up aloft on my 'bus, alone,
At gaze from its glass on the shimmering highway,
  Cried on myself: — 'Not sheep! They are stone!' —

Sarsen outcrops shelved by the glaciers?
  An aeon of darkness, ice and snow?
Beings bewitched out of far-away folk-tales?
  Prodigies such as dreams can show? . . .

The mind — that old mole — has its hidden earthworks:
  Blake's greybeard into a thistle turned;
And, in his childhood, flocking angels
  In sun-wild foliage gleamed and burned.

Illusions . . . Yet — as my 'bus lurched onward,
  Beech trees, park-land and woodland gone,
It was not sheep in my memory lingered
  But, strangely indwelling, those shapes of stone.

THE CREEK

Where that dark water is,
A Naiad dwells,
Though of her presence
Little else
Than her own silence tells.

Her twilight is
The pictured shade
Between a dream
And the awakening made.

Stranger in beauty she must be —
Cold solemn face and eyes of green —
Than tongue could say,
Or aught that earthly
Sight hath seen.

Human touch,
Or gaze, or cry
Would ruin be
To her half-mortal frailty;
As to the surface of her stream
A zephyr's sigh.

THE BROOK

Here, in a little fall,
From stone to stone,
The well-cool water drips,
Lips, sips,
And, babbling on,
Repeats its secret bell-clear song
The whole day long.

From what far caverns,
From what soundless deep
Of earth's blind sunless rock
Did this pure wellspring seep —
As may some praeternatural dream
In sleep?

ABSENCE

When thou art absent,
Grief only is constant,
My heart pines within me
Like the sighing of reeds
Where water lies open
To the darkness of heaven,
Voiceless, forsaken.

The bird in the forest
Where silence endureth,
The flower in the hollow
With down-drooping head —
Ah, Psyche, thy image! —
My soul breathes its homage;
But cold is this token,
Cold, cold is thy token,
When from dream I awaken,
By sorrow bestead.

THE RAINBOW

Stood twice ten thousand warriors on green grass
Ranked in that loop of running silver river,
The bright light dazzling on their steel and brass,
    Plumed helm, cuirass,
Tipped arrow, ivoried bow, and rain-soaked quiver;

And from these April clouds the blazing sun
Smote through the crystal drops of rain descending;
And, ere an instant of mere time was run,
    Or tongue could cry, *It's done!*
There spanned the east an arch all hues transcending:
Why, *then* would twice ten thousand dye the skies —
A different rainbow for each pair of eyes!
Oh, what a shout of joy might then be sent
From warrior throats, to crack the firmament!

But only a child was there — by that clear stream,
Reading a book, in shelter of a willow.
He raised his head to scan the radiant scene,
    His gaze aloof, serene,
    Smiling as if in dream;
And, sleeping, smiled again that night — his head upon
    his pillow.

[485]

THE GNOMON

I cast a shadow. Through the gradual day
Never at rest it secretly steals on;
As must the soul pursue its earthly way
 And then to night be gone.

But Oh, demoniac listeners in the grove,
Think not mere Time I now am telling of.
No. But of light, life, joy, and awe, and love:
 I obey the heavenly Sun.

EMPTY

The house by the sand dunes
Was bleached and dark and bare;
Birds, in the sea-shine,
Silvered and shadowed the air.

I called at the shut door,
I tirled at the pin:
Weeks — weeks of woesome tides,
The sand had drifted in.

The sand had heaped itself about
In the wefting of the wind;
And knocking never summoned ghost;
And dreams none can find

Like coins left at full of flood,
Gold jetsam of the sea.
Salt that water, bitter as love,
That will let nothing be

Unfevered, calm and still,
Like an ageing moon in the sky
Lighting the eyes of daybreak —
With a wick soon to die.

What then was shared there,
Who's now to tell?
Horizon-low the sea-borne light,
And dumb the buoyed bell.

LOVERS

There fell an hour when — as if clock
Had stayed its beat — their hearts stood still
At challenge of a single look,
Rapt, speechless, irretrievable.

Once, before lips had dreamed of kissing,
They languished, mind and soul, to see
Each the loved other's face; that missing,
In no wise else at peace could be.

Sleep, wherein not even dreams intrude,
Heart's haven may be from all that harms;
'Twere woe to the selfless solitude
They find in one another's arms.

Fantastic miracle, that even,
Though now all else seems little worth,
Would sacrifice the hope of heaven
    While love is theirs on earth!

'SAID FLORES'

'If I had a drop of attar
And a clot of wizard clay,
Birds we would be with wings of light
And fly to Cathay.

'If I had the reed called Ozmadoom,
And skill to cut pen,
I'd float a music into the air —
You'd listen, and then . . .

'If that small moon were mine for lamp,
I would look, I would see
The silent thoughts, like silver fish,
You are thinking of me.

'There is nothing upon grass or ground,
In the mountains or the skies,
But my heart faints in longing for,
And the tears drop from my eyes.

'And if I ceased from pining —
What buds were left to blow?
Where the wild swan? Where the wood-dove?
Where *then* should I go?'

NOT ONE

Turn your head sidelong;
 Gentle eyelids close;
In their small darkness
 Be all night's repose;
Weaving a dream — strange
 Flower and stranger fruit —
Wake heart may pine for
 But the day gives not.

Rest, folded lips,
 Their secret word unsaid;
Slumber will shed its dews,
 Be comforted:
Whilst I my vigil keep,
 And grieve in vain
That not the briefest moment — yours or mine —
 Can ever come again.

THE BRIBE

Ev'n should I give you all I have, —
From harmless childhood to the grave;
Call back my firstborn sigh, and then
Rob heaven of my last *Amen*;
Even if travailing back from Styx,
I brought you Pilate's crucifix;
Or, lone on Lethe, dredged you up
Melchior's golden Wassail cup;
Or Maacha's jewelled casket where
She shrined a lock of Absalom's hair;
Or relic whereon Noah would brood —
Keepsake of earth before the Flood;

Or flower of Adam's solitude;
The smile wherewith unmemoried Eve
Awoke from sleep, her fere to give,
And he, enravished, to receive;
Yes, and the daisy at her foot
She gazed at, and remembered not:
Nay, all Time's spoil, in dust put by,
Treasure untold to glut the eye —
Pining, and wonder, and mystery,
Rare and precious, old and strange,
Whithersoever thought can range,
Fish can swim, or eagle fly,
Harvesting earth, and sea, and sky;
And yours could be the empery: —
   What use?
There is no power or go-between or spell in time or space
Can light with even hint of love one loveless human face.

NOT YET

'Not love me? Even yet!'— half-dreaming, I
  whispered and said.
Untarnished, truth-clear eyes; averted,
  lovely head:
It was thus she had looked and had listened — how often —
  before she was dead.

DIVIDED

Two spheres on meeting may so softly collide
They stay, as if still kissing, side by side.
Lovers may part for ever — the cause so small
Not even a lynx could see a gap at all.

TREASURE

Reason as patiently as moth and rust
  May fret life's ardours into dust;
But soon — the sun begins to shine, and then —
Undaunted weeds! — they up, they spring, they spread
  — romp into bloom again.

[489]

CUPID KEPT IN

When life's wild noisy boys were out of school,
And, for his hour, the usher too was gone,
Peering at sun-fall through the crannied door,
I saw an urchin sitting there alone.

His shining wings lay folded on his back,
Between them hung a quiver, while he sat,
Bare in his beauty, and with poring brows
Bent o'er the saddening task-work he was at.

'*Which means she? — Yes or No?*' his problem was.
A gilding ray tinged plume and cheek and chin;
He frowned, he pouted, fidgeted, and wept —
Lost, mazed; unable even to begin!

But then, how could (Oh, think, my dear!), how *could*
That little earnest but unlettered mite
Find any meaning in the heart whose runes
Have kept me tossing through the livelong night?

What wonder, then, when I sighed out for shame,
He brought his scribbled slate, tears in his eyes,
And bade me hide it, until you have made
The question simpler, or himself more wise?

SCHOLARS

Logic does well at school;
And Reason answers every question right;
Poll-parrot Memory unwinds her spool;
And Copy-cat keeps Teacher well in sight:

The Heart's a truant; nothing does by rule;
Safe in its wisdom, is taken for a fool;
Nods through the morning on the dunce's stool;
And wakes to dream all night.

THOU ART MY LONG-LOST PEACE

Thou art my long-lost peace;
All trouble and all care,
Like winds on the ocean cease —
Leaving serene and fair
The evening-gilded wave
Above the unmeasured deep —
When those clear grave dark eyes
Call to the soul, in sleep —

In sleep. The waking hour —
How sweet its power may be!
Lovely the bird, the flower,
That feigns Reality!
But further yet, there is
A spirit, strange to earth,
Within whose longing lies
What day can not bring forth.

So I, though hand and lip,
Being body's, pine for thine,
Watch from my dreams in sleep
What earthly clocks resign
To cloaked Eternity:
Then weeping, sighing, must go
Back to his haunt in me,
In rapture; and in woe.

THE UNDERCURRENT

What, do you suppose, we're in this world for, sweet
    heart?
What — in this haunted, crazy, beautiful cage —
Keeps so many, like ourselves, poor pining human
    creatures,
As if from some assured, yet withholden heritage?
Keeps us lamenting beneath all our happy laughter,
Silence, dreams, hope for what may *not* come after,
While life wastes and withers, as it has for all mortals,
    Age on to age, on to age?

[491]

Strange it would be if the one simple secret
Were that wisdom hides, as beauty hides in pebble,
  leaf and blade;
That a good beyond divining, if we knew but where to
  seek it,
Is awaiting revelation when — well, *Sesame* is said;
That what so frets and daunts us ev'n in all we love
  around us
Is the net of worldly custom which has penned us in and
  bound us;
    That — freed — our hearts would break for joy
    Arisen from the dead.

    Would 'break'? What do I say?
Might that secret, if divulged, all we value most bewray!
    Make a dream of our real,
    A night of our day,
      That word said?
Oh, in case that be the answer, in case some stranger
  call us,
    Or death in his stead;
    Sweet Nought, come away, come away!

OUTER DARKNESS

'The very soul within my breast . . .'
'Mute, motionless, aghast . . .'

Uncompanioned, forlorn, the shade of a shade,
From all semblance of life I seemed to have strayed
To a realm, and a being — of fantasy made.
Where the spirit no more invokes Reason to prove
An illusion of sense it is cognisant of.
  I was lost: but aware.
  I had traversed the stream
By that nebulous bridge which the waking call dream,
And was come to an ultimate future that yet
Was the dust of a past no remorse could forget —
  Heart could covet no more,
    Nor forget.

[492]

Wheresoever my eyes might forebodingly range
They discerned the familiar disguised as the strange, —
Relics of memoried objects designed
To enchant to distraction an earth-enthralled mind,
   A sense-shackled mind.
The door was ajar when I entered. And lo!
A banquet prepared for one loved, long ago.
But I shunned to peer close, to detect what was there,
As I stood, lost in reverie, facing that chair.
In anguish and dread I dared not surmise
What fate had befallen those once ardent eyes,
The all-welcoming hands, the compassionate breast,
 And the heart now at rest,
 Ev'n from love now at rest.

The glass she had drunk from beamed faintly. Its lees
Were as dry as the numberless sands of the seas
In a lunar volcano parched up by the sun
Ere the Moon's frenzied courtship of Earth had begun.
Once, the flame of that candle had yearned to retrace
The heart-breaking secrets concealed in her face —
 Gentle palace of loveliness: avid to steep
With its motionless radiance cheek, brow and lip;
And in innocent scrutiny striving to win
Through the windows now void to the phantom within,
 To the spirit secluded within.

Now its refuse was blackened. The brass of its stick —
The virginal wax guttered down to the wick —
Was witch-hued with verdigris. Fret-moth and mouse
 Had forsaken for ever this house.
As I moved through the room I was frosted with light;
 Decay was here Regent of Night.
It clotted the fabric of curtain and chair
Like a luminous mildew infesting the air;
An æon had waned since there fell the faint call
Of the last mateless insect at knock in the wall.
The once rotten was dry — gone all sense of its taint;
The mouldings were only the shell of their paint,
 Though their valueless gold
 Glimmered on, as of old:
So remote was this hush: where none listens or hears;
By all sweetness deserted for measureless years,
 The wilderness mortals call years.

[493]

And I?

And I? Ghost of ghost, unhousel'd, foredone —
Candle, fleet, fire — out of memory gone.
Appalled, I peered on in the glass at the face
Of a creature of dread, lost in time, lost in space,
Pilgrim, waif, outcast, abandoned, alone,
In a sepulchred dark, mute as stone.
Yet of beauty, past speech, was this region of Nought
And the reflex of images conjured by thought —
Those phantoms of flow'rs in their pitcher of glass
Shrined a light that no vision could ever surpass.
In that sinister dusk every leaf, twig and tree
Wove an intricate web of significancy;
And those hills in the moonlight, a somnolent green,
Still awakened a yearning to scan the unseen,
    To seek haven within the unseen.

Alas, how can anguish and grief be allayed
    In a soul self-betrayed?
Yet that emblem of Man, in its niche by the door,
Limned a passionate pathos unheeded of yore,
A wonder, a peace, disregarded before,
    A grace that no hope could restore.

I had drunken of death. The night overhead
Was a forest of quietude, stagnant as lead;
Starless, tranquil, serene as the dead;
    The last love-stilled look of the dead.
Cold, as the snow of swan in her sleep
On pitiless Lethe to heart and to lip,
Was the void that enwrapped me — by slumber betrayed;
    Ecstatic, demented, afraid:
In a zero, forsaken, marooned: not a sigh.
An existence denuded of all but an I;
    And those relics near by:
    Neither movement nor sigh.

Till a whisper within, like a breath from the tomb,
Asked me, 'Knowest thou not wherefore thus thou art
    come
    To this judgement, this doom?'
And my heart in my dreams stayed its pulsings: 'Nay,
    why?'

But Nothingness made no reply.

[494]

OUT OF A DREAM

Out of a dream I came —
Woeful with sinister shapes,
Hollow sockets aflame,
The mouth that gapes
With cries, unheard, of the dark;
The bleak, black night of the soul;
Sweating, I lay in my bed,
Sick of the wake for a goal.

And lo — Earth's close-shut door,
Its panels a cross, its key
Of common and rusting iron,
Opened, and showed to me
A face — found; lost — of old:
Of a lifetime's longing the sum;
And eyes that assuaged all grief:
    'Behold! I am come.'

JOY

This little wayward boy
Stretched out his hands to me,
Saying his name was Joy;
Saying all things that seem
Tender, and wise, and true
Never need fade while he
Drenches them through and through
With his sweet mastery;
Told me that Love's clear eyes
Pools were without the sky,
Earth, without paradise,
Were he not nigh;
Even that grief conceals
Him in a dark disguise;
And that affliction brings
    All it denies.

[495]

Not mine to heed him then —
Till fell the need — and Oh,
All his sweet converse gone,
Where could I go?
What could I do? —
But seek him up and down,
Thicket and thorn and fell,
Till night in gloom came on
Unpierceable?
Then, when all else must fail,
Stepped from the dark to me,
Voiced like the nightingale,
Masked, weeping, he.

THE VISION

O starry face, bound in grave strands of hair,
Aloof, remote, past speech or thought to bless —
Life's haunting mystery and the soul's long care,
Music unheard, heart's utter silentness,
Beauty no mortal life could e'er fulfil,
Yet garnered loveliness of all I see,
Which in this transient pilgrimage is still
Steadfast desire of that soul's loyalty;

Death's haunting harp-string, sleep's mandragora,
Mockery of waking and the dark's despair,
Life's changeless vision that fades not away —
O starry face, bound in grave strands of hair!
Hands faintly sweet with flowers from fields unseen,
Breasts cold as mountain snow and far waves' foam,
Eyes changeless and immortal and serene —
Spent is this wanderer, and you call him home!

WHITENESS

I stay to linger, though the night
Is draining every drop of light
From out the sky, and every breath
I breathe is icy chill as death.
Not so much colour now there shows
As tinges even the palest rose;
Nor in this whiteness can be seen
The faintest trace of hidden green.

Scarlet would cry as shrill as fife
Here where there stirs no hint of life.
A child in rare vermilion,
Come out to wonder at the snow:
Like Moses' burning bush would show —
Its bonfire out, when he is gone!

Yet in this pallor every tree
A marvel is of symmetry,
As if enthralled by its own grace —
A music woven of silentness.
Dense hoarfrost clots the tresses of
That weeping elm's funereal white,
Biding the sepulchre of night
To whisper — 'It is cold, my love!'
To Winter, witless nihilist,
Who, the day long, has kept his tryst
With mistress no less mute than he,
And tranced in a like rhapsody.

As though from vacant vaults of space
Darkness transfigured haunts his face;
And, she, for spell to wreathe her brow,
Has twined the Druid mistletoe.

What viol in this frozen air
Could for their nuptials descant make?
What timbrels Eros bid awake?
Ask of those solemn cedars there!

SOLITUDE[1]

When the high road
Forks into a by-road,
And that drifts into a lane,
And the lane breaks into a bridle-path,
A chace forgotten
Still as death,
And green with the long night's rain;
Through a forest winding on and on,
Moss, and fern, and sun-bleached bone,
Till only a trace remain;
And that dies out in a waste of stone
A bluff of cliff, vast, trackless, wild,
Blue with the harebell, undefiled;
Where silence enthralls the empty air,
Mute with a presence unearthly fair,
And a path is sought
In vain. . . .

It is then the Ocean
Looms into sight,
A gulf enringed with a burning white,
A sea of sapphire, dazzling bright;
And islands,
Peaks of such beauty that
Bright danger seems to lie in wait,
Dread, disaster, boding fate;
And soul and sense are appalled thereat;
Though an Ariel music on the breeze
Thrills the mind with a lorn unease,
Cold with all mortal mysteries.
And every thorn,
And weed, and flower,
And every time-worn stone
A challenge cries on the trespasser:
Beware!
Thou art alone!

[1] A very different earlier version of this poem called 'The Journey' was published in the American edition of *Bells and Grass*, 1942, and in *Rhymes and Verses: Collected Poems for Young People*, New York, 1947. See opposite.

THE JOURNEY

When the high road
Forks into a by-road,
And this leads down
To a lane,
And the lane fades into
A bridle-path,
Green with the long night's rain,
Through a forest winding up and on —
Moss, fern, and sun-bleached bone —
Till hardly a trace
Remains;
And this thins out
Into open wild,
High under heaven,
With sunset filled,
A bluff of cliff,
Wide, trackless, wild;
And a path is sought
In vain. . . .

It is then that the Ocean
May heave into sight,
A gulf enringed
With a burning white,
A sea of darkness,
Dazzling bright;
And Islands — peaks
Of such beauty that
A secret danger lies in wait,
And soul and sense are afraid thereat;
And an Ariel music
On the breeze
Thrills the mind
With a lorn unease;
And every thorn, and bird, and flower,
And every time-worn stone
A challenge cries on the trespasser,
Beware! Thou art alone! . . .

It is then that the air
Breathes strangely sweet,
And the heart within
Can scarcely beat,
Since the Journey
Is just begun:
The Journey
Is nearly done.

THE UNRENT PATTERN

I roved the Past — a thousand thousand years,
Ere the Egyptians watched the lotus blow,
Ere yet Man stumbled on his first of words,
Ere yet his laughter rang, or fell his tears;
And on a hillside where three trees would grow —
    Life immortal, Peace, and Woe:
    Dismas, Christ, his bitter foe —
Listened, as yesterday, to the song of birds.

DUST

Sweet sovereign lord of this so pined-for Spring,
How breathe the homage of but one poor heart
With such small compass of thy everything?

Ev'n though I knew this were my life's last hour,
It yet would lie, past hope, beyond my power
One instant of my gratitude to prove,
    My praise, my love.

That 'Everything'! — when this, my human dust,
    Whereto return I must,
Were scant to bring to bloom a single flower!

PROBLEMS[1]

'Gone! Where? My glasses!' the old quidnunc cries;
    And still the blinder grows,
Until (the problems life solves in this wise!)
    He finds them on his nose.

THE OLD AUTHOR

The End, he scrawled, and blotted it. Then eyed
Through darkened glass night's cryptic runes o'erhead.
'My last, and longest book.' He frowned; then sighed:
    'And everything left unsaid!'

[1] Included in *The Burning-Glass and Other Poems*, New York, 1945, but omitted from the English edition at the page-proof stage.

[500]

The Traveller (1945)[1]

'"*I saw that the universe is not composed of dead matter but is ... a living presence.*"'
'*Le soir vient; et le globe à son tour s'éblouit*
  Devient un œil énorme et regarde la nuit . . .'
'*Not in lone splendour hung aloft the night*
  But watching . . .'

This Traveller broke at length, toward set of sun,
Out from the gloom of towering forest trees;
Gasped, and drew rein: to gaze, in wonder, down
A bow-shaped gulf of shelving precipices.

The blue of space dreamed level with his eye.
A league beneath, like lava long at rest,
Lay a vast plateau, smooth as porphyry,
Its huge curve gradual as a woman's breast.

In saline marshes Titicaca lies —
Its ruins fabulous ere the Incas reigned:
Was this the like? A mountain sea? His eyes
Watched like a lynx. It still as death remained.

Not the least ripple broke the saffron sheen
Shed by the evening on this wild abyss.
Far countries he had roved, and marvels seen,
But never such a prodigy as this.

No. Water never in a monstrous mass
Rose to a summit like a rounded stone,
Ridged with concentric shadows. No morass
Were vast as this, or coloured zone by zone.

Vague relics haunted him of mythic tales,
Printed in books, or told him in his youth —
Deserts accursed; 'witched islands; sunken bells;
Fissures in space . . . Might one yet prove the truth?

Or, in his own sole being long confined,
Had he been lured into those outskirts where
A secret self is regent; and the mind
Reveals an actual none else can share? —

---

[1] See Bibliographical Appendix, p. 898.

Prospects enchanting, dread, whereof as yet
No chart has record shown, could bearings tell;
Such as some fabulous Afreet might beget:
Clear as mirage, ev'n less attainable?

Stealthy in onset, between wake and sleep,
Such scenes, more moving than the earth can show,
May, self-created, in mutation sweep,
Silent and fugitive as April snow.

Or had he now attained the true intent
Of his unbroken pilgrimage? The sum
Of all his communings; and what they meant?
Was life at length to its Elysium come?

So flows experience: the vast Without;
Its microcosm, of the Soul, within;
Whereof the day-distracted eye may doubt,
But doubts no more as soon as dreams begin.

Thus mused this Traveller. Was he man or ghost?
Deranged by solitude? Or rapt away
To some unpeopled limbo of the lost —
Feint that the light of morning would betray? . . .

At verge of this huge void he camped for days;
Months of slow journeying from the haunts of men;
Till awe of it no longer could amaze,
And passion for venturing urged him on again.

Down, down into the abysm his mare, on hooves
Nimble as mountain-bred gazelle's, pricked on
From steep to steep, until through bouldered grooves
And shallowing streams she trod, their safety won —

An Arab lean and sleek, her surf-like mane
Tossed on a shoulder as of ivory made;
Full in the moonrise she approached the plain,
Was, with her master, in its beams arrayed.

He had scanned that lunar landscape when of old,
Tranced at a window as a child he had sat —
The Face, the Thorns, those craters grisly cold,
Volcanic seas now parched and desolate;

While from afar the bird of night bewailed
Her cruel ravishment. Even then he had pined,
Ere hope abandoned him, or courage failed,
To seek adventure, safety left behind.

Chilled by his travel in the shrewd clear air,
With wind-strown kindling-wood he built a fire;
Scant pasturage for man or beast was there,
And dreams but transiently assuage desire.

His supper done, he crouched beside the blaze,
Sharp-cheeked, wide-browed, and lost in reverie;
Flamelight and moonshine playing on his face,
The crackle of logs his only company.

When the dark tent of night at daybreak wanned,
He rose, remounted, and surveyed the vast
Convex of bloodshot stone that swept beyond
In arc enormous to the skies at last.

Great mountains he had ranged that lift their snow
In peaks sublime, which age to age remain
Unstirred by foot or voice; but here, a slow
Furtive foreboding crept into his brain

Of what yet lay before him — this Unknown;
In subtle feature so unlike the past
Havens of exile he had made his own,
Been restive in, or wearied of at last.

Soon as the risen sun rilled down its heat,
A dewy mist, in this huge hollow pent,
Washed like a sea of milk his Arab's feet.
And rainbows arched before him as he went.

The call of waters kept his ears a-cock —
Creeks fed by cataracts now left behind.
Forests of fungi in the lichened rock
Showed ashen wan and grey as withy-wind;

Spawn of a gendering hour, yet hoar with age,
They stood sun-bleached, ephemera of the night,
And — thing past even speculation strange —
Growths never grazed till now by human sight.

[503]

What tinier atomies of life were bred
Beneath their skin-thin gills, tents, muted bells,
Eye could not guess — as procreant a bed
As is man's body with its countless cells.

The furtive mist, these clustered funguses —
Minutest stirrings of primeval slime,
The empty heavens, aloof and measureless,
Illusions seemed, not only of space, but time.

From microscopical to the immense —
Mere magnitude of little moment is;
But violent contrast shakes man's confidence
Even in what lies plain before his eyes.

Birds of rare flight and hue, of breed unknown,
Rose, wheeled, fled onward, mewling as they went —
And left him — more forsaken and alone;
Sun for sole guidance in his slow ascent.

But borne not far upon the windless air,
The fickle fleet-winged creatures turned anon;
Came stooping backward on his face to stare:
Broke out in cries again; again, were gone:

Curious, but fearless of what never yet
Had on these mighty slopes been seen to appear;
With soft-tongued jargoning they his way beset,
Sadder than love-lorn pewit's on the ear.

Nor was it only stone that made reply.
Their sweetness echoed in his heart. Delight
And love long pent in fadeless memory
Welled to his eyes. He watched them out of sight.

What meaning harbours in a bird's lone note
Secret as music is; ineffable:
With Song of the Sirens it has been forgot:
But long he journeyed on beneath its spell.

Westward to eastward, wide as gaze could scan,
Shallowly troughed, the void savanna swept:
The dead of all the armies doomed by Man
Might, biding ransom, in its folds have slept.

[504]

And, hollow as sinister beating of a drum
The rock resounded when, with sudden bound,
His beast beneath him, on the treacherous scum,
Slipped, and, with snort of fear, her balance found.

That night, while yet in darkness lapped, it seemed
He had leapt from sleep, that instant made aware
The rock beneath had trembled while he dreamed,
Bleached of a sudden by the lightning's glare.

Foreboding perils unconceived before,
He woke when dawn again suffused the sky.
His earth, once stable, now proved insecure:
He sat and watched it with unwinking eye;

While chattering voices wrangled in his head:
'Alas, what horror of the soul is this?'
'Beware! Away!' 'Far better thou were dead
Than face the ordeal that now before thee lies!'

A plaintive whinny in the early air,
For company calling, solace brought. He smiled.
And in sweet converse with his timorous mare
Soothed her disquiet, and his own beguiled.

Towards noon an arid wind from out the East
Waxed, waned; and failed as they approached — these two,
In close companionship of man and beast,
To where the plain they paced lapsed into blue.

His aching eyes rejoiced. No more there showed
Branched veins of sanguine in a milk-pale stone;
An ever deepening azure gloomed and glowed
In shine and shadow as they journeyed on:

Turquoise, and sapphire, speedwell, columbine.
When clouds minute, like scales of fish, are seen
Dappling an April daybreak, then, divine
As Eros' eyes, there shows a blue between,

Tranquil, wan, infinite. So, pale to dark,
A dark as dazzling as the tropic deep,
Loomed now the prospect toward his distant mark,
When yet again he laid him down to sleep.

In this oblivion he dreamed a dream: —
He dreamed the transitory host of men,
Debased by pride, lust, greed and self-esteem,
Had gone their way; that Earth was freed again.

Their minds had brewed a poison in the blood;
The sap of their own nature had decayed.
They had chosen evil, had resigned the good;
False, faithless, pitiless, and of nought afraid.

Nature, released from this vile incubus,
Had wooed into being creatures of other kind,
Resembling those long since deemed fabulous,
As exquisite in aspect as in mind.

Beings, too, once adored for beauty and grace,
Who had left but echoes in the mirroring air,
Had sought again their bygone dwelling-place;
As happy birds in springtime homeward fare.

And he? — the sport of contraries in sleep! —
To childhood had returned; gone grief and woe;
That Eden of the heart, and fellowship
With innocence, that only children know;

And in a garden played, serene, alone;
Bird, flower, water, shining in his eyes;
And magic hidd'n in even the tiniest stone . . .
When, suddenly, a Trumpet rent the skies:

To Judgement had been called the Sons of Light,
The stellar host, the Sun and all his brood:
Rank beyond rank, height above heavenly height,
Within the eternal peace of God they stood,

Hymning his glory. And, alas, he knew
That, chosen envoy of the Earth, he had come,
Garbed in her beauty, and enraptured too;
But, though he had yearned for joy, his soul was dumb.

And by unuttered edict exiled thence,
He had fallen, as Satan fell, in leaden dismay,
And thus had wakened to the rock-land whence
His spirit, in fantasy, had winged away . . .

On high a dwindling, sun-bedazzled moon
Paled in the homeless solitudes of space,
Casting gaunt shadow here — his vision gone —
For void companionship in this bitter place.

He, Envoy of the Earth! — that mothering breast;
Those Suns and Sons, what meaning could he find? —
A cold satanic irony at best,
Or scoff of that mocking-bird in sleep, his mind.

Oh, that he had but one bright candle here
To pierce the double-dark of body and soul!
Could but a strain of music reach his ear
To ease this heartsick wretchedness and dole!

From lifted brow his leaden-lidded eyes
Searched the vast furrows of unanswering stone
To where the cedar-arc'd abyss must rise
Whence he had journeyed to this end, alone.

Gazing, he mused, beset by mystery,
Mere Sentience in the silence of the night;
Could Earth itself a living creature be,
And he its transitory parasite? —

A frosted incubus, by the cold congealed,
Doubting his senses, vacantly aware
Of what already instinct had revealed —
His deadliest danger now was blank despair.

Like an old zany, he seemed, who, year by year,
The slave has been of an Excelsior,
Its goal Eureka; and when that draws near
Hears fleshless knuckles on his chamber-door!

Or like a doting lover who at last
By one whose source had seemed of heavenly grace
Forsaken is, in outer darkness cast,
Her cheating blandishment a Lamia's face.

Meagre his saddlebag as camel's hump
When, sand-marooned, she staggers to her doom.
As shrunken too, his Arab's ribs and rump
Showed taut as vellum stretched upon a drum.

He strove in vain to reason, numbed with sleep,
But conscious that at first faint token of dawn,
Wraiths at whose beauty even the blind might weep,
Wooed to his solitude, had come, and gone —

Wraiths all but lost to memory, whose love
Had burned in hearts that never more would beat;
Of whose compassion sense could bring no proof,
Though solace 'twas beyond all telling sweet —

Like flowers that a child brings home; to fade.
Alas, alas, no longer could restore
Life to the faithful by neglect betrayed!
Too late for ransom; they'd return no more —

Had left him, like a castaway adrift,
Lashed to a raft upon a chartless sea,
His only motion the huge roller's lift,
Its depths his only hope at peace to be.

'Sea'! when this waste of stone in which he lay
Like night-blue porcelain was, untinged with red.
But when his cracked lips stirred, as if to pray,
He caught but leaf-dry whisper of what they said.

So tense was this his solitude — the sky
Its mute and viewless canopy — that when
His grieved 'O God!' was followed by a sigh,
It seemed eternity had breathed amen.

Ay, as if cock, horizon-far, had crowed,
His heart, like Peter's, had been rent in twain.
At pang of it his grief again up-flowed,
Though its 'Who's there?' called only in his brain . . .

On, and still on he pressed — scorched heel to nape,
Hunched in his saddle from the noonday's glare —
Watched by a winged thing, high in heaven, agape
To ken aught stirring in a tract so bare,

Which leaf or blade of grass could never yield.
A vitreous region, like a sea asleep,
Crystalline, convex, tideless and congealed,
Profounder far than Tuscarora Deep,

Further than sight could reach, before him lay.
Head bent, eyes fixed — drowsed by recurrent stroke
Of tic-tac ice-like hoof-beats, wits astray,
He slipped again from real to dream: awoke

To find himself marooned beneath a dome
Of star-pricked vacancy, and darkness near;
His breast bespattered with his Arab's foam,
And — trotting at his heels — the spectre, Fear:

Whose fell pursuit, unhastening, pace for pace —
Like Lama of Tibet in waking trance —
His very soul for quarry in the chase,
Forbade all hazard of deliverance:

A shapeless shape of horror, mildew-blue,
With naked feet, blank eyes, and leprous face,
Insane with lust, that ever nearer drew,
Tarrying for midnight and the dread embrace.

Foes of the soul there are, corrupt, malign,
Taint of whose malice is so evil a blight
That ev'n the valiant must hope resign
Unless God's mercy give them means for flight.

Witless as wild bird tangled in a net,
He dared not turn his head, but galloped on,
Spurs red at heel, his body drenched with sweat,
Until, with nerve renewed, but strength nigh gone,

He slowed his pace to listen; gasped, fordone;
Drew rein, dismounted . . . But, the peril past,
His cheek was fallen in like that of one
Whom mortal stroke of fate has felled at last;

And in a moment aged him many years —
Edict beyond the mind to comprehend.
Plaiting cramped fingers in the elf-locked mane,
'Come, now,' he muttered, 'we must rest, my friend.'

The creature's sunken eyeballs, scurfed with rheum
And mute with misery, returned his gaze;
And thus they communed in the gathering gloom,
Nought but the love between them left to graze.

She pawed the unnatural ice, tossed her small head,
By inarticulate alarm distressed;
Baring her teeth, squealed faintly, smitten with dread;
And, snuggling closer, lipped her master's breast.

His breath rasped harshly — wind in blasted wheat;
Through fret of her coarse mane his sun-parched eyes,
Their swol'n lids blackened by the daylong heat,
Swept the dim vacuum of earth and skies.

'Quiet, dear heart! The end is nearing now.
Into disaster thou hast been betrayed.'
He smoothed her gentle muzzle, kissed her brow.
'Nought worse than one more night to live,' he said.

'We both are mortal, both have fallen at last
Into disgrace. But had I swerved aside,
And safety found, what peace, the danger past,
Is his who sleeps with Terror for his bride?

But one night more. And then must come what may.
But never mistress held man's life in fee
As mine has been. And how could speech convey
The woe, forlorn one, that I feel for thee!'

So grieved he in his heart. This comrade dear!
His gentle hand upon her shoulder lay
Though still she shivered, twitching flank and ear,
In this drear wilderness so far astray.

Long stood he motionless, while overhead
The circling constellations, east to west,
Misting the infinite, their effluence shed —
Friends long familiar on how many a quest!

From this dark timeless absence of the mind
It seemed an inward voice had summoned him: —
'See! See!'— a whisper fainter than the wind
Or ripple of water lipped on Lethe's brim.

For now — the zenith darkening — opal-pale,
As if the earth its secret well-spring were —
Softly as flowers of night their scents exhale —
A strange and deepening lustre tinged the air,

Gentle and radiant. So, from off the sea
May mirrored moonbeams, when calm waters lave
A rock-bound coast, steal inward silently,
Blanching the sombre vaultings of a cave.

Not rock his roof-tree here, but hollow sky;
Not reflex moon-ray, but a phantom light,
Like hovering, pervasive reverie
Of Mind supreme, illumining the night.

Rapt in this loveliness, his spellbound face,
To travail the while, and famine, reconciled,
Of fret and weariness shed every trace,
As sleep brings comfort to a tired-out child:

Sleep to a body so pure and exquisite
Like manna it is, at gilding sunrise seen;
The senses so untrammelled that as yet
No more than frailest barrier lies between

Soul and reality. Thus beauty may
Pierce through the mists that worldly commerce brings,
Imagination's blindness wash away,
And — bird at daybreak — lend the spirit wings.

Even the little ant, devoid of fear,
Prowling beneath the shadow of a man,
Conscious may be of occult puissance near,
Whose origin it neither recks, nor can.

So, though he too was now but vaguely aware
Whence welled this boon of benison and peace,
In awe of a mystery so divinely fair,
Tears gushed within him, not of grief but bliss.

Courage revived, like greenness after rain.
Slowly he turned; looked back. And in amaze —
A waif self-exiled from the world of men —
Trembled at sight of what now met his gaze: —

The hushed and visionary host of those
Who, like himself, had faced life's long duress,
Its pangs and horrors, anguish, hardship, woes,
Their one incentive ever on to press,

[511]

Defying dread and danger — and in vain:
Not to achieve a merely temporal goal,
Not for bright glory, praise, or greed of gain,
But in that secret craving of the soul

For what no name has; flower of hidden stem: —
The unreturned of kindless land and sea;
Venturers, voyagers, dreamers, seers — ay, them
The Angel of Failure hails with rhapsody.

Him, too, for some rare destiny designed,
Who, in faith and love, has ranged; unmarked, alone;
Though means to share it he will never find
Since its sole language is unique — his own:

Great deeds win sweet renown: the hope forlorn
May perish, and none know what fate it braved;
The self content, at ease, has yet forsworn
The scope that still awaits the soul that's saved:

Faith in a love that can no respite have,
Being its sole resource and anodyne —
Impassioned love, its goal beyond the grave,
However short it fall of the divine.

Ay, even though Man have but one earthly life,
Cradle to grave, wherein to joy and grieve?
His grace were yet the agony and strife
In quest of what no mortal can achieve.

'Angel', forsooth! Bleak visage, frigid breast,
Passionless Nemesis, the heart for prey,
She goads her votary with insane unrest
And smiles upon him when she stoops to slay!

Strange beauty theirs, this host — in rapt array,
Spectral and motionless, intent, and dumb,
Laved in light's loveliness they stretched away
Homage ironic to his Kingdom Come!

Less a mere castaway of flesh and bone,
Defenceless, lost, whom Fate will overwhelm,
He now appeared, than — child of genius — one
Who explores pure fantasy's unbounded realm;

And being at length confronted by ordeal
No human consciousness could comprehend,
A preternatural ecstasy can feel —
Life's kiss of rapture at life's journey's end.

'All hail!' he muttered; paused; then laid him low,
His crazed head pillowed on his Arab's flank;
Prostrate with thirst and weariness and woe,
Into a plumbless deep of sleep he sank.

What visitants of earth or air drew near
Rider and horse in these stark hours of night —
Sylphs of the wilderness or demon drear,
Gazed long and softly, and again took flight,

No sense ajar revealed; nor echo of
Music ethereal, pining sweet and shrill
Of voices in the vaults of heaven above,
The angelic solitudes of Israfel . . .

When daybreak moved above the hushed expanse,
By ague shaken, he awoke. Aware
Nought now could shield him from life's last mischance,
With tranquil mind he breathed the scentless air.

This sterile world! — no weed here raised its head;
No bird on dew-plashed wing, his ear to bless,
Flew up to greet the dayspring; but instead,
A tense unfathomable silentness

Engulfed the enormous convex, stony-still,
Of hueless, lucent crystal where he lay,
Shivering in fever in the sunless chill,
Its centre now scarce half a league away.

He rose; the rustle of his raiment seemed
A desecration of the quietude
Brimming its vacancy; as if there dreamed
A presence here where none had dared intrude

Since waters from waters had divided been,
World from the heavens, the land from ocean freed;
And fruitful trees sprang up, with leafage green,
And earth put forth the herb that yieldeth seed.

[513]

'Come, now', he whispered softly; paused; aghast,
Deeming his faithful one had found reprieve;
Had fled away, all tribulation past,
Where even the soul-less languish not nor grieve;

But green-grey willows hang their tresses down;
The heron fishes in his plashy pool;
There, in her beauty floats the silent swan —
Shady and verdurous and calm and cool:

Meadows where asphodel and cowslips blow,
And sunlit summer clouds dissolve in rain —
Her earthly paradise! At length! But no;
The gentle creature heard, had stirred again.

Scrabbling her fore-hoofs on the treacherous waste,
She rose, stood trembling; with sepulchral sigh
Turned her night-blinded eyes, her master faced;
And patiently, piteously set out to die.

To eyried bird above, now rosed with light,
Of insectine dimensions they appeared;
Like emmet creeping, or the weevil-mite
That in a mouldering ship at sea is reared.

Sable in plumage, ruff, and naked head,
Superb in flight, and poised upon his shelf
Of viewless air, he tarried for the dead,
And watched, indifferent as Death himself.

Though the great globe around them grudged them tomb,
Feast they would be for both these ravening foes —
Horseman and Arab, who had dared to roam
Beneath these mountains' never-melting snows.

Halt, maimed and impotent, still travelling on,
O'er very Eye of Earth they made their way,
Till rimmed into the east the risen sun
Flooding its orbit with the joy of day —

That Eye of Heaven, mansion of secret light,
Whose beams of all that's lovely are the shrine,
Procreant, puissant, arbiter of Sight,
Emblem and symbol of the light divine —

So brilliant the least flaw beneath their feet
A tiny shadow cast where nought there was
Taller than locust in the rilling heat
To check the splendour of this sea of glass.

And if pure radiance could pure music be,
And quiet supreme its tabernacle were,
This orb, now blazing in its majesty,
With a sublime Hosanna rent the air.

Moved by an impulse beyond wit to scan,
His poor rags stirring in a fitful breeze,
This worn, outwearied, errant son of man
Paused, bowed his head, fell down upon his knees;

And, with a faint and lamentable cry,
Poured hoarsely forth a babble of praise and prayer,
Sun on his brows, above the boundless sky,
No living soul to hear or heed him there . . .

A self there is that listens in the heart
To what is past the range of human speech,
Which yet has urgent tidings to impart —
The all-but-uttered, and yet out of reach.

Beneath him an immeasurable well
Of lustrous crystal motionlessly black
Deeped on. And as he gazed — marvel past words to tell —
It seemed to him a presence there gazed back:

Rapt, immaterial, remote; ev'n less
In substance than is image of the mind;
And yet, in all-embracing consciousness
Of its own inmost being; elsewise blind:

Past human understanding to conceive;
Of virgin innocence, yet source of all
That matter had the power to achieve
Ere Man created was, ere Adam's fall:

And in its midst a mote scarce visible —
Himself: the momentary looking-glass
Of Nature, which a moment may annul,
And with earth's hosts may into nothing pass:

The flux of change. Ay, this poor Traveller too —
Soon to be dust, though once erect, elate,
From whose clear gaze a flame divine burned through;
A son of God — no sport of Time or Fate:

It seemed his heart was broken; his whole life long
Concentred in this moment of desire;
Its woe, its rapture, transient as the song
The Phoenix sings upon her funeral pyre.

'Alas', he gasped — his journey now at end;
Breathed softly out his last of many sighs;
Flung forth his hands, and motionless remained,
Drenched through with day; and darkness in his eyes . . .

Head drooped, knees sagging, his forsaken jade —
Her stark hide gilded by the eastern sun,
Her abject carcass in its glory arrayed —
As though in fear to break his prayers, drowsed on.

But, as an acid frets its way through steel,
Into her sentience at length there crept
A deeper hush no silence could conceal —
And Death for long has never secret kept,

Though shadow-close it mime its sister, Sleep.
The creature nearer drew — reluctant, slow,
As if, like motherless child, to sigh and weep,
Too young the import of its loss to know.

Ears pricked, reins dangling, thus a while she stayed —
Of that in watch above full well aware:
'See, now, dear master, here I wait!' She neighed,
And stooping, snuffed the rags, the matted hair;

Then, of a sudden, in panic dread, upreared,
Plunged, wheeled, drew back, her eyeballs gleaming white,
And urged to frenzy by the thing she feared
From all that love had left on earth took flight . . .

Sweet is that Earth, though sorrow and woe it have,
Though parched, at length, the milk within its breast;
And then the night-tide of the all-welcoming grave
For those who weary, and a respite crave:
Inn at the cross roads, and the traveller's rest . . .

Inward Companion:
Poems (1950)

HERE I SIT

Here I sit, and glad am I
So to sit contentedly,
While with never-hastening feet
Time pursues the Infinite;
And a silence centuries-deep
Swathes my mind as if in sleep.
Passive hand, and inward eyes
Press on their transient enterprise;
As, across my paper's white
Creeps the ink from left to right,
Wooing from a soundless brain
The formless into words again:
So I sit, and glad am I
So to sit contentedly.

UNWITTING

This evening to my manuscript
Flitted a tiny fly;
At the wet ink sedately sipped,
Then seemed to put the matter by,
Mindless of him who wrote it, and
His scrutinizing eye —
That any consciousness indeed
Its actions could descry! . . .

Silence; and wavering candlelight;
Night; and a starless sky.

FUCHSIAS

I envied the droning, idle bee,
  Sucking his nectar sweet —
In that palace of light suspended there
  By his hooked piratical feet.

No care, no trouble, no conscience his!
  And what of my lot, instead?
It seemed an absurd futility
  Till the notion entered my head: —

Poor wretch, my flowers are no flowers to him,
  Only his daily bread!

MARTINS

'*Chelidon urbica urbica!*'
  I cried on the little bird,
Meticulously enunciating each syllable of each word;
  '*Chelidon urbica urbica!*'
  Listen to me, I plead!
There are swallows all snug in the hayloft,
I have all that your nestlings can need —
Shadow and sunshine and sweet shallow water —
Come, build in my eaves, and breed!

Fly high, my love! My love, fly low!
I watched the sweet pretty creatures go —
Floating, skimming, and wheeling so
Swiftly and softly — like flakes of snow,
'Gainst the dark of the cedar-boughs, to and fro: ...
    But no!
    But no!
  '*Chelidon urbica urbica!*'
None paid me the faintest heed.

JACKDAWS

This dry old dotard lived but to amass
Old prints, books, pictures, porcelain, and glass —
As some hoard Wealth, Fame, Knowledge. Such he was.
There pottered in Another, and peered round:
But he his treasures buries underground.

[518]

IZAAK WALTON

That lucent, dewy, rain-sweet prose —
 Oh! what a heaven-sent dish
Whereon — a feast for eye, tongue, nose,
 Past greediest gourmet's wish —
To serve not tongues of nightingale,
Not manna soused in hydromel,
Not honey from Hymettus' cell,
Garnished with moly and asphodel —
 But Fish!

HENRY VAUGHAN

So true and sweet his music rings,
 So radiant is his mind with light
The very intent and meaning of what he sings
 May stay half-hidden from sight.

His flowers, waters, children, birds
Lovely as their own archetypes are shown;
Nothing is here uncommon, things or words,
 Yet every one's his own.

POETRY

In stagnant gloom I toil through day,
All that enchants me put away.
No bird decoyed to such a breast
Could warble a note, or be at rest;
From the old fountains of delight
Falls not one drop to salve my sight.

Yet — Thou who mad'st of dust my face,
And shut me in this bitter place,
Thou also, past the world to know,
Did'st hinges hang where heart may go
After day's travail — vain all words! —
Into this garden of the Lord's.

THE CHANGELING

Come in the dark did I —
The last stars in the sky,
Foretelling, 'Daybreak's nigh'.
Out of the brooding West,
Safe in my mother's breast
Love sheathed my wings in rest.

Twilight my home is, then,
In this strange world of men;
And I am happier when
The sun in flames and light
Sinks from my dazzled sight,
Leaving me sleep, and night.

So, now: only with thee
My homesick heart can be
Stilled in like mystery;
Long did life's day conceal
This tender dream and spell:
　　Now all is well.

BELATED

Once gay, now sad; remote — and dear;
Why turn away in doubt and fear?
I search again your grieved self-pitying face;
Kindness sits clouded there. But, love? No, not a trace.

What wonder this? Mine not to scold.
You, in so much a child; and I, how old!
Who know how rare on earth your like must be:
There's nought commensurate, alas, in age or me.

Bare ruined choirs — though time may grace bestow
On such poor relics in eve's after-glow;
And even to age serenity may bring,
Where birds may haven find; and peace, though not to sing.

But ah, blest Light-of-Morning One,
Ev'n though my life were nearly done?
Ev'n though no mortal power could that delay?
Think of the lightless journey thither — you away!

UNMEANT

Oh, if I spoke unkindly, heed it not:
Had it a language, my wild heart you'd hear
Weeping the love a frantic tongue forgot:
Think not mere spindrift is the sea, my dear!

SHE SAID

She said, 'I will come back again
        As soon as breaks the morn.'
But the lark was wearying of the blue,
        The dew dry on the thorn;
        And all was still forlorn.

She said, 'I will come back again,
        At the first quick stroke of noon.'
But the birds were hid in the shade from the heat
        When the clock tolled, *No: but soon!*
        And then beat slowly on.

She said, 'Yes, I'll be back again
        Before the sun has set.'
But the sweetest promises often made
        Are the easiest to forget,
        No matter grief and fret. . . .

That moon, now silvering the east,
        One shadow casts — my own.
Thought I, My friend, how often we
Have shared this solitude. And see,
        Midnight will soon draw on,
When the last leaf of hope is fallen,
And silence haunts heart's vacancy,
        And even pining's done.

THE HOUSE

The rusty gate had been chained and padlocked
  Against the grass-grown path,
Leading no-whither as I knew well,
  In a twilight still as death.

Once, one came to an old stone house there,
  Wheels crunched in those scarce-seen ruts;
A porch with jasmine, a stone-fringed garden —
  Lad's-love, forget-me-nots.

A happy house in that long-gone sunshine;
  And a face in the glass-bright moon,
And a voice at which even memory falters,
  Now that the speaker's gone.

I watch that image as I look at the pathway —
  My once accustomed zest,
As the painted gate on its hinges opened,
  Now locked against the past!

A true face too, yet scant of the future —
  A book that I never read . . .
Nor shall now, since I soon must be going
  To another old house instead.

THE ROSE

He comes to where a seeding rose
Has scattered her last petals on
  The stones about her stem.
Beyond the louring hills a moon
Among the stars of heaven goes,
  Stealing their light from them.

His eyes shine darkly in his head —
A face that dream has scrawled upon.
  He trembles, listening there.
Once — before Winter had snowed up
His heart — one loved had hither sped,
  His solitude to share.

HERE

Forgave I everything —
The heart's foreboding unless she were near
Who all things lovely made even lovelier;
The baffled hopes, the care, dismay, desire,
The mocking images that feed love's fire;
The glut of leaden days, the futile dream,
Night's stagnant brooding by its sluggish stream:
Yes, every anguished sigh, and unshed tear,
Pang of foul jealousy, the woe, the sweat. . . .
    But how forgive, forget,
    In this bleak winter sere —
      That she is here?

NO

A drear, wind-weary afternoon,
Drenched with rain was the autumn air;
As weary, too, though not of the wind,
    I fell asleep in my chair.

Lost in that slumber I dreamed a dream,
And out of its strangeness in stealth awoke;
No longer alone. Though who was near
    I opened not eyes to look;

But stayed for a while in half-heavenly joy,
Half-earthly grief; nor moved:
More conscious, perhaps, than — had she been there —
    Of whom,— and how much,— I loved.

USURY

'Let be, unreasonable heart, let go;
Why struggle so
Vainly and foolishly? A day will come
When failing eyes, with infinite regret,
Their farewell, heartsick gaze will set
On this, your earthly home;
And what you now death-dark afflictions deem
Only the shadows of its joys may seem.

[523]

'What now you crave
Nought mortal ever gave;
Nor within earthly bounds lies where you'd range.
Give, and give yet again
The utmost love you have,
Ev'n though it be in vain,
It's usury to ask it in exchange.

'Did toil and seeking find
The sealed and secret fountains of your mind?
Can you, by dipping bucket in a well,
Dredge up the riches of the imaginable?
Like some small wild flower, open in the sun,
Did *you* your heart the nectar give
By which alone that very love can live?
Did you your eyes make see
The beauty and grace of wake and dream whereon
Your soul has feasted, and content should be,
Seeing that all things temporal stay
Only their transitory day?

'Never. From some unknown
Source inexhaustible the seeds were sown
Whence blooms the fleeting dayspring of delight;
And, were your being never dark with night,
Where then the cockcrow of another morn?
As well go seek a rose without a thorn
As, famished with desire,
To aught that's flawless on this earth aspire. . . .'

So argued on and on
My tedious censor — sermon never done;
While yet a haggard exile in my heart
Cared not a jot
For what he would impart;
But, pining still for what the while was gone,
Wept, like a thwarted changeling, for the Moon!

THE LAST GUEST

Now that thy friends are gone,
And the spent candles, one by one,
Thin out their smoke upon the darkening air;
Now that the feast's first flowers
Flagged have irrevocably in these latening hours,
With perfumes that but tell how sweet they were;
Turn now — the door ajar —
See, there, thy winter star,
Amid its wheeling consorts wildly bright,
Herald of inward rapture, never of rest!
Still must thy threshold wait a laggard guest
Who comes, alone, by night.

BEYOND

On such an evening — still; and crystalline
With light, to which the heavens their fairness owe,
What wakes some changeling in the heart to pine
For what is past the mortal to bestow?

Ev'n in the shallow, busy hours of day
Dreams their intangible enchantments weave;
And in the dead of dark the heart may crave
A sleep beyond sleep, and for its visions grieve.

For that strange absence nothing can atone;
And every hope is servant to desire;
The flower conceals a beauty not its own,
And echo sighs from even the silent wire.

OCCLUDED

Chilled is the air with fallen rain,
Flood-deep the river flows;
A sullen gloom daunts heart and brain,
And no light shows.

Yet, in a mind as dark, a hint may steal
Of what lies hidden from an earth-bound eye:
Beyond the clouds the stars in splendour wheel,
The virgin huntress horns the silent sky.

[525]

THE BURNING LETTER

The saffron flames, edged with that marvellous blue,
Creep through the paper, blackening as they move.
So senseless time robs heart and memory too
Of what was once their very life and love.

Oh, marvel, if in some unearthly May
The wintering bee its wings again should beat,
And, waking, rove the hive death hid away,
Its wax–celled honeycomb no whit less sweet!

THE PLASTER CAST

It called to mind one now long out of sight,
Whom love still treasures with its secret grace:
That cast — half-hidden there — sepulchral white,
A random moonbeam on its peaceful face.

FEBRUARY 29

Odd, waif-like Day, the changeling of
Man's 'time' unreckoned in his years;
The moon already shows above
    Thy fickle sleet — now tears!

As brief thy stay has been as though
Next Spring might seal our tryst again.
Alas, fall must four winters' snow
    Ere you come back. And then?

I love thy timid aconite,
Crocus, and scilla's deep-sea blue;
Hark, too, that rainbird, out of sight,
    Mocking the woodland through!

But see, it's evening in the west:
Tranquil, withdrawn, aloof, devout.
Soon will the darkness drape your breast,
    And midnight shut you out!

Sweet February Twenty Nine! —
This is our grace-year, as I live!
Quick, now! this foolish heart of mine:
    Seize thy prerogative!

[526]

DELIVERANCE

Starched-capped, implacable, through the slow dark
    night
She had toiled; and through a dawn she had not seen,
To bring into the world this shapeless mite.
Cheeks cold with sweat, strong hands, eyes kestrel-keen,
She had coaxed, and wheedled: 'Patience, now; push hard.
Strive on! I'm travailing too. Oh, have no fear!
See, I am come to comfort, help, keep guard.
Deliverance soon will come, swift, sure, my dear!'...
A last gasped wrenching groan; a gnatlike wail,
Shrill, angry, sweet, all human cries above:
'Thank God,' she sighed, 'Who did not let me fail!'
And sighed again — for pity, grief, and love.

A SNOWDROP

Thou break'st from earth. Thy beauty of dust is made.
Light called thee, trembling, from the sod's cold shade,
While yet bleak winter's blast its snow outspread.

Dark storm thy swaddling was, and freezing sky.
O dauntless loveliness, may Spring, on high,
Yet shed her balm, and sing thee lullaby!

THE SLEEPING CHILD

Like night-shut flower is this slumbering face,
    Lamplight, for moon, upon its darkness spying;
That wheat-stook hair, the gold-fringed lids, the grace
    Of body entranced, and without motion lying.

Passive as fruit the rounded cheek; bright lip;
    The zigzag turquoise of that artery straying;
Thridding the chartless labyrinths of sleep,
    River of life in fount perpetual playing.

[527]

Magical light! though we are leagues apart,
My stealthiest whisper would at once awake thee!
Not I, thou angel thing! At peace thou art.
And childhood's dreams, at least, need not forsake thee.

RARITIES

Beauty, and grace, and wit are rare;
        And even intelligence:
But lovelier than hawthorn seen in May,
Or mistletoe berries on Innocent's Day
The face that, open as heaven, doth wear —
With kindness for its sunshine there —
        Good nature and good sense.

TO CORINNA, FROWNING

Dark, historied eyes,
Head of Hypnotic grace,
Lips into silence sinking,
Brows deep as midnight skies,
Wisdom beyond surmise, —
Why shallow, sharpen, darken so lovely a face —
Well, with this 'thinking'?

DAYS AND MOMENTS

The drowsy earth, craving the quiet of night,
Turns her green shoulder from the sun's last ray;
Less than a moment in her solar flight
Now seems, alas! thou fleeting one, life's happiest day.

'LOVE'

Children — alone — are grave,
Even in play with some poor grown-up's toy;
Solemn at heart, and wise:
Whence else their secret joy?
And the deep sleep they crave?

So Love is pictured — with his bandaged eyes,
To veil the blinding beauty of his skies —
And laughs out, naked, like a little boy.

THE TWO LAMPS

Two lights well over this old oak table —
The lamp I have read by, the risen sun;
In a brimming flood through the windowed gable,
As I turn to the day's work, scarcely begun.

As if in ineffable peace together,
They mingle their beams in a mutual bliss;
And I marvel at both, who am little able
To measure their ultimate loveliness.

With the lamp's alone a miracle enters
The transient life which on earth I have spent —
Whose utmost fringes this frail mind centres —
Yet a life that resembles a banishment,

When challenged like this by such sudden splendour,
That Eastern glory of rose and gold;
And out of my darkness and dwindling winters
I weep at the sight, like a child grown old!

THE RISEN SUN

I lay a while, exulting in its light,
My Druid heart drenched through with awe and praise;
Then into darkness turned a dazzled sight,
    That dared not meet its gaze.

SECOND-HAND

Courage, poor fool! Ripe though thy tare-crop be,
Love, over its bonfire, still may smile on thee.
Yes; and, perhaps, when that rank seed was sown,
Some herb of grace was there, though not thine own.

THE LAST SWALLOW

The robin whistles again. Day's arches narrow.
Tender and quiet skies lighten the withering
    flowers.
The dark of winter must come. . . . But that tiny
    arrow,
Circuiting high in the blue — the year's last
    swallow,
Knows where the coast of far mysterious sun-wild
    Africa lours.

ANOTHER SPRING

What though the first pure snowdrop wilt and die?
What though the cuckoo, having come, is gone?
Clouds cold with gloom assail the sun-sweet sky,
And night's dark curtains tell that day is done? —
This is our earthly fate. Howe'er we range,
Life and its dust are in perpetual change.

What though, then, Sweet, as welling time wins on,
The early roses in thy cheeks shall ail?
When they have bloomed, it's not thyself shall wan,
Nor for lost music shall thy heart-strings fail.
That Self's thine own. And all that age can bring
Love will make lovely. Then another Spring!

THE SPOTTED FLYCATCHER

Gray on gray post, this silent little bird
Swoops on its prey — prey neither seen nor heard!
A click of bill; a flicker; and, back again!
Sighs Nature an *Alas*? Or merely, *Amen*?

[530]

THE IDOL OF THE WORLD

I saw the Idol of the World descend
To lave herself in the slow stream of *Time*.

Bespangled with bright stars in highest noon,
The soundless water flowed, and reflex gave
To the wild beauty of her sweet-tongued throng,
As one by one they stooped; and one by one,
Doffing their raiment even lovelier showed.

    The swans that float
On vaulted branchings through the wild ravines
Of that dark other river, *Sleep*, cast not
Such marvellous whiteness on the unrippling flood;
And these, past all pure white, incomparable,
Had tinged their beauty with the rose's dye;
And in the wind's breath as they stirred their heads
Shook out like banners, trembling, serpentine,
The incomputable riches of their hair:
Out on the wind, and out too over the water,
Flowing, in silence, these bright phantoms by.

But I, in vision, marvelled more to see —
While these, her nymphs, Wealth, Fame, Lust, Glory,
    Power,
Painted the wave with their bare loveliness,
And wakened Echo to take tongue and sing —
Her of the World, pranked in her pomp, step down,
Her face a spectral ort beneath its hood,
Her hands concealed and stiff beneath her gloves,
Her very shape and substance swathed and farced —
A monstrous formlessness on fire with gems —
And cast herself into their virgin arms.
Thus was she there disported, and made clean!

Wherefore I know not what her semblance is,
Know not the likeness of her form and face,
Nor what gross life stirred in those monstrous clouts,
Nor any charm in her, nor any lure,
Who seemed a rottenness scarce aught at all.

[531]

THE RUINOUS ABBEY

Stilled the meek glory of thy music;
  Now only the wild linnets wing
Along the confusion of thy ruins,
  And to cold Echo sing.

Quenched the wan purple of thy windows,
  The light-thinned saffron, and the red;
Now only on the sward of thy dominion
  Eve's glittering gold is shed.

Oh, all fair rites of thy religion! —
  Gone now the pomp, the ashen grief;
Lily of Easter, and wax of Christmas;
  Grey water, chrism, and sheaf!

Lift up thy relics to Orion;
  Display thy green attire to the sun;
Forgot thy tombs, forgot thy names and places;
  Thy peace for ever won!

THE BOMBED HOUSE

Daughters of Joy lived here —
  Glazed, watching, sleep-drugged eyes;
    reluctant feet.
Now, from these shattered, shuttered windows, dark
  and drear,
      They ghost the abandoned street.

PRIDE HATH ITS FRUITS ALSO[1]

What shades are these that now oppress my eyes,
And hang a veil of night on burning day?
I see the Sun through shadows; and his clouds
Clothed in their mutable magnificence
Seem to some inward sorrow moving on.

What meaning has the beauty of the earth?
And this unageing sweetness of the Spring —
Her trees that once, as if from paradise,

---

[1] First published as 'Pride' together with 'The Truth of Things' in *Two Poems* in a limited edition of 100 copies, Dropmore Press, July 1946.

Borrowed their shining simpleness; her flowers,
Blowing where nothing but the bleak snow was,
Like flames of crystal brightness in the fields?

Once I could gaze until these seemed to me
Only my mind's own splendours in disguise.
But now their inward beauty is lost and faded:
They are the haunts of alien voices now —
An alien wonderment of light beams forth —
No more the secret reflex of my soul.

'INCOMPREHENSIBLE'

Engrossed in the day's 'news', I read
Of all in man that's vile and base;
Horrors confounding heart and head —
Massacre, murder, filth, disgrace:
Then paused. And thought did inward tend —
On my own past, and self, to dwell.

Whereat some inmate muttered, 'Friend,
If you and I plain truth must tell,
Everything human we comprehend,
    Only too well, too well!'

'SEE, HERE'S THE WARRANT...'

The day has foundered, and dead midnight's here:
As dark this spirit now with doubt and fear.
Doused is the candle of celestial fire,
    Lighting my secretest desire.

Put up the board! This house of life's to let.
Cold-chimneyed, void, its mouldering parapet
Surveys lost forests and a tongueless sea;
Gone joy, light, love, fire, hospitality.

Moons may perpetually wax and wane,
And morning's sun shine out again;
But when the heart at core is cold and black,

No cock, all earth for ear, will ever crow
    Its witching wildfire back.

[533]

LOST WORLD

Why, inward companion, are you so dark with
    anguish?
A trickle of rancid water that oozes and veers,
Picking its sluggish course through slag and refuse,
Down at length to the all-oblivious ocean —
What else were apt comparison for your tears?

But no: not of me are you grieving, nor for me either;
Though I, it seems, am the dungeon in which you dwell,
Derelict, drear, with skeleton arms to heaven,
Wheels broken, abandoned, greenless, vacant, silent;
    Nought living that eye can tell.

Blame any man might the world wherein he harbours,
Washing his hands, like Pilate, of all its woes;
And yet in deadly revolt at its evil and horror,
That has brought pure life to this pass, smit through
    with sorrow,
Since he was its infamous wrecker full well he knows.

Not yours the blame. Why trouble me then with your
    presence?
Linger no instant, most Beautiful, in this hell.
No touch of time has marred your immutable visage;
Eros himself less radiant was in his dayspring! —
Or nearer draw to your heartsick infidel!

THE DUNCE

And 'Science' said,
'Attention, Child, to me!
Have I not taught you all
You touch; taste; hear; and see?

'Nought that's true knowledge now
In print is pent
Which my sole method
Did not circumvent.

'Think you, the amoeba
In its primal slime
Wasted on dreams
Its destiny sublime?

[534]

'Yet, when I bid
Your eyes survey the board
Whereon life's How, When, Where
I now record,

'I find them fixed
In daydream; and you sigh;
Or, like a silly sheep,
You bleat me, *Why?*

'"Why is the grass so cool, and fresh, and green?
The sky so deep, and blue?"
Get to your Chemistry,
You dullard, you!

'"Why must I sit at books, and learn, and learn,
Yet long to play?"
Where's your Psychology,
You popinjay?

'"Why stay I here,
Not where my heart would be?"
Wait, dunce, and ask that
Of Philosophy!

'Reason is yours
Wherewith to con your task;
Not that unanswerable
Questions you should ask.

'Stretch out your hands, then —
Grubby, shallow bowl —
And be refreshed, Child —
Mind, and, maybe, soul!

'Then — when you grow into
A man — like me;
You will as learnèd, wise,
And — happy be!'

ANOTHER WASHINGTON

'*Homo*? Construe!' the stern-faced usher said.
　　Groaned George, 'A man, sir.' 'Yes.
Now *sapiens*?' . . . George shook a stubborn head,
　　And sighed in deep distress.

HERE LIES A TAILOR

Here lies a Tailor, well-loved soul!
Whether but ninth, or one man whole.
Yet of our loss the world to tell
There tolled but one cracked funeral bell.

Cross-legged we'd see him, early and late.
Now he must in that garment wait
Wherein to ease their earthly rest
Slumbers unstirred Death's every guest.

His was by his own needle made —
And not a stitch but sang his trade.
Good woollen too. For well knew he
What scarecrows most men naked be.

THEOLOGIANS

They argued on till dead of night —
'"God"' *versus* '"God"'— till ceased to shine
The stars in cold Olympus: and
Daybreak their very faces proved divine!

FALSE GODS

From gods of other men, fastidious heart,
You thank your stars good sense has set you free.
Ay. But the dread slow piercing of death's dart?
Its, 'Why, *my* God, have I forsaken *thee*.'

PALE-FACE

Dark are those eyes, a solemn blue:
Yes, silent Pale-face, that is true;
But I — I watch the fires that sleep
In their unfathomable deep,
Seeming a smouldering night to make
Solely for their own shining's sake.

It's common talk you're beautiful:
But I — I sometimes wonder, will
Love ever leave my judgment free
To see you as the world doth see —
'All passion spent'. No more to know
The very self that made you so.

FRESCOES IN AN OLD CHURCH[1]

Six centuries now have gone
Since, one by one,
These stones were laid,
And in air's vacancy
This beauty made.

They who thus reared them
Their long rest have won;
Ours now this heritage —
To guard, preserve, delight in, brood upon;
And in these transitory fragments scan
The immortal longings in the soul of Man.

BENIGHTED

'Frail crescent Moon, seven times I bow my head,
Since of the night you are the mystic queen:
May your sweet influence in her dews be shed!'

So ran by heart the rune in secret said:
Relic of heathen forbears centuries dead?
Or just a child's, in play with the Unseen?

[1] Stowell Park, Gloucestershire.

[537]

BLONDIN

With clinging dainty catlike tread,
His pole in balance, hand to hand,
And, softly smiling, into space
He ventures on that threadlike strand.

Above him is the enormous sky,
Beneath, a frenzied torrent roars,
Surging where massed Niagara
Its snow-foamed arc of water pours:

But he, with eye serene as his
Who sits in daydream by the fire,
His every sinew, bone and nerve
Obedient to his least desire,

Treads softly on, with light-drawn breath,
Each inch-long toe, precisely pat,
In inward trust, past wit to probe —
This death-defying acrobat! . . .

Like some old Saint on his old rope-bridge,
Between another world and this,
Dead-calm 'mid inward vortices,
Where little else but danger is.

JONATHAN SWIFT

That sovereign mind;
Those bleak, undaunted eyes;
Never to life, or love, resigned —
How strange that he who abhorred cant, humbug, lies,
Should be aggrieved by such simplicities
As age, as ordure, and as size.

DOUBLE DUTCH

That crafty cat, a buff-black Siamese,
Sniffing through wild wood, sagely, silently goes,
Prick ears, lank legs, alertly twitching nose,
And on her secret errand reads with ease
A language no man knows.

[538]

THE FOREST

'Death-cold is this house. Beasts prowl at its threshold;
A forest of darkness besieges its gate,
Where lurks the lynx, Envy; the leopard named
    Malice;
And a gaunt, famished wolf, padding softly, called
    Hate.

'So when that fair She, there — slant eyes and slim
    shoulders,
Voice stealthy with venom — our solitude shares,
I sit with my sewing away from the window,
Since it's thence that the wild cat called Jealousy glares.

'But supposing ajar were that door — she alone here?
And my whisper the black stagnant forest lipped
    through? . . .
No, she sips of my wine; breaks bread; has no notion
It is I, the despised one, those bolts might undo.'

ALL HALLOWE'EN

It was not with delight
That I heard in the dark
And the silence of night
The little dog bark.

It was not for delight
That his master had come
That so shrill rang his bark;
And at dawn, cold with rain,
That he yelped yet again:

But for fear, fury, fright
At the softness, the swiftness, the waft of the sprite,
    Doomed to roam
    Through the gloom,
As the vague murk of night
Gave cold, grudging birth
To daybreak, on earth —
Wanning hillside and grove,
Once his lodgement and love:
    And now, poor soul,
    Hieing off home.

[539]

SLIM CUNNING HANDS

Slim cunning hands at rest, and cozening eyes —
Under this stone one loved too wildly lies;
How false she was, no granite could declare;
Nor all earth's flowers, how fair.

'IT WAS THE LAST TIME HE WAS SEEN ALIVE'

'You saw him, then? . . . That very night?'
'A moment only. As I passed by.

'The lane goes down into shadow there,
And the sycamore boughs meet overhead;
Then bramble and bracken everywhere,
Moorland, whin, and the wild instead.
But the jasmined house is painted white
And so reflects the sky.

'He was standing alone in the dwindling dusk,
Close to the window — that rapt, still face,
And hair a faded grey —
Apparently lost in thought; as when
The past seeps into one's mind again,
With its memoried hopes and joys, and pain,
And seduces one back . . .

'He stirred, and then
Caught sight, it seemed, of the moon in the west —
Like a waif in the heavens astray —
Smiled, as if at her company;
Folded his old hands over his breast;
Bowed: and then went his way.'

THE VACANT FARMHOUSE

Three gables; clustered chimney-stacks; a wall
Snowed every Spring with cherry, gage, and pear,
Now suckered, rank, unpruned. Green-seeded, tall,
A drift of sullen nettles souring near —
Beside a staved-in stye and green-scummed pond,
Where once duck-dabbled sunshine rippled round.

Dark empty barns; a shed; abandoned byres;
A weedy stack-yard whence all life has fled;
A derelict wain, with loose and rusted tyres;
And an enormous elm-tree overhead . . .

That attic casement. . . . Was there flaw in the glass? . . .
I thought, as I glanced up, there had peered a face.
But no. Still: eyes are strange; for at my steady stare
Through the cool sunlit evening air,
Scared silent sparrows flew up out of the ivy there
Into an elder tree — for perching-place.

FLOOD WATER

What saw I — crouching by that pool of water
    Bright-blue in the flooded grass,
Of ash-white sea-birds the remote resort, and
    April's looking-glass? —
Was it mere image of a dream-dazed eye —
That startled Naiad — as the train swept by?

HAUNTED[1]

'The roads are dangerous.'

    'What? What? . . . "The roads"!
I sit at *home.* And what my heart forebodes
Is not . . . mere death — to catch me unawares,
But Life, which ever in at window stares;
Life that still drives me on, and edges by
Perils perpetual, and not transitory.
Knife-edged the daily precipices I tread,
By trotting footfall of the unseen misled:
Abysses of time; vile scenes illusions breed;
Fear that like fungus sprouts from viewless seed.

'You say, *This is.* The soul cries, *Only seems.*
And who, when sleeping, finds unreal his dreams? . . .
That hill; those hollows; sloping into shade.
The spawning sun; the earth for night arrayed;
The listening dark; the Fiend with his goads. . . .
"The roads are dangerous"? . . .
      'Oh, yes: "the roads".'

[1] First published as Linden Broadsheet No. 4, Linden Press, 1939.

THE OTHERS

'*Friendly?*'
   'Perhaps!'
     '*Say, neutral?*'
       'How to tell?'
'*Not* hostile!'
     'Well — who then would intercede?'
'*And do you rap? Or crystal-gaze? Or set*
Traps in the dark? Glass? Ouija? Or planchette?
A Madame Medium pay? Book — candle — bell?'
      'Oh, no; I sit and read.'
'*Or merely sit?*'
     'Sometimes. Why not? The air,
Wild Ariel's air, must thrill with secrecies
Beyond the scope of sense. . . . Ev'n we two share
Our thoughts and feelings chiefly by surmise.
You speak: I watch and listen. But faith alone
Vows that the well-spring of your life's my own.
And when Goodbye is said, and comes the night,
What proof has each of either — out of sight?

'Yes, even now — to eyes of love how clear! —
It is the ghost in you I hold most dear.
When, then, you urge me — mockery or dismay —
For evidence, for proof, I can but say,
The deeper my small solitude may be
The surer I am of unseen company . . .
It haunts with loveliness this silent night.'

'*Evils?*'
   'They too may prowl. 'Gainst them we had best
Guard unrelentingly both mind and breast.
I cannot answer, No, then. Only pray
Fortress of life and love the soul shall stay.
And Good-Night come — well this must be confessed:
It grieves me to the heart when, blessing the blest,
I have to add, Alas! For, truth to say,
  They are the happier when I'm away.'

COMPANY

There must be ghosts, I think, in this old house.
　　Often, when I am alone,
　　The quiet intensifies;
The very air seems charged with mute surmise;
I pause to listen, with averted eyes;
As if in welcome. And a passionate rapture,
As if at some thing long since pondered on,
Wells suddenly up within me. . . . Then is gone.

ENIGMAS

I weep within; my thoughts are mute
With anguish for poor suffering dust;
Sweet wails the wild bird, groans the brute:
Yet softly to a honied lute
Crieth a voice that heed I must;
　　Beckons the hand I trust.

O from nefarious enigmas freed
Shall all that dies not live at last,
Obedient as the seeding weed
Unto fruition come indeed,
　　Its perilous blossoming past!

AN ANGEL

Oh, now, Alexander's Angel,
Whither are thy pinions winnowing,
On what swift and timeless errand
Through the wilds of starry splendour
That to mortal eyes are merely
Points of radiance pricked in space?
Earthly minds can see thee solely
In the semblance of their bodies,
Winged with light thy locks of glory,
Streaming from thy brows gigantic,
Brows unmoved, and feet of crystal,
Heaven reflected in thy face!

[543]

THE TOWER

There were no flowers among the stones of the
    wilderness.
I was standing alone by the green-glazed tower,
Where among the cypresses winds went wandering,
Tinged now with gold-dust in the evening hour.

What goddess lingered here no tablet recorded;
Birds wild with beauty sang from ilex and yew;
Afar rose the chasms and glaciers of mountains,
The snow of their summits wax-wan in the blue —

In the blue of the heights of the heavenly vacancy —
My companions the silence, the relics, the lost;
And that speechless, divine, invisible influence,
Remote as the stars in the vague of the Past.

GO FAR; COME NEAR

Go far; come near;
You still must be
The centre of your own small mystery.
Range body and soul —
Goal on to further goal,
Still shall you find
At end, nought else but *thee*.
Oh, in what straitened bounds
Of thought and aim —
And even sights and sounds —
Your earthly lot is doomed to stay!

And yet, your smallest whim
By secret grace
To look the simplest flower in the face
Gives an inevitable reflection back,
Not of your own self only,
But of one
Who, having achieved its miracle,
Rests there, and is not gone;
Who still o'er your own darker deeps holds sway
Into whatever shallows you may stray.

[544]

Whatever quicksands loom before you yet,—
Indifference, the endeavour to forget,
Whatever truce for which your soul may yearn,
Gives you but smaller room
In which to turn,
Until you reach the haven
Of the tomb.

'The haven'? Count the chances . . . Is that so?
You are your Universe. Could death's quick dart
Be aimed at aught less mortal than the heart?
Could body's end,
Whereto it soon shall go,
Be end of all you mean, and are, my friend?

Ah, when clocks stop, and no-more-time begins,
May he who gave the flower
Its matchless hour,
And you the power
To win the love that only loving wins,
Have mercy on your miseries and your sins.

A DAYDREAM

In a daydream, all alone,
Shone another sun on me,
Where, on cliffs of age-cold stone,
Harebell, thyme and euphrasy,
Seraphs came that to the air
Blew a music water-sweet;
And, as I watched, in reverie,
Danced with flowerlike soundless feet.

With what joy each instrument
Answered their sweet mouths. How burned
Their tranquil heads in ardour bent,
While, in peace unfaltering, turned —
Turned they their strange eyes on me,
Blue in silver of the morn.
But in leaden slavery
Lay my limbs, and I forlorn
Could but watch till faint and wan
Waned their beauty, and was gone.

[545]

O my heart, what eyes were these?
What viols theirs, that haunt me so? —
Those faint-sunned cliffs, those leaf-still trees,
Heavily hanging, shade o'er shade,
Where flowers of coral, amber, pearl,
In a burning stillness laid,
Coloured the clear air with light? —
O too happy dreams that furl
Their day-fearing petals white;
And vanish out of sight!

FRIENDS

When on my bed I lie,
To sleep and rest,
My two hands loosely folded on my breast,
As all men's are when they the long sleep share,
It seems they are closer friends than ever I guessed
They even in childhood were!

SOLITUDE

Space beyond space: stars needling into night:
Through rack, above, I gaze from Earth below —
Spinning in unintelligible quiet beneath
A moonlit drift of cloudlets, still as snow.

MIRACH, ANTARES . . .

Mirach, Antares, Vega, Caph, Alcor —
From inch-wide eyes I scan their aeon-old flames,
Enthralled: then wonder which enchants me more —
They, or the incantation of their names.

THE CELESTIAL LIBRARY

'THE SECRETS OF ALL HEARTS', I read. And sighed.
   That vast cold gallery. Tomes in endless line.
'"All"!' mused the Stranger, standing at my side;
   'These contain only thine.'

WINTER EVENING

Over the wintry fields the snow drifts; falling, falling;
   Its frozen burden filling each hollow. And hark;
Out of the naked woods a wild bird calling,
   On the starless verge of the dark!

BLOW, NORTHERN WIND

Blow, northern wind; fall snow;
And thou — my loved and dear,
See, in this waste of burthened cloud
   How Spring is near!

See, in those labouring boughs,
Buds stir in their dark sleep;
How in the frost-becrumbling ruts
   The green fires creep.

The dreamless earth has heard
Beneath snow's whispering flakes
A faint shrill childlike voice, a call —
   Sighs, ere she wakes . . .

What Spring have we? Turn back! —
Though this be winter's end,
Still may far-memoried snowdrops bloom
   For us, my friend.

THE KISS

In the long drouth of life,
Its transient wilderness,
The mindless euthanasia of a kiss

Reveals that in
An instant's beat
Two souls in flesh confined
May yet in an immortal freedom meet.

[547]

From those strange windows
Called the eyes, there looks
A heart athirst
For heaven's waterbrooks.

The hands tell secrets.
And a lifted brow
Asks, 'O lost stranger,
Art thou with me now?'

All stumbling words are dumb;
And life stands still;
Pauses a timeless moment; then resumes
The inevitable.

WORDS

Were words sole proof of happiness,
How poor and cold the little I have said!
And if of bitter grief, no less
    Am I discomfited.

The lowliest weed reflects day's noon of light,
Its inmost fragrance squanders on the air;
And a small hidden brook will all the night
Mourn, beyond speech to share.

INCOMPUTABLE

Think you the nimblest tongue has ever said
A morsel of what may ravish heart and head?
Think you the readiest pen that ever writ
Has more than hinted at what makes life sweet?

As well assume old Thames — eyot, meadow, copse —
Sums, as he disembogues, his waterdrops:
That beechen woods count up their countless leaves;
Furrows the birds once nurtured on their sheaves.

See, now, the stars that mist the Milky Way;
The hosting snowflakes of a winter's day;
Count them for tally of what life gives, thus shown,
Then reckon how many you have made your own!

[548]

DAY[1]

Wherefore, then, up I went full soon
And gazed upon the stars and moon —
The soundless mansion of the night
Filled with a still and silent light:

And lo! night, stars and moon swept by,
And the great sun streamed up the sky,
Filling the air as with a sea
Of fiery-hued serenity.

Then turned I in, and cried, O soul,
Thank God thine eyes are clear and whole;
Thank God who hath with viewless heaven
Drenched this gross globe, the earth, and given,
In Time's small space, a heart that may
Hold in its span all night, all day!

---

[1] The original version was written as a prologue to *Henry Brocken* (1904), though
it was not finally included there.

Winged Chariot (1951)

'Is every subject apt for rambling rhyme? —
Some are intractable, and some sublime:
Only Eternity could master Time.'

'As I sat by myself, I talked to myself,
And myself replied to me . . .'

'I, whom thou seest with horyloge in hande,
Am namèd Tyme, the lord of very howre . . .'

. . . Why this absurd concern with clocks, my friend?
Watching Time waste will bring no more to spend,
Nor can retard the inevitable end.

Yet when, the old wide staircase climbed once more,
Your bag in hand, you attain its second floor,
Turn the Yale key in lock, sigh, open the door

And into these familiar rooms you slip —
Where even Silence pauses, finger on lip —
Three emulous metal tongues you wake from sleep.

Do they suffice you? No, you pause again.
And (as if mechanisms made by men
The Truth could tell) you search each face. And then,

Though every minute of your life's your own,
Though here you are 'master' and at ease, alone —
You ring up *TIM*; consult the telephone.

The *telephone*! . . . Then, these precautions past,
Time made in Greenwich safely yours at last,
You set all three some fifteen minutes fast.

Psychopathist might guess the reason why
You indulge your wits in this mendacity.
Think *you* Man's 'enemy' is thus put by?

Think you so fleet a thing — that madcap hare
You daily waken from its nightlong lair —
Time, would consent such stratagems to share?

Or is it that you reassurance seek,
Deeming the Future will appear less bleak
Now that your clocks will 'go' a whole long week?

[551]

'. . . "O, it came ore my eare, like the sweet sound
That breathes upon a banke of Violets;
Stealing, and giving odours . . ." '

If Time's a stream — and we are told it's so,
Its peace were shattered if you check its flow;
What Naiad then ev'n fingertip would show? —
Her imaged other-world in ruins? . . . No:

Should once there haunt your too-attentive ear
A peevish pendulum, no more you'll hear
The soundless thunder of the distant weir

Which is Eternity. . . . Blest reverie:
When, from the serfdom of this world set free,
The self a moment rapt in peace may be;

Not void; but poised, serene, 'twixt praise and prayer,
Such as the flower-clocked woods and meadows share,
Lulled and fed only by day's light and air.

How punctual they! But to no *tic-toc* rune.
Theirs is an older code than 'May' and 'June';
As testifies 'Jack-go-to-bed-at-noon';
Airiest of ghosts, he goes to bed at noon!

'. . . *Jocond day stands tiptoe on the mistie mountaine's top* . . .'

Nimbused in his own song at dawn of day,
From earth's cold clods the skylark wings his way,
Into the sun-gilt crest of heaven to stray.

Housed in the dark of sleepy farms below,
At their own hour the cocks craned up to crow,
Their harems hearkening in obsequious row.

But wheel and barrel, ratchet, pawl, and spring?
Dear heart alive, how dull and dead a thing,
Compared with any creature on the wing,
Wherewith to measure even a glimpse of Spring.

Or, 'splitting seconds', to attempt to mete
The thrill with which a firefly's pinions beat.
Yes, or the languor, lingering and sweet,

When, lulled in the embraces of the sun,
The rose exults that her brief course is run
And heat-drowsed honey-bee has come; is gone.

[552]

Last night, at window idling, what saw I
Against the dusky summer greenery? —
Midges, a myriad, that up and down did fly,
Obedient to the breezes eddying by —
Sylphs scarcely of Time but of mere transiency:

An ovoid of intricate *winged* things, beautiful;
As on some sea-breeze morning, sunned and cool,
One may peer down upon a wavering shoal —
Like eddying weed in ebb-tide's lap and lull —
Of tiniest fish-fry in a rock-bound pool.

'. . . *Among which the elephant is the greatest and commeth nearest in wit and
capacitie to men* . . .'

The sage, slow elephant, night-scampering mouse,
Snug-wintering tortoise in his horny house,
To cark of frost and snow oblivious —
Share they, think you, our sense of time with us?

And that old sly close-fisted cockatoo —
Whose private life's a furtive *entre nous*,
What temporal lens did *his* round eye peer through
Whilst five kings reigned, and died — ere he died too?

Or, destined denizen of perpetual night,
She, of the termites? Bloated, teeming, white,
Huge and scarce motionable: yet her hosts' delight?

A-drowse in the ocean in an Arctic gale —
What clock ticks Vespers to the suckling whale?
And bids Aurora her heavenly face unveil?

'. . . *Whannè thet Aprille with his shourès sote
The droghte of Marche hath percèd to the rote* . . .'

What jewelled repeater edged the cuckoo's wing,
Lovesick from Africa, to flit in Spring?
Only one ding-dong name to say and sing —
And dower our pipits with a fosterling?

Oh, what a tocsin has she for a tongue;
How stealthy a craft to jilt her eggs and young,
And put them out to nurse their whole lives long! —

[553]

This heiress of the primeval. How learned she
Time, season, mileage and the momentary? —
Two idle summers and a sundering sea;
And all small honest birds for enemy.

If ev'n we share no thought with our own kind
But what with voice, face, words may be defined,
How shall these quicksands of Nature be divined?
How fathom the innate by means of mind?

Reason strives on to bridge the vague abyss
Sev'ring the human from the languageless,
Its countless kinds and spheres of consciousness.

Insight delights in heavenly mysteries
And loves the childish game of *'Well, now, guess!'*

*'. . . Love is from the eye: but . . . more by glances than by full gazings; and so
for envy and malice . . .'*

See, now, that dwindling meteor in space
Which with its ruin illumed the night's hushed face:
As well *time* headlong Lucifer's disgrace!

And, fleeter ev'n than flickering lightning's glow,
Transfiguring hidden landscapes hushed below,
Imaged ideas through consciousness may flow:
Fruit raised from seed before ev'n leaf could show!

And feeling races thought. *One* stricken glance
At some, till then, scarce dreamed-of countenance —
The very soul's at gaze, as if in trance:

Poised like a condor in the Andean night,
When scarp and snowdrift, height to pinnacled height,
Transmute with wonder the first morning light.

So, in its innocence, love breaks upon the sight.

Hatred, dread, horror, too. As books relate: —
Thyestes when his own son's flesh he ate;
First stare at his iron cage of Bajazet;
And Œdipus — when parricide's his fate.

'... *By which there sat an hory*
Old agèd Sire, with hower-glasse in hand,
Hight Time ...'

Dogged morn till bed-time by its dull demands,
The veriest numskull *clock*-cluck understands,
Eked out by solemn gestures of its hands:

A subtler language stirs in whispering sands:

That double ovoid of translucent glass;
The tiny corridor through which they pass,
Shaping a crescent cone where nothing was,

Which mounts in exquisite quiet as the eye
Watches its myriad molecules slip by;
While, not an inch above, as stealthily,

Those rocks minute might fall of waters be
Pouring themselves as imperturbably
Into the crystal of their central sea.

A tiny shallowing on the surface seen
Sinks to a crater where a plane has been.
Could mutability be more serene?

Invert the fragile frame; and yet again
Daydream will rear a castle built in Spain.
'Time' measured thus is dewfall to the brain.

Water-clock, clepsydra, candle-flame and day-break.

So, out of morning mist earth's flowers arise,
Reflecting tintless daybreak in the skies;
And, soon, the whole calm orient with its dyes.

And even in bleak Winter one may go
Out of night's waking dreams and see the snow
In solemn glory on the fields below.

How happy he whose 'numbers' well as sweet,
Their rhythms in tacit concert with their feet,
And measure 'time', with no less hushed a beat. . . .

And clepsydra — the clock that Plato knew,
Tolling the varying hours each season through;
Oozing on, drop by drop, in liquid flow,
Its voice scarce audible, bell-like and low
As Juliet's communings with her Romeo.

More silent yet; pure solace to the sight —
The dwindling candle with her pensive light
Metes out the leaden watches of the night.
And, in that service, from herself takes flight.

'. . . The Sun's light when he unfolds it,
Depends on the Organ that beholds it . . .'

Ah, after vigil through the hours called small,
Earth's dumb nocturnal hush enshrouding all,
When dread insomnia has the soul in thrall,
To see that gentle flame greet sunrise on the wall!

Clocks fuss along, the lackeys of a spring;
Slaves of escapements; chime, but never sing:
Snow-soft as ghost-moth is *Time's* winnowing wing;
Though even to granite it some change must bring;

And to all else that's temporal. Which is yet
Nothing corrupt, but merely change. And that
On goal supreme — through change — its course may set.

And ev'n if ruin Nature's face betray,
Time was not cause thereof, but mere decay,
Slow as renewal, wending its wonted way.

'. . . One thinks the soul is air; another fire;
Another, blood diffused about the heart,
Another saith, the elements conspire.
And to her essence each doth give a part . . .'

When restless thought lulls low, as winds may cease
On dune and marram-grass, and there is peace,
The self becalmed may be by a loneliness

That pays no heed to time; and may attain
What Reason mocks at as the 'intense inane';
Though little one covet to come back again.

Sea-gulls home this way in the setting sun,
When — lowered lamp — his winter is begun.
He dyes their plumes with his vermilion,
As, in their idling squadrons, they wing on.

Under this roof, when, motionless and dense,
Silence beleaguers every nerve and sense,
Self-solitude is made the more intense.

Head turned on shoulder then, the straining ear
Dreads and yet conjures up the voice of Fear.
An inward sentry cries, 'Who's listening here?' ...

Could fancy alone in this old thick-walled house,
When nothing stirs, not even a wainscot mouse,
Thus haunt mere matter with the ominous?
    And these misgivings rouse?

Midnight beyond that shutter broods. The rain
Its lully whispers in the towering Plane
Whose presence canopies my complete domain —

Whose every twig breathes freshness in the air,
And mottled boughs five-fathom tresses wear,
In May-time dangling like a Siren's hair.

*'... In the Desarts of Africa, you shall meet oftentimes with fairies appearing
in the shape of men and women, but they vanish quite away like phantastical
delusions ...'*

Phantoms draw nearer then of the unseen.
They pause in silence at the entering-in;
Eyes, raiment, wraithlike faces, vapour-thin —

Heeded perceptions of a secret mind
Less closely to the physical confined:
Like flowers in their beauty to the blind.

And every soul draws ever toward its own
Viewless associates as it journeys on;
Is never less alone than when alone.

When, then, I leave this haunt, as soon I may,
Will not some homesick relic of me stay —
Unseen, unheard? And while — what? ... *Time*, away!?

'Are they shadows that we see? ...'

Hearken the heart must if it seem to share
A rarer presence yet than light or air;
Visage serene, calm brows, and braided hair —

More real even than what imagining
Into the confines of the eye may bring;
Tranquil as seraph, with half-folded wing.

[557]

Would I her scholar were in poetry!
No toil in vain then. Nothing to weary me.
Alas, these halting rhymes — that cannot be.

Yet, when, a child, I was content to rove
The shingled beach that I was Crusoe of,
All that I learned there was akin to love.

The glass-clear billow toppling on the sand,
Sweet salt-tanged air, birds, rock-drift — eye, ear, hand;
All was a language love could understand.

'. . . *Those steps of stone* . . .'

Yet there was mystery too: those steps of stone —
In the green paddock where I played alone —
    Cracked, weed-grown,
Which often allured my hesitant footsteps down

To an old sun-stained key-holed door that stood,
The guardian of an inner solitude,
Whereon I longed but dreaded to intrude;
Peering and listening as quietly as I could.

There, as I knew, in brooding darkness lay
The waters of a reservoir. But why —
In deadly earnest, though I feigned, in play —
Used I to stone those doors; then run away,
Listening enthralled in the hot sunny day

To echo and rumour; and that distant sigh,
As if some friend profaned had made reply, —
    When merely a child was I?

'. . . *Love is a malady apart, the sign*
And astrolabe of mysteries Divine . . .'

Nor is this *love* a jewel in one plane.
It many facets has: mind, soul; joy, pain:
And even a child may to this truth attain.

Secret and marvel too the body is,
And exquisite means of earth's infrequent bliss;
But love foresees Love's everlastingness.

[558]

Had passion voice, why then the strange delight
Ev'n an hour may bring would pæans indite;
And, seeing no words these mercies could requite,
Age pines, in talk, to skirt the infinite;
As birds sing wildlier when it draws towards night.

'Whoe'er she be . . .'

She whom I vision many masks has worn,
Since, in this world, half-alien, I was born;
And every one has left me less forlorn.

And though pure solitude may be utmost grace,
And leagues from loneliness, a loved-one's face
Quadruples happiness in any place.

Time shared then's not time halved. Yet if it be
Spent in that loved one's fleeting company,
It flies even swiftlier than the caught set free.

Leaving an empty cage? . . . May heaven forbear!
Blank absence then would greet us everywhere —
A *wilderness*, called Time, bereft and bare
Be the slow tedium left however fair.

'. . . There mournful cypress grew in greatest store,
And trees of bitter gall, and Heben sad,
Dead-sleeping Poppy, and black Hellebore,
Cold coloquintida . . .'

However fair. . . . But cracked may be love's bells;
Mirage its lode-star, and disaster else;
As (countless cantos) this old fable tells: —

THE PALACE OF TIME

'A self-sick wanderer, in the leprous light
Of death-drear forest at the fall of night
Came out on no less derelict a sight: —

'Its walls slant-shadowed by the dwindling shine
Of day, a mansion — bleached, gaunt, saturnine,
With windows gaping 'gainst the evening green
As though by fire-flames charred their mullions had been.

'It called to mind a dream he once was in. . . .

'That broken turret; fallen roof — were these
The prey of *age*? Weather's slow ravages?
Or sudden blasting stroke of destiny's?

'When what is beautiful is that no more,
Except as memory may its grace restore,
One's very heart stands listening at the door;

'And self-arraigned, the fatal charge must meet:
"Wilful neglect; betrayal; self-deceit."
And no defender left to answer it.

'. . . *And we watered our horses at the pool of Siloam* . . .'

'What though once-Eden now is sour morass,
The abode of croaking frogs and venomous flies,
      Yet, which of us, alas,
Can not in his own visage darkly trace
      That blighted Seraph's face?

'And when, companionless, at night we fare,
Ascending our own private corkscrew stair,
Is't never Darkness that awaits us there? . . .

'Down the chill chace he paced . . . Where once the deer
Browsed in the dappling sun devoid of fear,
And supped the conduit's waters rippling clear;

'Where wooed the turtle-dove; and all dark long
Creatures nocturnal in its woods would throng,
And nightingales mock passion with their song;

'Now effigies, in guise of life, of stone —
Grief, woe, despair their broken faces on,
Some as though smiling — in the dusk-line shone.
All else seemed foundered in oblivion.

'And *Silence* mouldered there; aloof, alone.
Ev'n should the sun now shine and gild the tips
Of motionless cypresses in this wide ellipse,
His beams were shorn of power, as in eclipse.

'And formless shapes of rock that seemed to brood
On lost primordial secrets, crouched or stood,
Lifeless, yet menacing, margining the wood.

[560]

'... *The lady rade, True Thomas ran,*
Until they cam to a water wan;
O it was night and nae delight,
And Thomas wade aboon the knee.'

'Yet no thing living showed, save where it seemed
The stone-work of a dial vaguely gleamed;
And there, though not asleep, one lay and dreamed.

'*It was dark night, and nae starlight,*
And on they waded lang days three,
And they heard the roaring o a flood,
And Thomas a waefou man was he ...'

'Sickened with expectation, close he drew,
The sun-warmed turf beneath his feet; and knew
Eyes glassy-cold as serpent's watched their thin lids through —
    Lids fringed with gilt, and eyes of sleep-glazed blue.

'*Palace of Time*, he had heard these ruins named;
Once seat of Pride and Pomp, but long ill-famed,
Since Pride had fallen, and venging fire had flamed.

'... *Side by side, jarring no more,*
Day and night side by side,
Each by a doorless door,
Motionless sit the bridegroom and bride
On the Dead-Sea-shore. ...'

'She, then, was Witchcraft, and on evil bent,
Foe of the abandoned, lost, and malcontent,
And doomed to ruin whithersoever they went?

'The tarnished dial, its gnomon shorn away,
Worn steps, now shattered, with cankering lichen grey,
Told of phantasmal night, past hope of day.

'A lunar dial? Astarte's wizardry?
Secret, adored, cold, wanton in perfidy;
The bygone haunt of ancient revelry?

'And he, this wanderer? What fate was his?'...
So runs this ancient legend of dole and Dis;
Whereof no end's recorded beyond this.

'Like one who, victim of a malady,
Having its name, yet knows not what it be,
Seeking for light in some old dictionary,
Meets *caput mortuum's* cold scrutiny ...'

*   *   *

[561]

'*. . . Feed apace then, greedy eyes, On the wonder you behold! . . .*'

Love is life's liberty. 'Time' will snare remain
Until to peace of mind and heart we attain,
And paradise, whose source it was, come back again.

Inscrutable Nature in her own slow way
Seems even in labour to be half in play;
With hyssop in wall will dally a whole long summer's day.

She takes her time: and, the rich summer gone,
Through autumn mists and winter cold dreams on
Till, Phoenix-like, her beauty is re-won.

. . . How often comes to memory—silly sooth!—
That tiny bird I took to be a moth . . .

Yes, and with what élan her creatures live,
How in their kinds, crafts, busyness they thrive!
The tribute lovely, wanton, odd they give

To all that nurtures them — the viewless air,
The Sun in dazzling bounty circling there,
Rivulet, bosoming hill and woodland fair.
Her faintest change each in its kind must share;

Unique, exultant beings of infinite zest,
Preying or preyed on, and supremely blest
In that by human cares they are unoppressed.

'*. . . If things of Sight such heavens be,*
What heavens are those we cannot see? . . .'

How ponder quickly enough on what one sees
To realise this beauty's mutableness? —
Its range is one of infinite degrees.

Stir not your gaze, but let it so remain,
In all its quietude, in eye and brain;
Of its own nature it will soothe, and sain.

A plain wood panel will the whole long day
In light and shadow change with every ray.
No eye will *watch* that loveliness away.
Alas, that nothing can less briefly stay!

[562]

The moment is annulled — however dear —
Sooner than raptured tongue can utter, *'See, it's here!'*
Shrill from his midden-top whoops Chanticleer,
Scratches — and priceless gewgaws disappear.

Nor is some strangeness absent from the seen,
However usual, if there intervene
The unageing mind. Its hidden life has been
This edge of contrast to the day's routine.

Jasmine, and hyacinth, the briar rose
Steep with their presence a whole night; nor close:
Time with an infinite gentleness through them flows.

Fantastic growths there are too — flower and scent —
In earth's occult alembic strangely blent,
To some obscure decree obedient,
And as of sorcerous or divine descent.

Mist, dew and rainfall keep these trystings sweet,
And light, with ghosting shadow, dogs our feet;
Day in, day out, thrums on heart's secret beat,
Calmly refusing to conform with it.

While none of these then can 'pure time' bespeak,
Which every eager intellect should seek,
Each mind its time-piece has. And that's unique.

'. . . Time was: Time is: Time is not . . .'

Time was: Time is: Time is not, runs the rune.
Hasten then. Seize that *is*, so soon begone.
As well subtract the music, keep the tune!

For no 'time' ever yet in storage lay,
Sun-ambered, weathered, sweet as new-mown hay,
Waiting mind's weaving — Rumpelstiltskin's way: —

Time 'real'; time rare; time wildfire-fleet; time tame;
Time telepathic, out of space, and aim;
Time starry; lunatic; ice-bleached; of flame;
Dew-transient, yet immutably the same;
Meek-mild as chickweed in a window-frame;

Tardy as gathering dust in rock-hewn vault;
Fickle as moon-flake in a mirror caught
At pause on some clear gem's scarce-visible fault . . .

And how moves Time in triple darkness hid,
Where — mummied 'neath his coffered coverlid —
Sleeps on the Pharaoh in his pyramid:
Time disincarnate — and that sharp-nosed head?

Even though suave it seem as narded oil,
Fatal to beauty it is, and yet its foil.
It is of all things mortal the indifferent soil.

Eye scarce can tell where, the whole spectrum through,
Orange with yellow fuses, green with blue;
So Time's degrees may no less diverse show,
Yet every variant be its fraction true.

'... And over them Arachne high did lift
Her cunning web, and spred her subtile net. ...'

Grey with their dust, cribbed in with facts and dates,
On foundered centuries the historian waits.
Ashes in balance, he sifts, weighs, meditates.

Unlike the astronomer in the heavens at play,
Through Time defunct, not Space, he elects to stray.
Stars of a magnitude his chosen prey,
He spends less leisure on its Milky Way,
Man's millions in its *Coalsack* stowed away.

Much he may look for which he is like to find;
And to its worst may be at length resigned:
'The follies, crimes, misfortunes of mankind.'

Transmuting facts into his truth, rejecting none,
Rapt in seclusion, he toils gravely on;
Crypt, arch, pier, buttress, roof; and fickle moon —
A noble structure when the building's done:
But of wild coarse sweet positive *life*, no breath — not one.

Yet, let disciple read him with delight —
In Time interred, a fellow-anchorite —
It is as though into the gloom of night
Scapegrace Aladdin chanced to come in sight,
And rubbed his lamp. ... The change is infinite.
Shadows take bodies; blood begins to beat;

And through this inky ichor softly rills
The Jinnee's magic, and each cranny fills
With scene, thought, action, as the context wills;
And very life itself his record thrills.

[564]

So too in fane of Time's memorial stones —
In crisscross framework of poor human bones,
Isis, Baal, Ormuzd on their scaling thrones —
The scutcheons glimmer of the great Unknowns . . .
    And now — their withered *Once!*

. . . Sup humbly. All things compassed, near or far,
Are — for ourselves — but what we think they are:
The Web of Seeming holds us prisoner . . .

They touch us to the quick, these far events,
Looming beyond mere mortal instruments;
Omens of destiny, of Providence:
Their dust long fall'n, but not their influence.

But no rune's yet recalled Time's lost and gone —
Only its ghosts. And theirs is *dies non*.
All is in flux; nor stays, but changes on.
No sunrise hymns the self-same orison.

The unique's unique — assort it as we please;
Every oak's acorns will sprout differing trees.
So many lives, as many mysteries.

Nor do the morning stars together sing
One only *Laus* to *Alleluias'* ring,
When shout the sons of God before their King.

'. . . O tell me mair, young man, she said,
This does surprise me now;
What country hae ye come frae?
What pedigree are you? . . .'

Were moments seeds, we then therein might say
What hidden kind, hue, value, beauty lay,
Virtue and quality. But, these away,

Theirs only quantity, mere measurement,
Sans substance, pattern, form, shape, taste and scent —
Flimsier than bubble, and more transient.

Should, then a Stranger from another Sphere
Enquire, *'This Time, of which so much I hear?*
Light — dark; heat — cold; void — solid: these are clear;
But TIME? What is it? Show me some, Monsieur!'

[565]

What should we choose for semblance? A flake of snow?
A beach-brine bubble? A tiny shell or two?

Poised in the sun, pure diamond of dew?
Or whisper, '*Look! a clock! Now watch Time flow;
It's a Machine, you see. It makes it go.*'

Bland face; sly jerking hands: staring he'd stay,
Dumbly astonished. And then turn, and say,
*Closer to Nothingness could nothing stray!
And now, pray, make Time flow the other way!*'

'. . . *O fairest flower, no sooner blown than blasted,
Soft silken primerose, fading timelesslie* . . .'

'Moments', like sun-discs on a rippled sea,
No heed paid to them merely cease to be,
Leaving no trace of their identity:

Mere litter stowed in Time's packed Lumber-Room —
Moth, spider, mildew, rust, star-raftered gloom;
Vast as moon-crater, silent as the tomb,
Not even a death-watch for a pendulum.

But mark Self summing up what's really his —
Glimpses of childhood, friendship, bygone bliss —
Those fumbling fingers, that impassioned kiss!
Dear beyond words are relics such as these.

And who, in his dark hours, dulled, overcast —
At envy, hatred, malice, cant aghast —
Would not abscond a while from this worn temporal waste;
Into another world of being haste,
And, maybe, meet the idolised at last?
Chaucer? Keats? Marvell? Wyatt? Drayton? — Oh
Any long-lov'd and true enthusiast!

'. . . *Some nameless stuff* . . .'

Lost in that company the spirit may range
A rarer, deeper, closer interchange
In the imagination, rich and strange —
A Mariana in a moated grange.

At shut of dusk, 'neath timbered roof, worn stone,
Dark at the window-glass, and all life gone,
In hush of falling dust and mouldering bone,

Inward, still inward let the round ear lean!...
Time's not of moments made. It's hidden in
Some nameless stuff that oozes in between....

'..."*I stand like one*
That long hath ta'en a sweet and golden dream,
I am angry with myself now that I wake"...'

Yet, friend, (once more), when you are here again,
Do you *possess* this quiet? The Silence drain?
Give thanks for boons withheld from other men?
A Paternoster breathe — and then count ten?

No, like some light-o'-love, away you chase
Straight to that *chit-chat* in the china case
You bought in Woodbridge — 'Fitz's' native place.
Then comes 'Susanna', with her prim round face;

Next your much-prized old dial, inlaid with brass,
Sun-pendulum'd in gilt. And next....
                                        Alas,
Still will the hours for you melt much too fast!

Not for the world that I would mock at what
Have 'timed' the countless godsends of my lot;
And still might miss, most earthly things forgot.

'...*Keeping time, time, time*
To a sort of runic rhyme...!'

Even as 'child of Paules', when brood I would
At thunder of its bell — Night: Solitude —
(And slow-coach was I always, doomed to plod),
I must have fallen in love with clocks for good.

Tompion, Bréguet, Knibb, Ellicot, Cole, Quare,
How featly chime the names of those who were
Masters in this sweet art; famed everywhere:
Timepiece-artificers beyond compare.
And each of sovereign Harrison the heir,
    With his supreme chronometer.

Bell-tinkling *watch*-craft too, tiny as bees,
Set bezel-wise, may match great clocks with ease —
And, no less punctually, the Pleiades.

And should you wish to meditate; then, where
A grandpaternal timepiece crowns the stair,
Pause as you go to bed; to listen; and share
The unhastening monologue it ponders there.

'. . . *But at my back I alwaies hear*
Times winged Charriot drawing near . . .'

To Julius and Gregory be praise,
Who bade the Calendar amend its ways.
But when from such dull durance fancy strays —
How beautiful is the procession of the days.

With each cold clear pure dawning to perceive
The Sun's edge earlier; and, at fall of eve,
When the last thrush his song is loth to leave,
To mark its latening, however brief!

Nor is the marvel of his burning rose,
Bronze, saffron, azure, discontinuous;
He takes his splendour with him as he goes.

So thought the poet, Fabre d'Églantine,
(When his sweet France had licked the platter clean).
Brumaire . . . . Nivôse . . . . Vendémiaire — things *seen*
In Terra's tilt, from virgin white to green:

Snow . . . . Rain . . . . Wind . . . . Bud . . . . Flower . . . . Grape
    make richer sense
Than our pastiche of dead-alive events —
Janus to Juno, and December thence.

Sick unto death must Woden be of Thor;
Deaf Saturn yells at Frig, '*We have met before!* . . .'
Sun unto Moon, '*Would God weeks were no more;*
Or that to Man He would his wits restore!' . . .

'. . . *And yonder al before us lye*
Desarts of vast Eternity . . .'

Still: dangling keys 'twixt clumsy finger and thumb,
You bustle your punctual way from room to room,
And into senseless tongues transform the dumb.

You wind the docile things — run-down or not;
You set them fast, as cautious mortals ought;
And are at once in TIM's sly coggery caught.

Yet hopes, joys, prayers will tell much more that is
In this strange world of ours of bale and bliss.
Ev'n specks of sand secrete eternities:
Sit down then; listen to their confidences.

Think you, indeed, benumbed by grief or pain,
Or lost in some dread labyrinth of the brain,
An earth-bound clock will set you free again?

Why pause not *now*? To ponder, unoppressed?
The halcyon come again. And in your breast
The brief Elysium of a soul at rest?

'. . . *As that fair flower Adonis, which we call an anemone flourisheth but one month*. . . .'

An opening flower, night's furthest nebulae
In mind supreme must be contemporary.
In one same moment they might cease to be.

And that faint eastern star —'light-years' gone by
Its beams have ranged which pierce the evening sky,
To find their haven in a human eye;
On human heart to shed tranquillity.

And though with his ingenious Optick Glass
The mind of man may map the wastes of Space,
Thence he may yet return in joy to trace
The light of welcome in a human face.

Merely material things hark back again
To their unknown, unknowable origin;
As, to death-darkening gaze, the world of men.

Those rocks green-capped, round which the sea-mews whine,
Reared up aloft, wide-gullied from the land,
Are no more stable in the wash of Time
Than lost enchanted palace in the sand.

Sun-bleached, slim, delicate bones of wings at rest,
And whispering thrift that trembles in the blast
Tell of the transiency of earthly dust
To which even adamant must return at last.

There falls a night, of myriads gone by;
A starless tempest raves; the wildering sea
Storms in. And daybreak lifts a heavy eye
For what has gane its gaite, and ceased to be.

So, to day's eye, destruction shows — void space
Where towered massive majesty and grace,
Coped by the foam-flowers of sea-wilderness.

'. . . *So did this noble Empire waste,*
Sunk by degrees from glories past. . . .'

Engirdling the great World these waters flow,
To charred wan moon obeisant, to and fro.
But swang she nearer? . . . Chaos and overthrow:
Which of our marvels then were left for show

Of all Man's pomp and power? Of aught achieved
Whereby his reign on earth might be believed;
Or his superb effrontery be conceived?

That he — of all God's creatures niggling-nice,
Yet seamed with pride, conceit, and racked with vice;
Dove-gentle; saintlike; evil as cockatrice —

Should thus have edged his way from clime to clime
In a mere millionth of terrestrial 'time',
And talked of Truth, of Wisdom, the Sublime!

Once, a bold venturer, perched on his '*Machine*',
Broke out (Man's history over) on a scene
Of Sun stark still, and leprous sea brine-green.
And, for sole witness of life's Might-have-been,
A tentacled crustacean, vast, obscene!

'. . . *But things to come exceed our human reach* . . .'

Now — in a patch of sea-turf may arise
Low mounds secreting the packed enterprise
Of empires past all sapience to assize —
The latest of a myriad dynasties.

And when the heat of summer wells into
Their chambered queens, then their dark galleries through
Swarm they with their sheened courtiers up into the blue —

To glut the sea-gulls, or creep back to shed
Their cheating gnawed-off pinions; or, instead,
To blacken for miles the sea-sands with their dead . . .

Time? May God help us! Better a few years
Of casual change than slavery such as theirs:
Where all are pitiless, and none shed tears.

Once was a hidden country, travellers say,
(Due East-by-West of North-by-South it lay),
Designed to serve as a Utopia;
Where all things living lived the selfsame way.

Its flowers were scant and scentless (like our musk);
One weight of ivory was each tooth and tusk;
On every nut there swelled the same-sized husk;
Noonday to night there loomed perpetual dusk.

Fate was appalled. Her See-Saw would not stir.
Man sat dead-centre and grimaced at her.
Her prizes? None could shine where none could err;
So every artless dunce was a philosopher . . .

'. . . *This infant world has taken long to make,*
Nor hast Thou done with it, but mak'st it yet,
And wilt be working on when death has set
A new mound in some churchyard for my sake . . .'

Still in long clothes was I when learnèd men
Tracked down the 'atom'. They as busy had been
On evidences of a distant When
That mite had ape for kith and kin. Amen.

Once did the tiny shrews lemurs beget;
And they the tarsier, starred with eyes of jet;
And that the wistful little marmoset:
At length came Man; with Fate for martinet.
And *Time*? How could it else but aid, abet?

Still, there was other route. One no less free:
A virgin, visionary Earth to see,
Seed of supreme potentiality
Of man with God and love at peace to be.

Were life a poem we have to improvise
(Facing the stubbornest of all prosodies)

[571]

An Epilogue might close the enterprise;
And all else seem a mere parenthesis.
Which — when Earth's 'actual' thins — we know it is.

As when in pangs of death a hermit lay —
Cave, rill, rock, leaf-shagged tree — and from the sky,
Blue above sand, a seraph hovered nigh,

And set his foot there. Like a god's, his face
Shone in the shadow, smiling in its grace,
And shed infinity in that narrow space.

'The riddle nature could not prove
Was nothing else but secret love. . . .'

Cry on the dead: — *'Beseech thee! wake! Arise!'*. . .
Impassive waxen visage, fast-sealed eyes
Sunken past speculation or surmise:
And, for response, not even the least of sighs.

How, then, can he we knew and loved be *there*?
Whose every thought was courtesy; whose one care
To show his friendship, and to speak us fair:

Gentle and steadfast. Why, but three days since
We talked of life; its whither and its whence;
His face alert with age's innocence.
He smiled an *au revoir* when he went hence . . . .

Oh, ev'n should folly bring Man's world to woe,
Out of its ashes might a sweeter show.
And what of the life beyond, whereto we go?

Even were that of this a further lease
It yet might win to a blest state that is
Past thought — transcending scope of clock-time's bliss.
More simple, passionate, and profound than this.

'. . ."O Lord! methought what pain it was to drown!
What dreadful noise of water in mine ears!". . .'

Dazed by mere 'Space' void-universes-wide,
Where All-that-is has Nought-that-thinks for bride,
The mind rebels. It's Reason's suicide . . . .

[572]

That dream I had of old — when, gazing sheer
Down verge of an abysm of stagnant air,
Senses as sharp as insect's, I could hear
Time's Ocean, sighing on the shingle there:

A whispering menace that chilled brain and blood;
Enormous, formless. Agonised I stood,
Tongueless with horror of what this forbode;

Yet lured on ever closer to its brim;
The night-long plunge; the gulf, vast, vaporous, dim;
That vault of Nothingness, the Nought of dream.

Ah, well I knew the doom in wait for me —
Lost in that quagmire of Sleep's treachery —
Drowning, to thirst for death; but never die. . . .

'. . . Be able to be alone . . . Delight to be alone and single with Omnipresency.
He who is thus prepared, the Day is not uneasy nor the Night black unto him. . . .'

Yet never fiend that trod Earth's crust could break
Man's steadfast soul while he was ware and wake,
Though God Himself should seem him to forsake —
Unless, 'twould seem, such fiend took human shape.

And never in Matter, surely, shall we find
Aught that is wholly inconsonant with a Mind
That thus conceived, evoked, informed its kind?
Else to forlorn Unreason we are confined.

Why, then, so closely pry? Consider, too —
Despite the earth-bound lenses we look through —
At exquisite equipoise rests what is true;
'All knowledge is remembrance' . . . 'Nothing's new.'

Oh, with what joy an ignorant heart may steal
From dry-as-dust abstractions to a 'real',
Where what we think is blent with what we feel.

That star, which through the window spills its ray
On sheet and pillow when in dream we stray —
That's not a myriad light-years far away!

No further (if mere distance be at all),
Than is the ultramicroscopical —
The goddess who electrons has in thrall.

[573]

. . . What! 'island universes'! — thick as dew?
When even of huge Betelgeuse it's true
That distance lends enchantment to the view! . . .

Will ever indeed have tongue the power to tell
All ev'n a taper discloses in a well?
If Truth's it be, it's clean impossible.

Thick too as motes that in a sunbeam drift
Day's dreamlike images may swirl and shift
Too instantaneous for clock to sift.

Strive then to give them words. The wits fall numb;
Into a *cul-de-sac* thought seems to come;
A timeless semi-conscious vacuum.
And how long wait will they a lip that's dumb?

No more than stream till it is stayed in ice
Will with its waters glass the same scene twice
Can we recall Time's content as it flies.

Clear be its well-spring, then; its tide slow, deep.
Rich in reflection, let the quiet mind steep.
Peace comes but seldom, let not one crumb slip.

'. . . And all put on a gentle hue,
Hanging in the shadowy air
Like a picture rich and rare . . .'

Transient the loved may be. The ripple flows;
So is perfected — falls the wreathed musk-rose.
'Tis his own rainbow with earth's traveller goes.

One unique journey his. His dial tells
His own sun's passive shadow, nothing else;
Though nought its splendour, when it shines, excels.

And if in the familiar, prized, serene —
Green hill, and woodland, pool in twilight seen,
House we have loved, shared, treasured, talked, been
            happy in —
Our wonder and delight have always been,

Strange paradox it were, if it were true,
That, when the sight goes, then the see-er goes too.
What? For *that* finis a long life's ado?

[574]

Whence was that whispering — as if secretly?
A scarce-heard utterance, followed by a sigh: —
'*Some there may be who when they die, they die.*'
'*And their whole world goes with them?*' came reply.

'*Why, it might chance he leaves some tale behind*
Whose radiant aim had left him all but blind,
Which yet none living could for reader find.
So evanescent may prove all mankind:
Though ghost with ghost still commune; mind with mind.'

'*. . . Her rest shall not begin nor end, but be;*
And when she wakes she will not think it long . . .'

Yet, even if, dying, we should cease to be,
However brief our mortal destiny,
Were this for having *lived* outrageous fee?

For having loved, laughed, talked, dreamed, toiled, endured
        our dree;
Ev'n cut *one* birthday-cake — with candles three?

That were to mere good sense clean contrary;
As well might once-green skeleton leaf upbraid its
        Springtide tree.

Days there may come that wish there were no morrow,
No night of weeping, nor a dawn of sorrow;
Yet only out of bonds as bleak and narrow,
Can we the rapture of forgiveness borrow.

Swift-falling flower, slowly fretting stone
Clock on unheeded those who lie alone,
Whose quiet dust in darkness may dream on
The more serenely if they peace have won —

And in earth's sempiternity awake
The annual yew-buds that above them break,
And to the winds their incense-pollen shake.

[575]

'. . . Sometimes Death, puffing at the doore,
Blows all the dust about the floore:
But while he thinks to spoil the room, he sweeps . . .'

Strange prodigy is Man. Of so short stay,
Yet linked with Vega and with Nineveh.
Time — Space: what matters it how far away,
In this strange Hall of Mirrors through which we stray?

Life's dearest mysteries lie near, not far.
The least explored are the familiar;
As, to a child, the twinkling of a star;
As, to ourselves, ourselves — who know not what we are!

Subtler than light, *Time* seems our eyes to steep
With beauty unearthly as things age; and slip
Into the timelessness Lethean of Sleep.

The Trumpet sounds. The listening arise;
Host beyond host the angelic hierarchies
Dome with their glory the once-empty skies. . . .

'An Old Wives' tale . . .'? We smile; or yawn: refuse
Credence to fables which no more amuse
Wits braced and pregnant with the morning's News.

'Tale' if it be, 'twas by no idiot told
Of some far Golden Age to an Age of Gold,
Whose chief pursuit concerns the bought and sold.

Would you your cranium case of clockwork were?
Its mainspring cleverness, its parts all 'spare';
Its key mere habit, yet each tick, *Beware!*?

'. . . When yet I had not walkt above
A mile or two, from my first love . . .'

Better than that, it were to stay the child
Before 'time' tamed you. When you both ran wild
And to heaven's *Angelus* were reconciled.

Host of all sun-blest things by nature his,
His mind imagines all on earth he sees,
His heart a honeycomb of far resemblances —
Ere fall the shadows, shams, obliquities.

The streams of air that throng his timeless sky
Toss the green tree-tops, and not even sigh

In the slim nid-nod grass that seeds near by,
Or rob by a note his blackbird's lullaby.
And when the day breathes cold, and winds are high,
To watch the autumnal jackdaws storm the sky! —
Meal-dusty polls, glossed plumage, speedwell eye —
Ere cold of winter come; and Spring draw nigh.

And though the beauty both of bird and song
May pass unheeded in the press and throng,
In its own small for-ever it lived long.

Not by mere age, renown, power, place, or pride
The heart makes measurement. Its quickening tide
Found once its egress in a wounded side:

Love is its joyful citadel. Its moat
A lake of lilies, though they wither not.
Beyond our plummet's reach lies where they float.

Yet may we sound that deep as best we can,
And, unlike dazed Narcissus, there may scan
Reflections of the inestimable in man:

All that of truth is in its mirror shown;
And, far beneath, the ooze life feeds upon,
Whose *rot* breeds evil, jealousy and scorn.
A nature merciless, a mind forsworn.

'. . . He promised he'd bring me a basket of posies,
A garland of lilies, a garland of roses . . .'

Love on; and faithfully. Death hath his pace.
No past inveigles him. That timeless face
Ev'n of the future shows no faintest trace;

But what far-beckoning mysteries hide there,
In those phantasmal sockets, bleak and bare?
Visions frequent their dark; but not *Despair*.

Mere fictions? . . . Still, how sweet upon your ear
Was always, 'Once upon a time, my dear . . .' —
Robbing both night and morrow of all fear.

[577]

Ev'n this enchantment soon as come was gone
To swell that 'once'. And so you morrowed on.
Is *that* why clocks set 'fast' you choose to con?

Just to seduce the dotard with his glass
By damming back his sands a while? Alas,
A specious trick, poor soul! — But let it pass.

Dog in the manger, Master Yea–and–Nay,
You pine for time to hasten, yet bid to stay —
Creature of contraries for ever at play.

As seems the moon — when clouds in legion lie —
'Gainst the wild wind to race; till, suddenly,
Her full effulgence floods a tranquil sky.
And both are good — wind, and tranquillity —
That vault of Silence, and the hoot-owl's cry.

'Change lives not long, time fainteth and time mourns,
Solace and sorrow have their certain turns. . . .'

And what worse fate were there than the decree: —
'Thy days shall pass in changeless impotency —
Sand, salt, grey mist, stark rock and wash of sea —
Thy one conundrum, How to cease to be?'

Only the impotent grieve —*'The hours drag by.'*
Self is their burden. That's a bond-slave's cry.
Will it be *clock*-time, think you, when you die?
Or body's zero; soul's eternity?

Immeasurable aeons ere the sun
Sprayed out the planets, as a fish its spawn,
Clotho her fatal tissue had begun

Which lured you to this instant. And, know this:
Eve fell; the King looked up; cock crew; ywis
Woe, of a moment, was the traitor's kiss.

All in a moment Eros shoots, and flies;
Corroding hatred gazes from the eyes;
The heart is broken. And the loved one dies.

No wonder, then, that soon as day's begun,
Shadow foretells the course that it will run —
Cast by that radiant Prince of Time, the Sun;

Whom our dull clouds conceal; whom Earth forsakes,
And skulking denizens of the dark awakes.
It is her own withdrawal midnight makes.

'. . . Man is the shuttle, to whose winding quest
And passage through these looms
God ordered motion, but ordained no rest. . . .'

Journeying swiftly on, she makes no stay;
'A thousand years are but as yesterday':
By candle Alfred set his hour to pray:
And, once, Man merely Sunned his life away.

Now we devices have so accurate
They tell the exigent enquirer what
Sheer millionth of a second he is at —
Or *was*, if one must really get it pat.

Would they might pause instead! . . .
            Or slow, or fast,
Time's falling waters grieve,
            This cannot last!
In mere momentum merging with the Past.

Back to our homely hour-glass let us go.
It tells us nothing till we wish it to;
And, even then, in dosage smooth and slow. . . .

'. . ."O Time! thou must untangle this, not I.". . .'

Ponder the problem how we may, and can,
Time has enigma been since Time began,
The subtlest of confusions known to Man;

One no less baffling than it is to say
How came what we call Consciousness our way;
Whence flows the wellspring that keeps life in play;
Or, this dilemma solved, where then 'twill stray.

Where Mind is not, there Time would cease to be,
All expectation, hope, and memory;
Without a warp how weave a tapestry?

Let there be Chaos! was the first decree;
And one of infinite potentiality.

[579]

Apart then from the whither and the whence —
What *is* this 'time' but term to mark our sense
Of life's erratic sequence of events,
Though not their scope and range or consequence;

And we its centre and circumference?

They fleet along, as if by Fancy led,
Like flotsam on a brook, and we its bed —
The world without; the mind-world, in our head —
Urgent, sweet, shattering; forlorn, half-dead.

Three score and ten . . . Like leaves our lives unfold;
Hid in the telling moves the tale untold.
It is not wishing makes the heart grow cold.
And saddest of all earth's clocks is Others growing old:
The silvering hair that once was palest gold.

'. . . But most she loathed the hour
When the thick-moted sunbeam lay
Athwart the chambers, and the day
Was sloping toward his western bower. . . .'

Watched pots are loth to boil, old bodies prate;
Snail-slow moves *everything* for which we wait:
The craved-for news; the kiss; the loved-one, late;
The laggard footfall at the fast-locked gate;
Yes — and a dead man's shoes, if that's our bait.

All that we long for, languish, pray for — Oh,
Never moved Car of Juggernaut so slow.
It comes — and hours into mere moments flow:
For even on Innocents' Day the blade may show
Of Snowdrop piercing through the crudded snow,
Snell though the starving blasts of winter blow.
    It's bidden, and wills it, so.

But drifts of living, eventless, feelingless,
Lapse out unmemoried into nothingness.
Instant and timeless are our ecstasies.

And should events be swift, wild, urgent — then
No cranny shows for clock-time to creep in;
Life leaps to action, even the sun unseen.

*'. . . The mind, that Ocean where each kind
Does straight its own resemblance find;
Yet it creates, transcending these.
Far other Worlds, and other Seas . . .'*

Not less remote that tick when one's engrossed
In arduous treasure-hunt on Fiction's coast,
Called El Dorado: with one's self for ghost.

Thus celled — aurelia in its cocoon —
In thrall of this strange make-believe, alone,
Phantoms appear, in seeming flesh and bone.
They breathe; live; move; they *are* — one's very own.
Scene, story and intent web softly on . . . .

You pause; look up: *'Good heavens; the morning's gone!'*

And as for Coleridge, spellbound with his *Rime* —
Whose music, radiance and strangeness seem
Real as the simulacra of a dream —

Four several 'times' he mingled in his theme: —
His clock's, his mind's, the ship's that had no name,
The Sun of genius', regnant over them. . . .
And *Kubla Khan?* — when one from Porlock came?

*'. . . Life is a Terrace-walke with an Arbour at one end, where we repose, and
dream over our past perambulations. . . . The Soule watcheth when wee sleepe. . . .'*

Throughout the day throbs on this inward loom;
Though little heeded be its whirr and thrum.
Comes then the dark. And, senses lulled and numb,
The sleeper lies; defenceless, passive, mum.

Hypnos awaits him, and what dreams may come;
The Actual faint as rumour in a tomb.

Stealthy as snow, vicissitudes drift by —
Watched, without pause, by some strange inward eye —
Lovely; bizarre; inane; we know not why!
Nor what of Space and Time they occupy,
Who's their deviser, or whence his puppetry.

Once, dreamer dreamed (his candle just puffed out)
He'd travelled half earth's oceans round about,
Stormed-on, becalmed; wild chance-work and unsought;
To sea-wind's whine, surf's hiss, and dolphin's snort
Days, weeks, his ship had sailed from port to port;

[581]

Sweeping the tides for wonders she had run
A moon's five phases; whirlwind and typhoon;
Islands galore . . . .
                    At length, his voyaging done,
He woke — to find his wick still smouldering on!

Had he been gone two minutes, or — well, none?

He who in slumber deep doth lie
Is that far in eternity.
Near clock may strike; no heed pays he —
Time' — less in his non-entity.

So may a drowning man his past descry;
Softly, yet softlier falls his lullaby.
And Lethe? . . . Much may hap twixt that last sip and sigh.

Head nods. Lids droop. What then may *not* befall
In realms where nothing's four-dimensional?
Where nothing's real, yet all seems natural;
And what seems ages is no time at all?

Even the Sycamore with her thousand keys
Could not force locks as intricate as these,
Nor Argus ravel out such mysteries.

'. . . Sweet Swan of Avon! what a sight it were
To see thee in our waters yet appeare,
And make those flights upon the bankes of Thames,
That so did take Eliza *and our* James! *. . .'*

So, wake to sleep; and sleep to wake we stray;
And genius early treads the two-fold way: —

Sun in the willow trees, Avon's placid stream:
And there, a Child, caught up 'twixt wake and dream:

Learning, with words, two wonders to condense —
A marvellous music, and a matchless sense.

Say that this came of the air — what matter that?
Desert, or tarn? Rocks where the Sirens meet?
Between the stars? Or where the Nameless sit?
Or wrenched from adversity? — It's no less sweet.
It cannot be gotten for gold, nor is silver the price of it.

Ideas thus pent may like bright diamonds be,
Of a scarce-earthly diuturnity,
Their facets drenched with light's transparency
Of every hue we in the rainbow see:
Yet each gem single in its unity.

   Alas, ev'n these too must
Of Wisdom itself be but the crystalline dust:
Their archetypes the Immortals have in trust.

'. . . O could my spirit wing
Hills over, where salt Ocean hath his fresh headspring! . . .'

Friends have these ever been of Poetry's.
Unlike the plant called 'everlasting', this,
Never straw-dry, sapless, or sterile is;
And since its virtue in the simple lies,
The unlearned may share its essence with the wise.

Vision and reverie, fantasies, ecstasies,
No hours 'keep' they, when, ranging as they please,
Over the hills we fare . . . over the seas . . . .
Senses celestial, mind's antipodes,
Nought Reason can invoke, or Logic seize;
No chime but sea-bell's dallying in the breeze:
To where the sovereign Muses dwell — the *Hesperides*.

And any mortal whom They shall enchant
Their happy secret myrtle groves may haunt;
Nor Time, nor Age, nor Death the soul to daunt . . . .

'. . . An Ecstacy is a kind of medium between waking and sleeping, as sleep is a
kind of middle state between life and death . . .'

But reef your sails upon the Sea called Dead:
Quicksands where *Ennui* skulks; and, visage dread,
Dumb *Accidie* awaits you, heavy as lead:
Salt-marsh, blind wilderness, and skies blood-red;
Your horologe a vulture overhead . . . .

When Dürer, rapt in *Melencolia* sat,
Did ladder, rainbow, the disconsolate,
The child no voice could rouse, no sleep could sate,
In that unfathomable silence prate
Of *time*? . . . Did bat squeak, 'Albrecht Dürer, it grows
  late!'?

[583]

Only the soul these symbols could portray —
That comet-stricken sea, those flames at play,
Midnight, bell, hound asleep; and — turned away —
That face, of woe and speechless grief the prey.
Timeless, in torpor of Despair are they.

'*Then it was Music that enchanted you?*'

Yet, while we gaze, a rapture is achieved,
As in the hush when music is conceived;

'*Ah, yes, Sir. Music; which at times I hope I heard*
(*As if of water, instrument, or bird*)
Echo in my "poor rendering of the word".'

Its very beauty mourns it is bereaved:
Is grieved
The embrace that gave it birth can never be retrieved.

All things — by sorrow and truth thus tinctured even,
And so transfigured — this rare grace are given;
From life's poor temporal deceits are shriven . . . .

'*. . . And Ruben wente out in the wheat harvest and found mandragoras in the
felds . . .*'

Even a drug may thus delude and cheat —
One word, 'assassin', is a proof of it.
Muffle your brain with hashish: and the beat
Of clock falls slow as echo in the night
In some primaeval cavern hidden from sight —
Stalactite whispering to stalagmite.

Hues as of Ishtar's Garden cheat the eye.
Into the distance slips the inert, near by;
The far recedes into infinity.
And — if it listen — ear will magnify
The querk of cock to Roc's appalling cry.

Or dare those deserts where no zephyr stirs,
And coins gleam on, which age-gone travellers
Dropped from their camel-caravans. And theirs
The dog whose tracks have stayed unblurred for years.

Come sudden danger, dread, the soul stands still;
An ice-cold vigilance freezes mind and will;
And every pulse-beat seems immeasurable.

No less intent, as the doomed Russian said,
Are they who keep appointment with the dead,
And, their last journey, towards the scaffold tread.

'. . . *Fancy, and I, last Evening walkt,*
And, Amoret, *of thee we talkt* . . .'

But would you bid Time *hasten* — race?
                                        Then sit
In fancy again with Chloe — once-loved chit;
By the clear stream, where may-fly used to flit,
The copse of hazel and the young green wheat —

That rose-pale cheek, loose hair, and eager tongue
Sooth as a willow-wren's the leaves among;
The silence as the water rippled along.

How feveredly you watched the shadows grow
Longer and darker in the deepening glow
Of sun to set so soon. So soon . . . . 'No, no!
        You shall not, cannot go!'

Drave the wheels heavily when last look and kiss
Left you forsaken of all earthly bliss?
A fleeting moment's paradise — then this?

The loved, the loving; idol or worshipper —
Which hated Time the most, as you sat there?
She, the so young, so heedless and so dear,
Or you who mourned her absence —.she still near?

'. . . *How could it be so fair, and you away?*
How could the Trees *be beauteous,* Flowers *so gay?* . . .'

So Michael Drayton grieved; lorn, melancholy;
His mistress absent; her sweet company
Lost for a while, leaving him solitary: —

'Of every tedious hour you have made two,
All this long winter here, by missing you:
Minutes are months, and when the hour is past,
A year is ended since the clock struck last.'

[585]

'... *Did'st thou ever see a lark in a cage? Such is the soul in the body* ...'

And so must once have felt the little maid,
Needling until the light began to fade,
My cross-stitch sampler-rhyme, so often read,
Words all but meaningless in her small tired head: —

> *Short is our longest stay of life;*
> *And soon its prospect ends:*
> *Yet on that day's uncertain date*
> *Eternity depends.*

And what — his life's loved labour at an end —
Chose Robert Burton for farewell to send
His hypochondriac votaries? This, my friend: —

> 'When I go musing all alone,
> Thinking of divers things foreknown,
> When I build castles in the air,
> Void of sorrow and void of fear,
> Pleasing myself with phantasms sweet,
> Methinks the time runs very fleet.

> All my joys to this are folly,
> Naught so sweet as melancholy.

> 'When I lie waking all alone,
> Recounting what I have ill done,
> My thoughts on me then tyrannize,
> Fear and sorrow me surprise,
> Whether I tarry still or go,
> Methinks the time moves very slow.

> All my griefs to this are jolly,
> Naught so sad as melancholy ....'

'... *Parvula* ... *formica* ... *haud ignara ac non incauta futuri* ...'

See that small bird — sand, water, groundsel, seed —
How tender seems its captor to its need.
Yet may its prisoned heart for freedom plead.

'... *To effect the same exactly it is beyond the Arithmetic of any but God,*
himself. ...'

As may one's own — this *Cage* that we are in —
Dangling in Time, though Time itself's unseen,
If the beyond-it is our true demesne,
Alike its issue, and its origin.

[586]

Queer are its inmates. Though brief age they attain,
They cackle, argue, imprecate, complain —
As though some Moloch 'kept' them, for pure gain!

Whether we mope or warble, soon learn we
Mood, mind, and clock were ever at enmity.
What truth one tells the others falsify —
Prolong our griefs, give pleasure wings to fly.

If, then, Time Present goes so often awry,
Where seek the skill to judge the Future by? —

That void pretentious region where no time is,
Only incessant possibilities,
Haunting and sweet-sick half-expectancies,
Flowers of envy, desires and reveries
Which may fall sterile, or fruit quite contrariwise.

Yet — daring its vast vague uncertainty,
Defying chance, and blind fatality,
Man's noblest acts and works achieve did he.
All was 'imagined' ere it came to be;

That marvellous coral in Time's unstable sea: —
Wells, Ely, Fountains, Gloucester, Lincoln, Canterbury.

And on that verge — its echoing arch, its restless to and fro —
Two Worlds resort; the one called Dream and this — our weal and woe.

But cheating mirage, too, when most serene,
    The Future's ever been —
An Ocean, as it were from cockboat seen;
With in-shore drifts of islets witching-green.

'Golden', or 'grim', or 'menacing' — in a trice
We paint the ineffable figment of its skies —
And are in Purgatory, or Paradise.

And every 'moment' we thus waste or spend,
Waiting on what we cannot comprehend,
Has it for sequel; and, no less, for end.

Day-dream, and night-, may richest pasture be —
There strays the Unicorn called Fantasy.
But why become so readily the prey —

Clean contrary to true sagacity —
Of spurious futures we shall never see?
How seldom foresight and the facts agree!

Plague on the blank forebodings, heart-ache, dole,
The grim chimæras which our wits cajole,
The signs and omens that never reach their goal;

The fears, the follies hung upon an *'If'*! . . .
Surely, of foes to peace, joy, love, belief,
Is not this Time Apocryphal the chief?

'. . . She glode forth as an adder doth . . .'

In mien how soused in guile. No hairspring *he*,
Buzzing brisk seconds busier than a bee.
He *glides*. . . . As stealthily and remorselessly
As did the Serpent to Eve's apple-tree.

'Time' sheened the splendour that was Absalom's hair;
Time stilled the Garden; seduced Judas there;
Sped the avenging blade for Robespierre;
Dogged Marx, in reverie drowned, through Bloomsbury
      Square.

Give Ruin room, Time cries, *my brother, Space!*
Whether Man win to glory or disgrace,
Things still corrupt, corrode, and leave no trace.

And with its aether-silent, deadening flood,
Which robs the unfolding flower of its bud,
Time cheats us of our loveliest for good.

All is in flux, the coming and the gone.
This massive globe rotates, zone on to zone;
5.59 at *B* at *C*'s 6.1;
Its every sunrise leaves a day just done;
So, bland automaton, it circles on.

Cowed by the spectre which 'for no man waits',
Obsequious hireling of the witless Fates,
Time pins down ev'n Dictators to their 'dates'.

'You who never sate with your wings folded. . . .'

Still, *if* it's 'time' alone we hold in fee,
Why, load its every rift with ore, *pardie!*
At least be lively Ephemeridae.

[588]

Else, days may rot, like apples in the grass,
Sick worthless windfalls, once good fruit, alas,
Which even rootling pigs unheeded pass.

Now — with its whole penumbra, clear to dim,
Abject with misery or with bliss a-brim —
Is our Sun's universe, to its utmost rim.

'. . . *Doth not our chiefest bliss then lie*
Between thirst and Satiety,
In the midway? . . .'

We know no other's 'now', though guess we may —
And in that guessing while our own away;
And 'nows' innumerable make up our 'day':

Beads, baubles, gems, strung close; and we the string;
Each one a reflex of the everything
Around it. As may rain-drop mirror Spring;
Or foxed old hand-glass, Winter, on the wing.

. . . And never was there myth in guise more ghast
Than gluttonous Chronus, without pause or rest
Gorging his progeny to glut the Past . . .

And with each *Now* a rivulet runs to waste,
Unless we pause to stoop; to sip; to taste;
And muse on any reflex it may cast:

Its source a region of mountains, east to west,
High snows, crag, valleys green, and sunken fens —
                    a region called the Past.

Elusive Memory's concealed demesne
Wherein all relics of the Once-has-been
In viewless treasury unchanged remain.
And yet a livelong novelty retain.
Breathe *Sesame!* and make it yours again.

With caution, lest ajar the door she set
Where lurks the half-conscious one had best forget.
Vast is her cellarage. Beware of it.
Only the winds of heaven can keep it sweet.

Ah, wastrel, Memory. Hear her laugh — or weep;
Casual, erratic; and how fond of sleep;
Life's league-wide cornfields — and one sickle, to reap!

Lift up thy face, thy guileless face, my child!
The grey beard wagged; the dim, bleached, blue eyes smiled:
I am the Past. And thou, Time undefiled.

There, for the while, may silent phantoms tread,
Vivid with light and life, though long since dead;
With whom we commune, yet not one word said. . . .

'. . . *With "Hey my little bird, and ho my little bird,*
And ho but I love thee dearly". . .'

I see a low square house. It's dusk. Within,
Half-crazed with dread as shades of night begin,
I stand in watch: and so for hours have been.

Behind me voices drone, where sit at tea
My guardians, mindless of my misery:
'*A silly homesick child! All fiddlededee!*'

Footsteps approach; pass by. And still not She.

Could she forget? Not care? Forbear to come?
Illness? Ev'n death? Alas. My heart falls numb.
Gone then for ever — mother, peace, and home . . . .

So, in a flash, my heaped-up years I span
To fill *this* Now, as, with uplifted pen,
I match that child with this scarce-changed old man;

Espy, as then, along its close-shorn edge
The longed-for bonnet top the hated hedge:
Anguish to joy — how brief that slender bridge.

'. . . *In a valley of the restless mind*
I sought in mountain and in mead . . .'

Isles in oblivion such scenes remain;
Poignant and vivid and passionate. And then
Life's piecemeal picture-book shuts-to again.

Oh, for pure attar, for one drop of TIME —
Essence Hesperidean of morning-prime;
How lustrously would it enrich this rhyme.

What gem would it resemble? Brilliance? Hue?
What, if — like *Ægypt's* pearl — dissolved in dew,
It lay on the tongue, then swept the whole self through?

[590]

But where's the Druggist with his Bottles three —
'*Time dead and gone*', '*Time Now*', '*Time soon to be,
For use in any grave emergency?*'
What is his price *per* minim?

                        Search, and see!

'. . ."*I do account the world a tedious theatre,
For I do play a part in't against my will.*". . .'

    From London's swarm of clocks — Bow's to Big Ben —
    Our darting eyes extort 'the' time. And then,
    Back to the day's routine we turn again.

    In much that matters most whole centuries slow,
    Lashed to its creaking treadmill on we go;
    Its inmost purpose past our wits to know.

    Cribbed in by diaries, with their fume and fret;
    Chained to an almanac, lest we forget
    To tell the Moon when she must rise and set;

    Mock-solemn creatures, with our jackdaw airs,
    Our Loans, Exchanges, Markets, stocks and shares,
    And — squinting two-faced monsters — Bulls-and-Bears;
    Boredom and bankruptcy our recurrent cares;
    And Nobody, poor souls, to hear our prayers:

    How *thus* win liberty? How thus to come,
    With these poor fractions, to a sovereign sum?
    Ensure ourselves our own continuum?
    Dance with the stars in their choragium?

    Ring the bells backwards! Ay, no pause; no ease!
    There looms on high the Sword of Damocles,
    Dangling by hair now hoar as Destiny's
    Over the labyrinth of days, like these.

    Tyrannies deadlier than of Syracuse
    Slowly insidiously undermining us —
    The heart's debasement, and the mind's misuse.

    Man gone, his clocks gone, *Time* might fall asleep?
    A halcyon brooding on the Pacific Deep;
    That huge, slow swell — sans wrack or sign of ship —
    Which from the heavens seems scarcely even to creep . . .

'Les Chinois voient l'heure dans l'œil des chats.'

ONCE

'*Once*', runs the tale, 'in the lost isle of Lyncke,
A Cat, long poised on Instinct's very brink,
Crossed it by chance: and found that she could think.

'No previous venture could her feat excel.
At one swift leap she'd borne away the bell;
Pouncing on notions past all count to tell,
Quick as a kitten with a ball of wool.

'High in her Monarch's kitchen, snug on shelf,
Half-hidd'n by ancient pots resembling Delf,
She'd sit, for hours, colloguing with herself.

'*. . . Then gan she wondren more than before*
A thousand fold, and down her eyen cast;
For never sith the time that she was bore,
To knowen thing desirèd she so fast. . . .'

'Motionless eyes upon the scene below —
Jars, bowls, pots, platters, dishes, stew-pans in a row;
All creature comforts man and feline know,

'Cream by the gallon, a ceaseless to and fro,
Copper, brass, crystal, silver, twinkling and a-glow,
Scullions a score, and Cook in cap of snow —
Her thoughts welled on. And all were apropos.

'Logic for Law, she ranged from A. to Z.,
Never deluding her now brass-bright head,
By speculation, or mere fancy led,
With chance-wise ray that might on it be shed
Had she roved off at *N.*, *Q.*, *X.*, instead.

'She mused on Space and Time, on Mind and Brain;
The 'isms and 'ologies that to them pertain;
On Will, Fate, Fortune: then turned back again
To dredge what in her Unconscious might remain
And purged its sediment of the faintest stain . . . .

'She sniffed at ideologies — was sick;
Pondered on "policy" and "politic" —
Yawned, and enwreathed her chops with one long lick.

'Once, ev'n, ejecting a contemptuous look
Down on the Scene below, a vow she took
She'd some day learn these Humans how to cook.

'And so, alack, the years thus spent
Failed to benumb her with sublime content.
A mewling voice kept nagging vague dissent:
"What, now they're over ma'am, precisely have they meant?
Are you the wiser for this banishment?" —

'And all those vats of choicest knowledge hers!
The mischief done by inward Whisperers! . . .
Dead-weary of her Past (the tale avers)
And even of the great philosophers,

'She supped: on tipsy-cake, to be precise;
Re-crossed her Rubicon; and, in a trice,
Resumed her sport of catching rats and mice:
Then slept; and dreamed; and slept. 'Twas paradise.

'. . . So in peace our task we ply,
Pangar Bán, my cat and I;
In our arts we find our bliss,
I have mine and he has his . . .'

'Then, winter come; and snow; and wassailing;
Crouched on the Jester's knee, she'd purr, (he'd sing),
Runes strange and secret upon Everything,
Gazing meanwhile intently at the King . . . .'

Ah, had she learned to swim; to sail a boat;
Tread water — anything to keep afloat,
She might have reached the Mainland — though remote;
Been broken in to live by rule and rote;
Timed, taped, stampeded by the siren's hoot.

'No; old yet wise, and come to where she'd be,
Throughout Life IX all tranquilly lived she —
"Puss by Appointment to His Majesty".'. . .

'Nothing on Earth, no thing at all
Can be exempted from the thrall. . . .'
'. . ."And lest that I should sleep,
One plays continually upon a drum". . .'

'*Breakfast at eight.*' '*Adjourned till April 2.*'
'*Au revoir.*' '*No flowers.*' '*Of a son.*' '*Na-poo!*' —
Thus Man clocks in, clocks out, his whole life through.

[593]

His Struldbrugg *Father Time* — starved, bald, and daft,
Must limned have been — scythe, hour-glass, fore and aft —
By him who blinded Eros; and then laughed.

Emblems like this were cuts on every page
In Abel's hornbook — Adam's heritage:
They'll serve, perhaps, until Man comes of age.

Meanwhile we grope — as might the withy-wind
Striving around the ecliptic to be entwined.
Clocks 'right', but differing, found us still resigned,
Till, seventy years ago, we changed our mind:
And Act of Parliament *the* 'time' defined.

'O sisters, too,
How may we do
For to preserve this day? . . .'

Yet once, the kings being gone, as Scripture tells,
Heaven's host now silent, star-shine on the hills,
Came, with his coral and its silver bells,

To lull both Mother and Son to their first sleep —
Safe, for the while, in stable with the sheep,
Nor any carking Cross wherefore to weep —

None else but *Time* himself: once more a child;
The youngest of the Cherubs, and less wild;
Hawk paired with turtle-dove, and reconciled.

So still he sate, being both young and wise —
Poised on the verge 'twixt two eternities —
Beauty itself he seemed, in earthly guise;
And daybreak-blue the colour of his eyes . . . .

'Sing levy dew, sing levy dew, the water and the wine,
The seven bright gold wires and the bugles they do shine . . . .'

To me, one cracked old dial is most dear;
My boyhood's go-to-bed, its Chanticleer;
Whose tick, alas, no more enchants my ear.

Dumb on the wall it hangs, its hands at noon;
Its face as vacant as a full-blown moon;
The mainspring broken, and its wheels run down —

A kitchen chattel. No fit theme for rhyme;
That case encrusted with a century's grime.
And yet, it taught me 'how to tell the time'.

I knew a bank. . . . Ah, then was Time indeed.
Ere life's first buds had bloomed, and gone to seed —
And none unloved; least so, the lowliest weed.

Harebell, moss, pimpernel; a swift in flight;
The star of evening on the verge of night —
One's heart stood still for wonder and delight:

And in that pause to a far island came
Of strangest semblance, and without a name;
For ever changing, and yet still the same.

Flame was its beauty, and the sea its bliss;
Its every sound a secret music. Yes,
An island such as in *The Tempest* is —

Imaged in words, but Thulë of a mind,
Not only Shakespeare's, but of all mankind:
That which blest Poetry alone can find . . . .

'. . . *Motionless as a cloud the old Man stood* . . .'

'What *is* this Poetry,' self whispered self,
'But the endeavour, faithfully and well
As speech in language man-devisèd can,
To enshrine therein the inexpressible?

'See, now, the moon's declining crescent slim;
Thridding the stars in heaven she goes her way:
Yet doth she silver-tinge the virgin white
Of that clear cluster of jasmine on its spray.

'Ay, and my cheek her finger touched. I turned,
Through window scanned the seed-plot I could till,
And called a garden: and my heart stopped beating,
So marvellous its darkness, and so still . . . .'

[595]

'..."*Long thou for love never so high,*
My love is more than thine may be"...'

Ours is that wine; that water clear and cool;
That very vineyard; and the troubled pool;
Wherewith to fill the thirsting spirit full.

Our utmost reach is what their content seems;
What mind surmises, and the heart esteems —
Ev'n though it be as transient as our dreams.

The true, the guileless, meaningful, and fair
Rest for their essence on our heed and care;
These are Earth's everything, Heaven's everywhere,
However small the commons we ourselves may share....

O Lovely England and Other Poems
(1953)

O LOVELY ENGLAND

O lovely England, whose ancient peace
    The direst dangers fret,
Be on the memory of your past
    Your sure devotion set;
Give still true freedom to fulfil,
    Your all without regret!

Heed, through the troubles that benumb,
    Voices now stilled, yet clear,
Chaunting their deathless songs — too oft
    To ears that would not hear;
Urging you, solemn, sweet, to meet
    Your fate unmoved by fear.

Earth's ardent life incites you yet
    Beyond the encircling seas;
And calls to causes else forlorn,
    The children at your knees:
May their brave hearts in days to come
    Dream unashamed of these!

THE MISSING WORD

'The glory that was Greece', I read;
    'The grandeur that was Rome';
And pondered:
            Love of Freedom? Justice?
    Good sense? Of children? Home?
A craving restless as the sea
    Uncharted seas to roam?
A shame-faced pining for poetry
    None worldly-wise could plumb? . . .

No. No one word to chime with *England* —
None to define, embrace, cage, brand her,
True both for those who have blessed or banned her,
Whereby her foes might understand her —
    Into my mind would come!

[597]

AN OLD CANNON

Come, patient rust;
Come, spider with thy loom,
Make of this enginery,
War's dateless tomb!

Frail bindweed, clamber, and cling,
And clog this motionless wheel;
Upon its once hot throat
Hoar-frost, congeal!

O, may its thunder have won
A last surcease,
And its dark mouth of woe
Ever yet hollower grow
In praise of peace!

FOR A CHILD

Now is the gentle moon on high,
And, clear as dewdrops, in the deep
Of dark blue space we call the sky,
Stars watch the walls of sleep —

When hungry, it is good to eat;
When thirsty, sweet to drink;
When tired, to bathe the weary feet;
When solitary, to think . . .

The men who roved this once-wild earth
Far back in time as Man can see,
As children, slept beside the hearth,
Were lapped upon a mother's knee —

Whether King Solomon, the wise;
Or Absalom, the vain and fair;
Samson, the strong, with blinded eyes;
Or Daniel in lions' lair;

Sidney, the soldier; mystic Blake;
Shakespeare, this England's starry Fame —
They laughed for simple laughing's sake
And knew a small child's fear and shame.

[598]

And Jesus too, lulled fast asleep,
By Mary in the manger lay;
She kissed his eyes when he did weep,
And soothed his little hurts away.

Once, even as I, they talked and played,
And learned their lessons, hard as mine;
And sat beneath the hawthorn's shade
And wreathed their heads with eglantine.

And when came night, how vext they were
To leave their toys, and go to bed:
How happy, on a pillow fair,
    To lay a tired head!

O God, remember me: and, in
Thy love, teach me the all I can
In mind and heart at length to win
The strength and grace to be a man.

ENGLAND

All that is dearest to me thou didst give —
Loved faces, ways, stars, waters, language, sea;
Through two dark crises in thy Fate I have lived,
    But — never fought for thee.

'WHY, THEN COMES IN...'

Long-idling Spring may come
With such sweet suddenness
It's past the wit of man
    His joy to express.

To see in the cold clods
Green weed 'twixt stone and stone!
The violet nod in flower
    Its frail stalk on;

[599]

To watch the wintry sky
Shed pallor from its blue:
And beams of purest light
    And heat pierce through!

To share, to live, to be
Merely a reflex of
Earth's old divine delight,
    And peace, and love!

SPRING

Now the slim almond tree
Tells April soon will be
Scattering her petals where
Snow still lies cold and bare.

Birds in its leafing boughs
Echoes of spring arouse.
Piercing the drowsy earth,
Crocus her flower brings forth —

Wooing the bees. And soon
Winter's ice-silvered moon
Shall melt, shall kindle on high
Springtime within the sky.

A FIDDLER

Once was a fiddler. Play could he
Sweet as a bird in an almond tree;
Fingers and strings — they seemed to be
Matched, in a secret conspiracy.
Up slid his bow, paused lingeringly;
Music's self was its witchery.

In his stooping face it was plain to see
How close to dream is a soul set free —
A half-found world;
And company.

His fiddle is broken.
Mute is he.
But a bird sings on in the almond tree.

REFLECTIONS

So much herself she is that when she is near
All love-delighting things are thrice as dear;
And even the thought of her when she is far
Narcissus is, and they the water are.

NO, NO, NO!

Had you loved me,
Earth had given
All that heart
Could wish of heaven;
That sigh entreats,
Past hoping even:
Had you loved me.

Yet love itself
Endure may not;
Best not harboured
Than forgot:
Lost, cold, faded —
Then — ah, what?
Even love itself?

No, no, no! —
Would summer miss
One wild flower
For cause like this!
Still must I crave
Where nothing is
But — 'No, no, no! . . .'

ARE YOU SO LOVELY?

Are you so lovely? Why, a drop of rain
Has all the beauty your clear eyes contain:
And when death calls you, as ev'n you he must,
How many roses will enhance your dust?

'A drop of rain'! Alas, what lie is this,
When in your eyes your very spirit is!
And 'death' — tak'n thus in vain! The perfidy! —
When life itself were dross, you gone from me.

[601]

INTERMITTENT FEVER[1]

Heaven help me! I'm in love again;
Befuddled past the wit of man!
A dupe, caught walking in his sleep,
A loon, to make the angels weep.

Never burned there fever yet
As wild as love's — for fools to get!
Pleasure, comfort, quiet, ease —
Gone all! — perfidious memories.
For this to count the world well lost —
To chase a maid, and catch a ghost!
Touch but her hand, 'tis to be pricked
With keener pangs than thorns inflict;
In a low, idle voice to hear
The knell of all things once held dear!
In a cold, sweet, indifferent face
To search in vain for hint of grace!
And Oh, to lie awake at night —
Those taunting eyes of all delight!
Or dream — and, waking, find her gone
Whose absence brought the anguish on!

Never again shall every sense
Be drugged by love's dark influence;
Never shall lips, whose wisest word
Folly alone with pleasure heard,
Befool this mind and heart to plan
Merely to prove her maid; me, man!

And yet — bright heaven, what else is worth
A single hour with her on earth!

THE DISGUISE

Dream-haunted face,
Still lips, and dark clear eyes,
So natural and sweet,
Few may perceive how wise.

[1] See also 'Never Again', Uncollected Poems, p. 653, an earlier version.

What wonder, then, if love,
In greeting of such grace,
'An angel!' cries?

An angel, yes! And yet,
Could aught more heavenly be earth's disguise?

THE ENIGMA

'Happy love'! When shall that be? —
Dark prey of idiot jealousy?
Envying even the breeze that blows
Faint with the fragrance of an unplucked rose! . . .

Giving all; demanding none;
Only thus may peace be won.
Passion cannot sleep, or rest,
For the Babel in its breast.
Pleading, pining, craving; yet
Powerless its need to get,
Knowing nothing earthly can.

Alas, then,
Misfortuned Man!
Ever with his soul at strife,
He makes himself the torment of his life . . .

'How came you here?' 'By heaven's grace.'
'Yet seek your heartbreak in a woman's face?'

'. . . ALL GONE . . .'

'Age takes in pitiless hands
All one loves most away;
Peace, joy, simplicity
Where then their inward stay?'

Or so, at least they say.

'Marvel of noontide light,
Of gradual break of day;
Dreams, visions of the night
Age withers all away.'

Yes, that is what they say.

[603]

'Wonder of winter snow,
Magic of wandering moon,
The starry hosts of heaven —
Come seventy, all are gone.

'Unhappy when alone,
Nowhere at peace to be;
Drowned the old self-sown eager thoughts
Constantly stirring in thee!'...

Extraordinary!
That's what they *say* to me!

SECOND THOUGHTS

Gone the promise, pains and care —
All I'd seemed to squander here!
Now I read what then I writ
Even sense has forsaken it.

Whither must my heart have flown,
Leaving head to drudge alone?
Whither can my wits have strayed
To let such lifeless things be said!

Oh, what mischief pen can make,
Scribbling on for scribbling's sake!
How such vanity condone?
Peacock shimmering in the sun!

The Muse, if ever present, gone!

'THE THRUSH'
[*a woodcut by Phyllis Taunton Wood*]

That speckled thrush, perched nimbly on its spray,
With open bill among its thorns and flowers,
Trills mutely as if pining to reveal
Its rapture in the rising of the day.

And I who have heard that echo of no tone,
As if from outer silence, and alone,
Strive on in vain to express what all hearts feel
    Yet words can never say.

NOW

The longed-for summer goes;
Dwindles away
To its last rose,
Its narrowest day.

No heaven-sweet air but must die;
Softlier float,
Breathe lingeringly
Its final note.

Oh, what dull truths to tell!
Now is the all-sufficing all
Wherein to love the lovely well,
Whate'er befall.

ABSENCE

'What, autumn, friend! And she not yet back?
The year is old, past her equinox;
Now, with their winds, come the tardier nights,
The laggarding mornings!' — Memory mocks.

'So the harvest moon may rise in vain
On one whom of old it could tranquillise
Merely by lighting his heavens. Alas,
How coldly then it will meet his eyes!

'Once-dear September: its sheaves and dew,
Seeding grasses . . . evening peace!
Strange, is it not, that things like these
May shed so ironic a tenderness?

'Absence will meet you everywhere —
Mute lips, dark eyes, and phantom brow.
I warned you not to invite in ghosts;
No power have I to evict them now.

'Yet the wildest longings, they say, burn down;
Wasted, as a candle its wax; are passed . . .'
Thus Memory taunts me, wishing me well! —
With, 'There's one Goodbye *must* be the last.'

REJECTED

When you in Paradise find grace,
And think no more of one who adored that angel face,
   Remember this small fountain . . . Here I knew —
   Searching your reflex in its mirroring blue —
What even hope of heaven could never annul —
   The losing you.

THE BOURNE

Rebellious heart, why still regret so much
A destiny which all that's mortal shares?
Surely the solace of the grave is such
That there naught matters; and, there, no one cares?

Nor faith, nor love, nor dread, nor closest friend
Can from this nearing bourne your footfall keep:
But there even conflict with your self shall end,
And every grief be reconciled in Sleep.

WHEN LOVE FLIES IN

When Love flies in,
Make — make no sign;
Owl-soft his wings,
Sand-blind his eyes;
Sigh, if thou must,
But seal him thine.

Nor make no sign
If love flit out;
He'll tire of thee
Without a doubt.
Stifle thy pangs;
Thy heart resign;
And live without!

INTRUDER

There were no clouds in the arch of the evening,
Mute were the heavens in transient gold;
Not a leaf stirring, not a bird twittering,
Dreamed the dark woodland, fold within fold.

Rose-green the light where a hermit knelt, praying,
His solitude verdurous, vision-like, still;
When of a sudden, frigid and burning
There pierced through his body an exquisite thrill —

Thrill, as when nightingale, crazed with repining,
Shakes a whole tree's clustered blossom with song;
Thrill, as when outcast in desert benighted
Hears Demon mocking him, hasting along. . . .

IN A CHURCHYARD[1]

As children, told to go to bed,
Puff out their candle's light,
Knowing earth's natural dark is best
Wherein to take their flight
Into the realms of sleep: — so we
God's summons did obey;
Not without fear our tired eyes shut,
And now await the day.

EPILOGUE

'Pining to live, I was constrained to die,
Here, then, am I.
Love was my maker, fountain of all bliss.
Now, only this.
The maze of thought and feeling that I was!
Of all earth's marvels the blest looking-glass!
The all desired, the little brought to pass!
Alas!'

'Poor soul; he suffered. But, at end, no child
Ever more gently fell asleep.
He smiled.
As if all contraries were reconciled.'

ECHO

'How like your mother, child!' I said.
'Those night-blue eyes, that stooping head.'
'How like her mother!' Echo sighed. And then,
'But neither grief nor love restores the lost again.'

[1] First published in *The Sunken Garden and Other Poems* (1917).

THE TRUTH OF THINGS[1]

'You might have told me the truth of things!' —
'"*The truth of things*", *my dear?*'
'How softly the wind, as if in ruth,
    Breathes in the willows here . . .
It may be a comfort at last to dream
    Where the dead their mole-mounds rear.'

'You might have told me the facts of life!' —
'"*The facts of life*", *my dear?*'
'How blazingly looked that stranger's wife
    With love. Why did he leer
And writhe from her clutching hand as if
    From a tainted shape on a bier?'

'You might have told me what's never told.' —
'"*What's never told*", *my dear?*'
'Those queer little gleams that were darkly rolled
    From mother's eyes, ere the day drew near
When they took her away for ever and aye. . . .
    Are mine as strangely clear?'

DAUGHTER TO MOTHER

I owe you life. Would I had owed you too
What, dumbly, gropingly, I craved from you,
      But never knew —
The death-sweet dangers I might journey through.
For when this poor crazed heart awoke from sleep
It was in solitude it faced the deep.

Not that I grieve, now deaf to tempests' shocks,
'Twas love that drove my vessel on the rocks.
There are worse shipwrecks. Yet, would I had known
You too had suffered; and, like me, alone,
And comfort giv'n. . . .
      But you are in your grave.
And the child love gave you, me it never gave.

[1] First published together with 'Pride Hath Its Fruits Also' in *Two Poems* in a limited edition of 100 copies, Dropmore Press, July 1946.

THIS IS THE END[1]

'This is the end': the anguished word
Scarce stirred the air. She bowed her head.
What token was mine that though I had heard,
I shared that bitter dread?

Above us loomed the night-black tree;
Beneath, a valley in shadow lay;
A waning moon beyond the sea
Cast a faint sickly ray.

Once, 'Oh, have courage!' had been my cry;
Now mutely aghast I gazed into
A face distorted, and caught the sigh
That shook her through and through.

No — no. Why further should we roam?
Since every road man journeys by
Ends on a hillside far from home
Under an alien sky!

Where souls disconsolate and sick
That Valley scan each treads alone —
That Sea whose menace leaves the quick
Colder than churchyard stone.

LETHE

Only the Blessed of Lethe's dews
    May stoop to drink. And yet,
Were their Elysium mine to lose,
Could I — without repining — choose
    Life's *sorrows* to forget?

[1] This is the revised version of the poem that appeared in *New Poems 1956*,
P.E.N. anthology, ed. S. Spender, E. Jennings and D. Abse, London, 1956.
It was originally called 'The End'.

THE CANDLE

Day unto day
Life wastes and wanes,
Like a candle
Burning its oils away,
Till naught but charred wick
Remains.

Well, content would I be,
With flame as still,
Some light to have given
Whereby One who can see
Might work his inscrutable
Will:

If, perchance, long eternities
Hence, that strange Mind
Might in trance
Of far-brooding memory turn,
To light me one instant — else,
Blind.

FEY

The branch of that oak jutting into the air
Is shaped like some fabulous beast, trampling there:
Raised, menacing paw, crouched head, dwelling eye . . .
Figment of night's obscure blazonry? —

Or mere play of fancy? . . . Well, seen, when I woke
From a sleep dream-morassed — in that time-crusted oak,
As I gazed through the glass, the mere sight of it there
Benumbed for a moment my heart with despair.

THE TRYST

'O whither are you faring to, my sweetheart?
How far now are you journeying, my dear?'
'I am climbing to the brink of yonder hill-top,
Naught human far or near.'

'And what will you be seeking there, my sweetheart?
What happy scene is thence surveyed, my dear?'
''Twill be night-tide when outwearied I come thither,
And star-shine icy-clear.'

'But what will you be brooding on, my sweetheart?
What fantasies of darkness will appear?'
'My self will keep a tryst there — bleak and lonely —
My own heart's secrets I shall share.'

'But what will be the manner of your greeting?
What word will you then whisper — no one near?'
'Ah, he who loved me once would know the answer,
Were he still true, my dear.'

THE REFLECTION

Empty and cold is the night without.
From this fire-lit room I peer through the pane:
Of starry assurance the dark breathes not;
My own face only peers back again.

I know those eyes, that brow, that mouth —
Mask, or mirror, the all I have;
But if *there* lay the Ocean and mine were the ship,
Not such for its Master would then I crave:

But a close friend rather; since love's clear rays
Are the light that alone makes man's dust divine,
And like his, the Unseen's — whose compassionate gaze
May not even yet have abandoned mine.

[611]

TARBURY STEEP

The moon in her gold over Tarbury Steep
    Wheeled full, in the hush of the night,
To rabbit and hare she gave her chill beams
    And to me on that silvery height.

From the dusk of its glens thrilled the nightjar's strange cry,
    A peewit wailed over the wheat,
Else still was the air, though the stars in the sky
    Seemed with music in beauty to beat.

O many a mortal has sat there before,
    Since its chalk lay in shells in the sea,
And the ghosts that looked out of the eyes of them all
    Shared Tarbury's moonlight with me.

And many, as transient, when I have gone down,
    To the shades and the silence of sleep,
Will gaze, lost in dream, on the loveliness seen
    In the moonshine of Tarbury Steep.

ONE SWALLOW

Strange — after so many quiet Springs,
Wherein the ever-dwindling sap uprose —
That swallow should return on death-dark wings,
Should bloom a cankered rose!

JENNY

I love her face —
    That long, flat cheek,
Those eyes, dark pools wherein the light
    Plays hide-and-seek;
    Lank, questing ears
    And soot-black lips —
    And yet a sight
Whereat an angel even might laugh outright,
And oh, that see-saw voice at dead of night!

    '*Stupid*'? — not she!
Look how sedate, calm, patient a soul
Peers out from that peaked wire-haired poll,
    And luminous eye!
And see, she's turned her gentle head,
    And there, her foal!

WE WHO HAVE *WATCHED*

We who have watched the World go by,
Brooding with eyes, unveiled and clear,
On its poor pomp and vanity,
Seen Mammon, vice and infamy
Cringe, bargain, jape and jeer —
What surety have we here?

We who have witnessed beauty fade,
And faces once divine with light
In narrow abject darkness laid,
Consigned with busy heedless spade
To clay from mortal sound and sight —
Where look we for delight?

We who have seen the tender child
Leap from its mother's breast, to rove
This earth; and soon, by fiend beguiled,
With wanton sickliness defiled,
Resign at last faith, hope and love.

What mercy dream *we* of?

SO IT WOULD SEEM

When, then, it comes at length to this —
The last of all earth's mysteries —
That moment when, heart breaking, I
Can only nod my last goodbye.

From its all-baffling brink may yet
My glazing gaze on you be set;
Strive still to acquaint you that you gave
What from the cradle to the grave
Has life's most strangest blessing been,
Prayer could entreat, or answer mean.

No more than beauty to the wind
Can speech reveal the secret mind.
Be then alone a while, and seek
In your own eyes and mouth and cheek
What only your glass can tell you of —
The face that mirrored all I love —
The self of my idolatry.

[613]

Grief and despair and dread; ah, yes;
Nothing on earth the heart to bless
Brings unremitting happiness.
Nor shall you from the spice-sweet gorse
Pluck any thornless bloom perforce;
So, all the rapture, all the care
As close as thorn and blossom were.

Every day through I lived in you,
Present or absent, the whole day through;
Nothing I saw, or heard, or felt
Might not its vivid instant melt
My very bowels with thought of thee:
Whisper then 'Lo!' Then, *Sesame!*

NEVER YET

Never yet I peaceful lay
With my face upturned to where
Fierce amid their glories play
The Great and Little Bear.

Yet in that quiet bed — my last —
They will surely range my bones
So my eyes to'rd heaven are cast
Between my tomb's stones.

Come, then; come, some quiet hour;
Over book, or needle, dream;
Gather here and there a flower —
Find thy self in them!

Surely then unto the East
Turn upon my side shall I;
Find at length my endless rest,
And, once more, happy, die!

UNCIRCUMVENTIBLE

Ah, if what energy I have
Be mine alone to get, and give! —
Though I should to my utmost strive,
    Whence then the means to live!

[614]

Secrets like these a flower might tell
Could air its honeyed language free;
Or drone at ease in a fuchsia-bell;
    They'll learn it not from me!

Soul's inward rain, the sun's sweet light,
Divining rod of questing man —
No pains or care will compass it,
    Since nothing human can.

Blow the Spring wind where it listeth, then;
And Night her ancient kingdom keep,
Since there the god, named Hypnos, sets
    The spirit free, in sleep.

IMMANENT

The drone of war-plane neared, and dimmed away;
The child, above high-tide mark, still toiled on.
Salt water welled the trench that in his play
He'd dug as moat for fort and garrison.

Lovely as Eros, and half-naked too,
He heaped dried beach-drift, kindled it, and lo!
A furious furnace roared, the sea winds blew . . .
Vengeance divine! And death to every foe!

Young god! — and not ev'n Nature eyed askance
The fire-doomed Empire of a myriad Ants.

THE CHINESE POT

Sunsets a myriad have flamed and faded
Since he who 'threw' this clay upon his wheel
With life-learned skill its hues and colours graded,
And in his furnace did its glaze anneal:

A Chinese, ages distant. Yet how clear —
In all of essence to our minds most dear —
This thing of beauty brings its maker near!

[615]

THE BIRTH OF VENUS

The tide lapped high, blue, tranquil and profound;
Apollo his bright car had steered to noon,
And paused exultant, flaming to the ground,
Whereon white wild flowers like a veil were strewn;

When, as it were, a sigh ran over the deep;
A shoal of fish on silver-sharpened fin
Sped round-eyed into gloomier secrecy;
The small birds trembled the sweet air within;

And from the woods against the shore arose
A warbling of faint multitudinous throats.
The leopard, mewing, to his covert goes.
A mist of gold before Apollo floats.

And — as when winter snowdrops, wakening,
Lift from the thin cold snow their pale delight —
From out the sea befell a lovelier thing —
Venus arose into the morning light.

Her eyes, made blue with dreaming in the deeps,
Pierced the shore's woods with April suddenly,
Her hair, like arching water where light sleeps,
Shook gold above the azure of the sea:

And one white foaming billow ran like flame,
Stayed, broke, and cried in ecstasy her name.

FROM AMID THE SHADOWS

Years gone I woke — from a dark dream — so terrified
    I lay a while like one stone-dead.
From out the Shades a voice had uttered Judgement:
    These were the words it said:

'This poor lost soul lead back to the World of Strife,
To serve its sentence *there*: — Eternal Life.'

ASTRAY

This is not the place for thee;
Never doubt it, thou hast come
By some dark catastrophe
    Far, far from home.

All that else were thine to prize,
Is yet with strangeness patened too;
Passion and pining haunt thy gaze,
    Yet tears thou look'st through.

Never one came loving thee;
Never loved thou one, now gone;
But some hapless memory
    Was left — to live on.

Echoes taunt thee night and day;
Shadows fall whence nothing is.
Silence hails thee, *Come away*,
    Here's not thy peace!

Ignis fatuus thou; and all
Earth can show is dream, and vain;
Whatsoever fate befall
    Mockery will remain.

I AM

I am the World . . . Unveil this face:
Of brass it is; cold — ice-cold hard;
It broods on the splendour of my disgrace —
Remorseless and unmarred.

I am the Flesh . . . With drooping lid
My eyes like sea-flowers drowse and shine
Unfathomably far. I bid
The lost all hope resign.

I am the Devil . . . *H'sst*, stoop close!
The hatred in my vulture stare
Thy doubting, fainting soul will dose
With cordials rich and rare.

[617]

I am the World . . . Come, enter, feast!
Look not too nearly — gilt, or gold?
Nor heed the wailing of man and beast,
The clamour of bought and sold!

I am the Flesh . . . Enormous, dim,
Dream doth invite thee, thick with fumes
Of burning gums. Faint visions gleam;
Sea's phosphor the vague illumes.

I am the Devil . . . Head askew,
And dwelling eye. See, how earth's straight
Distorted-crooked crocks. And through
Time's bars grins gibbering Fate.

THE MOURNER

'Nothing for him on earth went right,
    A destined outcast he,
A bastard hustled out of sight,
    A stark epitome
Of all betokening Fortune's spite,
    And human apathy.

'There lurked beyond his vacant eyes
    A soul in mute eclipse —
A sea named *Nothing*, harbourless,
    Sans wind, sans sun, sans ships;
Of will, of mind, of eagerness
    No trace in those loose lips.

'His bridgeless nose, his toneless cry,
    His clumsy hands, his gait,
Sheer satire of humanity,
    Proclaimed a loon's estate;
"Made in God's image" — ay, meant to be:
    This mommet, scorned of Fate.

'He was not even monstrous enough
    To extort a schoolboy's jeers;
Too tame to cause a fool to scoff,
    Or incite a woman's fears.
He lived beyond the reach of love —
    For thirty years!'

' "Beyond the reach of love"! You say?
    Whence then these scalding tears?'

[618]

ARITHMETIC

Those twittering swallows, hawking between the ricks —
The oddest theirs of all arithmetics!

Daring the seas, the cliffs of England won,
Two in late April came. . . . Their housework done,
They conned this simple problem: — (1×1).

And lo! — in the evening sunshine, gilding the ricks —
Four fork-tailed fledgelings, and the answer — *six!*

HARD LABOUR

This Prince of Commerce spent his days
In crafty, calm, cold, cozening strife:
He thus amassed a million pounds,
And bought a pennyworth of life.

PUSS

A sly old Puss that paused to cross the road,
  The dangerous venture did at length decline.
'A human may prize his life at what it's worth,'
 she mused;
    '*I* treasure *all* my nine!'

RATS

 'Foul vermin they,
 Both black and brown!
 Nothing's too vile
 To keep the wretches down!'
Yet smiled my Sam to see (he's in disgrace!)
 One, with its forepaws,
 Wash its whiskered face.

DR. MOLE

That Love's our earthly Light —
What man could doubt it? —
Until the Reverend Mole,
Yoked with his jet-black stole,
In his dogmatic role,
    Preaches about it?

SECOND CHILDHOOD

What! heartsick still, grown old and grey,
And second childhood on its way?
Still listening after ghosts that come
Only to find you far from home?
Not even your spectre there to tell
How loving, loved and lovable.

Still feigning that from outward things
Enduring consolation springs?
Still preening? Hopping perch to seed;
Mockery of song? As if your need
Were all in one small cage contained,
Nor hint of wilder bird remained.

In the long, arduous, bitter day
Scarce one half-audible Wellaway?
As though — alone — no strangled note
Rasped with affliction that dumb throat!
'Twill snap your very heart-strings soon;
Poor outcast, pining for the Moon! . . .

Lovely, she rides the quiet skies,
And glasses all grieved aching eyes;
She who ne'er yet, at any tide,
Revealed to earth her hidden side.
She who no night-bird ever taught
To sing, not what it must, but ought.

She sinks. The day breaks — mounts on high,
To gild with grace Man's bloodier dye,
His world in wreckage . . . Miriam, come:
Transfigure our hearts with trump and drum!
A harp, forsooth; and still to crave
For love, peace, joy! Beyond the grave?

[620]

OUTCASTS

There broods a hovel by a narrow way,
    Broken and overgrown;
Ay, though intemperately the sickle is thrust,
    Weeds seed, and flourish on.

Sunk in that garden is a broken well.
    Its waters hidden from sight —
Small comfort any bucket draws from thence,
    Ev'n though it dip all night.

A few lean fowls stalk, envious of the dust,
    A cock at midnight cries;
But from those fallow acres, near and far,
    No clarion replies.

The dog-day suns shower heat upon its thatch,
    Till sty and bog and dust
Breathe up a filthy odour to the heavens
    At every fitful gust.

The winter falls. With leaden nights; and days
    Frozen and parched and harsh;
Far in the valley-mist an idiot head
    Stoops o'er a sterile marsh.

His toil and travail are a fruitless gage
    Thrown down to Destiny;
His pleasure a besotted jest
    'Twixt sin and misery.

Hope in his eyes a phantasm in a tomb,
    Faith in his heart a flame
His masters dim with hatred and revolt,
    And sadden into shame.

He grunts and sweats, through the long drouth of noon,
    Broods, gazing into mud;
Till, suddenly, upon his spade shall stream
    A light as bright as blood.

Then shall he rise against his naked door,
    Fronting a fading West,
The wrath of God within his glassy eyes,
    And ruddy on his breast.

REUNION

Tyrants — the slaves of intermittent dread —
Prefer the undauntable securely dead;
Though dreams might give them pause — of how, and
    when
In deathless Hades they may meet again.

It is not vengeance they will there confront.
Not for the valiant the weapons wrought by fear!
Strike may the damned again as was their wont,
Yet not by barest inch bring safety near.

Saint may with fiend through outer darkness fare,
And not for hatred shun the filthy lice.
Hell is the heart that nought divine can share,
And all else verges towards paradise.

'LIFE LIVES ON LIFE'

Life lives on life — that stale old tale!
Ev'n beauty fades — to be
The new and tender loveliness
Of a mere transiency: —

So, with these thickly lidded eyes
I wandered in the maze,
And in such base and barren thought
Laid waste immortal days;

Till, suddenly on my body fell
A close and stinging dart,
And, for a time, my head, at peace,
Made converse with my heart.

Both had seen better days; and yet
This new communion
Brought back the simple clear good sense
Of a childhood past and gone;

And while they hob-nobbed, quietly enough,
In a world, insane, at war;
Theirs now a tale that had an end —
Like happier tales before.

And when in consort either chanced
To look on cheek, or rose,
Or time-worn hand, or shadow of bird,
None hinted former woes;

No, these two cronies — far from hale —
Lifted their mugs, and then,
Nodding towards their Host, gave toast:
'*This world of living men!*'

Yes, even from Death's latchless door
They gladly turned away,
Such blessed eyes looked peace on them,
And long-loved lips mused, Stay!

SHE

Stay, and hearken; low I lie,
And nothing here to know me by,
Nothing but a heap of earth,
Once my riches, now my dearth.
That damask rose with petals wan
Long since was back to briar gone;
The summer grass has dropped its seed;
Flowered now has every weed.

Yet these, if they had voices, might
Tell my love, though hidden from sight:
And if there came a woman — *She!*
In token of long memory,
And at my footstone musing stood . . .

Though doomed to silence, then I would,
Pointing a fleshless finger there,
Without a whisper of speech declare,
'Lo! the all that me possessed! —
          Thinkest thou I'm at rest?'

FOREBODING

Ev'n on the tenderest hour of love
A stealthy spectre may intrude,
And, with the wreckage of a dream,
    Daunt the day's solitude.

Then from a limbo in the mind
Fear lifts a haggard face and cries,
'Yours may the fate be to live on
    When cold in death she lies;

'And then to stay. And wait...' Alas!
I *see* you, silent in the grave
That rapes the heart of all it loved —
    To miss, to mourn, to crave.

THE CHALLENGE

I speak, none listens; but I hear
My own voice beating on my ear.
I love, but this wild love that yearns,
Foiled from its goal, in haste returns,
    And my own bosom burns.

Yet all that haunts me I bestowed.
Faint as a shadow on the road
That leads thro' evening into night
Thou wert, till dreaming made thee bright;
And the rich marvel of thy hair,
'Twas I hid all earth's darkness there:
Would I, then, harm what I have made?
    O be no more of me afraid!

WIRELESS

'When other lips . . .' — *that* old outmoded ballad!
Trolled in falsetto tenor, reeking of long-gone years!
And yet . . . Some grieved and cheated waif in me
      stirred and hearkened;
  My eyes were stung by tears.

DEADALIVE

My inward world is strangely still;
It seems the wintry fog without
Into one's very wits may steal
And shut light, hope, ev'n fancy out.

Not a mouse stirring; not a glim
Of Man's lost microcosm! Why,
A child with his toy panoram
    Is better off than I!

Yes, and some dolt's mislaid the map!
Life has forsaken this poor mind;
Ev'n Memory has shut up shop,
And then pulled down the blind.

Alas, through all Man's centuries
No wizard yet has forged the key
To unlock, at will, the cell where lies
The Mage of Dream, called Fantasy.

Worse; even with one's heart for bait,
The soul may stagnant be, and numb;
Love may stand weeping at the gate,
    And yet refuse a crumb!

ULLADARE

Down by thy waters, Ulladare,
  A cedar gloomy and profound
Bids the north wind awaken there
  How sad a sound!

No exile's harp-strings could entice
  Sorrow so heedfully as this
To wake with music memories
  Of bygone bliss.

Then what far peace, to me unknown,
  Seems, by that gently lipping wave,
That shrouded tree to brood upon,
  Unless the grave?

DE PROFUNDIS

The metallic weight of iron;
The glaze of glass;
The inflammability of wood . . .

You will not be cold there;
You will not wish to see your face in a mirror;
There will be no heaviness,
Since you will not be able to lift a finger.

There will be company, but they will not heed you;
Yours will be a journey only of two paces
Into view of the stars again; but you will not make it.

There will be no recognition;
No one, who should see you, will say —
Throughout the uncountable hours —

'Why . . . the last time we met, I brought you some flowers!'

IT IS A WRAITH

It is a wraith — no mortal — haunts my way,
Of a strange loveliness Time cannot snare,
Nor fretting of mortality decay,
Nor death defeat that feeds on all things fair.

What is desire but this one tryst to keep?
What my heart's longing but to await the hour
When to full recognition it shall leap,
As into summer flames the opening flower?

No mockery lurks within those steadfast eyes;
False words spring not from lips as mute as these;
Ages have learned that longing to be wise;
Love to survive life's cold inconstancies;
Have patience, Angel. With this dust's last sigh
Whisper my mouth thy name, and whispering, die!

THE OWL

Apart, thank Heaven, from all to do
To keep alive the long day through;
To imagine; think; watch; listen to;
There still remains — the heart to bless,
Exquisite pregnant Idleness.

Why, we might let all else go by
To seek its Essence till we die . . .

Hark, now! that Owl, a-snoring in his tree,
Till it grow dark enough for him to see.

[627]

2. UNCOLLECTED POEMS

THE COMPANION[1]

If I should from my grave arise
    To wander in the eventide,
Turn thou in thine old lovely wise;
    When at thy side
The meadowsweet a fragrance takes,
    Too full to be of earthliness,
And in dim boughs a song awakes
    Of ecstasies —
So wild thy very heart shall leap
    And sink again to its old peace,
And that arise that lay asleep
    More sweet than these.

LABYRINTH[2]

I marvelled at earth's glory, her grey seas
    Which stretch in light in confines of the sky,
    At her still mountains reared immovably,
The fear and wonder of her leafy trees;
Much more I marvelled, musing at my ease,
On man and all his curious history,
The scars and pangs of his antiquity,
The childlike splendour of his fantasies,

How, like earth's grass, he flourishes and goes —
    His grief, his love, his passion, and his fear,
His ant-like labours, his sublime repose —
    Yet finds no peace to be accomplished here.
O God, I said, who mewed me in this place,
How shall I through these dreams Thy realty trace!

[1] *Pall Mall Magazine*, September–December 1902.
[2] *Pall Mall Magazine*, September–December 1902.

IN DEEP SLEEP[1]

In deep sleep I had forgot
All that thou hadst taught of care;
Now, alas! remembered not
Is the dream I dreamèd there:
    Roses die
    When summer goes,
    Dream is but
    A fading rose.

O what sorcery is this —
Thou whom I have banished
Should into my sleep arise,
Yet by dawn have vanished!
    Waking, sleeping,
    This I know —
    Only thou
    Wouldst grieve me so.

LULLABY[2]

Shut now those slumber-haunted eyes,
'Tis but the lonely owl that cries,
    Tu-whit, tu-whoo!
And oh, its burden is — Come soon
Sleep to the drowsy little one!

Stir not thy hands! The wind that goes
To breathe the sweetness of the rose,
    Sighs softly through;
And oh, its whisper is — Come soon
Sleep to the drowsy little one!

Fold thy bright lips! The voice that wails
Is the far-echoing nightingale's,
    Lone to the moon;
And all her music is — Come soon
Sleep to the drowsy little one!

---

[1] *Pall Mall Magazine*, January–April 1903.
[2] *Living Age* (Boston), 28 January 1905.

AGE AND CHILDHOOD[1]

She stooped with serious eyes
    Where peace in shadow lay,
Searched in my frightened eyes, and smiled
    All fear away;

Pierced to my heart — my heart,
    All language else forgot,
Caught all the secrets love to love
    Refuses not;

Trembling, and dim, and weak,
    Took my cold, idle hand
That yearned, yet trembled to receive
    Her mute command.

Out of the dusk a bird —
    A leaf from the tossing tree —
Eyes in a fading mist of age
    Summoning me.

CHILDHOOD[2]

A pinch of spice, a crust of fairy bread,
With wild bees' honey and with comfits spread,
A stalk of cherries, a wild strawberry's stain,
And two small crumpled rose-leaves wet with rain; —
Such for her cheeks: but O, now for her hair,
What sunbeams cast such shadowiness, and where?
But for her eye, I think some woodland elf
Laughed in that looking-glass to see himself.
And when she sighed in dreams, a drowsy wren
Hopped her sweet mouth into from off her chin,
And in her throat entwined a tiny nest
Wherein to pipe the song a wren knows best . . .
Lo! then, the house where dwells, O, who can say —
A soul still winking at the break of day;
From those bright starry windows still to peep
And shut those shutters when 'tis time to sleep;
To op'n those scarlet doors, and learn to cry
How sweet a 'you', how wonderful an 'I'!

[1] *Blackwood's Magazine*, February 1905; *Living Age*, 25 March 1905.
[2] *Pall Mall Magazine*, vol. 4, new series, 1906; *Living Age*, 2 February 1907.

REUNION[1]

Where twilight broods o'er Acheron
A youthful face waits mine,
Care cannot make a whit more wan,
Or sorrow less divine.

By Styx, whose changeless asphodel
Blooms heavy with dew, is one
Who in his innocence keeps well
Our tryst till Time be done.

O eyes whose earthly light is hid,
Heart of my childhood be
Content to sleep, till Love have bid
Age turn again to thee!

ALONE[2]

No sound over the deep, only the desolate foam,
White in the evening mist, of the last wave home:
No sound over the fields, only the lonely cry
Of the last bird speeding to rest and nest 'neath the darkening sky.

I walk and I think of you here — your courage, your truth; I
know,
Though the lips and the heart be silenced, and the eyes into
darkness go,
These still may live within me, if I keep my truth, and am brave;
Nor mourn too sadly, wildly for one who mourns no more in the
grave.

Yet, yet, even you will forgive, if a grief, as still as the sea
With all its waters a flood at peace, call on hope's shores for thee;
You will forgive, if a late bird weary, 'neath a sorrow as dark as
the night,
Cry low, sad, keen, in so deep a peace, your dear name, once, in the
height.

UNFORGOTTEN[1]

When my heart wearies, and to rest are gone
The friends I loved in youth and leaned upon —
One after one, the faces bright life gave
Into the soundless nothing of the grave;

When only mothlike through my mind do flit
Age-shadowed memories to solace it:
Ev'n then, ev'n then, I think thine eyes will be
As dark, as tender, and as dear to me.

When my hand trembles, and no task remains
But needs more cunning than its palm contains;
When every step I take but echoes, 'Lo!
How lightly and gladly did we long-since go!'

Ay, when my head upon an arching spine
Nods in the glass unto a face scarce mine: —
Despite all these hard things, one dear shall be
Haunting my helplessness — the ghost of thee.

By feeble candle-light to rest I'll get
And in gray dreams walk where the violet
Blows sweet — where once a foolish boy grew hot
Lest thou, O dear and far, didst love him not:

I shall not know, in dream, what age hath done,
But turn to kiss a cheek for ever gone:
And I, perchance, shall take thy hand and say
Words whereof Death steals not the breath away.

[1] *Pall Mall Magazine*, vol. 11, new series, 1910; *Living Age*, 26 March 1910.

I WENT TO PLUCK A FLOW'R[1]

I went to pluck a flow'r,
To send it to my love,
But no bloom could I find
Perfect enough and fair
To set among her hair,
Or where the laces bind
Her bosom, or above
Her heart to lie an hour.

And so my choice prefers
An unpretentious bloom,
A simple meadow weed,
A humble blue-eyed thing:
Like the weak praise I sing,
It is to intercede
For one whose sighs presume
To beauties such as hers.

And when my offering
She sees, and reads my rime,
She'll gently lay it by,
She'll ponder for a while:
Then smile a little smile,
And sigh a little sigh,
And wonder that old Time
Has such a leaden wing.

TO A CHILD[2]

If I could but be happy,
    As you, dear, are happy! —
Like green fields in May
All my heart gay;
Like pure April skies
Clear light in my eyes;
Yes, and shake a small tongue
In sweet sallies of song,
And dance with my shadow
In the sun in the meadow,
And lie down to rest,
Joy in my breast!

[1] *Westminster Gazette*, 18 May 1914; *Saturday Westminster Gazette*, 23 May 1914; *Living Age*, 25 July 1914; *Literary Digest* (New York), 19 September 1914.
[2] *Pall Mall Magazine*, May 1914.

But alas and alack,
   Childhood will not come back.
Like snow Time's strange hours
Have o'er-topped its small flowers,
Have frozen its waters,
And silenced its rills
And clothed with cold cloud
The gold of its hills.

Yet this sadness I know
   Is but fancies of woe,
Heavy dreams that would break
If I could but awake
From the sleep I am in,
The dull sleep I am in;
If Youth would consent
To return to my door —
Call with the wild voice
It called me before;
I should slip off this heaviness,
Scorn anxious fear,
And gaze without grief
On your beauty, my dear.

A TRUE-BLUE BROADSIDE OF '14[1]

'And what's the news, Mr. Sergeant, what news, my soldier man?' —
'We're away and a-ship to Bel-gi-um as softly as ship can;
The Kaiser and his Lords of War have shook a mailèd fist,
And a hundred thousand Englishmen are off to keep the tryst.

'The Kaiser he's a gentleman, and eager for to dance
Across the floor of half the world from Petersburg to France;
"In gay Paree, we'll sup," says he, "so Moltke, call the page,
His name is little Bel-gi-um, and my pumps are in Liège."

' "Soft," says Sir Edward, calm and cool, "there's them across the seas
Are ready to take a turn, my lord, and join you, if you please;
They're not such folk as *wants* to jolt on any friendly toes,
They'll merely set to partners, sir, and that's a game they knows.

[1] *Saturday Westminster Gazette*, 22 August 1914.

' "With Dreadnoughts here, two kinds of French, the Rooshans at
 your heel,
They'll keep the ball a-rolling, sir, and face you keel to Kiel;
And when it comes to hornpipes, la, Britannia's learned the knack
Of dancing midnight down the sky and dancing morning back."

'So it's H'st, my lads, and Wh'st, my lads, the music's just begun,
The gals have brought their powder-puffs, and the world shall watch
 the fun;
There's Jellicoe to keep the row, and the Kaiser he shall prance
With a leetle more broth than he *meant* to spare 'twixt Petersburg and
 France.'

THE LADY GODIVA[1]

The Lady Godiva, all tender and fair,
On shoulders and bosom her loose gold hair,
With none but small birds flitting winsome to see,
Rode bare in her beauty through Coventry.

White was the palfrey Godiva did sit,
Shrill rang his bridle-rein, clear clankt his bit;
Youthful her cheek, and 'twas lovesomely bent
On the streets of the township all shuttered and shent.

Strange was that solitude. Strange 'twas to be
The only soul stirring in hushed Coventry.
And she blushed — and laughed out — when she chanced for to spy
Through the chink of a shutter poor Tom's peeping eye.

A child in his manners, how could he forbear
To watch utter loveliness taking the air?
Alas! — but so marvellous bright she did shine
There was naught left but dream in the dark of his eyne.

'Twas a secret between them; and false 'twere to say
That Tom was a sorrowful man from that day.
For pity brimmed deep in Godiva's clear mind,
And of folk to be pitied there's none like the blind.

---

[1] *New Statesman*, 8 September 1917.

THE TRYST[1]

'Are you very peaceful there, Thomas Nunn?'
    'O yes, for where I am laid
No deed of wickedness is done,
    Nor cruel word is said.

'I fall, I fall from dust to dust;
    But my spirit hovers near,
Obedient to God's simple "must",
    And unafraid of fear.

'I fall, I fall: quiet is my tongue;
    Darkened my eyes; but O,
My spirit haunts these stones among,
    And will not let me go.

'It whispers — whispers, "Come, Thomas Nunn!"
    But dust am I, and say,
"Wait on, thou Spirit, we must wait on,
    Until the Judgement day.

' "Then He who me from thee did break,
    And gave me peace to sleep,
Will bid thee stoop, and I shall wake,
    My tryst with thee to keep." '

GAMESTERS[2]

Three devils sate there, gloating on my sins,
In the dense music of thought's violins,
The whining, twining, pining violins.

Lean shone the tapers on them, chin and eye.
They diced and chaffered while the dark flowed by;
Hour after hour the dark and stars flowed by.

They saw me not. From that cold mask no sign,
No signal shook from this lone soul of mine;
Blind were their presences to hint of mine.

[1] *New Paths: Verse, Prose, Pictures 1917–1918*, ed. C. W. Beaumont and M. T. H. Sadler, London, 1918.
[2] *Athenaeum*, 9 May 1919, and *Living Age*, 14 June 1919, where it was called 'The Old Shrouders'; and it was later revised for *Atlantic Monthly* (Boston), November 1952, and *Poetry Review*, January–March 1954.

Rejoiced I was to leave them fingering there
The short swift record of my earthly care;
Life's hapless evil its insistent care.

And like a child, who plucks a flower that blows —
Moon-cupped convolvulus or the clear briar rose —
And happy, in beauty, for a moment goes,

So I, in mercy, freed them from all my sins,
Heard lapse the whining of the violins;
Heard silence lighten round the violins.

TO SOME MOST HAPPY MEN[1]

To some most happy men the grace is given
After long circuit to come back to heaven —
The heaven where they in childhood used to dwell;
Life is the school in which they have learned to tell,
After long labour, of the lovely and fair
In shape, form, colour that inhabit there,
Whose light celestial unchanging gleams
Only where innocence or wisdom dreams.
This happier child at peace in that first home,
As yet untravelled, need no further roam;
But over her paper and her colours bent
Can paint the bliss 'tis to be innocent.
Life, add thy wisdom, and at length bring us
Where springs the fountain of her genius.

THE MIGHT-HAVE-BEEN[2]

Parched were my lips with drought of noon,
   Broken my feet, in broken shoon,
     The sun shone fierce and leonine
      On the salt, salt sea.
But fell at length cool eventide
On barren wave, spread waste and wide,
On spike-grassed, whispering dunes of sand,
And soft-ebbed twilight on that land —
     The land of Might-have-been.

[1] Prefatory poem, *Babes and Fairies*, catalogue of an exhibition of drawings by Pamela Bianco, Leicester Galleries, London, May–June 1919.
[2] *New Statesman*, 28 June 1919; *Living Age*, 30 August 1919. See also 'An Interlude', *Memory and Other Poems*, 1938, p. 390, a shorter poem derived from this one.

Chill sighed the wind on cheek and hair,
A region bare and bleak, yet fair,
Fair with its sparse-strewn, dry-root flowers,
Its siren-singing haunted bowers,
The silence of those long, long hours
    That stuff no mortal year.
Of silver and untroubled sheen
Hung in the West's crystalline green
A planet ne'er by mortal seen,
    Named 'Never', sweet and clear.

A thin brook gushed o'er stones hard-by,
'Forsaken' it babbled; lone was I;
Night's oriental canopy
    Tented the eastern sky.
Shade that I was in dream waylaid,
Benighted, and yet unafraid,
I sate me there, all sorrows fled,
    And whispered to the sea
The thousand songs I had hoped to sing
When I on earth was wandering,
Whereof, alas! poor words could bring
Nought but a deadened echoing
    Of 'Benedicite!'

Sweeter than any note men hear
When, latticed in by moonbeams clear,
The bird of the darkness to its fere
    Tells out love's mystery,
Rose in my throat and poured its dew —
That hymn of praise — my being through;
Gave peace to a heart that never knew
    Peace until then, I ween.

No listener mine, mayhap; but ne'er
Trolled happier wight in heaven fair
    To a lyre of golden string.
Nought but a soundless voice was I
Beneath that deep, unvoyaged sky,
Silence and silence telling o'er
    What makes the stars to sing.

O vanity of age to mourn
What youth in folly left forlorn!
Doth not earth's strange and lovely mean
Only, 'Come, see, O son of man,
All that you hoped, the nought you can —
    The glory that might have been.'

[639]

SIX AND THIRTY YEARS GONE[1]

Six and thirty years gone,
Old friend, 'tis to-day
Since from June and her roses
Death called you away,
 In slumber, away.

Strange, perchance, was the dream
Ushered in such a guest,
Strange the notes of the night-birds
That lulled you to rest —
 Unawakened, to rest.

Yes, but one who in quiet
Found his music and love
In the nightingale's song
And the croon of the dove
 His roof-tree above,

Of the grave had to fear
No 'blue devil' breed
Worse than folly and strife,
Affectation and greed
 Of humanity's seed.

Haply 'idle' your ease;
But not '*seemingly* deep'
Is the time-heedless tide
That now stirs not your sleep,
 Where the green grasses creep . . .

Or is Youth again yours,
May we mortals surmise?
And do even the Shades
In wan daybreak arise —
 A faint sun in their eyes?

And at no 'polite circles'
Or new faces aghast,
Do you pocket your book,
And lapse into the past,
 Quite happy at last?

[1] Omar Khayyám Club menu, Pagani's, London, 25 March 1920; *The Second Book of the Omar Khayyám Club, 1910–1929*, London, 1931, limited edition of 125 copies. Edward Fitzgerald died on 14 June 1883.

Do, in meads, queerly sembling
Silly Suffolk's, you lie,
Where Jordan reflects
Deben's larks in the sky?
  And, musing near by,

Reclines dreaming Omar,
Far from home, but at ease?
And, at stone's throw, one fishing
With crumbs of cream cheese,
  A Greek, if you please: Sophocles?

Clucks water on bottle
(Inexhaustible bin!):
And impearled in the distance —
Where the palm-trees begin
  And the gates are asheen —

Step guests, well beloved,
In delicious 'confab' —
Calderon, Tacitus,
And compromised Crabbe,
  With conscience a-stab?

Green the bough, cool the shade?
And lo! But sweet Muse,
Ours the urgent To-day
We may spend — as we choose —
  But we cannot refuse.

Speed the bowl: toast the guest:
Yet, while hastes the feast on,
Breathe, friends, a prayer
For the poet that's gone,
  The philosopher gone! —

The fastidious recluse,
Gentle, faithful, austere,
Who in life as in books
Loved Man's best. Rare and dear:
  In spirit draw near!

PROLOGUE[1]

Summer is come — brisk pink, and wilding rose,*
And all the enchantment which this England knows,
When honeyed hours of sunshine clearly bright
Steal on in beauty to'rds how brief a night;
While yet the cuckoo calls her hollows through —
Two faltering grace notes, now, to every *'oo* —
Till the harsh piping of each nesting brood
Fall mute; and sweet-tongued from his solitude
The lingering nightingale in dingle or dell
Sings even the lovelier since he sings, Farewell.

Alas, that June should fade; that time should be
So rich yet fugitive a pageantry.
Forsake it then awhile, and with us fly
Into the past where nothing now can die:
Where even the young and lovely, old and staid,
Live on unchanged — of purest fantasy made.

Here, then, another pageant; take your ease,
Your hearts attuned to welcome refugees.
See; now they come — in semblance of a Masque —
Craving your credence — it is all they ask.
Charles is enthroned; the Plague is o'er, the Fire
That burned half London, in disaster dire,
Is smouldering out; yet not extinct all fears:
For lo, a child is lost, and still in tears!
Comfort will come to her full soon . . . But nay;
I'm telling secrets — *She* is in the Play;
A waif indeed, alas, but not from Love a-stray.

---

* For winter productions, the words 'Summer is come' should read 'When summer comes'.

---

[1] A prologue 'specially written by Walter de la Mare' for *When Charles was King: A Seventeenth Century Masque*. The author and date of the masque are not known, and the text has not been traced. A copy of the poem printed on a single sheet of paper was found among the de la Mare papers. It may have been written in about 1920.

THE HOSTAGE[1]

In dead of dark to the starry North
   St. Nicholas drew near;
He had ranged the World this wintry night,
   His elk-bells jangling clear.
Now bitter-worn with age was he,
   And weary of Mankind, for few
Had shown him love or courtesy.

His sacks lay empty — all save one;
   And this to his affright
Stirred as he stopped with fingers numb,
   Ablaze with hoar-frost bright.
Aghast he stood. Showed fumbling thumb,
   Small shoulder, a wing: What stowaway
Was this, and whence was't come?

And out there crept a lovely Thing —
   Half angel and half child: —
'I, youngest of all Heaven, am here,
   To be thy Joy,' he smiled.
'O Nicholas, our Master Christ
   Thy grief hath seen; and He
Hath bidden me come to keep His tryst,
   And bring His love to thee;
To serve thee well, and sing, Nowell,
   And thine own son to be.'

PROLOGUE[2]

'A good wine needs no bush' — Ay, so. No more
Than full moon riding heaven, an almanac,
Or April 'mid her bluebells, a town-crier.
Why then, I ask, comes interloping here
Betwixt the gustful reader and his dish
A prosy prologiser? He knows well
How even a learnèd preface, angel-sweet,
Far from persuading critics to be kind
May merely serve to make them less than kin.
Forfend *that* consummation!

[1] *Poetry* (Chicago), ed. Harriet Monroe, December 1921; then published by itself as *The Hostage* in a limited edition of 100 copies, London, 1925.
[2] Prefatory poem, *Christopher Marlowe: A Play in Two Acts*, Ernest Milton, London, 1924.

[643]

His one hope
Is but to whisper: — Lo, good friends, Romance!
'Sconced in 'the little nowhere' of your minds
Bid the imponderable curtains waft aside;
And on those spectral boards prepare to see
Wooed back to life from out the spacious days
Of proud Eliza, Shades — whose noble names
Give even a four-foot fancy Ariel's wings.
A feat to daunt the bravest.
But in truth
The wind has blown too long from out the east,
Over bleak naturalism's arid wastes.
We sit, like children in a dingy school,
Intent on copying some 'norm' of life —
The portrait of a visage chiefly warts.
Yet give the Imagination wing, she'll mount.
Her natural habitation is the Sun.
And though high-flying dare as sheer a fall;
Though every inch threat danger — o'er an abyss;
Who would not praise the courage of a man
Who — player himself of Shakespeare, root to crown;
Bearing a name only less famed than his —
Hath for first venture dared our low-fall'n stage
With tragic Marlowe for prodigious theme?

CHRISTMAS EVE[1]

Dark is the hour, long the night;
Hoarfrost sheds a shimmering light;
The wind in the naked woodland cries
A harplike music; the willow sighs.
But a marvellous quiet dwells in heaven —
Sirius, Markab, the faithful Seven —
For the Old Year's sands are well-nigh run;
This is the Birthday of the Sun.

No glint of dawn; but Chanticlere
Is crowing of Christmas, bugle clear.
In waxen hive, close-wintering,
Bees a slumbrous orison sing;

[1] *Harper's Monthly Magazine* (New York), January 1926.

[644]

Roused from their lair in dales of the snow,
Light-foot deer in procession go;
Cattle and sheep in byre and pen
Kneel in the darkness, unseen of men:
For the Old Year's sands are well-nigh run;
This is the Birthday of the Sun.

Now houses of humans with jargonings ring,
Hautboy and serpent and flute and string,
Voices in gruff-shrill carolling —
Men and boys hunched up in the cold.
Tinkles the ice on the frozen mould.
Hesper is shining — rime on thatch;
Stag-borne Nicholas comes — unlatch!
Children stir in their dream and then
Drowsily sigh and turn over again.
Airs of the morn in the orchard flow;
Lo, in the apple boughs, mistletoe!
For the Old Year's sands are well-night run;
This is the Birthday of the Sun.

Master and Man, the East burns red;
Drowse no longer in sluggard bed;
Garland the Yule log; scatter the wheat —
Feast for the starving birds to eat.
Mistress and maid, wax warm you shall —
Boar in oven, burned wine, spiced ale,
There's quiring in heaven; and Gabriel
Wings from the zenith his news to tell;
Shepherd and king fare forth again —
Peace on earth, goodwill to men —
For, loving and lovely, in manger laid,
Dreams o'er her Babe the Virgin Maid.
Kindle then candles for your soul;
Shake off the net life's follies bring;
Ev'n of the innocent death takes toll;
There is an end to wandering.
But see, in cold clod the snowdrop blows;
Spring's inexhaustible fountain flows;
Love bides in earth till time is done;
The Old Year's sands are well-nigh run;
This is the Birthday of the Sun.

COME![1]

Shrill trills the bird concealed in leaves;
A greening sunlight gilds the flower;
Enchantment in this woodland weaves
Her labyrinthine bower.
Follow then, sweetheart! Eye, scarce stir!
Peals six-belled bloom a phantom chime,
Calls a far voice — 'Come, Wanderer!' —
On zephyr faint with thyme.

WINTER[2]

Cold and raw the north wind doth blow,
Bleak in the morning early.
All the hills are covered with snow,
And winter's now come fairly.

THE EMPTY CHARIOT[3]

Amid the wood's delicious green
While I dreamed the noon away,
Saw I once how strange a scene! —
Fleet along the wooded way,
Rolling softly o'er the moss,
Drawn by fawns as white as may
Which upon the air did toss
Antlers white as mountain-spray,
A small silver chariot!
Empty it was, save for a bow,
And a quiver, freighted not
For that small and slack-stringed bow.

[1] *Two Poems*, privately printed for R. N. Green-Armytage in an edition of 100 copies, 1931.
[2] *Scholastic Magazine* (New York), 26 October 1935.
[3] *Saturday Review of Literature* (New York), 14 December 1935.

Whose it was, ah! who may say? —
Save the nightingale alone
That upon a shadowy spray
Mused this drowsy scene upon;
Called on love melodiously,
Sadly as a hollow stone,
Love, love, love where art thou flown?
Empty flits thy chariot by,
Warriorless, solitary.

GILBERT KEITH CHESTERTON[1]

Knight of the Holy Ghost, he goes his way,
Wisdom his motley, Truth his loving jest;
The mills of Satan keep his lance in play,
Pity and Innocence his heart at rest.

DR. WILLIAM HARVEY[2]

This mild geographer set not his mark
On unknown seas, lakes, rivers vast in flood;
He loved to ponder softly in the dark
   The motions of man's blood.

In caves, delved out at Combe, he'd meditate.
'Crack-brained,' said some. 'Yes, childish, it appears.'
Alack, not even he could stimulate
In fools the circulation of Ideas.

---

[1] *G.K.'s Weekly*, 23 July 1936; memorial card for Chesterton (beginning 'Of your charity Pray for the repose of the Soul of Gilbert Keith Chesterton Who ... died on June 14th 1936 ...'), no date; Maisie Ward, *Gilbert Keith Chesterton*, London, 1944, where it is suggested that the poem was originally written for 'a paper run by [Chesterton's] supporters for the Lord Rectorship of Glasgow University'; John Sullivan, *G. K. Chesterton: A Bibliography*, London, 1958.
[2] *London Mercury*, December 1936.

A PRODIGAL SON[1]

This weakling who, while yet a child,
Had heard of vice; crime; murder; rape:
Finding the 'Real' a thought defiled,
    Wrote poetry of escape.

At length, distrustful of his Star,
And tainted too with evil and sin,
He rattled at its padlocked bar:
    But none would let him in.

... 'MR. BLANK, IT APPEARS, WAS A WRITER OF SHOCKERS'...[2]

The fire had drowsed to a sullen heat;
But cold lay body, cold its guest.
He wiped the knife on her cotton sheet,
Rinsed off the darkening blood, and dressed.
Pausing to wipe away the sweat,
He flung out her clothes from the stained-deal chest;
Stole letters, mock pearls from a keyless drawer —
Then stonily listened, while in the street
A constable paced on his midnight beat:
On ... on ... and gone. He opened the door;
Skinned off his gloves; prayed; wiped his face;
And stared at the moonshine, bleak and hoar,
Curdling the snow now thinly at rest.

A wind from the east, as he turned west,
Palsied his bones in a stark embrace.
And an Imp — fallen mute for an hour or more —
Jeered, 'Strange, is it not, that never before
Have we mapped out a "plot" round a similar case!'

---

[1] *London Mercury*, December 1936; *The Year's Poetry 1937*, ed. D. K. Roberts and G. Grigson, Reader's Union, London, 1938.
[2] *Night and Day*, 2 September 1937. It was called 'The Shocker Shocked' there. The version above is a revised one made by de la Mare in the late 1940's which remained unpublished.

IF[1]

If this, or that, had else-wise been,
We who now part had never met:[2]
See, then, of that dark god called Chance
   This tiny statuette!
A taper let us burn to him,
And wreathe his brows with mignonette . . .

And he? — that smile oblique and sly!
The mocking urchin seems to say,
'Ifs' still upon the future wait —
   Wherever that may be!
Now is the all decreed by Fate:
   Why waste it on a sigh?
Why waste it on a sigh, says he;
   And looks the other way.

THE DUNCE[3]

Aetatis Sui 63

'Come, child! Say, nine times' seven!' Dunce was I.
Tongue-tied I stood, surveying frown, and stick . . .
Experientia docet. Now I sigh;
'Nine sevens, Sire? — the Grand Climacteric.'

AT THE ZOO[4]

Cowled with a news-sheet in his asphalt cage
A mateless Mandrill sulked, with sullen blink;
While one, among us gapers, with a cane,
Prod — prodded on; yet failed to make him shrink.
Black-coated he — less striking in *décor*,
As drab behind as he was drab before!
Closer I peered — glare, heat, bars, crowd and stink.
Bloodshot the ape's eyes watched me through a chink —
Able to feel, it seemed, if not to think.

Strange: when I turned to scan the Humans there,
There showed small semblance of a missing link!

[1] *Nash's Magazine*, September 1937; *Everybody's*, 9 August 1952.
[2] 'Alas, we two had never met.' *Nash's Magazine*, September 1937.
[3] *Poems*, privately printed at the Corvinus Press, December 1937. Omitted from the page-proofs of *Memory and Other Poems*, 1938, where it was to have served as a dedication.
[4] *Good Housekeeping* (New York), January 1938, where it was called 'The Mandrill'; revised version, *New Poems 1952*, P.E.N. anthology, ed. C. Dyment, R. Fuller, and M. Slater, London, 1952.

VOICES[1]

Rapture and sorrow
The bird of the darkness
Shares with the listening night;

A desolate cadence —
Its ecstasy over —
Closes the skylark's flight;

And under the hills
The curlews are calling —
Grief — grief, in the failing light.

Sweet, witless tongues,
Of an infinite solace —
If a pining heart could but listen aright!

I WONDER[2]

I wonder if Nile's *papyrus* grows
    On Acheron's brink —
That sullen stream whose water flows
    As leaden black as ink?
Then, maybe, stolen out of sight
(And scent) of Cerberus, I might
Of Lethe shun awhile to drink;
And, reed for pen, and worm for light,
Still for a little try to write —
    Where Time there will be to think.

---

[1] *Time and Tide*, 19 February 1938; revised version, *Atlantic Monthly*, February 1939.
[2] *Observer*, 3 April 1938. A slightly different version was omitted from the page-proofs of *Memory and Other Poems*, 1938.

'HERE LIES...'[1]

Think kindly of me. A Tasmanian snake
Clings so insensately to life, 'tis said,
That even its skin, dried, brined, will reawake
At secret lure, and spectral scalings shed.

Haply this falling dust beneath...? O friend,
Should'st thou some faint far sweetness here perceive,
Unwonted radiance, hush — its call attend:
The all of praise to God mere dust can give.

ULYSSES[2]

There was a high ship sailed the main,
Masts to the stars sailed she:
Not a wraith of foam 'neath her figurehead shone
So still was the sea.

Happier the landsman with care distraught
Than mariners winds may cheat,
While the mouths of the guileful sea-maids chant
Lament, and the sea-bells beat

A solemn resounding knell, and call
Their souls from their bodies, and wake
A thirst in the eyes no beauty on earth
Hath power to slake.

THINGS[3]

Things are the mind's mute looking-glass —
That vase of flowers, this work-box here,
When false love flattered me, alas,
Glowed with a beauty crystal clear.

Now they are hostile. The tulip's glow
Burns with the mockery of despair;
And when I open the box, I know
What kind of self awaits me there.

[1] *Poetry* (London), ed. Tambimuttu and Anthony Dickins, February 1939.
[2] *Ladies Home Journal* (Philadelphia), April 1940; *Spectator*, 5 July 1940;
Poetry Book Society Bulletin, July 1956.
[3] *Poetry* (Chicago), August 1940.

ANTIQUES[1]

Those quaint old worn-out words!
Fashions in miniature:
Pious, amiable, reserved, serene,
Modest, sedate, demure!
Mental poke-bonnets — and no less effete —
Why, even their meanings now are obsolete.

SECRET[2]

A hidden self rebels, its slumber broken;
Love, secret as crystal, forms in the spirit's womb;
The heart as faithfully beats, its vow unspoken;
All things to silence come.

A PORTRAIT[3]

Scarf and fillet, chaplet, gem
Hath she for fourfold diadem.
Bare breast, crimped ringlets, she sidelong gazes,
Turning her lips from the flowers she raises —
Violet, buttercup, opening daisies,
A wild-wood posy — she heeds not them:
A stealthy challenge haunts her eye,
'Lucrezia Borgia? . . . It is I.'

TINTERN ABBEY[4]

A frozen music, yes, this ruinous stone,
Which 'mid the drifting mist lowers cold and dark;
Yet whispers of man — noble — in ages gone;
And every weed in its cranny whispers 'Hark!'

---

[1] *Poetry* (Chicago), August 1940.
[2] *Poetry* (Chicago), August 1940; *Time and Tide*, 5 October 1940. See also p. 376.
[3] *John o'London's*, 13 September 1940.
[4] *Ladies Home Journal*, September 1940; *Poetry* (London), January–February 1941.

SOON[1]

Soon, soon must I forgotten be;
Frail is human destiny:
What's gone, again can never be.

Then mourn not, dear; remember too
The peace and joy of loving you
That ever deeper, sweeter grew.

Life would grow grievous, didst thou weep;
Be happy then, in safety keep,
   Till thou too sleep.

NEVER AGAIN[2]

Well, if I fall in love again,
God knows, I am a simpleton.
Never was there fever yet
As vexed as love for fools to get;
Pleasure, quiet, peace and ease
Gone! like vanished memories!
For this to deem the world well lost —
To chase a maid, and catch a ghost!
Touch but her hand, 'tis to be pricked
With keener pangs than thorns inflict;
Echo her laughter, 'tis to hear
The knell of all things once held dear.
And, oh, to lie awake at night —
Those taunting eyes of no delight!
Only to dream, and find her gone
Whose absence brought such folly on!
Never again shall every sense
Be drugged by love's dark influence·
Never shall lips whose wisest word
Folly alone with pleasure heard
Lure these dull wits and heart to plan
Only to prove her maid, me man. . . .
And yet — bright heaven, what else is worth
A single hour with her on earth?

---

[1] *Harper's Bazaar* (New York), 1 November 1940.
[2] *Harper's Bazaar* 1 November 1940. See also the later version called 'Intermittent Fever,' *O Lovely England and Other Poems*, 1953, p. 602

PASSION[1]

Passion's a flame that, leaping up apace,
Will in blind fury its own being efface;
Squand'ring its fuel in a deadening dust,
Not for the wishing, but because it must.

ENOUGH[2]

Pleasure early, pleasure late
Brings a fool to fool's estate:
Oh, the fields of tares that lie
When sickled Age goes hobbling by.

Toiling late and moiling early
Brings a sour heart and churly:
Oh, then, what a coil I'm in,
For to find the golden mean!

CROPS[3]

Farmer Giles has cut his rye;
    Oh my! Oh my!
Farmer Bates has cut his wheat;
    Och, the thieving hares in it!

Farmer Turvey's cut his barley;
    Ripe and early, ripe and early.
And where day breaks, rousing not,
    Farmer Weary's cut his throat.

[1] *American Mercury* (New York), December 1940.
[2] *Poetry* (Chicago), June 1941.
[3] *Poetry* (Chicago), June 1941.

THE VERY SELF[1]

Clear eyes, beneath clear brows, gaze out at me,
Clear, true and lovely things therein I see;
Yet mystery, past ev'n naming, takes their place
As mine stay pondering on that much-loved face.

JOHN BULL[2]

Based like a rock, he so abides;
He stands alone in his own stead.
'What I have said,' he says, 'I've said.'
  The blows of Fate
  May break his pate;
They will not shake Old Sober-sides.

He weighs, considers, and decides;
No flunkey of the powers that be.
His patient, stubborn 'Wait and see'
  Leaves ample room
  For what may come
From whencesoever to Sober-sides.

Byes he may bowl; no No's or Wides;
Pitch, length, pace he'll keep all day.
That square packed head, broad nose; the way
  He stands — fixed eyes,
  Shoulders and thighs;
'Get the man *out*!' says Sober-sides.

What stirs him to the bone he hides;
He has no use for sentiment.
He goes the way he always went.
  Others may range
  And veer and change
East — West: not so, Old Sober-sides.

[1] *Poetry* (Chicago), June 1941.
[2] *Poetry* (Chicago), June 1941; revised version, *The Book of the P.E.N.*, ed.
Hermon Ould, London, 1950. The earlier version was called 'A Character'

No point too nice his mind divides;
One thing a problem has — its *root*;
His Yea and Nay are absolute.[1]
   Shades, tints and hues,
   Fancies and views? —
'I am *convinced*,' says Sober-sides.

Nothing cares he what else betides.
Words are mere words; but facts are facts.
No fumbling doubts for him: he acts.
   Staunch, wideawake,
   The rack, the stake
He'd face unmoved, Old Sober-sides.

Simple and solid, he confides
The all he has in what he loves,
And that upon his pulses proves.
   Nature and Art
   May play their part;
His soul's his own, Old Sober-sides.

Blockheads like him the World derides.
Fools scoff. Vice spits, and turns away.
The clever look for easier prey;
   Or eye askance
   Such ignorance.
And he stares back — Old Sober-sides.

Age creeps; sands sink; time onward glides.
Unfaltering friend; unflinching foe;
The hour will strike when he must go.
   But if the grave
   A secret have,
He fears it not — Old Sober-sides.

Dogging life's high road, he bestrides
Horse Sense. . . . Alas, the loveliness
Wasting beyond the wayside trees;
   The dells, the dales,
   The nightingales,
The sweetness and grace — Old Sober-sides!

[1] 'His Nay is Nay, and absolute.' *Poetry* (Chicago), June 1941.

Man's heart — that sea! — has varying tides;
And these in service veer and move
Of other moons than that called Love.
  Still — full, sure, slow
  Great rivers flow:
And, at *one*'s source, sits Sober-sides.[1]

WELL, HERE'S[2]

Well, here's to a Tinker —
A rascally Tinker —
Here's to a Tinker died yesterday e'en;
Who never did worse
Than tipple and curse,
And now is, forsooth, where much better men been.

Lord, he could chaffer!
Could beat down half a
Dozen old women with tongues like a mill;
Such bargains be driving
He made fatter living
Than any Lord Bishop with sermons to sell.

His whetstone a-spinning,
He'd set folk a-grinning
At stories you wouldn't for parlour folk keep;
Blunt knives and old kettles
Kept his belly in victuals
And for drink — not a monarch has pockets so deep.

So, here's to a Tinker,
A raggle-taggle Tinker,
Who expired in his cups midnight yesterday gone,
And I give you fair warning
He'll sleep sound till morning
Where old Clootie will find him some jobs to be done.

[1] In *Poetry* (Chicago), June 1941, the last stanza read as follows:
  'Man's heart — that sea — has its own tides
  Which flow and ebb. And many move
  Obedient to a moon called love.
    But full, sure, slow,
    Great rivers flow;
  And, at their source, sits Sober-sides.'
[2] *Virginia Quarterly Review*, July 1941.

THE STONE[1]

Folded hands and darkened eyes —
    Here one loved too well now lies;
What her name was, Stone, declare;
    Thou could'st not say how fair!

LEAVES[2]

Even as my fingers snapped the stem
Of these bright leaves whose drooping now
Proves what a strange shadow leans over them,
An inward voice sighed, 'Pitiless thou!'

Their green-veined beauty was my prey —
Not their slow death I coveted:
Why, then, the question, 'Thou away,
What word for "beauty" will serve instead'?

PAINT[3]

A dumpy plain-faced child stands gazing there,
One hand laid lightly on a purple chair.
Her stuffed and stone-grey gown is laced with black;
A chain, with pendent star, hangs round her neck.
Red bows deck wrist and breast and flaxen hair;
Shoulder to waist's a band of lettered gold.
Round eyed, and cupid mouth — say, seven years old;
The ghost of her father in her placid stare.
Darkness beyond; bold lettering overhead:
LINFANTE. MARGUERITE, there I read;
And wondered — tongue-tied mite, and shy, no doubt —
What grave Velasquez talked to her about.

---

[1] *Virginia Quarterly Review*, July 1941. Cf. 'Slim Cunning Hands', p. 540.
[2] *Sunday Chronicle*, 5 November 1944.
[3] *Listener*, 17 January 1946. A later, much revised version of 'A Portrait' in *Memory and Other Poems*, 1938: see p. 382.

TU QUOQUE[1]

A frigid, mute, cold Christmas Eve
    Gilded the louring sky,
Yet a daisy showed in the winter grasses
    As I passed by,
Lovely as when in an age-gone springtime
    I saw them in infancy.

But a breeze set dancing the skeleton leaves,
    Sere now, and dry;
And at glimpse of them, out of a hollow heart
Came the question one can't put by —
    That 'Whither?' and that 'Why?'

KISMET[2]

Beneath the cold stone wherein cut is this Rhyme
Lie the bones of a human who wasted his Time.

Like a mildewed old book by some worthy long dead,
Now a larder for worms, never opened or read;
Like a well-spring of water no wayfarer drinks;
Like the thought of a thinker which nobody thinks;
Like a mute-bellied fiddle deprived of its bow;
Like a clock, with the key lost that made the clock go;

So, noonday and night-tide, compline and prime,
The Bones hugger-muggered here wasted their *Time*.

The one thing this wastrel would do with a minute
Was to yawn through the three-score brief seconds within it.
The sweetest of visions to him 'twas to see
His breakfast extend into *souper au lit*.
Did he ask, 'What's o'clock?' it was merely to know
Why its hesitant hands moved so painfully slow.
He would drowse like an owl through a sweet summer Sunday,
Rejoiced to perceive it had lapsed into Monday;
He scorned the brave Sun for pursuing its course
Round this Mill of a World like a blinded old horse;

[1] *Time and Tide*, 3 December 1949.
[2] *Everybody's*, 24 December 1949.

So maundered his day out, expired in his prime,
Having wasted, exhausted, the whole of his Time.

Consider, then, Stranger, how sadly he's placed
Who has passed to a Realm where there's no Time to waste!

Like some fabulous Croesus — with nothing to spend;
Like a tail-eating serpent sans entrance and end;
Like the bow of a fiddle no catgut will ease;
Like a wretch on a raft in salt tropical seas
Who may drink — drink — drink, till he madden, or burst,
Yet slake no iota his torment of thirst —
He sits: knowing *never* his hair will turn grey,
Or dusk gently settle on infinite Day:
Sits and sulks in Eternity's heavenly clime
And would barter his ALL for one moment of Time.

DESPISE IT AS I MAY[1]

Despise it as I may,
This old demoded heart will have its way;
Like a belated bee it still must flit
From shutting flower to flower, and find them sweet;
And even in shadow of a world in woe —
Like some frayed butterfly on an idle stone,
Once warmed by noonday's sun,
Poise, lost, alone;
And, though it soon must into darkness go,
Praise that sun's Heaven for his last afterglow.

TRUANTS[2]

This sabbath morning — all good folk in church —
I watched beneath the innocence of the sky
Two amorous butterflies flit blindly by;
And then, in the cold shadow of a tree,
Turning my head, I chanced to see
A spotted flycatcher on his well-worn perch.

---

[1] *Observer*, 1 January 1950.
[2] *Spectator*, 3 February 1950.

VISION[1]

'I see no sense in poetry,' says Glimm;
And poetry, it seems, stirs none in him.

THE STORM[2]

(after Crabbe)

Now evening's dusk in haze is muffled o'er;
Loud beats the wave upon the echoing shore.
All birds are mute, except the wheeling gull,
Crying 'twixt cloud and sea her sorrowful
Plaint to the billows. Now yet gloomier grow
Twilight and storm together. White as snow
Beams the last sun-ray from the murk behind,
And, through the dark East, goes a sighing wind.
The fly-vexed cattle beneath thick-boughed trees
Stand eyeing heaven in huddled companies;
Its topmost arch surmounting, blue and keen,
Streams the enkindled lightning on the scene,
And, rushing through the silence with a cry,
Wind, mixed with thunder, bellows in the sky.
Flash to bleak flash replies, till deepening night
Seems darkness manifest in blinding light;
And — as if sea for deeper sea were fain —
Cold-gushing stream the torrents of the rain.

THE WINNOWING DREAM[3]

I saw a Seraph, brighter than the East,
        Who held a rushing fan,
Wherewith, from best to worst, from first to least,
        He fanned the thoughts of Man.

[1] *Ladies Home Journal*, July 1950.
[2] *The Countryman*, summer 1950, where it was called 'A Storm (after Crabbe)';
New Poems 1952, P.E.N. anthology, ed. C. Dyment, R. Fuller, and M.
Slater, London, 1952.
[3] *Times Literary Supplement*, 1 September 1950; then published as an Ariel
Poem (No. 3, new series), *The Winnowing Dream*, London, 1954.

Like simple birds that tumble in the air,
    Thin ashes in the sky,
The scattered draff streamed up, unresting there,
    Blown through tempestuously.

Only upon the floor a little grain
    Of Truth lay, strange to see;
The which that Seraph gathered up for gain,
    Man's saving grace to be.

He turned away, mighty in weariness:
    And I in doubt drew near
To scan the little left poor man to bless
    'Gainst his last night of fear.

My heart fell in me, sickened and forlorn;
    Nothing of me or mine! —
Save a few things of love, not yet outworn,
    Sorrow had made divine:

Here, an old childish faith, in rueful state,
    There, lost simplicity;
Nought there of high account, deep, subtle, great —
    Nor valued even by me!

SONG FROM A PLAY[1]

Whirls now the wind with winter snow,
And trout-sweet brook is hard as glass;
Old bones full well that rigour know;
They pine for the South, but — let it pass.

'Why this pretence, No-longer-mine?
You gave; then took all back. Alas!
Straight to my face. "All hope resign!" '
So may a woman, but — let it pass.

[1] Omar Khayyám Club dinner card, Kettner's, London, 29 March 1951 (called 'Song (For a Play)' there); *Spectator*, 4 April 1952.

Wag the wry world then how it please —
Stark wilderness or sour morass;
Or sink of all iniquities:
Stare the thing out! And — let it pass.

Thought ebbs and flows. O blest full-tide!
Nothing more actual ever was
To Imagination in its pride
Worth pinch of dust; but — let it pass.

Love is life's sovereign fount of grace.
All else in the feast — a *demi-tasse*.
Place, Fortune, Fame — watch Wisdom's face!
None came my way; but — let it pass.

Sharp lust for earth's small hope for heaven.
How were I worth, good souls, one Mass?
Yet have I tasted sorrows seven:
Truth be my witness. Let it pass.

THE JACKET[1]

Things seen but once — ev'n by chance — may win
To a granite niche in the under-mind;
Dread, grief, terror have let them in,
Never, till death come, to be resigned:

A tear-racked face, and a high, laced boot;
A tethered body in Thames' high tide;
A huddle of rags, in the dust and soot;
The walker — called Jay — a suicide;

And, etched in detail, the when, the where,
The pang of horror, the inward knell —
As I gazed at the livery some must wear —
The waistcoat called strait, and the padded cell . . .

In my childhood's fancy the world was flat;
Its seas surged thundering into Space:
There are verges, too, of the mind, whereat
The soul recoils, sans hope, ev'n grace.
Alone — in an anguish unutterable —
The canvas jacket, the padded cell.

[1] *Modern Reading* (London), ed. R. Moore, winter 1951–1952.

DE MORTUIS[1]

Now that — his last word said —
This demagogue lies dead,
A silence never his own seeps stealthily in
And, not ev'n solely his, that now ingenuous grin.

WORK[2]

Work! Work apace! But only a heart at rest
Can rock the visiting halcyon on its breast.

POINTS OF VIEW[3]

This Satirist, well-meaning, makes a hubbub
In scorn of the benighted in a suburb;
And they, poor happy naturals, persist
In blissful ignorance of the Satirist.

ENGLISH FINGERPOSTS[4]

'A stubborn, barbarous race!' the alien vows,
'Shopkeepers, mutes, dull rural sheep and cows
Blinded to Art; *sans* wit, *esprit* and *ton*;
Gauche lackeys, yawning at Life's gay Salon!'

'So be it, Monsieur. Not all Shakespeares we! —
But may not a language whisper of Poetry?
A dialect, of not inglorious ghosts?
Ay, and had Jourdain scanned our fingerposts?'

[1] *New Statesman and Nation*, 26 July 1952.
[2] *New Statesman and Nation*, 26 July 1952.
[3] *Spectator*, 19 September 1952.
[4] *Spectator*, 3 October, 1952.

BUTTERFLIES[1]

'To be always seeking after the useful
does not become free and exalted Souls . . .'
Aristotle

Plato to his Utopia
    No poet would admit.
But they — his captives too — who make
Songs for mere joy and music's sake,
    Under his Pupil sit:
Their silly souls exalted, free,
    From flower to flower they rove,
Not seeking, like the honey bee,
    What only may useful prove,
But — unattainability! —
    The Muses' love.

FINISHED WITH[2]

Not less alone than when alone,
These two — leagues distant — sat.
Through the lamp's shine he gazed at her,
As Scullion may at Cat.

'Only one word, before I go!
You loved me — once? A day?'
Sidling her eyes, she smiled to herself;
But nothing would she say.

'Some proof, dark heart, I've touched your lips,
And never may again!'
She pouted; eyebrows arched to heaven;
But tongueless did remain.

'A nod, a whisper, we two have lain
Clasped in the selfsame bed.'
Fie! seemed her cherry mouth to shape,
Though never a word she said.

[1] *Spectator*, 3 October 1952.
[2] *Poetry* (Chicago), October 1952.

'Fool that I've been! Not even a hint.
Soul — pocket — spent their all?'
She tilted her round chin an inch,
But nothing could recall.

'You lovely thing! Stay motionless!
A ditch may mirror heaven!'
Her parted lips stirred sluggishly
But never whispered even.

'Shut those cold eyes, then, and say out,
"Perish in ice, for *me*!" '
The snake lids widened a little space,
But not as if to see.

'Ay? . . . Then I go to death and hell —
With broken heart and mind!' . . .
'Others have done the same. And, well —
Well, now they're more resigned!' . . .

Stark silence settled in the room.
The lamp-flame ducked; then shone
More brightly, calmly, softly now
That the night-wind's sigh was gone.

ANOTHER TONGUE[1]

The chimney swallows gossip: — '*This sullen weather!*' . . .
'*Those vulgar sparrows!*' . . . '*Eggs!?*' . . . '*The dearth of flies!*'
Or sibilant love-talk? . . .

Well, I know not whether
Than humans they are wiser, or less wise;
Only that as in daydream I sit and listen,
They seem to be syllabling of paradise!

[1] *Spectator*, 24 April 1953.

BOTH BARRELS[1]

If one can make it difficult
To grasp what one is writing
'Twill breed, perhaps, a privy Cult
Who'll find it most exciting.

And if one, now and then, indulge
In what is called the *curious*,
They will not rest till they divulge
What makes Philistia furious.

WENT THE MIND CLOCKTIME-WISE[2]

Went the mind clocktime-wise, then *genius* could
By taking pains achieve the all it would:
Six days hard labour, and the seventh found good.
Life's winds list otherwise. A power remains,
Only at hazard commensurate with the pains.

HOW WAYWARD[3]

How wayward one's exquisite taste may be!
One's judgement how deficient! —
To idolize efficiency,
Yet — not the efficient!

AFTERMATH[4]

How strange that Victory
May breed Defeat;
And the blood of the Vanquished well
So pure and sweet
That it falls like the dew of life, on the heart
Which had almost ceased to beat!

[1] *Spectator*, 24 April 1953.
[2] *Spectator*, 24 April 1953.
[3] *Spectator*, 24 April 1953.
[4] *New Statesman and Nation*, 16 May 1953.

ELIZABETH IS MY QUEEN[1]

Elizabeth is my queen,
England is my land,
Oh! may God let her people be
Countless as sand!

Through all the passing hours
The never silent sea
Upon her hollow-sounding shores
Shouts Liberty.

Old Drake my cousin is,
And Shakespeare's Elizabeth,
And Nelson — he whose fame
Shall outstay Death.

Ah! when with eager eye
I scan the centuries
And count this England's matchless men
My blood doth rise,

And burns upon my cheek,
And welters in my heart,
Urging me in their foot-tracks go
And do my part.

Sweet are her fields to me,
Sweet is her lovesome rose,
Sweet with the savour of the seas
Each wind that blows.

Elizabeth is my queen,
England is my land,
Oh! may God let her people be
Countless as sand!

[1] *Reader's Digest*, June 1953. A slightly different version of this poem called '1897–1953', and beginning 'Victoria is my queen', was omitted from the page-proofs of *O Lovely England and Other Poems*, 1953. The original six-stanza poem (no longer extant) was written in 1897, the year of Queen Victoria's Diamond Jubilee.

THE ARROWS[1]

All night Love lay on Stella's breast
  In slumber cool and sweet;
But, morning come — dreams gone their way —
  Her heart more wildly 'gan to beat,

Her heart to throb, and she to sigh;
  Till up he sprang, and said,
'By my own Mother's girdle, I
  Must seek a quieter bed!'

Poor Stella — pining too for rest,
  Sighed, 'Nay, thou fledgling dear;
Sleep on, else soon my stricken breast
  Will fall too still, I fear.'

Alas! — his pinions preened — he went.
  But was it kind, or fair,
Where he such harmless hours had spent,
  To leave his arrows there?

DILEMMA[2]

Un-numbered souls, life's day at end,
Have left their dust, and hied away.
How few, it seems, return to wend
Earth's haunts in spectral disarray!

Yes — and I wonder which would daunt *me* most —
To face this world again, as child, or ghost.

AN EPITAPH[3]

Would'st liefer be alive, or dead?
Grisly gray? Or rosy red?
Would'st liefer hear the marriage bell,
Or Sexton's one-note-knocking knell?

[1] *Time and Tide,* 4 July 1953.
[2] *New Statesman and Nation,* 31 October 1953.
[3] *New Statesman and Nation,* 31 October 1953. This poem was omitted from the galleys of *O Lovely England and Other Poems,* 1953.

Ah, friend, if thou have any care
To be abroad in light and air,
Get thee quick gone. No traffic have
Within the ambit of the grave.

TIME, LOVE AND LIFE[1]

I saw young Time with laughter in his eyes
And all a mist of sunshine in his hair,
He went with bow enarched where sweetly cries
The brook of tribulation dipping down
Into a place of solitude, and air
Made sad with falling roses overblown.

He stoop'd, he drank, and gathered up his mouth
As if with some old childish petulance;
And all the light unshaded of the South
Smote on his face; on, wild and ruinous,
The grey and ivy of his inheritance,
Myrtle and hearts-ease, lichen, and green moss.

And yet the gloom was fair as with a star
When his strange youthfulness on heedless foot
Came singing like a woodlark from afar,
The very waters with a silenced wave
Took gold in shadow at the willow-root,
And light unto the leaves his passing gave.

But in his solitude seemed still to brood
The songs of them who come no more to sing,
And in his cypresses a faint dream showed
Of other trees' first flowers passed away; —
Ev'n in his youth a thought of sorrowing,
And in his gold a twilight still and grey.

But always answered him amid his groves
A voice intense and wilder ev'n than his,
Whose sweet insistency showed me it was Love's,
Mocking young Time in labyrinthine glooms
From the strange borders of his Paradise,
Whither, too, Time only in echo comes.

[1] *National and English Review*, June 1954.

So, as it seemed, an echo and a dream
The voice of both was jargoning, half vain,
Half ever lovely; and their haunt did seem
Thorn, or all-silent moss, a vision seen
Soon before morning ere light fall again
On eyes that ev'n asleep toward morning lean.

Surely, too, following that water deep
And secret with unnumbered shadowiness,
Which, sleeping, seems but only mocking sleep,
Time shall at last with eyes Death cannot dim
Scan one close portal amid his cypresses,
And Death in solitude awaiting him.

Love calleth ever, tangled, and high, and sweet;
Life knows not whither, though he, following,
Run all the way with Time until he meet
Death too, and leave unfound his urgent quest,
Leave too his love-inhaunted sorrowing,
Leave all dreams else to take his little rest.

TARES[1]

The seeds of childhood and of youth
Come all to bloom at last;
Pansy, nettle, rosemary,
Nightshade, thistle, fleur-de-lys,
Where they were cast
Spring up in tears, in ice, in drouth.

No cloud, no tempest shall restrain
One wild unearthly flower;
Nor hath the nightbird any power
Nor parching sun, nor pelting rain,
To wither or profane
The buds that bless, the buds that stain.

Only the gardener may choose
To take fresh seed in hand;
To scatter balm for thistledown,
Myrtle for thorn; to stoop him down
O'er mire, o'er stone, o'er sand;
And in his sweat no time, no trouble, lose.

[1] *National and English Review*, July 1954.

And, Oh, the fever, fear, and fret
Of the dark tedious night,
Lest dawn surprise him, poppy-bound,
Cast down in sleep upon the ground,
And with red light
Reveal nought else than thorns and weeds in it!

No thicket shall for long withstand
That piercing ray; within
His deepest arbour he shall not be hid,
But must come out when he is bid,
Naked as when he entered in,
And give account of all his land —

This was to ravening bird resigned,
And that to wanton weed;
Trembling, he shows one sweeter root,
But there a hedge where carrion hoot,
And this a rose at seed,
And there only dry grass and wind.

While still the sky with hosts shall move;
And like a cloud the witnesses,
In fearful silence of the dawn,
Shall pluck their strings of harp and shawm
And heavenly psalteries,
While he, poor man, his all must prove.

I seem to hear a mocking note
Among my specious trees;
I catch the glint of glistening coils
Where ev'n the sweet bee toils;
And in my labour quake my knees;
And in my memory bleats a goat.

DERELICT[1]

As Captain Fleet, aloof, looked out,
And scanned unheeding night's starry scene,
His thoughts turned inward, and he sighed
At a lost might have been.

[1] *National and English Review*, July 1954.

He surveyed his Past, like a huddled field
Of wreckage dumped in a blazing sun,
Everything broken, rusted, dead —
Skeleton, sword and gun.

THE OTHER VOICE[1]

Sweet musician stay thine art,
Hush thy fretting melody;
There is that within my heart
    Importuneth me;

Crieth with a voice long still,
Like the soft autumnal rain
Wooing flowers faded all
    To blossom again.

Grievous wood, poor trembling string,
What incessant sorrow must
Pine in your souls to bring
    Sweetness out of dust!

THE WALL[2]

No more than house-wall without hole or glass
Will let a single ray of sunshine pass,
Can we by wisdom and beauty enravished be
Unless by Love we have been taught to see.

THE SLEEP-WALKER[3]

The wick lay wasting in its oil,
    Darkness was in the house,
The silence of night in every room,
    Save for the busy mouse,

But fell a foot-step, soft as snow,
    And into that gentle beam,
Came one whose eyes in faint surmise,
    Gazed out as if in dream.

[1] *National and English Review*, July 1954.
[2] *Saturday Night* (Toronto), 4 September 1954.
[3] *Time and Tide*, 4 December 1954.

So when the master of the house,
    Stepped tiptoe on the stair,
His heart stood still, it seemed he saw
    A phantom standing there.

Then, while he gazed with startled eye,
    He thought what jeopardy
This little child in slumber wild
    Would be in but for me.

To some dream world her soul is gone,
    I know not how remote,
While here her earthly body stays,
    Yet of that earth sees nought.

Who knows what birds unheard by men,
    She hearkens far and sweet?
Who knows what happy paradise,
    Thrid now her gentle feet?

Anon he softly called to her,
    And she no answer gave,
But dim and wistly thro' a mist
    Of sleep smiled, still and grave:

Her dark hair shadowing her brow,
    Her cheeks as crocus pale,
Her rounded lip as if't did sip
    Songs of the nightingale.

Her hands upon the dark air laid,
    Her gown a cloud did seem,
As if the moon shed thereupon
    Her light-at-evening beam.

'Florence!' he says again, and she
    Answers him unaware,
'Florence,' she says, and, still at gaze,
    Moved softly to the stair.

And presently she laid her down,
    With one oppressèd sigh,
Pressing her face into that place
    Where it was wont to lie.

And he, as if an echo 'twere,
    Answered her sigh with his,
And would to God his feet still trod
    Such paths of ecstasies.

[674]

DR. BROWNING AT BREAKFAST[1]

'Will ye take a scrambled egg, Dr. Browning, with your toast,
  Or p'raps the daintiest slice of ham or beef,
Or a snack of Finnan haddie (and ye'll pardon me the boast)
  O' dainties they Scots haddies are the chief;
There's porritch on the wagon, Dr. Browning, if ye wish,
  And devilled kidneys comin' from below
And if ye'd wet your whistle — o' coky take a dish —'
  'Cocoa! Mrs. Green, Cocoa!'

'Anchovies are beside ye and honey from the hive,
  And creases if ye'd like a bit o' green;
Or just look'ee at that lobster — in the pot at half past five;
  Or if it takes your fancy a sardine.
If furrin is your taste there's some Rooshan caviare
  Or them apricocks that Green himself did grow
La, and if ye'd wet your whistle there's coky, and to spare —'
  'Cocoa!! Mrs. Green, Cocoa!!'

'Have a mushroom or a muffin, all a-swimming in its grease
  Or a slice of brawn, a relishin' o' mace;
Just make yeself at 'ome, Dr. Browning, if ye please,
  I would like to see ye plumper in the face.
Grilled trout and seedy cake, peach preserve and prawns in pot,
  Fried sassage, bacon, ox tongue, and cod's roe;
Why, and if ye'd wet your whistle there's coky pipin' hot —'
  'Cocoa!!! Mrs. Green, Cocoa!!!'

WHEN ONE IS A GIRL[2]

When I was a girl, in a pretty green hat,
  Why, one laughs as much as one can!
And I hadn't a pleasure loved better than that
  Of kissing my strapping young man.

He'd a nose like a frigate, and eyes grey as glass,
  And his hair came down shaped like a fan:
It was being in heaven wherever he was —
  Just me, and my strapping young man.

[1] *Argosy*, August 1955.
[2] *Time and Tide*, 3 December 1955.

[675]

We'd sit and we'd talk, looking over the sea
  At some ship, sailing blue on its rim;
And never were sandboys as happy as we —
  I mean *me*, and my strapping — well, *him*!

Would ever ill fortune have darkened my way,
  Had life gone on as it began!
Had I kept my heart faithful, and open as day —
  And all for my strapping young man!

But the salt ocean took him — ay, over the sea;
  Too far for young fancy to scan.
God help me; I thought myself jilted to be;
  And that by my strapping young man!

I'm married; have money; and sweet children three;
  But the white bread's as tasteless as bran
When I gaze out of window, and wish I were free
  To go look for my strapping young man.

Long since I'm forgotten. His bones may lie low.
  Love's over. And Life's but a span:
But I shan't be less happy — when old, lone, and cold —
  When I think of my strapping young man!

THE LOST SELF[1]

Oh for the will to love no more
  One loved too well, in vain!
Or that mere wishing could restore
  My vanished self again!

Vain all repining; every vow,
  Sworn 'gainst thee in my heart,
Can but bring back more wildly now
  All that thou wert, and art.

[1] *Time and Tide*, 3 December 1955.

THE MORROW[1]

The moon doth fade that shone on Juliet,
Fades on her starry garden dark and sweet;
Happy and still she lies while dawn doth creep
Flooding the lovely margent of her sleep,
    Yet even now her tears in wonder flow
    From tired eyes that dream of Romeo.

The treason of sleep tells her the nightingale
Yet lingers in the moonlight dim and pale,
So ev'n her lips are curled again to kiss
Him who shall wake no more to earthly bliss;
    And now they stir as when still showers flow
    And roses waken, breathing 'Romeo'.

She wakes to see with slumber-haunted eyes
Her casement a bright field of Paradise;
And it beyond she hears in apple-boughs
Blackbirds and thrushes in a sweet carouse;
    And thro' this beauty like a flame doth flow,
    Love and delight of one named Romeo.

She lifts her hands as if in some amaze
To find them human in such beauteous ways;
And joy upon the threshold of her mouth
Stoops wondering like roses to the South;
    And one strange name on her heart's blood doth flow
    The echo of a faint name — 'Romeo'.

She is a child; else why doth she conceal
Her burning cheeks, and in that covert feel
Eyes bright as blue-bells scan her passionate tale,
And tongues of traitors mock the nightingale?
    'O heart, O heart!' she cries, her wild eyes close,
    She dreams she sleeps and dreams of Romeo's.

For piercing-clear his image haunteth her;
Her eyes perceive him howsoe'er she stir,
And, breathless, strive to banish him away;
Her lids are night, but her dark eyes are day:
    And tho' with all her heart she bids him go,
    That heart is refuge sure for Romeo.

[1] *Two Poems*, published privately by R. N. Green-Armytage in a limited edition of 50 copies, Bath, 1955.

She rises from her bed and opens wide
Her casement to the flowery country-side; —
The gloomy forests where young Adon sleeps,
A hunter moonstruck at the water-deeps —
　　Yea, on her eyes, as in a pool doth flow
　　Thro' every loveliness a Romeo.

It seems her childhood was a secret way
To lead at length to this unearthly day:
The dewy greenness of the grass is green
Only since there a Romeo hath been;
　　The honey-bees do only droning go
　　Along the paths where trespassed Romeo.

These crescent apple-leaves the moon and sun
Wrestle in radiance to shine upon;
The thrush may sing deeming himself a thrush,
But not of him her heart entreateth 'Hush!'
　　Surely the wind that thro' the garden blows
　　Will catch those iterated 'Romeos!'

So fear leers sidelong on her solitude;
And fear a keener gladness doth intrude,
Till Juliet wonders which this aching be,
Fear's or the pangs of love's bright archery:
　　But ever from bliss commingled she doth go
　　Back to the simple theme of Romeo.

It seems a marvellous simplicity
T'assuage the world's unkindness with a sigh,
Till even sorrow like a weeping child
Runs to love's bosom to be reconciled,
　　Till every usual thing her senses know
　　Leaps into beauty born of Romeo.

And like a lark unloosèd from the night
Her soul runs leaping up the morning-light,
Her body a discarded mask that life
Hath vext and sullied with continual strife:
　　Only her spirit is free, and upward goes
　　Singing to heav'n to be with Romeo's.

Till in the extreme delight of love for him
The very meaning of himself grows dim,
And back to earth she falls, tired and distrest,
To find Love weeping in her vacant breast;
　　And all her comfort were in wrath to go
　　And rail on him for being Romeo.

Ev'n for one passionate moment — Would that death
Might hide her worthlessness the dust beneath;
Would that, now all her joy on earth is done,
She might for ever lie at peace alone;
    For what is life but vanity I know;
    And vanity of vanities is Romeo.

But thus come back to life's reality,
Her raiment lures her into flattery;
Her sorrowful beauty in the glass doth bring
The secret in her breast to laugh and sing;
    The dusty sunshine the long casement thro'
    Streams like her tenderness of Romeo.

Would now that vain she were to shew how sweet
The earth might break to flowers at his feet:
Nought under Heav'n's so mean as Juliet
To tell her love for him and instance it:
    She can but unto Christ in agony go
    And offer her soul to service Romeo.

So her glad heart, like an untutored bird
Which the first cheeping of its young hath heard,
Leans toward the sun and glory of the day,
In some dim birdlike sweetness of dismay;
    From Joy's pure silence her glad notes o'erflow
    And consecrate the world to Romeo.

Like haunting incense ev'ry hour ascends,
Each meanest office to some splendour bends;
Wind, flow'r, bird, cloud, are in a strategy
To break her heart with too sweet ecstasy:
    Yea, like a river of pride her thoughts do flow
    Sweeping her self-disdained to Romeo.

What tho' the night a gloomy secret keep
And blind disaster stoop into her sleep,
Tho' all the stars with vext and ruddy beams
Light terror to the thicket of her dreams,
    Tho' the world wither and to dust she go
    'Twere lovely thus to pleasure Romeo!

But lo! 'Tis noonday in Love's rosery;
Birds white as lilies fill the archèd sky;
Far, far, and still lies Death's long cypress grove
Transfigured in the simpleness of love,
    Where she shall break earth's thorns most gently
        thro'—
    Flee to the everlasting peace of Romeo.

THE SUN[1]

O, after winter's wrath what loveliness
Hath the sweet sun in his new splendour then!
How he burns upward, quenchless, effortless,
In the dark regions of the sky again!
How wide he casts his white and trembling beams;
How he seeks leaves ev'n 'neath the hoarded snow;
How o'er the icy water-pools he streams;
How glories he in his arches to and fro!

The earth with shouting waves crieth to him;
The woods with pricking boughs clap out his praise;
Fly up the wild birds now, sing in the dim,
Ere yet his day beams on their pinions blaze;
He runs, trailing his splendour o'er the land,
Praise in his footprints, love in either hand.

NOT ONE[2]

We may, most dear, as bodies meet,
As bodies kiss; but when
Our hearts no more together beat
We are phantoms once again.

Nor — of those happy moments gone,
Whose rapture seemed to achieve
A peace beyond oblivion —
Can life even one retrieve.

---

[1] *Two Poems*, published privately in a limited edition of 50 copies, Bath, 1955.
[2] *Time and Tide*, 28 January 1956.

'ANALYSTS'[1]

They too came Nature's way;
　　And so
Did Shakespeare, Newton, Michelangelo.

　　Mind, body, spirit, they;
　　　And none
Of this strange trinity can the others shun —

　　A subtle and miraculous Three;
　　　Since even in dream
Their tri-twined influences twist and gleam.

　　Why, then, so dingily
　　　The theme perplex
By strum — strum — strumming on *one* note, called Sex.

THE OTHERS[2]

How few the human frailties we can never
With mere good-humour and a smile annul!
But how, sweet heaven! to exercise the clever?
How dodge the dread contagion of the dull?

THE RIFT[3]

'We argue on of gods, not God,
　And might all strife resign,
　If only I could find in yours,
　What you reject in mine.'

THE MINSTREL[4]

'Black night; small moon;
　Stars needle-clear.
　I sing a song:
　To bring you cheer.'

---

[1] *Poetry London–New York*, ed. Tambimuttu, March–April 1956.
[2] *Poetry London–New York*, March–April 1956.
[3] *Poetry London–New York*, March–April 1956.
[4] *Listener*, 19 April 1956.

'Away, away!
These walls are dumb —
Minstrel, not here
Song-singing come.'

'That voice sighs soft
As whispering bough?
Sing I more clearly —
Hearken, now!'

'Minstrel begone!
'Tis not night's breath
Sighs in thine ear:
I am death.'

ST. PAUL'S CATHEDRAL[1]

The ancient hills take the pale sun
With like divine serenity,
When the fierce heats of day are done;
And with a sad satiety
Evening to night sinks tranquilly.

Amid its blue on feathers light
Grey doves with soundless flutterings
Sweep on in solitary flight
Above the shadow of their wings,
And twilight deeper silence brings.

Yet haunts within its quiet vaults
A rumour marvellous, wild and faint
Of a vast host that never halts,
Nor flags, nor tires; without complaint
Labours regardless of its Saint.

And ever within shrill echoes roam,
Like jargoning birds in mountain dells,
Crying with long entreaty, 'Come!'
Here's water from the living wells;
Here the sweet peace of the far hills!

[1] *Choristers' Magazine* (St. Paul's Choir School), July 1956. In a letter to Mrs. Price dated 19 March 1956, printed opposite the poem, de la Mare wrote: '. . . With this comes . . . a copy of the verses on the Cathedral — probably written before Queen Victoria descended from the throne. . . .'

And evensong to morning-prime,
Ever upon its outer stone
The livelong iron pen of Time
Frets unimpassioned, gravely on,
Making its patient orison.

Like a foul stain on England's green
Stretches the darkness of the town:
Yet all-exultantly doth lean
The shadow of a great cross down
On smoke chaotically blown.

SHEPHERD'S WARNING[1]

Pleasant it was, once — once to stray
Through the antique woods,
The primeval May,
Heedless of morrow or yesterday;

Nor even to think,
As we went our way,
The World was skirting a Future's brink
That might shatter and wrench it link from link.

What cause to question? — to pause in surmise? —
Save that sullen red in the eastern skies?

EUREKA![2]

We failed to see, when we began,
With selfless assiduity,
Our quest for marvels hidden from Man,
Past tentacles of sense to scan,
That, having to the 'atom' come —
Infinitesimality —
We should no whit less curious be;
    And so conspire our doom.

Dowered in childhood with such gifts —
As might the Seraphim make weep;
Unheeding in this House of *Life*
What treasure genius can give,

[1] *Poetry Book Society Bulletin*, July 1956.
[2] *English*, English Association, summer 1956.

Free from all rancour, envy, strife —
A beauty, wonder and mystery,
   No Israfel could lip;

Like unimaginative brats,
Disdaining faith and love,
We squatted on the nursery floor,
Shrouded the windows, locked the door,
And everything in it to tatters tore.

Not to find joy in what it is *for*,
   But merely what made *of*.

Alas, sweet Nature! To have to say,
'Mother, beware! There'll come a day —
Gone all your once fond might-have-beens —
When we, the cleverest of your weans,
Shall teach the stupidest the means
To blow even You to smithereens!

   'Yes — we've found out the way!'

BY ORDER![1]

Slant sunshine and these naked fields once more;
Evening: the wayfarer now nearing home.
Once it was, 'Surely, I've been here before!'
Now, 'Why has all so strange to me become?'

Through crowds I wander, isolate and alone,
As if they were mere phantasmata of my mind;
As do the autumnal birds — a *whirr*; they are gone;

A listening solitude — dark fields, a gate;
Dusk, and a baffling sign-board — 'By Order, Fate.'

THE LAST STRAW[2]

I watched them troop through the gates of glory —
The children, the saints, the fools, the wise,
Lovers and lunatics keeping their trysts,
Haggard, ecstatic, young and hoary —
Finished their earthly enterprise.

[1] *New Poems 1956*, P.E.N. anthology, ed. S. Spender, E. Jennings and
D. Abse, London, 1956.
[2] *New Poems 1956*.

[684]

And I asked of the Angel with chrysoprase eyes,
Who had shut me out with a '*Very* sorry,'
As the sound of the Trump echoed out through the skies,
And I turned to the track that downward twists:
'So it's all come true, then, the old, old story?
But *must* I mix with the "moralists"?'

A LIFETIME:[1]
EPITAPH FOR WILLIAM BLAKE

I lived; I toiled — day in, day out,
Endless labour, shafts of bliss,
For three score years and ten,
   And then:
I watched, with speechless joy and grief,
My last and loveliest spring
   Take wing.

Think you, I grudged the travailing?
I, who am come to this?

[1] *The Divine Vision*, essays on William Blake, ed. Vivian de Sola Pinto, London, 1957 — for which it was specially written: *The Poets and their Critics*, ed. Hugh Sykes Davies, London, 1962.

Uncollected Verses

SLUMBER-SONG[1]

Lullaby, lullaby,
  Featherlids close,
Fold tiny-petalled hands,
  Mother's moss-rose.

Still in the twilight
The evening star looms,
Still in the twilight
The pale primrose blooms;
Droning and drowsy
Lolleth homeward the bee,
The linnet is hushed
In the quiet o' the tree;

From their green housen
The candle-flies creep;
And the owl hooteth drowsily
Out of his sleep.
Soon shall the glow-worm
Enkindle her torch,
And the cricket shrill clear
From the jessamined porch.

Lullaby, lullaby,
  Featherlids close,
Fold tiny-petalled hands,
  Mother's moss-rose.

Like little mice
Afraid of the light,
The stars shyly peep
From the casements of night.
'Hush,' saith the silence,
'O round-spinning earth;
Hush ye to slumber
Sweet children of mirth!'

[1] *Pall Mall Magazine*, September–December, 1900.

Then lull thee, ah, lullaby,
Babe of my breast,
Tranquil as Hesperus
Wan in the West.

THE SHELLFISH[1]

Here I saw the mist roll inland
Where the green brakes cease to stand,
Where the meadows turn to marshes
And the marshes change to sand;
Where the wash of mighty waters
Sliding back from off the shore
Sends a curious moaning echo
Mingling strangely with the roar.
Here I thought I heard the shellfish
As they danced in boisterous glee
Come by scampering, rejoicing
Mid the beating of the sea.

JOLLY LAUGHTER[2]

With strawberry jam and cream for tea,
Plum-cake a-following after;
It always seems, it seems to me
There's room enough for laughter,
        Jolly laughter.
Not that I'd ever think to make
A plea to eat for eating's sake,
But when a Scare-Bones takes his place
With a long, lean, sour, hungry face
And cannot even breathe a grace,
There couldn't be a denser, dafter;
And for his pains I take to laughter,
        Jolly laughter.

[1] *Christian Science Monitor*, 15 November 1920.
[2] *Saturday Review* (London), 5 December 1925; *Saturday Review of Literature* (New York), 26 December 1925.

I've sat beside a dainty Miss
And passed her that and them and this,
And when she *never* answers 'Iss,'
Why then, bless me, I've gently chaffed her
Until she *can't* resist for laughter,
  Jolly laughter.
And so I say, crowd round the table!
And eat as much as you are able!
Man's mouth is not so very wide,
There's plenty of old Earth outside —
And all the moon and stars abaft her
A-shaking of their sides with laughter,
  Jolly laughter.

TWINKUM[1]

Twinkum, twirlum, twistum, twy,
How many rooks go floating by,
Caw, caw, in the deep blue sky?

Twinkum, twirlum, twistum, twee,
I can listen though I can't see,
Seven sooty-black rooks there be.

Twinkum, twirlum, twistum, twoh,
Who can say what he don't know?
Blindman's in, and round we go!

ONE, TWO, THREE[2]

One I've loved, and two I've loved,
But three's the love for me;
Kate was slim and Nancy dark,
But both was Jessamy.

Stars may shine, and crystal too,
Yet lovelier things there be,
Brighter than Kate's and Nancy's are
The eyes of Jessamy.

---

[1] *Saturday Review of Literature*, 16 November 1929. For the later version of this poem called 'Blindman's In', see *Bells and Grass*, p. 409.
[2] *Bulletin*, Canadian Library Association (Ottawa), August 1955.

Dreams I have had, gay, solemn, sad,
'Twas slumber's sorcery.
One was of Kate, and one of Nan —
One woke to Jessamy!

One I've loved, and two no less,
But Oh, the luck in three;
Kate has Sam, and Nancy Jack,
But Jessamy chose me.

THE JOLLY HUNTSMAN[1]

There was a jolly huntsman
In coat of scarlet red;
All day he hunted fast and free
As fox or vixen led;
Then *Tallyho* rode home again,
To supper, and to bed.

No wife he had; but blankets
Of thick-spun Shropshire wool,
Which, summer come, he'd tumble off
To keep his leggen cool;
He did such wholesome things by chance,
No slave was he to rule.

And oft at nightfall passers-by
Would lean a listening ear
To hear a muffled mellow horn
A-tootling high and clear,
Perhaps, *A swain a-roving went*,
Perhaps, *Come, kiss me, dear*!

THE SHADOW[2]

Poor Fanny Thynne was much too lean
To please her aunt, Miss Grout;
'If I,' she'd say, 'could have my way,
I'd soon make Fanny stout.

[1] *Bulletin*, C.L.A., August 1955.
[2] *Bulletin*, C.L.A., August 1955.

[690]

'Fat pork, baked taties, duff and cheese,
Are what she needs for dinner;
Things else than these, for stick like she is,
Would only make her thinner.'

They did. They did. In vain she chid;
No sight could well be sadder;
Weaker and wan grew little Fan,
And faded to a shadow.

THE FACES[1]

The Sweep has such a sooty face
For six days of the week
His children, when they speak at all,
To all but a stranger speak.

But what a froth of suds he makes
In secret, Saturnight,
So that on Sunday all may view
Their father with delight.

THE FAITHFUL PIG[2]

Sir Jasper Ginger had a pig, sir;
He dressed it up in a yaller wig, sir;
He larned it to drive in a dingdong gig, sir;
To toot on the flute, and to dance a jig, sir.

When he was dead, they all burst out a-laughing
To see it come sobbing and gruffing and graffing —
Not caring a twist for their mocking and chaffing —
All the way after its old friend's coffin.

---

[1] *Bulletin*, C.L.A., August 1955.
[2] *Bulletin*, C.L.A., August 1955.

THREE[1]

Three little jimp little bodies there be —
Thimble and *Needle* and *Thread*;
They work together, gossip together,
And together they go to bed.

But supposing they all scuttled off to the moon —
Wouldn't the round World stare!
For all little girls would have nothing on,
And all little boys would go bare.

THE LITTLE HOUSE[2]

I built my dear a little house,
Little and low and lonely;
Where sweet-voiced birds would sing to us,
And green leaves whisper only.

Three rooms it had; a roof of thatch,
A chimney stack above, O;
A shed for wood, a run for hens,
An arbour for my love, O.

I took her with her golden hair,
And lips like ripened cherry;
We eat and drink, and laugh and sing,
Sleep, chatter, and are merry.

THE GLUTTON[3]

Pray, pity the poor glutton! —
Who yawns the hours away
From breakfast-time to dinner-time,
From dinner-time to tea!

Oh, pity the poor glutton,
Whose appetite is such
That he can never, never, never
Eat too much!

[1] *Bulletin*, C.L.A., August 1955.
[2] *Bulletin*, C.L.A., August 1955.
[3] *Young Elizabethan*, May 1956. This poem was selected for inclusion in *Bells and Grass*, 1941, but was finally omitted.

Oh, pity the poor glutton
Whose troubles all begin
In struggling on and on to turn
What's out into what's in.

THE THIEF[1]

Once was a Thief of London Town,
He sped with his spoil to Spain;
He poured out his pouch till all was gone,
Then dared the seas again.

He cried in his heart, 'Ay, all's forgot:
From this cheating land I'll be over.'
But they catched him aboard as the anchor dropped
By the bright chalk cliffs of Dover.

THOUGHTS[2]

The greenwood sighs
Beneath the sky
Music the winds bear
Sweeping by.

The billowing sea
On the rockbound shore
Shakes the air to the stars
With its hollow roar.

But these, my thoughts? —
O woods, O sea!
What wind, from whence
Wakes them in me?

[1] *Young Elizabethan*, May 1956.
[2] *Young Elizabethan*, May 1956.

ONCE[1]

As deep as sand in Egypt
In Muscovy's the snow;
And flashing bright with powdered ice
The ding-dong sledges go;
The Czar with horses three abreast
Glides, muffled to the chin,
To Petersburgh, 'neath boughs as black
As Springtime makes them green;
Oh, what a roar of smoke and flame
Must up his chimneys go,
When deep as sand in Egypt
In Muscovy's the snow!

---

[1] *Young Elizabethan*, July 1956.

3. UNPUBLISHED POEMS

BEFORE YOU CAME[1]

Before you came, the earth to me seemed wrapt
   In robe of sorrow grey,
A song of sadness where the waters lapped,
   And grief usurped the day.
No melody of song the thrushes sang,
   The flowers — no beauty fair;
The eternal deep with dirge of sorrow ran,
   And wildness of despair.

You rose, my star, and night seemed sleeping day,
   The rising sun brought joy;
The rippling waters trilled a joyous lay
   Of peace without alloy.
The birds poured forth their souls in anthems long,
   Each flower with love was crowned;
The seas with one supernal flood of song
   Did ceaselessly resound.

THE PORTRAIT[2]

Only thy fair small face I see,
The slenderness of palm and brow,
That hint of anonymity,
That shadow of a vow,
That half-sad languor of the eye,
   Lonely, and clear, and deep,
Of one who sees earth's dreams pass by
   Still in untroubled sleep.

LONG AGO[3]

Whatever sweetness this poor heart may keep,
Was brought long since by some sun-drowsy bee
Of heaven visiting our mutual sleep
   From you — most dear — to me.

[1] This was enclosed with a letter written to Elfrida Ingpen in 1894. The original manuscript had no punctuation.
[2] In a manuscript booklet of original verses and stories copied out and bound up with a sheet of vellum and a green ribbon by de la Mare, and given to Celia Newbolt as a girl — one of a series of such Christmas presents, and it should probably be dated 1903 or 1906.
[3] A poem referred to by de la Mare as 'very early', and revised long after its original composition.

[695]

Whatever silence in my solitude
Brings passing quiet to a mind distressed
Recalls a trouble-hearted child that stood
    Hushed, solaced, to your breast.

Ev'n now I trace your face in dreams by night;
Your eyes regard me, the lightening gloom
Summons the wanderer in the infinite
    Back to earth's transient home.

O gentle face Time only makes more sweet!
O place of peace, would, would that I could be —
A child at heart, and turn on happy feet
    To you — most dear — to thee.

IN VAIN MINE EYES THY BEAUTY SCAN

In vain mine eyes thy beauty scan,
Vainly I ponder in my thought
Why thou should'st waste on me, a man,
    The love, sans hope, I sought.

O stir not yet: still, still, most dear,
Tranced in thy loveliness, dream on;
Wake not the darkness that my fear
    Must face, thou gone.

WHEN A GREAT WATER SINKS TO PEACE

When a great water sinks to peace
Its surges cry awhile, then cease;
Though on a faint wave toss frail flowers of foam,
Soon all at length to a last quiet come.
Such storm that hour we shared,
Nor cared
Unto what shipwreck our two hearts should beat,
Nor in what wild of night our eyes go blind,
Seeking that other self no self can find,
Nor dreamed what strangers in that dark should meet.
What wonder, then, when each from each had gone,
The waves of life lulled low to rest
Within each breast,
Even memory tired and love itself did die,
Like spindrift faintly falling,
In a sigh?

ARE YOU ASLEEP? THEN LISTEN, DREAMER

Are you asleep? Then listen, dreamer, I
Keep still my watch in Time's eternity,
Still on the borders of your dark I give
To every thought that stirs a faint *Qui vive?*
In heedless solitude your body lies,
Not the less lovely now, with fast-sealed eyes,
And lips close-close, and hands laid slim and small
On that mute bosom's languorous rise and fall,
Your burden of gold upon your pillows spread
For Orient chaplet to a dreaming head:
So, now I see you; and with you I dream —
O beauties in the gloom that shelters them,
Far, far from your dear memory though I am
As in that last strange hour before you came.
And yet if coming softly I could win
My way to your sleep's quiet entering-in;
If I could touch your hand, and, stooping, press
Your sleep-cold mouth's faint archèd loveliness —
O what returning spirit would it be
Out of your waking dark would shine on me?

TO ROSE

Eat, drink and be merry, he said,
The wisest and saddest of men;
For the living at last shall be dead
And what shall it profit them then?

They knew, too — the ancients austere
When the last fumbled obol was paid,
How cold is the comfort, my dear,
Of being the shade of a shade.

And they told of a desolate stream
Whose treacherous waters commix
In a slumber, unlit by one dream,
With the silence and sorrow of Styx,

Called Lethe: cold is its tide;
One sip, and all memory is gone,
Love, hope, passion, jealousy, pride
And the beauty heart lavished them on.

Love me — my dear: ere 'tis night,
Ere deep death's oblivion flows
That can hardly with any delight
Raise up the *ghost* of a Rose.

TWELVE OF THE CLOCK

Twelve of the clock — lost hour when lovers' ghosts
Stir in their sleep towards breasts that held them dear,
To hide a shadowy head in spectral hands.
Shall I, too, wake when the whole moon reflects
Coldly on dew-dark yews the sheet of flame
An earth-obscurèd sun showers sweet through Space?
Can dead men's voices dead desires express?
Will you, O fair with beauty, hearken then?
Shall we keep tryst where thickset cypress shakes
To hear Pan's piping tremble upon the bell
That tolls for all at last a mute goodbye?

Come, sweet, you are asleep: shut out from me
By fast-closed lids and slumber-sealèd ears.
You would not quicken though I stoopt so near
The faint, pale roses of your cheek should burn
Softly against my secret lips: your mouth —
O, I would whisper lightly and be gone.

For what is waking but a deeper sleep
Into which Love cries its forlorn, Arouse!
What do our hearts when wildest in love's hope
But beat tattoo against the doors of dream?
Think, O dear thou! You thought a child was sighing
For the lost solace of its mother's arms,
When it was I, with wild and stubborn calling,
Made the still wood of your deep silence ring
With my poor dark despair. O, never heed!
We grope for Peace: peace but a moment stays.
From Sleep, to Sleep, to Sleep at last we go;
Then twelve of the clock — the hour for lovers' ghosts.

LONE MUST EVERY SPIRIT BE

Lone must every spirit be,
Cabined in a fast-shut house,
Peering from casement dim to see
Beauty and mystery,
Fair and far and ominous.

Strangers grace the quiet dust,
Distant voices music make,
Bright life wantons swift in lust,
All things sweet and lovely must
Dream themselves awake.

And the spirit restless too,
Turning inward, searches close
Every chamber, through and through,
For some sure and secret clue,
Refuge and repose —

Perchance at length in fear and doubt
Climbs a privy, tortuous stair,
From a high window looketh out
To see in evening crystal fair
Death shining there.

AN ANSWER

'When the love-bird leaves her nest,
Does she fly to the East? Or the West?'

Nay, she flies as fancy take her
Where some far isle's flowers shall wake her
Songs of grief and joy, and break her
Heart with that wild useless pining
Past even music's reconciling,
Which — when she hath left her nest
And flies her East and flies her West —
    Never here finds final rest
    Unless in earth's green breast.

A CHILD'S SONG[1]

A voice says, Come!
　　But my heart here
Keeps still its beat,
　　Serene and clear;
My spirit hearkens,
　　Yet fears to roam,
Though still that voice
　　Keeps calling, Come!

On to the day
　　When I shall be
A man 'midst men
　　It summons me;
Till, grown quite old,
　　And nearing home,
I hear again
　　That voice call, Come!

FATHER AND SON

Do you remember that evening, how, lost in silence,
We were crossing the meadow together — you and I;
And a low gray drift of clouds in the latening twilight
Moved with us, on, as we loitered slowly by,
And horses browsing there — shag, lumbering cart-horses —
Lifted their heads from the grass and crossed our way,
Two of them keeping close, as if friends the one of the other.
And we talked of the perilous times. And the cool night wind in our
　　nostrils
Breathed sweet of the new budded leaves and the growth of May,
Encanopied over with clouds — and we thought of England —
England, the old, and the dear, of my past, and of yours, and of you;
England the wise, the faithful, the near, the happy;
And evening's faint, dying breezes muttered, 'It's true, it's true.'

---

[1] Omitted from the page-proofs of *Peacock Pie*, 1913.

[700]

ALAS

Alas, dear wife,
In how sad grave
We have at last
Our lodging made!
Yet peace it is,
And aye will be,
Or quick, or dead,
To rest with thee.

THE VICAR OF THIS PARISH

Rest now, revered and gentle sir,
Robin and wren for chorister,
And earth's wild flowers for sepulchre.

Thy self, our livelong benison,
Fails us in no wise though thou art gone.

Whithersoever he may fare,
Who bringeth peace makes little stir.

Than love of God nought's quieter.

NOT BY THE CLOSEST SHAVE

Not by the closest shave
Could this old Barber skirt the grave:
Death watched him till of goodly years,
And then himself took up the shears.
And he who often others bled
      Now bloodless lies abed,
Razor and shears and cup laid down,
      And all his occupation gone.

LE JEU EST FAIT

Here lies a gambler, every trick now played —
Diamonds useless; his last Heart mislaid;
By some blind lank-faced Knave of Clubs betrayed;
      And only one card left, a Spade.

[701]

THE UNLOVING

When your strange beauty haunted every thought,
And love of you made even my miseries dear,
When to be with you was the one end sought,
And to be reft of you my only fear;
Then all I valued was of fathomless worth,
Seeing its meaning was by you bestowed,
Eden my garden was — you shared the earth;
The blessèd was three times blest if yours the road.

Ah, riddle! Tell me, now that you are gone
And love a fantasy seems of mocking sleep,
Or like a tale that once enticed me on
At which remembrance can nor smile nor weep,
Why all that's lost — though it was never given —
Has made the world a waste, and exiled heaven?

HOMECOMING

Wondrous that journeying o'er the Atlantic deep! —
The long-drawn days of wake; brief nights of sleep;
And, lo! these green, still fields and veils of rain:

And England come again!

'GATHER YE ROSES'

I that loved, now love again
Eyes as bright, and one as tender;
And for her once loved in vain? —
May Fate a truer lover send her!

I that sighed, sigh deeper yet
For one as like to prove as fickle.
What care I! New love is sweet,
Though destined for the selfsame sickle?

So, like a weathercock, I'll turn
Whithersoever fancy wander;
A heart, once kindled, bright may burn,
Nor care how oft Time change the tinder!

'TELL ME...'

Tell me why I am sad,
And I will say
Why blackest night besieges brightest day.

Tell me why still I grieve,
And I will prove
That there is human heart no plea can move.

Tell me why I despair,
And hope is dust —
Oh, 'tis because I love, since love I must.

PEACE

A heart to be at peace with,
Wisdom at peace to be;
To love no less though loved no more
Be all the hope in me.

I, FRIEND

I, friend, drink to thee, friend,
As my friend drank to me.
And I, friend, charge thee, friend,
As my friend charged me
That thou, friend, will drink to thy friend
As thy friend drank to thee.
   And the more we drink together
   The merrier we'll be.

DEAR BROTHER HORSE

I woke. Without, the full moon's light
Lay on the stubble white as snow,
And still and bare as far-off wastes
Where anxious travellers go.

[703]

Beyond them lay the gilded sea,
Unmoved by wave or swell.
A lighthouse shone on vacancy
And mutely signalled, 'All is well'.

There was no sound, nor wind nor bird
Brought life to the enchanted night;
Until all suddenly he came
As if created out of light:

Created out of light, as swift —
He leaped the wheatfield's border rail,
A horse escaped from Master Man,
Proud head raised high, and banner tail;

Then paused — I worshipped Beauty there,
For all life's loveliness was he,
Before he snorted, and was gone,
And left the empty night to me.

THE REVENANT[1]

It is late evening, and darkness wells into the low, domed theatre, in which muffled in fantastic disguise, sits the King. Beneath him the curtained proscenium of a stage is dimly visible. Above, in a gallery, and screened from sight by dark cloths, are seated his Musicians. Through the low windows that encircle the theatre, and beneath the delicate music, enters the sound of waves breaking on a remote shore, dimly discernible by a greenish watch-light that shines from far away.

The King is sunk in reverie, and sits as immobile as are the two soldiers, carved out of ebony, that in barbaric accoutrements, and with staring ivory eyes, keep watch on either side of his purple canopy. The music faints away into silence. Whereat the King stirs, and, slowly lifting his eyes, perceives stationed before him, her hands folded across her breast, and as if hovering in the air, the figure or phantom of a woman, her countenance so obscure in the fading light that he cannot discern whether her eyes are closed or not, whether she smiles or not, or whether her features show any change or movement. He has been muttering to himself and now resumes his soliloquy.

Thou art, then, come? Years are but days. But days
Eternity, when the close mind broods on,
Pining for witness of the dream it dreams.
The journey has been tedious, and its course

[1] A poem that was revised for publication in *The Burning-Glass and Other Poems*, 1945, but omitted from it at the galley-proof stage.

[704]

Beset by shapes of horror, gross or sweet,
Breathing delirious questions in my ear.
Through thought's black intertangled branches I
Have pressed, unseen of wandering moon or stars,
Seeking the brink of life, keeping that tryst
Which thou and I through countless ages of time
Have ever evaded till this last-struck hour . . .

So, so; thou answered not? Nor in this mirk
Can these my mortal eyes discern, perchance,
Thy curved lips stir, or those all-dwelling eyes
Lift for an instant their dark blinds to beckon:—
'I am She'.
Nay, the entranced far wailing of the strings,
The pauses immeasurable when the soul cries, Stay!
Suffice to make inaudible to me
The whisper of the air thou, smiling, breathest.
Smiling? Why, then, as I gaze on and on,
Does that vague face evoked from nothingness
Usurp the cold of stone, and lour in beauty
Like cliffs rock-shadowed o'er a waste of sea?
And yet, since at my bidding thou art come,
'Tis I that called thee from the untrodden verge
Where the stark real flow'rs out into the imagined?
Not so? Then stoop, until the words I lip
Thrill through the ichor which thy veins distil
And thou perforce take life. I tell a tale
Would still the sirens' song and bid pay heed
The broken-hearted in a world insane.

*The last airs of evening stir through the chamber, bringing the shadows of
night with them; and the instruments again break softly into music. With a
sidelong head intently watching the Woman, the King talks on as if in
self-communion.*

All men are Hunters, Phantom. Ay, even a child
Breaks from his dream of being to pursue —
Hovering in air, delighting in the sun —
The coloured fly; and with small feeble fingers,
Smeared with the powder of its myriad dyes,
Plucks wing and wing away. Men thirst for blood.
They have no pity on the piteous, lave
Cruel and trembling hands in the ebbing gush
That is the stream of life. Not mine this foulness.
    I to a darker fate came hither,
        My only quarry — Thou . . .

[705]

There lived a Princess, in the past that's dead,
Gentle as daybreak in a valley of flowers.
And I, as young as she, found in her face
The characters that spell what men call Love.
Imagine thou a fountain, thridding slim
Into the air on which it coolness pours,
Transfigured with the crystal of the dawn!
Then all is verdant, boskèd in with green
Of cedars and the everlasting yew
That tents the nothing of the sightless dead.
There in heaven's east faints to invisible silver
The planet couched on Aphrodite's breast.

Mock, mock, depraved! The child of that far day,
Fevered with vision of what cheating life
Weaves never into the semblance of the real,
Refreshed not lip but eye in that cold spring —
On verge of paradise sniffing at a bait
Tainted with venom that, in grot of earth
Whereto it crawls for dusk to heal its pangs,
Its tongue shall blister, and its heartstrings snap.

How should the unlearn'd that I was then tell o'er
The musicked syllables of a love unsmeared
By faintest tinge of an undreamed reward?
I gave; she thirsting sipped. Thou knowest the tale?
That lovelier-than-heaven in a child's clear eyes.
Well, taste deferrèd recompense! And learn
That daydreams may in woeful dark dream on! . . .

Ho, there, drive silence out, dumbed serfs of wind!
Straddle, you string-nicked thumbs, lest night shall hear
The warble air makes in a gut-thralled throat!
Ho, there, my stranglers, bring me screw and spit
And dangling fires to warm the skin that's cold,
    And hasten harmony in minds asleep . . .
No answer? . . . Nor bade I to my presence enter
The wind that cools their silk-embroidered stools.

So, then, I am alone. And I am I . . .
A mind distempered is a spirit at peace.
I hide beneath the wreckage of my thoughts
As do the drowned in belly of the deep.
In secret tongue I commune here with shades
Whose lightfoot tread no echo yet hath wakened

On the long flinty highways of the world . . .
What if poor touch do lie? — the sigh tells truth.
And, borne upon the cold deep of our dream,
The perfume of thy body haunts my sense.
Alas, strange heart, only fair friends are we,
Met only discourse of the happier past.
Ay, Sheba, thou'st kept late thy Solomon.
I am, 'tis said, so old I am scarce human.
Something in thy still scrutiny summons back
A tale told by a fool to an old king . . .

Ay, that there was a prince in the long-ago —
Proud as a stallion in the mettle of his blood;
Of languid black, sleek locks and narrow head
And gaze the hawk meets when perchance he stoops
Poised o'er the crystal mirror of a flood.
And in his coursing, one sweet stagnant eve,
When the unageing forests ranked their boughs
O'er gazelle-slimmed labyrinths of their sombre courts,
As if in stupor of the power divine,
He came — companioned by a tongue-parched hound
And nothing human — to a house of stone.
The racket of his harness smote the walls.
With liquid eye his horse tossed back its foam,
And snorted caution. One thin waft of smoke
Mounted from clustered chimney idly on.
Else cornice and gable and rooftree were heavy with age,
Painting desertion on the sightless air.
Our prince sate brooding, by a fancy guiled
That unseen hand, as if to track the forgot,
Had turned the pages of existence back,
And this were record of another life —
The scene, the motionlessness, the green, the blue,
Those windows vitreous with prolonged disuse.
O dark at the window now reveal this face! —
Lips all as mute as a night rose; and eyes
Lustrously dim as starry vault of space. . .
No, get thee gone. I weary of thy gaze.

Hush now. And presently I'll lift my head
And vacancy will lour where burned that brow;
And she, discourteously treated, shall be gone.
Stealthy, O King; glance sidelong, scarce stir hand . . .
Thou art not nothingness then? Thine own sense too
Heard into vacancy the strings die down?
And thou hast quaked at thought, *We are alone!*

Between us hangs an air suffused with dark
Laced only by the silvering of the stars.

I stretch my hand. Thou movest not. Within
A voice cries, 'Utter the secret word!' Would'st blanch!
These soldiers twain who guard my sacred chair
And ghost from out the blackness of their wood,
If I cried, Strike! would stir to life. And thou —
Hast thou no fear of soldierly courtesies?
O whence the flower wherewith I dower thy cheek?
Whence the desire, the solemn dream, the thirst —
As of a wilderness in bleak of noon
Shaken with heat above a grove of palms
That sets the goal of longing in thine eyes
And makes thy mouth the fruit of the Dead Sea? —
Stifling with ash the life and soul that yearn
For the immeasurable quiet of death.
Albeit, thy hands in semblance of a cross
Guard the serene cold founts of thy still breast.

Nay, see, I'll put thee to the tangible proof.
You shall perceive that separateness counts nought;
The form I've given thee shall substance take.
I rise, I stoop, I thrust out both my hands.
Making a hood, a cowl, a tent, a refuge
Of mine own self to haven thee at last.
Enter then, weave thyself, flesh, bone, into this frame,
And share the soul that brought thy Self to birth.
Come back, thou lovely and most harmless thing,
And be a child again, and innocent.

Nay, none
Can change the dread dark real of the past,
I cannot expiate my sins with hope.
There is no judge can ransom what is lost,
No love divine redeem what still I crave.
Know, then, thou art a phantom of the dead;
Spit I could execration and despair.
But thou'rt beyond me, and wilt still smile on
Until death loose me too, and I a shade
Pursuing thee, past capture, in the tomb.

THE INCANTATION[1]

Green drowsed the valley. Glassed the sun
    Noon's vacancy of blue.
Hollow in nowhere trolled a voice —
    Two echoless notes, *Cuck-oo*!

O incantation dark, malign,
    What ghost within me stirred and said,
'Ten thousand thousand Springs are mine,
    Would God that *you* were dead!'

A MODERN GADARA

Appalled, in dream, I watched the ravenous swine
Hustling in frenzy towards that fatal brim;
But when I peered — down — down — to search the surfy brine,
    Lo, every one could swim.

GRATITUDE

A poor word, *gratitude*! —
    When the tongue lacks grace
    Wherewith to shadow forth
    In mute embrace
The joy reflected ev'n in one loved face!

A cold word, *gratitude*! —
    When the mind would bless,
    Beyond all speech could tell
    Or even heart confess,
The Unseen that brought, untraced, unsought,
That one brief moment's inward happiness!

[1] Omitted from the page-proofs of *The Fleeting and Other Poems*, 1933.

THE TWO BIRDS[1]

Gentle bird of tender voice,
Sing and make my heart rejoice!
In that heart another bird
Has thy singing heard.

As I stand and listen here,
Each to each pipes low and clear;
And when thou hast ceased to sing,
Mine will still be echoing.

THE SNARE

Poets tell over to a lulling air
The time-charmed beauty of a lip, an eye;
Sing halting praises of the virgin breast
Their unborn children shall be nourished by;
Rant of their fears, their jealousy, their scorn;
Challenge the moon to shed as lovely a light
As long-gone races have bequeathed to a brow
Which age will soon unflatter in their sight.

Oh, what a short-lived memory is Man's
Who, lapped in rich imagination, lies;
Barters 'For ever' for a smile, a kiss;
Takes death's proud name in vain in amorous sighs.
Does he not know that love's a honeyed snare
Which limes man's feathers for a priceless bait —
That hidden desire to which as 'She' he raves,
That God made manifest the Worlds await.

YOU SAY YOU LOVE

You say you love, but will you ever know
A foolish heart's sweet wild, tempestuous pinings,
The helmless sport of all the winds that blow,
Veiling the beauty of the rock-isled sirens
        In spindrift cold as snow?

Yours the blest secret of a happy nature
Unvexed with storm, nor restless as the sea;
These tranquil eyes, that smile of flattered wonder
Tell only where the halcyon loves to be,
        No haven, alas, for me.

[1] For another version of this called 'A Warbler', see *Bells and Grass*, p. 410.

IN THE PUBLIC SERVICE

Body amorphous, head piled high with hair
A grease-glossed black, above that brazen stare;
A man's broad nose, an octopus's beak,
Voluptuous triple chin, and porcine cheek —
She squats in stupor, brooding over her prey,
Kept for the dark though netted in the day.

A spider she, who keeps alive her fly
For those she scorns to feast on and suck dry,
Maybe, poor wretches, to be poisoned by.
Reptile of womanhood, hell's toad, Black Bess,
A bawd's foul pussiecat, a procuress.

AT WAR

A world at war: and I sit here at peace!
Shame chills the cheek at such stark heedlessness.
Yet earth-life always is at war with woe,
Inward and outward. The same Fiend for foe
        Stalks this world's wilderness.
And were I not to my own evil blind,
How dread a shambles were my waking mind!

BLIND

His squalid beard floats on the wavering wind;
His hand is veined and gnarry as his old stick;
Clothed is his sharp white face with skin like rind
Of autumn-fallen apples, scarred and thick
With winter's usage. The mud of evil days
Stiffens his rags. In thin lament he cries
His beggary to the street, lifting a face
Bleak with the summons of two sightless eyes.

But who can tell what vivid visions lurk
Behind that dark? What things of sun and moon,
More gloriously arising in the murk
Bring him oblivion of his tuneless croon?

Dole him your penny, boy: he is blind and old.
But, in your pity, be not over-bold!

[711]

TAT FOR TIT

Shrill, glass-clear notes — 'Titmouse!' I sighed, enchanted;
Then looked for the singer ere its song should cease:
A wild-eyed gipsy pushing an old go-cart,
    Its wheels in need of grease.

THE CHINA CAT

You never stir, and heaven forbid,
Since, mutest companion, if you did —
A creature formed of clay and glaze —
Nature herself would stand at gaze,
Albeit it with an intent to flatter:
Man would have conjured life from matter —
If from your bowels there should befall
A low protracted caterwaul,
Those slanting eyes should open and pause,
Those pads eject their hidden claws.
No nightlong vigil I know well
Would consummate that miracle;
Yet even that passive attitude
Once did a questing dog delude.

EVEN AS THE HEART

Even as the heart — how stark the cost! —
May grieve that it grieves no more, in vain,
So love, its inmost impulse lost,
    Dies never to rise again.

STRANGE, IS IT NOT!

Strange, is it not! One aged — yea, seventy-five —
May every day exult in being alive!
When up to bed he bears his weary bones,
Or they bear him, 'tisn't with sighs and groans
(Not of intent) he mounts the stairs, to cry
With unaffected heart, and no one by,
    'Thanks be to God'.

What, yet another day in this still place,
His blissful haven for so full a space —
His silence company — his small resort
For friends, the loved, the found, the sought,
For talk, books, window-watch and inward thought!

WIDEN YOUR CALLS

Widen your calls, let TIM decant her spells —
She'll give you at least true clock-time, if nought else;
Or dial 999, and gain at once
Safety from fire, police and ambulance,
All those necessities at such extremes
When states remoter taunt the realm of dreams;
Or as a last resort plain O, poor dunce,
Will call the Controller to your aid at once.
Meekly I obey: a still small voice
Replies, What ails you, restless child? Rejoice
God gave you life. And love, its consort bliss,
Whether a sigh reveal it or a kiss,
Is your small all; squander it as you may,
Still there remains that all — to give away.
Keep nothing, not one mould-crust on the shelf;
The only fatal prison is yourself.
And as to velvet skin or stubborn bone,
Your sweetest safety is to be alone
And seek your wholeness in division.
That, child, forgone, what whit of you would stay
When, poor mute fugitive, you kneel to pray!
What would you — that the dewdrop should flame on,
Or into noon's vast nothingness be gone?
God made you out of dust, a living soul,
Else pre-annihilation were your goal;
Because you are severed by yourself and sin,
His infinite mercy pines to bring you in —
And that last lesson you alone can learn
When in your compass you as vainly yearn
And in a love-doomed face and human eyes
Discern the haven of life's whole enterprise.

IN RETROSPECT

Not for mere peace I sigh,
But for a mind that in impassioned rest
Might in tranquillity
Endure the worst, unwearied of the best;
And for a sentient heart whose love was such
Its only mortal grief could be
It loved too much.

Is it but youth that is gone?
Doth age from dark to dark lead on?
And will that 'death' which used to seem
Only the solemn wakening from a dream
Prove now a sigh of gratitude — that night
Will hide all cheating daybreaks out of sight
And lay limbs, wearied of, sans desire and strength,
In never-broken quietude at length?

Ah, if by secret bargaining
I could from the unseen assurance wring
That the pure spirit I in childhood knew
Were mine for purchase, swift and true,
At cost of all the wisdom yet in age's keeping —
How blest this night would be this body's sleeping!

LOST

A long life passes; but of all it gives
What in full fragrance of remembrance lives?
Imagination roves on eagle's wing,
But where the record of its journeying?
Vain are ev'n words of subtlest sound and sense
A single hour of ardour to condense,
Or, clear as raindrop trembling from a thorn,
To orb one moment of a summer's morn.

Unpublished Verses

THE PROMENADE
1880

See Master Humphrey, with his mother,
    Walking in the town
In velvet breeches, and his golden
    Curls streaming down.

His mother is attired in satin,
    Bonneted in lace;
And a smile of mild good breeding
    Creases her face.

She walks along with fragrant rustle
    In delicate boots,
And 'neath her parasol of lilac
    Her friends she salutes.

'There's Mr. Davis, with his daughters,
    Taking the air;
And see—dear Lady Ann Matilda
    (Humphrey, don't stare!).

'Why there's the Bishop, in his gaiters,
    With dear Dr. Fapp;
Poor gentleman, he's very feeble
    (Humphrey, raise your cap!).

'And Mrs. Sims! — so young a widow;
    Left very well;
And Captain Howe with his fiancée,
    Charming Miss Bell.

'I doubt 'twill be the gayest wedding!
    La, there's Mr. Grey!
And, on his arm, his ailing sister —
    Beautiful day!'

With Fashion, then, on either pavement,
    Between twelve and one,
Walk greeting their polite acquaintance
    Mother and son.

But now they must return to luncheon —
　　Roast lamb and peas,
New potatoes, tart and custard,
　　Biscuits and cheese.

MISS GOOTZ

Certain people one knows
　Must fall short, I suppose,
Of all that one hopes that such people should be.
　There is, for example,
　My neighbour Miss Gootz
Who lives, she has told me, entirely on roots —
　A limited fare, you'll agree!
Of a friend who subsists on swede, turnip and leek
One might in mere kindliness scruple to speak,
　Unless at sheer duty's decree.
And while poor Miss Gootz merely *fed* upon roots —
And went out to buy them in very old boots —
　The habit seemed one of degree.
But now I am certain, without any doubt,
That the neighbour I'm speaking of never goes out,
That her attics are bare, and she sleeps down below
In a cellar where not ev'n a radish would grow,
I feel that I *ought* to say something, and so
　I am saying it now, as you see.
Far worse: I have formed a suspicion that it's
Playing havoc at last with the poor creature's wits —
　This dumb subterranean craze.
She is old, she is feeble, she wanders, she says
That the one thing in life that she pines for and prays
　Is to win from this body to where
Out of dark of the grave she will surely uprise
And the spirit within her flower sweet in the skies,
　Just as primroses sweeten the air.
She seems to consider that what we are here
Saves up for this journey; I'm not very clear.
　And I hate talking out in the street.

Still, I think that's excessive, I feel that Miss Gootz
Has lived far too long on a diet of roots:
　A heathenish horrible fare.
I'm convinced some respectable clergyman should
Explain how one feels about this, if he could:

[716]

'On delusions like these it is wicked to brood';
   Say it kindly, of course, I agree.
How such notions occur I don't quite understand,
For though I have lived on the fat of the land,
   Not the faintest of reasons I see
For supposing *I*'m likely to blossom as sweet,
And I doubt if, *post mortem*, I'm anxious to meet
   My very odd neighbour Miss G.

'WILLIE!'

Willie, Willie!
I call and cry,
But Echo only
Makes reply.
Willie, Willie!
The birds are still,
The sweet sun shines
On the empty hill;
The brake stirs not,
The flowers seem
Half-folded in
An emptier dream.
Morning to dusk
I call in vain;
Comes but my own voice
Back again.

WHERE?

'Where, Oh, where is Alice Bates?
And where is Willie Wether?'
'Where the pretty partridge mates,
Inches deep in heather.
A golden ring he's promised her,
A kiss to him she's given,
And every breeze that stirs those bells
Rings sweet of earth and heaven.'

BUCK BUCK[1]

*Bucca, bucca, quot sunt hic?** —
Ten fat candles but no wick,
Thumb, and Toucher, Longman, Lechman, Little Man —
  or Little Dick.

Nine, eight, six, five, three — guess quick!
Or here I stay and here I stick,
Bucca, bucca, quot sunt hic? —
Tommy Tomkins, Billy Wilkins, Slim Long Larum,
  Betsy Bedlam, Tippety-Town-End — Little Dick.

SINGING AND DANCING[1]

That Day, that Day, that Gentle Day
We fairing went to *Rumblelow;*
We sang, sang we *Broom, Broom on Hill,*
And *Trolly lolly leman, dow.*

We danced *The Bace of Voragon,*
The Vod and the Val, The Bee, Leaves Green,
The Long Flat Foot of Garioch,
  We danced *The Loch of Slene.*

That Day, that Day, that Gentle Day
Was music wild at *Rumblelow;*
O Mine Heart, hey, this is my song,
Trolly lolly leman, dow.

---

* This is how the Roman boys, two thousand and more years ago, began the game of *Buck Buck,* which is still played in England in the same fashion. Toucher, Longman, etc. are old names for the five fingers.

---

[1]Selected for inclusion in *Bells and Grass* (1941), but finally omitted.

WORDS[1]

How I love the rhymes that I can dance to, sing to —
Sing to, dance to, and echoing with birds !
Rhymes that, like bells, the mind may chime and ring to,
Elf-bells, steeple-bells — sweet-tongued words.

Stranger than a fiddle they call into the heart, and
Silence itself says what speech has never known;
But oh, the joy and beauty that a voice may impart, and
The twice-sweet pleasure if that voice is one's own!

[1] Selected for inclusion in *Bells and Grass* (1941), but finally omitted.

PART II

1. POEMS FROM PROSE AND MISCELLANEOUS WORKS

Henry Brocken (1904)[1]

YOU TAKE MY HEART WITH TEARS

You take my heart with tears;
I battle uselessly;
Reft of all hopes and doubts and fears:
    Lie quietly.

You veil my heart with cloud;
Since faith is dim and blind,
I can but grope perplex'd and bow'd:
    Seek till I find.

Yet bonds are life to me;
How else could I perceive
The love in each wild artery
    That bids me live?

SIGHS HAVE NO SKILL

Sighs have no skill
To wake from sleep
Love once too wild, too deep.

Gaze if thou will,
Thou canst not harm
Eyes shut to subtle charm.

Oh! 'tis my silence
Shows thee false,
Should I be silent else?

Haste thou then by!
Shine not thy face
On mine, and love's disgrace!

[1] Subtitle: 'His travels and adventures in the rich, strange, scarce-imaginable regions of romance'.

[723]

ALL SWEET FLOWERS

All sweet flowers
    Wither ever,
Gathered fresh
    Or gathered never;
But to live when love is gone! —
Grieve, grieve, lute, sadly on!

All I had —
    'Twas all thou gav'st me;
That foregone,
    Ah! what can save me!
If the exorcised spirit fly,
Nought is left to love me by.

Take thy stars,
    My tears then leave me;
Thine my bliss,
    As thine to grieve me;
Take . . . .

PILGRIM FORGET

Pilgrim forget; in this dark tide
Sinks the salt tear to peace at last;
Here undeluding dreams abide,
    All sorrow past.

Nods the wild ivy on her stem;
The voiceless bird broods on the bough;
The silence and the song of them
    Untroubled now.

Free that poor captive's flutterings,
That struggles in thy tired eyes,
Solace its discontented wings,
    Quiet its cries!

Knells now the dewdrop to its fall,
The sad wind sleeps no more to rove;
Rest, for my arms ambrosial
    Ache for thy love!

FOLLOW THE WORLD

Follow the World —
  She bursts the grape,
And dandles man
  In her green lap;
She moulds her Creature
  From the clay,
And crumbles him
  To dust away:
    Follow the World!

One Draught, one Feast,
  One Wench, one Tomb;
And thou must straight
  To ashes come:
Drink, eat, and sleep;
  Why fret and pine?
Death can but snatch
  What ne'er was thine:
    Follow the World!

COLD TO BOSOM

There's a dark tree and a sad tree,
Where sweet Alice waits, unheeded,
For her lover long-time absent,
Plucking rushes by the river.

Let the bird sing, let the buck sport,
Let the sun sink to his setting;
Not one star that stands in darkness
Shines upon her absent lover.

But his stone lies 'neath the dark tree,
Cold to bosom, deaf to weeping;
And 'tis gathering moss she touches,
Where the locks lay of her lover.

DITTY

The goodman said,
"'Tis time for bed,
Come, mistress, get us quick to pray;
   Call in the maids
   From out the glades
Where they with lovers stray,
With love, and love do stray.'

   'Nay, master mine,
   The night is fine,
And time's enough all dark to pray;
   'Tis April buds
   Bedeck the woods
Where simple maids away
With love, and love do stray.

   'Now we are old,
   And nigh the mould,
'Tis meet on feeble knees to pray;
   When once we'd roam,
   'Twas else cried, "Come,
And sigh the dusk away,
With love, and love to stray."'

   So they gat in
   To pray till nine;
Then called, 'Come maids, true maids, away!
   Kiss and begone,
   Ha' done, ha' done,
Until another day
With love, and love to stray!'

   Oh, it were best
   If so to rest
Went man and maid in peace away!
   The throes a heart
   May make to smart
Unless love have his way,
In April woods to stray! —
In April woods to stray!

The Three Royal Monkeys (1910)[1]

[1] Originally called *The Three Mulla-Mulgars*. The title above was first used in 1935.

THE MULGARS' FAREWELL[2]

Far away in Nanga-noon
Lived an old and grey Baboon,
Ah-mi, Sulâni!
Once a Prince among his kind,
Now forsaken, left behind,
Feeble, lonely, all but blind:
Sulâni, ghar magleer.

Peaceful Tishnar came by night,
In the moonbeams cold and white;
Ah-mi, Sulâni!
'Far away from Nanga-noon,
Old and lonely, gray Baboon,
Is a journey for thee soon!
Sulâni, ghar magleer.

'Be not frightened, shut thine eye;
Comfort take, nor weep, nor sigh;
Solitary Tishnar's nigh!'
Sulâni, ghar magleer.

Old Baboon, he gravely did
All that peaceful Tishnar bid;
Ah-mi, Sulâni!
In the darkness cold and grim
Drew his blanket over him;
Closed his old eyes, sad and dim:
Sulâni, ghar magleer.

*Talaheeti sul magloon
Olgar, ulgar Manga-noon;
Ah-mi, Sulâni!
Tishnar sootli maltmahee,
Ganganareez soongalee,
Manni Mulgar sang suwhee:
Sulâni, ghar magleer.*

[2] Called 'Gar Mulgar Dusangee' in *Poems 1919–1934*, 1935 and 'Marching Song' in *Collected Rhymes and Verses*, 1944.

[727]

THE MULLA-MULGARS' JOURNEY SONG[1]

That one
Alone
Who's dared, and gone
To seek the Magic Wonderstone,
No fear,
Or care,
Or black despair,
Shall heed until his journey's done.

Who knows
Where blows
The Mulgars' rose,
In valleys 'neath unmelting snows —
All secrets
He
Shall pierce and see,
And walk unharmed where'er he goes.

ANDY BATTLE'S AND NOD'S SONG[2]

Once and there was a young sailor, yeo ho!
    And he sailèd out over the say
For the isles where pink coral and palm-branches blow,
    And the fire-flies turn night into day,
            Yeo ho!
    And the fire-flies turn night into day.

But the *Dolphin* went down in a tempest, yeo ho!
    And with three forsook sailors ashore,
The Portingals took him where sugar-canes grow,
    Their slave for to be evermore,
            Yeo ho!
    Their slave for to be evermore.

With his musket for mother and brother, yeo ho!
    He warred wi' the Cannibals drear,
In forests where panthers pad soft to and fro,
    And the Pongo shakes noonday with fear,
            Yeo ho!
    And the Pongo shakes noonday with fear.

[1] Also included in *Poems 1919–1934*, 1935.
[2] Also included in *Peacock Pie*, 1913, as 'Andy Battle', and in *Rhymes and Verses: Collected Poems for Young People*, New York, 1947, as 'Yeo Ho!'

Now lean with long travail, all wasted with woe,
    With a monkey for messmate and friend,
He sits 'neath the Cross in the cankering snow,
    And waits for his sorrowful end,
            Yeo ho!
And waits for his sorrowful end.

ANDY BATTLE'S SONG

Voice without a body,
Panther of black Roses,
Jack-Alls fat on icicles,
Ephelanto, Aligatha,
Zevvera and Jaccatray,
Unicorn and River-horse;
            Ho, ho, ho!
Here's Andy Battle,
Waiting for the enemy!

Imbe Calandola,
M'keesso and Quesanga,
Dondo, Sharamomba,[1]
Pongo and Enjekko,
Millions of monkeys,
Rattlesnake and scorpion,
Swamp and death and shadow;
            Ho, ho, ho!
Come on, all of ye,
Here's Andy Battle,
Waiting and — alone!

SHE'S ME FORGOT[2]

Me who have sailèd
    Leagues across
Foam haunted
    By the albatross,
Time now hath made
    Remembered not:
Ay, my dear love
    Hath me forgot.

[1] 'Sharammba' in all editions of *The Three Royal Monkeys*.
[2] Called 'Andy's Love Song' in *Poems 1919–1934*, 1935.

Oh, how should she,
　Whose beauty shone,
Keep true to one
　Such long years gone?
Grief cloud those eyes! —
　I ask it not:
Content am I —
　She's me forgot.·

Here where the evening
　Ooboë wails,
Bemocking
　England's nightingales,
Bravely, O sailor,
　Take thy lot;
Nor grieve too much,
　She's thee forgot!

THE MULGAR JOURNEY SONG[1]

In Munza a Mulgar once lived alone,
And his name it was Dubbuldideery, O;
With none to love him, and loved by none,
His hard old heart it grew weary, O,
　Weary, O weary, O weary.

So he up with his cudgel, he on with his bag
Of Manaka, Ukkas, and Keeri, O;
To seek for the waters of 'Old-Made-Young',
Went marching old Dubbuldideery, O,
　Dubbuldi-dubbuldi-deery.

The sun rose up, and the sun sank down;
The moon she shone clear and cheery, O,
And the myriads of Munza they mocked and mopped
And mobbed old Dubbuldideery, O,
　Môh-Mulgar Dubbuldideery.

He cared not a hair of his head did he,
Not a hint of the hubbub did hear he, O,
For the roar of the waters of 'Old-Made-Young'
Kept calling of Dubbuldideery, O,
　Call — calling of Dubbuldideery.

[1] Also included in *Poems 1919–1934*, 1935.

He came to the country of 'Catch Me and Eat Me'—
Not a fleck of a flicker did fear he, O,
For he knew in his heart they could never make mince-meat
Of tough old Dubbuldideery, O,
  Rough, tough, gruff Dubbuldideery.

He waded the Ooze of Queen Better-Give-Up,
Dim, dank, dark, dismal, and dreary, O,
And, crunch! went a leg down a Cockadrill's throat
'What's *one*?' said Dubbuldideery, O,
  Undauntable Dubbuldideery.

He cut him an Ukka crutch, hobbled along,
Till Tishnar's sweet river came near he, O —
The wonderful waters of 'Old-Made-Young,'
A-shining for Dubbuldideery, O,
  Wan, wizened old Dubbuldideery.

He drank, and he drank — and he drank — and he — drank:
No more was he old and weary, O,
But weak as a babby he fell in the river,
And drownded was Dubbuldideery, O,
  Drown-ded was Dubbuldideery!

THE WATER MIDDEN'S SONG[1]

  Bubble, Bubble,
  Swim to see
  Oh, how beautiful
  I be.

  Fishes, Fishes,
  Finned and fine,
  What's your gold
  Compared with mine?

  Why, then, has
  Wise Tishnar made
  One so lovely
  One so sad?

[1] Called 'Song of the Water-Midden' in *Poems 1919–1934*, 1935.

Lone am I,
And can but make
A little song,
For singing's sake.

POOR BEN, OLD BEN[1]

Wi'decks awas'
Widevry sea,
An' flyin' scud
For companee,
Ole Ben, por Ben
Keepz watcherlone:
Boatz, zails, helmainmust,
Compaz gone.

Not twone ovall
'Is shippimuts can
Pipe pup ta prove
'Im livin' man:
One indescuppers
Flappziz'and,
Fiss-like, as you
May yunnerstand.

An' one bracedup
Azzif to weat,
'Az aldy deck
For watery zeat;
Andwidda zteep
Unwonnerin' eye
Stares zon tossed sea
An' emputy zky.
Pore Benoleben,
Pore-Benn-ole-Ben!

---

[1] Called 'Nod's Old English Song: "Poor Ben, Old Ben!" ' in *Poems 1919–1934*, 1935, and 'Wi'decks awas' ' in *Collected Rhymes and Verses*, 1944.

ENVOY

Long — long is Time, though books be brief;
Adventures strange — ay, past belief —
Await the Reader's drowsy eye;
But, wearied out, he'd lay them by.

But, if so be, he'd some day hear
All that befell these brothers dear
In Tishnar's lovely Valleys — well,
Poor pen, thou must that story tell!

But farewell, now, you Mulgars three!
Farewell, your faithful company!
Farewell, the heart that loved unbidden —
Nod's dark-eyed, beauteous Water-midden!

The Return (1910)

STRANGER, A MOMENT PAUSE, AND STAY

Stranger, a moment pause, and stay;
In this dim chamber hidden away
Lies one who once found life as dear
As now he finds his slumber here:
Pray, then, the Judgement but increase
His deep, his everlasting peace!

Memoirs of a Midget (1921)

'TWAS A CUCKOO, CRIED 'CUCK-OO'

'Twas a Cuckoo, cried 'cuck-oo'
In the youth of the year;
And the timid things nesting,
Crouched, ruffled in fear;
And the Cuckoo cried, 'cuck-oo',
For the honest to hear.

One — two notes; a bell sound
In the blue and the green;
'Cuck-oo: cuck-oo: cuck-oo!'
And a silence between.

Ay, mistress, have a care, lest
Harsh love, he hie by,
And for kindness a monster
To nourish you try —
In your bosom to lie:
'Cuck-oo', and a 'cuck-oo',
    And 'cuck-oo!'

COME ALL YOU YOUNG MEN, WITH YOUR WICKED WAYS

Come all you young men, with your wicked ways;
Sow your wild, wild oats in your youthful days;
That we may live happy when we grow old—
Happy, and happy, when we grow old:
The day is far spent, the night's coming on;
So give us your arm, and we'll joggle along—joggle
    and joggle and joggle along.

[737]

AH, STRANGER, BREATHE A SIGH

Ah, Stranger, breathe a sigh:
  For, where I lie,
Is but a handful of bright Beauty cast:
  It was; and now is past.

Crossings:
A Fairy Play (1921)[1]

ARABY[2]

'Dark-browed Sailor, tell me now,
Where, where is Araby?
The tide's aflow, the wind ablow,
'Tis I who pine for Araby.'

'Master, she her spices showers
O'er nine and ninety leagues of sea;
The laden air breathes faint and rare —
Dreams on far-distant Araby.'

'Oh, but Sailor, tell me true;
'Twas Man who mapped this Araby;
Though dangers brew, let me and you
Embark this night for Araby. . . .'

Wails the wind from star to star;
Rock the loud waves their dirge: and, see!
Through foam and wrack, a boat drifts back:
Ah, heart-beguiling Araby!

THERE SATE GOOD QUEEN BESS

There sate Good Queen Bess, oh,
    A-shining on her throne.
Up, Jessie; down, docket;
    My money's gone!

[1] First performed on 21 June 1919.
[2] Title of the musical setting by C. Armstong Gibbs in *Crossings*, 1921.

NOW SILENT FALLS[1]

Now silent falls the clacking mill;
Sweet—sweeter smells the briar;
The dew wells big on bud and twig;
The glow-worm's wrapt in fire.

Then sing, lully, lullay, with me,
And softly, lill-lall-lo, love,
'Tis high time, and wild time,
And no time, no, love!

The Western sky has vailed her rose;
The night-wind to the willow
Sigheth, 'Now lovely, lean thy head,
Thy tresses be my pillow!'

Then sing, lully, lullay, with me,
And softly, lill-lall-lo, love,
'Tis high time, and wild time,
And no time, no, love!

Cries in the brake, bells in the sea:
The moon o'er moor and mountain
Cruddles her light from height to height,
Bedazzles pool and fountain.

Leap, fox; hoot, owl; wail, warbler sweet:
'Tis midnight now's a-brewing;
The fairy mob is all abroad,
And witches at their wooing . . .

Then sing, lully, lullay, with me,
And softly, lill-lall-lo, love,
'Tis high time, and wild time,
And no time, no, love.

HERE TO-DAY

Here to-day and gone to-morrow;
Nowt to buy with, nowt to borrow;
Come the nightshine, packs down all;
Ring poor Robin's funeral.

[1] The musical setting by C. Armstrong Gibbs in *Crossings*, 1921, was called
'Lullaby'.

NOW ALL THE ROADS[1]

Now all the roads to London Town
Are windy-white with snow;
There's shouting and cursing,
And snortings to and fro;
But when night hangs her hundred lamps,
And the snickering frost-fires creep,
Then still, O; dale and hill, O;
Snow's fall'n deep.
Then still, O; dale and hill, O;
Snow's fall'n deep.

The carter cracks his leathery whip;
The ostler shouts Gee-whoa;
The farm dog grunts and sniffs and snuffs;
Bleat sheep; and cattle blow;
Soon Moll and Nan in dream are laid,
And snoring Dick's asleep;
Then still, O; dale and hill, O;
Snow's fall'n deep.
Then still, O; dale and hill, O;
Snow's fall'n deep.

FOL DOL DO

Fol, dol, do, and a south wind a-blowing O,
Fol, dol, do, and green growths a-growing O,
Fol, dol, do, and the heart inside me knowing O,
    'Tis merry merry month of May.

Fol, dol, do, shrill chanticleer's a-crowing O,
Fol, dol, do, and the mower's soon a-mowing O,
O lovelier than the lilac tree, my lovely love's a-showing O,
    In merry merry month of May.

[1] Title as in *Poems for Children*, 1930. The poem was called 'Beggar's Song' in *Poems 1919–1934*, 1935, as was the musical setting by C. Armstrong Gibbs in *Crossings*, 1921.

THE FAIRY-PEDLAR'S SONG

Of your 'nevolent nature
    Spare a crust for a creature.
A drink and a dole,
    For a ho-omeless soul.

Of slumber but tossings—
    White the rime in bare Crossings;
Cold is shed, barn and byre, leddy,
    A coal from your fire, leddy!

And Oh, sleepy odours,
    The bosom to lull;
When the swart raven yells,
    And the taper burns dull!

THE FLOWER[1]

Listen, I who love thee well
Have travelled far, and secrets tell;
Cold the moon that gleams thine eyes,
Yet beneath her further skies
Rests, for thee, a paradise.

I have plucked a flower in proof,
Frail, in earthly light, forsooth:
See, invisible it lies
In this palm: now veil thine eyes:
Quaff its fragrancies!

Would indeed my throat had skill
To breathe thee music, faint and still—
Music learned in dreaming deep
In those lands, from Echo's lip. . . .
'Twould lull thy soul to sleep.

[1] Included in *The Veil and Other Poems*, 1921, and *Poems 1919–1934*, 1935, as 'Tidings', but called 'The Flower' in *Poems for Children*, 1930. The musical setting by C. Armstrong Gibbs in *Crossings*, 1921, was called 'Candlestick-maker's Song'.

Ding Dong Bell (1924)[1]

(EPITAPHS)

HERE LIES OLD BONES[2]

Here lies old bones;
Sam Gilpin once.

NO VOICE TO SCOLD

No Voice to scold;
    No face to frown;
No hand to smite
    The helpless down:
Ay, Stranger, here
    An Infant lies,
With worms for
    Welcome Paradise.

ANN HARDS

They took me in Death dim,
    And signed me with God's Cross;
Now am I Cherub praising Him
    Who but an infant was.

ALICE HEW

Sleep sound, Mistress Hew!
Birds sing over you;
The sweet flowers flourish
Your own hands did nourish;
And many's the child
By their beauty beguiled.
They prattle and play
Till night call them away;
In shadow and dew:
Sleep sound, Mistress Hew!

[1] Eighteen new epitaphs were included in the 1936 edition. These are the eighteen poems from 'Strangers and Pilgrims' appearing on pp. 751–756.
[2] This poem and the next eighteen are from 'Lichen'.

THOMAS GROAT

All men are mortal, and I know't;
As soon as man's up he's down;
Here lies the ashes of Thomas Groat,
Gone for to seek his Crown.

SAMMIE GURDON

Maybe, my friend, thou'rt main athirst,
Hungry and tired, maybe:
Then turn thy face by yon vane, due west;
Trudge country miles but three;
I'll warrant my son, of the *Golden Swan*,
Will warmly welcome thee.

THREE SISTERS

Three sisters rest beneath
This cypress shade,
Sprightly Rebecca, Anne,
And Adelaide.
Gentle their hearts to all
On earth, save Man;
In Him, they said, all Grief,
All Wo began.
Spinsters they lived, and spinsters
Here are laid;
Sprightly Rebecca, Anne,
And Adelaide.

SUSANNAH PROUT

Here lies my wife,
Susannah Prout;
She was a shrew
I don't misdoubt:
Yet all I have
I'd give, could she
But for one hour
Come back to me.

[744]

YE SAY: WE SLEEP

Ye say: We sleep,
But nay, We wake.
Life was that strange and chequered dream
For the waking's sake.

NAT VOLE

Here lieth Nat Vole,
Asleep now, poor Soul!
'Twas one of his whims
To be telling his dreams,
Of the Lands therein seen
And the Journeys he'd been!
La, if now he could speak,
He'd not listeners seek!

JOHN VIRGIN

If thou, Stranger, be John Virgin, then the
Corse withinunder is nameless, for the Sea
so disfigured thy Face, none could tell
whether thou were John Virgin or no:
Ay, and whatever name I bore
I thank the Lord I be
Six foot in English earth, and not
Six fathom in the sea.

FANNY MEADOWS

'One, two, three'—
O, it was a ring
Where all did play
The hours away,
Did laugh and sing
Still, 'One, two, three,'
Ay, even me
They made go round
To our voices' sound:
'Twas life's bright game
And Death was 'he'.
We laughed and ran
Oh, breathlessly!
And I, why, I

[745]

But a maid was then,
Pretty and winsome,
And scarce nineteen;
But 'twas 'One — two — three;
And — out goes she!'

NED GUNN

Where be Sam Potter now?
Dead as King Solomon.
Where Harry Airte I knew?
Gone, my friend, gone.
Where Dick, the pugilist?
Dead calm — due East and West.
Toby and Rob and Jack?
Dust every one.
Sure, they'll no more come back?
No: nor Ned Gunn.

JOHN SIMPSON

'Is that John Simpson?'
    'Ay, it be.'
'What was thy age, John?'
    'Eighty-three.'
'Was't happy in life, John?'
    'Life is vain.'
'What then of death, friend?'
    'Ask again.'

DIG NOT MY GRAVE O'ER DEEP

Dig not my grave o'er deep
Lest in my sleep
I strive with sudden fear
Toward the sweet air.

Alas! Lest my shut eyes
Should open clear
To the depth and the narrowness —
Pity my fear!

Friends, I have such wild fear
Of depth, weight, space;
God give ye cover me
In easy place!

[746]

TOM HEAD

I rang yon bells a score of years:
　Never a corse went by
But they all said — bid old Tom Head
　Knoll the bell dolesomely:
Ay, and I had a skill with the rope
　As made it seem to sigh.

A POOR NATURAL

Here lieth a poor Natural:
The Lord who understandeth all
Hath opened now his witless eyes
On the Green Fields of Paradise.

Sunshine or rain, he grinning sat:
But none could say at who or what.
And all misshapen as he were,
What wonder folk would stand and stare?

He'd whistle shrill to the passing birds,
Having small stock of human words;
And all his company belike
Was one small hungry mongrel Tyke.

Not his the wits ev'n joyed to be
When Death approached to set him free —
Bearing th' equality of all,
Wherein to attire a Natural.

THE MIDGET

Just a span and half a span
From head to heel was this little man.
Scarcely a capful of small bones
Raised up erect this Midget once.
Yet not a knuckle was askew;
Inches for feet God made him true;
And something handsome put between
His coal-black hair and beardless chin.
But now, forsooth, with mole and mouse,
He keeps his own small darkened house.

[747]

THE BOY

Finger on lip I ever stand;
  Ay, stranger, quiet be;
This air is dim with whispering shades
  Stooping to speak to thee.

M.O.R.S.[1]

Stranger, where I at peace do lie
Make less ado to press and pry!
Am I a Scoff to be who did
Life like a stallion once bestride?
Is all my history but what
A fool hath — soon as read — forgot?
Put back my weeds, and silent be.
Leave me to my own company!

SUSANNAH FRY

Here sleep I,
Susannah Fry,
No one near me,
No one nigh:
Alone, alone
Under my stone,
Dreaming on,
Still dreaming on:
Grass for my valance
And coverlid,
Dreaming on
As I always did.
'Weak in the head?'
Maybe. Who knows?
Susannah Fry
Under the rose.

[1] This poem and the next ten are from ' "Benighted" '.

HERE LIES MY HUSBANDS

Here lies my husbands; One, Two, Three:
Dumb as men ever could wish to be.
As for my Fourth, well, praise be God
He bides for a little above the sod.
But his wits being weak and his eyeballs dim,
Heav'n speed at last I'll wear weeds for him.
Thomas, John, Henry, were these three's names
And to make things tidy, I adds his — James.

CHRYSTOPHER ORCHERDSON

Here restes ye boddie of one
Chrystopher Orcherdson.
Lyf he lived merrilie;
Nowe he doth deathlie lie:
All ye joye from his brighte face
Quencht in this bitter place.
With gratefull voice then saye,
Not oures, but Goddes waye!

NED VAUGHAN

A Shepherd, Ned Vaughan,
'Neath this Tombestone do bide,
His Crook in his hand,
And his Dog him beside.
Bleak and cold fell the Snow
On Marchmallysdon Steep,
And folded both sheepdog
And Shepherd in Sleep.

ELIZA DREW AND JAMES HANNEWAY

Here rest in peace Eliza Drew and James Hanneway
whom Death haplessly snatched from Felicity.
Eliza and James in this sepulchre tarry
Till God with His trumpet shall call them to marry.
Then Angels for maids to the Bride shall be given,
And loud their responses shall echo in Heaven.
And e'en though it be that on Paradise Plains
A wife is no wife; spinster spinster remains;
These twain they did tarry so long to be wed
They might now prefer to stay happy instead.
Howe'er it befall them, Death's shadows once past,
They'll not laugh less sweetly who learn to laugh last.

SAM LOVER

Poor Sam Lover,
Now turf do cover;
His Wildness over.

JULES RAOUL DUBOIS

Here sleeps a Frenchman: Would I could
Grave in his language on this wood
His many virtues, grace and wit!
But then who'd read what I had writ?
Nay, when the tongues of Babel cease,
One word were all sufficient — Peace!

[750]

THE VIRGIN

Blessed Mary, pity me,
Who was a Virgin too, like Thee;
But had, please God, no little son
To shower a lifetime's sorrows on.

J.T.

Here's Jane Taylor,
Sweet Jane Taylor,
Dark,
Wild,
Dear Jane Taylor.

BE VERY QUIET

Be very quiet now:
A child's asleep
In this small cradle,
In this shadow deep!

HERE LIES — HOW SAD THAT HE IS NO MORE SEEN[1]

Here lies — how sad that he is no more seen —
    A child so sweet of mien
Earth must with Heaven have conspired to make him.
    As wise a manhood, 'tis said,
    Promised his lovely head;
    As gentle a nature
    His every youthful feature.
But now no sound, no word, no night-long bird —
Not even the daybreak lark can hope to awake him.

---

[1] This poem and the next seventeen are from 'Strangers and Pilgrims'.

EMMANUEL

Here lies a strangely serious child,
Called on earth Emmanuel.
Never to laughter reconciled,
This day-long peace must please him well;
He must, forsooth, in secret keep
Smiling — that he is so sound asleep.

THE WIDOW

Art thou a widow? Then, my Friend,
By this my tomb a moment spend,
To breathe a prayer o'er these cold stones
Which house-room give to weary bones.
And may God grant, when thou so lie,
Dust of thy loved one rest near by!

WILLIAM HACKLE

Here's an old Taylour, rest his eye:
    Needle and thredde put by.

SILAS DWIGHT

Though hautboy and basoon may break
This ancient peace with, Christians, Wake!
We should not stir, nor have, since when
God rest you, merry Gentlemen!
He of the icy hand us bid,
And laid us 'neath earth's coverlid.
Yet oft did Silas Dwight, who lies
Under this stone, in cheerful wise
Make Chancel wall and roof to ring
With Christmas Joys and Wassailing;
And still, maybe, may wind his horn
And stop out shrill, This Happy Morn.

WILLIAM PARR

He that lies here was mortal olde,
All but a hundred, if truth be told.
His pinpricke eyes, his hairless pate,
Crutch in hand, his shambling gaite —
All spake of Time: and Time's slow stroke,
That fells at length the stoutest Oke.
Of yeares so many now he is gone
There's nought to tell except this stone.
His name was Parr: decease did he
In Seventeen Hundred Sixty Three.

THREE SCORE YEARS I LIVED

Three score years I lived; and then
Looked for to live another ten.
But he who from the Hale and Quick
Robs the pure Oile that feeds the Wick
Chanced my enfeebled frame to mark —
Hence, this unutterable Darke.

SIR WILLOUGHBY BRANKSOME

Alas! Alack!
We come not back.
Adieu! and Welladay!
Yet, if we could,
No wise man would;
What more is left to say?

JOB HODSON AND HIS FOUR WIVES

Here rests in peace, Rebecca Anne,
Spouse of Job Hodson, Gentleman.

Here also Henrietta Grace,
Destined to lie in this same place.

And Jane, who three brief years of life
Did bear the honoured name of wife.

Here also Caroline (once Dove).
And him, the husband of the above.

[753]

TIMOTHY BLACKSTONE

O Death, have care
Only a Childe lies here.
A fear-full mite was he,
My last-born, *Timothy*.
Shroud then thy grewsome face,
When thou dost pass this place;
Lest his small ghoste should see,
And weep for me!

O.A.

Who: and How: and Where: and When —
Tell their stones of these poore men.
Grudge not then if one be bare
Of Who, and How, and When, and Where.

Such is nought to them who sigh
Still with their last breath, Why?

SON OF MAN[1]

Son of man, tell me,
Hast thou at any time lain in thick darkness,
Gazing up into a lightless silence,
A dark void vacancy,
Like the woe of the sea
In the unvisited places of the ocean?
And nothing but thine own frail sentience
To prove thee living?
Lost in this affliction of the spirit,
Did'st thou then call upon God
Of his infinite mercy to reveal to thee
Proof of his presence —
His presence and love for thee, exquisite creature of his
    creation?

[1] Title used in *The Burning-Glass and Other Poems*, 1945.

To show thee but some small devisal
Of his infinite compassion and pity, even though it were as
   fleeting
As the light of a falling star in a dewdrop?
Hast thou? O, if thou hast not,
Do it now; do it now; do it now!
Lest that night come which is sans sense, thought, tongue,
   stir, time, being,
And the moment is for ever denied thee,
Since thou art thyself as I am.

RICHARD HALLADAY

Each in place as God did 'gree
Here lie all ye Bones of me.
But what made them walke up right,
And, cladde in Flesh, a goodly Sight,
One of hostes of Living Men —
   Ask again — ask again!

O ONLIE ONE, FARE-WELL!

O onlie one, Fare-well!
Love hath not words to tell
How dear thou wert, and art,
To an emptie heart.

HE WHO HATH WALKED IN DARKEST NIGHT

He who hath walked in darkest night,
Stars and bright moon shut out from sight,
And Fiends around him cruel as sin,
Finds welcome even the coldest Inn.

SUSANNA HARBERT, SPINSTER

Let upon my bosom be
Only a bush of Rosemary;
Even though love forget, its breath
Will sweeten this ancient haunt of Death.

[755]

TRAVELLER, FORBEAR

Traveller, forbear
To brood too secretly on what is here!
　Death hath us in his care.
　There is no Fear.
But thou, in life — Oh, but I thee implore,
Stray thou amidst these dangerous shades no more!

N.F.

See now, if thou have any heed
For thine own soul, now hence make speed!
Here in this waste of briar and thorn
Sojourns one hungry and forlorn,
Self-murdered, unassoiled, unshriven,
Haunting these shades twixt Earth and Heaven.
O get thee gone; no biding make;
Lest the Unsleeping find the Wake!

STRANGER, A LIGHT I PRAY![1]

Stranger, a light I pray!
Not that I pine for day:
Only one beam of light —
　To show me Night!

I WAS AFRAID

I was afraid,
Death stilled my fears:
In sorrow I went,
Death dried my tears:
Solitary too,
Death came. And I
Shall no more want
For company.

[1] This poem and the remaining eleven in this section are from 'Winter'.

CORPORAL PYM

This quiet mound beneath
Lies Corporal Pym.
He had no fear of death;
Nor Death of him.

THOMAS LOGGE

Here lies Thomas Logge — A Rascally Dogge;
A poor useless creature — by choice as by nature;
Who never served God — for kindness or Rod;
Who, for pleasure or penny, — never did any
Work in his life — but to marry a Wife,
And live aye in strife:
And all this he says — at the end of his days
Lest some fine canting pen
Should be at him again.

JACOB TODD

Here be the ashes of Jacob Todd,
Sexton now in the land of Nod.
Digging he lived, and digging died,
Pick, mattock, spade, and nought beside.
Here oft at evening he would sit
Tired with his toil, and proud of it;
Watching the pretty Robins flit.
Now slumbers he as deep as they
He bedded for ye Judgement Day.

ALICE CASS

My mother bore me:
My father rejoiced in me:
The good priest blest me:
All people loved me:
But Death coveted me:
And free'd this body
Of its youthful soul.

[757]

ALICE RODD

Here lyeth our infant, Alice Rodd;
    She were so small,
    Scarce aught at all,
But a mere breath of Sweetness sent from God.

Sore we did weepe; our heartes on sorrow set.
    Till on our knees
    God sent us ease;
And now we weepe no more than we forget.

THE SPANIARD

Laid in this English ground
A Spaniard slumbers sound.
Well might the tender weep
To think how he doth sleep —
Strangers on either hand —
So far from his own land.
O! when the last Trump blow,
May Christ ordain that so
This friendless one arise
Under his native skies.
How bleak to wake, how dread a doom,
To cry his sins so far from home!

ANN POVERTY

Stranger, here lies
    Ann Poverty;
Such was her name
    And such was she.
May Jesu pity
    Poverty.

ASRAFEL HOLT

Here is buried a Miser:
Had he been wiser,
He would not have gone bare
Where Heaven's garmented are.
He'd have spent him a penny
To buy a Wax Taper;
And of Water a sprinkle
To quiet a poor Sleeper.
He'd have cried on his soul,
'O my Soul, moth & rust! —
What treasure shall profit thee
When thou art dust?'
'*Mene, Tekel, Upharsin!*'
God grant, in those Scales,
His Mercy avail us
When all Earth's else fails!

ISAAC MEEK[1]

Hook-nosed was I, loose-lipped; greed fixed its gaze
In my young eyes ere they knew brass from gold;
Doomed to the blazing market-place my days —
A sweated chafferer of the bought and sold.
Fawned on and spat at, flattered and decried —
One only thing men asked of me — my price.
I lived, detested; and deserted, died,
Scorned by the virtuous, and the jest of vice.
And now, behold, blest child of Christ, my worth;
Stoop close: I have inherited the earth!

O PASSER-BY, BEWARE!

O passer-by, beware!
Is the day fair? —
Yet unto evening shall the day spin on
And soon thy sun be gone;
Then darkness come,
And this, a narrow home.
Not that I bid thee fear:
Only, when thou at last lie here,
Bethink thee, there shall surely be
    Thy Self for company.

[1] As printed in *The Fleeting and Other Poems*, 1933.

Come Hither (new edition 1928)[1]

STARS[2]

If to the heavens you lift your eyes
When Winter reigns o'er our Northern skies,
And snow-cloud none the zenith mars,
At Yule-tide midnight these your stars:
Low in the South see bleak-blazing Sirius;
Above him hang Betelgeuse, Procyon wan;
Wild-eyed to West of him, Rigel and Bellatrix,
And rudd-red Aldebaran journeying on.
High in night's roof-tree beams twinkling Capella;
Vega and Deneb prowl low in the North;
Far to the East roves the Lion-heart, Regulus;
While the twin sons of Zeus to'rd the zenith gleam forth.

But when Midsummer Even in man's sleep-drowsed hours
Refreshes for daybreak its dew-bright flowers,
Though three of these Night Lights aloft remain,
For nine, if you gaze, you will gaze in vain.
Yet comfort find, for, far-shining there,
See golden Arcturus and cold Altaïr;
Crystalline Spica, and, strange to scan,
Blood-red Antares, foe to Man.

PRECIOUS STONES[2]

Ruby, amethyst, emerald, diamond,
Sapphire, sardonyx, fiery-eyed carbuncle,
      Jacynth, jasper, crystal a-sheen;
Topaz, turquoise, tourmaline, opal,
      Beryl, onyx and aquamarine: —
Marvel, O mortal! — their hue, lustre, loveliness,
Pure as a flower when its petals unfurl —
Peach-red carnelian, apple-green chrysoprase,
      Amber and coral and orient pearl!

---

[1] First published in 1923, with the sub-title, 'A collection of rhymes and poems for the young of all ages'.
[2] First published as part of note 466 in *Come Hither*, 1928, without titles. The titles in *Old Rhymes and New*, 1932, were 'Christmas Stars' and 'A Bag of Gems'.

On the Edge: Short Stories (1930)

THERE RODE A MILLER ON A HORSE[1]

There rode a Miller on a horse,
A jake on a jackass could do no worse —
With a Hey, and a Hey, lollie, lo!
Meal on his chops and his whiskers too —
The devil sowed tares, where the tare-crop grew —
With a Hey, and a Hey, lollie, lo!

MY MIDNIGHT LAMP BURNS DIM WITH SHAME[2]

My midnight lamp burns dim with shame,
    In Heaven the moon is low;
Sweet sharer of its secret flame,
    Arise, and go!

Haste, for dawn's envious gaping grave
    Bids thee not linger here;
Though gone is all I am, and have —
    Thy ghost once absent, dear.

THERE WAS SWEET WATER ONCE

There was sweet water once,
Where in my childhood I
Watched for the happy innocent nonce
Day's solemn clouds float by.

O age blur not that glass;
Kind Heaven still shed thy rain;
Even now sighs shake me as I pass
Those gentle haunts again.

[1] From 'A Recluse', which was first published in Lady Cynthia Asquith's *Ghost Book*, London, 1926.
[2] This poem and the remaining fourteen poems in the book are from 'The Green Room', which was first published in *Two Tales* in a limited edition of 250 copies, London, 1925. All the poems in the story were supposed to have been written by a young woman with the initials E.F. who had killed herself.

LULLAY, MY HEART, AND FIND THY PEACE

Lullay, my heart, and find thy peace
  Where thine old solitary pastures lie;
Their light, their dews need never cease,
  Their sunbeams from on high.

Lullay, and happy dream, nor roam,
  Wild though the hills may shine,
Once there, thou soon would'st long for home,
  As I for mine!

GOODBYE[1]

Do you see? Oh, do you see? —
Speak, and some inward self that accent knows
  Which bids the East its rose disclose
  And daybreak wake in me.

Do you hear? Oh, do you hear? —
This heart whose pulse like menacing night-bird cries?
Dark, utter dark, most dear, is in these eyes,
  When gaunt Goodbye draws near.

THE LOOKING-GLASS AND THE GARDEN[2]

This is my window: here I see
The self within my dazzled eyes,
To secret garden summoning me,
And thine its radiant skies.

Come soon, that twilight dusky hour,
When thou thyself shalt enter in
And take thy fill of every flower,
Since thine they've always been.

[1] As printed in *O Lovely England and Other Poems*, 1953.
[2] A late, revised version of the poem, with a title, found in typescript form, and clearly intended for publication (like 'Goodbye' and 'Have Done!'). The original first stanza read thus:
  '"There is a garden in her face:"
  My face! Woe's me were *that* my all! —
  Nay, but my *self*, though thine its grace,
  Thy fountain is, thy peach-bloomed wall.'

No rue? No Myrrh? No nightshade? Oh
Tremble not, spirit! All is well.
For Love's is that lovely garden, and so
There only pleasures dwell.

WHEN YOU ARE GONE, AND I'M ALONE

When you are gone, and I'm alone,
From every object that I see
Its secret source of life is flown:
All things look cold and strange to me.

Even what I use — my rings, my gloves,
My parasol, the clothes I wear —
'Once she was happy; now she loves!
Once young,' they cry, 'now carked with care!'

I wake and watch when the moon is here —
A shadow tracks me on. And I —
Darker than any shadow — fear
Her fabulous inconstancy.

That sphinx, the Future, marks its prey;
I who was ardent, sanguine, free,
Starve now in fleshly cell all day —
And yours the rusting key.

YOUR MADDENING FACE BEFOOLS MY EYES

Your maddening face befools my eyes,
    Your hand — I wake to feel —
Lost in deep midnight's black surmise —
    Its touch my veins congeal.

What peace for me in star or moon?
    What solace in nightingale!
They tell me of the lost and gone —
    And dawn completes the tale.

YOUR HATE I SEE, AND CAN ENDURE, NAY, *MUST*

Your hate I see, and can endure, nay, *must* —
Endure the stark denial of your love;
It is your *silence*, like a cankering rust,
That I am perishing of.

What reck you of the blinded hours I spend
Crouched on my knees beside a shrouded bed?
Grief even for the loveliest has an end;
No end in one whose soul it is lies dead.

I watch the aged who've dared the cold slow ice
That creeps from limb to limb, from sense to sense,
Yet never dreamed this also is the price
Which youth must pay for a perjured innocence.

Yours that fond lingering lesson. Be content!
Not one sole moment of its course I rue.
The all I had was little. Now it's spent.
Spit on the empty purse: 'tis naught to you.

LINES ON OPHELIA

She found an exit from her life;
She to an earthly green-room sped
Where parched-up souls distraught with strife
Sleep and are comforted.

Hamlet! I know that dream-drugged eye,
That self-coiled melancholic mien!
Hers was a happy fate — to die:
Mine — her foul Might-have-been.

TO-MORROW WAITS ME AT MY GATE

To-morrow waits me at my gate,
While all my yesterdays swarm near;
And one mouth whines, Too late, too late
And one is dumb with fear.

[766]

Was this the all that life could give
Me — who from cradle hungered on,
Body and soul aflame, to *live* —
Giving my all — and then be gone?

O sun in heaven, to don that shroud,
When April's cuckoo thrilled the air!
Light thou no more the fields I loved.
Be only winter there!

HAVE DONE![1]

Have done with grieving, idiot heart!
If it so be that Love has wings,
I with my shears will find an art
    To still his flutterings.

Wrench off that bandage too, will I,
And show the Imp he's blind indeed.
Hot irons shall prove my mastery;
    He shall not weep but bleed.

And when he is dead and cold as stone,
Then in his mother's books I'll con
The lesson none need learn alone,
    And, callous as both, play on.

AND WHEN AT LAST I JOURNEY

And when at last I journey where
All thought of you I must resign,
Will the least memory of me be fair,
Or will you even my ghost malign?

I plead for nothing. Nay, Time's tooth —
That frets the very soul away —
May prove at last your slanders *truth*,
And me the Slut you say.

[1] As printed in *O Lovely England and Other Poems*, 1953.

ONCE IN KIND ARMS, ALAS, YOU HELD ME CLOSE

Once in kind arms, alas, you held me close;
Sweet to its sepals was the unfolding rose.
Why, then — though wind-blown, hither, thither,
I languish still, rot on, and wither
Yet *live*, God only knows.

ESTHER! CAME WHISPER FROM MY BED

Esther! came whisper from my bed.
Answer me, Esther — are you there?
'Twas waking self to self that's dead
Called on the empty stair.

Stir not that pit; she is lost and gone.
A Jew decoyed her to her doom.
Sullenly knolls her passing bell
Mocking me in the gloom.

LAST NIGHT[1]

Last night, as I sat here alone,
Thimble on finger, needle and thread,
Light dimming as the dusk drew on,
I dreamed that I was dead.

Motionless, waxen, inert, ice-cold,
My black hair plaited, hands on breast,
Eyes shut, mouth stilled — beneath the mould,
I sank from rest to rest,

[1] A late, revised version of the poem, with a title, found in typescript form, and clearly intended for publication. The original version read thus:

Last evening, as I sat alone —
Thimble on finger, needle and thread —
Light dimming as the dusk drew on,
I dreamed that I was dead.

Like wildering timeless plains of snow
Which bitter winds to ice congeal
The world stretched far as sight could go
'Neath skies as hard as steel.

From dark to dark: — what mattered it?
This body — once all thine — no more,
With pangs unutterably sweet,
    Thy mastery could restore.

And you I loved, who once loved me,
Who shook with woe this mortal frame —
Were sunken to such an infamy
    That when I called your name,

Its knell so chilled my senseless clay
That my lost spirit, lurking near,
Wailed, like the damned, and fled away,
    And woke me — stark with fear.

Lost in that nought of night I stood
And watched my body — brain and breast
In dreadful anguish — in the mould
    Grope to'rd its final rest.

Its craving dreams of sense dropped down
Like crumbling maggots in the sod:
Spectral, I stood; all longing gone,
    Exiled from hope and God.

And you I loved, who once loved me,
And shook with pangs this mortal frame,
Were sunk to such an infamy
    That when I called your name,

Its knell so racked that sentient clay
That my lost spirit lurking near,
Wailed, like the damned, and fled away —
    And woke me, stark with *Fear*.

The Lord Fish [1933]

THE PARCHMENT

Thou who wouldst dare
To free this Fair
From fish's shape,
And yet escape
O'er sea and land
My vengeful hand: —
Smear this fish-fat on thy heart,
And prove thyself the jack thou art!

With tail and fin
Then plunge thou in!
And thou shalt surely have thy wish
To see the great, the good Lord Fish!

Swallow his bait in haste, for he
Is master of all wizardry.
And if he gentle be inclined,
He'll show thee where to seek and find
The Magic Unguent that did make
This human maid a fish-tail take.

But have a care
To make short stay
Where wields his sway,
The Great Lord Fish;
'Twill be too late
To moan your fate
When served with sauce
Upon his dish!

The Wind Blows Over (1936)

AND THERE, MAYBE TO MOCK THE EYE[1]

And there, maybe to mock the eye,
Goes fluttering by a butterfly.
But mark, dear Pilgrim, mark with me,
How *rational* is the honey bee!

THERE WERE LEAVES ON THE BRANCHES LIKE SILVER[1]

There were leaves on the branches like silver,
And dew thick as frost on the grass,
And nought but the moon in the shimmery-shammery,
And me staring out through the glass.

TOO-WHIT OR TOO-WHOO[1]

Too-whit, or *too-whoo,*
Come now, or come soon,
You won't miss the sun
If you look at the moon.

IT'S JOYS AND CARES AND STRIFE[1]

It's joys and cares and stri-i-ife
I'm singing to you of,
And some they call it li-i-ife,
And some they call it lov.

---

[1] From the short story called 'Miss Miller'.

[773]

COME WHAT COME MAY[1]

Come what come may; go what go will,
There *is* such a thing as must.
Then why be philo-so-sophical
So long as one tries to be just?

IT MIGHT BE A LUMP OF AMBER[1]

It might be a lump of amber, ma'am,
It might be a stick of coral;
But what we have to remember, ma'am,
Is to keep our eye on the moral.

---

[1] From 'Miss Miller'.

Pleasures and Speculations (1940)[1]

BOOKS

Books! —
        for the heart to brood on; books for peace;
From the dull droning of the world release;
A music snared, a spring distilled of Spring;
At one spare board to feast on Everything! —
Plain, wholesome, racy, various and rare;
And yet — like Bird of Paradise — on air.

Books! — whose sweet witchery retrieves again
All that the heart of childhood may retain;
Its wonder, ecstasy; grief, terror, woes —
Salved by the leechcraft age alone bestows;
All youthful braveries, too, Time plucked away,
When Hope's clear taper could out-dazzle day.
Books — to intoxicate, to storm, to press
The soul insatiate to unearthliness;
To summon heaven where an attic high
Gleams in communion with a starless sky;
To entice pure Eros from his realm above,
To kneel, palm arched o'er lute, and sing of love;
To make men smell of laurel, and to be
Of wild romance the rue and rosemary;
And, with a truth by art alone divined,
To bare the close-kept secrets of the mind.

Books — laced with humour, and shot through with wit,
Pungent in irony, by wisdom lit,
Life to reveal, and purge, and quicken it,
Probe and explore, dissect and scrutinise,
Mirror its real, unmask its sophistries,
And leave it, fearless, where seraphic Death
Sits with his sickle, and none answereth.

Thought, fleet as errant fancy, comes and goes
As transient as the light upon a rose;
The visioned eye for but a moment sees

[1] A 48-line version of this poem appeared in *The Bookman*, July 1906.

All heart hath craved for, in life's long unease;
Imagination, on its earth-bound quest,
Seeks in the infinite its finite rest;
Wrapt close in dark cocoon the Ego weaves
What of philosophy the mind conceives;
And night-long slumber, deep as Lethe's stream,
Rears evanescently the walls of dream:
And — like a dial by the sun forsook —
Their one enduring refuge is a book.

Eden the radiant, Crete, Athens, Rome
Shared have with Babylon the self-same doom,
All have to little more than paper come.
The age-long story of how men plan, act, think —
To be at last dependent upon ink!
Monarch and conqueror, Caesar, Napoleon —
Stilled are their trumpets; here they echo on:
Ay, Tyrant! ink alone, thy spectre gone,
Will blacken thy infamy — else, oblivion.
What, though long years the peaceful poet dote,
How thin a trickle keeps his name afloat! —
One line, of myriads — for Dull to quote.
Still, *one* — when most men from life's wheat-tare crop
Win no more record than a mute full-stop.

Stones fall, brass cankers, mummy thins to dust,
The voiceless grave stills frenzy, pride and lust;
The very gods that mete out shame and fame,
Save for the written word, were but a name.
All the bright blood by fevered passion spilt
Finds reflex only in unfading gilt;
And noble selfless friendship — nought again
But the pure vellum which that gold doth stain.
Helen's long centuries of peerless praise
Else had the wonder been of nine brief days;
An empty rumour, Sappho, Socrates,
Wind-spoil of nights foregone — O leafless trees!
Shakespeare a crumbling clot of wisdom left
In old men's cranies, of all else bereft.
The Star, Gethsemane, the stock of wood,
The garbled rune of an immortal good;
Saints, martyrs, mystics — Oh, what dust would lie
On their lean bones, sole-shrined in memory!
Nay, earth's strange Universe — that hive of suns —
Books gone, the enigma were of brute and dunce;

[776]

And Man — scarce witting of his grace and power,
Gone like a sunbeam in a winter hour;
Since mind unaided, though it knowledge breeds,
And blooms in splendour, yet can leave few seeds;
And memory, like wasting waterbrooks,
Needs reservoirs to rest in. These are books.

Abiding joy is theirs; rich solitude,
Where mortal cares a while no more intrude;
Here, by the day's sweet light, or candle-beam,
The waking sense finds solace in a dream;
And self flits out, like wild bird from a cage,
To preen its wings in a lost hermitage —
Gardens of bliss, whose well-springs never stay,
Where founts Elysian leap and fall and play;
And lo, a nimbus, from a further sun
Colours them with enchantments not their own.
Yet every word is void of life and light
Until the soul within transfigures it —
Then sighs, for rapture, wildly pines to see
Who wakes this music, under what strange tree —
And pines in vain; for it is Poetry.

2. VERSES WRITTEN TO ILLUSTRATIONS

A Child's Day:
A Book of Rhymes (1912)[1]

I SANG A SONG TO ROSAMOND ROSE

I sang a song to Rosamond Rose
Only the wind in the twilight knows:
I sang a song to Jeanetta Jennie,
She flung from her window a silver penny:
I sang a song to Matilda May,
She took to her heels and ran away:
I sang a song to Susannah Sue,
She giggled the whole of the verses through:

But nevertheless, as sweet as I can,
I'll sing a song to Elizabeth Ann —
The same little Ann as there you see
Smiling as happy as happy can be.
And all that my song is meant to say
Is just what she did one long, long day,
With her own little self to play with only,
Yet never once felt the least bit lonely.

SOFTLY, DROWSILY

Softly, drowsily,
Out of sleep;
Into the world again
Ann's eyes peep;
Over the pictures
Across the walls
One little quivering
Sunbeam falls.
A thrush in the garden
Seems to say,
Wake, little Ann,
'Tis day, 'tis day!
Faint sweet breezes
The casement stir,
Breathing of pinks
And lavender.

[1] See Bibliographical Appendix, p. 890.

[779]

At last from her pillow,
With cheeks bright red,
Up comes her round little
Tousled head;
And out she tumbles
From her warm bed.

LITTLE BIRDS BATHE

Little birds bathe
In the sunny dust.
Whether they want to,
Or not, they *must*.
Seal and Walrus
And Polar Bear
One green icy
Wash-tub share.
Alligator,
Nor Hippopot-
Amus ever
His bath forgot.
Out of his forest
The Elephant tramps
To squirt himself
In his gloomy swamps.
On crackling fins
From the deep sea fly
Flying-fish into
The air to dry.
Silver Swans
In shallows green
Their dew-bespangled
Pinions preen.
And all day long
Wash Duck and Drake
In their duckweed pond —
For washing's sake.
So, in her lonesome,
Slippety, bare,
Elizabeth Ann's
Splash — splashing there;
And now from the watery
Waves amonje
Stands slooshing herself
With that 'normous sponge.

Puma, Panther, Leopard, and Lion
Nothing but green grass have to dry on;
Seals and Walruses in a trice
Flick their water-drops into Ice;

Back to his forests the Elephant swings
Caked in mud against bites and stings;
As for the plump Hippopotamus,
He steams himself dry to save a fuss;
And the bird that cries to her mate Quack, Quack!
Is oily by nature if not by knack,
So the water pearls off *her* beautiful back.

But sailing the world's wide ocean round,
In a big broad bale from Turkey bound,
All for the sake of Elizabeth Ann
This towel's been sent by a Mussulman,
And with might and main she must rub — rub — rub —
Till she's warm and dry from her morning tub.

NOW TWELVE ABOVE

Now twelve above,
And twice six beneath,
She must polish and polish
Her small, sharp teeth.
The picture, you see,
Entirely fails
To show how nicely
She's nipped her nails.
But it's perfectly clear
With what patient care
She has drawn back neatly
Her smooth brown hair.
All *tiresome* things,
I'm bound to say,
For beasts just scratch
Their claws away.
And never from Egypt
Up to Rome
Walked monkey using
An ivory comb.
But there, Ann dear,

[781]

You'd rather be
A slim-tailed mermaid
In the sea:
And she has only
One small care —
To sleek and sleek and sleek
Her hair.

HERE ALL WE SEE

Here all we see
Is Ann's small nose,
A smile, two legs,
And ten pink toes,
Neatly arranged
In two short rows.

THE QUEEN OF ARABIA, UANJINEE

The Queen of Arabia, Uanjinee,
Slaves to dress her had thirty-three;
Eleven in scarlet, eleven in rose,
Eleven in orange, as every one knows;
And never was lady lovelier than she —
The Queen of Arabia, Uanjinee.

Yet — though, of course, 'twould be vain to tell a-
Nother word about Cinderella —
Except for a Mouse on the chimney shelf,
She put on her slippers quite — quite by herself,
And I can't help thinking the greater pleasure
Is to dress in haste, and look lovely at leisure.
Certainly summer or winter, Ann
Always dresses as quick as she can.

AND THERE SHE IS
(ON THE OTHER SIDE)

And there she is (on the other side),
The last button buttoned, the last tape tied.
Her silky hair has perched upon it
A flat little two-stringed linen bonnet.
Each plump brown leg that comes out of her frock
Hides its foot in a shoe and a sock.

[782]

But what we wear — O dearie me! —
Is naught but a patch upon what we *be*.
And rags and tatters often hide
A brave little body bunched up inside.
And one thing's certain; nobody knows
The Good from the Wicked by just their Clothes.

ENGLAND OVER

England over,
And all June through,
Daybreak's peeping
At half-past two.
Roses and dewdrops
Begin to be
Wonderful lovely
At half-past three.
Gulls and cormorants
On the shore
Squabble for fishes
At half-past four.
The great Queen Bee
In her golden hive
Is sleek with nectar
By half-past five.
The ravening birds
In the farmer's ricks
Are hungry for luncheon
At half-past six.
While all the pigs
From York to Devon,
Have finished their wash
Before half-past seven.
But Elizabeth Ann
Gets up so late
She has only begun
At half-past eight
To gobble her porridge up —
Hungry soul —
Tucked up in a bib,
Before her bowl.

THOUSANDS OF YEARS AGO

Thousands of years ago,
  In good King George's isles,
Forest — to forest — to forest spread,
  For miles and miles and miles.
All kinds of beasts roamed there,
  Drank of Teviot and Thames,
Beasts of all shapes and sizes and colours,
  But without any names.
And snug and shag in his coat,
  With green little eyes aglare,
Trod on his paws, with tapping of claws,
  The beast men now call Bear;
Lurched on his legs and stole
  Out of the rifts in the trees
All the sweet oozy summer-sun comb
  Of the poor little bees;
Sat in the glades and caught
  Flies by the hour,
Munched 'em up, just like a dog,
  Sweet with the sour.

But Time, she nods her head —
  Like flights of the butterfly,
Mammoths fade through her hours;
  And Man draws nigh.
And it's ages and ages ago;
  Felled are the forests, in ruin;
Gone are the thickets where lived on his lone
  Old Bruin.

WHEN SAFE INTO THE FIELDS ANN GOT

When safe into the fields Ann got,
She chose a dappled, shady spot,
Beside a green, rush-bordered pool,
Where, over water still and cool,
The little twittering birds did pass,
Like shadows in a looking-glass.
Ann slily looked this way, and that;
And then took off her shady hat.
She peeped — and peeped; off came her frock,
Followed in haste by shoe and sock.
Then softly, slowly, down she went

[784]

To where the scented rushes bent,
And all among the fishes put
Like a great giant, her little foot,
And paddled slowly to and fro
Each little tiny thirsty toe.
Then dabbling in the weeds she drew
Her fingers the still water through,
Trying in vain with groping hand
To coax a stickleback to land;
But when she had nearly housed him in,
Away he'd dart on flickering fin,
The softly wavering stalks between.

WHEN SHE WAS IN HER GARDEN[1]

When she was in her garden,
And playing with her ball,
Ann heard a distant music
On the other side of the wall —
A far-off singing, shrill and sweet,
In the still and sunshine day,
And these the words were of the song
That voice did sing and say: —

'Happy, happy it is to be
Where the greenwood hangs o'er the dark blue sea;
To roam in the moonbeams clear and still
And dance with the elves
Over dale and hill;
To taste their cups, and with them roam
The fields for dewdrops and honeycomb.
Climb then, and come, as quick as you can,
And dwell with the fairies, Elizabeth Ann!'

Ann held her ball, and listened;
The faint song died away;
And it seemed it was a dream she'd dreamed
In the hot and sunshine day;
She heard the whistling of the birds,

[1] Stanzas 2 and 4 were included in *Down-Adown-Derry*, 1922, as a separate poem entitled 'Happy, Happy it is To Be'.

The droning of the bees;
And then once more the singing came,
And now the words were these: —

'Never, never, comes tear or sorrow,
In the mansions old where the fairies dwell;
But only the harping of their sweet harp-strings,
And the lonesome stroke of a distant bell,
Where upon hills of thyme and heather,
The shepherd sits with his wandering sheep;
And the curlew wails, and the skylark hovers
Over the sand where the conies creep;
Climb then, and come, as quick as you can,
And dwell with the fairies, Elizabeth Ann!'

And just as Ann a-tiptoe crept,
Under the old green wall,
To where a stooping cherry tree
Grew shadowy and tall;
Above the fairy's singing
Hollow and shrill and sweet,
That seemed to make her heart stand still,
And then more wildly beat,
Came Susan's voice a-calling 'Ann!
Come quick as you are able;
And wash your grubby hands, my dear,
For dinner's on the table!'

THERE WAS AN OLD WOMAN
WHO LIVED IN THE FENS

There was an old woman who lived in the Fens
Who had for her breakfast two nice fat hens.

There was an old woman who lived at Licke
Whatever she gobbled up gobbled up quick.

There was an old woman who lived at Bow
Who waited until her guests should go.

There was an old woman who lived at Ware
Supped on red-currant jelly and cold jugged hare.

There was an old woman who lived at Bury
Who always ate in a violent hurry.

There was an old woman who lived at Flint
Fed her sheep on parsley, her lambs on mint.

There was an old woman who lived at Cork
Lunched with her nevvy on pease and pork.

There was an old woman who lived at Greenwich
Went out with a candle to cut herself spinach.

There was an old woman who lived at Hull
Who never stopped eating till she was full.

There was an old woman who lived at Diss
Who couldn't abide greens, gristle, or grease.

There was an old woman who lived at Thame
Who ate up the courses just as they came.

There was an old woman who lived at Tring
At meals did nothing but laugh and sing.

There was an old woman who lived at Steep
Who still munched on though fast asleep.

There was an old woman who lived at Wick
Whose teeth did nothing but clash and click.

There was an old woman who lived at Lundy
Always had hash for dinner on Monday.

There was an old woman who lived at Dover
Threw to her pigs whatever was over.

THIS LITTLE MORSEL
OF MORSELS HERE

This little morsel of morsels here —
Just what it is is not quite clear:
It might be pudding, it might be meat,
Cold, or hot, or salt, or sweet;
Baked, or roasted, or broiled, or fried;
Bare, or frittered, or puddinged, or pied;
Cooked in a saucepan, jar, or pan —
But it's all the same to Elizabeth Ann.
For when one's hungry it doesn't much matter
So long as there's *something* on one's platter.

Now fie! O fie! How sly a face!
Half greedy joy, and half disgrace;
O foolish Ann, O greedy finger,
To long for that forbidden ginger!

[787]

O Ann, the story I could tell! —
What horrid, horrid things befell
Two gluttonous boys who soft did creep,
While Cook was in her chair asleep,
Into a cupboard, there to make
A feast on stolen tipsy-cake —
Which over night they had hid themselves,
On one of her store cupboard shelves;
They ate so much, they ate so fast,
They both were sadly stuffed at last.
Drowsy and stupid, blowsed and blown,
In sluggish sleep they laid them down,
And soon rose up a stifled snore
From where they huddled on the floor.
And, presently, Cook, passing by,
Her cupboard door ajar did spy,
And that all safe her stores might be,
Turned with her thumb the noiseless key.
Night came with blackest fears to wrack
Those greedy knaves (named Dick and Jack).
They woke; and in the stuffy gloom
Waited in vain for Cook to come.
They dared not knock, or kick, or shout,
Not knowing *who* might be about.

The days dragged on. Their parents said,
'Poor Dick and Jack; they must be dead!'
Hungrier and hungrier they grew;
They searched the darksome cupboard through;
Candles, and soda, salt, and string,
Soap, glue — they ate up everything:
Nothing but shadows they seemed to be,
Gnawing a stick of wood for tea.
At length, at last, alas! alack!
Jack looked at Dick; and Dick at Jack;
And in his woe each famished brother
Turned in the dusk and ate the other.

So when Cook came to open the door,
Nothing was there upon the floor;
As with her candle she stood there,
Ceiling to floor the place was bare;
Not even a little heap of bones
That had been two fat brothers once!

And see! That foolish Ann's forgot
To put the cover on the pot;
And also smeared — the heedless ninny —
Her sticky fingers on her pinny.
And, O dear me! without a doubt,
Mamma has found the culprit out.
And Ann is weeping many a tear;
And shame has turned her back, poor dear;
Lonely and angry, in disgrace,
She's hiding her poor mottled face.
But ginger now will tempt in vain,
She'll never, never taste again.

ANN, UPON THE STROKE OF THREE

Ann, upon the stroke of three,
Half-way 'twixt dinner-time and tea,
Cosily tucked in her four-legged chair,
With nice clean hands and smooth brushed hair,
In some small secret nursery nook,
Sits with her big Picture-book.

There Puss in Boots, with sidelong eye
And bushy tail goes mincing by;

Peering into an empty cupboard
With her old Dog stoops Mother Hubbard;

Beside a bushy bright-green Wood
Walks with the Wolf Red Ridinghood;

In their small cottage the Three Bears,
Each at his bowl of Porridge stares;

There's striking Clock — and scampering Mouse;
The King of Hearts' cool Counting-house;

There a Fine Lady rides all day,
But never, never rides away;

While Jack and Jill for ever roll;
And drinks to his Fiddlers Old King Cole.

And though Ann's little busy head
Can't quite get down from A to Z,
She is content to sit and look
At her bright-coloured Picture-book.

[789]

AS SOON AS EVER TWILIGHT COMES

As soon as ever twilight comes,
  Ann creeps upstairs to pass,
With one tall candle, just an hour
  Before her looking-glass.
She rummages old wardrobes in,
  Turns dusty boxes out;
And nods and curtseys, dances, sings,
  And hops and skips about.
Her candle's lean long yellow beam
  Shines softly in the gloom,
And through the window's gathering night
  Stars peep into the room.

Ages and ages and ages ago,
Ann's great-grandmother dressed just so;
In a big poke-bonnet, a Paisley shawl,
Climbed into her coach to make a call;
And over the cobble-stones jogged away,
To drink with her daughter a dish of tay.

Then nice little boys wore nankeen breeches;
And demure little girls with fine silk stitches
Learned to make samplers of beasts and birds
And ever so many most difficult words.
Then Anns and Matildas and Sams and Dicks
Were snoring in blankets long before six.
And every night with a tallow candle,
And a warming-pan with a four-foot handle,
The maids came up to warm the bed
(And burnt a great hole in the sheet instead).
Then pretty maids blushed, and said, 'My nines!'
At hundreds of thousands of Valentines.
Then never came May but danced between
Robin and Marion, Jack-in-the-Green;
Then saged and onioned, and stewed in its juice,
To table on Michaelmas Day sailed Goose;
Gunpowder Treason and Plot to remember
Bonfires blazed on the fifth of November;
And never the Waits did a-carolling go
In less than at least a yard of snow.

So — poor little Ann a sigh must smother
Because she isn't her great-grandmother.

NOW, DEAR ME!

Now, dear me!
What's this we see?
A dreadful G —
H — O — S — T!
A-glowering with
A chalk-white face
Out of some dim
And dismal place.
Oh, won't poor Nurse
Squeal out, when she
Comes up, that dreadful
Shape to see!
She'll pant and say,
'O la! Miss Ann,
I thought you was
A bogey-man!
Now! look at them
Untidy clo'es!
And, did you ever,
What a nose!
If you was in
A smock, Miss Ann,
They'd take you for
The Miller's man.
To see the mischief
You have done,
And me not twenty minutes gone!'

NOW, MY DEAR, FOR
GRACIOUS SAKE

'Now, my dear, for gracious sake,
Eat up this slice of currant cake;
Though, certain sure, you'll soon be screaming
For me to come — and find you dreaming.
In *my* young days in bed we'd be
Once we had swallowed down our tea.
And cake! — we'd dance if mother spread
A scrap of butter on our bread!
Except my brother, little Jack,
Who was, poor mite, a humptyback.
But there! times change; he's grown a man;
And I'm no chick meself, Miss Ann.

[791]

Now, don't 'ee move a step from here,
I shan't be gone for long, my dear!'

But soon as Nurse's back was turned
Ann's idle thumbs for mischief yearned.
See now, those horrid scissors, oh,
If they should slip an inch or so!
If Ann should jog or jerk — suppose
They snipped off her small powdery nose!
If she should sneeze, or cough, or laugh,
They might divide her quite in half;
They might this best of little daughters
Slice into four quite equal quaughters.
And though she plagues her nurse, poor soul,
She'd much prefer Miss Mischief whole,
Would wring her hands in sad distraction
O'er each belov'd but naughty fraction.

This then had been our last, last rhyme,
Had Nurse not just returned in time.
For when Ann heard her on the stairs
She hid in haste those wicked shears;
And there as meek as 'Little Jimmie'
Was seated smiling in her shimmie.

THE KING IN SLUMBER WHEN HE LIES DOWN

The King in slumber when he lies down
Hangs up in a cupboard his golden crown;
The Lord High Chancellor snores in peace
Out of his Garter and Golden Fleece;
No Plenipotentiary lays him flat
Till he's dangled on bedpost his gold Cockhat;
And never to attic has Page-boy mounted
Before his forty-four buttons are counted;

But higgledy-piggledy
Slovenly Ann
Jumps out of her clothes
As fast as she can;
And with frock, sock, shoe,
Flung anywhere,
Slips from dressedupedness
Into her bare.

Now, just as when the day began,
Without one clo', sits little Ann,
A-toasting in this scant attire
Her cheeks before the nursery fire.

Golden palaces there she sees,
With fiery fountains, flaming trees;
Through darkling arch and smouldering glen
March hosts of little shimmering men,
To where beneath the burning skies
A blazing salamander lies,
Breathing out sparks and smoke the while
He watches them with hungry smile.

THE WORLD OF DREAM[1]

Now, through the dusk
With muffled bell
The Dustman comes
The world to tell,
Night's elfin lanterns
Burn and gleam
In the twilight, wonderful
World of Dream.

Hollow and dim
Sleep's boat doth ride,
Heavily still
At the waterside.
Patter, patter,
The children come,
Yawning and sleepy,
Out of the gloom.

Like droning bees
In a garden green,
Over the thwarts
They clamber in.
And lovely Sleep
With long-drawn oar
Turns away
From the whispering shore.

[1] Title in *Down-Adown-Derry*, 1922.

Over the water
Like roses glide
Her hundreds of passengers
Packed inside,
To where in her garden
Tremble and gleam
The harps and lamps
Of the World of Dream.

LOB LIE BY THE FIRE[1]

He squats by the fire
On his three-legged stool,
When all in the house
With slumber are full.

And he warms his great hands,
Hanging loose from each knee,
And he whistles as soft
As the night wind at sea.

For his work now is done;
All the water is sweet;
He has turned each brown loaf,
And breathed magic on it.

The milk in the pan,
And the bacon on beam
He has 'spelled' with his thumb,
And bewitched has the dream.

Not a mouse, not a moth,
Not a spider but sat,
And quaked as it wondered
What next he'd be at.

But his heart, O, his heart —
It belies his great nose;
And at gleam of his eye
Not a soul would suppose

He had stooped with great thumbs,
And big thatched head,
To tuck his small mistress
More snugly in bed.

[1] Also included in *Down-Adown-Derry*, 1922.

Who would think, now, a throat
So lank and so thin
Might make birds seem to warble
In the dream she is in!

Now, hunched by the fire,
While the embers burn low,
He nods until daybreak,
And at daybreak he'll go.

Soon the first cock will 'light
From his perch and point high
His beak at the Ploughboy
Grown pale in the sky;

And crow will he shrill;
Then, meek as a mouse,
Lob will rouse up and shuffle
Straight out of the house.

His supper for breakfast;
For wages his work;
And to warm his great hands
Just an hour in the mirk.

SADLY, O SADLY, THE SWEET BELLS
OF BADDELEY[1]

Sadly, O sadly, the sweet bells of Baddeley
Played in their steeples when Robin was gone,
    Killed by an arrow,
    Shot by Cock Sparrow,
Out of a Maybush, fragrant and wan.

Grievèdly, grievèdly, tolled distant Shieveley,
When the Dwarfs laid poor Snow-white asleep on
    the hill,
    Drowsed by an apple,
    The Queen, sly and subtle,
Had cut with her knife on the blossomy sill.

[1] Also included in *Down-Adown-Derry*, 1922.

THIS BRIEF DAY NOW OVER

This brief day now over;
Life's but a span.
Tell how my heart aches,
Tell how my heart breaks,
To bid now farewell
To Elizabeth Ann.

Lullay O, lullaby,
Sing this sad roundelay,
Muted the strings;
Since Sorrow began,
The World's said goodbye, Ann,
And so too, must I, Ann;
Child of one brief day,
Elizabeth Ann.

Flora:
A Book of Drawings (1919)[1]

MISERICORDIA!

Misericordia!
Weep with me.
Waneth the dusk light;
Strange the tree;
In regions barbarous
Lost are we.

I, Glycera,
And Silas here,
Who hath hid in sleep
His eyes from fear;
Wan-wide are mine
With a tear.

Misericordia!
Was I born
Only to pluck
Disaster's thorn?
Only to stray
Forlorn?

MORNING TOILET

'Tis sure eleven by the sun,
And now, her morning toilet done,
Perfumed and powdered fair,
My Madame Dives, smooth and bland —
The richest lady in the land —
Reclines upon her chair.

Languidly hangs her idle wrist
In those great beads of amethyst;
Steadily her head
Turns its two eyes, as if to say,
Well, well, and here's another day
To fatten and be fed.

[1] See Bibliographical Appendix, p. 892.

Honeycomb, cream and dainty fruit
Have plumped her cheek, and silked her throat
And ringleted that wig.
And only princes' minions know
Where blooms like these are made to blow —
A thousand crowns a sprig.

LISTEN!

Quiet your faces; be crossed every thumb;
Fix on me deep your eyes;
And out of my mind a story shall come,
Old, and lovely, and wise.

Old as the pebbles that fringe the cold seas,
Lovely as apples in rain;
Wise as the King who learned of the bees,
Then learned of the emmets again.

Old as the fruits that in mistletoe shine;
Lovely as amber, as snow;
Wise as the fool who when care made to pine
Cried, Hey and fol lol, lilly lo!

Old as the woods rhyming Thomas snuffed sweet,
When pillion he rode with the Queen:
Lovely as elf-craft; wise as the street
Where the roofs of the humble are seen. . . .

Ay, there's a stirring, there's wind in the bough;
Hearken, a harp I hear ring:
Like a river of water my story shall flow
Like linnets of silver sing.

THE MOTH[1]

Isled in the midnight air,
Musked with the dark's faint bloom,
Out into glooming and secret haunts
The flame cries, 'Come!'

[1] Also included in *The Veil and Other Poems*, 1921.

Lovely in dye and fan,
A-tremble in shimmering grace,
A moth from her winter swoon
    Uplifts her face:

Stares from her glamorous eyes;
Wafts her on plumes like mist;
In ecstasy swirls and sways
    To her strange tryst.

AS I DID ROVE

As I did rove in blinded night,
Raying the sward, in slender ring,
A cirque I saw whose crystal light
Tranced my despair with glittering.

Slender its gold; in hues of dream
Its jewels burned, smiting my eyes
Like wings that flit about the stream
That waters Paradise.

Sorrow broke in my heart to see
A thing so lovely; and I heard
Cry from its dark security
A 'wildered bird.

I GO HOME

My mistress dreams — and me forgot;
For parlour silks I cannot care;
    Abroad she will not roam.
But birds invite to sandy grot;
Good warren folk await me there;
    So *I* go home.

Her human sprite's flown out of house;
Her shoe scarce prints the painted mat;
    She dreams of fay and gnome,
And such as in full moon carouse:
So, soft, tap this foot, softlier that —
    And *I* go home.

[799]

THE PATH

Is it an abbey that I see
Hard-by that tapering poplar-tree,
Whereat that path hath end?
'Tis wondrous still
That empty hill,
Yet calls me, friend.

Smooth is the turf, serene the sky,
The timeworn, crumbling roof awry;
Within that turret slim
Hangs there a bell
Whose faint notes knell?
Do colours dim

Burn in that angled window there,
Grass-green, and crimson, azure rare?
Would, from that narrow door,
One, looking in,
See, gemlike, shine
On walls and floor

Candles whose aureole flames must seem —
So still they burn — to burn in dream?
And do they cry, and say,
'See, stranger; come!
Here is thy home;
No longer stray!'

FORGIVENESS[1]

'O thy flamed cheek,
Those locks with weeping wet,
Eyes that, forlorn and meek,
On mine are set.

'Poor hands, poor feeble wings,
Folded, a-droop, O sad!
See, 'tis my heart that sings
To make thee glad.

'My mouth breathes love, thou dear.
All that I am and know
Is thine. My breast — draw near:
Be grieved not so!'

[1] Also included in *The Veil and Other Poems*, 1921.

[800]

THE COQUETTE

Yearn thou may'st:
Thou shalt not see
My wasting love
For thee.

Lean thy tresses;
Fair that fruit;
Slim as warbling bird's
Thy throat.

Peep thou then:
Doubt not some swain
Will of thy still decoy
Be fain.

But I? In sooth —
Nay, gaze thy fill!
Scorn thee I must,
And will.

DIVINE DELIGHT

Dark, dark this mind, if ever in vain it rove
The face of man in search of hope and love;
Or, turning inward from earth's sun and moon,
Spin in cold solitude thought's mazed cocoon.
Fresh hang Time's branches. Hollow in space out-cry
The grave-toned trumpets of Eternity.
'World of divine delight', heart whispereth,
Though all its all lie but 'twixt birth and death.

BITTER WATERS[1]

In a dense wood, a drear wood,
    Dark water is flowing;
Deep, deep, beyond sounding,
    A flood ever flowing.

There harbours no wild bird,
    No wanderer stays there;
Wreathed in mist, sheds pale Ishtar
    Her sorrowful rays there.

Take thy net; cast thy line;
    Manna sweet be thy baiting;
Time's desolate ages
    Shall still find thee waiting

For quick fish to rise there,
    Or butterfly wooing,
Or flower's honeyed beauty,
    Or wood-pigeon cooing.

Inland wellsprings are sweet;
    But to lips, parched and dry,
Salt, salt is the savour
    Of these; faint their sigh.

Bitter Babylon's waters.
    Zion, distant and fair.
We hanged up our harps
    On the trees that are there.

'SUPPOSE'

'Suppose . . . and suppose that a wild little Horse of Magic
Came cantering out of the sky,
With bridle of silver, and into the saddle I mounted,
To fly — and to fly;

'And we stretched up into the air, fleeting on in the sunshine,
A speck in the gleam
On galloping hoofs, his mane in the wind out-flowing,
In a shadowy stream;

[1] Also included in *The Veil and Other Poems*, 1921.

'And, oh, when at last the gentle star of evening
Came crinkling into the blue,
A magical castle we saw in the air, like a cloud of moonlight,
As onward we flew;

'And across the green moat on the drawbridge we foamed and we
    snorted,
And there was a beautiful Queen
Who smiled at me strangely; and spoke to my wild little Horse,
    too—
A lovely and beautiful Queen;

'And she cried with delight — and delight — to her delicate
    maidens,
"Behold my daughter — my dear!"
And they crowned me with flowers, and then to their harps sate
    playing,
Solemn and clear;

'And magical cakes and goblets were spread on the table;
And at window the birds came in;
Hopping along with bright eyes, pecking crumbs from the
    platters,
And sipped of the wine;

'And splashing up — up to the roof tossed fountains of crystal;
And Princes in scarlet and green
Shot with their bows and arrows, and kneeled with their dishes
Of fruits for the Queen;

'And we walked in a magical garden with rivers and bowers,
And my bed was of ivory and gold;
And the Queen breathed soft in my ear a song of enchantment —
And I never grew old . . .

'And I never, never came back to the earth, oh, never and never . . .
How mother would cry and cry!
There'd be snow on the fields then, and all these sweet flowers in
    the winter would wither, and die . . .

'Suppose . . . and suppose . . .'

FIVE OF US

'Five of us small merry ones,
And Simon in the grass.
Here's an hour for delight,
Out of mortal thought and sight.
See, the sunshine ebbs away:
We play and we play.

'Five of us small merry ones,
And yonder there the stone,
Flat and heavy, dark and cold,
Where, beneath the churchyard mould,
Time has buried yesterday:
We play and we play.

'Five of us small merry ones,
We sang a dirge, did we,
Cloud was cold on foot and hair,
And a magpie from her lair
Spread her motley in the air;
And we wept — our tears away:
We play and we play.'

DEAR DELIGHT

Youngling fair, and dear delight,
'Tis Love hath thee in keeping;
Green are the hills in morning light,
A long adieu to weeping!

The elfin-folk sing shrill a-ring;
Children a-field are straying;
Dance, too, thou tiny, lovely thing,
For all the world's a-maying.

Droop will the shadows of the night;
Quiet be thy sleeping.
Thou youngling fair, and dear delight,
'Tis Love hath thee in keeping.

GAZE, NOW

Gaze, now, thy fill, beguiling face,
Life which all light and hue bestows
Stealeth at last from youth its grace,
From cheek its firstling rose.

Dark are those tresses; grave that brow;
Drink, happy mouth, from Wisdom's well;
Bid the strange world to sigh thee now
All beauty hath to tell.

THE COMB

My mother sate me at her glass;
This necklet of bright flowers she wove;
Crisscross her gentle hands did pass,
And wound in my hair her love.

Deep in the mirror our glances met,
And grieved, lest from her care I roam,
She kissed me through her tears, and set
On high this spangling comb.

THE BIRD SET FREE

'No marvel, Sweet, you clap your wings
In hunger for the open sky;
I see your pretty flutterings,
Will let you fly.

'But O, when in some shady grot
You preen your breast in noonday's blue,
Be not your Susan quite forgot,
Who hungers too!'

[805]

MOURN'ST THOU NOW?[1]

Long ago from radiant palace,
Dream-bemused, in flood of moon,
Stole the princess Seraphita
Into forest gloom.

Wail of hemlock; cold the dewdrops;
Danced the Dryads in the chace;
Heavy hung ambrosial fragrance;
Moonbeams blanched her ravished face.

Frail and clear the notes delusive;
Mocking phantoms in a rout
Thridded the night-cloistered thickets,
Wove their sorceries in and out. . . .

Mourn'st thou not? Or do thine eyelids
Frame a vision dark, divine,
O'er this imp of star and wild-flower —
Of a god once thine?

THE SNOWFLAKE[2]

See, now, this filigree: 'tis snow,
Shaped, in the void, of heavenly dew;
On winds of space like flower to blow
In a wilderness of blue.

Black are those pines. The utter cold
Hath frozen to silence the birds' green woods.
Rime hath ensteeled the wormless mould,
A vacant quiet broods.

Lo, this entrancèd thing! — a breath
Of life that bids Man's heart to crave
Still for perfection: ere fall death,
And earth shut in his grave.

[1] Also included in *The Veil and Other Poems*, 1921.
[2] Also included in *The Fleeting and Other Poems*, 1933.

FLOTSAM[1]

Screamed the far sea-mew. On the mirroring sands
Bell-shrill the oyster-catchers. Burned the sky.
Couching my cheeks upon my sun-scorched hands,
Down from bare rock I gazed. The sea swung by

Dazzling dark blue and verdurous, quiet with snow,
Empty with loveliness, with music a-roar,
Her billowing summits heaving noon-aglow —
Crashed the Atlantic on the cliff-ringed shore.

Drowsed by the tumult of that moving deep,
Sense into outer silence fainted, fled;
And rising softly, from the fields of sleep,
Stole to my eyes a lover from the dead;

Crying an incantation — learned, Where? When? . . .
White swirled the foam, a fount, a blinding gleam
Of ice-cold breast, cruel eyes, wild mouth — and then
A still dirge echoing on from dream to dream.

ALAS

One moment take thy rest.
Out of mere nought in space
Beauty moved human breast
To tell in this far face
A dream in noonday seen,
Never to fade or pass;
A breath-time's mute delight:
A joy in flight:
The aught desire doth mean,
Sighing, Alas!

---

[1] Also included in *The Veil and Other Poems*, 1921.

CRAZED[1]

I know a pool where nightshade preens
Her poisonous fruitage in the moon;
Where the frail aspen her shadow leans
In midnight cold a-swoon.

I know a meadow flat with gold —
A million million burning flowers
In moon-sun's thirst their buds unfold
Beneath his blazing showers.

I saw a crazèd face, did I,
Stare from the lattice of a mill,
While the lank sails clacked idly by
High on the windy hill.

THULE

Green-cupped the acorn, ripened the pear,
Grass, lily, jonquil sweeten the air;
Tendrilled convolvulus softly doth clamber;
To his Dame steps Sir Coney, with balm for her chamber;
Cry echoes cry — would my tongue could remember!

Away on his errand, in secret, runs Joy,
That wistful, naked, bud-ankleted boy.
Though never a feather in shade is seen,
Thin jargoning music wells out of the green.

On high in those branches bird-glancings espy
Foamed blue of ocean imbowled by the sky.
There the lustrous-locked sun in chair sits a-flame,
Illuming a region no sailor can name. . . .

Thule? Atlantis? Arcadia? . . . .

---

[1] Also included in *The Veil and Other Poems*, 1921.

MASTER RABBIT

As I was walking,
Thyme sweet to my nose,
Green grasshoppers talking,
Rose rivalling rose:

Wings clear as amber,
Outspread in the light,
As from bush to bush
The Linnet took flight:

Master Rabbit I saw
In the shadow-rimmed mouth
Of his sandy cavern
Looking out to the South.

'Twas dew-tide coming,
The turf was sweet
To nostril, curved tooth,
And wool-soft feet.

Sun was in West,
Crystal in beam
Of its golden shower
Did his round eye gleam.

Lank horror was I,
And a foe, poor soul —
Snowy flit of a scut,
He was into his hole:

And — *stamp, stamp, stamp*
Through dim labyrinths clear —
The whole world darkened:
A Human near!

INNOCENCY

In this grave picture mortal Man may see
That all his knowledge ends in mystery.
From mother's womb he breaks. With tortured sighs
Her racked heart sweetens at his angry cries.
Teaching his feet to walk, his tongue to express
His infant love, she pours her tenderness.
Her milk and honey he doth taste and sip;
Sleeps with her kiss of kindness on his lip.
But with the vigour mastering time doth yield
He exults in freedom; ventures him afield;
Down to the sea goes, and in ship sets sail,
Crazed with the raving of love's nightingale,

And trumps of war, and danger's luring horn,
And dark's faint summons into dreams forlorn.
Pride in earth's vanquished secrets fills his breast;
Yet still he pines for foregone peace and rest,
And prays in untold sorrow at last to win
To a long-lost Paradise an entering-in.
O yearning eyes that through earth's ages scan
The 'glorious misery' 'tis to be a man;
Secure in quiet arms that Saviour be,
Whose name is Innocency.

MIRAGE[1]

. . . And burned the topless towers of Ilium

Strange fabled face! From sterile shore to shore
O'er plunging seas, thick-sprent with glistening brine,
The voyagers of the world with sail and heavy oar
    Have sought thy shrine.
    Beauty inexorable hath lured them on:
Remote unnamèd stars enclustering gleam —
Burn in thy flowered locks, though creeping daylight wan
    Prove thee but dream.

[1] Also included in *The Veil and Other Poems*, 1921.

Noonday to night the enigma of thine eyes
Frets with desire their travel-wearied brain,
Till in the vast of dark the ice-cold moon arise
    And pour them peace again:
    And with malign mirage uprears an isle
Of fountain and palm, and courts of jasmine and rose,
Whence far decoy of siren throats their souls beguile,
    And maddening fragrance flows.

Lo, in the milken light, in tissue of gold
Thine apparition gathers in the air —
Nay, but the seas are deep, and the round world old,
    And thou art named, Despair.

SEPHINA

Black lacqueys at the wide-flung door
Stand mute as men of wood.
Gleams like a pool the ball-room floor —
A burnished solitude.
A hundred waxen tapers shine
From silver sconces; softly pine
'Cello, fiddle, mandoline,
To music deftly wooed —
And dancers in cambric, satin, silk,
With glancing hair and cheeks like milk,
Wreathe, curtsey, intertwine.

The drowse of roses lulls the air
That's wafted up the marble stair.
Like warbling water clucks the talk.
From room to room in splendour walk
Guests, smiling in the silken sheen;
Carmine and azure, white and green,
They stoop and languish, pace and preen
Bare shoulder, painted fan,
Gemmed wrist and finger, neck of swan;
And still the plucked strings warble on;
Still from the snow-bowered, link-lit street
The muffled hooves of horses beat;

[811]

And harness rings; and foam-flecked bit
Clanks as the slim heads toss and stare
From deep, dark eyes. Smiling, at ease,
Mount to the porch the pomped grandees
In lonely state, by twos, and threes,
Exchanging languid courtesies,
While torches fume and flare.

And now the banquet calls. A blare
Of squalling trumpets clots the air;
And, flocking out, streams up the rout;
And lilies nod to velvet's swish.
And peacocks prim on gilded dish,
Vast pies thick-glazed, and gaping fish,
Towering confections crisp as ice,
Jellies aglare like cockatrice,
With thousand savours tongues entice.
Fruits of all hues, too, shape and bloom —
Pomegranate, quince and peach and plum,
Nectarine, grape, and cherry clear[1]
And knotted pine — each leaf a spear . . .

And lo! — 'La, la!
Mamma, mamma!

---

[1] The text of a variant edition of *Flora*, 1919, reads as follows down to 'Couched on the staircase overhead':

'Mandarine, grape, and cherry clear
Englobe each glassy chandelier,
Where nectarous flowers their sweets distil —
Jessamine, tuberose, chamomill,
Wild-eye narcissus, anemone,
Tendril of ivy and vinery.

Now odorous wines the goblets fill;
Gold-cradled meats the menials bear
From gilded chair to gilded chair:
Now roars the talk like crashing seas,
Foams upward to the painted frieze,
Echoes and ebbs. Still surges in,
To yelp of hautboy and violin,
Plumed and bedazzling, rosed and rare,
Dance-bemused, with cheek aglow,
Stooping the green-twined portal through,
Sighing with laughter, debonair,
That concourse of the proud and fair —
      And lo! "La, la!
      Mamma . . . Mamma!"
Falls a small cry in the dark and calls —
      "I see you standing there!"
Fie, fie, Sephina! not in bed!
Crouched on the staircase overhead,'

More marvellous lovely than a star
I see you standing there! . . .'
'Fie, fie Sephina! not in bed!'
Couched on the staircase overhead
Like ghost she gloats, her lean hand laid
On alabaster balustrade,
And gazes on and on;
Down on that wondrous to and fro
Till finger and foot are cold as snow
And half the night is gone;
And dazzled eyes are sore bestead,
Nods drowsily the sleek-locked head:
And, faint and far, spins, fading out
That rainbow-coloured, reeling rout
And, with faint sighs, her spirit flies
Into deep sleep. . . .
Come, Stranger, peep!
Was ever cheek so wan?

This Year: Next Year (1937)

THE PICTURE-BOOK

Dear Reader, prythee, stay, and look
At this delightful Picture-Book!
Others like it you'll have seen,
For eye and mind to linger in,
But surely none, for tints and tones,
Lovelier than this — by Harold Jones?
Is there a colour — earth, sky, sea,
Which from his box can missing be?
Even a Rainbow might whisper, Hush!
In envy of his paints and brush.

See with what heedful skill and grace
His patient pencil fills his space;
How stroke by stroke, and stage by stage,
He fits his pattern to the page,
And shows in every hue and line
Not only joy in his design,
But all that he takes such pleasure in.
Even his commonest objects tell
His love for what he sees so well.
And such is the delight he shows —
In stool or table, bird or rose —
That, sharing them, one hardly knows
Which for pleasure gives richer cause —
What he draws, or *how* he draws.

Things far and near so real are seen
You'd think the air flowed in between;
Yet touch of finger shows us that
The page itself is paper-flat!
Look once: again: and yet again —
Some fresh delight will still remain.
And though (I should confess betimes),
There was no need at all for rhymes,
'Twas yet the more a joy to tell,
If only in headlong doggerel,
What rich and lively company
This Picture-Book has been to me.

DAYBREAK

The curtains of the solemn night
  Draw back; and daybreak fair
Shines on these tulips cold with dew,
  And fills with light the air.
No child stands tiptoe yet to sip
Clear water from the fountain's lip;
  Nothing stirs anywhere,
But the birds in the dust, the leaves in the breeze,
The nut-brown squirrels in the trees;
  And empty is every chair.

DUCKS

See, now, a child must this way come —
  And early out of bed! —
Who, still with dreams in his bright eyes,
  Has filled a bag with bread,
And scampers down to feed the Ducks,
  All flocking to be fed.

The tiny man in that tiny boat,
Upon the placid lake afloat,
Is looking back, and so can see
Many now hidden from you and me;
And these, like ours, no doubt he finds
Of several sizes, shapes and *kinds:*—

The Farmyard Duck is white as snow;
  And quacks a merry quack;
  The Tufted wears a topknot;
  The Labrador is black;
The Pochard, and the Goldeneye
  As soon as seen are gone:
Like fish-with-wings they cruise beneath
  The water else they are *on.*

The wild, wild Mallard in chestnut flies,
    Steel-blue, and emerald green;
Low head outstretched, and bead-dark eyes,
He arrows through the empty skies,
    As evening dusk sets in.
The Pintail whistles to the wind;
The Shoveller calls 'puck-puck';
The downy Eider an island loves
    And shares a sailor's luck;
The wary Widgeon will talk all day,
    Then sleep on a stormy sea;
But the Teal nests inland, and at peace —
    A loving mother she.
And one a bill has like a hook;
    And one like a flattened spoon:
They gossip, paddle, dive and bask —
    Pond, ocean, stream, lagoon:
On snails or plants or fishes feed,
Worms, insects, frogs, or water-weed,
As does, according to his need,
    The lovelorn Mandarin.

All these are *kinds*. But every Duck
Himself is, and himself alone:
Fleet wing, arched neck, webbed foot, round eye,
    And marvellous cage of bone.
Clad in this beauty a creature dwells,
Of sovran instinct, sense and skill;
Yet secret as the hidden wells
    Whence Life itself doth rill.

THE THRUSH

Even earlier yet this listening thrush —
    Alone on her leafy bough —
Trilled out her brier-sweet song of praise
To greet the risen sun; and now,
With glittering eye and speckled breast,
Peeps this way, that way, then at nest,
As though, for joy, she is not sure
If it hold one egg less — or more,
    Since last she counted *four*.

[817]

How strange that one, of shade the lover,
Has chosen a tree so spare in cover!
But had she built to shield her brood
In laurel bush, or ivy-tod,
Her plaited nest so plainly seen
Would hidden out of sight have been.
Nor could a watch be kept so well
When her first young one cracks its shell;
Nor on all four when, fledged, they fly,
And — later eggs being hatched — will try
To help her feed her family!

BOOKS

A boy called Jack, as I've been told,
Would sit for hours — good as gold —
Not with a pie, like Master Horner,
And plums, for dainties, in his corner,
But silent in some chosen nook,
And spell-bound — by a story-book!
Whether the dawn brought sun or rain,
Back to its pages he'd hasten again;
He had even wheedled from his friends
A secret hoard of candle-ends,
And — slumber far from his round head —
Would read, till dead of night — in bed!

How often his mother would sigh, and cry —
'Up Jack, and put that trumpery by!
    See, Spring is in the sky!
The swallow is here, the thorn's in blow —
Crimson, pink, and driven snow;
Lambs caper in the fields; and there,
Cuckoo flies calling through the air;
    Oh, why stay in? Oh, why?'

And Jack would smile . . . No wonder! He
In books found marvellous company,
Wonder, romance, and mystery.
He pined to follow, on and on,
Sailors on strange adventure gone;
With travellers to rove, and scan
Regions untrodden by mortal man.

[818]

Eyes shining, breathless, cramped, stock-still,
Lost in these dreams he'd crouch until
The fancied all but seemed the real.
Tales old or new he read with zest,
But some he loved beyond the rest:—

That other Jack's, whose magic Beans
Led skyward to a Giant's demesnes —
His Money Bags, Harp — centuries old,
The Hen that laid him eggs of gold:

And starving Dick's who ran away,
But heard Bow Bells up Highgate Way,
Entreating him turn back again.
The which he did. And not in vain!
Since close behind him, sleek and spruce,
Came trotting on his faithful Puss.
'Twas she who rid the soot-black Chief
Of rats in myriads past belief,
Which, when he lay in deep repose,
Would nip his fingers, gnaw his toes;
And while at meat he sat, in State,
Would drag the beef bones off his plate!
A mort of money, in coffers fat,
This Moor paid down for such a Cat.
These shipped, Dick then sailed home at once,
With casks cram-full of precious stones;
And, having given her all he had brought her,
Won for his bride his master's daughter
(A lass as sweet as she was fair),
And thrice was London's loved Lord Mayor.

Gulliver, too; who, shipwrecked, woke,
Arms, legs pegged down by pygmy folk,
With needle arrows, bows of gut,
Who fifteen hundred horses brought,
And dragged him off to Lilliput.
When two explored his box of snuff
They nearly sneezed their cranies off.
Pitching a ladder against his side,
They rambled over him, far and wide —
As emmets on a pumpkin creep.
They fed him fat on tiny sheep;
Startled, like birds, at every wink,

[819]

Poured puncheons down his throat for drink.
Church-high he paced along their streets;
For handkerchiefs they gave him sheets;
And when they went to War, then he
Tugged their whole Navy out to sea.

He sailed once more, was wrecked again,
And seized by a Brobdingnagian,
Huge as an oak, his shoes to match,
And hair as thick as farmyard thatch,
Teeth like small milestones, eyes beside,
Like green glass marbles a cubit wide.
These towering bumpkins roared to see
A human imp minute as he;
Made him a mock, a toy — and worse,
Gave him a child to be his Nurse,
Fifty feet high. Her plaits of hair
Swung like gold hawsers in the air,
Her ribbons fluttered wide and far
Like pennons on a ship of war.
She loved him dearly — gentle soul,
Far more than even her favourite doll;
And made two boxes for the waif,
To carry him and keep him safe.
The woes he faced! — the horrid Ape
Which dandled him upon its lap,
Then snatched him up and scuttled off
To sport with him upon a roof
Whose rain-pipes when in overflow
Poured down five hundred feet below.
Perils beset him everywhere;
'Twas death to topple off a chair.
In nick of time he pinked a rat
Ferocious as a tiger-cat;
And, like Duke Clarence, drowned did seem
When rescued from a bowl of cream.
But courage will on danger thrive;
Not only cowards come home alive!

And Sindbad — tranced on Indian deep,
When shades of night began to creep —
Who took for land a Whale, asleep!
And, pushing off in a small boat,
To where this Monster lay afloat,
With his three shipmates, scrambled up
Its steep and slippery side — to sup.

There, having heaped the sun-dried wrack,
They lit a bonfire on its back.
A whisper through the Creature ran —
'Beware! Arouse thee! Danger! Man!'
It stirred; it woke; its drowsy eye
Fixed on the flame-flushed company —
Turban, sash, and matted hair —
Feasting, singing, carousing there.
There came a swirl of flukes and fin —
And then was nought where Whale had been!
Only a watery waste of sea
Where a strange Island had seemed to be!
And in its moonlight one black head —
Sindbad's, aghast with terror and dread,
His boon companions — drowned — and dead.
Ay, and 'twas Sindbad, too, who found —
When on a real isle marooned,
A Roc's egg — fifty paces round.
Teeth chattering, blanched with fear, he heard
The wing-beats of the mother-bird,
Like distant thunder on the air;
And — darkening day — her shadow there,
In heaven. Down she swooped to rest,
A riot of splendour, on her nest.
Nearer, at length, he dared to draw,
And tied his body to her claw,
Scaled as with mail, its talons trim,
But broader than a weaver's beam.
She rose, soared high, and alighted in
A valley where a stream had been —
A gaunt and haunted wild abyss,
Scarped with a dizzying precipice.
And Sindbad stood, like one who is stunned,
At sight of a huge diamond —
Flashing its lightnings through the air.
Nay, thousands of blazing gems were there
In heaps — like apples in a pie.
And lo! aloft, against the sky,
Wheeled screaming eagles, starved for meat.
And merchants came . . .

　　　But every bit
Of these strange voyages Jack knew
All but by heart; and Crusoe's, too.
Bandage his eyes, I vow he would
Not falter in *his* Solitude! —

The wreck, the footprint, the stockade,
Cave, parrot, cats; the pots he made.
'Neath its great stars at will he'd rove
Hill and valley, creek and cove.
So close and often the tale he had read
He knew the Island as Friday did;
As if from home himself he'd run,
Worn Crusoe's goatskins, fired his gun.

Our Jack loved *all*. As dear to him
The tales of Andersen and Grimm.
He had roamed their pages through and through —
The Seven Swans; Rapunzel, too;
The Gnome whose secret was his name;
Hansel and Gretel, who weeping came
To a cottage of cake and sweetmeats made,
Which, for a trap, a Witch had laid.
And Snow-White, whom the Dwarfs took in
To guard her from the wicked Queen.
She, envious of her lovely face,
Came, painted, to her hiding-place,
With poisoned comb, and bodice-lace.
'Taste Sweet!' her wheedling tongue besought,
When she the fatal apple brought —
Pleasant to eye and sweet to lip.
One morsel; and in trance-like sleep —
A dreamless slumber, heavy as lead —
Poor Snow-White lay like one who is dead.
At evening from their copper mine
The merry Dwarfs came home to dine.
They found their Snow-White cold and still
As a wraith of flowers on an April hill.
Oh bitter grief! Alas! Alas!
They made her a coffin of crystal glass;
There to this day aswoon to lie,
Had not a Prince come riding by,
Who, marvelling at her loveliness,
Stooped low, and waked her — with a kiss.
Poetry, too, was Jack's delight;
He even rhymed in dreams at night;
Roving where every stream and tree
The haunt was of divinity;
Where lorn Esnalda, lost, astray,
In a wide forest, green with May,
Was found by an Elfin, and rode away
Pillion, upon a dapple-grey.

Knee-deep in flowers, sweet and wan,
He heard the enticing pipes of Pan;
And — where the waves in foam of snow
Shine in the gilding after-glow —
Hearkened, afar, that echoing
Shrill song the lovely sirens sing,
At eve in their rock-bound solitude.
Well, well — so Jack would sit and brood.
Book-crazed was he, and still read on;
His heart was where his eyes were gone.
Friends would come knocking might and main,
Make faces through the window-pane,
Call, whistle, taunt him — all in vain.
He hardly heeded what they said,
Lowered an inch or two his head,
And once more read — and read — and — read.
Ev'n finish a tale he would, and then
Devour it, every word, again!
All which is how, one might suppose,
A Jack into a *bookworm* grows —
A wretched thing, of paper made,
Timid, half-blind, caged-in, afraid;
And quite unable to enjoy
What pleases any other boy.

Never believe it! What Jack read
Refreshed his senses, heart, and head.
Words were to him not merely *words* —
Their sounds rang sweet as bells, or birds;
Nor could he tell, by any test,
Whether he loved — he once confessed —
Their music, or their meaning, best.
And all they pictured clearer was
Than things seen in a looking-glass
Like an old pedlar with his pack,
As light as air upon his back —
His story finished, through and through,
Its scenes still sweet in memory, too,
He'd shut his book, a moment sit,
Inwardly musing over it,
Then stretch his legs, forsake his seat,
Blink his bright eyes, glance up and see
Perhaps a flower, bird, or bee,
Or green leaves dancing in a tree —
Would stand an instant, mute and dazed,
Then out he'd run, as if half-crazed,

[823]

Shouting and leaping with delight;
Yes, even at the commonest sight —
Hedgerow in leaf, or finch on twig,
As glad and merry as a grig.
He loved to lie, his daydream eye
Fixed on a blue, or starry sky,
Watching the clouds, or listening
To every note a wren can sing,
To every caw a rook can caw,
Ravished at what he heard and saw —
The green of moss, a radiant drop
Of water in a bramble-cup.
Which pleased him most no tongue could tell —
To look or listen, taste or smell! . . .

This seems to me at least to hint,
That if we give what wits we have
To Books, as Jack himself them gave —
To all we read a willing slave —
The while we dream, delight, and think,
The words a precious meat and drink,
And keep as lively as a spink,
There's not much harm in printer's ink.

ESMERALDA

Plump Mrs. Brown, we may suppose,
With basket and umbrella goes
Shopping. Why? Because she knows
That rain will pelt till dark comes down —
On wood and meadow; street and town;
That rain's set in till shut of day,
And the watery world is hidden away:
What use then still indoors to stay?

She sallies out with her small daughter:
These two young urchins following after,
Snailed in as snug as snug can be —
With rainy nose and blinking eye
Jack-boots, sou'wester, cap-à-pie —
Like sailors, in a gale at sea;
And aching fit to burst with laughter
At watching Mrs. Brown forget
Her Esmeralda's getting wet!

THE ROOM

Pot on the mantel; picture; clock —
A naked, marble Cupid — look!
  And, in the grate, a fire,
Whose wild bright flames in pallid smoke
  Branch higher yet, and higher:
A leather pouffe beside a chair,
  Its cushion striped with blue;
A pair of slippers on the kerb;
  And logs laid ready — two.
And see — a portrait hanging there,
  Dark hair, and darker eyes,
Above a pitcher filled with flowers
  Whose Springlike incense lies
In drifts of sweetness on the air —
  Proving the loved may find
That even when they are far from sight
  They are not out of mind.

ASLEEP[1]

Sister with sister, dark and fair,
Slumber on one pillow there;
Tranced in dream their phantoms rove —
But none knows what they are dreaming of.
Lost to the room they love, they lie
Their hearts their only lullaby.
Whither that cloud in heaven is bound
Can neither tell. No scent, no sound
Reaches them now. Without avail
Warbles the sweet-tongued nightingale.
Oh, how round, how white a moon
Streams into this silent room!
Clothes and curtains gleam so gay
  It might be day.
But see, beyond that door ajar,
  Night's shadows are;
And not a mouse is stirring where
  Descends an empty stair.

[1] The original poem had these additional lines:
      'Oh, how round, how white a moon
      Streams into this silent room!
      Clothes and curtains gleam so gay
            It might be day.'   (*This Year: Next Year*, 1937)

HOLIDAYS

Dobbin's in the stable, pigs are in sty —
Norfolk Dumpling and Twinkle-eye —
  And milking time is come.
Four cows stand drowsing, head to tail,
Waiting for Moll with her stool and pail,
  And two are trotting home.
The sea lies flat as a pane of glass;
  Languid and faint the air,
The shadows lengthen in the grass —
  Was ever day so fair?
The wheat's in sheaf, a clucking hen
  Pecks supper for her chicks;
(And if not one is out of sight,
  She has precisely six).
The engine puffs, the people sit,
  And out of window gaze
At lank-legged Peggy with the switch
She cut at dawn — the switch with which
  She wooed her beasts to graze;
And (since he's hidden behind the cows)
They hear an unseen dog's bow-wows!

What wonder in a scene so bright
Their hearts are brimming with delight,
Welling with songs of joy and praise!
What wonder! Why, this very night
  Begins the Holidays!

AWAY GO WE

One, two, three,
And away go we!
Shingle, starfish,
Sand, and sea!
Wind on cheek,
Clear sun on skin;
The tumbling waves
Sweep out, sweep in.

A magic, broken
Music calls
In the water
As it falls;
Voices, a sigh,
A long-drawn *hush*,
As back — in myriad
Bubbles — gush
The green-grey ripples,
Flecked with snow —
A music solemn,
Sweet, and low.

THE GARDEN

That wooden hive between the trees
Is Palace of a Queen — of Bees.
With seed-black eyes, and hidden stings
Sentries, at entry, beat their wings
To cool the night-dark gallery
Where waxen-celled Princesses lie;
And drones — their grubs — sleep snug near by,
While busier bees store honey.

From the bright flowers in the bed —
Ripening pippins overhead —
Some pollen cull to kneed bee-bread,
Or nectar still — for life and love,
Love on both sides, not money.

Soon the two doves in the pale green grass
With whirr of wing
Will airward spring
And perch upon the table;
Then tapping beaks
Will peck the cakes,
And nibble, nibble, nibble;
For no-one's peering from the door
Or peeping from the gable.

HAYMAKING

Bill's on the hay-wain
Sam's below,
And Simon's up on the stack;
Jeremy Joe
Is behind — and so
He must be at the back!
Tiny Tim,
By the horse (that's him),
Gives him a wisp to munch;
But Little Boy Blue
We can't see you —
Snuggled asleep, maybe, under a wall,
Cows and sheep far out of call,
Or eyeing what's there, for lunch.

THE POOL IN THE ROCK

In this water, clear as air,
Lurks a lobster in its lair.
Rock-bound weed sways out and in,
Coral-red, and bottle-green.
Wondrous pale anemones
Stir like flowers in a breeze:
Fluted scallop, whelk in shell,
And the prowling mackerel.
Winged with snow the sea-mews ride
The brine-keen wind; and far and wide
Sounds on the hollow thunder of the tide.

MR. PUNCH

A screech across the sands;
A drum's dull thump;
Oh, wicked Mister Punch,
Hook-nose and hump!
What corpse is this lies here? —
An infant dear;
And Judy listening
In grief and fear,
Knowing the Hangman
With his rope draws near!

While lean Dog Toby yawns —
Ruff, paws, and tail —
And now at starfish blinks,
And now at pail.

A screech across the sands!
That sullen thump!
Oh, wicked Mr. Punch,
Belled cap, hook-nose
and hump!

THE TENT

How cool a tent!
How leafy a shade!
And, near at hand, a heap of sticks.
The kettle waits,
The cloth is laid —
With fruit and bread and Banbury cakes.
Cows rove the meadows; in woods afar
Steals out a listening fox:
I wonder where the campers are,
And what is in that box.

OVER THE DOWNS

A stick between his knees, sits Pat,
And sugar-loaf in shape's his hat;
But Phil, his friend, has neither,
Unless to cool his fevered brow,
His hidden hat is off just now,
For warm in sooth's the weather.
Though Denton's seven miles away,
How sweet it is a while to be
At rest in this green solitude
Of peace and mystery! —
So still the very hares creep close,
As if in hope they can
By leaning their lank listening ears
His secrets share with Man.
What lies beyond that broken fence
When on we journey? Well,
The motionless bird upon the post
May know: he does not tell.

[829]

HARVEST

Poppy, cornflower, nid-nod wheat,
    The sheaves are ripe for rick.
And perched aloft in the dusty glow
    Toils on hot, red-faced Dick.
A sultry and enormous sun
    Sinks slowly in the West;
Another harvest day is done;
And soon — these humans homeward gone —
    The fields will be at rest.
Soon, when the moon shines honey-pale
    On the wide world's round breast,
Silv'ring the cherries of the dwale
    And that green woodland's crest,
These horses will in stable be,
    This silent bird in nest.

HIGH

Fly, kite!
    High!
Till you touch the sky!
  Stoop, whistling in the wind;
And whisper down the quivering string
  If, as you soar, you find
The world we tread is like a ball —
With mounds for hills, and ponds for seas,
Its oxen small as creeping bees,
  Mere bushes its huge trees!

But ah, the dew begins to fall,
  The evening star to shine,
Down you must sink to earth again —
  An earth, I mean, like mine.

APPLE-FALL

Rosy the blossom that breaks in May;
    Autumn brings the apple;
Jackdaws in the belfry tower,
    Jackdaws in the steeple.
Comes a wind, blows a wind,
    Headlong down they tumble;
But bloom and berry share the sprig
    Of the prickly bramble.

THERE WAS AN OLD WOMAN
OF BUMBLE BHOSEY

There was an old Woman of Bumble Bhosey —
    Children she had forty;
Half of them sang hymns all night;
    Half of them were naughty;

Twenty went to Botany Bay;
    Ten of them on crutches,
And the last of them nimmed the clouts that lay
    A-bleaching on the bushes!

THE LITTLE SHOP

The Whistler on the whistle
    Asks a penny — and is gone;
The scampering dog behind the lamp
    Hies off to thieve a bone;
'Williams & Sons' at Ninety-two
    Stay open — till they are shut,
Sell balls, bears, boxes, beads and barrows,
    Masks and fireworks — BUT:—

The *oldest* Shop, to the ends of the earth,
    Is in Little Old Nowhere Street;
Where rivers of Eden, named Now and Then,
    Sing, as their waters meet;
And the ribs of the coracle bleach in the sand
Wherein Nemo, the Sailorman, came to land.

Shem, Ham, Japheth, the wise declare,
    Found a booth where its bell now clinks;
The sun that gilded Absalom's hair
    Through its bottle-glass window blinks;
Here a child named Caesar bought lumps of lead —
To melt and to mould into soldiers, he said.

An all-sorts shop; where Alfred tasted
    His first little sip of mead,
Five years, at least (a child of six)
    Before he was taught to read;
Hither came Stephen, hawk on wrist;
In its garden Prince Hal a sweetheart kissed.

[831]

A bottle of lollipops loved by Bess
    Stood apart on a window shelf.
When William, her poet, came in as a child,
    He smiled, and he helped himself;
And, munching at counter, carved his name
Where little Dan Chaucer had done the same.

Here Raleigh first peered at a Map of the World.
    And from over the snow on the wold
A wean, called Francis Bacon, came —
    Not a day over six years old,
So parched with the blast, he could scarcely speak:
'I want, so it please you, some books in Greek.'

The two doomed children who asked for bread,
    Were given, alas, a stone.
Their uncle, whom folk called Crookback, had
    Sneaked in through the dusk — alone.
'Bird-lime', he mumbled. But Francis Drake
Bought marbles; and tackle, a ship to make.

A long-faced prince, not five foot tall,
    A Sceptre and Crown bespoke,
But the Crown his dark head failed to fit,
    And the golden Sceptre broke.
Another Prince Charlie, with ringleted hair,
Chose beads — for a lassie he loved to wear.

A huge black cat on the counter drowsed
    In the sunshine, hot through the glass,
Blinking his yellow eyes, narrow as slits,
    At the geese outside in the grass,
When he spied a boy, his face like a hawk's,
Who in for a penn'orth of powder stalks,
    And muttered, 'My "name"? 'Tis Fawkes.'

Dolls, knives, string, and things to eat —
    Ginger-bread, buns, mince-pie,
Cram that bottle-glass window in Nowhere Street,
    Enticing the passer-by.
Not a child in the world but has flattened its nose
On its panes, gazing in, its small face in a muse,
Pining, wondering what to choose —
From Helen of Troy down to Margaret Rose. . . .

Nights in summer — how wan her stars!
    Her dark — how brief, and sweet!
Voices, past human wits to follow,
    Are heard where those waters meet.
The song of the bird in the silent hills
    Into the moonshine rills.

Old as they is that dark little house;
    But little a child can need
Is not to be bought there, for pennies, or love;
    And in gilded, outlandish screed,
Over its shutters — as if to rhyme! —
    Is the name of the Shop-keeper — TIME.

ALL THE FUN

Here's all the Fun of the Fair! Come buy!
Chute, and swing, and a penny a shy!
    And the lamps will blaze at night —
The dangling lamps that drip and hiss
Where peppermint, candy and liquorice,
Bull's-eyes, hardbake, coconut-ice,
    Are a farthing, or less, a bite.

The gilded organs blare and groan,
Jack rides the skewbald, Ruth the roan,
    Finger and knee clutched tight.
Giddily galloping on they course . . .
But who is it sits the little blue horse?
What stranger straddles that dark little horse,
    Half hidden out of sight?

And when, all silent, dark, and still
Are tent and tree-top, meadow and hill,
    Merry-go-round and man,
When the autumn stars shine faint above,
And the barn owl hoots from her secret grove,
And the shades of night begin to rove,
I wonder what he'll be dreaming of —
    The gypsy-boy in the Van.

[833]

THE HUNT

Tallyho! Tallyho! —
Echo faints far astray,
On the still, misty air,
And the Hunt is away!
Horsemen and hounds
Stream over the hill;
And, brush well behind him,
Pelts with a will
Old Reynard the Fox —
As in conscience he may,
For hot at his heels
Sweep Trim, Trap and Tray;
Chestnut, and black,
And flea-bitten grey.
But the Crafty One knows
Every inch of the way!
Thicket and spinney,
Gully and dell,
Where the stream runs deep,
And the otters dwell —
Hemlock, garlic,
Bog asphodel —
He'll lead them a dance,
Though they ride like hell.
And — wily old animal,
Cunning as they! —
He'll live — to go hunting —
Another fine day.

'PLEASE TO REMEMBER'

Here am I,
A poor old Guy:
Legs in a bonfire,
Head in the sky;

Shoeless my toes,
Wild stars behind,
Smoke in my nose,
And my eye-peeps blind;

Old hat, old straw —
In this disgrace;
While the wildfire gleams
On a mask for face.

Ay, all I am made of
Only trash is;
And soon — soon,
Will be dust and ashes.

THE SNOW-MAN

What shape is this in cowl of snow?
    Stiff broom and icy hat?
A saffron moon, half-hidden, stares —
    But what is she staring *at?*

The knocker dangles on the door,
    But stark as tree and post
He blankly eyes the bright green paint,
    Is silent as a ghost.

But wait till belfry midnight strike,
    And up to the stars is tossed
Shrill cockcrow! — *then*, he'll gadding go —
    And, at his heels, Jack Frost:

Broom over shoulder, away he'll go,
Finger-tips tingling, nose aglow,
Dancing and yodelling through the snow,
    And, at his heels, Jack Frost!

[835]

ICE

The North Wind sighed:
And in a trice
What was water
Now is ice.

What sweet rippling
Water was
Now bewitched is
Into glass:

White and brittle
Where is seen
The prisoned milfoil's
Tender green;

Clear and ringing,
With sun aglow,
Where the boys sliding
And skating go.

Now furred's each stick
And stalk and blade
With crystals out of
Dewdrops made.

Worms and ants,
Flies, snails and bees
Keep close house-guard,
Lest they freeze;

Oh, with how sad
And solemn an eye
Each fish stares up
Into the sky.

In dread lest his
Wide watery home
At night shall solid
Ice become.

'ALL HOT'

Brooding he stands,
And warms his hands
In this chill moonlit spot;
Cold to his feet
Is the cobbled street
And cold the north wind blows.
But his fire of coke —
Like rubies, look,
In Ali Baba's grot! —
Glows still and clear;
And children hear —
As dancing home from school they near —
His, 'Chestnuts! Hot! All hot!'

That dog, called Jinks, who quietly blinks,
While toasting back and side,
Sits on in silence while he thinks,
And can at need *decide!*
He loves his slim Jemima,
But his collar can't abide.

So, one dark eye on her small thumb,
He waits his moment, sure to come,
When, tail and lead behind him,
With yelp of rapture off he goes,
Where nothing but his own sharp nose
Can ever hope to find him!

LOGS

This tree, by April wreathed in flowers,
That sheened with leaves the summer hours,
In dappling shine and shade,
Now all that then was lovely lacks,
Is vanquished by the saw and axe,
And into firewood made.

[837]

How happy and gentle a daybreak song
Whispered its solemn boughs among,
    At sigh of morning stirred;
It braved the dangerous lightning; rose
In splendour, crowned with winter's snows;
    And sheltered every bird
That perched with slender claw and wing
To preen, to rest, to roost, to sing,
    Unseen — but not unheard.

But came the Woodman with his axe
    Into the sun-sweet glade;
And what was once all beauty and grace
    Is into firewood made.

NOWEL

Holly dark: pale Mistletoe —
Christmas Eve is come, and lo,
Wild clash the bells across the snow,
Waits in the dark streets carolling go;
'Nowel! Nowel!' they shout — and, oh,
    How live out the day!
Each breath I breathe turns to a sigh;
    My heart is flown away;
The things I see around me seem
Entranced with light — as in a dream;
The candles dazzle in my eyes,
And every leaping fireflame tries
    To sing, what none could say.

THE SECRET

Open your eyes! . . . Now, look, and see!
Those starry tapers in the tree
Keep a promise 'twixt you and me:
Every toy and trinket there
In our secret has a share:
The Fairy on the topmost spray
Hears every single word I say:
I love — and *love* you: and I would
Give you my life, too, if I could.

SANTA CLAUS[1]

'Hast thou, in Fancy, trodden where lie
Leagues of ice beneath the sky?
Where bergs, like palaces of light,
Emerald, sapphire, crystal white,
Glimmer in the polar night?
Hast thou heard in dead of dark
The mighty Sea-lion's shuddering bark?
Seen, shuffling through the crusted snow,
The blue-eyed Bears a-hunting go?
And in leagues of space o'er-head —
Radiant Aurora's glory spread?
Hast thou?' 'Why?' 'My child, because
There dwells thy loved Santa Claus. . . .'

THE FEAST

Crackers, meringues, and pink blomonge —
    Eat not for eating's sake!
But where mincepies and turkey went,
    A corner keep for cake.
See, dear Mamma's best silver too —
    And all for Christmas' sake!

While we sit snug within; without,
    The frost bites bitter sharp.
Bleak is the tune cold Winter sings,
    As shrilly rings his harp.
And dawn will whiten on a waste
Of wintry hills, and woods at rest,
Where stript of fruit are rose and thorn,
And famished birds flit mute, forlorn.
No, not a morsel good to taste,
Nor drop to drink — unless there come
Some friendly human, with fingers numb,
To bring them dainties — such as these:
Crusts, hemp-seed, marrow-bones and cheese.

---

[1] The original poem had a first stanza which read:
    'On wool-soft feet he peeps and creeps,
        While in the moon-blanched snow,
    Tossing their sled-belled antlered heads,
        His reindeer wait below.
    Bright eyes, peaked beard, and bulging sack,
        He stays to listen, and look, because
    A child lies sleeping out of sight,
        And this is Santa Claus.'   (*This Year: Next Year*, 1937)

THE PANTOMIME

Were those fine horses once white Mice,
    Their Coachman an old Rat,
And the coach itself of the shape of a melon,
    There'd be good reason that
My pen should now attempt to tell a
    Tale entitled 'Cinderella'.

We see, it's true, a gentle face,
    As on the haughty henchmen pace;
But nowhere any hint, alas,
    Her two small slippers are made of glass.

It may be then the Stage is set
For quite a different Play; that this
Vast Castle, with its moated walls,
    The wild Aladdin's is —
Which, in the Scene that follows, may
Be magicked off to Africa.
Or Puss in Boots? Or Bluebeard's fell?
Or valiant Mollie Whuppie's? Well,
    We guess, but cannot tell.

Or are these pennons, this wild array
To welcome one who rode away,
Pillion upon a dapple-grey,
In the flush of the morning, in month of May?
    We ask, but cannot say.

FAREWELL

Ah me! That pen should be where mine is —
That F-I-N-I-S spells FINIS!
It means — oh, sad! — our Book is over,
And all its Pictures, excepting one
You'll find, dear Reader, on the cover —
Of starlings feeding in the sun.

There, *open* stands a shining door;
To let us out — but in, no more.
There glides a stream. A linden tree
Dreams of the Spring. The distant woods
Hear the south wind sigh, 'This is She!' —
And into leaf unfurl their buds.
Listen! that far, faint clarion! . . .
Farewell! All blessings! I am gone.

3. NONSENSE VERSES

Stuff and Nonsense, and So On
(1927)[1]

THE MOUSE

In a snug little house
Which I shared with my Fanny,
Lived a mite of a mouse,
And we called it Magnani.

MOONSHINE

There was a young lady of Rheims,
There was an old poet of Gizeh;
He rhymed on the deepest and sweetest of themes,
She scorned all his efforts to please her:
And he sighed, 'Ah, I see,
She and sense won't agree.'
So he scribbled her moonshine, mere moonshine, and she,
With jubilant screams, packed her trunk up in Rheims,
Cried aloud, 'I am coming, O Bard of my dreams!'
And was clasped to his bosom in Gizeh.

THE BONNET

There was a young man in a hat,
And by went Miss B. in a bonnet;
When he saw her, he smiled at the lat-
ter: ay, and the roses upon it.
But when, by and by —
As blue as the sky —
He detected her eye
'Neath its brim; well, oh my!
He wished that fair cheek was well under his hat.
And his own half-concealed in her bonnet.

[1] See Bibliographical Appendix, p. 893.

THE TULIP

There was an old Begum of Frome,
There was an old Yogi of Leicester;
She sent him a tulip in bloom,
He rolled his black eyes and he blessed her.
How replete with delight
Is a flower to the sight!
It brightens the day and it sweetens the night.
Oh! if all the old ladies grew tulips in Frome,
How happy the Yogis in Leicester!

A PAIR

There's a stealthy old gaffer named Time;
There's a nimble rapscallion called Cupid;
They have often been put into rhyme
By poets one should not call stupid:
Yet never shall Man,
Ponder deep as he can,
Get the hang of that hour-glassed old younker named Time,
Who mows down the lovely from Compline to Prime,
And at work must have been before loving began,
Who yet by this amorous fledgling is duped —
A sly, blindfold rascal (with arrows) called Cupid.

DEAR SIR

There was an old Rabbi of Ur;
He loved a Miss Beaulieu.
She sent him a letter: 'Dear Sir . . .'
Then a stone-cold 'Yours truly.'
Now what she could mean
By the dots in between
Is not plain to be seen.
We can but infer the Rabbi of Ur
Enquired of Miss Beaulieu.

THE DUET

There was a young lady of Tring,
There was an old Fellow of Kello;
And she — she did nothing but sing,
And he — he did nothing but bellow:
    Now I think (and don't you?)
    That the best thing to do
    Were to marry these two:
Then maybe the one would sing no more in Tring,
    Or the other not bellow in Kello.

THE RUBY

There was an old Bhoojah of Ghât,
Who wore a prodigious great Ruby —
'Out of sight,' it is said, 'when he sat.'
But how can this possibly true be?
I've pondered and pondered, and sometimes have felt
That the gem in discussion reposed in his belt,
For 'tis there if sheer sitting has made one too fat,
And — being a Bhoojah — one sits on a mat,
    There *might* blaze unseen a great Ruby.

MISS PHEASANT

There was an old man with a gun,
Who espied an old lady named Pheasant;
She sat on a seat in the sun,
And he stared, and he stared: most unpleasant!
    But at last, drawing near,
    He made it quite clear
That he had no *intention* so rude to appear,
    But was merely confused, being out with his gun,
    At espying a lady named Pheasant.

HOPPING

There was an old widow of Wapping;
There is a sweet pretty country in Kent:
She heard that her friends had gone hopping,
And thought she'd go too. So she went.
　　Now this simple old dear,
　　Who was sixty — and plump,
　　Thought a hop, it is clear,
　　Is a one-lègged jump;
And thus she progressed — *hop-hop-hop* — *hop* —
　　through Wapping,
　　On — on — into sweet pretty Kent.

DUSK

There was an old person named Fish
Who descried in the twilight a Finn;
Then the eyesight's not all one could wish,
And the shadows of nightfall begin.
His greeting was frigid. He said, 'I declare
Such fractions are vulgar. Yes, quite. I don't care
To perceive mere excrescences taking the air,
Whether dorsal, or ventral, or caudal. So there!
Let a stark monosyllable serve, namely, Pish!'
Said that peevish, self-centred old person named Fish
　　Who'd descried in the twilight a Finn.

GREEN

There was an old grocer of Goring
Had a butter assistant named Green,
Who sank through a hole in the flooring
And never was afterwards seen.
　　Did he look in his cellar?
　　Did he miss the poor fellow?
　　Not at all. Quite phlegmatic,
　　He retired to an attic,
And there watched the moon in her glory o'er Goring —
　　A sight not infrequently seen.

[846]

THE LADY McTAGGART

The Lady McTaggart preferred to recline
(Not to sit on a chair) when she went out to dine;
And, if she approved of the victuals, she would,
When she sank on the sofa, sigh, 'So far, so good.'

J. J.

There was an old vicar of Sinder
Had a sexton named Jeremy Jones,
He'd watch him from out of his winder —
And smile at him digging up bones;
    Then, hid in a curtain,
    To make sound uncertain,
He'd holla, 'Hello, there! OLD JONES! J. Jones!'
    And Jones, like an owl,
    Would peer o'er his showl,
And wonder from which of his old friends in Sinder
Had burst out that muffled, 'Old Jones!'

BUTTONS

There was an old skinflint of Hitching
Had a cook, Mrs. Casey, of Cork;
There was nothing but crusts in the kitchen,
While in parlour was sherry and pork.
So at last, Mrs. Casey, her pangs to assuage,
Having snipped off his buttonses, curried the page;
And now, while that skinflint gulps sherry and pork
    In his parlour adjacent to Hitching,
To the tune blithe and merry of knife and of fork,
    Anthropophagy reigns in the kitchen.

MEAT

From out his red and sawdust shop
This butcher, born to chepe and chop,
Surveys without a trace of grief
Perambulating tombs of beef.
From an unmoved and pale-blue eye,
He gloats on these sarcophagi —
Whether they're walking or riding in 'busses
He gloats on these sarcophaguses,
And as he gloats (with greedy eye)
He says, 'Buy! Buy! Buy! Buy! Buy! Buy!'

It's probable we never shall
Convince him that an animal
Is not mere layers of lean and fat;
He may have butched too much for that.
But still; some day we may be able
To wean him to the vegetable.
Turnip, potato, parsnip, swede —
If only upon these he'd feed,
One beast the fewer then might bleed
He'd be less butcherous than of yore
And help the greengrocer next door.

FISH

In June it must be very nice
To bask about a block of ice —
And watch the World go broiling by
Under a hot and windless sky;
Then turn aside, and, sniffing, see
Perennial mounds of shrimps for tea;
How genial, too, when fancying dab,
To slip one from one's marble slab;
Or, when the stars begin to twinkle,
To broach an unofficial winkle;
Or to descend in morning slipper
And not to have to *buy* a kipper.
This must be very pleasant, and
As pleasant, too, to understand,
When you have cod — are dining off it —
You're only eating so much profit.
Solacing thoughts like these must stir
The musings of the Fishmonger.

[848]

IRON

It is the gentle poet's art
In pleasing diction to impart
    Whatever he thinks meet:
And even make the ugly bloom
    In splendour at our feet.
But neither Shelley, Keats nor Byron
Sang songs on Zinc, or odes to Iron:
    Impracticable feat!

When passing, then, I always bow
To him who makes (I know not how)
A living out of nails, pans, pails —
    I bow across the street —
Just bow: and then my courage fails:
    I beat a swift retreat.

For who can help but ponder on
His awful state when, Sunday gone,
    At daybreak bleak and chill,
He turns the shop-key in its lock,
Stares in upon his ghastly stock
    And opens Monday's till.

THE BARDS

My agèd friend, Miss Wilkinson,
    Whose mother was a Lambe,
Saw Wordsworth once, and Coleridge, too,
    One morning in her p'ram'.*

Birdlike the bards stooped over her —
    Like fledgling in a nest;
And Wordsworth said, 'Thou harmless babe!'
    And Coleridge was impressed.

The pretty thing gazed up and smiled,
    And softly murmured, 'Coo!'
William was then aged sixty-four
    And Samuel sixty-two.

> * This was a three-wheeled vehicle
>   Of iron and of wood;
>   It had a leather apron,
>   But it hadn't any hood.

[849]

THE TANK

'If I had a little money,' mused the Reverend Philip Fish,
'And could buy (without a scruple) any little thing I wish,
I would purchase an Aquarium, some moss and ferns and sand,
Some pretty shining pebbles, branching coral, seashells, and
At centre, a small cistern — made of glass — and placed, well, *so*:
    And filled with what in France is known as *eau*.

'It's really very singular; as soon as I'm asleep,
My dreams at once commit me to the wonders of the deep;
I wallow with the whale, or in profundities obscure
Disport with shapes no waking eye for terror could endure.
At times I am an octopus; at times I am a sprat;
    And there *is* a lot of ocean for a little fish like that!

'I had an uncle — Phineas Fish; but now that he's deceased
All hope of a small legacy has practically ceased.
But if a rich parishioner should tactfully suggest,
"Now, tell me, Father Fish, what little present you'd like *best*,"
Although I wouldn't *think* of it — could only smile my thanks,
    I'm *sure*, you know, my thoughts would turn to tanks!'

BISHOP WINTERBOURNE

The Reverend William Winterbourne,
    When walking in the Mall,
Tired of genteel pedestrians,
    Much yearned to meet a *pal*,
Or, failing an old crony,
        His best gal.

Beelzebub decoyed that wish up.
The Reverend William's now a bishop.
Now, when he fares down Piccadilly,
His blameless Conscience — willy-nilly —
So archepiscopally staid is,
He never gives a thought to ladies.
Heedless of impious scrutinies
The curious fix on all D.D.'s,
His gaiters 'neath his apron wend;
His steps in one direction bend;
His heart, as right as reverend,
Has for desire one only end —

To wit, to join the wild Te Deum
That echoes through the Athenaeum.

THE BUN

The muffin and the crumpet are
    When adequately done
A dish to make a curate wish
    To excel in feats of fun;
A Canon booms, 'tis said, when fed
    On toasted Sallie Lunn;
E'en Deans, I ween, plum cake being seen,
    Have been observed to run:
But, Ah! a Bishop come to tea!
    He takes the Bun.

HYSSOP

Said Judge Jessop,
    'The hyssop
You *think*'s in your wall
    Correctly
    And strictly
Isn't hyssop at all.'
'Isn't hyssop?' says I;
'Isn't hyssop,' says he;
'By no means — not hyssop at all.'

    'If my hyssop,
    Judge Jessop,
Isn't hyssop at all,
    Tell me truly
    And duly
Why it grows on my wall!'
'Why it grows on?' says he.
'Yes, it grows on,' says I;
'Why it grows and it grows on my wall.'

    'On the Bisop,'
    Said Judge Jessop,
'(With the h out), we'll call,
    And straightly,
    Sedately,
We'll resort to your wall.'
'With a ladder?' says I,
'With a ladder,' says he;
'And we'll ask him — "What's *that* in the wall?" '

[851]

So the Bisop,
Judge Jessop
And me — three in all —
Hell and leather
Together
Climbed up on my wall.
'What's that there?' says I.
'What's what where?' says he;
'Why, house-leek,' said the Bisop. That's all.

MISS CLEGG

Miss Clegg was accustomed to do as she wished,
  Upon Fate she was never a waiter;
And whenever she came upon water she fished,
  And always attired in a gaiter.

The word has a singular look, I agree,
  Yet is apt in the case of Miss Clegg;
Since from birth she a monopode happened to be,
  And you can't wear a pair on one leg.

Her foot was her basis then, while with her float
  She dangled a worm 'neath a willow;
Or, far out to sea, stood erect in a boat,
  And awaited a bite from the billow.

THE MONSTER

There was an Old Man with a net.
He heard of a Fish in the sea.
He sighed, 'It is strange I forget
The spot where the monster should be.'
      But ev'n as he yearned,
      His back being turned,
The leisurely Behemoth swam up behind
In a manner by no means ostensibly kind,
      And not pausing to gloat
      Neatly swallowed his boat —
Its oars and its rowlocks (the whole of the set),
The Old Man in his sea-boots, Sou'-wester, and net;
Leaving nothing at all, to be viewed with regret,
No touching memento at which one might fret —
      No, Nothing at all: merely Sea.

[852]

THE LADY GODIVA

The Lady Godiva Godolphin, of a blood by the centuries
blued,
  Flowing back, I believe,
  To Adam and Eve,
 Had a rooted disdain of the *nood*.

'Sheep are clad,' she would cry, 'in their woollies; the
buffalo's hirsute, though rude;
  Apart from their tails,
  Even flounders have scales;
 Not a shrimp in the ocean swims nood.

'The ruff has a ruff, though a ruff's not enough; the sea-
lion, I'm told, has a hood;
  The lobster a back,
  It's an effort to crack,
 And the zebra with stripes is imbrued.

'The oyster is shelled, and the goat has a coat, whether
wild, or domestic or Zoo'ed.
  From a bee to a bear —
  You can look, you can stare —
 But in nature *no* creature is nood.'

Pelisses and petticoats, tippets and jupes, she wore
by the gross (when she could),
  She would ride in her gig
  In nine fronts and three wig,
 And smile when the little boys boo'ed.

Her tables and chairs and her bedsteads — lest even their
toes should obtrude —
  She sewed up in chintz
  Trimmed with calico, since,
 Thus upholstered, they couldn't look nood.

The Cherubs, that graced the Godolphins at rest in the
Church of St. Jude,
  She said, looked less bloated,
  When trousered and coated,
 And at all events none remained nood.

[853]

When her bath-tub was brought by a handmaid (who at
  no time desired to intrude),
      She would paddle, splash, plunge —
      In a sark made of sponge,
  And not, as do most of us, nood.

Now it's whispered the Lady Godiva was the least little
  bit of a prude;
      I really can't say,
      She long since passed away,
  And what matter if nobody knoowed?

AN IDLE WORD

I used to wear a diamond ring,
A small but valuable thing,
A souvenir of how and when
I had succeeded up till then.
I used to wear it day and night.
I polished it to keep it bright.
I never took it off. I'd sit
For hours at home and look at it.
For years and years I'd had to wait
To make it mine. It kept me straight.

When, too, in shops I've sat at tea,
People would stare at it, and me —
Not knowing *who* I might not be.
I'd just call, 'Miss!' — the waitress would
Scamper to bring me drink and food.
Then with my hand I'd smooth my hair,
Knowing my diamond safely there.

Often, when walking in the street,
'Aha!' I've thought (the thought was sweet),
'They little guess what's lying hid
'Beneath this glove!' (of suède or kid).

If only I'd been let alone,
I'd have stayed happy with that stone.
But no. In this world there are them
   Who envy even a gem.
One day I heard a lady say —
And as she spoke, she looked my way:
'A diamond is a vulgar thing
To see corusking in a ring;
And, like as not, as I've been told,
They're only glass — in brass: not gold.'

I rose. I felt, without a doubt,
My very life-blood trickling out.
I sold the ring, at awful loss,
To one I knew named Isaac Moss.
And now in life no hope I see;
Its bottom's fallen out for me.

My situation's gone; I owe
Not less than twenty pounds or so;
Outside a Public House I stand,
With loafers upon either hand;
And if a Constable draws near,
My skin goes cold and stiff with fear;
He knows I know he's but to wait
And some dark cell will be my fate.

It only proves — what good men teach —
We should be cautious in our speech.
If that proud lady had not said
My diamond of glass was made,
Should I be drifting in my prime
Into a *cul-de-sac* of crime?
One heedless, scoffing word — and see!
What the old vixen's done for me!

HORSES

I never see a coach go by
Without remembering that I
Shall some day take a ride in one
With horses not allowed to run.
They'll step on leisurely to where
A hole gapes in the open air,
Then turn and look, to see if they
May now enjoy a munch of hay,
Or any other kind of meal.

It's odd how little horses feel.
Half their delight on earth one knows is
To have us humans pat their noses.
And when at last we go our way,
They don't so much as breathe a Nay;
But, if permitted, on will pass,
To graze upon our funeral grass.

BAH!

When I chanced to look over the wall in the glade —
    I was taking a walk with Mamma —
I saw an old ewe sitting down in the shade,
    And she opened her mouth and said, 'Bah!'

That's always what happens when sheep I come near,
    They watch me approach from afar,
And out of the turnips and clover I hear
    A horrid ironical 'Bah!'

What can I have done? I can't understand —
    The cantankerous creatures they are!
I never throw stones, I hold dear Mamma's hand,
    And I don't think they *ought* to say 'Bah!'

ARCHERY

To place one's little boy — just *so* —
    An apple on his head,
Then loose an arrow from one's bow
    And not to shoot him dead: —

That is a feat requiring skill,
    And confidence as well;
As any archer would have told
    The man who tolled the bell.

The luck must hold; the child stand still:
    This William befell;
But just how close was core to corse
    Could only William tell.

SAID JANE

Said Jane to the old Fisherman,
    'I cannot understand
Why ever little fishes swim
    So close up to the land;
If *I* knew of those horrid hooks
    I'd keep away from *sand.*'

That Fisherman, he scratched his head
    ('Twas sunset o'er the lea),
Then twisted of his quid, and said,
    'What, missie, boffles *me*
Is why the little warmits keep
    A sight too far to sea.'

And there the problem must remain —
    Beyond the wit of man —
As posited by little Jane
    And by the Fisherman,
Leaving it still precisely as
    When they their talk began.

THE WAIF

There lived a small hermaphrodite beside the silver Brent,
A stream meandering not in maps of Surrey, Bucks, or Kent;
Yet jealous elves from these sweet parts, this tiny mite to vex,
Would tease, torment, and taunt, and call him, 'Master Middlesex!

He lived on acorns, dewdrops, cowslips, bilberries, and snow —
A small, shy, happy, tuneful thing, and innocent of woe;
Except when these malignant imps, his tenderness to vex,
Would tease, torment, and taunt, and call him, 'Master Middlesex!'

He ran away; he went to sea; to far Peru he came.
There where the Ataquipa flows and odorous cinchona
     blows and no one knows his name,
He nests now with the humming-bird that sips but never pecks;
And silent slides the silver Brent, and mute is Middlesex.'

THE SEA-NYMPH

There was an old mariner
Heard 'mid his dunes
A swallow-tailed sea-nymph
Decanting of tunes.
Trill, grace-note, cadenza,
And high in the treble,
She warbled as sweet
As a sea-nymph is able.

He hearkened, he pondered,
He said, 'I'm aware
Of the strains of a sea-nymph
Seducing the air;
No doubt she sits combing
And sleeking her hair.

'She sings like a linnet,
I assume she is fair,
And she *may* be supposing
That *I'm* lurking near!
But of music I've little;
Of voice I have none;
I can merely applaud
When the aria is done.'

[858]

So he sate on the dunes
By the fringe of the deep,
And, lulled by her warblings,
He fell fast asleep.
When he woke, 'twas cold night
With huge stars overhead,
But all silent the sands
Of his barbarous bed.

He sighed — oh, sighed softly:
'My applause will come late,
For I see that the sea-nymph
Was unable to wait;
Still, good manners must not by
Inaction be sapped';
So he clap-clap-clap-clap-clap-
Clap-clap-clap-clap-clapped.

NO!

Full oft I've stood at winter dusk alone upon the strand,
Watching the breakers thundering in for leagues across the sand,
And smiled up at my friend in heaven, the Moon, so
   pale and wan,
      Amused within that wise men say
      'Tis she who, gliding on her way,
       'Tis *She* — who leads them on!

No, no. And when at dead of dark — and that sweet
   orb's at rest —
I muse for hours on Rigel, Deneb, Spica, and the rest
Of Night's clear candles gleaming there like glow-
   worms in the grass,
      I laugh aloud to think of those
      Who, peering through a tube, suppose
       They're pits of boiling gas!

Away with them! I dance and sing; but could not sing at all,
Believing me mere matter on a rotatory Ball.
Such horrid thoughts confuse my mind, they fill my soul
   with woe;
      But when in meadows green I stray,
      Between the dawning and the day,
      And hear the lark's shrill roundelay,
       I *know* I KNOW I KNOW.

[859]

OLD B.

To sit under a tree,
No humans near by,
And to gaze on and on, up, up, into the sky,
Was from breakfast to tea
The delight of old B.;
And sometimes he'd smile, or he'd sigh.

Yes, such was his bent,
And it's just to declare
Quite apart from the fragrance and joy of fresh air,
If his days were so spent,
With a tree for a tent,
He may have found something of interest there:

A vagabond crow,
A lark o'er the lea,
A nest with its little birds, possibly three,
A voluminous cloud sailing off to the sea,
A balloon with its basket gone off on the spree:
Mere sky, as we know,
May stay blank as an O . . .
Still, no matter that. There he'd sit 'neath his tree;
And that's about all that is known of old B.

ANN'S AUNT AND THE BEAR

It filled Ann's Aunt Maria with rage
To see a wild thing in a cage.
At sight of creature, winged or furred,
Confined by bars, by chains deterred,
She'd melt with pity. In a word —
'Pore thing,' she'd cry, 'you pore, *pore* thing!'
At which the dainty dear would sing
A little soft sad song, or cheep,
Or turn a curious eye to peep
At her great face, and brow, and bonnet —
Like a cathedral perched upon it.

'Twas just her kindly, friendly humour:
She'd grieve as much o'er lion or puma,
And gloat upon their keepers when
They chanced their heads within its den.
'Pore thing!' she'd mutter. Not 'Poor Men!'

One afternoon her aunt and Ann
(Who'd gone to see a nursery-man
About a leaky watering can),
As they were moving gently home,
On a most horrid scene did come:
Two foreigners (with longish hair)
Were leading on a chain a Bear,
A bushy, bright-eyed, thirsty beast,
Who had trudged a score of miles at least
In heat and dust — at least a score,
And danced perhaps as many more;
Yes, danced — and growled — and danced again
Whene'er these long-haired foreign men
Should in their cruelty think proper
To try and earn an English copper,
Or tuppence, even, if any dunce
Should want the dance danced more than once.

Yes, there, beneath a chestnut's shade,
This parched-up beast was being made
To caper and to growl a noise
To please a pack of errand boys;
It danced and gruffed, it breathed vast sighs,
Its half-bald head a maze of flies;
Its claws went tic-tac in the dust,
And still it danced, for dance it must;
While the two Frogs in hope of gain
Stood grinning by and tweaked its chain.

When Ann, and Ann's aunt, Aunt Maria,
Saw this, Ann's aunt's eyes flashed with fire;
She said, 'Pore thing! you pore, pore thing!'
And then she raised a stout umbrella,
And *turned* upon the nearest fellow.
French or Italian, Greek or Dutch,
She simply couldn't thwack too much;
Sound thumping thumps she laid full many on,
Then up and smote his dazed companion.

And there you see kind Aunt Mari',
Her bugled bonnet all awry,
And plump cheek flushed with her exertions
Against these parasitic Persians;
While Ann, now lost in rapture, stands
Clapping her little mittened hands,
And butcher's, baker's, grocer's boy
Yell out their rude barbaric joy.

Alack! what evil chance we find!
Her wrath made Aunt Maria blind:
In compassing his tyrants' ruin,
She didn't notice their poor Bruin,
Who, having wriggled off his muzzle,
Was shuffling in to join the tussle,
And, rather giddy in the head,
In gratitude for what she had said
And done to that cruel Bruin-baster,
Went sidling up, and then — embraced her!

It's sad indeed to have to tell
What then this kind, kind soul befell —
Ann's Aunt Maria. So sharp B's squeeze
Ann hadn't time to whisper, 'Please,
You're cuddling my dear aunt so close
You must be treading on her toes,
I cannot even see her nose!'

And when at length the Bear had shown
That gratitude goes to the bone,
Nothing the caitiffs then could do
Would bring his cold protectress to.
They could but rub their hands. They said,
'We 'ave ze fear, ze ladee's dead!
She do not breathe, nor any ting;
Pore zing, pore zing, ze pore, *pore* zing!'

'Tis said all clouds are silver-lined;
This one small fact then keep in mind:
Had quite, quite base been either man,
They might have fed the Bear on Ann.

THE WARMINT

Oh, she was just a little thing
    A slim thing, a narrow thing,
A pig-tailed, dark and black-eyed thing,
        Not five span.
She didn't care a fig, a fig,
For any creature, small or big,
Gander, turkey, cow, or pig,
        Woman or man.
She set papa a booby-trap
    It tumbled on his head;
She dived into the water-butt;
    Lit fireworks in the shed;

The bed they call an apple-pie
   She made poor cook for Sunday;
Played with the bunnies under the moon
   Through half the night to Monday.
Oh, she was just a little thing,
A starry, dark, mischievous thing,
An imp of mischief, out and in,
   A terror, tax and torment.
Mamma called her her precious lamb;
Cook cooked her custards, tarts and flam;
The gardener, whose name was Sam,
Wild strawberries grew to make her jam;
The nurse who wheeled her in her pram,
   And stitched her many a garment,
No peace a moment ever knew;
And yet they loved her through and through —
   This wicked little warmint.

THE EVENING

Happy was Edward in the love
   Of beauteous Esmeralda;
And one fair evening in a grove
   His ownest own he call'd her.

Upon his meek and manly breast
   She hid her eyes cerulean,
While modesty her cheek expressed
   Like some small shy chameleon.

But ah! a Panther spies them there,
   Deep-tranced in speechless rapture;
He gloats on such inviting fare,
   How easy, too, to capture.

Supple and gay, he sleeks his way,
   And — gollops up poor Edward.
'Oh, Esmeralda, shun delay,
   And hasten quickly bedward!'

Alas! she lingers; and too long.
   A pounce, a far, faint squealin',
The young and fair are now the strong,
   And much refresht's the feline.

[863]

ERGO

There was an old man said, 'I am:
And therefore, O rapture! I think!'
They retorted, 'H'm, h'm?' and 'H'm, h'm!'
And each at the rest winked a wink.
    Yet it may be, you know,
    That he *fancied* it so —
    That he'd taken to heart
    The words of Descartes,
Who, hoping and hoping for *some*thing to come,
At last had exclaimed, '*Cogito, ergo sum.*'
Yes, it may be he had not intended a cram,
    Or to give an occasion to wink,
When he piped up in ecstasy, 'Neighbours, I am:
    And therefore I think!'

VERY

There was a young lady of Bow,
A dandy there was, too, of Derry;
'How sweetly the hawthorn trees blow!'
    He murmured. And she replied, 'Very.'
    Then she glanced, and she smiled,
    And she tapped with her shoe;
    Then slid her eyes sidelong,
    And both were pure blue;
    And the longer the silence,
    The deeper it grew:
    Till he said, 'If 'twere kissing,
    I'd like to kiss *you*.
Would it be very naughty to do — well — like — so?'
She thought him a goose, yet she didn't cry, 'Bo!'
But blushed, tittered, sighed, and said, 'Very!'

TOBAGO

There was an old man with delight
Heard his father was born in Tobago;
For now it seemed perfectly proper and right
He should be such a prey to lumbago.
    The old gentleman, too,
    Had been known to complain —
    In terms, some might think,
    Too extreme — of the pain:
To hear, then — we won't say, the reason — but rhyme,
For this state of affairs was a triumph sublime:
He looked at his sire with the utmost delight,
    And wrote a long ode to Tobago.

THE EEL

There was an old person of Dover
Who called on his sister in Deal,
With a sack hanging over his shoulder
In which was a whopping great eel.
It leapt down the area, scuttled upstairs.
It golloped up bolsters and wash-jugs and chairs,
Her boots, shoes, and slippers, in singles and pairs;
    And alas! when this Ogre
    Had finished its meal,
    There was no one of Dover
    With a sister in Deal.

THE BLACKBIRDS

There was an old man, in reproof
Of the blackbirds hob-nob in his cherries,
Cried: 'Be off now, you rascals, be off!'
But the rogues never stirred from the berries.
    They knew that his wits
    Were a little astray;
    They knew on old fogeys it's
    Easy to prey.
So they merely sang sweeter to drown his reproof,
And louder he called at them, 'Rascals, be off!'
    The merrier they in his cherries.

[865]

THE PENNY

A person of Abergavenny
Met an old man from Bromley-by-Bow;
He said, 'Would you lend me a penny?'
And she, she replied, 'I don't know.'
Now strangers are dangerous, that we agree;
And with money in public best not be too free.
Still, perchance 'twere less caustic to say, 'Well, I'll see,'
    Than that vague 'I don't know,'
When asked for a penny in Abergavenny
By an old man from Bromley-by-Bow.

FRECKLES

There was a young lady of Beccles,
Who had a twin sister in Crete,
She was dappled all over with freckles,
    From her top-knot right down to her feet;
For round about Gnossos the sun is so hot
One sits in a torpor, complexion forgot,
    And basks in the bountiful heat.
Now the Beccles young damosel, being a twin,
Soon reflected the state her poor sister was in,
    Though never a word came from Crete;
        But she being taller,
        The freckles were smaller,
    And stopped inches short of her feet.

KANT

There was an old Lawyer of Diss,
There was an old Doctor of Bicester;
They argued, if *that* there is *This*,
Then the Thing-in-Itself is a twister.
    When an agèd old aunt,
    Of philosopy scant,
    Said such talk was all cant:
Then her nephews indulged in contortions of bliss,
    And one of 'em up and, yes — kissed her.

THE FLY

There was once an old parson named Next
  Saw a fly in his pulpit.
The instant he gave out his text
  He detected the culprit.
It winged up and up, paused to stare in his eye;
Betwixt neck and neck-band proceeded to pry;
It traversed his sermon on six tufted toes;
Buzzed up in his face and then perched on his nose.
Expelled from this organ, it made a swift pass
To sip of the water that stood in his glass,
Lost its balance — fell in . . . O, alas and alas!
      And he? Parson Next?
      Distressed and perplexed,
      He stopped in his pulpit —
      He just couldn't help it —
      And proceeded to gulp it:
Yes, insect and all, and disposed of the culprit.
So if ever kind Fate should a see for him dish up,
It may, in due season, reside in a Bishop.

WOOL

There was an old lady of Poole
Who called at a mercer's in Whitting,
And ordered £10 worth of wool,
When 'twas *weight* she required — for her knitting.
    Now her nephews and nieces
    Look like sheep in their fleeces;
    Their feet sound like trotters,
    When out with their mothers;
    When they're drinking and eating,
    Their talk is all bleating;
And many a glutton has thought of boiled mutton
When watching their capers in school.

THE SHUBBLE

There was an old man said, 'I fear
That life, my dear friends, is a bubble,
Still, with all due respect to a Philistine ear,
A limerick's best when it's double.'
When they said, 'But the waste
Of time, temper, taste!'
He gulped down his ink with cantankerous haste,
And chopped off his head with a shubble.

VENDETTA

An enemy of Dr. Drake's,
Who, after many worse mistakes,
Prescribed him tar for stomach-aches,
Bought four and twenty duck.
Stowed in a sack
On the carrier's back,
He crept next door to a tumbledown shack
And dumped them in the muck.

They turned the doctor's head, they did;
He often now saw red, he did;
Ev'n fees became a tax.
'That Dr. Drake,' his patients said,
'There's word he's taken to his bed,
No doubt he'll very soon be dead;
He can't endure their *Quack*(s)!'

MEDDLING

Says James to his second cousin, he says,
'Fair mystery, John, it be,
Where them that thinks get the thoughts they thinks —
What they calls philosophee;
I sits on these sands for days at a stretch,
Staring out at the deep blue Sea,
But, pickle me, Coz, if a glim there comes
Of the thoughts what they thinks to *me*.'

Says John, nodding solemn, 'There's men and there's men,
    And there's some keeps their minds on the latch;
But if ever you pines for to fish down deep,
It's got to be done when you're half asleep,
    And with tackle and hook to match.
And I warn you, James, when you gets a bite,
    It's turrible things you'll catch;

'Fishes with goggle eyes, fishes with wings,
Fishes with beards and electric stings,
Shapeless, elastic and jellified things,
    No Christian could despatch.

'What's worse,' says he, 'and I've seed it in books
    On *most* peculiar themes,
If you hankers to know what a willain you are,
    Keep a werry sharp eye on your dreams.
Look at 'em close, James, and you'll find
You've got a fair horrible sink of a mind,
    Like a bog in a fog that steams.

'But never no good come of meddling, James.
    There's things as is *hid*, I say.
Take it or leave it, then, just as you please,
There's nothing what's round us here — he's or she's —
But lives on a soo-per-fish-i-es,
    And there I intend to stay.'

THE ACCOMPANIMENT

The man in the hat (whom you see in the picture)
    Mused softly one evening: 'I sit in this copse,
And the birds warble sweetly, for sweet is their nature;
    Yet they sing at haphazard, then — every one stops.

'Yes, as if at the lift of a baton or finger,
    The love-notes, *pu-wees* and *too-witta-woos* cease,
Not a pause for applause, not a wing seems to linger,
    The forests fall mute — the whole world is at peace.

'I marvel. I marvel. For take, now, the linnet —
    That sociable haunter of charlock and gorse,
There is no sweeter throat with a melody in it,
    Still, *solo* he pipes as a matter of course!

'God forbid that with drum, cornet, triangle, cymbal,
    We should drown the wee cherubs: assuredly not.
Still, my dear sister Jane on the harp is still nimble,
    Nor have I my old skill with the fiddle forgot . . .'

So now, as the sun in the West is declining,
    The twain to that hill hie, the birds hie there too;
Rings the plucking of harp-strings, the catgut's sweet pining,
    And a chorus *orchestral* ascends to the blue.

Besides which, a host of all small kinds of beasties
    (They are shown on the cut, though Miss Jane's out of sight),
Having learned the harmonic a marvellous feast is,
    Troll out an *Amen* ere they part for the night.

WHY!

'Dear Father, tell me, Why are Worms?'
    Tim questioned me; and I —
Mute as a fish, stared on and on
    Into the empty sky.

'Father, dear, tell me, *Why* are Worms?'
    Tim questioned me. Poor me!
In vain, in vain, I gazed, gazed, gazed
    Over the vacant sea.

'O Father, father! How are Worms?
    And When? — and What? — and Where?'
I scanned the mute and wintry blue,
    The cloudlets floating there;
I scanned the leafless trees that tossed
    Their twiglets in the air;

I marked the rooks and starlings stalk
    Up — down the furrows bare;
I passed an unresponsive hand
    Over my hatless hair;

But when these eyes encountered Tim's
    Mine was the emptier stare.

SUPPOSE

Suppose the year were but a month,
  And that a week,
  And that a day:
At thought of it I scarce can speak;
  The *difference*, I say!
In four-and-twenty hours to see,
Like phantoms in a dream flit by,
Between the smiling earth and sky,
A whole year's birds, flowers, seasons fair,
Packed in a space so small, so spare,
  The gross rapidity!
It simply makes my head go round,
It lifts me dizzy from the ground,
  The mere idea, *per se*.

PONJOO

My Uncle Jasper in Siam
Once breakfasted on Ponjoo jam.
This Ponjoo is a fruit, I find,
That has its pulp outside its rind,
  In colour a pale puce.
Within it lurks a heart-shaped stone
As hard as granite, iron, or bone,
  And round it wells its juice.

Now Uncle was a man of fashion
  Just visiting Siam;
And when he stripped away the pulp
And took the kernel at a gulp,
He flew into a furious passion
  And said the bad word '————!'

The Emperor, whose palace stood
Within the fragrant Ponjoo wood,
Sitting at lattice, stooped and heard
My uncle use this wicked word,
  And to his menials said:
'Convey that Pagan to a cell
Where never Echo's voice shall tell
The language that just now befell,
  And there strike off his head.'

And that is why our Family,
At early breakfast, lunch, or tea,
And I, where'er I am,
If on the table we see laid
A pot of Ponjoo marmalade,
Say, 'Drat it,' to the parlourmaid,
But never, never '————!'

ODD MAN OUT

'Have you ever fought in a battle, Tom?'
Tom stared; and thought: and said,
'Fought in a battle once did I . . . knee-deep
in dead . . .
The sun was downlike — over there; the night's
first murk was up,
And leaf-still woods was all around. We was
caught-like, in a cup;
The Regiment gone. Just me, and Sam,
shouldered against a stack;
And the Enemy come on in sheaves; and we —
we kept 'em back.

'I sees their shakoes now — mole-gray; and
their faces scowling — *so;*
Their mouths a hubbub of shouts and squeals,
a-rocketing to and fro.
They come in droves with bright bare swords —
guns was a coward's game;
And every head we see — sun-red, we — well —
sliced off the same.
At last Sam says, he says, "Fight on! I'm
wounded seven times o'er."
And I, I says to Sam, "That's me; and saturate
with gore."

[872]

'Groan, Oh, we did! And the dew dripped down,
 and 'undreds and 'undreds still
I sees like grass before the wind come sweeping
 up that hill . . .
I s'pose it were turned half-past-nine, and a
 high and starry night,
When me and Sam climbed arduous out, no living
 soul in sight.
And I — I dragged Sam's tunic off; Sam did the
 same by me;
And we bound up our wounds and broken bones with
 strips of hankerchee.

'And then we takes a mattock each; a trench —
 sixteen by ten —
We dug afore old midnight struck, to bury them
 poor men —
Born Sodgers like ourselves, but now, corpses
 as cold as clay:
'Underd and fifty seven in rows we laid 'em
 neat away;
And scrabbled back the good leaf mould, and
 beat it flat and trim:
And Sam in the moonshine looks at me; and I —
 I looks at him.

' "I ain't much shakes at sums," he says, "but
 one-five-seven by two
I reckon leaves one over, Tom. Did I kill
 he — or you?"
Says I, a-smiling soft and meek, "The night,
 lad's, getting late,
But if you wants your total, Sam, I *counted*
 seventy-eight . . ." '

'But did you really, *really*, Tom?' Tom drove
 deep down his spade;
'That were Sam's score, sir. Odd man out I
 took for mine,' he said.

THE SPECTRE

The moment I glanced at the mirk-windowed mansion
    that lifts from the woodlands of Dankacre, Lincs.,
To myself I said softly: 'Confide in me, pilgrim, why is
    it the heart in your bosom thus sinks?
What's amiss with this region? It's certainly England;
    the moon, there, is rising, and there Vega blinks.'

A drear wind sighed bleakly; it soughed in the silence;
    it sobbed as if homesick for Knucklebone, Notts.;
The moon with her mountains showed spectral and sullen;
    the corncrake and nightjar craked, jarred, from their grots;
And aloft from its mistletoe nest in an oak-tree, a
    scritch-owlet's scritch froze my blood into clots.

I called on my loved one asleep 'neath the myrtles whose
    buds turn to berries in Willowlea, Herts.;
I mused on sweet innocent scenes where in summer the
    deer browse, the doves croon, the butterfly darts;
But, alas! these devices proved vain, horror loured, my
    terror was such as no metre imparts.

For afar o'er the marshes the booming of bitterns, like the
    bitterns that boomed once from Bootle in Lancs.,
Came mingled with wailings from Dowsing and Dudgeon
    of sea-gulls lamenting o'er Bluddithumbe Banks —
My bowels turned to water; my knees shook; my skin
    crept; and the hairs on my cranium rose up in hanks.

And lo! from an attic, there peered out a visage, with
    eyes like brass bed-knobs and beak like a hawk's;
And it opened the casement, and climbed down the ivy,
    with claws like a trollop's, on legs like a stork's;
And I screamed and fled inland, from mansion and moon-
    shine, till I saw the sun rising on Pep-y-gent, Yorks.

BONES

Said Mr. Smith, 'I really cannot
    Tell you, Dr. Jones —
The most peculiar pain I'm in —
    I think it's in my *bones*.'

Said Dr. Jones, 'Oh, Mr. Smith,
　　That's nothing. Without doubt
We have a simple cure for that;
　　It is to take them out.'

He laid forthwith poor Mr. Smith
　　Close-clamped upon the table,
And, cold as stone, took out his bones
　　As fast as he was able.

And Smith said, 'Thank you, thank you, *thank* you,'
　　And wished him a Good-day;
And with his parcel 'neath his arm
　　He slowly moved away.

THE JILT

When, in her shift, poor Delia Swift
　　Heard footfall on the stair,
She whispered low into the house
　　　'Who's there?'

Her blood stood still from cheek to heel,
　　When, softer than a sigh,
Sang in her ear, forlorn and drear,
　　　''Tis I!'

'What have you come for? Oh, for whom?'
　　The quiet stagnant grew:
And a voice like the wind in the chimney wailed,
　　　'For *you!*'

The room fell bitter cold, her bed
　　Multangular became;
The zig-zag pattern on curtain and wall
　　Jigged in the candle flame;
And Delia, now to panic moved,
Mindless of what a jilt she'd proved,
Cried out on all the loves she'd loved,
　　　By name.

On — on — she pleaded; vowed; and wept.
　　She pleaded, wept, in vain.
The Spectre catched her, came a lift,
And never seen was she (or shift)
　　　Again.

[875]

FALSE DAWN

My old friend, Lord O., owned a parcel of land —
A waste of wild dunes, rushes, marram and sand —
With a square Tudor mansion — not a bush, not a tree —
Looking over salt flats a full league to the sea;
    And at his demise he bequeathed it to me. . . .

It was dusk as I entered. A gull to its mates
Cackled high in the air as I passed through the gates,
And out of the distance — full twenty miles wide —
Came the resonant boom of the incoming tide:
    Gulls' scream and groundswell, and nothing beside.

In the cold of the porch I tugged at the bell,
Till the bowels of the house echoed back like a knell.
I hearkened; then peered through the hole in the lock;
And a voice, cold and clammy, inquired, 'Did you knock?'
    And there was Lord O. — in his funeral smock.

In silence he watched me, then led me upstairs
To a room where a table stood, flanked by two chairs;
For light but a dip, in an old silver stick,
With guttering grease and a long unsnuffed wick;
    And he said, 'If you're hungry, eat quick.'

So I sipped his cold water and nibbled his bread,
While he gazed softly out from the holes in his head:—
'You would hardly believe, Brown, when once I was gone,
How I craved for your company — where there is none;
    Shivered and craved — on and on.

'This house, I agree, may seem cheerless to you;
But glance from that window! By Gad, what a view!
And think, when we weary of darkness and rats,
We can share the long night with the moon and the bats,
    And wander for hours on those flats.

'And when in the East creeping daybreak shows wan,
You'll excuse me, I know, if I have to be gone,
For as soon as sounds cock-crow, the red and the grey,
It's a rule with us all — even peers must obey —
    We all have to hasten away.'

So that is my fate now. The small hours draw near,
We shall stalk arm-in-arm in that scenery drear;
Tête-à-tête by blanched breakers discuss on and on
If it's better to be flesh and blood or mere bone,
 Till it's time for Lord O. to be gone.

Yet, doubtless he means well. I would not suggest
To shun peers with property always is best.
But insomnia, nightmare, tic-douloureux, cramp,
Have reduced me to what's little short of a scamp;
For I've hung in my hen-roost a very large lamp.
And now, well, at least two full hours before day,
 Lord O., he hears cock-crow, the red and the grey;
 Sighs; stares at the ocean — and hastens away.

THE JOLLIES

The Captain, he said to his Passenger, ''Twill-a be Full
 Moon to-night,
And at Six Bells sharp, by yon transom and the trucks!
 the Jollies will heave in sight;
And if I was a man and a Christian as would deign for to
 cargo be,
I'd scuttle to my cabin and I'd down and say my prayers,
 for the Jollies is a sight to see!'

The Passenger looked at the Captain, his cheek grey,
 green, and white,
And he stuttered at the scuppers, 'Oh, thank you, Captain
 Stingo, I should much enjoy the sight';
Then descended, like cold suet, to his cabin, and sate in
 the dusk on his bunk,
And (if the English language here admitted of it) he
 thunk and thunk and *thunk.*

And at Five Bells sharp of that there Middle Watch, that
 ship she gave a lurch,
With a noise like the falling of a steeple with all that
 hangs inside it on a church.
And the Passenger ran like a rabbit, his whiskers stiff as
 bristles on his cheek,
And he peered with his eyes above the binnacle, and he
 hadn't very far for to seek.

[877]

For to larboard and to starboard was the Jollies — wan,
    green waves mountain-high,
All silvery and haggard, and a-roaring and a-screaming
    under the pitch-black sky;
Boiling like a pot full of snow-bright broth with a rim
    full nine miles wide;
And the green Moon gloated on the Passenger while he
    stared at the Jollies — and cried.

And the Captain, he said to the helmsman, 'One course
    I've ever took,
And that breast-forward, like R. Browning in the poem;
    so keep her by the book.'
And the Captain, he said to his Passenger, 'Look around,
    and you'll agree,
There seems to be a Jonah stowed away aboard this vessel;
    and by Davy, thou beest he!'

And the Passenger, now past hollering, from his
    waistcoat took his fountain pen,
And wrote, 'I leave the all I have to Stingo, kindest
    and best of men.'
And Stingo, having long since a conviction that where
    there's a Will there's a Way,
Stood a-smilin' and a-smilin' till the ship was on her
    beam ends, and then he yelled, 'Belay!'

'Good-bye,' he sobbed, 'my *dear* Mr. Robinson, it's sad
    to think that parting is so near,
I hoped you might be staying on to breakfast; no
    chance of that, I fear.'
And the Bo'sun piped shrill upon his whistle; and a
    four-foot-thick A.B.
Just lifted Mr. Robinson as gently as a babby, and
    dropped him into the sea.

And a Mermaid swimming quiet by the combings, where
    the keelson hawse-pipe yares,
Inwedged him to her bosom like a porpoise at its
    weaning, and soothed away his cares;
And Stingo, thus bereft of Mr. Robinson, yelled, 'Ho,
    there, lay her by!
For by Davy and by Golly she's a match for any Jolly,
    and there's Rum for them that's dry!'

THE PRETENDER

In the greens of the wilds of Seringapatam
Is the haunt of an ancient redoubtable ram,
  With sharp-pointed horns on its head;
When it snuffs out a Brahmin it scoops with its hooves,
Till the jungle around it is jungle in grooves,
  And then it pretends to be dead.

O White Man beware of such tactics as these,
For if in compassion thou sink to thy knees,
  All thought of mere safety forgot,
With a jerk of its horns the fell creature comes to,
And smiles, as if saying, 'Ah, friend, is it you?'
  When there's none to reply, 'It is not.'

AHKH

At full moon in cold Khamchatka,
  Where the Wheelagheelah flows,
That aquatic fowl, the Vhatka,
  Softly tippets on its toes
(Inebriate with her love-light,
    I suppose).
It is then the astute Khamchatkan
    Fowling goes.

But when her dwindling quarter
  Has to dark her disc resigned,
'Tis a job, by Gob, to slaughter
  A fowl no eye can find —
And his '*Ahkh*,' his '*Ahkh*' is nothing
    But a blind.

Now it's nearer, sweeter, clearer;
  Now it wails and wanes and dies;
Now the night-beleaguered hearer
  Hears it *ahkhing* in the skies;
When, in sooth, it's nesting snugly in a nest
    not half its size,
Hidden in the reeds and rushes, scarce a hand's-
    breadth from his eyes!

So the Fowler should go fowling,
  Armed with candle, book, and bell,
When Khamchatka's gleamy crescent
  Casts a beamy, dreamy spell
O'er a forest vaguely pleasant
  With the Oomatonga's smell,
And for leagues around him amorous *'Ahkhs!'*
  Cacophonously swell:
With luck he'll bag a Vhatka!
      Who can tell?

QUICKELS

The Quickel-fish a-quiver in Parana-tinga river never
  shiver when they hear the shrill 'A-veisse!'
Of the brave to his old squaw, as he pads on muffled paw,
  up the slopes bestrown with porphyry and gneiss;
For they see the rose a-blowing, hear the paddles to-and-
  froing, and they know that's quite impossible in ice.

But when mute upon the mountains fall the well-springs
  and the fountains, where the chamois o'er the
  glacier nimbly sports;
When through snow-embowered crevasses gallop squadrons
  of wild asses, seeking herbage 'mid the jasper and
  the quartz;
Ah then, ah then, alas! their haunts congeal like glass —
  gelidified to crystal are their courts.

O brief, sweet day thus ended! In a marvellous trance
  suspended, they shine like gouts of gold in shimmering ore —
Like frozen clots of light, amber, opal, malachite —
  while their turquoise eyes in terror scan the shore;
For like cats come Indians stalking; sounds a baleful
  tomahawking; they chop them out in blocks — and
  thirst for more!

GOAT

Leaving his cave secure and tidy,
See Crusoe, with his trusty Friday —
While low in heaven the crescent floats —
Have sallied out in search of goats.
In skins, close-skewered, Robinson,
His Pretty Poll perched thumb upon,
And shag umbrella to the skies —
Since dews descend when mists arise —
Is treading soft as soft can be
The track his black can plainly see;
Whose round and glaring eyes, you'll mark,
Were no less useful in the dark.

Now, more in joy than wonderment,
Man Friday is on knee down-bent,
And with an unmistaken hand
Points to the hoof-prints in the sand.
It's likely they will lead at last
To where, replete from his repast,
On ground, which looks a little hilly,
An unsuspecting handsome Billy,
With calm and pensive bearded face,
Awaits the huntsmen and the chase.

See, cloud has dimmed the moonbeams wan —
'Tis Fortune's self now leads them on!
Good sport to you, brave Robinson!
Where'er you fare, or how, or whoso,
A thumping bag, beloved Crusoe!
And when goat's bubbling in the pot,
All weariness by F. forgot,
May man and master hob-a-nob,
With Puss a-purring on the hob;
While for his share of supper-meat
Shrieks the bedizened parakeet.

AH, MOMOTOMBO!

Ah, Momotombo, would I might
  Thy distant mountains scan!
Were green Managua's groves in sight —
  How pleasing then life's plan!

Atlas in hand, I watch and wake,
Pining to hear the billows break
  On Desolado's shore.
Sweet were to me their wild refrain —
A deep, a sad, a solemn strain —
  They'd roar it o'er and o'er.

Alas! 'tis not my fate to roam,
Not *there* for me is hearth, heath, home;
  I stay but where I am.
Yet never sighs the halcyon breeze
That tells not of thy tim-tam trees,
  The yookoos in thy yams,
Thy merry little chickadees,
  And clutemnacious clams.

I sleep, I creep where, fathoms deep,
  El Paraiso flows;
Exultant climb at morning-prime
  Tegucigalpa's snows.
With dream-tranced eyes I watch the flies
  Cloud inland, rank on rank.
Borne on the breeze that thrills the seas
That sweep with ease the Caribees,
They swarm with parched proboscides,
Protruding eyes and folded knees,
  Athwart Mosquito Bank.

Alas! sweet Momotombo — and
  Solentiname's Isle!
But though my grief is past relief,
  And innocent of guile,
Whene'er, with open Gazetteer,
My own enchanting voice I hear
Lisping in accents shrill and clear —
'Agguapadalpo, Yali, Za —
Catacoluca, Paundma,
Chalatenango . . .' — well, la, la!
  I *can't* refrain a smile.

[882]

FOXES

Old Dr. Cox's
Love of foxes
Led his steps astray;
He'd haunt the woods and coppices,
And lure the beasts away,
Into a bright green private park,
In safety there to *stay*.

Now Dr. Cox's
Dodge with foxes
Was simple as could be;
For first of all he'd find an earth,
And mark it with a T
(Just T for Trapper); then he'd wait
Till dusk; just wait and see.

For Dr. Cox's
Way with foxes
Needed but a *hush;*
When seated on a bank of loam,
Beneath a tree or bush,
He'd tootle-ootle on a comb,
And each would bring its brush.

THE LION-HUNTER

The lion-hunter is a man
Who lives to hunt the lion;
He'd gladly hunt him might and main,
Through France and Portugal and Spain,
And back to old Albíon.

But where there's Negroes in the place
The sun shines hot and dry on —
'Tis there, with spy-glass to his eye,
He takes his camp-stool, no one by,
And spies about — and spies about — just spies about
for lion.

Yes, there he sits, with hat on head —
The only hat he'd try on —
His hat (I mean) of pith with peaks,
And flaps, both sides, to shield the cheeks,
Wherein he hunts the lion.

From one oasis to the next,
  He packs his bag to hie on,
And sometimes his pyjamas share
That bag with hanks of tawny hair —
And these were once — yes, these were once — yes, these
    were once a lion.

Perchance, at last, this happy man
  Will hunt his way to Zion —
With a golden harp and most beautiful wings
  To play on and to fly on.
But now and again when the music's done,
He'll hie to some nook of sand and sun,
And there you'll find him (with his gun)
  Colloguing with a lion.

QUACK-HUNTING

When evening's darkening azure
    Stains the water crystal clear,
It's a marvellous sweet pleasure
    A small coracle to steer
To where, in reeds and rushes,
    Squeak and chuckle, sup and suck
A multitudinous company
    Of Duck.

There silver-shining Hesper
    Smiles at Mars — a solemn red;
The myriads of the Milky Way
    Are circling overhead;
But even though the dusk's too dim
    To sheen their wings — with luck
I catch those button eyes and know
    They're Duck.

Not mine the dismal fowling-piece,
    The *living* duck for me!
I strow upon the water crumbs
    Which they, that instant, see;
They paddle in like steamboats, with
    Their tails behind their backs;
And I? I simply sit and count
    Their quacks.

One sigh in that great silence —
Wild-winged creatures, they'd be gone!
But me — I scarcely breathe, I don't,
But softly sidle on;
And while the dears are feeding, with
Their tails behind their backs,
I make my nightly score, I count
Their quacks.

MARCH HARES

'The best way to go,' said my muffled-up friend, 'is to look in
its *form* for a Hare, you know';
So, with gun over shoulder, we sallied out early, the bushes all
hunched up with snow, you know;
The dawn was still under the eastern horizon, and O but the
morning was rare, you know;
The elms and the oaks were a-dangle with ice, that swayed in
the breeze to and fro, you know —
Icicles half a yard long at the least, that tinkled and rang in the
air, you know;
'A marvellous music,' said I to my friend; and he, he never
said, No, you know.

The snow had been falling for days, there were drifts full
fifteen feet deep, and so fair, you know,
Aurora herself might have looked to her blushes, and Cupid
have trimmed up his bow, you know;
And when o'er the rim of the World came the Sun, and with
eye like a topaz did glare, you know,
We stood for a while as if blinded with Paradise, dumb in that
wonderful glow, you know;
We coughed, and we shifted our guns, and went on — no more
than a cough could we dare, you know,
For moment by moment we couldn't tell where we should
come within sight of the foe, you know.

And, all of a sudden, my friend, he said, 'Ssh!' and I looked
and I listened; and there, you know —
Not half a shot off, with his ears and his scut, crouching close in
the lily-white snow, you know,
And his eyes like two blazing bright marbles of glass — sat
staring and glaring a Hare, you know!
The sun it shone brighter, the blue it grew bluer, the heavens
like an infinite O, you know,
And a breeze out of nowhere rang sweet as a bell rings, and
stirred in our whiskers and hair, you know.

My friend — then — he — up — with — his — gun — to — his —
shoulder — and tugged at the trigger: but lo! you know,
In his kindness of heart he'd forgotten to load, for for slaughter
he didn't much care, you know;
We laughed, oh! laughed we; and, my ghost! if old Watt
didn't up with his nose and cry, 'Ho!' you know;
And stamped for his brothers and sisters to come; and they
hopped up in scores from their lairs, you know.
They danced, they fandangoed, they scuttered, they sang,
turned somersaults, leapfrogged, and so, you know
We trudged back to breakfast with nothing to jug, which
wasn't *exacaly* fair, you know,
   Which *wasn't* exacaly fair.

WEA

If I were the Beadle of Weston Weaton,
   A happy old Beadle I'd be,
Sitting up there in my two-pair-back,
   Looking out on the deep blue sea;
While a bellying cloud on the West Wind comes
And splashes my scarlet geraniums;
      And the honey-bee hums,
      As I twiddle my thumbs
And smile at the gables of Wea.

If I were the Beadle of Weston Weaton,
   I'd have a stuffed dog in a case,
A woolly-haired, brown, retriever dog,
   With amber eyes in his face.
Under the picture of widgeons he'd stand,
Looking into the parlour, mute and bland,
      On fine yaller sand,
      Stuffed by Indy Shand,
   10, High Street, Weston Wea.

As soon as my Birthday (June 9) came round,
   I'd give all the children a treat —
Infants like angels at tables on trestles,
   And flags blazing out in the street;
Cherries and gingerpop, buns and plum-cake,
Lord! what huzzaing and clapping they'd make;
      While their little hearts break,
      As my way I'd take,
   Smiling and bowing through Wea!

On Sundays I'd sprightly step off to the Kirk —
  Neat pepper-and-salt, in tweed,
With a springside boot, silk cravat at my throat,
  Stiff collar — intoning the Creed.
With the ladies and little tots all in a row,
I'd troll out the hymmums and Psalms, and throw
    A languishing glow
    On a widow I know —
  Mrs. James, of the *Chequers*, in Wea.

And I'd thank my stars, as I climbed the stairs,
  I was born in the parish of Wea,
Where the Burghers are solid respectable folk,
  And the Lord of the Manor's a Ffeogh;
And me be angry with Edward Lear
For his Cheadle limerick? — Lor, no fear!
    I'd toast him, I know it,
    For a man and a poet,
  If I were the Beadle of Wea.

WITCHCRAFT

A parson I knew in the village of Eard —
Himself like a solemn bespectacled bird —
  Had a witchcraft I've never seen beat,
For attracting around him small creatures with wings;
Whatsoever on earth hops, nests, flutters and sings,
  Would flit at his call to his feet.

A whistled decoy-note, and out there would hie,
From the tops of his trees, stables, chimneypots, sky,
A host of small birds, and, all twittering, come,
Not in hope of cheese, fat, worms, seed, water or crumb,
But merely for joy of himself, and to share
In the open of heaven his company there.

I've sat with my friend in the twilight and seen
The whimbrels at play in the glim,
And owls large and small hooting out of the green,
And it seemed they were calling to him,
And he'd sidle his head o'er his book, and you knew
That its print now said naught but Too-whit and to-hoo:
  And it couldn't say sweeter to him.

And often, with candle in hand, he has said,
As we climbed up the staircase to go off to bed,
'I like, Jones, to think they'll sing on when I'm dead.
   And wherever I happen to be,
Should it chance but an echo of music should come
Such as now I delight in, I'll post away home —
   I couldn't resist it, you see.

'Besides, Jones, a secret,' he muttered it low,
In the gleam his round spectacles all of a glow,
'Soft down's on my shoulder-blades sprouting, I vow;
And even the primaries stirring, and so,
   The flight will come easy to me!'
With a chuckle he clutched at my elbow, and I —
   I confess I was bound to agree.

So we laid him to rest where, in green month of May,
A group of young hawthorns would sweeten the day,
   And there, if you happen to pass,
You will hear morn and evening, and middle-day too,
The wild birds lamenting the friend they all knew;
   And even when midnight's o'erhead,
In the midst of the may-blossom — silent as snow —
When all throats are hushed, sobs a voice sweet with woe —
   The nightingale's voice, it is said.

FINIS

   This Mouse is here
   (As the cut makes clear),
For to prove, whatsoever else fails,
   That Providence sends
   The mite *two* ends —
The tip of his snout and his tail's.

BIBLIOGRAPHICAL APPENDIX[1]

1. SONGS OF CHILDHOOD (1902)

The first edition, by 'Walter Ramal', contained 47 poems. The second edition of 1916 contained 48 poems and had substantial alterations: four poems, 'The Grey Wolf', 'The Night-Swans', 'Cecil' and 'Envoy' (beginning 'There clung three roses to a stem') were omitted; five new poems, 'A-Tishoo', 'The Rainbow', 'The Fiddlers', 'The Funeral' and 'Envoy' (beginning 'Child, do you love the flower') were included; and 'The Gnomies' was re-titled 'Sleepyhead'. Nearly a third of the poems had been revised in this edition, some heavily — especially 'The Pedlar', 'The Ogre', 'The Pilgrim', 'The Gage', 'The Phantom', 'Down-Adown-Derry', 'The Isle of Lone', 'As Lucy Went a-Walking' and 'Lullaby'. There were also alterations in the 1923 edition, which had 51 poems — 'The Night-Swans', 'Cecil' and 'The Grey Wolf' having been restored from the 1902 edition. There are, therefore, three distinct early versions of the book from the point of view of text and contents; and there were further changes in text and contents later on, too. The 1935 edition, the last of the four editions published by Longmans, omitted the three poems restored in 1923. The final separate edition was first issued in 1942 by Faber and Faber, who had taken over the publication rights. This corresponded to the 1916 edition as regards actual choice of poems, but sometimes the text of poems that had been revised at various stages was now the same as it had been originally in the 1902 edition. The poem 'Cecil' was omitted from CRV (1944). Because *Songs of Childhood* is so complicated bibliographically and textually, no textual variants at all have been given in this volume.

2. HENRY BROCKEN (1904)

Described in its sub-title as 'His travels and adventures in the rich, strange, scarce-imaginable regions of romance by Walter J. de la Mare ("Walter Ramal")', this novel included seven original poems. None of them have been reprinted elsewhere, and none had titles. (See also p. 549.)

3. POEMS (1906)

Poems (1906) consisted of 73 poems, 16 of which were omitted from CP (1942) — that is, 'Juliet', 'Desdemona', 'Casca', 'Come',

---

[1] *Collected Poems* (1942) and *Collected Rhymes and Verses* (1944) are abbreviated to CP (1942) and CRV (1944) respectively.

'The Winter-Boy', 'Even Rosemary', 'Coup de Grâce', 'Messengers', 'Irrevocable', 'Winter Coming', 'Omniscience', 'Youth', 'The Voice of Melancholy', 'Portrait of a Boy', 'Unpausing' and 'The Seas of England'. The last four lines of 'The Birthnight: To F.' were used as a dedication in *Inward Companion* (1950).

The book was originally divided into five sections: 1. 'Characters from Shakespeare', 2. [no title], 3. 'Sonnets', 4. [no title], 5. 'Memories of Childhood'. The arrangement, contents and titles of the five sections in *Poems 1901 – 1918* (1920) (vol. 1) were slightly different. The first two were called 'Lyrical Pieces' and 'Descriptive Pieces', and the remaining three had the titles of 1, 3 and 5 above.

4. THE THREE ROYAL MONKEYS (1910) (originally called *The Three Mulla-Mulgars* and re-titled in 1935)

Of the nine poems in this story written for de la Mare's children, 'The Mulla-Mulgars' Journey Song', 'Andy Battle's and Nod's Song' (also called 'Andy Battle' and 'Yeo Ho!'), 'She's Me Forgot', ('Andy's Love Song'), 'The Mulgar Journey Song' and 'Envoy' (beginning 'Long — long is Time, though books be brief') were omitted from CRV (1944). 'Andy Battle's and Nod's Song' appeared in the 1913 edition of *Peacock Pie* (as 'Andy Battle') and in the American edition of CRV (*Rhymes and Verses: Collected Poems for Children*, 1947) (as 'Yeo Ho!'), and 'The Mulla-Mulgars' Journey Song', 'The Mulgar Journey Song' and 'She's Me Forgot' in *Poems 1919–1934* (1935), the latter as 'Andy's Love Song'.

5. THE RETURN (1910)

This novel contained a poem which has not been reprinted elsewhere.

6. THE LISTENERS AND OTHER POEMS (1912)

The Listeners consisted of 51 poems. 'Spring', 'Ages Ago' and 'Home' were omitted from CP (1942).

7. A CHILD'S DAY: A BOOK OF RHYMES (1912)

A Child's Day consisted of 24 photographs illustrating a day in the life of a small child for which de la Mare wrote 23 rhymes. Until 1947, only three complete rhymes, 'Lob Lie by the Fire' (beginning 'He squats by the fire'), 'The World of Dream' (1922 title) and 'Sadly, O Sadly' were included elsewhere — they appeared in *Down-Adown-Derry* (1922), two stanzas of 'When She Was in Her Garden' also being included there as a separate poem, 'Happy, Happy it is To Be'. In 1947, a slightly revised version of *A Child's Day* was included at the end of the American edition of CRV, three poems ('Now Twelve Above', 'Here All We See' and 'And

There She Is (On the Other Side)') and twelve lines (six from 'When Safe into the Fields Ann Got', four from 'Ann, Upon the Stroke of Three' and two from 'This Brief Day Now Over') being omitted. This version has been used here, except that the three missing poems have been restored; 'Lob Lie by the Fire' has been given back its title, which had been omitted (it was in fact the only poem given a title in the original 1912 edition); and the American version had no titles.

8. PEACOCK PIE: A BOOK OF RHYMES (1913)

Like *Songs of Childhood*, this collection of rhymes has an involved bibliographical history. The 1913 and 1916 editions consisted of 82 poems, of which one, 'Andy Battle's and Nod's Song' (or 'Andy Battle', its earlier title), came from *The Three Royal Monkeys* (1910). The 1924 edition 'with embellishments by C. Lovat Fraser' had 10 additional poems, 'Kings and Queens', 'Not I!', 'Snow', 'Mr. Alacadacca', 'The Horseman' (beginning 'There was a horseman rode so fast'), 'The Sea Boy', 'Must and May', 'Late', 'Blind Tam' ('The Penny Owing') and 'Groat nor Tester'. There were further issues of the 1913 edition (each reset) in 1925, 1936, 1941 and 1946. Of the 10 additional poems (1924), which were all included in the 1969 edition of *Peacock Pie*, 'Kings and Queens', 'Mr. Alacadacca', 'The Sea Boy', 'Must and May', 'Late' and 'Groat nor Tester', did not appear in CRV (1944), though 'Kings and Queens' was included in the American edition of CRV (1947). 'The Horseman' turned up again in *Bells and Grass* (1941); and 'Blind Tam' was re-titled 'The Penny Owing' in *Poems for Children* (1930). (See also p. 700.)

The book was originally divided into eight sections called 'Up and Down', 'Boys and Girls', 'Three Queer Tales', 'Places and People', 'Beasts', 'Witches and Fairies', 'Earth and Air' and 'Songs'.

9. THE SUNKEN GARDEN AND OTHER POEMS (1917)

The Sunken Garden appeared in a limited edition of 270 copies, of which 20 were printed on vellum, and had 24 poems. All were included in *Motley and Other Poems* (1918) with the exception of 'In a Churchyard', which was also omitted from CP (1942), but was later published in a revised version in *O Lovely England and Other Poems* (1953).

10. MOTLEY AND OTHER POEMS (1918)

Motley consisted of 48 poems, including 23 from *The Sunken Garden* ('The Little Salamander', 'The Sunken Garden', 'The Riddlers', 'Mrs. Grundy', 'The Empty House' ('The Dark House'), 'Mistress Fell', 'The Stranger', 'Music', 'The Remonstrance', 'The Exile', 'Eyes', 'The Disguise' ('The Tryst'), 'The Old Men', 'The

Dreamer', 'Motley', 'To E.T.: 1917', 'The Fool's Song', 'Clear Eyes', 'Alexander', 'The Flight', 'The Two Houses' ('Nostalgia'), 'For All the Grief' and 'Fare Well'), the single poem 'The Old Men' having first been published in 1913 as a 'Flying Fame' broadsheet decorated by C. Lovat Fraser. Two poems, 'Happy England' and 'The Two Houses', were omitted from CP (1942); but the latter was published in a revised version called 'Nostalgia' in *The Burning-Glass and Other Poems* (1945).

11. FLORA: A BOOK OF DRAWINGS (1919)

Flora was a book of drawings by the 12-year-old Pamela Bianco, with 27 illustrative poems by de la Mare. There are at least five variants of the book due to last-minute changes in the text and illustrations. Seven poems, 'The Moth', 'Forgiveness', 'Crazed', 'Mirage', 'Flotsam', 'Mourns't Thou Now?' and 'Bitter Waters', were later reprinted in *The Veil and Other Poems* (1921); and one, 'The Snowflake', in *The Fleeting and Other Poems* (1933). Three poems, 'Morning Toilet', 'I Go Home' and 'Thule', were omitted from both CP (1942) and CRV (1944). (See also pp. 638, 897.)

12. POEMS 1901—1918 (1920) (2 vols.)

A collection of 273 poems, 149 of them in the first volume, and 124 in the second. The first contained 57 poems from *Poems* (1906), 47 from *The Listeners and Other Poems* (1912), and 45 from *Motley and Other Poems* (1918); and the second 44 poems from *Songs of Childhood* (1902) and 80 from *Peacock Pie* (1913).

13. MEMOIRS OF A MIDGET (1921)

This novel contained three original poems none of which have been reprinted elsewhere.

14. STORY AND RHYME (1921)

Story and Rhyme was a selection from his writings made by de la Mare himself for schools and colleges. The poem 'Sam's Three Wishes or Life's Little Whirligig' was first collected in this volume (see also p. 219). It appeared again in 1922 in *Down-Adown-Derry*.

15. CROSSINGS: A FAIRY PLAY (1921)

This fairy play with music by C. Armstrong Gibbs, which was first performed by the boys of the Wick School at Hove on 21 June 1919, contained eight original poems. One of them appeared again in *The Veil and Other Poems* (1921) as 'Tidings', a title which was later changed to 'The Flower'. 'Now Silent Falls' appeared in *Selected Poems*, New York, 1927, as 'Wild Time'. Only the four musical settings originally had titles and only one of these, 'Araby', was retained in CRV (1944) (see *Crossings* section, pp. 739–742).

16. THE VEIL AND OTHER POEMS (1921)

Of this collection of 53 poems, seven, 'The Moth', 'Forgiveness', 'Crazed', 'Mirage', 'Flotsam', 'Mourns't Thou Now?' and 'Bitter Waters', had already been included in *Flora* (1919), and one, 'The Flower' ('Tidings'), in *Crossings* (1921).

17. DOWN-ADOWN-DERRY: A BOOK OF FAIRY POEMS (1922)

Down-Adown-Derry was a collection of 61 so-called fairy poems from *Songs of Childhood* (1902), *Poems* (1906), *The Listeners and Other Poems* (1912), *A Child's Day* (1912), *Peacock Pie* (1913), *Motley and Other Poems* (1918), *Story and Rhyme* (1921) and *The Veil and Other Poems* (1921). Five poems, 'The Stranger', 'The Enchanted Hill', 'The Little Creature', 'The Old King' and 'The Double', had not been published previously. The four poems from *A Child's Day* (see above) were not reprinted in CRV (1944).

18. COME HITHER (1923)

This collection of rhymes and poems 'for the young of all ages' included none of de la Mare's own verse before the appearance of the enlarged and revised second edition of 1928, which contained two unsigned and untitled rhymes (finally called 'Stars' and 'Precious Stones') in the notes. These rhymes were reprinted in *Old Rhymes and New* (1932) and CRV (1944); and 'Precious Stones' also appeared in *Pleasures and Speculations* (1940).

19. DING DONG BELL (1924)

Ding Dong Bell originally consisted of three short stories around epitaphs called 'Lichen', ' "Benighted" ' and 'Winter'. A fourth story called 'Strangers and Pilgrims', containing 18 epitaphs, was added in the 1936 edition after ' "Benighted" ' (see p. 751). All 42 of the original epitaphs in the text and the 18 new ones were written by de la Mare. None of them, except the poem from 'Winter' which reappeared (revised) in *The Fleeting and Other Poems* (1933) with the title of 'Isaac Meek', were reprinted in CP (1942). The poem beginning 'Son of man, tell me' (1936 edition) was reprinted in *The Burning-Glass and Other Poems* (1945) as 'Son of Man'. None of the poems originally had titles, and the other titles in this volume that are not simply the first lines of poems are derived from the stories themselves.

20. STUFF AND NONSENSE, AND SO ON (1927)

A collection of 60 limericks and nonsense rhymes. The second, revised edition of 1946 contained 13 additional rhymes ('The Mouse', 'A Pair', 'Dusk', 'The Lady McTaggart', 'The Bun', 'The Monster', 'Archery', 'Old B.', 'The Warmint', 'The Fly' (beginning 'There was once an old parson named Next'), 'Vendetta', 'Odd Man Out' and 'Goat'). Of the 60 original rhymes only three, 'March Hares', 'The Accompaniment' and 'Quack-hunting', were reprinted in CRV (1944). A further one, 'Foxes', was reprinted in the American edition of CRV (1947).

The first edition was illustrated by Bold and was divided into six sections: 'Twiners', 'Meat, Fish, Etc.', 'Animated Nature', 'More Twiners', 'Thinkers and Spectres' and 'Far and Near and Finis'. One or two of the rhymes appear to have been altered to refer to Bold's woodcuts.

21. Poems for Children (1930)

Poems for Children consisted of nearly all the poems in *Songs of Childhood* and *Peacock Pie*, four poems from *Poems* (1906), one from *Motley and Other Poems* (1918), nine from *Flora* (1919), four from *Crossings* (1921), one from *Story and Rhyme* (1921), and one from *Down-Adown-Derry* (1922), with 21 new poems: 'The Fleeting', 'The Four Brothers', 'Thames', 'Wild are the Waves', 'Echoes', 'The O.M.O.R.E.', 'Babel', 'Seeds', 'The Holly', 'Who Really?', 'Puss', 'Hi!', 'Lone', 'As I Went to the Well-head', 'Eden', 'She in Thy Dreams Watch Over Thee' ('Lullaby'), 'To Bed', 'The Apple Charm', 'Jenny Wren' (beginning 'That farthing bird, J. Wren,'), 'Crumbs' and 'The Robin' — the last four of which were omitted from CRV (1944), though they were included in the American edition of CRV (1947). 'The Fleeting' was later the title poem in *The Fleeting and Other Poems* (1933) — with which it has been kept in this volume — and so was also omitted from CRV (1944), and included in CP (1942) instead. It, too, appeared in the American CRV (1947).

22. On the Edge: Short Stories (1930)

A collection of short stories, two of which contained poems or rhymes: 'A Recluse' had one rhyme, and 'The Green Room' 15 poems. None of them (except 'Lines on Ophelia') had titles, and none appeared in CP (1942) or CRV (1944). But 'Goodbye' and 'Have Done!' ('The Green Room') appeared — with these titles — in *O Lovely England and Other Poems* (1953).

23. The Fleeting and Other Poems (1933)

Of the 68 poems in *The Fleeting*, 'I Sit Alone' (original title 'Alone'), 'Self to Self', 'The Snowdrop', 'News' and 'Lucy', had previously been published as single poems in the Ariel Poems series; 'The Snowflake' had appeared in *Flora* (1919); 'Isaac Meek' in *Ding Dong Bell* (1924); and 'The Fleeting' in *Poems for Children* (1930). 'A Ballad of Christmas' had been issued as a separate poem in 1924, and 'Thus Her Tale' in 1923. Six poems, 'On the

Esplanade', 'Reconciliation', 'The Captive', 'The Snail', 'The Strange Spirit' and 'To K.M.', had previously been published in an American collection, *The Captive and Other Poems* (1928), in an edition limited to 600 copies. 'The Snowdrop' and 'Lucy' were revised for *The Fleeting*. 'Karma', which had appeared again (revised) in *Bells and Grass* (1941) as 'Full Circle', was omitted from CP (1942), and was later included in CRV (1944). (See also p. 709.)

In his prefatory note, the author writes: 'The poems included in this volume range over a good many years, but only a very few — which have been revised — were written before the publication of *The Veil* in 1921. Of the rest, many are recent . . .'

24. THE LORD FISH (1933)

A collection of short stories, illustrated by Rex Whistler. The story called 'The Lord Fish' contained a poem which has not been reprinted elsewhere.

25. POEMS 1919—1934 (1935)

A collection of 182 poems, all but eight of them from previous books. All the poems in *The Veil and Other Poems* (1921) and *The Fleeting and Other Poems* (1933) were there, together with six from *The Three Royal Monkeys* (1910), 16 from *Flora* (1919), four from *Crossings* (1921), the five new ones in *Down-Adown-Derry* (1922), three of the new ones in the 1924 edition of *Peacock Pie*, the two poems in the 1928 edition of *Come Hither* and the 21 new poems in *Poems for Children* (1930) (one of them being 'The Fleeting'). It contained seven new poems, 'Winter', 'Romance', 'An Epitaph' ('Afraid'), 'A Stave', 'Oh, Yes, My Dear', 'Quack' and 'Seen and Heard'; and also a poem which had been published in 1926 as one of two poems in a compilation with the title of *St. Andrews* (the other was by Rudyard Kipling), and which was called 'A Memory' there and in this collection, but later re-titled 'St. Andrews' in *O Lovely England and Other Poems* (1953). These eight new poems were not included in CP (1942) or CRV (1944). 'An Epitaph' and 'Seen and Heard' were printed again in *Inward Companion* (1950) in slightly different versions, the former with a new title, 'Afraid'.

26. THE WIND BLOWS OVER (1936)

A collection of short stories, one, 'Miss Miller', containing seven rhymes by de la Mare. None of them appeared in CP (1942) or CRV (1944).

27. THIS YEAR: NEXT YEAR (1937)

These 34 poems for children were written to drawings by Harold

Jones. Eleven poems, 'The Thrush', 'Esmeralda', 'The Room', 'Holidays', 'Haymaking', 'The Tent', 'Over the Downs', 'There Was an Old Woman . . .', 'The Feast', 'The Pantomime' and 'Farewell', were omitted from CRV (1944); though all of them except 'Farewell' were included in the American edition of CRV (1947).

28. MEMORY AND OTHER POEMS (1938)

A collection of 74 poems. (See also pp. 638, 649, 650, 658.)

29. PLEASURES AND SPECULATIONS (1940)

A collection of essays. It was prefaced by a poem 'Books' which has not been reprinted elsewhere.

30. BELLS AND GRASS: A BOOK OF RHYMES (1941)

A collection of 91 rhymes, of which one, 'The Horseman', had already appeared in *Peacock Pie* (1924), and one, 'Full Circle', in *The Fleeting and Other Poems* (1933) — as 'Karma'. 'Where' (beginning 'Houses! houses! — Oh, I know') was not included in CRV (1944). The American edition (1942) contained an earlier version of 'Solitude' (in *The Burning-Glass and Other Poems* (1945)) called 'The Journey'. Both 'Where' and 'The Journey' were included in the American edition of CRV (1947). (See also pp. 689, 692, 710, 718, 719.)

In his introduction, the author makes it clear that a considerable number of the rhymes were written before the end of 1906, and most of the rest a year or two before publication.

31. COLLECTED POEMS (CP) (1942)

This was a collection of 342 previously published poems. In his prefatory note, the author writes:

'This volume contains the Collections entitled *Poems* (1906), *The Listeners, Motley, The Veil, The Fleeting* — as these were reprinted in *Poems: 1901 to 1918* (Volume I) and in *Poems: 1919 to 1934* — and *Memory*. Nothing from *Songs of Childhood, Peacock Pie, Bells and Grass*, and no other rhymes primarily intended for children have been included; nor is there anything from *Ding Dong Bell*. I have made very few revisions.

'Nor have I attempted to sift out what I should prefer to exclude, and certainly not what would have been left to blush unseen by a finer taste and judgment. The one enterprise would have revealed in detail *how* fond a paternal affection may be; the other, even if it had been practicable, might have resulted in — well, the slimmest of pamphlets, and that all but wholly compassionate. Time will soon see to all that . . .'

Sixteen poems from *Poems* (1906), three from *The Listeners and*

Other Poems (1912), two from *Motley and Other Poems* (1918), one from *The Fleeting and Other Poems* (1933), and the eight new poems in *Poems 1919 – 1934* (1935) were omitted. The book was divided into twelve sections. The American edition of CP, published in 1941, included the poem from *The Fleeting* omitted in CP (1942) and was grouped according to collections.

32. COLLECTED RHYMES AND VERSES (CRV) (1944)

Of this collection of 306 poems, mainly intended for children, two poems, 'Kings' and 'Noon', had not previously been published. In his prefatory note, the author writes:

'This collection of rhymes and verses includes the complete contents of *Songs of Childhood*, of *Peacock Pie* and of *Bells and Grass*; most of the rhymes in *This Year: Next Year*; a few others (not in these volumes) from *Down-Adown-Derry*, and from *Poems for Children*; a few from *Flora*; a few songs from *Crossings*, a Play, and from *The Three Royal Monkeys* . . .; three rhymes from the Notes in *Come Hither*; two from *Stuff and Nonsense*; and two that have not hitherto appeared in print . . .

'Most of the volumes here referred to were intended for children — and there is little need to say how ambitious and hazardous any such intention is. Children are unflinching critics. They know usually beyond a doubt what they like, and make no allowances. And that is a chastening reflection. To what degree and in what precise respect the contents of this volume differ from the contents of *Collected Poems* are little problems which I will not attempt to explore. Somewhere the two streams divide — and may re-intermingle. Both, whatever the quality of the water, and of what it holds in solution, sprang from the same source. And here, concerning that — nor will I even venture on an Alas — silence is best.'[1]

One poem from *Songs of Childhood*, six poems from *Peacock Pie* (all of them new in the 1924 edition), and one from *Bells and Grass* (1941) were in fact omitted; and also 11 from *This Year: Next Year* (1937), five of the 21 new poems in *Poems for Children* (1930), and five of the nine poems in *The Three Royal Monkeys* (1910). CRV (1944) has *two* poems from *Come Hither* (1928 edition) and *three* from *Stuff and Nonsense, and So On* (1927). All eight poems in *Crossings* (1921), the five new poems in *Down-Adown-Derry* (1922), and 16 of the 27 poems in *Flora* (1919) were included (eight of the remainder had appeared in CP (1942)).

The book was divided into 10 sections: 'Green Grow the Rashes, O!', 'All Round About the Town', 'Soldiers: Sailors: Far Countries: and the Sea', 'All Creatures Great and Small', 'Fairies: Witches: Phantoms', 'Winter and Christmas', 'Books and Stories',

[1] See also the long introduction in *Poems for Children* (1930).

'Moon: and Stars: Night: and Dream', 'Odds and Ends' and 'Somewhere'. The enlarged CRV of 1970 contained 358 poems. The American edition of CRV called *Rhymes and Verses: Collected Poems for Children* (1947) had 366 poems. It contained 22 poems from CP (1942), all but one from *This Year: Next Year* (1937), all but three from *A Child's Day* (1912), and nine other additional poems: one more from *The Three Royal Monkeys* (1910), *Peacock Pie* (1924 edition) and *Stuff and Nonsense* (1927), four more from *Poems for Children* (1930)[1], and two more from *Bells and Grass* (1941 and 1942: one of them only appeared in the American edition of 1942). 'Sambo' was omitted.

33. THE BURNING-GLASS AND OTHER POEMS (1945)

Of the 74 poems in *The Burning-Glass*, one, 'Son of Man', had previously been published in the story 'Strangers and Pilgrims' in the 1936 edition of *Ding Dong Bell*. An early version of 'Nostalgia' called 'The Two Houses' had been published in *The Sunken Garden and Other Poems* (1917) and *Motley and Other Poems* (1918); and an earlier version of 'Solitude' called 'The Journey' had been included in the American edition of *Bells and Grass* (1942). 'The Chart' appeared again in *Inward Companion* (1950). The American edition of *The Burning-Glass* (1945) also contained the first-published version of *The Traveller* (see below), and a poem called 'Problems'. (See also pp. 500, 704.)

In his prefatory note, the author writes: '. . . Some of [the poems] were written many years ago, and have since been revised; others recently . . .'

34. THE TRAVELLER (1945) (first separate edition, 1946)

This long poem was first published in New York in 1945, in the Viking Press edition of *The Burning-Glass and Other Poems*. It was not included in the Faber edition (see above), and was brought out on its own in England in 1946. There are numerous differences in the English and American editions — so many in fact that to have noted even only the important ones would have been beyond the scope of this volume. Among other things, stanzas 8, 9, 33, 53–57 (these five replace stanza 50 in the American edition), 81, 101, 102 and 124 in the English edition, used here, are new. The poem was reprinted in *Selected Poems*, ed. R. N. Green-Armytage (1954).

35. INWARD COMPANION: POEMS (1950)

Of the 81 poems in *Inward Companion*, two, 'Afraid' ('An Epitaph') and 'Seen and Heard', had previously been published in *Poems 1919–1934* (1935); one, 'Haunted', as a broadsheet in 1939;

---

[1] Not including 'The Fleeting', already counted among the CP (1942) poems.

one, 'The Chart', in *The Burning-Glass and Other Poems* (1945); and one, 'Pride Hath Its Fruits Also' — as 'Pride' — in *Two Poems*, a limited edition, in 1946.

In his prefatory note, the author writes: 'One or two of the poems . . . were written as many as fifty years ago; others during the last few years, and most of these are recent. All of them have been revised . . .'

In America, *Inward Companion* was published together with *Winged Chariot* in 1951 as *Winged Chariot and Other Poems*.

36. WINGED CHARIOT (1951)

De la Mare's longest published poem — nearly three times as long as *The Traveller*. For the American edition, see *Inward Companion* (1950) above. It was reprinted in *A Choice of de la Mare's Verse*, ed. W. H. Auden (1963).

37. O LOVELY ENGLAND AND OTHER POEMS (1953)

Of the 69 poems in *O Lovely England*, 'St. Andrews' had been previously published under the title of 'A Memory' in *Poems 1919 – 1934* (1935); 'In a Churchyard' in *The Sunken Garden and Other Poems* (1917); 'Goodbye' and 'Have Done!' — without titles — in *On the Edge* (1930) in the story called 'The Green Room'; and 'The Truth of Things' in *Two Poems*, a limited edition, in 1946. (See also pp. 653, 668, 669.)

In his prefatory note, the author writes: '. . . Many of these pages were written years ago, some of them as far back as the second decade of this century . . .'

38. SELECTED POEMS (1954)

A selection of 175 poems made by R. N. Green-Armytage including *The Traveller*.

39. A CHOICE OF DE LA MARE'S VERSE (1963)

A paperback selection of 149 poems made by W. H. Auden, with a full-length critical introduction, and including *Winged Chariot* (1951). Only 29 of the poems were the same as poems included in *Selected Poems* (1954).

Walter de la Mare: A Checklist, prepared by Leonard Clark for the exhibition of de la Mare books and MSS held at the National Book League in April–May 1956 (University Press, Cambridge, 1956), has been an important source of information in the compilation both of this appendix and of the present volume.

Index of Titles

(Secondary references are in italics)

[913]

Index of First Lines

[917]

[927]

Quiet your faces; be crossed every thumb; 798

Rachel sings sweet — 107
Rare-sweet the air in that unimagined country — 246
Reason as patiently as moth and rust, 489
Rebellious heart, why still regret so much, 606
Rest now, revered and gentle sir, 701
Rest, rest — there is no rest, 133
'Return from out thy stillness, though the dust, 87
Roofless and eyeless, weed-sodden, dank, old, cold — 370
Rose, like dim battlements, the hills and reared, 53
Roses are sweet to smell and see, 211
Rosy the blossom that breaks in May; 830
'Rouse now, my dullard, and thy wits awake; 225
Ruby, amethyst, emerald, diamond, 761

Sad is old Ben Thistlethwaite, 102
Sadly, O sadly, the sweet bells of Baddeley, 795
Said Jane to the old Fisherman, 857
Said Judge Jessop, 851
Said Mr. Smith, 'I really cannot, 874
'Sailorman, I'll give to you, 9
Sand, sand; hills of sand; 96
Says James to his second cousin, he says, 868
Scan with calm bloodshot eyes the world around us, 461
Scarf and fillet, chaplet, gem, 652
Scatter a few cold cinders into the empty grate; 309
Screamed the far sea-mew. On the mirroring sands, 807
See Master Humphrey, with his mother, 715
See, Master Proud-Face! 406
See, now, a child must this way come — 816
See now, if thou have any heed, 756
See, now, this filigree: 'tis snow, 806
See this house, how dark it is, 195
Seven sweet notes, 415
Shadow and light both strove to be, 108
'Shall we help you with your bundle', 24
She found an exit from her life; 766
She had amid her ringlets bound, 67
She in thy dreams watch over thee! 274
She said, 'I will come back again, 521
She stooped with serious eyes, 631
She will not die, they say, 198
Shrill, glass-clear notes — 'Titmouse!' I sighed, enchanted; 712
Shrill rang the squeak in the empty house, 271
Shrill trills the bird concealed in leaves; 646
Shut now those slumber-haunted eyes, 630
Sighed the wind to the wheat: — 251
Sighs have no skill, 723
Silly Sallie! Silly Sallie! 408

[941]

Index of Books,
Periodicals and Sections[1]

[1] Broadsheets and pamphlets are included. The periodicals are those referred to
in the Uncollected Poems section.

[945]